THE LEICA AND LEICAFLEX WAY

THE LEICA AND LEICAFLEX WAY

The Leica and Leicaflex Photographer's Companion

ANDREW MATHESON

Eighth Edition

FOCAL PRESS - LONDON - NEW YORK

SBN 240 50670 7

First published: December 1953
Second edition: May 1954
Third edition: June 1955
Fourth edition: July 1957
Fifth edition: December 1959
Sixth edition: February 1963
Seventh edition: May 1966
Eighth edition: June 1968

ALL ENQUIRIES

relating to this book or to any photographic problem are answered by the Focal Press without charge if a stamped addressed envelope is enclosed for reply

French Edition:
LA PRATIQUE DU LEICA
Publications Paul Montel, Paris

German Edition:
DAS GANZE LEICA SYSTEM
Verlag Wilhelm Knapp, Düsseldorf

Spanish Edition:
GRAN MANUEL LEICA No. 2
Ediciones Omega, S.A., Barcelona

Printed in Great Britain by W. & J. Mackay & Co. Ltd Chatham
1968

CONTENTS

In view of the constant development of the Leica camera and accessories, certain models and items are being replaced all the time by new designs. Large numbers of obsolete and discontinued pieces of equipment are, however, still in use. For the sake of completeness, these are therefore fully described, but printed (just as are some paragraphs of more theoretical interest) in smaller type than the main text.

THE PIONEER MINIATURE

Some hundred years ago cameras were usually large and weighty. Since then negative sizes have decreased as camera designers tried to make photography a more convenient hobby.

Not unnaturally the progress of photography brought out many freaks: cameras taking pictures as small as 1 inch or even ½ inch square were known from the very beginning. Although some of these were popular for "secret" photography, especially with fiction thriller authors, the most common camera sizes around fifty years ago were quarter-plate (3¼ × 4¼ inches), 9 × 12 cm., and 2½ × 3½ inches. The smaller models were in advance of their time, for the quality of the results they produced left much to be desired. Neither lenses nor current sensitive materials were good enough to yield really enlargeable miniature negatives.

That was also the experience of Oskar Barnack, who eventually designed the Leica. At the beginning of the century he was experimenting with methods of taking multiple shots of fifteen to twenty miniature pictures side by side on a 5 × 7 inch plate. His incentive was the fact that a 5 × 7 inch plate camera with plate holders and supplies of plates was rather heavy to carry about on walking tours. Those attempts were a failure; the small negatives were too grainy and not sharp enough.

The Original Leica

Barnack then approached the problem from the direction of cinematography. Cine film was much finer in grain than ordinary plates, and small enlargements from an 18 × 24 mm. cine frame were quite acceptable.

The degree of enlargement was still limited, so Barnack doubled the height of the negative—the width was fixed by the standard width of the cine film—to produce the 24 × 36 mm. format. For it he built a camera to take perforated 35 mm. cine film: the original Leica of 1912.

In its basic design this camera (which had at that time no

LEICA HISTORY

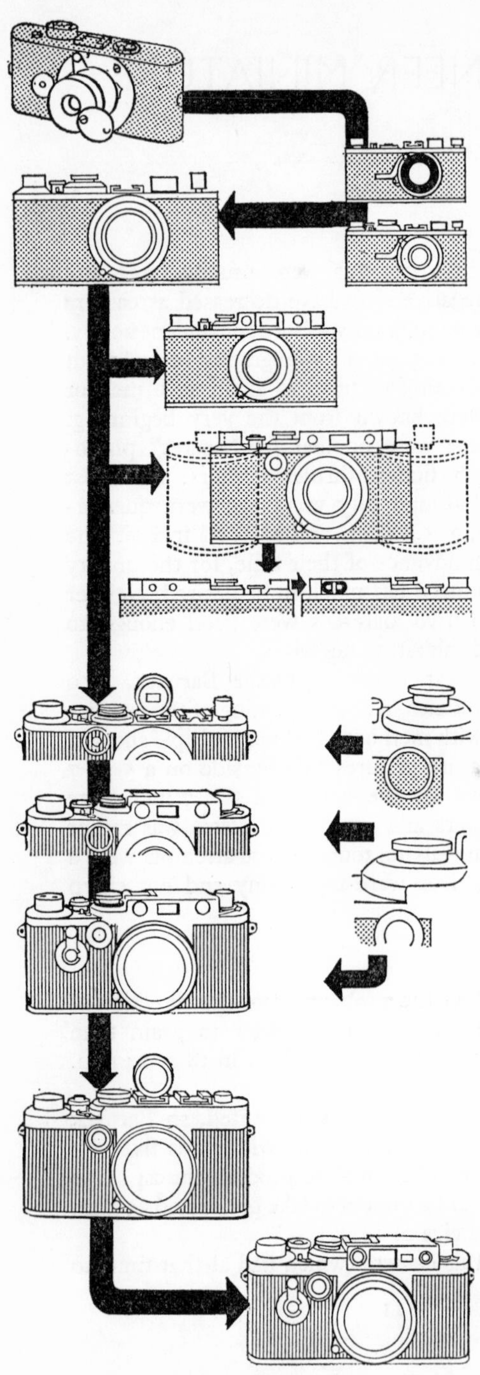

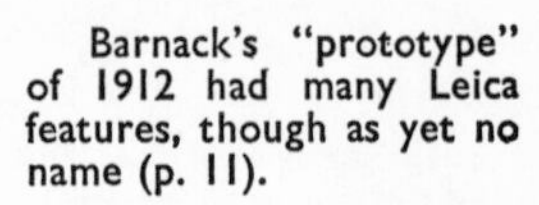

Barnack's "prototype" of 1912 had many Leica features, though as yet no name (p. 11).

The Leica of 1925 appeared in two versions, with a focal plane and with a Compur shutter. This was the forerunner of the Leica I models of 1930 and 1932 (p. 14).

In 1932 the Leica II came out with the coupled rangefinder (p. 14).

The Leica III and IIIa of 1933 had a range of slow speeds, and (model IIIa), a top speed of 1/1000 second. The Leica 250 (dotted) was a IIIa with extra large spool chambers (p. 60).

The Leica IIIb of 1938 was fitted with twin eyepieces for the view and rangefinders (*right*).

In the post-war series, the Leica If of 1952 features flash synchronization as well as being more up to date in other respects. Its forerunner, the Ic, was identical except that it had no provisions for flash (*right*).

The Leica IIf of 1951 similarly developed via the IIc without flash (*right*).

The Leica IIIf of 1950 has flash synchronization and a full range of shutter speeds from 1 to 1/1000 second. Again an earlier version without flash appeared in 1939 (IIIc).

The Leica Ig and IIIg of 1957 were the last models with screw-mounted lenses, with a revised viewfinder (IIIg) and flash system. The screw-mounted Leica cameras were finally discontinued in 1960.

LEICA M HISTORY

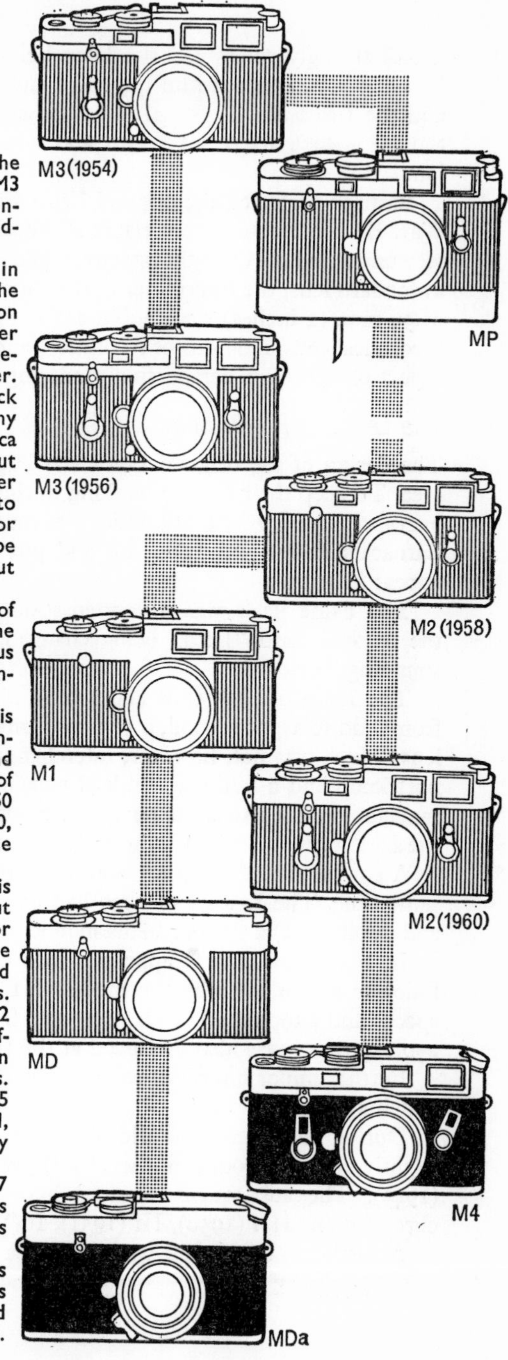

The first model of the Leica M series was the M3 of 1954 with bayonet mounted lenses and rapid winding lever.

This was followed in 1956 by a special model, the Leica MP with a built-on Leicavit rapid-winding lever and a slightly different design of the film counter. This model had an all-black camera body, without shiny chrome parts. The Leica MP had no self-timer, but was fitted with a finder frame selector lever to enable the finder frames for different focal lengths to be brought into view without changing the lens.

An improved model of the M3 of 1956 also has the same selector lever plus certain slight internal changes.

The Leica M2 of 1958 is a derivative of a MP, without Leicavit attachment and with a different selection of viewfinder frames (35, 50 and 90 mm. instead of 50, 90 and 135 mm., as on the M3.)

The Leica M1 of 1959 is a simplified model without rangefinder, self-timer, or finder frame selector. The viewfinder shows fixed frames for two focal lengths.

Since 1960, Leica M2 models have a built in self-timer and show certain other slight design changes.

The Leica MD of 1965 has no finder system at all, being intended primarily for scientific work.

The Leica M4 of 1967 has rapid loading facilities and a rewind crank plus other minor changes.

The Leica MDa of 1967 is similar to the MD but has the simplified loading and the rewind crank of the M4.

name) strongly resembled the later Leica models. It had a focusing lens, coupled film transport and shutter tensioning, and the Leica-shape body. It also had a focal plane shutter, though with a fixed slit width and adjustable spring tenion.

Barnack perfected the original Leica after the First World War. He constructed the variable slit focal plane shutter, the viewfinder and the daylight cassette, while Max Berek designed a standard lens, the forerunner of the Elmar. The focal length of 50 mm. (2 inches) was chosen as the ideal one, both from theoretical considerations of resolution, and from the practical aspect of optimum perspective rendering.

The Leica in Production

The design of the original Leica was largely Barnack's own idea. To keep their factory working during the economic upheavals in the 1920s, Leitz decided to manufacture a camera. Barnack's design was taken up and put into production to appear in 1925.

The name itself was a condensation of LEitz-CAmera; the original form "Leca" being changed later to the better sounding "Leica".

The Leica of 1925 thus had a focal plane shutter, speeds from 1/20 to 1/500 second, a 50 mm. Elmax (later Elmar) *f*3.5 lens (which was not, however, interchangeable), a film transport knob and a built-in standard viewfinder. There was no rangefinder, but a separate rangefinder was available to fit into the accessory shoe on top of the camera.

A similar model, with a Compur shutter, appeared at the same time. The Leica I of 1930 had an interchangeable lens and (after 1933) a standard lens mount.

In 1932 the Leica II appeared with coupled rangefinder, followed a year later by the models III and IIIa with slow speeds and a top speed of 1/1,000 second. A special model for 250 exposures was also produced at the time.

Further minor improvements were made in the Leica IIIb which appeared in 1938.

During the Second World War the Leica models were slightly altered, producing the IIIc (1939), IIc (1948) and Ic (1949). The subsequent versions have built-in flash synchronization: IIIf (1950), IIf (1951), If (1952).

A further modification was the Leica IIIg (1957) with a

reflected frame viewfinder similar to the M3 model (p. 15), and automatic flash synchronization, as well as a new range of shutter speeds.

The Leica Ig (1957), replacing the If, had the IIIg features except for the finder system and the self-timer.

A special model which appeared in 1954 in small numbers is the Leica 72; this takes seventy-two exposures 18 × 24 mm. and is designed for microfilm copying.

The first radical change in the design of the Leica was the model M3 (1954), with a range of modern features such as a rapid-winding transport lever and bayonet-mounted lenses. For a time, while the traditional style Leica models of the f and g series were still available (until 1960), the models of the M range were regarded as an alternative to the traditional style. Eventually—and inevitably—the latter ceased production.

The M2 appeared in 1958 and differed from the M3 mainly in the viewfinder and in the film counter and other minor features. The M1, produced in 1959, is similar to the M2, but has no rangefinder.

The MD, produced in 1965, is similar to the M1 and M2, but has no finder system at all (and no self-timer). A special feature is the provision of a slot for the insertion of lettering slides along one edge of the film opening. This permits automatic registration of reference data on the film during the exposure.

An intermediate version between the M3 and the M2 appeared in 1956 as the Leica MP. This was designed especially for Press photographers, providing increased speed of action with the Leicavit MP rapid-winding base plate.

The M4 in 1967 brought further innovations in the form of a greatly simplified quick loading system and a rewind crank in place of the traditional knob. This model takes over various features (such as the finder and the film counter) from both the M2 and the M3 which it will eventually replace.

The MDa of 1967 is an MD with the rapid loading facilities and rewind crank of the M4.

The basic concept of the Leica had always been that of a rangefinder camera, though certain models had no rangefinder. The Leicaflex, introduced in 1965, represented the first departure from this principle. The Leicaflex, a single-lens reflex camera with eye-level pentaprism finder, is thus a distinctly different camera type and is being produced parallel with the Leica M series. It is therefore described separately in this book.

The Accessories

The Leica interchangeable lenses developed parallel with the first cameras. Beginning with the Elmars of 35, 105, 90 and 135 mm., the range covered some ten lenses of focal lengths from 28 to 200 mm. by the early 1930s. Further lenses are still being added and existing ones replaced by improved ones of new design.

Since 1954—with the advent of the Leica M models—lenses appeared with either screw or bayonet mounts, for the two types of Leica camera.

Screw-mounted lenses continued to be available for a time even after the screw-mounted Leica camera series was discontinued. No screw-mounted lenses are produced any longer and the more recent Leica lens designs were never made available in a screw mount. But the tele-lenses of the Telyt range intended exclusively for use on the reflex housing come in a screw mount which does not fit the camera directly.

The Leicaflex also takes bayonet-mounted lenses, but with a different mount specification. This camera therefore has a different lens range designed specifically for it. Certain Leica M lenses and close-up units can be fitted on the Leicaflex with the aid of a special adapter ring.

As the number of lenses grew from the beginning, accessories of all types were produced at the same time to adapt the camera to a variety of purposes: the Leica camera became the Leica system.

The development is not complete even today; it goes on continuously in all directions. The multitude of 35 mm. miniature cameras that followed the Leica, and even imitated it, proved the soundness of the Leica method of photography. And although it was a pioneer, the Leica system is today still the most complete and versatile of its kind.

A WAY OF PHOTOGRAPHY

**Leica photography calls for careful picture taking and processing technique to get the most out of the small negatives.
With its versatility the Leica can, however, cover subjects and make use of opportunities which are outside the scope of any other type of camera.**

The pioneers of the Leica were obliged to experiment with numerous methods of exposure and development to overcome the inherent shortcomings of materials available at the time. Gradually they evolved a rational technique of miniature photography to make the best of the thirty-six tiny negatives on a strip of Leica film, and to obtain prints which could compare in quality with those from larger negatives.

Nowadays there is nothing unusual in using small negatives to produce larger prints. Modern photographic procedure in general has absorbed many of the methods evolved originally for miniature negatives. But they call for careful technique of picture taking and processing. The latitude of treatment we can tolerate with large cameras is much reduced when we deal exclusively with negatives which are no more than $1 \times 1\frac{1}{2}$ inches in size.

The Miniature Image

As Leica negatives will invariably be much enlarged to yield prints of an acceptable size, the image must be of the best possible quality.

The slightest unsharpness, usually invisible in the negative, shows up disturbingly as soon as we enlarge it some six or eight times—by no means uncommon for miniature shots. And if we think in terms of 12×15 inch prints, we have to look critically at our equipment as well as at our technique.

This demands first of all a high degree of mechanical and optical precision of the camera and lens. The film must be accurately positioned in the focal plane of the camera; a deviation of $\frac{1}{500}$ inch either way would seriously upset the definition of the image. Similarly, the focusing movement, the lens mounting, and the design of the lens itself must be perfected to the same standard of accuracy.

For successful miniature photography, therefore, we need a camera of the precision of the Leica.

The Miniature Film

The second point of importance is the film on which we produce the picture. When we enlarge the Leica negative some eight or ten times, we get a very close view of the image structure itself. Normally we see the detail of how the film builds up the picture only under a powerful magnifying glass. In Leica photography we are in fact doing just that all the time, and we are therefore operating near the limits of sharpness set by the grain and resolution of the film.

These two factors determine the smallness of the detail that the film will reproduce. With large negatives we rarely have to worry about either; they do not as a rule interfere with normal photography. To get the most out of a miniature negative we have to choose a film of sufficiently high resolving power and fine grain.

In addition, we must adjust our technique to make the best of the advantages of using a fine-grain film. This calls for accurate exposure; we cannot utilize the latitude which ordinary films have.

We have to be equally careful over processing. Miniature films other than the slowest need fine-grain development, preferably in special developers, to keep down the grain of the image. And the negative has to be correctly developed within comparatively fine limits, or we lose most of the advantages gained by miniature processing.

Handling miniature film also demands utmost cleanliness. Fingermarks, spots due to dust and chemicals, both in the camera and the enlarger, show up disturbingly when enlarged.

Miniature Technique

With a load of thirty-six exposures in the Leica, single processing and compensation for exposure errors are out of the question. Usually we develop the whole film in one. The individual exposures not only have to be correct, they have to suit the processing conditions—so accurate work is essential.

As a result, the technical side of miniature photography has grown into a standardized, and in a way scientific, way of producing pictures. There is little room for guesswork or rule-of-thumb methods; the whole process, from determining exposures to processing the film, becomes a more or less mechanical procedure.

All this has, however, tended to make miniature photography simpler rather than more complicated. It is considerably easier to follow a set of laid-down rules than to decide on the procedure from case to case.

The apparent difficulty of the miniaturist is to make up his mind which of a bewildering number of authoritatively recommended procedures he should adopt as his own method. That may be a matter of trial and error or of careful comparative testing. But once he has decided on a procedure, he can more or less regard it as settled once and for all.

There may be much controversy as to whether such an almost automatic technique is a good thing or not, but in fact it has come to stay. And for all its technicality, miniature photography has shifted its emphasis from the darkroom to the art of picture taking. With the Leica we can look at life.

The Miniature Camera

The chief tool of miniature photography, the Leica, is a miniature camera. While this makes, as we have seen, great demands on precision in construction, it has several advantages.

The Leica is always ready for action. Being small and handy, it is easily carried about and we can take pictures at a moment's notice. And by virtue of its design and range of accessories, the Leica could be made as versatile as required at any time.

One feature to widen its scope is the series of interchangeable Leica lenses. As the Leica negative only covers an area of 1½ square inches, we must utilize this area as fully as possible. By using different lenses we fully control the scale of the image even if we cannot go close enough to, or far enough away from, the subject.

Rangefinder and Reflex

While the Leica was the first commercially successful 35 mm. camera, it was also typical of its kind: the miniature with a direct-vision optical finder and (slightly later) rangefinder. In the meantime another miniature camera type evolved and grew immensely popular: the single-lens reflex with a swing-away mirror in the optical path. This diverts the light to a viewing screen which is observed via an eye-level finder system incorporating a pentaprism unit. This is the form which the Leicaflex takes.

This parallel development does, however, present a choice

between the two camera types which compete on different terms in different fields. The rangefinder Leica is particularly good at rapid focusing with short to medium long-focus lenses, while the Leicaflex reflex is best for accurate focusing and viewing at close range and with lenses of very long focal length. The accuracy of viewing with the Leicaflex is superior with all lenses and focal lengths. The finder image shows just what the film will record, irrespective of the lens used and of the subject distance. There is thus no parallax error, and no viewing error.

Focusing with the reflex camera is a little slower with lenses from about 35 to 135 mm. than with the rangefinder. On the reflex camera the eye has to judge changes from unsharp to sharp, while in the rangefinder it only has to observe the fusion of image outlines. And the latter is a more positive visual operation.

Reflex-camera focusing is more convenient where the rangefinder either ceases to become useful (below the near limit of the normal focusing range) or it is no longer sufficiently accurate—at longer distances where precise focusing becomes important with long-focus lenses. This is also why for these applications the reflex housing is recommended with the rangefinder Leica.

The rangefinder Leica is also more compact and lighter than the Leicaflex. The latter also needs special lens designs to accommodate the mirror movement of the Leicaflex between the lens and the film.

This a further result: In the Leicaflex the image disappears from the finder for a fraction of a second while the picture is being taken. In the rangefinder Leica the finder shows the picture all the time.

On the other hand with the reflex system, exposure measurement through the lens also becomes possible. This is used on the Leicaflex SL where part of the light going through the lens to the finder is deflected into a meter cell. We shall come back to that in due course.

Miniature Subjects

Getting back to the concept of the miniature camera, we may recall that the Leica (and the Leicaflex) is derived from the cine camera and uses the same size of film.

When in old-time photography the conventional camera user went after comparatively carefully arranged subjects, the

Leica can shoot almost on the run. What we see, we perceive instantly without much preparation. The miniature captures what it sees with equally few preliminaries.

Thus the Leica was the first champion of the candid picture. Its immediate readiness to shoot with the help of the comparatively great depth of field (p. 206) of the normal lenses and the rapid operation of the camera, makes it specially suitable for that kind of photography.

Admittedly, we have to allow for a certain amount of hit-and-miss shooting.

Like the cine camera, the Leica has to cover a slice of time, a series of instants instead of a single moment, and we can then select the best of a row of shots. In candid photography we don't secure pictures by ponderous preparation, and the film is cheap.

Miniature Limits

As an action camera, the Leica inevitably had to sacrifice some of the adjustability of more cumbersome apparatus.

This is the first limitation of the miniature. We can control the scale of the image but little else, and have to take the photograph as we see it, whether we like it or not.

The second limitation of the miniature camera is its image size. In the last resort the smallest image detail that the film can resolve or separate depends on the physical characteristics of the sensitive layer. The smaller the image, the smaller will be its finest detail. In the miniature image some of this detail will disappear when it would still be visible in a larger image.

We can partly overcome this drawback by using long-focus lenses where necessary to fill the negative with the subject.

The Miniature System

The Leica is above all a many-sided camera. It owes its versatility to the wide range of accessories which adapt the camera to a large number of specialized purposes.

To be more precise, we should say that the Leica outfits are adaptable. The camera itself is no more versatile than any other high-class amateur instrument. It is the combination of the Leica and its accessories which shows a certain systematic idea.

So let us have a closer look at this train of thought.

A SYSTEM OF EQUIPMENT

The Leica system is based on a precision camera with an immense range of lenses and accessories to adapt the basic instrument for many specialized purposes.

The Leica not only started a revolutionary method of photography; it also introduced a new system of equipment.

The Unit Principle

The principle of this system was to build up the photographic apparatus for any type of subject from a number of standardized units, each designed for a particular purpose. Instead of using a different kind of camera to cover each task, the Leica employs a different interchangeable component which is best suited to tackle the job in hand. Where portrait photography demanded a studio camera, and, for instance, copying a process camera, changing the lens and fitting close-up accessories converts the portrait Leica into a copying Leica.

The part that exposes the negative—the camera body—remains the same, but the part that produces a portrait image, or a close-up shot, changes. The components all fit together in the fashion of a Meccano set; different combinations of parts will add up to different sets of specialized tools for different jobs.

The idea of using accessories, or even interchangeable lenses, was, of course, not new when the Leica appeared. But the Leica developed it into a rational system of hitherto unknown magnitude. Other cameras soon followed both the Leica method of miniature photography and the Leica system of interchangeable equipment on the unit principle, but the Leica today still has the widest range of general and specialized accessories.

The Universal Camera

This unit principle has several important merits.

Firstly it is based on a comparatively simple camera with a general field of application. It holds the film, has normal provision for exposing it, but no special features to complicate handling. It remains thoroughly manageable.

Secondly, the Leica with its range of accessories can cover

LEICA EQUIPMENT

Flash equipment and similar gear enable the camera to tackle subjects under unfavourable conditions (p. 246).

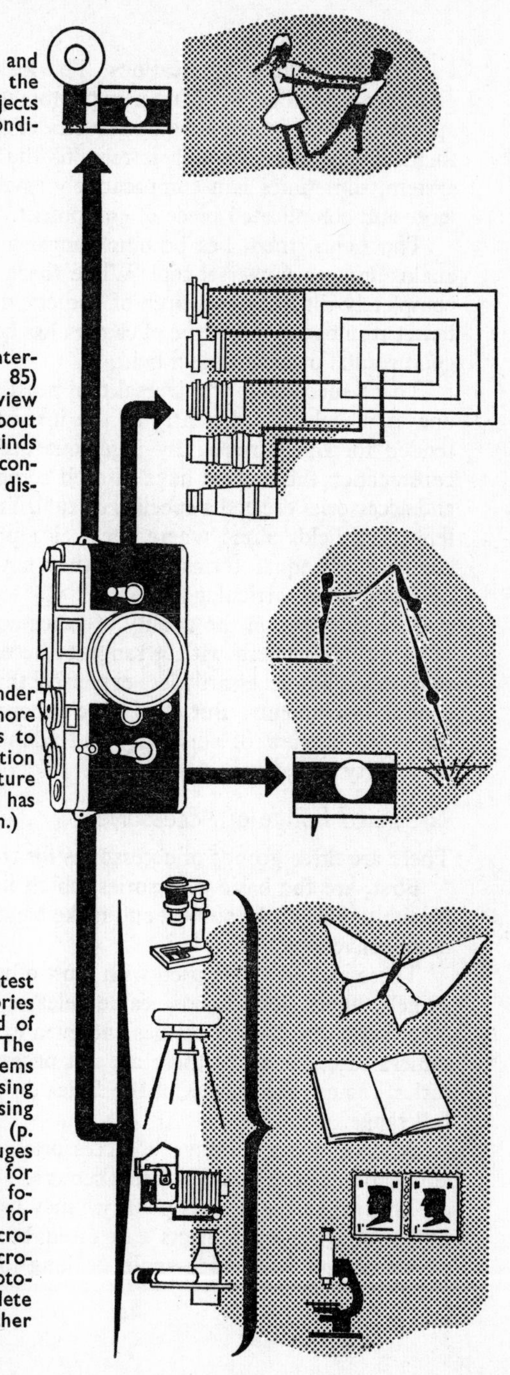

The wide range of interchangeable lenses (p. 85) will cover a field of view from 82° down to about 5°, for shots under all kinds of circumstances, in confined quarters, and for distant views.

The Leica rapid winder (p. 346)—and even more the motor—enables us to cope with quick-action sequences and picture series. (The Leica MP has its rapid winder built-in.)

Perhaps the greatest range of Leica accessories is devoted to the field of close-up photography. The equipment includes items like the close-up focusing mounts for near focusing with the rangefinder (p. 368), the distance gauges and extension tubes for copying (p. 364), the focusing bellows (p. 376) for various types of macrophotography, the micro-attachment for photomicrography and complete close-up outfits for other specialized tasks.

an immense field of applications. The makers have, in fact, endeavoured to deal with any new photographic problems that appeared by designing new accessories to adapt the Leica to them. The camera, though it remains the key to the whole system, sometimes is a comparatively small component in a large and complicated piece of equipment.

The Leica, then, has become almost a universal camera, analogous to a universal tool. While there are cases where a completely different principle of camera design might yield better results, no other type of camera has been able to achieve good results over so wide a field.

To be successful, a universal tool must be able to do any one of its jobs as efficiently as the instrument specially intended for the purpose. By ingenious design and precision construction the makers have in each combination of camera and accessories created a specialized tool. Yet they have wisely left those fields alone where the Leica principle could not compete on equal terms with other equipment expressly designed for a particular job.

As a sidelight on the quality of Leica equipment, the idea of using one camera with a range of accessories for special purposes is not necessarily less expensive than using a range of special instruments. But it is much more convenient from the point of view of versatility and adaptability, as well as portability and storage.

The Leica Range of Accessories

There are three groups of accessories for the Leica.

First, are the basic accessories which help to compensate for limitations of the subject and make handling of the camera more convenient.

These include items used with most other cameras as well, namely filters, lens hoods, cable releases, also tripods and other supports, camera cradles and even exposure meters and camera cases. Some of these are not necessarily Leitz accessories, though the makers of the Leica do provide almost the full range.

Second, are a number of accessories which extend the application of the unaided Leica camera.

Thus when the light is poor, we may use flash equipment. Different types of subjects can often be more successfully photographed with wide-angle or long-focus lenses (which have special viewfinders to go with them), and for sequence shots the rapid winder is useful.

The Visoflex reflex housing turns the Leica into a reflex camera. In conjunction with the Visoflex the current M models become almost as versatile as any other miniature reflex camera, with the added advantage of retaining the handier rangefinder operation whenever the subject calls for that.

Third, there are certain accessories which convert the Leica into a special-purpose camera for a particular type of task.

Some of these accessories are comparatively simple like the stereo system for three-dimensional photography, or the near focusing gear with extension tubes or supplementary lenses which can easily be fitted to the Leica for close-ups. With these the camera does not require much adaptation.

Other specialized accessories are more complex, and the camera becomes a minor—though still fundamental—part of a specialist outfit. Many of these outfits are largely used in scientific and medical photography, like the universal focusing bellows, the focusing stage, the Reprovit equipment for macrophotography and copying, or the micro attachment for photomicrography.

Some of these fields require a highly specialized photographic technique, and often the Leica becomes just an accessory of the scientific instrument used.

The Leicaflex Range of Accessories

While the Leica camera contains only the basic elements for general photography and uses accessories for everything else, the Leicaflex is a more flexible instrument requiring fewer specialized accessories. Thus the reflex system does away with the need for a reflex housing or special finders for close-up and telephotography. The Leicaflex lenses themselves have an extended focusing range with a nearer focusing limit for close-ups. This also makes the basic camera a little bigger.

The more basic accessories have their equivalents in the Leicaflex system. The latter can also use certain Leica lenses.

To help in ordering, all Leica cameras, lenses, accessories and other pieces of equipment for many years used to have a code word. Nowadays this is replaced by a catalogue number, but some items became so well known by their code word that the latter was more characteristic than the description of the accessory itself. Whenever applicable, such items will therefore still be referred to by this code word in the text.

THE LEICA ITSELF

The current Leica models feature interchangeable lenses, a flash-synchronized focal plane shutter with speeds from 1 to 1/1000 second, built-in coupled rangefinder, and coupled film wind and shutter tensioning.

Having examined the Leica system of equipment, let us turn to the cameras in particular and see exactly how they work.

The Leica Models

We can find the principle of the Leica system of equipment already in the construction of the camera itself.

There is a basic body which is common to the current Leica models and contains the shutter and film transport mechanism. Not only the lenses and outside accessories but also some of the built-in features like the rangefinder, self-timer, etc., are extensions of this basic body. They are absent, for instance, in the Leica M1 or MD, but can be built in subsequently. That then converts the M1 into an M2, with the cost of conversion being merely the difference between the list prices of the two models.

Within each range (the current bayonet-mount types and the earlier screw-mount models) the differences are systematic rather than design variations. That means that within each range all accessories fit nearly all models. Moreover, certain accessories for the screw-mount models are still available; so Leica owners who bought their camera thirty years ago can utilize nearly all the latest accessories and in this way keep up to date.

These are the current models of the Leica range:

Leica M2.—Introduced in 1958, this model has the Leica body with a focal plane shutter providing speeds from 1 to 1/1000 second and B. It has an automatically coupled film-transport and film-winding mechanism, operated by a single lever. It takes all the interchangeable lenses with the quick-change bayonet mount. All shutter speeds are set on a single knob which can be coupled with the Leicameter MR (as well as the MC or M) exposure meter (p. 221). The Leica M2 further has a coupled rangefinder combined with the view-finder. The latter shows reflected image frames for the 35, 50 and 90 mm. lenses. The image frames are individually selected on inserting the appropriate lens in the camera. Alternatively, a special selector lever brings the required image frame into view, even when the standard lens is fitted on the camera. The rangefinder field also incorporates a visual depth of field indicator.

The camera is loaded from the base, but the camera back opens to make loading easier. The camera is synchronized for flash photography at all shutter speeds. The Leica M2 is available either with the metal parts finished in chrome or black enamel. The latter version is popular with press and feature photographers who prefer to have their camera looking less conspicuous.

Current models of the M2 have also a built-in self-timer; earlier models did not have this, but the self-timer can be fitted subsequently. An M2 model without self-timer was marketed in the U.S.A. as the model M2s.

Leica M3.—This original model in the M range first appeared in 1954, and underwent slight modifications later. The viewfinder is different from the M2, giving a larger full-size image with individually selectable field frames for 50, 90, and 135 mm. lenses. The M3 also has a self-timer and a different film counter which resets itself automatically on loading. The Leica M3 is again available in chrome or black finish. Early models of the M3 had no finder frame selector lever, and the film-transport lever required two strokes instead of one to advance the film by one frame.

Leica M4.—Appearing in 1967, this is scheduled to be the standard M model. Its main improvement over the previous versions is a greatly simplified loading system with a built in take-up spool which obviates all film threading. The Leica M4 thus follows the current trend to easy loading systems using standard 35 mm. cassettes. The rewind knob is replaced by a crank. The viewfinder is similar to that of the M2, but indicates the image field for the 135 mm. lenses as well as focal lengths of 35, 50 and 90 mm. The film counter resets itself automatically on opening the base plate. Minor changes are in the finish of some of the operating levers including the winding lever.

Leica MD.—This is a model introduced in 1965 for certain fields of scientific photography where the camera is used exclusively with a reflex housing or on a microscope. The MD therefore has no viewfinder or rangefinder at all (and obviously no finder frame selector), nor a self-timer. All mechanical

LEICA M4 CONTROLS

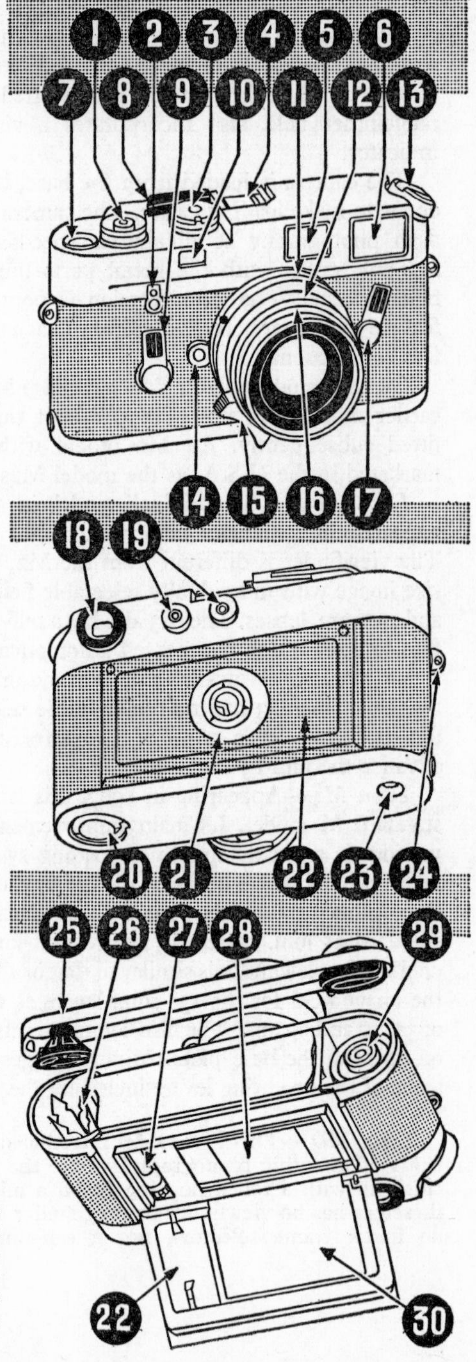

1. Release button.
2. Reversing lever.
3. Shutter speed dial.
4. Accessory shoe.
5. Illuminating window for finder frames.
6. Viewfinder window.
7. Film counter.
8. Transport lever with hinged tip.
9. Self-timer lever.
10. Rangefinder window.
11. Bayonet lens mount.
12. Distance and depth of field scales.
13. Rewind crank.
14. Lock of bayonet lens mount.
15. Focusing lever.
16. Aperture ring.
17. Selector lever for viewfinder frames.
18. Finder eyepiece.
19. Flash sockets (co-axial type) for electronic flash and bulbs.
20. Base plate lock.
21. Film type indicator.
22. Camera back.
23. Tripod bush.
24. Eyelet for carrying strap.
25. Retaining flange for quick loading take-up core, built into base plate.
26. Rapid loading take-up spool core.
27. Transport sprocket.
28. Film aperture.
29. Film cassette.
30. Film pressure plate.

The Leica MDa is similar in appearance and features but does not have a range-finder, viewfinder, self-timer or finder frame selector lever (items 10, 5, 6, 18, 9 and 17).

LEICA M3 CONTROLS

1. Release button.
2. Reversing button.
3. Shutter speed dial.
4. Accessory shoe.
5. Illuminating window for finder frames.
6. Viewfinder window.
7. Film counter.
8. Transport lever.
9. Self-timer.
10. Rangefinder window.
11. Bayonet lens mount.
12. Distance and depth of field scales.
13. Rewind knob.
14. Lock of bayonet lens mount.
15. Focusing lever.
16. Aperture ring.
17. Selector lever for viewfinder frames.
18. Finder eyepiece.
19. Flash sockets for electronic flash and bulbs.
20. Eyelet for carrying strap.
21. Base plate lock.
22. Film indicator.
23. Camera back.
24. Tripod bush.
25. Take-up spool.
26. Transport sprocket.
27. Film track.
28. Film cassette.
29. Film pressure plate.

The Leica M2, MD and M1 are similar in appearance to the M3, with the following features changed:

5, 6, and 18. The Leica MD has no finder system.

7. Film counter: manually set disc underneath transport lever on MD, M1 and M2.

8. Self-timer absent on MD, M1 and early models of M2 (but can be fitted).

10. The rangefinder is absent on the MD and M1.

14. Lock of bayonet mount simpler in appearance (but identical in action) on MD, M1 and M2.

17. Selector lever for viewfinder frames missing on Leica MD and M1 (35 and 50 mm. finder frames permanently reflected in finder of M1).

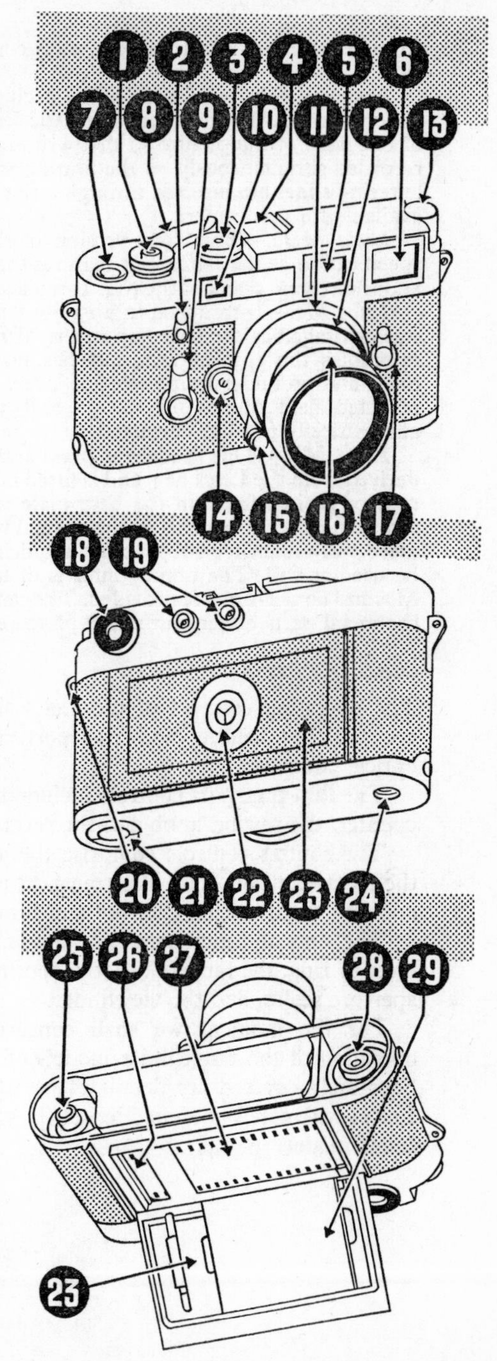

features (shutter, film transport, etc.) correspond to the Leica M2.

A special feature of the MD is a channel in the film path which permits the insertion of plastic lettering slides in front of one edge of the picture so that written reference data can be recorded simultaneously on the film during an exposure. These lettering slides are inserted through a slot in a special baseboard available for this camera.

Lecia MDa.—This 1967 version of the MD has the same specification as the latter, but features the rapid loading system and the rewind crank of the M4. It replaces the MD.

Leica M1.—Introduced in 1959, but now discontinued, this was envisaged as the first step in the M range. The M1 closely resembles the current M2, but has no rangefinder, no self-timer and no finder frame selector lever. The viewfinder shows reflected field frames for the 35 and 50 mm. lenses and is automatically parallax corrected.

Leica MP.—This model for press and news photography is derived from the Leica M3, and is fitted normally with a Leicavit type of rapid winder in the base plate for maximum speed of film transport. Either this or the normal winding lever (which is more convenient for subjects not requiring fast sequences) can be used at will. The film counter is of the same design as the M2, and no self-timer is provided. The camera was available with the metal parts either chromium plated or enamelled black.

Leica Operation

The operating controls of the Leica fall into three general groups: film loading and transport, the shutter, and the optical controls.

The film transport controls include the transport, the film counter, the rewind knob and the reversing lever.

The shutter controls comprise the speed setting dial and the release button. The film transport tensions the shutter in addition to advancing the film and film counter.

The optical components are the lens itself, the focusing lever or ring, the rangefinder, the depth of field, distance, and aperture scales, and the viewfinder.

For the moment we shall concern ourselves with the operation of the rangefinder models of the current M series. Separately covered are details of manipulation of the earlier Leicas with screw-mounted lenses (p. 57) and of the Leicaflex reflex models (p. 148).

HANDLING THE LEICA

Learn how to operate the Leica until it becomes second nature.
Carry the camera in its ever-ready case to protect it, yet keep it instantly ready for action.
Practise holding the Leica perfectly steady, both for horizontal and vertical pictures.

The Leica is a delicate piece of machinery. Ignorant use may damage it, and will certainly waste film.

Therefore learn how to handle the Leica: how to hold it and how to shoot with it. This is far from difficult; despite its complicated construction the Leica is almost fool-proof.

Practise working the camera until all its operations become almost second nature. Then load it (p. 72) and simply go out to take pictures.

Carrying the Camera

Modern Leica models are fitted with eyelets at the ends of the body, to take a carrying strap. This allows the camera to be carried round the neck or over the shoulder.

The safest type of strap attaches to the eyelets via a split ring, hanging directly in a loop of the leather strap. Spring hooks with metal swivels look more elegant, but easily break.

When not in use, cover the lens with the lens cap for protection against injury.

The Ever-Ready Case

For normal use, carry the Leica in an ever-ready case. This protects the camera against all the everyday knocks and shocks which would in time mark the body. It also helps to keep out dust, dirt, and even occasional rain. If the Leica should ever be accidentally dropped, it will be less likely to suffer serious damage inside a case.

The Leica can remain in its case for shooting from the hand. To open the lid, simply pull off the flap from the press stud at the back, and fold down the top and front, exposing the lens and all the controls. The only time the camera has to be removed is for loading and unloading, or when the Leica is to be used with some of the specialized accessories.

On the other hand, the ever-ready case is not always as ready as its name implies. In particular it makes the camera more bulky to hold and slows down operation if we want to shoot fast-action sequences. So it is always useful to have the separate carrying strap. Then, before a shooting session, take the camera out of its case and hang it round the neck by the strap. That really does keep it ready at an instant's notice. But use it in the case for occasional shots where the greater handiness of the camera without its case is not so vital.

To fit the Leica into the case, open the lid, insert the camera and fasten by screwing in the tripod screw attached to the case. This prevents the camera from falling out. The Leica, together with the case, may even be mounted firmly on a tripod since the tripod screw of the case itself carries a tripod bush. To remove the camera, unscrew the tripod screw on the bottom of the case.

There are various types of ever-ready cases. When a more comprehensive Leica outfit has to be carried, a holdall case or gadget bag is useful (p. 147).

When carrying the camera in its ever-ready case adjust the neck strap so that the camera lies comfortably on the chest, either with the strap going round the neck only or going under one arm and over the other shoulder (p. 36). Avoid carrying the Leica hanging behind the hip; in that position it is not so easy to bring up for shooting, and it is much more easily stolen in a crowd.

Special soft cases are also available for the Leica, to provide protection of the camera while it is carried, yet to leave it unencumbered for shooting.

Holding the Leica

Apart from focusing, an absolutely steady hold of the camera during the exposure is important for sharp results. Camera movement or shake while taking the picture spoils more negatives than any other single fault.

The correct way of holding the Leica is therefore the one which allows the camera to be held as steadily as possible yet with the maximum comfort. To some extent this will depend on personal preference and the size of one's hands.

There are several good ways of supporting the Leica, both orthodox and unorthodox. Whichever is chosen, with or without individual modifications, practise it and keep releasing the shutter (with the camera empty) until the Leica is really steady during the exposure.

LEICA HOLDS

The standard hold uses the right index finger to release, and the left index finger to work the focusing lever.

With long-focus lenses which have no focusing lever but a ring this has to be modified. One method is to work the focusing ring with the tips of the second finger of the left hand and the second or third finger of the right hand.

Alternatively, grip the focusing mount with the left hand.

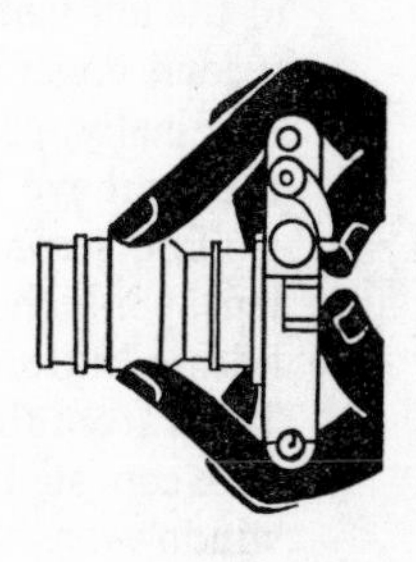

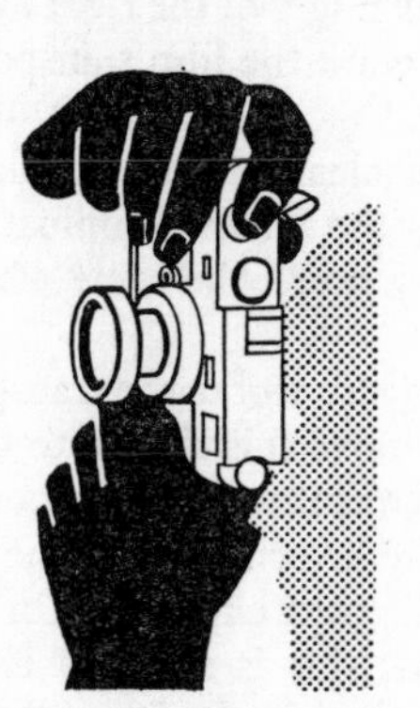

For vertical shots there are two alternatives. One uses the right thumb to press the release and support the weight of the camera.

The other vertical hold is derived from the standard horizontal position, by bringing the right hand up and the left hand down.

When holding the Leica in its ever-ready case for vertical shots, swing the flap of the case downwards so that it is out of the way and cannot swing in front of the lens.

To advance the film move the thumb up to the transport lever and swing the latter out all the way.

(Avoid touching the rewind crank on the M4 while advancing the film.)

Horizontal Shots

Place the right hand round the right-hand end of the camera body (i.e. the end carrying the winding lever), with the thumb pointing diagonally across the back to the accessory shoe. Curl the index finger over the top of the body and rest it on the release button. The second and third fingers, bent at right-angles, press against the front of the body. The bottom right-hand end should fit snugly into the palm of the right hand.

Place the thumb of the left hand across the camera back to meet the right thumb, and press the left index finger, bent at right-angles, against the camera front. Tuck the third finger of the left hand underneath the base plate, and stretch out the second finger so that its tip rests on the focusing lever.

Finally, press the left hand against the right cheek, so that the right eye is opposite the finder eyepiece.

The second finger of the left hand therefore focuses the lens, while the index finger of the right hand is free to press the release button and work the film transport without taking the Leica from the eye.

Keep all fingers clear of the viewfinder and rangefinder windows, as well as the finder-illuminating window.

This hold is very much the same when the Leica is in its ever-ready case.

The right thumb also works the transport lever. After every exposure therefore move this thumb to the right and push the transport lever as far as it will go. On current Leica M models one full swing of the lever advances the film and tensions the shutter ready for the next exposure. On early M3 models two swings are required; this is slightly slower, but only a little less convenient. On the M4 also keep all fingers of the left hand clear of the rewind crank while advancing the film.

The transport lever also has a very short "dead" movement. That is to say, it really starts operating the mechanism only when it has swung out by about ½ inch from its rest position. The purpose of this is to give a better grip on the lever while shooting sequences.

Alternatives

Several modifications are possible.

With the Leica M1, which has no rangefinder, the lens has to be set to the right distance beforehand. When exposing, therefore, tuck the second finger underneath the lens mount.

With longer-focus lenses which have no focusing lever press the tips of the second finger of the left hand and the third finger of the right hand against the milled focusing ring, and rotate the latter with these two fingers.

Alternatively, grip the focusing mount with the left thumb and index finger (bent double) and focus that way. The left-hand end (i.e. that carrying the rewind knob) of the Leica then rests with the base plate against the ball of the left hand and the camera back is pressed directly against the right cheek.

Some people may prefer to use their left eye for viewing. In that case the nose is best placed underneath the angle formed by the two thumbs in the middle of the camera back as described before.

Another possible hold for the left hand is to press the left thumb against the end of the camera body, with the second finger supporting the Leica from underneath. The left index finger is then free to work the focusing lever. This method is quite useful for fairly distant subjects and is also easy for changing over from horizontal to vertical shots. For close-ups the position of the focusing lever is not so convenient. It does not work with long-focus lenses, which are not fitted with a focusing lever.

With the Leica MP the left hand supports the camera and grips the rapid winder in the baseplate. Pulling the lever fully from the right to left advances the film by one frame. If this winder is folded away, the camera is, of course, held normally.

Vertical Shots

For vertical pictures there are two alternative ways of holding the Leica, depending on personal preference.

With the first method the right hand supports the transport end of the Leica from underneath. Bend back the second and third fingers and support the camera on the second finger. The right index finger goes across the camera front, and the thumb bears against the release button. To advance the film and tension the shutter, the right thumb then reaches over to the transport lever and pulls it down as far as it will go. It may be desirable to lift the camera away from the face slightly while doing this.

The left thumb and index finger grip the left-hand or rewind end of the camera, with the second finger on the focusing lever. The camera back is pressed against the nose and forehead to steady it, so that the right eye is behind the eyepiece.

When using long-focus lenses without a focusing lever, grip the focusing mount with the thumb and second fingers of the left hand, and use the left index finger to press the camera against the forehead. Keep all fingers clear of the rewind crank on the M4 while advancing the film.

If the use of the left eye is preferred for focusing and viewing, press the camera against the left cheek.

The above method and its variation are equally good with the camera in its ever-ready case, or with accessory viewfinders. When using the ever-ready case for vertical shots swing the lid round so that it hangs down out of the way of the lens.

Another Way

The alternative vertical position may be more suitable for people with small hands.

Grip the camera with the right hand as for horizontal shots: thumb across the back, second and third fingers against the front, and index finger on the release button.

Turn the camera vertical, and support it against the left thumb, or, if more convenient, against the ball of the left hand with the thumb across the top of the rangefinder. The second and third fingers of the left hand help to grip the Leica, while the index finger works the focusing lever.

Press the left thumb against the forehead, and the wrist of the left hand against the chin to steady the camera. Use the left eye for viewing and focusing.

The grip is much the same again with the camera in its ever-ready case. As before, the third and last fingers of the left hand hold the lid out of the way of the lens.

With long-focus lenses, support the rewind end of the camera on the palm of the left hand, and turn the focusing mount with the left thumb and index finger. But keep the fingers clear of the viewfinder and rangefinder windows.

Using the Camera Strap

Often the strap of the ever-ready case will provide an additional means of steadying the camera.

The strap is adjustable; shorten it sufficiently to give just enough room to get the head and the left arm comfortably through the loop. When carrying the camera it should lie

STANDS AND SUPPORTS

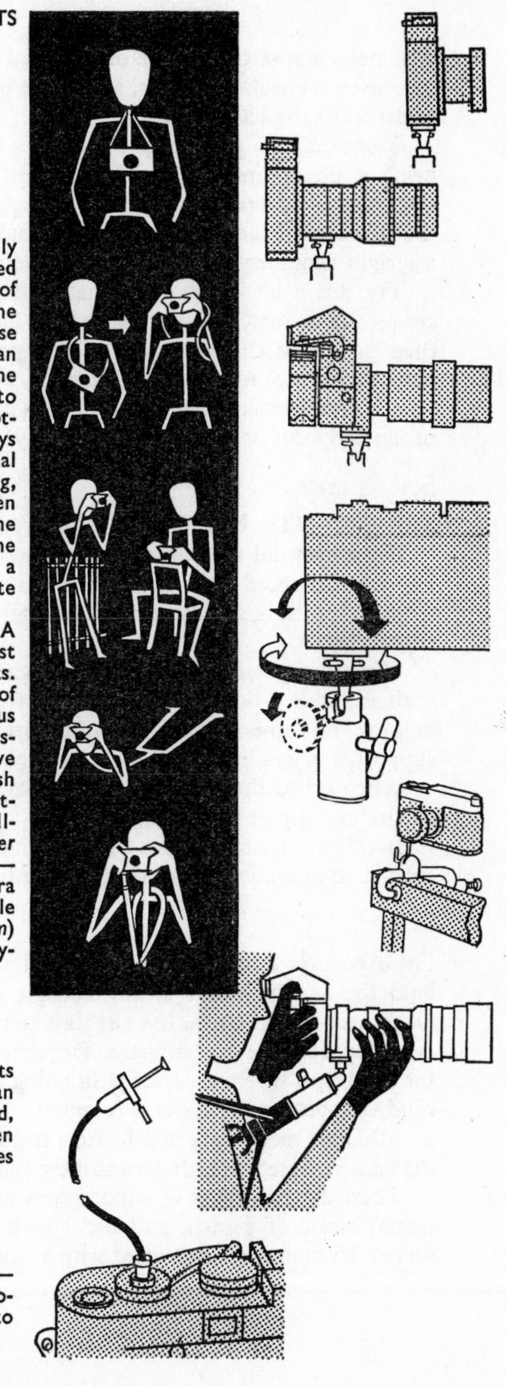

Black panel: Normally the Leica is best carried round the neck by means of the camera strap or the strap of the ever-ready case (*top*). The camera strap can also be used to steady the camera (*upper centre*) and to bring it quickly into shooting position (p. 36). Always look round for additional supports—a fence, railing, tree, wall, chair, or even the ground—to steady the camera (*lower centre*). The unipod may serve as a useful tripod substitute (*bottom*).

Right-hand column: A tripod is one of the most versatile camera supports. It screws into the bush of the Leica (*top*). Long focus lenses and the reflex housing (*upper centre*) have their own tripod bush to balance the camera set-up more evenly. A ball-and-socket head (*lower centre*) makes levelling—or angling—of the camera more convenient, while the camera clamp (*bottom*) fixes the Leica almost anywhere (p. 40).

The table tripod with its ball-and-socket head can also serve as a chestpod, steadying the camera when used with long-focus lenses (p 40).

The cable release—essential for time exposures (p. 44)—screws into the release button.

diagonally across the middle of the chest with the strap running over the right shoulder, across the back, and coming up underneath the left armpit.

When taking a picture, grip the Leica with the right hand, bring it up to the eye, and bring up the left hand. While holding the camera, press the left hand against the strap, and the face against the camera back. This tightens the strap from the right shoulder to the left armpit and steadies the camera.

Try this a few times first, lengthening or shortening the strap as necessary. Getting the camera into shooting position then takes less than a second. Some people may prefer to hang the camera over the left shoulder, working in reverse.

A carrying strap fixed directly to the camera by the eyelets in the body can be used in the same way.

Body Stance

The stance of the body is equally important.

For horizontal shots, tuck both elbows well into the body. For vertical shots press the arm which supports the camera from underneath, against the body. Stand with the feet placed slightly apart.

Whenever possible lean the body against something firm, such as a wall, a door, a lamp-post or a tree. A further help to holding the camera steady is to prop up the elbows on some support, e.g. a railing, wall, a table, or even the arms of a chair.

When sitting down on the floor, the knees can often provide a suitable support for the elbows.

In this way sharp pictures without camera shake are possible even at comparatively slow shutter speeds.

Tripods

For exposures longer than 1/30 second it is rarely possible to hold the camera really steady enough in the hand. When using long-focus lenses, the slightest camera movement produces appreciable unsharpness. For time exposures and also for close-ups, where accurate positioning is important, a really rigid support for the Leica is essential.

All Leica models are fitted with a tripod bush at the end of the camera base plate, underneath the film transport.

There are two types of tripod screw and bush: the Continental screw of $\frac{3}{8}$ inch, and the $\frac{1}{4}$ inch English Whitworth screw. To mount a Leica fitted with a Continental bush on an

English tripod or vice versa, suitable adapters may be used. Some tripods have reversible heads with both Continental and English screws.

The smaller and lighter the tripod, the less firm it is likely to be. Generally a normal folding tripod is quite satisfactory for the Leica with standard lenses. With long-focus lenses, and especially with the reflex housing, a much heavier tripod is necessary to keep the camera steady.

To set up the Leica, thread the screw of the tripod into the bush on the camera, and extend the legs of the tripod to the required height. The camera may be levelled by moving one of the tripod legs in or out, or sideways.

A ball-and-socket head which is screwed between the tripod and the camera makes the levelling of the camera even easier. It also allows the lens to be tilted in any direction, or even pointed vertically downwards.

The Leitz heavy-duty ball-and-socket head (No. 14121) holds the camera rigidly at any angle. To mount the camera, slack off the large wing locking nut and turn the camera plate with the tripod screw to screw it firmly into the camera bush. Then line up the camera (with the ball-and-socket head mounted on the tripod) in the required direction and tighten the wing nut to lock the head in place. The camera can even point vertically up or down.

The Leitz ball-and-socket head has reversible threads at both ends, accessible on unscrewing the milled rings at the top and bottom.

The ball-and-socket head can also be used on the Leitz table tripod when a reasonably flat solid surface is available on which to stand it. Ball-and-socket heads and table tripods of other makes can also be used, provided they are firm enough.

With the heavy long-focus lenses the strain on the tripod bush at the end of the Leica would be too heavy as the camera becomes unbalanced. These lenses (e.g. the 135 mm. Elmarit) therefore carry their own tripod bush which should be used in place of the camera bush. For the same reason the reflex housing used with the Telyt lenses or certain close-up gear has its separate tripod bush.

To improve the balance of the camera on the tripod even with the normal lens there are several camera cradles (not made by Leitz). These consist of a U-shaped casting, velvet lined inside, which takes the camera body, holding it in position by means of a movable clamp. The cradles have tripod bushes in the middle of the base and also in one side, to hold the Leica horizontally or vertically.

Emergency Supports

Where the use of a tripod is not practicable we can still considerably steady the camera by means of a unipod or chestpod.

The unipod is a single leg which screws into the tripod bush, and supports, but does not hold, the camera on the ground.

The chestpod is a short unipod (most unipods are collapsible and can be used as a chestpod) which supports the camera against the user's chest. Sometimes the leg of the chestpod may fit into a special leather cup held in place on the chest by a neck strap.

The Leitz table tripod with the ball-and-socket head also makes a useful chestpod. The table tripod consists of three swivelling legs which rotate around the central stem. To open it up, slack off the nut at the bottom and bring the legs out at approximately 60 deg. to each other, then tighten the nut. Mount the ball-and-socket head on the table tripod, and the camera on the head. Brace the table tripod against your chest, and adjust the camera position so that you can comfortably view through the finder (or reflex housing if used). The right hand, holding on to the winding lever and the release button, now steadies the camera while the left hand rotates the focusing mount of the lens. If you lean against a wall, tree or similar support while shooting, hand-held and comparatively shake-free exposures of $\frac{1}{15}$ and even $\frac{1}{8}$ second are perfectly feasible in this way.

When using this arrangement for direct viewing through the Leica finder it is usually more convenient to view with the right eye.

Camera clamps are also made which clamp on to suitable chair backs, doors, fences, and the like. The clamps carry tripod screws, and may be used in conjunction with a ball-and-socket head to level or incline the camera in any direction.

Yet another method is to use a chain or loop of string hanging down from a screw screwed into the tripod bush. In use, step on the bottom end of the chain, and pull the Leica upwards against the chain to steady it.

THE LEICA M CONTROLS

The aperture, set on the lens, controls the amount of light passing through. The shutter controls the time for which the light is admitted to the film.
The rangefinder determines the subject distance, and is coupled with the lens focusing movement.

To take a picture with the Leica, first pull out the lens if it is collapsible. Check by the film transport whether the shutter is tensioned.

Next set the lens aperture and the shutter speed to produce the required exposure.

Then focus the subject through the rangefinder or set the distance. Check the view in the viewfinder and press the shutter release to take the picture.

Finally, wind on the film ready for the next exposure.

These are all perfectly simple and straightforward operations and should not take longer than a few seconds. But let us look at them in detail.

Setting the Aperture

The Leica lenses are all fitted with an adjustable iris diaphragm which controls the aperture of the lens. It thus regulates the amount of light passing through the lens. Each number on the aperture scale corresponds to a greater or lesser amount of light. The numbers are arranged in such a way that changing from any one aperture figure (or stop) to the next higher number halves the amount of light coming through the lens. In reducing the aperture we are said to be "stopping down" the lens. Similarly, going from any one aperture to the next lower number doubles the light that the lens can pass (p. 214). The lowest aperture figure (largest lens opening) marked on the lens is sometimes an exception to this rule. The aperture also affects the depth of field (p. 206).

To set the aperture, turn the milled ring nearest the front of the lens until the index line or a red dot points to the required number.

Most modern Leica lenses have click stops; the aperture ring clicks into place at each setting (spaced out on a linear scale), allowing the aperture to be adjusted by touch only.

A few of the Leica lenses are collapsible (for example the 50 mm. Elmar *f*2.8 and one version of the 90 mm. Elmar *f*4).

To get the lens ready for use pull out the lens barrel by its front ring as far as it will go and then turn a little to the right to engage the lock. To collapse the lens, turn the barrel slightly anti-clockwise and push it back into the body.

Before shooting also remember to remove the lens cap (keep it on the lens when the camera is not in use).

The Shutter

The Leica cameras have a focal plane shutter, consisting of two rubberized cloth blinds which pass close to the film.

On pressing the shutter release button, the first blind starts to uncover the film, and, after it has travelled a certain distance, the second blind follows and covers up the film again. In effect, the two blinds form a slit which travels across the film plane, exposing the negative in strips from end to end.

The point at which the second blind is released, and the width of the slit thereby formed, determines the time for which the negative is exposed.

If the second blind starts to move 1/60 second later than the first one, and therefore covers each point of the film 1/60 second after the first blind has uncovered it, the effective exposure time becomes 1/60 second. If the second blind starts 1/500 second later than the first one, the effective slit is much narrower, and the time will only be 1/500 second.

In practice, the exposure time depends both on the speed with which the blinds move, and on the distance between them. The speed of the blinds is the same for all shutter speeds. However, towards the end of their travel the blinds, which are spring driven, accelerate. This would mean that the blind would pass the last portion of the film appreciably faster than the first, and that part of the negative as a result would receive less exposure.

For this reason the separation between the two blinds on current Leica models increases as the shutter runs down to compensate for the loss of light.

The rollers carrying the blind move in ball bearings to make the action of the shutter as smooth as possible.

Setting the Shutter Speeds

The shutter speed setting dial on top of the Leica—next to the release button—controls the distance between the blinds.

The shutter speed dial carries a series of figures corresponding to the exposure times. The figures are: 1000, 500, 250, 125, 60, 30, 15, 8, 4, 2, 1 (early M3 models: 1000, 500, 250, 100,

M SHOOTING DRILL

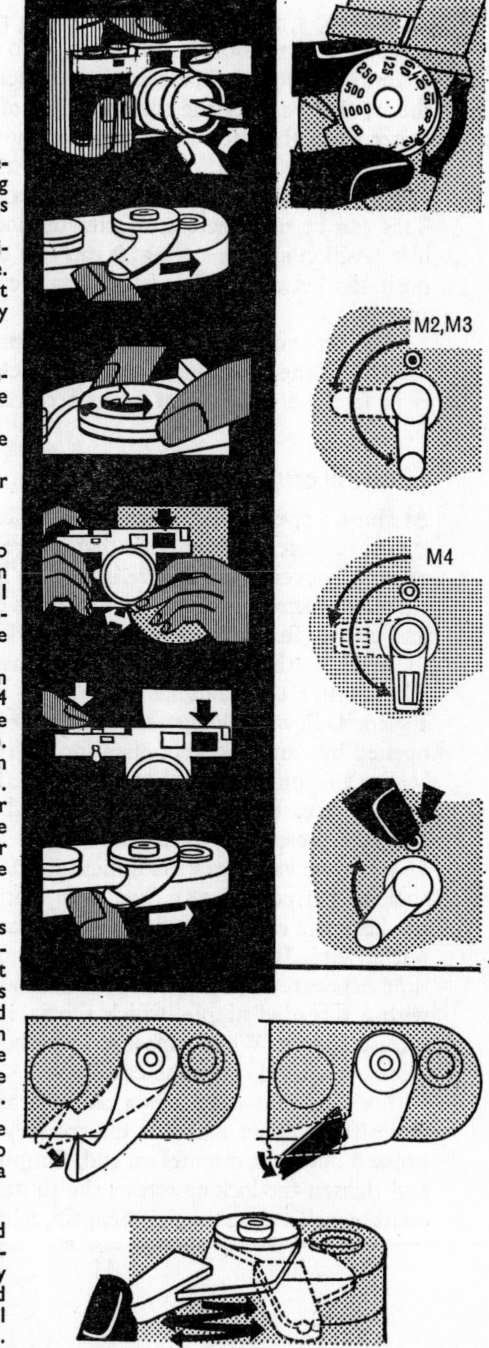

Black panel: The sequence of picture taking with the Leica M models is (*from top to bottom*):

Pull out lens (if collapsible) and set the aperture.

Wind the transport lever (if not already wound).

Set the shutter speed.

Focus by the rangefinder (on the MI set the distance by hand).

View the subject in the finder and expose.

Pull the transport lever to advance the film.

Right-hand column: To set the shutter (*top*) turn the shutter speed dial until the required speed is opposite the index mark on the accessory shoe.

For delayed action shots, on the M2 to M4 pull down the lever on the front of the camera (*centre*). Then press the button above the lever (*bottom*). The shutter will go off after about 10 seconds with the lever fully pulled down, or after 5 seconds with the lever horizontal (*dotted*).

The transport lever has two positions. In its working position it sticks out towards the back and is then easily worked to and fro. In its rest position (*dotted*) it lies against the shutter speed dial to make the camera more compact.

On the M4 (*right*) the plastic tip of the lever also swivels outwards to give a better grip.

To advance the film and wind the shutter the transport lever has to be fully pulled to the right and allowed to fly back. Several short strokes will also do.

50, 25, 10, 5, 2, 1), and B. The figures represent fractions of a second; thus 1000 stands for 1/1000 second, 60 for 1/60 second, and so on. There is also a notch between the 2 and the 4; this engages the setting wheel of the Leica exposure meter when the latter is mounted on the camera (p. 221).

To set the speed, turn the dial till the required figure is opposite the line engraved at the side of the accessory shoe. This can be done before or after tensioning. The dial clicks into position at each setting; it can also be set to intermediate positions between 1/60 and 1/1000 second for intermediate speeds.

The broken arrow mark (like a lightning symbol) between the 30 and the 60 settings serves for electronic flash shots (and is in fact the setting that ensures correct synchronization—p. 258).

Time Exposures

At shutter speeds of 1/30 second and slower (in other words exposure times longer than that figure) the shutter blinds open fully every time. There is thus no longer a question of a slit moving across the film; the first blind opens, and the second one closes after an appropriate delay. The latter depends on the speed setting and is controlled by the built-in mechanism. The shutter thus automatically times exposures as long as 1 second. For still longer exposure times the shutter must be opened by hand and kept open for the required time.

For this purpose set the shutter speed dial to B. On pressing the release button, the shutter will open and stay open until the pressure is removed.

For time exposures the camera must be on a firm support such as a tripod (p. 38). Such a support, however, still does not keep the camera steady enough when pressing the release button directly on the Leica. So always use a cable release for time exposures. The Leica M models take a standard release, with a threaded nipple, which screws into the centre of the release button. When exposing keep the release slack; a taut release may still shake the camera.

For long time exposures a cable release with locking screw is desirable. That makes it unnecessary to keep the plunger pressed down for minutes on end. Simply depress the plunger and tighten the locking screw; the shutter then remains open on its own. To close the shutter again, release the locking screw.

The longer the cable release, the less the risk of camera shake; 12 to 18 inches is a good length.

Viewing Through the Finder

A view through the eyepiece at the rear of the camera shows the subject field taken in. The image is the right way round and the actual picture area recorded on the film is outlined by a white optical frame image which appears to float in space.

When viewing, keep the eye close to, and straight behind, the eyepiece. Even when viewing at an angle the image frame still outlines the correct field of view, but the whole frame will not then be visible.

The finder frame visible in the Leica M2 to M4 viewfinder with the 50 mm. lens in place corresponds to the view of that lens. On fitting instead a 90 mm. lens, a smaller frame appears to show the reduced field of view of the long-focus lens (see also p. 47). Yet another finder frame can be brought into view with a further focal length. This, however, differs with the various Leica M models.

With the Leica M2 and M4 the brilliant frame for the 50 mm. lens disappears on fitting a 90 mm. or a 35 mm. wide-angle lens. In the first case a smaller frame appears to take in the 90 mm. view, and in the second case a larger frame shows the field taken in by the wide-angle lenses. This frame also appears on fitting a 135 mm. lens, and on the M4 small corner marks in the centre of the image show the field of the 135 mm. lens. The viewfinder itself shows the whole field of view in about three-quarters visual size. In other words, objects in the finder appear about 25 per cent smaller than they do on looking directly at the scene with the unaided eye (for example on glancing over the top of the camera). For lenses of other focal lengths special finders are required.

The Leica M3 shows the finder view in virtually natural size. There the scene through the finder appears in more or less the same scale as seen directly. The three focal lengths accommodated by the finder are here 50, 90, and 135 mm. The finder frame for the 50 mm. lens remains visible all the time; the reduced frame for the appropriate long-focus lens appears in addition.

To obtain the correct view with a 35 mm. wide-angle lens on the Leica M3, the lens has to have a special finder attachment. Wide-angle lenses are accordingly available either with this attachment (for Leica M3 models) or without (for the Leica M2, M4 and M1).

The Leica M1 shows two image frames simultaneously in the finder for the 35 mm. (outer frame) and 50 mm. lenses.

The Finder Frame Selector

The Leica M2 to M4 models (also the MP) carry a finder frame selector. This is the lever beside the lens on the camera front, just below the main viewfinder window. This lever also controls the image frame in the finder, and does so independently of the lens that is fitted into the camera. This means that we can try out the effect of the different focal lengths without actually changing the lenses. When the selector lever points upwards, and the 50 mm. lens is in the camera, the 50 mm. frame is visible. On pushing the selector lever inwards—towards the lens—the 90 mm. frame appears. Pushing the lever outwards (away from the lens) brings the 135 mm. frame into view on the Leica M3, the 35 mm. frame on the M2, or the 35 mm. and 135 mm. frames on the M4. This is useful for pre-judging of the most suitable lens.

When one of the other lenses is in the camera, the selector lever changes its position accordingly. Thus with the 90 mm. lens the lever points inwards; to bring the 50 mm. lens into view, push the lever so that it points straight upwards, and for the 135 mm. (or 35 mm.) lens push the lever fully out.

The frame selector lever does not, however, provide the correct effect when a 35 mm. lens is used on the Leica M3 together with the finder attachment. Then the lever in the 90 mm. position shows the approximate field of view (actually slightly reduced) for the 50 mm. lens, and in the 135 mm. position for the 90 mm. lens.

The finder frame selector system also switches to the 90 mm. frame when the 135 mm. Elmarit is mounted on the camera (p. 107). The finder attachment fixed to this lens then magnifies the finder view.

The Rangefinder

The Leica models M2 to M4 have a coupled rangefinder, combined with the viewfinder. The rangefinder field is visible in the viewfinder as a small rectangular area in the centre of the view. Within this area the outlines of objects in the scene appear double as long as the lens is incorrectly focused.

M2/M3/M4 FINDER

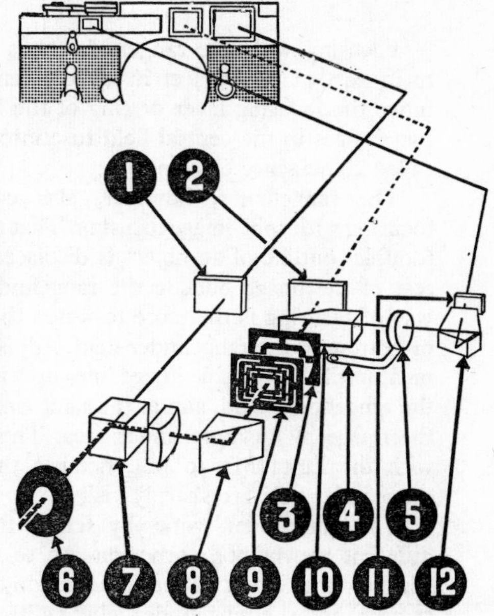

The optical system of the M2 to M4 finder consists of:

1. Main finder window showing the full view of the subject.
2. Illuminating window for the frame plate 9.
3. Movable frame mask uncovering the additional finder frames for long focus lenses in the frame plate 9. The frame plate and frame mask also move together to compensate for parallax.
5. Swinging lens coupled to the camera lens barrel through the focusing mechanism 4.
6. Eyepiece.
11. Rangefinder window providing the central rangefinder image reflected into the eyepiece by the prisms 7, 8, 10, 12.

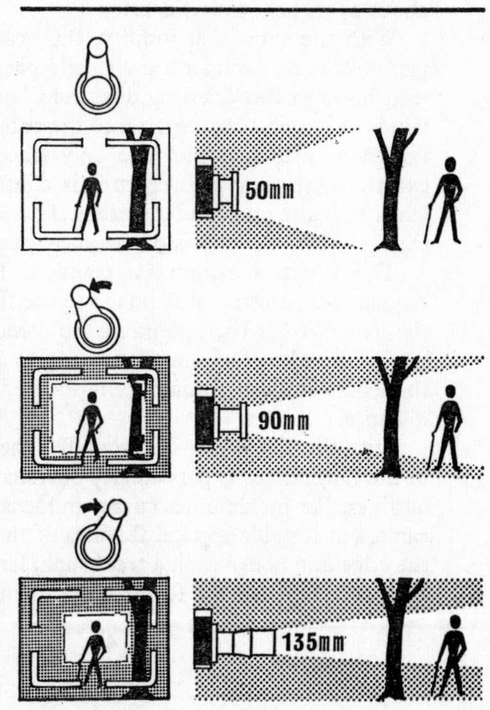

The white image frame shows the correct view for the standard 50 mm. lenses.

When the 90 mm. long-focus lens is fitted into the bayonet mount, a smaller image frame appears within the large frame, showing the reduced field of view.

With the 135 mm. lens in position, an alternative still smaller frame indicates the correct picture area (p. 46).

Either frame also appears on moving the frame selector lever next to the lens.

On the M2 the frames cover 35, 50 and 90 mm. fields, but work in the same way.

On the M4, frame marks show the 135 mm. field together with 35 mm.

Focusing with the rangefinder thus involves getting the main part of the subject inside the rangefinder field. Then move the focusing lever or ring of the lens (p. 51) until the two images in the central field fuse into one. This is the so-called coincidence principle.

The rangefinder, however, also combines coincidence focusing with split-image focusing. That means that the second (double) outline of an object is displaced with respect to the rest of the image outside the rangefinder field. The easiest way of focusing is therefore to watch the image near the top or bottom of the rangefinder field. Adjust the focusing movement until the movable image lines up with the outline outside the rangefinder field, and at the same time fuses into one with the image in the rangefinder area. This is particularly easy with the Leica M2 to M4, because the boundaries of the rangefinder field are sharply visible.

The rangefinder works by seeing the subject from two different viewpoints, corresponding to the main viewfinder window (the largest of the three windows on the front of the camera) and the rangefinder window itself (the small window just below the shutter speed knob). These two windows are about 2¾ inches (7 cm.) apart.

With the subject at infinity, the beams reaching the two parts of the rangefinder are virtually parallel. For nearer subjects however the "viewing directions" of the two rangefinder windows have to converge on to the subject. The rangefinder images as seen fuse into one only when the convergence is exactly right. This convergence is controlled by a swinging lens inside the rangefinder system. The movement of this lens thus provides the means of measuring the distance.

The Leica rangefinder is coupled. That means that the rangefinder adjustment is linked to the focusing movement of the lens. We get the two images to coincide by adjusting the lens itself: when the rangefinder images are correctly lined up the lenses are also automatically focused at the exact subject distance.

With the Leica held horizontally, the double-image effect in the rangefinder is particularly obvious with vertical subject outlines. For maximum accuracy in focusing therefore aim the camera at suitable vertical features of the scene—for instance the edge of a house wall, a tree trunk, lamp-posts, etc. Where the prominent subject features are mainly horizontal lines—

RANGEFINDER

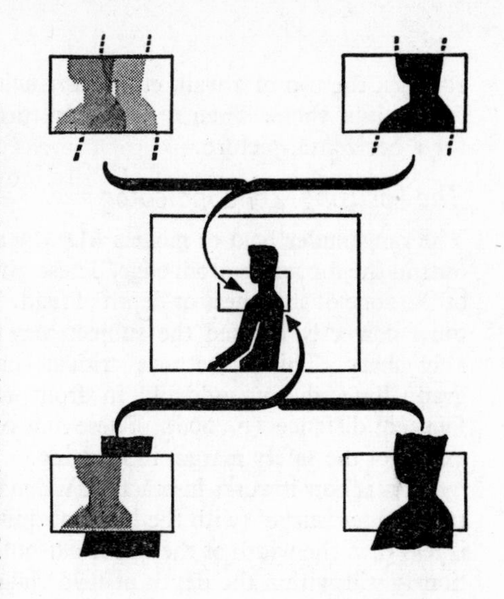

The coupled rangefinder of the Leica M2 to M4 works both by the coincidence and by the split-image system. In the central rangefinder field the image appears with double outlines as long as the lens is not accurately focused.

At the same time the boundaries of the central field are sharp; so it is possible to check the accuracy of focus by noting whether the outlines of the second rangefinder image are continuous with the outlines of the surrounding area. Combining these two methods makes rangefinder focusing particularly accurate.

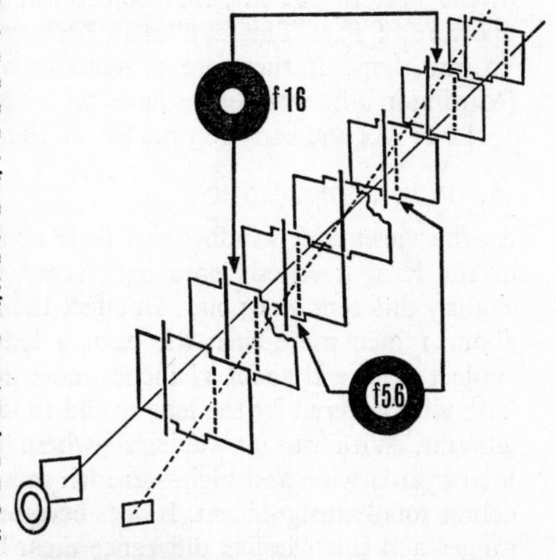

The rangefinder field of Leica models M2 and M3 incorporates its own zone focus indicator. There are two small cut-outs at the top and bottom of the rangefinder field respectively. If the separation of double outlines within the rangefinder field does not exceed the length of the bottom cut-out, the subject will be within the depth of field zone at *f*5.6. Similarly, if the separation of such outlines due to incorrect focusing does not exceed the width of the top cut-out, the subject is within the zone of sharpness with the lens stopped down to *f*16. This applies in all cases to the standard 50 mm. lens.

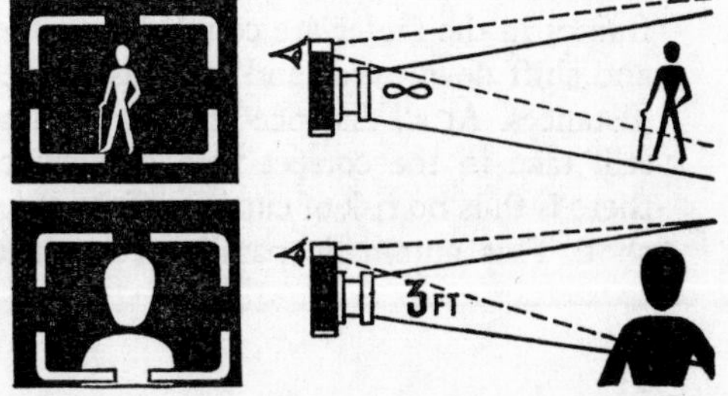

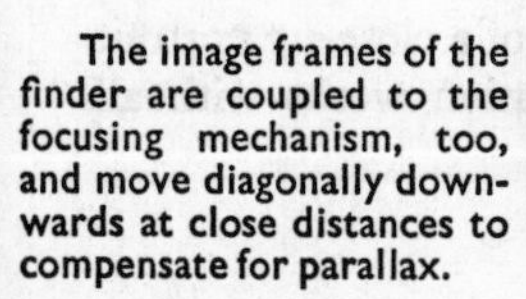

The image frames of the finder are coupled to the focusing mechanism, too, and move diagonally downwards at close distances to compensate for parallax.

railings, the top of a wall, etc.—focus with the Leica held as for upright shots. Then if necessary turn the camera round for a horizontal picture.

The Focusing Zone Indicator

The rangefinder field of models M2/M3 also carries two cut-outs in the top and bottom edge. These give a visual indication of the zone of sharpness or depth of field. When the lens is not quite correctly focused the subject may still appear acceptably sharp. This is because critical sharpness deteriorates gradually and not suddenly in front of, and behind, the focused distance (p. 206). These cut-outs thus show the extent of the safety margin in focusing.

This is how it works in practice. When the separation of the rangefinder images (with the lens not quite correctly focused) is less than the width of the upper cut-out, the object in question is still within the depth of field range at *f*16. Similarly, if the separation of the rangefinder images is less than the width of the bottom cut-out, that object will still be sharp at an aperture of *f*5.6. This applies in both cases to the standard 50 mm. lens. It therefore provides a convenient means of focusing in a hurry—for instance, with action subjects.

Leica M4 and early M3 models do not have this feature.

Parallax Compensation

As the viewfinder window is a little above and to one side of the lens, it strictly speaking "sees" the subject from a slightly different viewpoint. In effect the finder view takes in about 1 inch more than the camera lens at the top of the subject field, and about 1¼ inches more at the left-hand side. The view covered by the lens would thus be reduced by this amount. With distant subjects—where the subject field is many yards wide and high—an inch or so more or less is of course totally insignificant. It does become important at closer ranges and this parallax difference must be compensated for.

In the Leica M models this is done automatically. The image frames in the finder are coupled with the focusing movement and shift downwards and inwards as the lens is set to nearer distances. At all distance settings the finder frames therefore still take in the correct field of view covered by the lens; there is thus no risk of cutting off the top of a close-up portrait shot. This automatic parallax compensation works with all

Leica M models—even with the M1, which has no rangefinder.

At really close distances, below the near focusing limit of the lens, separate parallax compensation may be necessary. With the near focusing adapters this is often taken care of by the rangefinder attachment (p. 368). For really close shots with one of the Visoflex reflex housings, the latter shows directly the view covered by the lens and no parallax problems arise (p. 375).

Focusing

To focus the Leica lenses, screw the lens in or out by turning the milled focusing mount. This mount also carries a set of figures indicating distances, marked in either feet or metres or both. They range from infinity (∞) down to about 3½ feet or 1 metre in the case of the standard 50 mm. lenses.

To set the lens for a given subject distance, turn the focusing mount until the required distance figure is opposite the focusing mark (usually a triangle △).

Most standard and wide-angle Leica lenses have a lever attached to the rotating focusing mount, to make focusing more convenient.

There is a catch at the infinity position; to focus the lens for nearer distances, press in the knob of the focusing lever first to release the catch.

Long-focus lenses (p. 105) have no focusing lever, since the focusing movement is much greater, and the lever would at some settings obstruct the viewfinder or rangefinder window.

Where the lens is collapsible, it must be extended before focusing. Some of the collapsible Leica lenses cannot, in fact, be focused until they are properly extended and locked into position. If the infinity catch does not engage positively while extending or retracting the lens, hold the focusing lever with one finger.

The Coupling Movement

The coupling between the lens and the rangefinder consists of a spring-loaded coupling lever with a roller inside the camera. The roller bears on the rear focusing barrel of the lens. During focusing this barrel moves in or out, with the coupling lever following. It thus adjusts the direction of the two image beams to the subject focused on (p. 48).

The rear focusing barrel is connected to the lens itself by

means of a differential helical screw mount. This compensates for variations in the focal length of the lens. The actual forward movement of the rear focusing barrel is thus always the same for the same focusing range, even though the forward movement of the different lenses will vary with the focal length. In this way every lens (except the 125 mm. Hektor and the Telyts—p. 108) is automatically and accurately coupled with the built-in rangefinder at all focusing distances.

The roller of the coupling lever is made of specially hardened steel to reduce wear to a minimum and preserve the high accuracy of the coupling mechanism.

Releasing

To make the exposure, press the release button in the centre of the transport lever.

The Leica release button works very smoothly and needs little force to press. All the same, press it gently, so as not to jerk the camera.

When holding the camera horizontally the right index finger releases the shutter. To do this, slowly bend down the tip of the finger, squeezing the button, rather than pushing it. Never jab at the release.

Alternatively squeeze the index finger and thumb together, with the latter underneath the base plate.

With the camera held vertically, either the right index finger or the right thumb may work the release. In the latter case the second finger of the right hand should press against the camera base. This is to counteract the pressure of the thumb and avoid moving the camera.

After the exposure advance the film by one frame. To do this press the right thumb against the transport lever and push it outwards as far as it will go. Let it fly back again. Alternatively, advance the film by several short strokes of the transport lever until the latter locks. (On earlier M3 models push out the lever fully *twice* to advance one frame.)

This advances the film in the camera by an exact frame interval, and also tensions the shutter again for the next shot. The Leica is therefore instantly ready to shoot again, and can take picture sequences at a rate of a shot a second. A fast shutter speed with such rapid sequences minimizes the risk of camera shake.

The film counter in the window next to the transport lever on the M3, MDa and M4 (or on top of the body on the MD, M1 and M2) moves on by one division at the same time. The film counter indicates the number of the frame ready for the next exposure. Thus after ten exposures, advancing the film brings the film counter to No. 11.

The release button is always locked until the film is fully advanced.

During shooting it is convenient to keep the transport lever sticking out towards the back. This is the "dead" movement already mentioned (p. 34). When the camera is in its case, fold the lever into its rest position so that it lies against the speed dial.

The film itself is transported by a sprocket wheel on a shaft inside the camera. The shaft is also connected to the take-up spool, which is, however, held by a friction coupling that acts like a slipping clutch. As more film is wound up on the spool, the spool diameter increases. Without the slipping coupling it would tend to pull more film out of the cassette than is needed for each exposure. This sprocket transport, moving a definite number of perforations of the film each time, ensures even spacing of every shot on the film.

The Self-timer

The Leicas M2 (except early models) to M4 have a built-in self-timer or delayed-action release. This is the large lever on the camera front, next to the bayonet lock for lens changing.

The self-timer delays the opening of the shutter by about 10 seconds after release, thus enabling the photographer to appear in his own picture (e.g. for self-portraits or groups).

To use the self-timer pull down the lever outwards (away from the lens). Then press the little button above it on the camera front. The delayed action mechanism now comes into operation and the lever gradually moves back towards its starting position to the accompaniment of a faint whirring noise. Just before the lever reaches its original position the shutter is released. There is no need to press the shutter release.

The delayed action mechanism works with all shutter speeds from 1 to 1/1000 second (but not the B setting). The shutter must of course be tensioned first.

The delay time is adjustable. With the lever fully pulled down it is about 10 seconds, while the minimum delay (with the lever horizontal) is 5 seconds.

The self-timer is equally useful for releasing the shutter when the Leica is not very firmly supported—where *any* contact with the camera during exposure might shake it. It is also a help for slow exposures (from 1 to 1/15 second) with the camera held in the hand. In that case pull down the lever to its minimum delay—until it just engages when it is approximately horizontal. The mechanism then releases the shutter automatically about 5 seconds after pressing the self-timer release button (above the lever).

Double Exposures

Since the transport lever tensions the shutter at the same time as it advances the film, double exposures are impossible in the normal way. There is no need to remember whether the film was advanced after the last shot or not. If the transport lever is free to move it must be moved before releasing; when it locks it cannot be moved until the shutter has been released.

Intentional double exposures are, however, still possible. This is useful for trick photography, or if the shutter has been accidentally released with the lens cap in position.

To make a double exposure (to tension the shutter again without advancing the film), first turn the rewind knob or crank in the direction of the arrow engraved on it to take up any slack on the film in the cassette. Then hold on to this knob (for example with the thumb of your left hand while holding the Leica) during the following operations. Depress the reversing lever or button after the first exposure. This is the small lever on the camera front, just above the self-timer lever. Move this down to the position marked R or press it in on early M2 models. Keep the lever in the R position (or the button depressed) while tensioning the shutter again with the transport lever. Manipulating the reversing lever in this way disengages the transport lever from the transport shaft inside the camera; the film thus remains in the same place.

When tensioning the shutter only with the transport lever the take-up spool in the camera does, of course, still tend to rotate. That is why it is necessary to tension the film first, so that the slipping clutch movement really slips without pulling a little of the film along.

Registration of Data with the Leica MDa and MD

The data registration feature of the Leica MDa and MD permits the introduction of a narrow plastic strip, carrying lettering, reference data, etc., into the camera before every exposure. This

MDa and MD DATA REGISTRATION

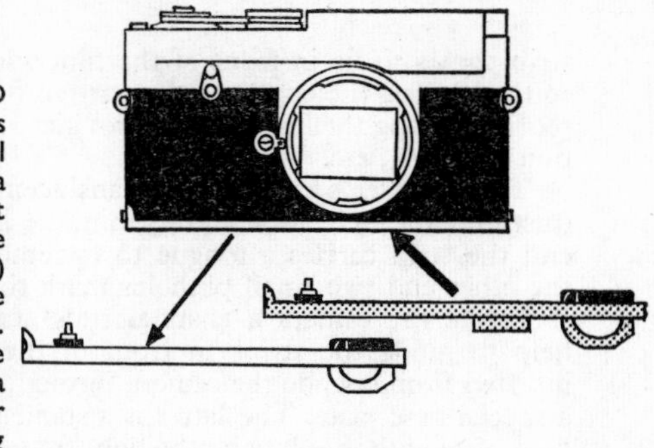

The Leica MDa and MD has no finder optics, but has instead a built-in channel for the inserion of data registration strips in front of the film. For this purpose the normal base plate (*left*) is replaced by a special base plate with light-trapped slot. Shown here is the MD; the base plate of the MDa carries a locating flange for the built in quick-loading take-up spool, while the camera itself also has a rewind crank.

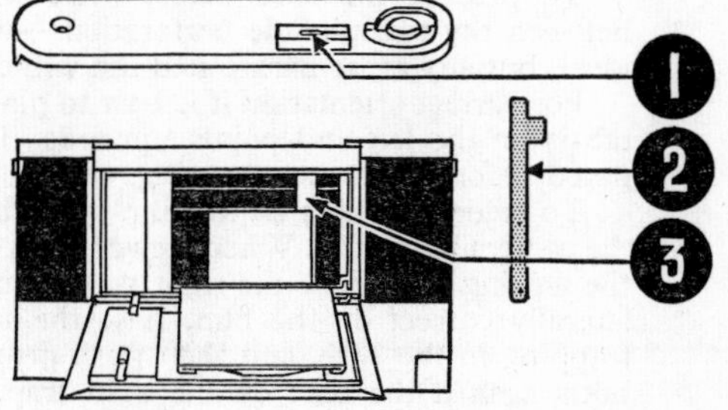

Data registration features of the Leica MDa/MD:

1. Light-trapped slot in base plate.
2. Data strip channel.
3. Plastic data strip.

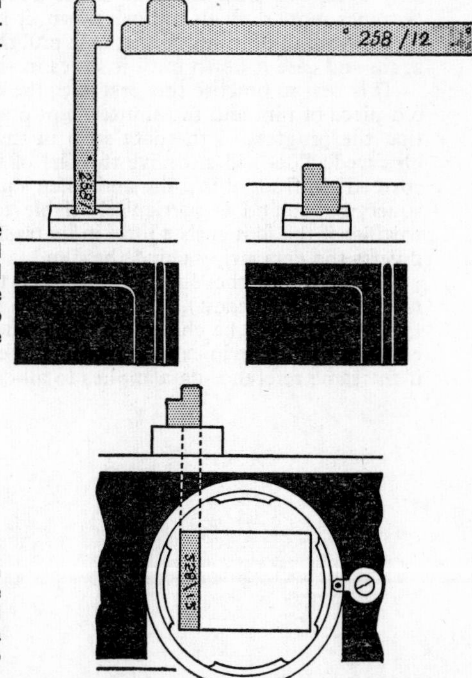

The data are written on the strip in the area between and below the perforated pinholes.

When inserting the strip the writing should read the right way round as seen from the back of the camera (*left*). Push the strip fully home, but make sure that it slides in easily.

The data strip sits in front of the film along one side of the image frame and reduces the image area from 24 × 36 mm. to 24 × 32 mm.

strip comes to lie in front of the film within the image frame, so that during the exposure the written data are simultaneously recorded along the image. This provides self-contained information for filing, etc.

The data strips are pieces of translucent grey plastic, 5.5 mm. (just under $\frac{1}{4}$ inch) wide and 65 mm. ($2\frac{5}{8}$ inches) long. Near one end the strip carries a tongue to facilitate manipulation. Near the other end two small pinholes mark the area for writing.

Inside the camera a channel runs across the film track to help to guide the strips in front of the film. The strips are inserted from outside the camera through a light-trapped slot in a special base plate. The latter is a standard Leica M4 or M2/3 base plate with the slot and the light trapping added.

To prepare the data strips, write on them—in the space between the two pinhole perforations—with ink. Indian ink is ideal, but any other dark-toned ink will do.

For correct orientation it is best to place the strip so that the tab is on the left and points upwards. The strips can be prepared before or during shooting.

To record the data on the film push the strip into the slot in the camera base plate. When viewed from the back of the camera the writing should be the right way round. It will then appear laterally correct on the film. Ease the strip through the light trapping in the base, and then push gently down until the tab butts against the base on the light trap. The strip must feed down smoothly; if there is a resistance just before the second pinhole disappears in the light-trapped slot, this means that the strip is encountering the edge of the film. If after that the strip becomes more difficult to push down, it has strayed behind the film instead of in front. In that case pull the registration strip up again and ease it down until it slides in smoothly.

It is best to practise this first with the camera loaded with an old piece of film and the shutter kept open on the B setting so that the progress of the data strip in the film window can be observed. This will also give the feel of the strip when sliding correctly in front of the film and when squeezing behind it. The squeezing behind is particularly liable to happen in very dry weather if the film curls a little in its track so that the film edge diverts the data strip behind the film.

If the strip catches slightly before it is fully home (against the top of the film window), ease it to and fro gently to push in fully.

The strips can be changed in the camera before or after any exposure or one strip can stay in the camera for a series of shots if the same reference data applies to all of them.

THE OLDER LEICAS

Leica models with screw-mounted lenses differ from the M series in a number of respects, especially the shutter settings, rangefinder operation, etc.
Operation is generally a little slower, but just as simple.

The Leica M models discussed so far are the last word in streamlined camera operation. For about thirty years all the Leicas available were of the earlier design taking screw-mounted lenses, and which are now discontinued. The differences mostly affect certain details of manipulation, without, however, changing the fundamental principle of shooting with a Leica. So we shall list here primarily the points in which the earlier series of Leica cameras deviate from the M models.

Let us first look at these camera types in greater detail.

The Screw-lens Leica Models

While the earlier Leica types differ from the M models in a considerable number of features, the most important—especially from the point of view of accessories—is the fact that they take interchangeable lenses fitted with a screw-mount instead of a bayonet mount. For that reason they are conveniently referred to as the screw-lens or screw-mounted Leica cameras.

Leica IIIg.—This model, appearing in 1957, is the last and most advanced of the screw-mounted Leicas. It has a focal plane shutter with speeds from 1 to 1/1000 second and B, the shutter speeds being set with two separate dials on the camera top and camera front. The film transport and shutter tensioning mechanism is coupled and operated by a transport knob instead of a lever. The coupled rangefinder is separate from the viewfinder and shows an enlarged view of the central subject field. The viewfinder has reflected field frames for the 50 and 90 mm. lenses, and automatic parallax compensation. For all other focal lengths accessory finders are necessary (p. 119). The viewfinder and rangefinder also have separate eyepieces, mounted next to each other at the rear of the camera. This model is synchronized for flash shots at all shutter speeds, the correct synchronization being selected with the shutter speed setting. The camera back of the Leica IIIg (and of all other screw-mounted Leicas) is solid and does not have the opening panel of the M models.

Leica Ig.—This is a simpler version of the IIIg, also introduced in 1957. It resembles the IIIg in all respects, but has no built-in rangefinder or viewfinder. Instead there is an Albada-type detachable viewfinder fitted in one of the two accessory shoes on top of the camera. The finder can be supplemented by a separate rangefinder (p. 68). There is no self-timer.

LEICA Ig, IIIg

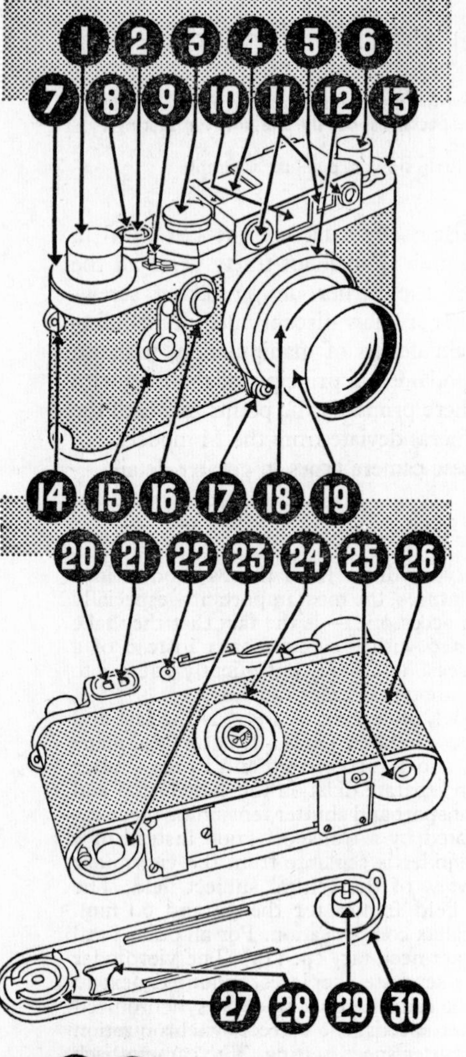

The outside features of the Leica IIIg are shown below.

1. Transport knob.
2. Release button.
3. Main speed dial.
4. Accessory shoe.
5. Illuminating window for finder.
6. Rewind knob.
7. Film counter.
8. Release guard.
9. Reversing lever.
10. Viewfinder window.
11. Rangefinder.
12. Distance and depth of field scales.
13. Focusing lever of rangefinder magnifier.
14. Strap eyelet.
15. Self-timer.
16. Slow shutter speed dial.
17. Focusing lever.
18. Lens barrel.
19. Aperture ring.
20. Rangefinder eyepiece.
21. Viewfinder eyepiece.
22. Flash socket.
23. Film cassette.
24. Film indicator.
25. Take-up spool.
26. Camera body.
27. Base plate lock.
28. Film guide finger.
29. Locating peg.
30. Base plate.

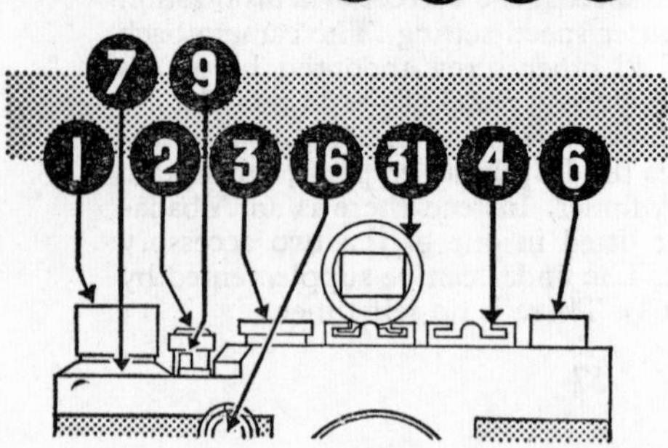

The Leica Ig has no rangefinder and no self-timer but two accessory shoes, the central one carrying a special brilliant finder.

4. Second shoe.
31. Brilliant viewfinder.

LEICA If, IIf, IIIf

The main features of the Leica f models are:

1. Film indicator.
2. Release button.
3. Main shutter speed setting dial.
4. Accessory shoe.
5. Viewfinder window.
6. Rewind knob.
7. Film counter.
8. Shutter release guard.
9. Reversing lever.
10. Flash synchronizing dial.
11. Rangefinder windows.
12. Distance and depth of field scale.
13. Focusing lever of rangefinder magnifying eyepiece.
14. Eyelet for carrying strap.
15. Film transport knob.
16. Self-timer (only on the last IIIf models).
17. Slow shutter speed dial (not on models If or IIf).
18. Focusing lever.
19. Lens barrel (collapsible with some of the 50 mm. lenses).
20. Aperture ring.
21. Rangefinder eyepiece.
22. Viewfinder eyepiece.
23. Flash socket.
24. Film cassette.
25. Take-up spool.
26. Camera body.
27. Baseplate lock.
28. Film guide finger (not on earlier models).
29. Locating peg.
30. Base plate.

The Leica If has no coupled rangefinder, and no slow shutter speeds nor self-timer. A special brilliant viewfinder is provided in the central accessory shoe, while a second accessory shoe is available for other gear.

4. Second accessory shoe.
23. Flash socket on front of camera.
31. Brilliant viewfinder.

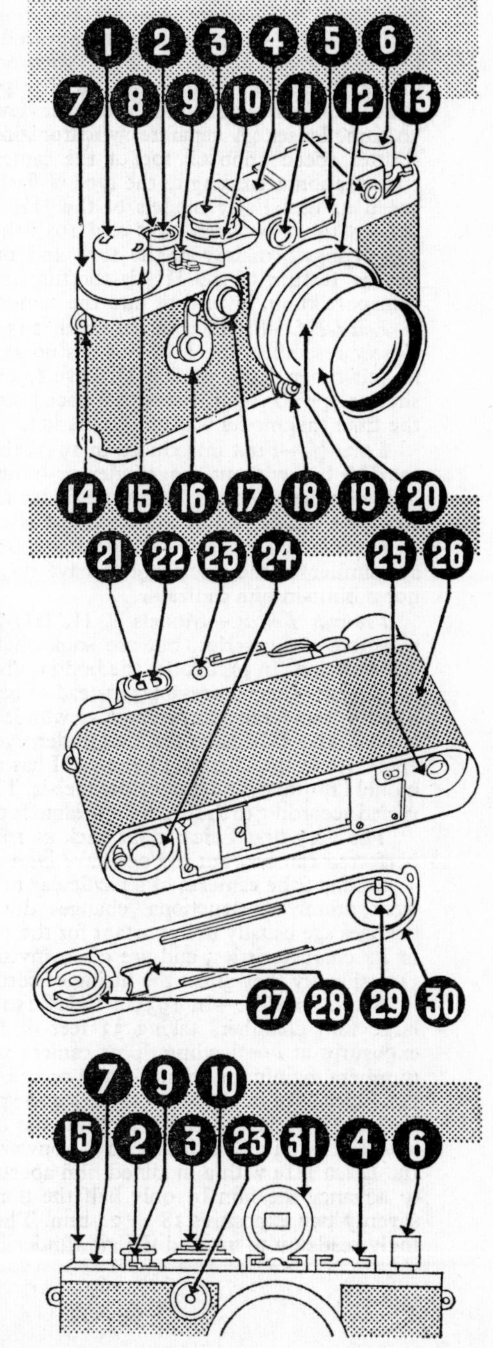

Leica IIIf.—This model first appeared in 1950 and is similar to the IIIg except for the flash synchronization and the view-finder. The latter incorporates neither parallax compensation, nor finder frames; it shows the correct view only for the standard 50 mm. lenses. A separate synchronizing dial below the fast shutter speed knob on top of the camera sets the flash synchronization according to the type of flash bulb and the shutter speed in use. Early models of the IIIf had no self-timer. At various times between 1950 and 1957 the shutter speed range was changed, mainly in the slow and intermediate speeds. A further feature of the IIIf is the film indicator built into the transport knob, instead of into the camera back.

Leica IIf.—Produced from about 1951 to 1957, this camera closely resembles the IIIf, but has no slow shutter speeds and no self-timer. Early models IIf have 1/500 second as the fastest shutter speed. Again the actual speed settings changed during the time this model was on the market.

Leica If.—First introduced in 1952, this camera is similar to the IIf, but without rangefinder or built-in viewfinder. It has instead a detachable Albada type finder in one of its two accessory shoes. The fastest shutter speed is 1/500 second.

Leica IIIc, IIc and Ic.—Appearing first in 1940, these models are similar to the f series, but have no flash synchronization, nor a built-in film indicator.

Pre-war Leicas.—Models I, II, III, IIIa and IIIb largely resemble the c series, but are somewhat different in internal construction. In particular, the body is about ⅛ inch shorter and is built up of metal pressings instead of being die-cast. The IIIb has the same rangefinder and viewfinder system as the IIIc; the III and IIIa have the two finder eyepieces spaced farther apart. As in the c series, the Leica II has no slow speeds and the model I no rangefinder nor slow speeds. The shutter speedranges varied according to the time of appearance of the different models.

The very first Leica as far back as 1925 was already a fully perfected camera, but did not have interchangeable lenses.

Some of the cameras of a particular model (e.g. IIIc) underwent minor constructional changes during the years. These changes are usually unimportant for the operation of that model or its characteristics, and are often invisible from the outside. Occasionally they affect the fitting of certain accessories.

Special models.—In 1935 a Leica 250 appeared with extra-large film chambers taking 33 feet of film and yielding 250 exposures at one loading. This camera was produced in small numbers mainly for scientific and recording work. It resembles the Leica IIIa in all other features and specification.

A more recent special model was the Leica 72 assembled for a year or two in Canada from 1954 onwards. This was based on the Leica IIIa with a modified film aperture and film transport to advance the film by only half the normal amount, yielding seventy-two exposures 18 × 24 mm. The film counter accordingly reads up to 72, and the viewfinder is masked down to the smaller size. The camera is fully synchronized like the Leica IIIf. The Leica 72 was intended for microfilm copying, making half-frame film strips, etc., rather than general photography.

Shooting Drill

The basic shooting drill with a screw-lens Leica is the same as with the Leica M (p. 41):

Pull out the lens (where collapsible).
Check that the shutter is tensioned.
Set the lens aperture and shutter speed.
Focus through the rangefinder (where fitted).
View and expose.
Wind on the film.

The controls relating to the lens (aperture—p. 41; focusing—p. 51) are the same as for the Leica M models. The shutter setting, rangefinder and viewfinder are radically different.

Holding and Viewing

The camera holds for the screw-lens Leica models are basically the same as for the M series. It becomes necessary, however, to change the eye over from the viewfinder to the rangefinder eyepiece between viewing and focusing; a slight movement of the head is usually sufficient for this. On the prewar models (except IIIb) this movement is rather greater, since the two eyepieces are set about ¾ inch apart.

The viewfinder of the Leica IIIg shows the subject within a white frame which outlines the field recorded on the film. Hold the camera close to the eye to see the whole field. Four corners within the field of view mark the limits of the area covered with a 90 mm. lens. For other focal lengths a separate viewfinder is needed. This frame is again coupled with the focusing movement for automatic parallax compensation.

The finder of the Leica IIf and IIIf as well as earlier models uses no suspended frame, nor does it show the view of the 90 mm. lens. The subject area covered by the film is everything that is visible in the finder. It is important in this case to look straight through the finder to see the correct view.

At close distances with models other than the IIIg estimate the parallax compensation visually. In effect this involves treating a small area at the top and at the left of the finder view as "dead" space; when arranging the subject in the finder frame therefore keep it well away from the top or left-hand edges of the finder.

The angle of view of any lens changes slightly with the subject distance. It is somewhat greater at infinity than at close-up distances when the lens is farther away from the film. The standard finder shows the exact field of view at about 10 feet. With distant subjects it will therefore include slightly less, and with near subjects 3½ feet (1 metre) away slightly more than will appear on the film. The difference is however negligible in

USING THE FINDER

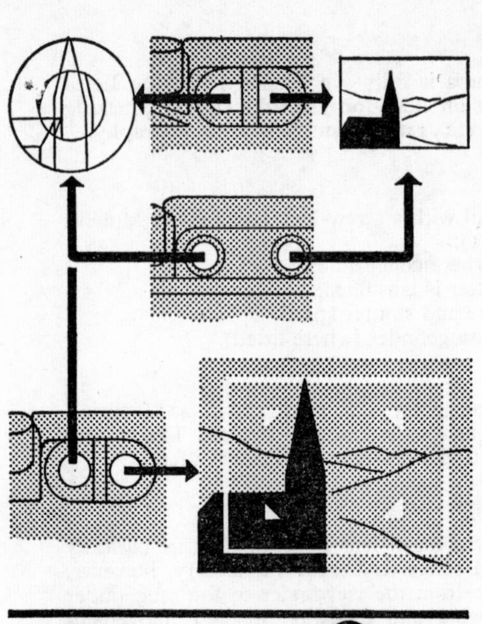

The twin eyepiece of the later series II and III Leicas incorporates the rangefinder on the left, and the viewfinder on the right. It permits rapid changing over from the one to the other. On earlier Leicas the eyepieces were separate.

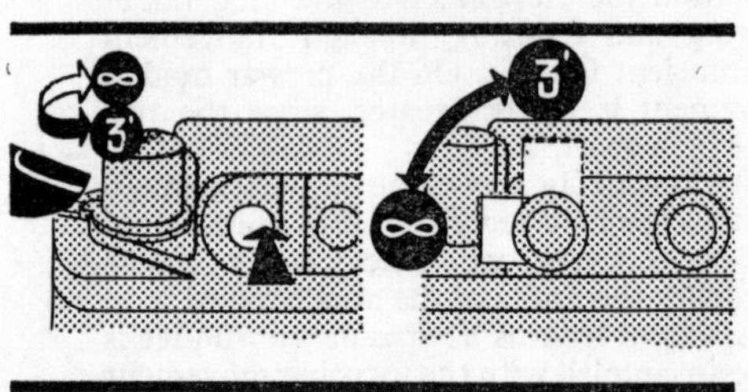

The finder eyepiece of the Leica IIIg shows the subject outlined by a brilliant suspended frame; this moves during focusing to compensate for parallax; the white corners mark the field of the 90 mm. lens.

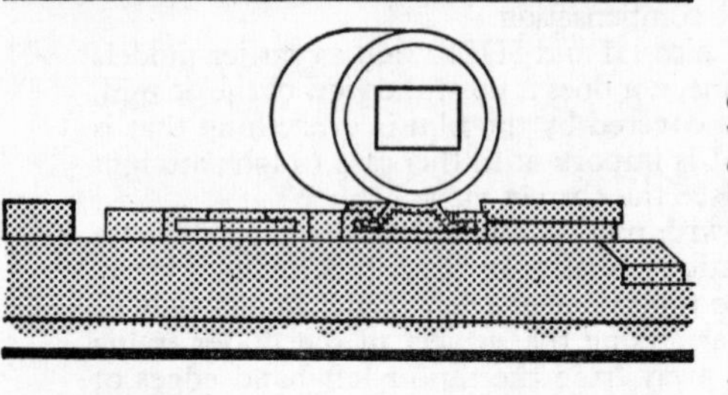

The rangefinder eyepiece has a built-in magnifier which can be focused for near or distant subjects by means of a lever below the rewind button (*left*). On older models (*right*) the focusing adjustment is fitted at the back to the eyepiece itself (p. 67).

Leica Ig, and Ic models carry a detachable brilliant viewfinder (p. 57) in one of the two accessory shoes. Earlier Leica I and Standard models have a permanently mounted optical finder.

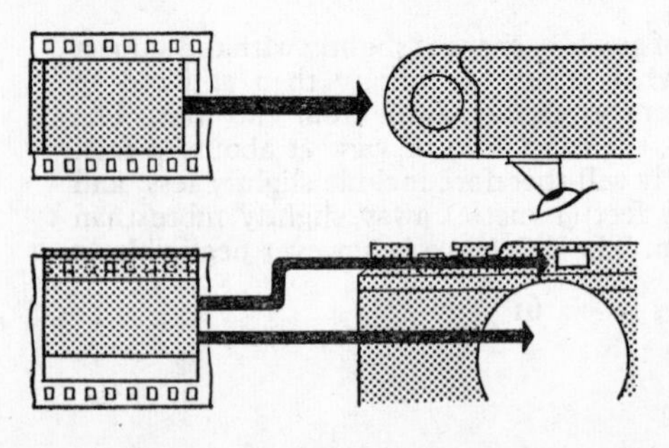

Look squarely through the finder; with the Leica IIf and earlier models viewing obliquely will not show the true field of view (p. 61).

As the finder is above the lens, it will on models other than the IIIg include slightly more of the top of the subject than the film. Allow for this parallax error with close shots (p. 61).

SHOOTING DRILL

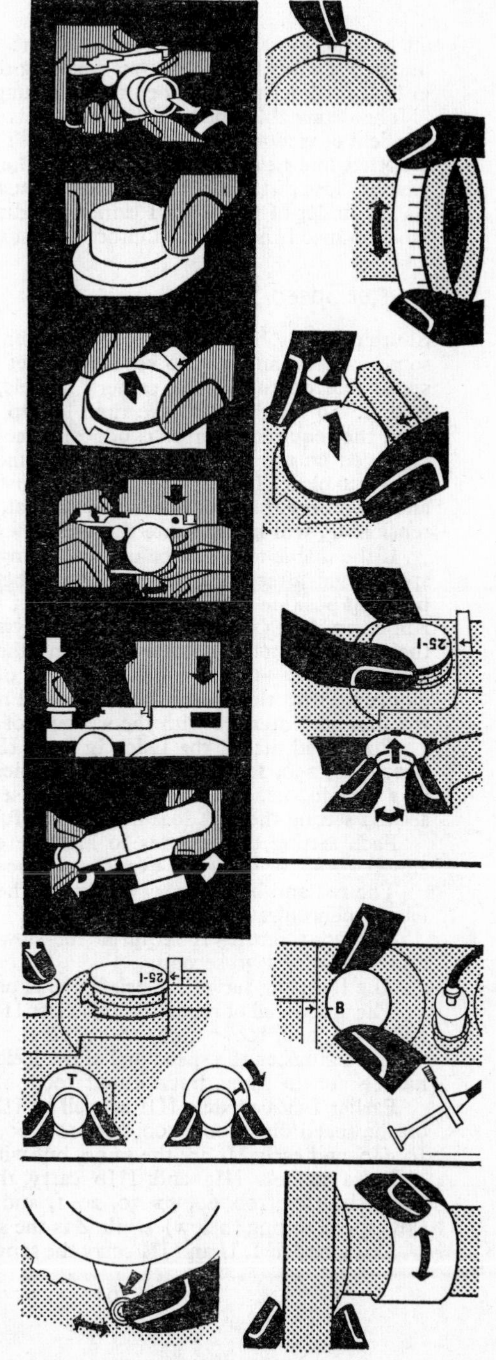

Black panel: The sequence of picture taking with the Leica models up to IIIf is (*from top to bottom*):

Pull out lens (if collapsible) and set aperture.

Wind transport knob (if not already wound).

Set shutter speed.

Focus by rangefinder.

View the subject and expose.

Advance film.

Right-hand column: Set the lens aperture (*top*) by moving the pointer, or appropriate mark on the aperture ring, to the required figure (p. 41). To set the shutter speed (*centre*), lift up the speed dial and turn to the desired speed (p. 64). For slow speeds (*bottom*) turn to 30–1 or 25–1, and set the speed on the slow speed dial. Depress the small lock first (p. 66).

For time exposures set the main speed dial to 30–1 or 25–1, the slow speed dial to T (*left*). Releasing opens the shutter; to close it turn the slow speed dial away from T (p. 67). Alternatively, set B, and use a cable release (*right*).

To focus the standard or wide-angle lenses (*left*) depress the infinity catch and move the focusing lever (p. 51). On long-focus lenses (*right*) turn the focusing ring.

all but the most exacting work. (On the Leica M models the finder is correct for the nearest focusing distance and the film, in fact, includes more at the infinity setting.)

The detachable finder of Leica models Ic to Ig again shows the field of view within a brilliant frame. This frame also carries a dotted line near the top to indicate the limit of the field of view at close distances. This is thus a visual parallax correction. As the finder of the series I cameras is directly above the lens, no allowance is necessary at either side of the finder frame.

Shutter Speed Settings

Shutter speeds between 1/30 second (1/25 or 1/20 second on some models) and 1/1000 second are set by the main shutter speed dial on top of the camera models, next to the release button. To set the exposure time lift up this dial and turn it until the required number is opposite the small line or pointer engraved on the side of the accessory shoe. Then let the dial drop into place. This should be done *after* tensioning the shutter and advancing the film. Otherwise the dial, which rotates during tensioning, will not indicate the correct exposure time.

If the dial is to be set before tensioning (or for checking the speed used after releasing) determine beforehand the corresponding position of the shutter speed set when the shutter has run down. Mark this on the camera body. To set the dial when the shutter is not tensioned—bringing the speed opposite this auxiliary mark—turn the dial clockwise only. Turning it anti-clockwise with the shutter not tensioned may partially advance the film and interfere with the working of the film transport.

The speed dial of the Leica Ig and IIIg carries the figures: 1000, 500, 250, 125, 60, 30–1, and B. These represent fractions of a second, i.e. 500 stands for 1/500 second. At the 1/1000 second setting the dial does not drop in fully.

Each setting corresponds to half the exposure of the next slower speed, or twice the exposure of the next higher one.

The red and black arrow marks on the speed dial serve for flash synchronization (p. 259).

The 30–1 setting is required for slow speeds (below) and also stands for 1/30 second.

The B setting serves for brief time exposures.

The speed dial of model IIf (also last IIIf) carries the figures 1000, 500, 200, 100, 75, 50, 25–1, and B.

The figures on the speed dial of the Leica If and pre-1954 IIf models are the same, but without 1000.

Earlier Leica models IIIf as well as IIIc carry these figures on the speed dial: 1000, 500, 200, 100, 60, 40, 30–1, B. Models Ic, IIc, and early IIf are the same, but without 1000.

Leica models IIIa and IIIb carry the following figures: 1000, 500, 200, 100, 60, 40, 30, 20–1, and Z. Here 20–1 is the slow speed setting (below), while Z is the same as B.

Leica models I, II and III carry the same figures, but without

SHUTTER AND FILM

Black panel: The components of the focal plane shutter are:

1. Tape of first blind.
2. Tape of second blind.
3. First blind.
4. Rollers.
5. Shutter speed dial.
6. Second blind.
7. Main drum.
8. Gears to transport mechanism.

Right-hand column: The exposure times are controlled by the distance between the blinds (*top*), moving past the film at a set speed. In practice the distance increases towards the end of the travel to compensate for the acceleration of the blinds (*bottom*).

For delayed action shots with the IIIg and last IIIf (*left*), pull down the self-timer lever and press the button next to it. With older models (*right*), a delayed action attachment screws over the release button. To use it, wind the disc and lift the button top (p. 68).

For double exposures the shutter must be retensioned without advancing the film (p. 71). Depress the release button, keep it depressed, and rotate the speed dial to wind the shutter. Then let go of the release button while still holding the speed dial.

For quick sequence shooting press the side of the index finger against the transport knob, and pull to the right (*left*). Use the thumb in similar manner (*right*) when taking upright shots (p. 71).

1000. On some early Leica I and II models there is no 20–1 mark, but only 20. Either stands for 1/20 second.

Setting Slow Speeds

Leica models of series III as well as the Leica Ig have a second shutter speed setting dial on the front of the body next to the lens. This serves for slower shutter speeds (longer exposure times).

When the main speed dial is set to 30–1 the first blind fully uncovers the film before the second blind begins to cover it. With the slow speed dial we can delay the closing of the second blind, by an escapement mechanism, up to 1 second.

To set the slow speeds, first set the main shutter speed dial to 30–1 or 25–1. Then depress the catch above the slow speed setting dial and turn the latter from 30 to the required speed.

The slow speed dial on the Leica Ig and IIIg carries the figures 30, 15, 8, 4, 2, 1 and T. The T setting is for long time exposures (p. 67).

On the older models of the IIIf as well as on the IIIc the figures are 15, 20, 30, 4, 2, 1 and T; on the later IIIf 10, 15, 25, 5, 2, 1, and T. The slow speed setting dial on Leicas III, IIIa, and IIIb carries the figures T, 1, 2, 4, 8 and 20.

While the speeds on the main dial have to be set exactly to the marked values, those on the slow speed dial can be set to intermediate values except between 1 and T (not always possible on IIIf and earlier models).

To change from a slow to a fast speed, simply change the setting of the main speed dial; the position of the slow speed dial is immaterial at any speed faster than 1/30 second, although this is not always the case with earlier models.

Unlike the fast speeds, the slow speed dial shows the correct shutter speed after, as well as before, winding the shutter.

A special method of making hand-held slow exposures uses the self-timer (p. 53).

The Slow Speed Attachment

For making exposures between $\frac{1}{8}$ and 1 second with Leica series I and series II models (which have no slow speed dial) a special slow speed attachment was produced (now discontinued).

Before fitting the slow speed attachment, tension the shutter and advance the film (p. 70), and set the main speed dial to B (or Z). Unscrew the guard on the release button and screw the shaft of the attachment over the release button.

Wind the delay mechanism of the attachment by twisting the lever with the two milled knobs clockwise as far as it will go.

To set any of the slow speeds, lift up the longer end of the winding lever and turn it until the index line points to the required speed.

When releasing, press the button at the side of the attachment, and keep it depressed until the shutter has run down. This button also has a thread similar to the release button on the camera itself, and will take a cable release.

With some early Leica models the setting screw inside the shaft of the attachment may need adjustment to operate the release properly.

Time Exposures

For time exposures longer than 1 second, set the main shutter speed dial to B. On pressing the release button, the shutter will open and stay open as long as the button is depressed.

The slow speed dial should be set to 30 or 25.

When the slow speed dial is set to, for instance, 1 second, the shutter will close 1 second after letting go of the button, instead of immediately. Similarly, with the slow speed dial set to 1/4 second, the shutter will close 1/4 second after releasing the pressure on the button.

For long time exposures on series III Leica models, set the main speed dial to 30–1 or 25–1 and the slow speed dial to T. On pressing the release button, the shutter will open and stay open even without pressure on the button. To close it again, turn the slow speed dial towards 1 (anti-clockwise on Leica models Ig, IIIg as well as on III, IIIa, and IIIb; clockwise on Leica models IIIc and IIIf).

Rangefinder Focusing

The built-in rangefinder of Series II and III Leicas consists of a fixed mirror and a movable prism, behind the two circular rangefinder windows on the front of the camera. The view through the eyepiece again shows two images, one seen direct through the left-hand semi-silvered mirror, and the other an image reflected by the movable right-hand prism and the fixed left-hand mirror. It is the movement of the right-hand prism which is here coupled to the coupling lever and hence to the focusing barrel of the lens.

The principle of rangefinder focusing with the screw-mounted Leicas is the same as with the M models. With the screw-mounted Leica the rangefinder, however, shows the central section of the subject enlarged as a circular field. The greater part of this circular field (except the very rim) is thus the rangefinder image. Within this field the double outlines of the subject must fuse into one on focusing the lens correctly.

Although the base length of the rangefinder on series II and III Leicas is shorter than that of the M models, the optical magnification of the rangefinder image increases the focusing accuracy to that of the Leica M2 and M3.

In Leica models IIf and IIc as well as on series III models the rangefinder image can be visually focused for more comfortable observation. For this purpose there is a focusing lever underneath the rewind knob (on Leica models III and IIIa the adjustment is in the eyepiece mount).

When using the rangefinder for distant subjects, set the lever to infinity (∞); for near subjects move it in the opposite direction. It also helps to compensate for minor variations of eyesight. Slightly shortsighted users will find that the image is sharper with the eyepiece focusing lever set to ∞ even for close subjects, while slightly farsighted photographers may be able to focus easier with the eyepiece lever set for close-ups, even with distant subjects.

For greater defects of individual eyesight, including astigmatism, correction lenses are available to fit into the eyepiece of the rangefinder and viewfinder.

A further rangefinder accessory is an orange glass which fits over one of the rangefinder windows on the camera front (next to the shutter speed dial). The two rangefinder images are then visible in two different colours and so are easier to differentiate.

A separate rangefinder is also available for series I models and fits into the accessory shoe. It works in the same way as the coupled rangefinder, but the reading obtained from the rangefinder scale has to be transferred to the distance scale on the lens mount. When fitting this rangefinder it goes into the shoe upright. The single eyepiece and large focusing wheel should face towards the back of the camera. (A still earlier type of rangefinder was horizontal, and swivelled on its base to permit access to the shutter speed dial. With this rangefinder the viewfinder of the Leicas Ig, If or Ic must first be removed.)

Releasing the Shutter

Press the release button gently to make the exposure. While releasing, keep all fingers clear of the main speed dial. This revolves while the shutter runs down, and any contact with it will cause wrong exposures.

The reversing lever must always be pushed fully to position A. If it becomes accidentally displaced towards R, the transport is locked; on earlier Leica models the shutter may run down without opening at all, or again give wrong exposure times, particular at slow speeds.

The screw-mounted Leica models need a special cable release which screws over the release button. To fit the release, screw the milled fixing nut over the button, pushing the hollow tube between the guard and the button.

On earlier Leicas other than types g, f and c, the guard is screwed directly over the release button and must be unscrewed first. The release button rotates during the film transport, so unscrew the guard after winding the transport knob. The same applies to unscrewing the cable release after the exposure.

The Self-timer

The Leica IIIg and last Leica IIIf models have a built-in self-timer, similar to that of the M3 and M2 (p. 53). This is again a lever on the camera front just below the slow speed dial.

RANGEFINDER

The optical parts of the Leica finder system in series II and III models are:

1. Rangefinger eyepiece.
2. Rangefinder magnifier.
3. Fixed mirror.
4. Rangefinder window.
5. Viewfinder window.
6. Movable prism.
7. Second rangefinder window.
8. Viewfinder eyepiece.
9. Viewfinder prism; reflected frame system of Leica IIIg not shown here.
10. Coupling levers of rangefinder mechanism.
11. Roller.
12. Rear focusing barrel of lens.

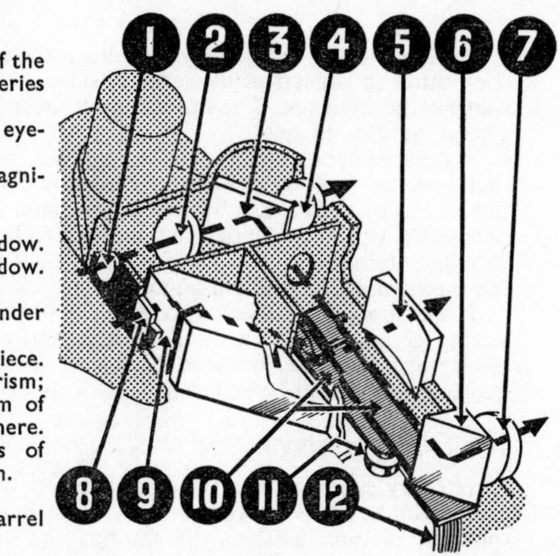

When the rangefinder is not focused correctly, two images are visible in the eyepiece (*left*).

Focusing the lens swings the movable right-angle prism coupled to the lens barrel, so that the views of both rangefinder windows converge on the subject, and the two images fuse into one. At this point the lens is sharply focused.

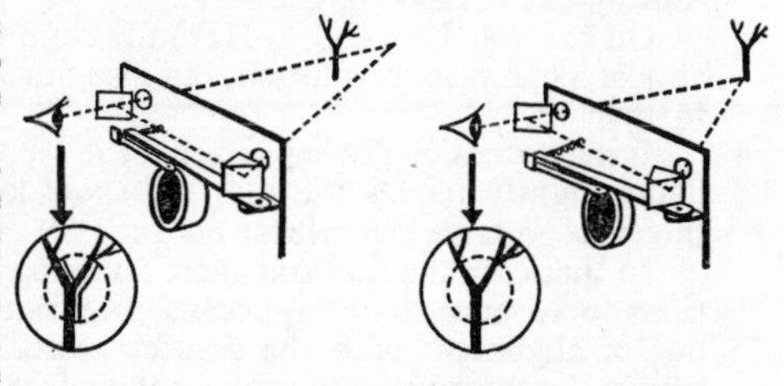

While the Leica rangefinder has only a comparatively short base length (p. 67), the built-in magnifier increases its accuracy to that of a finder of a much longer base.

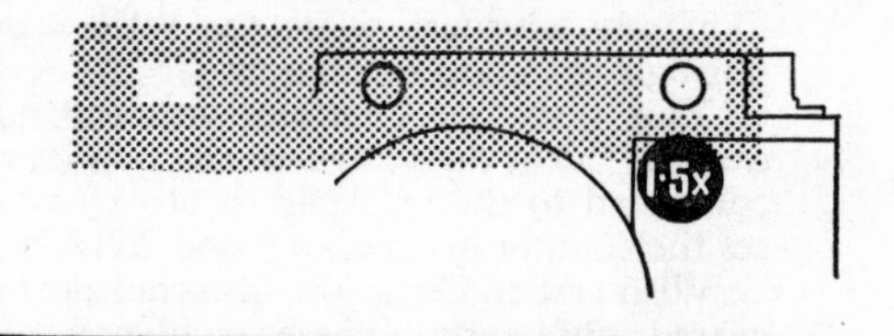

The series I models of the Leica have no built-in rangefinder, but will take a separate rangefinder in the accessory shoe (p. 68). This is just as accurate, though slower, to use. The distance is first measured with the rangefinder (*left*) and the lens then set to the distance found (*right*).

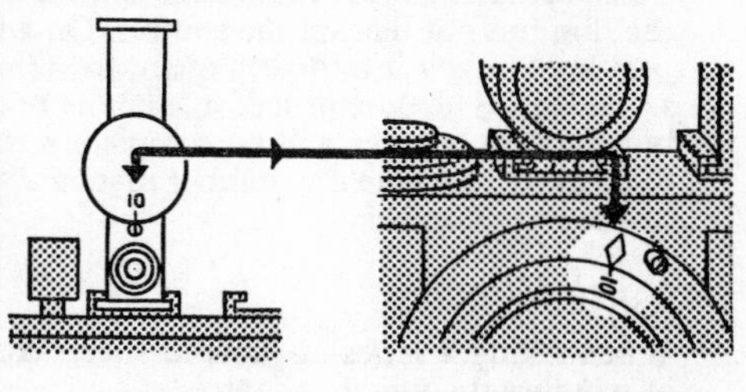

Older models of the separate rangefinder were mounted horizontally (*bottom right*) and swivelled on the mounting to allow access to the speed dial.

To use the self-timer, fully pull down the lever. Then press the button to the left of the lever to start the mechanism, and wait for the exposure. The self-timer on these cameras does not give an adjustable delay.

A delayed action attachment can be used with Leica models that have no built-in self-timer. This attachment screws over the thread of the release button in the same way as the cable release. After fixing the delayed action attachment, wind it by turning the milled disc clockwise as far as it will go. To start the mechanism, lift the top knob.

If the attachment does not release the shutter, screw out the setting screw inside the hollow shaft anti-clockwise. If the release acts too soon, screw in clockwise. A one-eighth to one-quarter turn should be sufficient.

The Film Transport

After every exposure turn the film transport knob in the direction of the arrow as far as it will go. This advances the film for the next picture, tensions the shutter, and also advances the film by one division of the scale.

On pre-war Leicas (I to IIIb) the counter disc turns through almost a complete revolution, but also finishes one scale division further on.

It may occasionally happen that the second finger of the right hand slightly moves the film transport knob while the index finger is pressing the release button.

In that case the film transport knob may require two revolutions to advance the film, because the transport knob has come out of alignment with the shutter gears. The first revolution brings the transport knob into gear again, while the second turn winds the film and tensions the shutter in the usual way. The film only advances while the release button is rotating, i.e. during the second revolution.

This does not interfere with the normal working of the camera, but it does advance the film counter (which is directly connected to the transport knob) by two divisions. Therefore set the counter disc back by one division.

With earlier Leicas the film transport and release button are geared differently. There accidental movement of the film transport knob, while the release button is depressed, will shift the film but not tension the shutter. On winding the film transport knob to get it into gear again, the film will be advanced by 1½ frames. This loss of half a frame is not particularly serious, but the film counter will be completely wrong (by 19½ frames, to be exact.) So note the number first, and then reset the counter to the next number.

Quick Winding

When taking a series of shots in succession, use this quick way of winding the film and shutter.

After each exposure take the camera from the eye, grip the transport knob with two fingers of the right hand (holding the Leica with the left hand). In one movement twist the left and right wrists simultaneously in opposite directions. Get hold of the camera again with the right hand, and bring it up to the eye for the next shot. With a little practice this need take no longer than about half a second.

For even quicker transport without moving the Leica from shooting position, stretch out the right index finger in front of the camera so that the tip rests on top of the lens. Press the side of the finger against the milled side of the knob, and pull back the finger, pressing it against the knob all the time.

When holding the camera vertically and operating the release with the thumb, pull back the thumb, press it against the transport knob behind the camera, and push upwards to turn the knob.

Special accessories are available for really rapid sequence shooting (pp. 346ff.).

Double Exposures

To tension the shutter without transporting the film, depress the release button and turn the shutter speed dial anti-clockwise as far as it will go (without lifting it up). Then let go of the button before releasing the dial. Now proceed in the normal way for the second exposure.

With some Leica models this procedure may open the blinds slightly if the shutter is set to a slow speed. It is therefore best to do this with the lens cap over the lens.

When tensioning the shutter this way, the release button may not come out again fully, but remain in a half-way position. If that happens, hold the speed dial (to stop the shutter from being released) and press in the release button, twisting it a little, until it fully emerges again. (This applies only to type f and type c models.)

LOADING AND UNLOADING

The Leica uses special self-opening cassettes or standard 35 mm. film cassettes.
Be sure to trim and fix the film correctly when loading.
Partly exposed films or short lengths can be unloaded and re-loaded easily for changing from one film type to another.

We can load the Leica with either standard 35 mm. cassettes (p. 181) or Leitz N cassettes (not for Leicaflex) containing up to a thirty-six exposure length of film. Both types of cassette can be loaded into the camera in daylight.

This, however, does not mean direct sunlight, always load the Leica in subdued daylight either indoors or in some suitable shady spot outside. The cassettes are normally light-tight, but a certain amount of light may find its way in and spoil the first negative or even more. We shall invariably discard the first two exposures to be on the safe side, but careless handling may even affect subsequent exposures. For that reason also, do not leave a loaded cassette lying about either before or after exposure; store it in its metal box.

The risk of light leakage is greater with standard cassettes than with Leitz cassettes. The light trapping is much more efficient with the latter, since they do not open until they are inside the camera and the base is closed.

The Leica is loaded from the bottom. The spools and film track are less easily accessible that way, but this does not appreciably complicate loading.

Some screw-mounted Leicas have a finger projecting from the inside of the base plate. This helps to keep the film properly aligned in the film track when the camera is closed.

Before opening the Leica, make quite sure there is no film in it. Check by turning the rewind crank or knob in the direction of the arrow; if it turns freely the camera is empty. If it does not turn, there is still a cassette with film inside, and the film must be removed first (p. 80).

To open the Leica, lift up the locking key in the base plate and turn in the direction of the arrow pointing to "auf—open" or "auf" until the arrow on the key itself points to "auf". Lift up the base plate by the locking key and unhook from the peg at the other end. Put down the base plate, inside upwards, on a clean surface. Don't put it, inside downwards, on the ground, or it may pick up dirt or grit.

LOADING THE M4

Loading is particularly quick and simple:

After opening the base plate drop the film into its channel so that the leader lies between the prongs of the take-up spool (*right*).

Refit the base plate and lock it (*left*). Release the shutter and wind the film twice until the film counter shows No. 0 (*right*) ready for the first exposure.

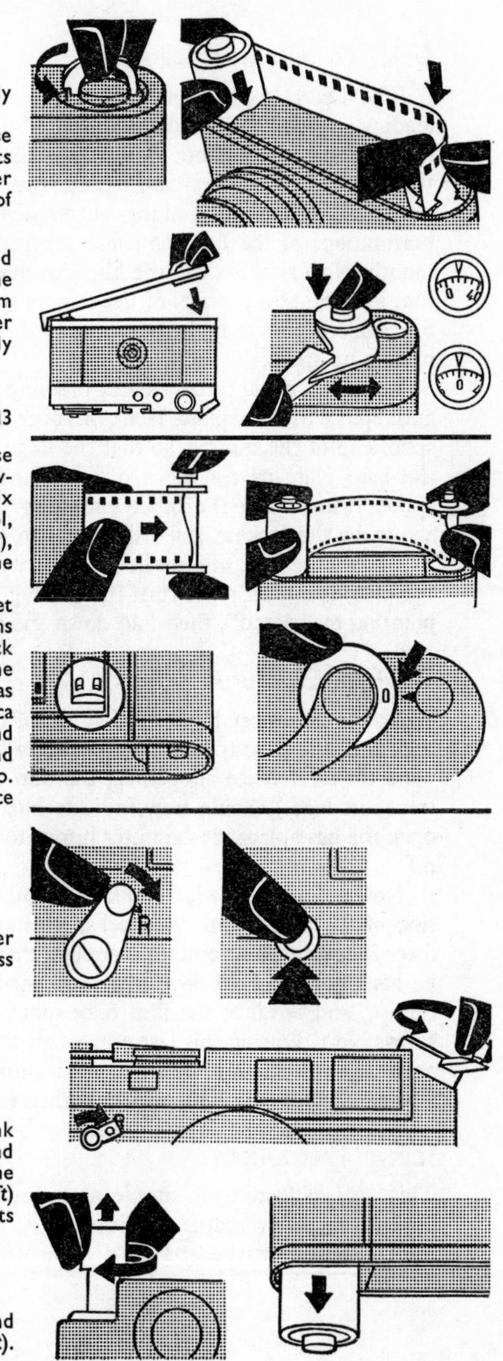

LOADING THE M1 TO M3

After opening the base plate and back and removing the take-up spool, fix the film end to the spool, emulsion outwards (*left*), then insert the film in the film channel (*right*).

Check that the sprocket engages the perforations (*left*) then close the back and base plate. Advance the film to the first exposure as with the M4; with the Leica M1 and M2 make two blind exposures after loading and set the film counter to No. 0 (*right*). Advance once more for the first shot.

UNLOADING THE M

Set the reversing lever on the front to R or press the reversing button.

Turn the rewind crank of the M4 or pull out and turn the rewind knob of the other models (*bottom left*) to rewind the film into its cassette.

Open the base plate and remove the cassette (*right*).

Quick Loading with the M4

The Leica M4 and MDa have a particularly easy quick-loading system. This is how it works. With the camera open as just described, pull about $4\frac{1}{4}$ inches of film out of its cassette. With a commercially available cassette (i.e. not a reloaded one—page 186) this means pulling out enough film so that three perforations of the *full film width* protrude from the cassette mouth. Now simply drop the film cassette with its protruding film into the film channel of the camera so that the end of the film leader comes to lie between two of the prongs of the built-in take-up spool.

Close down the camera back, pressing it against the body, and replace the base plate. Hook this over the peg at the take-up spool end of the camera, so that the large plastic wheel inside the base plate moves down over the prongs of the take-up spool. Bring down the other end fully. Make sure that the arrow on the locking key still points to the position "open" (otherwise the base will not fit over the camera properly). With the plate firmly in place turn the locking key in the direction pointing to "closed", then fold down the key.

The First Exposure

Work the transport lever until it locks, or press the shutter release if it is already locked. Alternately press the release and wind the lever twice altogether; the film counter (next to the transport lever) should now indicate No. 0. (Every time you open the base plate, this counter jumps to two divisions below 0.)

Now unfold the rewind crank and gently turn it in the direction of the arrow until you feel a resistance. On no account force it beyond this point; it is enough that the crank begins to be hard to turn. Fold down the crank again, press the shutter release, and advance the film once more so that the counter shows No. 1. During this last movement the crank should turn against the direction of its arrow—this indicates that the film is advancing properly. The camera is then ready.

Special Precautions

This way of loading is simple and almost foolproof. But it depends on a few simple conditions:

(1) There must be at least $\frac{1}{2}$ inch of film leader going in

between two of the prongs of the take-up spool. Pulling out the 4¼ inch film length mentioned above is the easiest way of ensuring this.

(2) The film must have a trimmed leader, but this need not necessarily be of the exact dimensions provided on commerical cassettes. The trimmed length should be at least 1 to 1½ inches (around 3 to 4 cm.) long and not wider than 1 inch (2.5 cm.) nor narrower than ½ inch (1.3 cm.). There is thus a certain amount of latitude if you trim the film end yourself (see also p. 189).

All films sold in commercial cassettes and as darkroom reloads (p. 181) have this trimmed leader—a shaped tongue about half the width of the film and some 4 inches long.

With the Leica M1 to M3 the trimmed leader is not really necessary, and when loading, for example, from bulk film it is perfectly permissible to cut off the film ends square. Trimming is, however, essential with the screw-mounted Leica models, since it is otherwise difficult to fit the film into the camera without getting it tangled up with the transport sprocket. This particular requirement of the traditional Leica models was, in fact, responsible for the universal provision of trimmed film leaders with all films sold for miniature cameras.

(3) The perforations on the film leader must be intact. Perforations may break if you hold the rewind crank while working the transport lever—so always keep your fingers well clear of the rewind crank. For the same reason do not try to tighten the film in its cassette by turning the crank until the film counter has advanced to No. 0.

It you have a torn perforation near the beginning of the leader, simply cut or tear off that bit of leader strip. If this leaves less than a 1½ inch length of narrow film at the beginning, re-trim the leader as described above or on p. 189.

(4) The film cassette must be properly in place. If necessary turn the rewind crank through a quarter turn to allow the cassette to be pushed home fully.

With standard cassettes the cassette mouth must point towards the slit of the camera back. When using Leitz N cassettes (the cassette should of course be closed) the cassette spring must be in the corner in the front of the camera.

(5) The Leica M4 (and all other M models) can only be used with the type N cassette. There is also an earlier version of this, a type B cassette which does not fit the Leica M models and would jam.

Loading the M1 to M3

With these models the loading procedure is a little more complex, for the film has to be attached to the removable take-up spool outside the camera.

Open the base plate (which here has no plastic wheel inside but only a holding shaft for the take-up spool) and the camera back, and pull out the take-up spool—carefully, to avoid fouling the release return spring next to the take-up spool camber.

Next pull out about 2 inches of the trimmed film leader from the cassette. Hold the take-up spool in the left hand and the cassette in the right, with the spool knobs of both pointing downwards. (While doing this place the camera, bottom up, on a level surface. Out of doors, wedge it between the knees.)

Insert the end of the film leader underneath the spring of the take-up spool (usually marked with an engraved arrow). The emulsion side of the film must *face away* from the core of the spool. Push the film end fully in. The perforated film leader edge must lie close against the take-up spool flange with the knob. Check that the film runs straight onto the spool core.

Pull out a little more of the film leader from the cassette until there is a 4 inch length (but no more) between the cassette and the take up spool.

Turn the cassette and and take-up spool over, so that both spool knobs point upwards. Now insert the film into the slit at the back of the camera—which should be held bottom up. Simultaneously push down both the take-up spool and the cassette into their respective film chambers.

Carefully ease the film round the sprocket next to the take-up spool chamber. Through the open back check that the film engages the perforations of the transport sprocket properly. Pull the transport lever slightly if necessary (after pressing the shutter release) to engage the sprocket in the perforations. The cassette must of course be located in the same way as when loading the model M4 (p. 75).

Finally close down the back, refit the base plate and lock it as with the M4.

Pull up the rewind knob and gently turn it in the direction of its arrow to tighten the film inside the camera. Push down the knob again.

Alternately advance the film with the winding lever and

press the release button until the film counter indicates No. 1 on the Leica M3. The counter of this model operates in much the same way as on the M4, but returns to its starting point on pulling the take-up spool out of the camera.

While advancing the film in this way check that the shaft of the rewind knob (not the knob itself) with the two red dots or the red line on it rotates at the same time.

If the rewind shaft does not rotate, the film may have left the take-up spool. Or, more likely, the sprocket has torn through the perforations and does not advance the film. In the latter case there may be a certain resistance to working the transport lever at first. The cause of this may be stiffness of the film in the cassette, particularly with standard cassettes which have been reloaded at home and bent in the process.

To deal with this, open the camera and take out the cassette and take-up spool. Cut off the trimmed tongue behind the damaged perforation and re-attach to the take-up spool. Hold the film end and tighten up the film in the cassette by gently turning the cassette knob anti-clockwise. Also try easing the cassette knob to and fro to make sure that it does not bind against its hole in the shell.

Then reinsert the take-up spool and cassette in the camera and proceed as before. Be particularly sure to check the proper engagement of the transport sprocket with the film perforations, by looking at the film through the open camera back.

With the Leica M1 and M2 advance the film twice (pressing the release button beforehand each time) and set the film counter to 0. This is the large disc below the transport lever. Turn it to bring the 0 opposite the mark by the little button next to the film counter.

Then press the release once more and advance the film, so that the film counter indicates No. 1.

These blind exposures at the beginning of the film take up the film length protruding from the cassette (which was already fogged during loading) and ensure that a completely fresh and unexposed film frame comes into position behind the lens.

It is not advisable to try and save film over these "blind" exposures. When advancing the film by less than the lengths just mentioned, there is always a serious risk of spoiling the first frame by fogging. Also, with colour films processed by service stations or manufacturers this length of film leader is often cut off and so the first exposure—whether spoilt or not—would be lost anyway.

The Film Indicator

The Leica models have a film indicator to show the type of film loaded in the camera.

On the Leica M cameras set the film indicator disc in the back of the camera by rotating the central knob with the tip of a finger pressed against it. Set one of the three pointers against the appropriate speed in ASA or DIN.

The three pointers correspond to black-and-white film (black-and-white chevron in centre), daylight type colour film (symbol of sun), and artificial light type colour film (symbol of lamp) respectively.

Since the film indicator is not coupled with the camera mechanism in any way, it can be set at any time.

Loading the Earlier Leica Models

The screw-lens Leica models are loaded similarly to the M models (other than M4). These earlier cameras have, however, no hinged back, so it is essential to get the film properly positioned in the film plane between the focal plane and shutter the camera back itself.

Open the Leica in the same way as with the M models, and again fix the film leader to the take-up spool removed from the camera. In this case the leader must be properly trimmed (p. 189).

Before inserting the film in the camera make sure that the reversing lever is set to A. Turn the transport knob as far as it will go, and press the shutter release button. Now carefully push the cassette and the take-up spool into their respective chambers, guiding the film into the slit at the back of the camera. Give the film transport knob a quarter turn to make sure that the film perforations engage the sprocket, and close and lock the base plate.

Then turn the transport knob until it locks and gently turn the rewind knob in the direction of the arrow to pull the film taut inside the camera. Press the release button, turn the transport knob, press again, and turn the transport knob once more. During this operation the rewind knob should rotate backwards to show that the film is advancing properly (if it does not, open the camera again, check for torn perforations, and reinsert the film properly.)

Set the film counter by turning the numbered disc underneath the transport knob anti-clockwise (get hold of it by the two projecting pegs) until No. 0 is opposite the arrow engraved on top of the camera. Finally turn the transport knob once more to bring the film into position for the first exposure.

The film counter can be set also after winding the transport knob for the last time; in that case set "1" opposite the arrow.

LOADING SCREW-LENS LEICAS

Black panel: The correct path (*top*) of the film runs from the cassette past the focal plane, over the sprocket, and, *emulsion side out*, on to the take-up spool. Make sure the Leitz cassette (*centre*) or standard cassette (*bottom*) is correctly inserted in the chamber.

Right-hand column: Open the camera by turning the base plate lock to "open" (*top*) and lifting off the base plate (*upper centre*). Withdraw the spool (*lower centre*) and attach the film leader to the core (*bottom*).

Make sure the reversing lever is at A, press the shutter release, and turn the transport knob.

Insert the cassette and take-up spool.

Close the base plate and lock by turning the key.

Press the release, and advance the film.

Check that the film is properly engaged by tightening the rewind knob.

Press the release again, advance the film, and set the counter to O. Press the release once more, and wind for a third time.

To set the film indicator (models If to IIIf only) pull up the transport knob and turn to bring the film type and speed into the cut-out (*right*). On the Leica IIIg turn the centre of the dial in the camera back to set one of the three pointers to the appropriate speed figure (*left*).

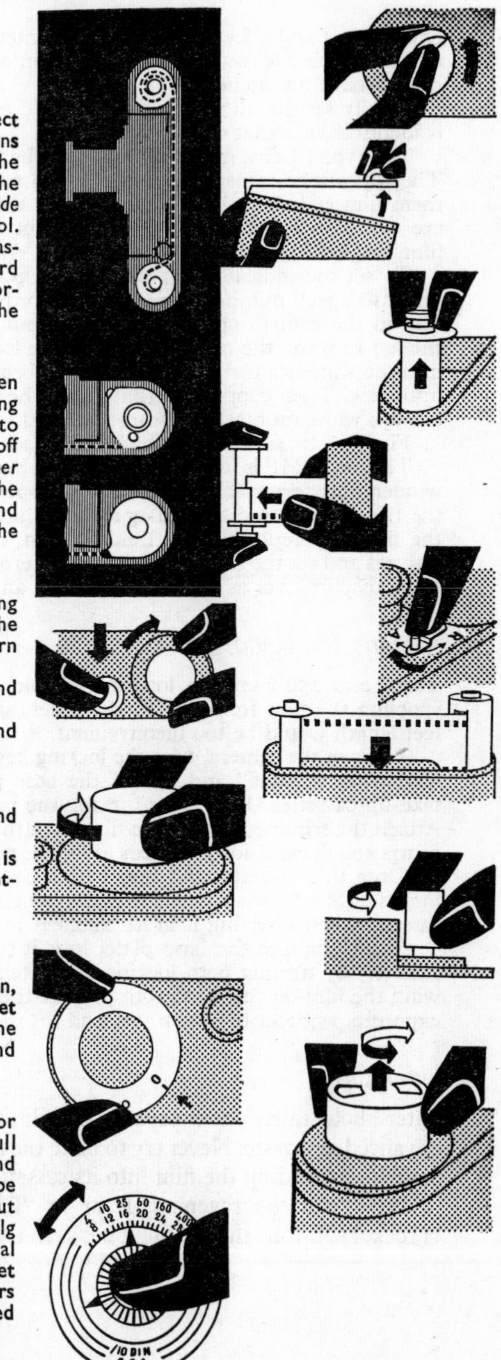

On type g, f and c Leica models the counter disc incorporates a ratchet which clicks while setting the film counter. Older Leica models have no ratchet.

Finally set the film indicator. On the Leica Ig and IIIg this is identical with that of the M models.

The type f Leica film indicator is in the film transport knob. The top of the transport knob has two cut-outs. Underneath them film speeds in ASA and DIN are engraved. The figures are white on black, with a black cut-out for black-and-white film, and red cut-out for colour film.

To set the indicator, lift up the transport knob and turn it until the speed number corresponding to the speed and type of film in the camera appears in the cut-out. Turn the knob to the left to bring the red cut-out with the letters ASA and DIN into the window; turn it to the right to bring the black cut-out into view. Then continue turning until the right speed number (always white on black) appears in the cut-out.

Finally let the transport knob drop back again.

The Leica MP is loaded similarly, but here the Leicavit rapid winder unit forms the base plate. To open, slide the lever at the tripod bush end to "auf-open", and lift off. After inserting the film and replacing the Leicavit unit, make two blind exposures and set the film counter disc underneath the shaft of the top transport lever as with the Leica M1 and M2.

Loading the Leica 250

The Leica 250 (now no longer available) uses two cassettes, spooling the film from one to the other, since rewinding a 33 feet length would be too inconvenient.

To open the camera, turn the locking keys at each end of the base plate to "auf" and lift off the base plate. Take out the take-up cassette. Open it by turning the inner shell clockwise. Attach the trimmed end of the film from the full cassette to the centre spool, emulsion outwards as for the normal take-up spool.

Close this cassette, and insert both cassettes, with about 6 inches of film between them, into the camera. Slightly turn each cassette when inserting it in its chamber to push home.

Finally replace the base plate, lock it (thereby opening the cassette) by turning both locking keys. Release the shutter and wind the film on three times to prepare the camera for the first exposure, as described on p. 78, and set the film counter.

Unloading

After about thirty-six exposures the film transport cannot be advanced any more. Never try to force the transport; this is the time for rewinding the film into its cassette.

First turn the reversing lever to "R" to disengage the sprocket and thus the coupling between the film transport and

UNLOADING SCREW-LENS LEICAS

Black panel: The sequence of unloading (*from top to bottom*) is (p. 80):

Set the reversing lever to R.

Turn the rewind knob to rewind the film into its cassette.

Open the base plate.

Lift out the cassette.

Close the camera.

Right-hand column: When unloading partly exposed films (*top sequence*) advance the film and make a note of the number of the last exposure. Rewind the film, and mark that number on the film leader. When reloading the film (*bottom sequence*) insert in the usual way, then cover the lens with the lens cap, and press the release and wind the film successively until the counter shows the next number to that noted. Remember to allow for the same number of initial blind exposures.

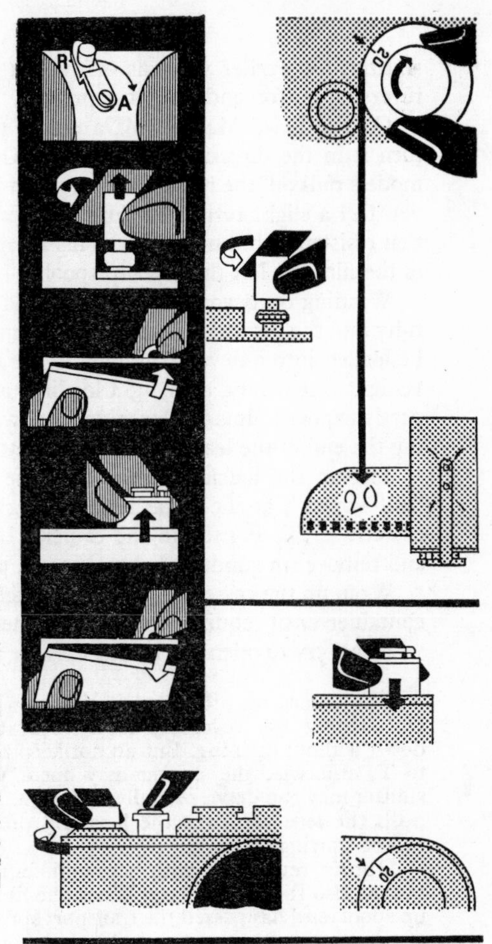

To unload short lengths, advance the film, then take the Leica into the darkroom. Open the base plate, and push the film cutting knife down the back near the cassette. Wind the transport knob twice and pull out the take-up spool. Unwind the exposed film from the spool, wrap it up light-tight, and retrim the cassette leader to reload the remaining length into the Leica.

shutter. On earlier versions of the M1 and M2 depress the reversing button and keep it depressed.

On the Leica M4 and MDa unfold the rewind crank and turn it in the direction of the arrow. On the other Leica M models pull out the rewind knob to turn it. Keep turning until you feel a slight resistance during rewinding. Wind just past that resistance, but no farther. This means that the beginning of the film has left the take-up spool.

Winding on beyond this point would draw the film leader fully into the cassette. That would not matter if the film had to be loaded into a developing tank in the dark. But it is inconvenient when using a daylight loading tank or when changing partly exposed films (below) since that would involve extricating the end of the leader from the cassette in total darkness.

Lift up the locking key on the base plate and turn it to "auf—open", at the same time closing the slit of the Leitz cassette if this is used in the camera. Lift off the base plate and remove (in subdued light). Finally, pull out the cassette.

Wrap up the cassette light-tight or keep it in its aluminium container until required for re-use or development.

Never try to open the loaded cassette in daylight.

The unloading procedure is similar with screw-lens Leicas. On turning the reversing lever to R the shutter may run down without opening. But do not keep the slow speed dial set to T, otherwise the shutter may open. With early Leicas the shutter may run down partially and open. To be on the safe side, push the lens cap over the lens and press the release button before starting to rewind.

During rewinding with screw-mounted Leicas the release button also turns clockwise. When the film end leaves the take-up spool (and has passed the transport sprocket) the button stops turning, as can be seen from a black dot on its rim. At this point stop rewinding.

This procedure for unloading is identical for all Leica models (though the rewind knob does not pull out with the Leica I) except the Leica 250. Here no rewinding is necessary. When the end of the film is reached, wind on past the resistance to free the film end from the spool of the feed cassette, wind for two more turns, open the camera and finally take out both cassettes, one full and one completely empty.

Changing Partly Exposed Films

Sometimes we may want to change from one type of sensitive material to another (e.g. black-and-white to colour, or vice versa) in the middle of a film. This is quite easy, though it entails sacrificing one frame during the change-over.

Before changing over, wind the film to the next exposure (if this has not already been done) and make a note of the number on the film counter. Now rewind the film as described above, taking great care not to draw the beginning of the leader into the casette. Then unload the camera. Mark the number of the next exposure noted above on the protruding film.

To reload a partly exposed film, proceed exactly as described on p. 72, but cover the lens with the lens cap when making the preliminary blind exposures.

Set the film counter in the usual way. With the lens still covered, keep on releasing the shutter and advancing the film until the film counter indicates one exposure after the number noted when unloading the film.

The most important point about reloading partly-exposed films is that the cassette spool should turn smoothly and that the perforations of the film leader should not be damaged. Otherwise the film will not reload properly.

Retrimming the film leader (p. 189) would ruin the first one or two exposures. If this should become necessary reload the film in total darkness. Advance it to two or even three frames beyond the number noted when unloading.

Alternately, to be on the safe side, advance the film altogether four times instead of three when loading it for the first time (and, of course, allow for the same number of blind exposures before setting the film counter when reloading).

Cutting Off Exposed Lengths

When 36 exposures are too long to wait before developing a few important shots, it is usually easiest to unload the film and waste the unexposed part. It is rarely worth going to the trouble of locating a darkroom and going through the cumbersome procedure for cutting off an exposed portion and then reloading the rest. With reversal colour film, the manufacturer's laboratories generally only accept uncut complete films for processing. Where cutting off of exposed lengths is really necessary, proceed as follows.

The simplest way is to advance the film for the next exposure, and release the shutter. Take the Leica into the darkroom, open it without rewinding the film, and cut off the exposed length. To do this, remove the base plate and open the back. Use one finger to push the film gently from the back towards the take-up spool, to disengage the perforations from the sprocket.

Then carefully pull up the take-up spool a little, edging the film up from the back of the camera. Pull out both the cassette and the take-up spool, removing the film from the camera altogether. Cut off the film near the cassette with a pair of scissors, unwind the film from the take-up spool, and wrap up light-tight.

Then reload the film remaining on the cassette in the usual way.

Naturally, the film will be finished well before the thirty-sixth exposure; therefore, do not force the transport knob.

There is also another way. Advance the film twice after the last exposure, and then open the shutter on the B setting. Unscrew the camera lens and stick a small piece of adhesive cellulose tape on the face of the film visible through the open shutter. Then close the shutter and rewind the film.

Take the cassette into the darkroom, and unwind the film, feeling carefully for the tape in the dark. Cut off beyond that point. Clean hands are absolutely essential for this job. While it is normally not a good idea to touch the film surface with the fingers, this trick is quite useful in emergencies.

With the screw-mounted Leicas a special cutting knife is available for cutting off the film in the camera. After opening the base plate in the darkroom, push the end of the knife between the camera back and the film near the cassette mouth. Turn the knife so that the cutting edge bears on the film, and carefully push the knife down to cut off the film, leaving a narrow strip protruding from the cassette if possible. Release the shutter, still in total darkness, and turn the film transport knob two or three times until the cut off piece is fully wound up on the take-up spool. Carefully pull out the latter, taking care not to scratch the film. Remove the cut off portion and wrap up light-tight.

With the Leica 250, where we more likely want to cut off exposed lengths, the process is greatly simplified. Make four blind exposures, open the base plate, and take out both cassettes. Cut off the film close to the take-up cassette, reshape the film leader, and attach it to the centre spool of a new take-up cassette. Then simply reload. All this can take place in ordinary (subdued) daylight.

LEICA LENSES

Wide-angle lenses take in a larger subject area than the standard lens, but image detail is smaller.
Long-focus lenses take in a narrower field of view, but show detail on a larger scale.
Use a lens hood, especially for against-the-light shots.

The versatility of the Leica is to a large extent due to its range of interchangeable lenses. The current series of twenty lenses covers focal lengths from $\frac{7}{8}$ inch (21 mm.) to 22 inches (560 mm.), and in the standard lenses, maximum apertures up to *f*1.2 (And the Leicaflex has its own series of lenses!)

This seems at first sight a bewildering collection; yet each lens has its specific applications, to enable the Leica to get the most out of almost any subject.

What, then, are the features which make a lens specially suitable for its task? Which lens shall we use for a particular purpose? Let us look at them in turn.

Focal Length

The fundamental specification of a lens is its focal length or focus. This is the distance between the optical centre of the lens and the image plane (in practice the film) when the lens forms a sharp image of a distant object. Each Leica lens is marked with its nominal focal length in millimetres.

The focal length determines the scale of the image: the shorter the focal length, the smaller the scale. A short focal length will therefore give a small image of the subject. When used with a given negative size, such a lens can pack a large part of the scene in front of it into the negative area. In other words it has a wide angle of view.

A long-focus lens, on the other hand, gives a larger image. Accordingly it will fit a smaller part of the subject into the negative. It has a narrow angle of view.

Somewhere between the two there should, of course, be something we could call a normal angle of view. While this is to some extent arbitrary, the standard focal length for a Leica negative is taken as 2 inches or 50 mm. Lenses with a shorter focus are regarded as wide-angle lenses, and those of a longer focal length as long-focus lenses.

Telephoto lenses (p. 108), though of somewhat different

optical construction also give the same type of result as long-focus lenses, and are in the same category.

The angles quoted for Leica lenses apply to the lens focused on infinity. They are slightly smaller with nearer subjects, and appreciably smaller when the lens is used for large close-ups and macrophotography.

The angles quoted in this book (p. 461) are horizontal and vertical image angles; they refer to the view taken in by the length and height respectively of the Leica frame.

Exact Focal Lengths

The focal lengths quoted for each type of lens are nominal ones. They are marked on the lens either in cm. or (since 1958) in mm. The true focal length of an individual lens may deviate slightly (up to 2 per cent either way).

This may be important in highly accurate scientific work and also in exact photo-surveying. The current Leica lenses therefore carry code numbers beyond the infinity end of the focusing scale, usually next to the metres or feet mark. These represent the last two digits of the focal length in tenths of a millimetre. For example, a 50 mm. lens with the code number 16 indicates an actual focal length of 51.6 mm.; or a 90 mm. lens with the code 95 has an actual focal length of 89.5 mm. Where the lens unit unscrews from the focusing mount, a similar code number may be scratched on the inner lens barrel itself. This provides an instant check that the lens is mounted in the correct focusing mount, since the latter has to match the exact focal length of the lens.

Earlier Leica lenses either have the actual focal length scratched on the inner lens barrel of the lens unit proper or a code letter or number stamped into the underside of the focusing lever on certain standard lenses. The exact focal length, where not clear from the coding, can be ascertained on inquiry from the makers.

Lens Speed

In addition to the focal length the front mount of the Leica lenses also indicates the maximum aperture or speed. This measures the light-gathering power of the lens.

The lower the aperture number, the more light the lens will admit; thus a maximum aperture of *f*1.4 (generally marked as 1 : 1.4 on the Leica lens front) is much faster than one of *f*3.5. It is in fact nearly 6½ times as fast. The former can therefore be used to take fast shots under poor lighting conditions.

The larger the maximum aperture, the more versatile the lens becomes when we are up against difficult subjects.

Names of current Leica lenses in focal lengths between 28 and 135 mm. tend to indicate the maximum aperture of the lens. Thus all Elmarit units are *f*2.8 lenses, all Summicrons are *f*2, and Elmar signifies *f*3.5 or *f*4. (The 50 mm. Elmar *f*2.8 is an older exception.)

The aperture is, of course, variable; we can make it smaller (stop the lens down) by means of a lever or ring on the barrel which works the iris diaphragm.

Lens Quality

In theory a lens should reproduce every point of the subject as a perfect image point on the film. In practice the image points are really small discs. If they are small enough to be invisible even on enlargement of the negative, the image will appear sharp. But as they get larger, they increasingly overlap. And if they are comparable in size to details of the image, such details will no longer be recognizable—the lens cannot resolve them.

This power to resolve fine detail gives some indication of the quality of the lens. The practice in testing a lens used to be to photograph sets of parallel lines of different size. The finest set of lines (i.e. with the most lines per millimetre) that the lens can separate on the film then measures the limit of its resolving power under the conditions of the test.

In practice the visual sharpness of an image depends not only on the resolution of fine detail but also on the contrast with which such detail is recorded. A simple resolving power figure, though a rough yardstick of the optimum performance of a lens, therefore provides only incomplete information.

Performance is nowadays specified more thoroughly by a curve which plots relative image contrast against resolution, and which goes under various names such as modulation transfer function, contrast transfer function or optical transfer function. Though its concept is more complicated, it can be measured automatically by certain instruments. The modulation transfer function of a final picture depends also on the film, the enlarger optics and even the conditions of viewing or projection of the print or transparency.

Although no lens is perfect, modern Leica lenses usually produce a sharper image than the film can record. Only the Thambar lens (p. 112) is purposely designed to yield slightly unsharp images for special pictorial effects.

Another aspect of the over-all optical performance of the lens is the evenness of illumination. The older high-aperture, and also wide-angle, lenses show some falling off of image brightness near the corners of the negative.

One of the reasons for this is that the lens barrel has a certain depth. Rays of light passing through the lens obliquely at an angle may thus be cut off before they can reach the film.

In addition, the lens opening, as seen from the corner of the negative would no longer appear circular, but as an ellipse with a smaller area, thus passing less light. In practice the latter phenomenon—which applies to all lenses of orthodox design—is rarely disturbing. The corners of the negative are frequently left out, anyway, in making enlargements, and the enlarging lens tends to have a similar effect which compensates for the uneven illumination of the camera lens.

These imperfections as well as residual lens aberrations largely disappear as lenses are stopped down one or two stops below their maximum aperture. Further stopping down increases the depth of field (p. 206), but tends to decrease the maximum sharpness of the image due to diffraction. Hence where great depth of field is not essential it is not good practice to stop the lens down extensively.

The third main practical defect of lenses, namely distortion (i.e. showing straight lines curved near the edges of the image) is virtually absent in most Leica lenses.

Air Bubbles

Occasionally a lens may contain a few very minute air bubbles. These arise in the smelting of the optical glasses used in lens making. They are not, as often claimed, a hall-mark of high-quality glass. They have nothing to do with quality, but in the course of the process of manufacture they are more difficult to avoid with such types of glass.

A few odd bubbles do not affect the performance of the lens in any way. Their only result is to reduce the speed by a minute amount due to light being lost by diffusion. The effect is considerably smaller than the already very close tolerances in the manufacture of these lenses.

Infra-Red Focusing

The Leica lenses, particularly those of newer design, are also fully colour corrected. This means that they focus light of all visible colours in the same plane and give uniformly sharp pictures of coloured subjects. That is of special importance for colour photography.

This colour correction does not, however, extend into the region of infra-red radiation which is sometimes used in photography (pp. 195, 453). The infra-red image is therefore formed very slightly behind the normal image, and in infra-red photography we have to re-focus the lens.

A convenient way is to use the right-hand *f*5.6 line of the

THE SCOPE OF LENSES

The different focal lengths of the Leica lenses provide us with many different angles of view. We can utilize this range to select just how much we want to include of the subject, either covering a wide over-all view (*above*), or closing in on the scene to pick out salient details on a progressively larger scale and to fill the picture area with them (*below*).

This choice of wide or narrow views is a particular asset where we cannot move about with the Leica.

The wide angle lens takes in a bigger view than we do when we look at the subject normally; the picture therefore conveys spaciousness as well as depth. It is a depth not only in sharpness, but also of perspective, from the dominating size of the foreground objects (*top*) to the diminutive people and surroundings in the distance.

The narrow view of the long-focus lenses concentrates interest on more distant subjects, bringing them closer for examination. The results appeal not by their impressiveness, but by rich close-up detail like the elaborate craftsmanship of the decorative work on the tabernacle from Aachen Cathedral (*left*).

The choice of lenses opens up great picture making possibilities.

We can approach the subject closely and still cover sufficient of it to show the overpowering perspective of the foreground pattern. With the normal focus lens the width of the view which creates the dramatic impact of the huge pipes in the factory workshop (*top*) would to a large extent be lost.

When the real element of the picture is just a small area of our field of view, we have to rely on the long-focus lens to lift the parts we really want to see out of their surroundings. We need its telescope-like probing into details we could hardly see with the naked eye like the activities of the bridge repair workers (*bottom*)—to bring the subject to our attention.

The contrast between foreground and background depends similarly on the lens.

With a short-focus lens we can look at individual features of the subject from close by and still include enough to identify the whole, as with the Albert Memorial in London (*above*).

Familiar themes like the Scott Memorial in Edinburgh (*opposite top*) exhibit new angles.

With the standard and longer focus lenses the foreground dwindles in importance, becoming more of a scenic frame for a building (*opposite bottom*) or for a view of a whole town like Whitby (*below*).

With the help of various close-up accessories we can really get at features that would not be otherwise accessible. The continuous range of subject distances covered from infinity to same-size or even enlarged reproduction brings a wide variety of subjects within our reach. We can record details of architecture and sculpture, like the Essen Madonna (p. 94), and miniature works of art (p. 95), of all sizes on almost any scale we like.

Perspective (p. 96) depends on the camera position. The nearer we go to the subject, the more prominent the perspective will be. To keep the size of the main subject constant on the film, we have to use longer focus lenses as we go back. As the focal length of the lens and the required taking distance increase, the background comes nearer, while the apparent separation between the planes in the scene gets smaller and the perspective more subdued.

Page 89: Image scale with 35, 50, 90, 135, 200 and 400 mm. lenses, Photos: *A. Tritschler*.

Page 90: 35 mm. lens, 1/30 sec., *f*9 (*top*), and 200 mm. lens in reflex housing, 3 secs., *f*18 (*bottom*). Fine grain pan film. Photos: *A. Tritschler*.

Page 91: 35 mm. lens, 1/20 sec., *f*6.3 (*top*), and 200 mm. lens in reflex housing, 1/100 sec., *f*9 (*bottom*). Fine grain pan film. Photos: *A. Tritschler*.

Page 92: 35 mm. lens, fast pan film, deep yellow filter, 1/200 sec., *f*11 (*top*), and 85 mm. lens, fast pan film, 1/200 sec., *f*8 (*bottom*). Photos: *J. Sadovy* and *D. Potts*.

Page 93: 35 mm. lens, fine grain pan film, light yellow filter, 1/30 sec., *f*12.5 (*top*), and 50 mm. lens fine grain pan film, 1/100 sec., *f*5.6 (*bottom*). Photos: *O. Marcus* and *A. Tritschler*.

Page 94: 135 mm. lens in reflex housing, fine grain pan film, 1 sec., *f*12.5. Photo: *A. Tritschler*.

Page 95: 135 mm. lens in reflex housing and focusing bellows, fine grain pan film, 1/5 sec., *f*12.5. Photo: *A. Tritschler*.

Left: Perspective with 35, 50, 90, 135 and 200 mm. lenses from increasing distances, chosen to record the car in the foreground on the same scale every time. Photos: *A. Tritschler*.

depth of field indicator as the focusing index (or between *f*4 and *f*8). Focus normally, then set the distance opposite the central focusing index against the right-hand *f*5.6 mark.

Many of the more modern Leica lenses (but not the current types) carry a special focusing index marked R for this purpose. That index line is usually a little to the right of the normal focusing mark. No infra-red index is provided, nor necessary, on the wide-angle lenses.

When using infra-red films, focus the Leica in the usual way (e.g. by rangefinder). Then reset the lens so that the distance mark originally opposite the focusing mark comes opposite the line with the R index.

Coated Lenses

The current Leica lenses all carry an anti-reflection coating on each glass/air surface. This coating largely eliminates the reflection and scattering of light which occurs whenever a ray enters or leaves a lens component. Such reflected light may appear on the negative as a weak over-all veil, and slightly reduce brilliance and contrast of the image in the shadows. In colour photography it may lead to desaturated colours.

If the subject includes particularly bright light sources either within or just outside the picture area, as in outdoor night shots, the inter-lens reflections may also appear as flare spots. These are ghost images—weak circular or star-shaped spots—in the darker parts of the picture.

The coating prevents this reflected light from being diverted from its proper path and lost. Consequently, a coated lens actually transmits more light than an uncoated one.

Older Leica lenses can be coated either by the manufacturers or by any reliable repair firm.

Coating—or the lack of it—does not affect the definition or colour correction of the lens in any way. It may affect the colour rendering in terms of the exact degree of warmth or coldness of a colour transparency. This, of course, also depends on the film and colour of the prevailing daylight.

The lenses themselves differ very slightly in colour rendering due to the varying number of elements and different glasses used. The choice of the coating often aims to compensate these variations.

The Choice of Lenses

For normal subjects one of the standard 50 mm. lenses is the ideal focal length.

The choice of any particular aperture will depend on the type of work to be done. Thus for average requirements the *f*2.8 Elmar or the *f*2 Summicron is the best all-round lens.

The $f1.4$ Summilux lens is useful for sports where fast shutter speeds are needed, or in poor light (circus, theatre, indoors, etc.); and with slow films, especially colour.

In a confined space—e.g. indoors—a wide-angle lens is handy. This takes in more of the subject when we cannot get far enough back to cover it all with the standard lens. The broad view also helps to give the picture depth and perspective.

Where we cannot get close enough to the subject to fill the negative with it, we need a long-focus lens. Its rather narrower angle of view cuts out the unwanted picture areas and instead produces an enlarged view of only the subject itself.

Long-focus lenses have a special use in portraiture, as they enable us to go farther away from the subject. We thus have more room in which to operate and set up lights. The more distant viewpoint yields a more pleasing perspective (p. 324).

The long-focus lenses are also valuable for unobserved shooting from a distance; we can watch the subject as we might through binoculars.

Other applications include pictures of sports and games, particularly action shots where we could not possibly get near enough to the action to show it on a sufficiently large scale (e.g. cricket or football pictures).

The magnification of the long-focus lenses is progressively greater with increasing focal length. Thus the 90 mm. lenses will be useful for moderate distances, while the 135 mm. lenses will give the same effect with more distant subjects.

A special lens unit was available for stereo (p. 443).

Bayonet and Screw Mounting

The Leica M models have a bayonet lens mount which takes lenses with a similar bayonet mount, thus making lens changing rapid and positive. The earlier Leica series up to IIIg have a screw flange which has been standardized since 1931. There the lens screws into the camera, a procedure which takes a little longer, but is also perfectly accurate.

As the flange-to-film distance on the M models is 1 mm. shorter than on the screw-mounted Leicas, screw-mounted lenses can be used on the M models with the aid of an adapter ring (p. 113).

Bayonet-mounted lenses cannot be used on any screw-mounted Leica.

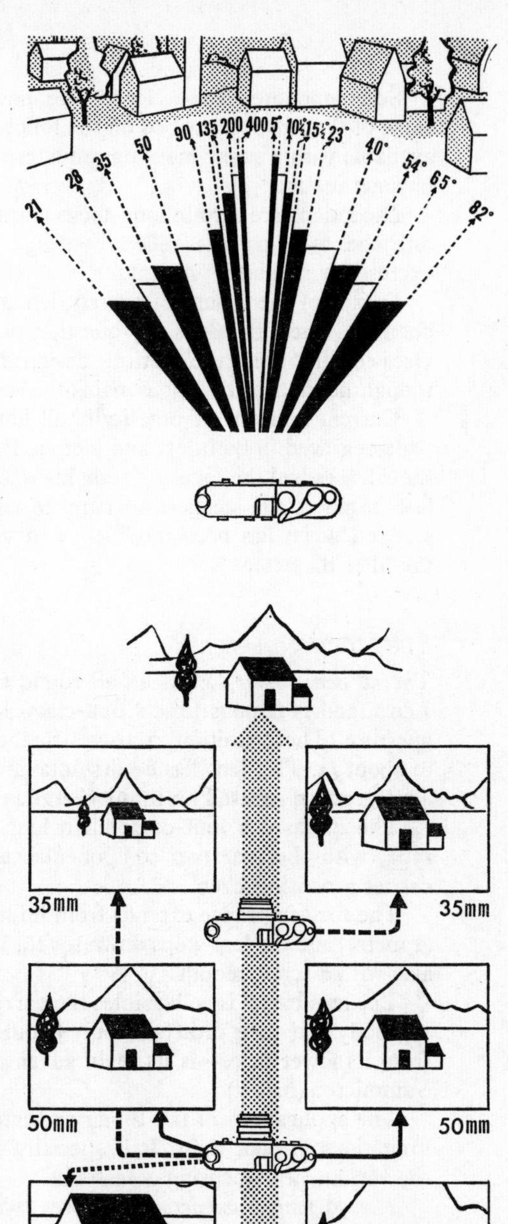

The range of interchangeable lenses for the Leica covers focal lengths from 21 to 560 mm. (shown here to 400 mm.), to take in horizontal image angles from 82 to just over 3½ degrees.

By choosing the appropriate focal length, with the camera at a given viewpoint, we can thus cover more of the subject on a smaller scale, or less of it on a larger scale (*left-hand column*). As long as the viewpoint is fixed, the angle of view only changes; the perspective—in effect the size relationship between different objects in the scene—remains the same (see also p. 89).

We can also control the perspective by varying both the camera distance and the focal length of the lens. In this way a selected main object can remain at the same scale throughout, but change in importance relative to a diminishing or growing background scale (*right*; see also p. 96).

Screw-mounted Leica lenses are now discontinued, but some of the lenses described on the following pages used to be available with a screw mount as an alternative to the Leica M bayonet mount.

Exceptions are certain long-focus and tele lenses which can only be used on the reflex housing. These are available exclusively in a screw mount.

Details of the mount of current lenses have in some cases changed since the lens in question was first introduced. Occasionally even the optical design has been improved, though nominally the lens remains the same.

Current versions of practically all lenses carry a focusing scale engraved in both feet and metres. Earlier versions of the same lenses had the focusing scale in *either* feet *or* metres. In a few instances the smallest aperture to which a lens could be stopped down has been modified, and very occasionally also the filter diameter.

The Standard Lenses

The 50 *mm. Elmar f*2.8 is an all-round standard lens for the Leica, and is famous for its first-class definition even at full aperture. The definition improves further on stopping down to about *f*4. This lens has a horizontal angle of view of nearly 40 deg. when focused on infinity, and 27 deg. vertical.

The Elmar is a four-component lens of the Cooke triplet type, with the rear two components cemented together. It carries a focusing lever.

The focusing range extends from infinity to 3 feet 4 inches (1 metre) and the lens stops down to *f*16. It used to be available also with a screw mount.

The lens barrel is collapsible; the barrel can be pushed into the body and then protrudes only about ¾ inch. This—apart from its lower price—is its main advantage over the 50 mm. Summicron (below).

The applications of the Elmar are extensive, though it has limitations in poor light. It is specially suitable for use with the various near-focusing accessories.

The 50 *mm. Summicron f*2 passes twice as much light at full aperture as the Elmar *f*2.8, and is the ideal universal lens for the Leica. It is derived from a symmetrical construction, consisting of seven components and utilizes modern

The wide-angle lenses for the Leica are the 21 mm. Super Angulon *f*3.4, the 28 mm. Elmarit *f*2.8, the 35 mm. Summaron *f*2.8 (*bottom left*), the 35 mm. Summicron *f*2 (*top right*), and the 35 mm. Summilux *f*1.4 (*lower right*). They all couple directly with the rangefinder of the Leica M2 and M3.

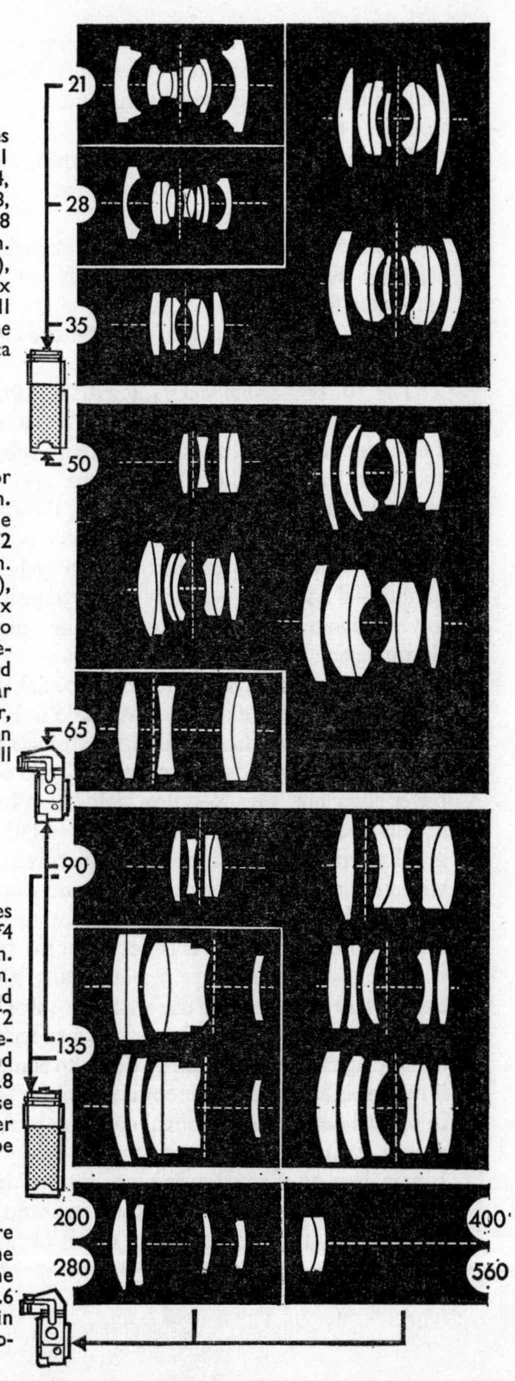

The standard lenses for the Leica are the 50 mm. Elmar *f*2.8 (*upper left*), the 50 mm. Summicron *f*2 (*centre left*), the 50 mm. Summilux *f*1.4 (*upper right*), and the 50 mm. Noctilux *f*1.2 (*lower right*). They also couple with the rangefinder. Almost a standard lens is the 65 mm. Elmar *f*3.5, which is, however, used only in conjunction with the Visoflex II or III reflex housing.

The long-focus lenses are the 90 mm. Elmar *f*4 (*top left*), the 90 mm. Elmarit *f*2.8; the 90 mm. Tele-Elmarit *f*2.8; and the 90 mm. Summicron *f*2 (*right*), the 135 mm. Tele-Elmarit *f*4. (*centre left*), and the 135 mm. Elmarit *f*2.8 (*bottom left*). All these couple with the rangefinder of the Leica, but can also be used with the Visoflex.

The long tele-lenses are the 200 mm. Telyt *f*4, the 280 mm. Telyt *f*4.8 and the 400 and 500 mm. Telyt *f*5.6 These can only be used in conjunction with the Visoflex housings.

highly refracting optical glasses. It has a specially large front lens ($1\frac{1}{4}$ inches diameter) to reduce loss of light near the picture edges through vignetting and to ensure even illumination over the whole negative.

Focusing is by a lever or by turning the focusing mount. The nearest focusing distance is 3 feet 4 inches (1 metre) and the lens stops down to *f*16.

The front unit of the 50 mm. Summicron lens unscrews for separate use (p. 370). A special version of this lens has an extended focusing range for near shots between 3 feet and 19 inches (p. 370). This lens (but not the close-up version) was available also in a screw mount.

The 50 *mm. Summilux f*1.4 with its ultra-wide aperture—twice the speed of the Summicron—is the most versatile of the Leica lenses and will tackle almost any subject. It is useful for sports and action where fast shutter speeds may call for the maximum aperture, and night shots, theatre pictures, etc.

The 50 mm. Summilux is a seven-element symmetrical derivative and in its current version yields as good an image quality—if not better—as any of the 50 mm. lenses. The focusing range and smallest aperture are the same as for the 50 mm. Summicron.

The 50 *mm. Noctilux f*1.2 is a special ultra-speed lens for applications where extreme lens speed is essential. Some of its six lens elements use aspherical surfaces; this has made a very much higher degree of optical correction possible with fewer elements. The Noctilux yields high image brilliance even at full aperture and is particularly suitable for night photography with light sources in the picture, which are rendered without distortion and without reducing the general image contrast. As however this lens costs about three times as much as the 50 mm. Summilux, it is very much a specialist's unit.

The 65 *mm. Elmar f*3.5 is virtually a standard lens, but exclusively designed for use with the Visoflex II and III reflex housings, where it provides—with a special focusing mount—a focusing range from infinity down to some 13 inches (p. 127). The lens is a four-component unit similar to the 50 mm. Elmar in optical design. The optical elements are well set back in the mount, which thus acts as its own lens hood. The 65 mm. Elmar has no focusing mount, but it does have a pre-set aperture system (useful in focusing and viewing with the Visoflex—p. 132) and can stop down to *f*22.

The Wide-Angle Lenses

The Summicron f2, of a focal length of 35 mm. or 1⅜ inches, takes in a subject field approximately twice as large in area as the 50 mm. lenses, and has a 40 per cent greater angle of view (horizontal 54½ deg., vertical 38 deg.). This makes the Summicron a useful lens for indoor shots in confined quarters and also for architectural photography.

The Summicron is a symmetrical eight-element lens with specially large front and rear components. Its size reduces vignetting and ensures an even light distribution over the whole of the negative.

A further use of the Summicron is for candid snapshooting, where viewing and focusing with the rangefinder would attract too much attention. The method is to point the camera in the direction of the subject and shoot without bringing it up to the eye at all. The wide angle takes care of mistakes in aiming while the depth of field takes care of errors in focusing.

The Summicron is focused by means of a focusing lever and stops down to *f*16.

*The Summaron f*2.8 of 35 mm or 1⅜ inches focal length is a slower wide-angle lens (half as fast as the Summicron *f*2) but is a less expensive lens for more modest requirements. It is a six-element symmetrical derivative.

The 35 mm. Summaron is focused by a focusing lever, and stops down to *f*16.

The 35 *mm. Summilux f*1.4 is the fastest wide-angle lens in the Leica range, and is twice as fast again as the Summicron *f*2. It is a seven-element symmetrical derivative, again with a smallest stop of *f*16.

All three 35 mm. lenses are available in two versions. One is the lens by itself for the M1, M2 and M4, where the finder of the camera incorporates a field frame for the 35 mm. field of view. The other version for the Leica M3 carries a viewfinder attachment which increases the image angle of the M3 finder to the view of the 35 mm. lens. This attachment is automatically positioned in front of the finder windows on inserting the lens in the camera.

The two versions of these lenses also have different focusing ranges. With the 35 mm. Summaron and Summicron the lens for the M4 and M2 focuses from infinity down to 28 inches (0.7 metres) while the version for the Leica M3 with finder attachment comes down to 26 inches (0.65 metres). The 35 mm. Summilux on the Leica M4 and M2 focuses only down to 40 inches (1 metre).

The Summaron and Summicron also used to be available with a screw mount—of course, without finder attachment.

*The Elmarit f*2.8 of a focal length of 28 mm. or $1\frac{1}{8}$ inches is an extreme wide-angle lens with an angle of view of 65 deg. horizontally and 46 deg. vertically. Its application is accordingly somewhat more specialized and limited. It is useful mainly for interior shots of small rooms where even the view taken in by the 35 mm. lens is not sufficient.

Optically, the 28 mm. Elmarit is a nine-element ultra-wide-angle lens of six components. It is remarkably free from distortion, and straight lines even at the edges of the picture area are still virtually straight in the image. It focuses from infinity down to 28 inches (0.7 metres), but the rangefinder coupling only goes down to 40 inches on the Leica M3; below this the distances must be set by estimation (the rangefinder movement stops following the focusing movement of the lens). The smallest aperture is *f*22, and the lens comes complete with its own lens hood (see also p. 118).

*The Super-Angulon f*3.4 with a focal length of 21 mm. or $\frac{7}{8}$ inch represents the shortest-focus lenses produced for a 35 mm. miniature camera. With its image angle of 82 deg. horizontally and 60 deg. vertically, this is a lens of very specialized applications, such as certain fields of industrial and advertising photography. It also yields immense depth of field: from 6 feet to infinity at full aperture.

It is a symmetrical eight-element design arranged in four components. The definition and illumination is reasonably even over the whole negative, and distortion reduced to a minimum for such an extreme image angle. A certain amount of geometric distortion does, however, arise which has nothing to do with lens corrections or design, but is an inevitable result of covering such an extreme angle of view (p. 196).

The Super-Angulon is focused by a focusing lever, and focuses down to 28 inches (0.7 metres). Again, the coupled focusing range with the range-finder of the Leica M3 only goes down to 40 inches (1 metre) The smallest aperture is *f*22. This lens also comes with its own lens hood (identical with that of the 28 mm. Elmarit).

As the Leica viewfinder cannot cover the field of view of

either the 21 or the 28 mm. lenses, special brilliant finders (No. 12002 and No. 12007 respectively) have to be used in the accessory shoe on the camera.

The Long-Focus Lenses

The Elmar f4 with a focal length of 90 mm. or 3½ inches is the all-round long-focus lens for the Leica. It is also a useful second lens for the Leica outfit, as it is comparatively small and easy to carry around. It is suitable for semi-distant and distant views with which the standard 50 mm. lens would include more of the subject than necessary.

The 90 mm. lens leaves out much of this unwanted space, particularly foreground matter, thus reducing the degree of enlargement required to produce a print showing the main subject in any given size.

This lens is equally useful for portraits (p. 278). The angle of view is 23 deg. horizontally, and 15 deg. vertically. A further advantage in portraiture is the smaller depth of field which helps to throw the background out of focus.

The 90 mm. Elmar has the same optical construction as the 50 mm. Elmar; it is a triplet type of lens consisting of four elements. It is nominally the oldest surviving lens in the Leica range. Current 90 mm. Elmar lenses are, however, optically rather improved on the earlier versions, and differ in a variety of details concerning the lens mount (distance scale, filter fittings, etc.). This lens was thus available for a long time in a screw mount.

The lens is focused by rotating the focusing ring, and the focusing range goes down from infinity to 3 feet 4 inches (1 metre). The lens stops down to *f*32.

Some of the earlier 90 mm. Elmars have an infra-red focusing mark (p. 88); this is between the *f*5.6 and *f*8 far distance depth of field lines on the depth of field scale. The *f*6.3 line can be used for infra-red focusing with older models of this lens which have no specially engraved mark.

The 90 mm. Elmar consists of the lens itself and the lens tube which carries the focusing mount. The lens can be unscrewed by turning the second milled ring from the front; this is useful when the Elmar is to be used with the Visoflex (p. 123) or the focusing bellows (p. 386).

An alternative version of the 90 mm. Elmar lens (only with Leica M bayonet mount) is fitted with a collapsible barrel, similar in principle to that of the 50 mm. Elmar. When pushed in, this 90 mm. Elmar can be left on the camera even with the ever-ready case closed. This lens also has an infinity lock in the form of a button on the focusing ring. The button must be depressed before focusing, but this is only possible when the lens is extended and locked in position.

The Elmarit f2.8 with a focal length of 90 mm. or 3½ inches has the same applications as the 90 mm. Elmar, but is twice as fast.

The Elmarit is also a triplet type design, but with a total of five elements instead of four. The lens unit again unscrews from the focusing mount for use on close-up accessories, and especially with the Visoflex III and II reflex housing (p. 123).

Rotating the focusing mount focuses the lens; the focusing range is the same as for the 90 mm. Elmar, and the smallest aperture is *f*22.

The Tele-Elmarit f2.8 with a focal length of 90 mm. has the same applications as the 90 mm. Elmarit, but is considerably more compact. It is a five-element system with five separate components and is a true telephoto design. It protrudes only about ½ inch more in front of the Leica than the 50 mm. Summicron, and will (with a little pushing) even fit into the normal ever-ready case with the camera.

The focusing range is the same as for the 90 mm. Elmarit, but the smallest stop is *f*16. The optical unit of this lens is *not* intended to be unscrewed from its mount and cannot thus be used with the Visoflex or other close-up gear in the same way as the 90 mm. Elmarit.

The Summicron f2, 90 mm. or 3½ inches in focal length, is a high-speed long-focus lens for sports and press photography in poor light, where its high speed (four times that of the 90 mm. Elmar) makes it particularly versatile. The angles of view and focusing range are the same as for the 90 mm. Elmar and Elmarit. The lens stops down to *f*22 (earlier versions to *f*16). It used to be available—like the 90 mm. Elmarit—also with a screw mount.

Optically, the 90 mm. Summicron is a six-element symmetrical derivative. The lens unit unscrews from the focusing barrel, and can be used with the focusing bellows. An alternative short focusing mount is also available for using this lens directly with the Visoflex II or III reflex housing. The difference in length between the standard and the short barrel compensates for the depth of the Visoflex II or III, preserving the normal focusing range from infinity to 3½ feet.

A special feature of this lens is the built-in lens hood. When required, simply pull the front rim of the lens forward.

The Tele-Elmar f4 with a focal length of 135 mm. or 5⅜ inches, has a horizontal angle of view of 15 deg. and a vertical angle of 10 deg. This also is a telephoto lens and therefore comparatively compact, considering its focal length. It is a five-element lens of three components and is the longest focal length among Leica lenses which is still coupled to the Leica rangefinder. It focuses from infinity down to 5 feet (1.5 metres) and stops down to *f*22.

The lens is finished in black, with white scales (the distance scale in feet is in red).

The lens unit unscrews and can be used, with a special focusing mount, on the Visoflex II or III reflex housing or on the focusing bellows.

On the Leica M4 and M3 the smallest of the finder frames shows the field with this lens. The viewfinder of the Leica M2 does not cover this focal length, and a separate reflecting finder is therefore needed.

*The Elmarit f*2.8 of 135 mm. focal length has the same angle of view as the Tele-Elmar, but is twice as fast. The focusing range is the same, but the smallest aperture is *f*32. This lens is also finished in black and has a built-in lens hood which—similar to that of the 90 mm. Summicron—extends forward when required.

The 135 mm. Elmarit carries a viewfinder attachment which locates itself in front of the camera finder of the Leica M2 to M4. With the M2 and M4 this enlarges the finder view to approximately natural size, and the 90 mm. field frame then indicates the correct field of view.

With the Leica M3 the finder image is magnified approximately one and a half times.

The lens unit itself unscrews and can be used on the focusing bellows and on the Visoflex II and III reflex housings. For use on the Visoflex housings this lens is fitted into a short focusing mount, giving a focusing range from infinity down to 5 feet or 1.5 metres. The short mount (No. 16462) is identical with the current short mount (but not earlier versions) of the 90 mm. Summicron (p. 106).

The 135 mm. Elmarit is a comparatively heavy lens and the camera should if possible be mounted on a tripod by the bush on the lens barrel to minimize the risk of camera shake. This bush carries two tripod threads for $\frac{1}{4}$ inch and $\frac{3}{8}$ inch tripod screws.

Alternatively a chestpod can be used for hand-held shooting (for example the Leitz table tripod in the manner described on p. 40).

The Telyt Lenses

Of the four Telyt lenses, the focal lengths of 200 and 280 mm. ($7\frac{7}{8}$ and 11 inches) with maximum apertures of *f*4 and *f*4.8 respectively are true telephoto lenses. The 400 and 560 mm. ($15\frac{3}{4}$ and 22 inch) Telyt *f*5.6 units are comparatively simple and straightforward long-focus lenses. The 200 mm. lens gives an image 4 × magnified compared with the standard 50 mm. lens, while the magnification of the 560 mm. Telyt is over 11 × normal.

The horizontal angles are $10\frac{1}{2}$, $7\frac{1}{3}$, $5\frac{1}{2}$ and $3\frac{1}{2}$ deg. respectively, the vertical angles 7, 5, $3\frac{1}{2}$ and $2\frac{1}{2}$ deg.

Despite its effective focal length of 200 mm., the smaller Telyt extends altogether only just over 180 mm. from the plane of the film; with an orthodox long-focus lens the distance would be more like 220–230 mm.

With the Telyt lenses the depth of field is so limited, that even focusing with the Leica rangefinder is no longer precise enough. In addition, the barrel would appreciably obstruct the view of both the viewfinder and rangefinder. For that reason the Telyt lenses are focused with the help of the Leica reflex housings (p. 123).

The 200 and 280 mm. Telyt lenses have a screw mount to fit directly into the Visoflex I housing or—via the adapter ring No. 16466—into the Visoflex II and III. The depth of the reflex housing (and adapter ring) is part of the lens extension in front of the film.

The 280 to 560 mm. Telyt lenses can also be used on the rapid focusing Televit mount. This—and the detailed use of tele lenses—is described extensively on p. 423.

The Telyt lenses have built-in lens hoods which pull forward when required to shield the lens. Always use this hood when shooting.

Older Leica Lenses

In addition to the current Leica range of lenses described so far, many older lens types are still in use. These were mostly rendered obsolete by the introduction of newer lenses of similar focal length and aperture, but with improved definition and optical quality. Apart from this, the earlier lenses were designed for the same applications as the current types.

The 50 mm. Elmar f3.5 was for over thirty-five years the most famous standard lens of the Leica, until the Elmar *f*2.8 replaced it. The screw-mounted version existed in slightly different forms over the years (arrangement of the distance scale, range of lens apertures, etc.). Unlike the other Leica lenses, the Elmar *f*3.5 has a small slide on the front for setting the apertures. The bayonet-mounted version closely resembles the Elmar *f*2.8.

The later models have an infra-red focusing index; with older models use the far-distance *f*6.3 line on the depth of field scale.

The 50 mm. Elmax, f3.5, the predecessor of the 50 mm. Elmar, was fitted on the very first Leica models. It was not interchangeable.

The 50 mm. Hektor f2.5, with twice the speed of the *f*3.5 Elmar, was the first large aperture lens for the Leica. The definition at full aperture is inferior to later high-speed lenses.

The 50 mm. Hektor carries a focusing lever and has a collapsible barrel. It has no infra-red focusing mark (p. 88) but the far distance *f*6.3 line of the depth of field scale can be used.

The 50 mm. Summar f2 is similar in optical design to the 50 mm. Summitar and the Summicron which followed it, but has only six lens elements instead of seven. The front element is smaller (26 mm. as against 33 mm. of the newer lenses) and at full aperture the Summar shows a slight degree of vignetting of the corners of the negative. The definition is best at *f*6.3.

The lens barrel is collapsible and does not rotate during focusing. The lens carries a focusing lever, and some of the later models have an infra-red focusing mark, coinciding with the far distance *f*2 line on the depth of field scale.

The 50 mm. Summitar f2 was the predecessor of the Summicron. It yields images of nearly the same quality as the Summicron and is similar in appearance and handling. All Summitar lenses have an infra-red focusing mark, but no click-stops.

The 50 mm. Hektor, Summitar and Summar lenses were made only for the screw-mounted Leica cameras.

The 50 mm. Summicron f2 in a collapsible mount, similar to that of the 50 mm. Elmar, preceded the current rigid version of this lens. On the collapsible Summicron the lens unit itself is not removable from the lens assembly, and cannot thus be used separately. Optically this lens is identical with the later 50 mm. Summicron, and was available with either a bayonet or a screw mount.

The 50 mm. Summarit f1.5 was the immediate predecessor of

the Summilux *f*1.4 of the same focal length. It is not quite as modern a design as the Summilux, and is also a seven-element symmetrical derivative. The lens was made with either a bayonet or a screw mount, and has a rigid lens barrel fitted with a focusing lever on the mount. The Summarit lenses have an infra-red focusing mark engraved on the barrel (p. 88).

The 50 *mm. Xenon f*1.5 was up to about 1947 the fastest standard Leica lens; its place was then taken by the Summarit lens with improved definition and resolving power. It was made only with a screw mount.

The 21 *mm. Super Angulon f*4 was the immediate predecessor of the current Super Angulon *f*3.4, and slightly slower as well as a little different in design. This lens was made with either a screw or a bayonet mount.

The 28 *mm. Summaron f*5.6 was the predecessor of the 28 mm. Elmarit. It was, however, only one-quarter as fast. This lens has a very slight degree of distortion (straight lines near the extreme edge of the picture area may appear a trifle curved) and gives optimum definition on stopping down to about *f*8. It was made only with a screw mount, requiring a bayonet/screw adapter ring for use on Leica M models.

The 28 *mm. Hektor f*6.3 is similar in application to the *f*5.6 Summaron, but is a little slower. This lens also was made only with a screw mount.

The 35 *mm. Summaron f*3.5 was similar to the 35 mm. Summaron *f*2.8, but a little slower. Like the Summaron *f*2.8, this lens was made with either a bayonet or a screw mount, and the bayonet-mounted lens existed in two versions with and without finder attachment, for the Leica M3, and M1 and M2 respectively.

The 35 *mm Elmar f*3.5, although identical in application to the Summaron lens is completely different in design, and is a triplet type containing four elements. At full aperture, this lens tends to vignette the extreme corners of the picture area. It was made only with a screw mount.

*The Summarex f*1.5 with a focal length of 85 mm. or 3⅜ inches is a long-focus lens with a slightly wider angle of view than the 90 mm. units (horizontal angle 24 deg., vertical angle 16 deg.). The Summarex with its maximum aperture of *f*1.5 is really a specialist lens, designed mainly for action shots in limited light. It is also particularly useful as a moderate long-focus lens for Press photographers who have to cope with highly unpredictable lighting conditions. Its function has now been taken over by the 90 mm. Summicron *f*2, which is slightly slower but more versatile, since it can be used with the reflex housing, etc.

The Summarex is a symmetrical type, five-component, seven-element lens. The definition is on the soft side at full aperture, but reaches optimum sharpness at about *f*4. It was produced with a screw mount only.

*The Hektor f*1.9 with a focal length of 73 mm. or 2⅞ inches has the same uses as the later high-speed Summarex *f*1.5; it is specialist lens for theatre and sports photography in poor light. Its focal length is slightly shorter (horizontal image angle 27½ deg., vertical angle 18½ deg.)

The definition of the 73 mm. Hektor is a little soft at full aperture which is useful for soft-focus portraiture. It was made only with a screw mount.

The 105 *mm. Elmar f*6.3 was an early all-round and light-weight long-focus lens of slightly longer focal length than the 9 cm. Elmar. It is of similar optical construction and gives very good definition. It is limited by its comparatively small aperture, however no serious drawback in outdoor landscape work. It was made only with a screw mount.

The horizontal angle is 19½ deg., vertical 13 deg.

The 125 *mm. Hektor f*2.5 was specially intended for portraiture. It is not coupled to the rangefinder of the camera, and has a short barrel for use with the Visoflex reflex housings only. The lens thus existed only with a screw mount. The horizontal angle of view is 16½ deg., and the vertical angle 11 deg.

At full aperture the 125 mm. Hektor yields a slight degree of intentional softness—hence the special application in portrait work—but the definition becomes pin sharp on stopping down to *f*4.

The 135 *mm. Elmar f*4 preceded the 135 mm. Tele-Elmar, and has the same angle of view, focusing range and smallest aperture. The 135 mm. Elmar *f*4 is, however, not a telephoto lens and is rather longer in construction than the Tele-Elmar. For that reason the lens has its own tripod bush on the lens barrel for more balanced tripod mounting of the lens and camera assembly.

The 135 mm. Elmar was originally made with either a bayonet or a screw mount. The lens unit can again be unscrewed from the focusing barrel, and then used, via an extension tube and universal focusing mount, on the Visoflex II and III reflex housings. Alternatively, a short focusing barrel is available for use of this lens on the Visoflex I. The lens unit itself can also be used on the focusing bellows with the aid of appropriate adapter rings.

The 135 *mm. Hektor f*4.5 was the predecessor of the 135 mm. Elmar *f*4, being slightly slower and older in design. It exists with a screw or bayonet mount, and can also be fitted with a short focusing mount for use on the reflex housing—in the same way as the later 135 mm. Elmar. The screw-mounted version existed in two forms: an early one with 36 mm. front mount to take push-on filters, and a later version taking larger screw-in filters like the bayonet-mounted 135 mm. Hektor.

The 135 *mm. Elmar f*4.5 was the predecessor of the 135 mm. Hektor, and is similar in its applications, but inferior in definition. Like the Elmar *f*4, it can be unscrewed from its focusing barrel and used with a short barrel on close-up equipment. It was made only with a screw mount.

The 200 *mm. Telyt f*4.5 is similar in application to the current 200 mm. Telyt *f*4, but consists of only four air-spaced lens elements. It stops down to *f*32 (the current Telyt only goes down to *f*22) and does not have the preselector aperture feature.

The 400 *mm. Telyt f*5 is similar in application to the current 400 mm. *f*5.6 unit, but consists of four air spaced elements and is a true telephoto lens. Its nearest focusing distance is 25 feet (8 metres), and it can be used either directly on the Visoflex housings or the lens unit on its own will fit the Televit (p. 425) mount.

The Thambar Lens

Although the 90 mm. Thambar *f*2.2 (now discontinued) is a long-focus lens, it is fundamentally different in application from the 90 mm. Elmar. It is specially designed for pictorial soft-focus effects (p. 325).

The Thambar is purposely computed to produce a spherically uncorrected image. The image formed by rays passing through the outside portions of the lens does not coincide with that produced by rays passing through the centre. At full aperture this lens therefore gives a noticeably soft image, with the highlights of the subject spreading over into the shadows.

The soft-focus effect can be controlled by utilizing the centre and the margins of the lens in a varying degree to form the picture. As we stop down the Thambar, the marginal rays are gradually cut out, and the image becomes sharper.

In addition, a detachable central stop is fitted. This covers the centre of the lens only, and increases the softness of the image still further by cutting out the central rays forming the basic sharp picture. It also distributes the softness evenly over the whole picture area. The central stop enables the Thambar to produce a soft image even when stopped down to about *f*4.5.

At apertures smaller than *f*9 the Thambar yields a perfectly sharp image without any softness. The central stop must not be used below *f*6.3, since it would obstruct the actual lens opening left free by the aperture.

The central stop naturally reduces the light passing power of the lens. The Thambar carries a second aperture scale, engraved in red, which gives the effective aperture with the central stop in position.

The Thambar is rather tricky to use, since the effect obtained depends on quite a number of additional factors such as lighting and subject distance. It needs appreciable experience to master the variables, and the results tend to be unpredictable in the hands of a beginner.

Changing Lenses

To attach a bayonet mounted lens to a Leica M, place it over the camera mount with the red dot opposite the catch on the body (also marked by a red dot). Push the lens in, and turn to the right to lock.

To remove the lens, press the catch on the body, and turn the lens mount to the left. Then lift out the lens. This system makes lens changing specially quick.

Be sure to place the lens squarely against the camera mount when fitting it, and also remove it straight, rather than prising it off the camera. Any use of force can damage the bayonet flanges and possibly upset the accuracy of the lens mounting on the camera.

Before lifting the lens off the camera, the red dot on the lens mount must be *exactly opposite* the bayonet catch of the camera. It is sometimes possible to turn the lens (anti-clockwise) a fraction beyond the correct release position, when it becomes difficult to lift off.

Screw-mounted lenses (except some very first models) are fitted with a standard screw barrel of 1½ inches (37 mm.) diameter. To fit a lens, place it squarely over the camera flange, turn slightly to the left (about a quarter turn) until the thread engages, and moderately firmly screw it into the camera until the lens flange is flush against the camera flange. There is no need to use force; when screwed home, the lens is automatically at the correct distance from the film to give the maximum image sharpness.

The lens unit itself of the 90 mm. Summicron and the 135 mm. Elmar *f*4 and Hektor *f*4.5 for the Leica M must only be used on its own bayonet-mounted M focusing barrel, while the lens unit for Leicas I to IIIg goes only with its own screw-mounted focusing barrel. This is because each lens unit is matched to its focusing barrel for rangefinder coupling and should not be changed to another barrel. Either lens unit can, however, be used in the short focusing barrel for use on the Visoflex housing, where the image is focused on the screen (pp. 123, 128).

Screw-mounted lenses can be used on the Leica M by first inserting a bayonet/screw adapter. Different versions of this are used for the 50, 90 and 135 mm. lenses. The adapter is inserted in the same way as the bayonet mount of a lens.

The 90 mm. adapter also serves for using the 85 mm. Summarex on the Leica M. The finder field then includes a trace less than will appear on the film.

The 135 mm. adapter also serves for the 35 mm. lenses with

the Leica M4 and M2. In all these cases insertion of the bayonet adapter ring also selects the appropriate finder frame in the Leica M2 or M3 viewfinder.

For lenses of other focal lengths (21 and 28 mm., also 35 mm. with the Leica M3) the 50 mm. adapter ring is used. In this case the finder does not show the correct frame; a separate accessory finder is in any case needed with these lenses.

Both the bayonet mount and the screw mount position any Leica lens absolutely accurately in relation to the film.

When changing lenses do not expose the shutter blinds to direct sunlight; change the lens in the shade, or at least in the shadow of the body. The blinds are light-tight under all normal conditions. But in very bright light some light may get through where the two blinds overlap, and fog the film.

Prolonged exposure to sunlight may eventually cause the rubberized cloth of the blind to perish.

Before removing or inserting any of the lenses with a collapsible barrel, pull the lens out and lock it in the taking position first (p. 41). Otherwise, with careless handling, the retracted barrel may knock against the rangefinder lever and in time upset the accuracy of the coupling.

The 21 and 28 mm. ultra-wide-angle lenses also have a barrel protruding somewhat beyond the back of the bayonet mount. Here it is again important to place the lens in position—or lift it out—carefully to avoid knocking against the rangefinder lever.

Special care is needed when screwing the earlier 200 mm. Telyt in or out of the reflex housing. The rear element of the Telyt projects very slightly beyond the end of the lens barrel when set to infinity, and may thus easily get scratched. Before changing the lens, therefore, set it to a nearer distance first.

The Care of Lenses

A dusty or dirty camera lens, like dirty spectacles, impairs the vision of the camera. Therefore keep the lens scrupulously clean at all times.

That does not mean that the lens should be cleaned at every opportunity. High-quality optical glass is comparatively soft and constant rubbing may in time destroy the high polish.

Avoid, therefore, any chance of dirt getting on to the lens. Never touch the lens surfaces with the fingers; moisture is particularly liable to attack the anti-reflection coating.

LENS CHANGING

To remove the bayonet mounted lens of the Leica M models, press the release catch next to the lens mount and turn the lens anti-clockwise to remove.

To fit a lens, line up the red dot on the lens mount with the red dot next to the bayonet release catch (*left*). Place the lens in position and turn clockwise in its mount until the catch engages (*right*).

To fit any of the lenses for the screw mounted Leica models simply screw in as far as it will go. To remove, just unscrew.

Screw mounted lenses can also be used on the Leica M, by first fitting a bayonet/screw adapter ring.

LENS HOODS

The lens hoods for the Leica M lenses, where not built in, are conical in shape and fit on to the rim of the lens. The short inverted hood (*left*) is used for the 35 and 50 mm. lenses, the long hood (*right*) for the 90 and 135 mm. lenses.

The 21 and 28 mm. ultra-wide-angle lenses (as well as 35 mm. *f*1.4) have a square-fronted shallow hood.

Lens hoods for the screw mounted lenses are mostly tubular in shape, and clamp to the front lens rim. There is also an extendible hood to cover several focal lengths (*right*). A few lenses have rectangular hoods.

Cover the lens with the lens cap when not in use. In addition, each lens is supplied with a protective lid for the back of the barrel. When the lens is not on the camera, fit this lid over the rear mount. These lids are available in screw and in bayonet versions. Some lenses, like the ultra-wide-angle unit, have a rear lid with a hollow well to accommodate the projecting inner lens barrel.

A protective bayonet or screw lid is also available for the camera body when stored without a lens.

When carrying spare lenses, keep them in proper containers. When several lenses are being used and constantly changed on a shooting session it is tempting—but not very wise—to put spare lenses into a pocket. Even if there are no hard objects in the pocket that can scratch the lens, there is practically always fluff and dust which gets inside the lens mount or barrel.

A special base-plate attachment for the Leica M models aids in parking lenses conveniently and safely. This fits over the camera base plate, hooking into the round peg at the camera side just above the base-plate lock. The other end of the base-plate attachment carries a tripod screw which screws into the bush in the camera base plate. On the attachment two bayonet rings take a couple of bayonet-mounted lenses. These simply lock into position in the normal way, and hang downwards when the camera is used for shooting.

To clean a lens, remove any dust with a soft brush, or a clean, soft and grit-free rag of chamois leather. Never breathe on the lens to clean it.

Any grease spots are best removed by wiping with cotton wool or a clean rag which is just dampened with spirit.

Never take a lens apart, except to change the complete lens unit of certain lenses. The components of the lens are very accurately aligned for maximum sharpness; even a skilled mechanic would not be able to realign them without a precision optical bench.

Lens Hoods

While each Leica lens covers a certain angle of view, light from outside this angle can still reach the front lens surface. Such light does not contribute to the picture, but if strong enough it can affect the image by being scattered inside the lens and reflected on to the film. It thus degrades the image and generally reduces its brilliance and contrast.

For really crisp pictures, therefore, the lens should be shielded with a lens hood. That is a tube which fits in front of the lens and screens off all outside light.

The lens hood is essential for against-the-light shots but will improve any picture, whatever the lighting. Therefore use it whenever possible.

The size of the lens hood we need depends on the lens on the Leica. The longer the focal length, the narrower its angle of view, and the deeper the lens hood can and should be.

The hoods for the wide-angle lenses are the shallowest. They will fit some of the long-focus lenses, but are less effective then. Too long a hood will, however, cut off or vignette the corners of the picture itself.

A special twin hood is provided for the Stemar stereo lens unit (p. 443).

Lens Hood Fittings

Most Leica lens hoods clip on to the outer front mount of the lens. To fit the hood, place it over the front of the lens, press in the two oblong spring buttons at the side, and push the hood home. To remove the hood, press the buttons and lift off. Each hood is marked with the focal lengths for which it is suitable. The hood of the standard lens can also be inverted over the lens and can remain on it in the ever-ready case.

The lens hood of the current 35 and 50 mm. lenses (except the Summilux) is an inverted truncated cone, with cut-away sections in the rim to avoid obscuring the finder view. This hood (No. 12585) is marked with the focal lengths—35 and 50 mm.—for which it is suitable. A similar (but correspondingly larger) hood—No. 12503—is available for the 50 mm. Noctilux *f*1.2 lens.

The hood for the 90 and 135 mm. lenses (except Summicron and 135 mm. Elmarit) is longer and flares slightly outwards. This also is marked with the focal lengths with which it can be used.

The Summilux lenses (35 and 50 mm.) come with their own hoods, which fit over the front in a similar way.

The hood for the 21 mm. *f*3.4 and 28 mm. *f*2.8 ultra-wide-angle lenses is rectangular, but the mounting ring fits on the front of the lens in the same way as the hood of the standard lenses. To orientate the hood correctly, line up the red dot on the hood rim with the red dot on front of the aperture scale on the lens. The hood will only go on in this position.

The 90 mm. Summicron, 135 mm. Elmarit and the Telyt lenses have an extending hood built in.

All lens hoods can be used together with a filter. With the ultra-wide-angle 21 and 28 mm. lenses of current design a series VII filter (p. 237) fits over the front of the lens and is held in place by the hood. In the same way the hood of the Noctilux will hold a series VIII filter over the lens.

Some lenses, especially older screw-mounted versions, take a hood with a clamping ring that grips the front lens mount.

The hoods for the 50 mm. Summicron (screw mount), Summitar, Summarit, Summar, and Xenon are rectangular; this permits them to be deeper without vignetting. Collapsible hoods are made for the Summicron, Summitar and Summar; they fold flat when not required.

An extendible hood is made for the earlier 50, 90 and 135 mm. Elmar and Hektor lenses. It consists of two tubes inside each other. The inner tube clamps on to the lens mount, while the outer tube can be pulled out or pushed in to vary the depth of the hood. A clamping screw fixes the positions of the extendible tube, while the inner tube carries markings to indicate the extension required for the different focal lengths.

The high-speed long-focus lenses (85 mm. Summarex, 73 mm. and 125 mm. Hektor, and 90 mm. Thambar) and earlier Telyts are supplied complete with hood. This hood can be reversed to fit snugly over the lens when not in use; the lens cap in turn fits over the bottom of the hood with these lenses.

LEICA VIEWFINDERS

The universal finder shows the view for all the lenses (except the Telyts) in the Leica range.
The brilliant and frame finders are useful for sports and action.
The reflex housing permits accurate screen viewing and focusing with the telephoto lenses.

The built-in optical viewfinder of the Leica shows the correct view of the subject as seen by the standard 50 mm. lens. In the Leica M4 the finder shows further the fields of view of the 35, 90 and 135 mm. lenses by means of image frames which automatically appear when the lens is fitted to the camera (p. 45). The M2 finder is similar, but does not show the 135 mm. frame.

The additional frames on the Leica M3 are those of the 90 and 135 mm. lenses. The field of the 35 mm. lens there appears in the finder on fitting the lens with the finder attachment (p. 46).

The viewfinder of the Leica M1 shows the field both of the 35 mm. and of the 50 mm. lenses.

The viewfinders of the screw-mounted Leica models only show the field of view of the standard lens; the only exception is the Leica IIIg, which also shows the 90 mm. field of view by special marks inside the finder.

There are, however, also a number of accessory Leica finders partly for use with lenses of different focal length, and partly for viewing under special conditions.

The alternative finders all fit into the accessory shoe. The shoe will take all finders with a standard 18 mm. base.

Since the accessory finders are situated well above the built-in finder, most special finders carry an adjustment to compensate for parallax at close distances.

The Leica accessory finders fall into two general groups: individual finders for standard or long-focus lenses, and universal or combination finders for several lenses.

The reflex housings occupy a special position. They serve as viewfinder and focusing finder for the long-focus and Telyt lenses, and also for close-up focusing.

The Brilliant Finders

The brilliant finder shows a brilliant white frame superimposed on the view in front of the camera. Both eyes can be kept open for viewing.

A brilliant finder is always needed when using the 21 and 28 mm. lenses. The 21 mm. finder shows the subject field at 0.3 times, the 28 mm. finder in approximately half natural size. The latter has a dotted line below the top of the frame, to indicate the limit of the view for subjects between 3 and 6 feet away (parallax correction).

Corresponding models are made for the 35, 50, 90 and 135 mm. lenses. Although these fields of view are mostly covered by the viewfinder of the Leica M models, the brilliant finders were originally intended for screw-mounted Leicas with their single finder. A brilliant finder for 50 mm. was included with the Leica Ig, If and Ic models; this was also useful as an alternative to the built-in finder of earlier series of II and III models, as it shows a larger image.

The 90 and 135 mm. models show no dotted lines to correct for parallax, but carry at the back a milled ring with a distance setting which tilts the whole finder down at near distances. Small white corners etched into the finder field show the reduced lens angle at close distances.

The focal length for which the finder is suitable is always engraved on the front.

The Universal Finder

This finder, formely known as the VIOOH finder, shows the exact field of view for all Leica lenses from 35 to 135 mm.

On looking through the eyepiece at the back, the subject appears upright and right way round, inside a black frame. The finder fits into the accessory shoe of the Leica, and carries a second shoe on top for further accessories (e.g. flash gun).

The universal finder has a milled ring round the middle portion, which moves past a scale engraved with the various focal lengths in centimetres of the Leica lenses.

On rotating the milled ring, the four sides of the black frame close in on, or move out from, the subject. To set the finder for any particular lens, turn the milled ring until the long index is in line with the index corresponding to the focal length of the lens in use.

On most models of the finder the ring engages with a click at each setting.

The second, shorter, index line should be used for close-up subjects, when the angle of view is slightly smaller.

To compensate for parallax error there is a small movable

LEICA FINDERS

Black panel: The current accessory finders are the brilliant finders (*top*), available as separate models (different in appearance) for all lenses from 21 to 135mm. Discontinued ones include the adjustable universal finder (*centre*); and the frame finder for 50, 90 and 135 mm. lenses (*bottom*).

Right-hand column: In the brilliant finder (*top*) a frame F is reflected by the silvered portions into the eye R. The eye therefore sees the image of the frame optically superimposed on the subject.

The universal finder changes the angle of view covered (*centre*) by a masking arrangement.

The parallax correction on the universal finder (*bottom*) tilts the whole finder downwards for close distances.

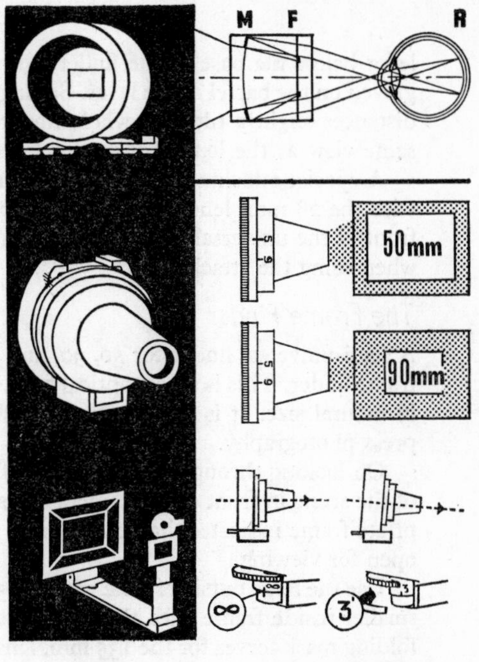

VISOFLEX III

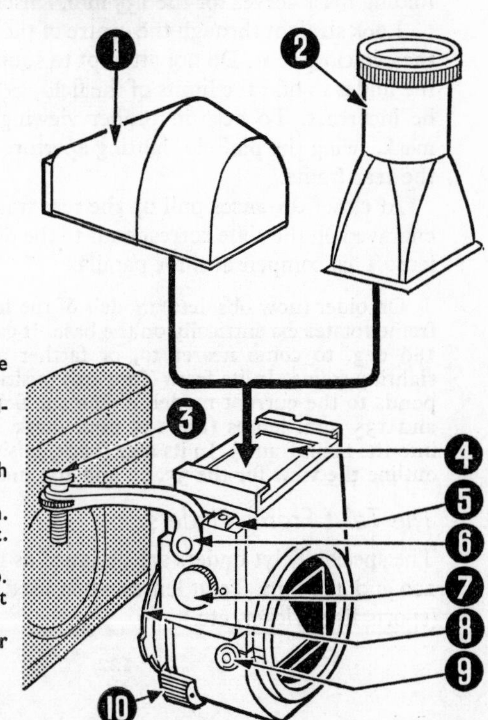

The components of the Visoflex III are:

1. Right-angle magnifier.
2. Vertical magnifier.
3. Release button with setting screw.
4. Ground-glass screen.
5. Cable release socket.
6. Release arm.
7. Mirror control knob.
8. Bayonet mount to fit on camera.
9. Locking button for lens or adapter unit.
10. Bayonet locking lever.

lever below the base of the finder, with distance settings engraved on the barrel of the lever. Setting the lever to the closer distances slightly tilts the whole finder forward, to cover the same view as the lens. Adjust this lever after focusing.

A special attachment converts the universal finder for use with the 28 mm. lens. This screws into the thread inside the front of the universal finder. Set the finder for 35 mm. lenses when using the attachment.

The Frame Finder

A semi-universal finder for 50, 90, and 135 mm. lenses is the frame finder. This is a non-optical type, and shows the subject in natural size. It is thus particularly suitable for sports and press photography.

On looking through the rear sight of the finder, the whole of the scene in front of the camera is visible, while the appropriate frame indicates the field of view. Both eyes can remain open for viewing.

Use the large outside frame with the 50 mm. lenses, and the smaller inside frame with the 85 mm. and 90 mm. lenses. A folding mask serves for the 135 mm. lenses.

Look straight through the centre of the rear frame and keep the eye close to it. Do not attempt to squint sideways through the finder to find the limits of the field, as the view would then be incorrect. To help in proper viewing with the 135 mm. mask, swing the pinhole sighting aperture centrally in front of the rear frame.

At closer distances pull up the rear frame so that the figure engraved on the slide corresponds to the distance setting of the lens. This compensates for parallax.

On older (now obsolete) models of the frame finder the front frame rotates excentrically on the base. It can be turned through 180 deg. to come nearer to, or farther away from, the rear sighting frame. In its front (forward) position the finder corresponds to the current model, giving the field of view for 50, 90 and 135 mm. lenses (the 135 mm. mask is separate and clips into the main frame). In its rear (back) position the three frames outline the view for the 35, 73 and 105 mm. lenses.

The Telyt Frame Finders

The special Telyt finders are designed as frame finders for the 200 and 400 mm. Telyt lenses when used for hand-held shots (sports like cricket, etc.).

They consist of a rectangular tube with a field frame set into its front end, and a small sighting aperture at the back. A milled ring, marked with the various distances, adjusts the position of the sighting aperture to compensate for parallax.

The special finder base fits only into the finder shoe of the Visoflex I reflex housing (p. 139) or of the extension tubes designed to replace the Visoflex I housing, but not into the accessory shoe of the Leica camera.

To fit the Telyt finder into the shoe, loosen the milled knob at the side of the base, push the base into the shoe, and screw the milled knob tight again.

The Visoflex III Reflex Housing

Basically the Leica M and screw-mounted models are rangefinder cameras. The rangefinder is the most rapid means of focusing, and is for wide-angle, standard and medium-long-focus units also the most accurate system. For longer-focus units, however—and also for large close-ups—ground-glass screen focusing is more convenient and sometimes more precise.

It is for that reason that the longest focal length coupled with the Leica rangefinder is 135 mm.

The Visoflex III housing provides the added versatility of reflex focusing on a screen. It fits in front of the camera in place of the lens, and in turn takes various lenses and extension tubes for close-up or normal photography. In effect it thus converts the Leica M models into a reflex camera—with the choice of eye-level or waist-level focusing—though it is not quite as convenient to handle for normal photography than the Leicaflex. Nor can it be used with wide-angle or even standard lenses (other than the 65 mm. Elmar).

The Visoflex III consists of a mirror housing with a swing-away mirror which diverts the light path from the lens to a ground-glass screen on the top of the housing. The mirror is controlled by a release lever which—when the Visoflex is mounted on the camera—positions itself above the Leica release button. Pressing the mirror lever swings the mirror out of the way an instant before releasing the camera shutter.

Two interchangeable viewing units are available. A pentaprism unit with 4× magnifier slides over the top of the ground-glass screen for an upright and right-way-round view of the image at eye level. With this arrangement the Visoflex and the camera form a reasonably handy assembly for single-lens reflex photography. In place of the eye-level finder a simple 5× magnifier permits looking directly down on to the ground-glass screen. This shows the image reversed left-to-right, and is useful when the Leica and Visoflex are mounted on a copying stand, as well as for low-angle photography.

The Visoflex III only fits the Leica M models; earlier Visoflex housings were available in versions for screw- and bayonet-mounted Leicas. The front mount of the Visoflex III is a bayonet ring to take certain bayonet-mounted lenses directly (others with the aid of intermediate rings); for screw-mounted lenses a bayonet/screw adapter (p. 113) is necessary.

The Visoflex II to III can be used for focusing over the whole range from infinity downwards with 90 mm. and longer focal length lenses, and also with the 65 mm. Elmar *f*3.5. The latter is virtually a standard lens, exclusively designed for use with this Visoflex. Its optical construction provides the full focusing range despite the extra depth of the Visoflex housing.

The 125 to 400 mm. long-focus and tele lenses can also be used with suitable intermediate rings, focusing from infinity downwards; 50 mm. and shorter-focus lenses permit close-up focusing, but do not cover the range to infinity.

Mounting and Using the Visoflex III

The Visoflex III can be fitted to the camera with either viewing magnifier and any of the lenses in position. To fit it, first push down the bayonet locking lever at the side, so that the red dot on the lever is opposite the red dot on the housing. Then place the Visoflex over the lens opening of the camera, so that the ground-glass screen and magnifier is on top. Check that the housing is properly seated against the camera front (ease it to and fro a little if necessary) and slide the bayonet-locking lever fully upwards. This secures the Visoflex to the camera housing.

Lenses and other fittings are inserted in the front bayonet mount of the Visoflex in the same way as on the camera. In other words, line up the red dot on the lens mount with the red dot on the catch on the Visoflex front. Push the lens home and turn clockwise to lock. To remove a lens, pull back the

USING THE VISOFLEX III

To fit the Visoflex III to the camera first bring down the bayonet locking lever before placing the reflex housing on the camera (*left*), then move this lever upwards (*right*) to secure the bayonet lock.

Fit the viewing magnifier by sliding it into the guide rails at the two sides of the ground-glass screen (*left*). To remove, press the button at the side before pulling off the magnifier.

Adjust the setting of the release lever (*right*) to match the mirror movement of the shutter (p. 126).

The Visoflex needs a steady hold, especially when working with a long-focus lens. For hand-held shots the upper left arm can provide a useful support for the assembly.

The Focorapid (p. 136) permits rapid focusing with the longer focus lenses on the Visoflex III and II. The main parts are:

1. Focusing knob with fine focus control.
2. Front barrel.
3. Click stop adjustments.
4. Infinity stop.
5. Catch for rotation of the mounting. This permits the Leica and Visoflex to be turned upright (*right*), without changing the hold on the Focorapid.

For rapid focusing slide the focusing knob with the left hand to click into place at preset distances. For fine focusing (e.g. when setting distance stops) turn the focusing knob itself.

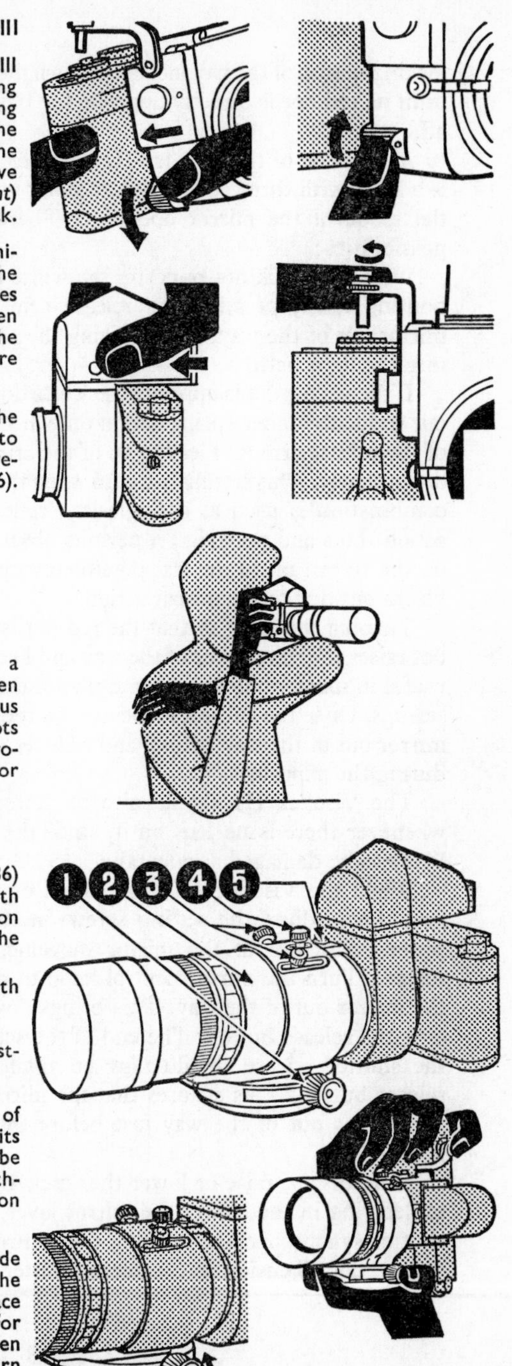

locking button of the bayonet catch, turn the lens anti-clockwise until its red dot is directly opposite the bayonet catch, and lift off.

At the side of the Visoflex III, just below the release lever, is a knob with three coloured dots along its rim. This controls the mode of the mirror operation. There are the following possibilities:

With the black dot opposite the white dot on the Visoflex housing itself, pressing the release arm smoothly lifts the mirror out of the way, and releasing the arm lets it drop back into the light path.

If the yellow dot is opposite the white dot, the mirror swings out suddenly under spring action only at the end of the travel of the release arm. On letting go of the arm, the mirror comes down slowly. This setting is useful when the Leica and Visoflex combination is used as a single-lens reflex for long-distance action shots and portraits; it permits observation of the image on the screen up to the last possible moment before the view blacks out due to the mirror action.

Turning the knob so that the red dot is opposite the white dot raises the mirror out of the way and keeps it raised. This is useful in macrophotography and photomicrography with fixed set-ups. Once the subject is focused on the screen, moving the mirror out of the way beforehand reduces the risk of vibration during the exposure.

The Visoflex III should also be stored in this condition whenever there is no lens on it, since the mirror is then less likely to be damaged accidentally.

When the Visoflex III is mounted on a Leica M for the first time, adjust the setting screw on the release lever for proper sequence of the mirror movement and the camera release. Turn the mirror control knob to the red dot, to raise the mirror out of the way. This brings down the mirror lever over the release button. The end of the screw which bears on the shutter release should now be about 1 mm. above the release button. This ensures that the mirror lever has moved the mirror out of the way just before the camera shutter is released.

If necessary, raise or lower the screw by turning the small milled ring in the end of the mirror lever. Check the mirror/shutter synchronism by turning the control knob back to the yellow dot. Tension the camera shutter—with the camera empty—and bring down the mirror lever. Two clicks should be audible, the first from the spring-powered release of the mirror, and the second from the shutter.

The interval between the two clicks depends of course also on the setting of the screw on the release lever. For fast shooting, where the lever is likely to be pressed down rapidly, it is better to make this interval longer when the adjustment is being tested—to eliminate all risk of accidentally tripping the shutter before the mirror is fully out of the way.

To release the mirror and camera with a cable release, screw the latter into the thread next to the Visoflex mirror lever. With the cable release the mirror rises slowly, whether the control knob is set to the black or the yellow dot. When screwing in the cable, pull the mirror lever down to make the cable socket more accessible. The cable release releases the camera shutter via the mirror lever of the Visoflex. (It is not possible to screw the cable release into the camera release button with the Visoflex III in position.)

Lenses for the Visoflex III and II

There are several combinations of lenses, focusing mounts and extension tubes to cover focusing ranges from infinity downwards with most Leica lenses of 65 mm. and longer focal lengths. The distances quoted below are all measured from the film plane (corresponds to the centre of the rear screws of the accessory shoe).

The 65 *mm. Elmar f*3.5 is used in a special helical focusing mount (No. 16464) to cover a focusing range from infinity down to 13 inches. The focusing mount fits into the front mount of the Visoflex, and the 65 mm. Elmar screws into the front of the focusing mount. Alternatively, an extension tube (No. 16471) can be interposed between the focusing mount and the Elmar lens. In that case the focusing range covers distances from 13 to 10½ inches (just under same-size reproduction).

The 90 *mm. Elmarit f*2.8 is used with the same focusing mount and (if required) extension tube as the 65 mm. Elmar. However, in this case the lens unit only of the Elmarit is needed. This unscrews from its barrel just behind the aperture ring, and simply screws into the helical focusing mount or extension tube for use on the Visoflex. The focusing range, with the (No. 16464) mount only, extends from infinity to just under 20 inches; with the (16471) extension tube subjects between just under 20 inches and 15½ inches can be covered, yielding just over half-size reproduction.

The 90 *mm. Elmar f*4 (not the collapsible version) needs a different helical focusing mount: (No. 16467). This takes the lens unit only of the 90 mm. Elmar and covers a focusing range from infinity down to 3¼ feet with a scale of 1 : 9.

To extend the focusing range an extension ring (No. 16468) fits between the Elmar lens unit and the focusing mount. One such ring covers a range from just over 3½ to just over 2 feet; two rings permit focusing down to a little under 20 inches. The scale of reproduction is then about one-third natural size.

For close-ups it is also possible to mount the 90 mm. Elmarit or Elmar on the front of the Visoflex III in its own normal focusing mount (p. 376).

The 90 *mm. Summicron f*2 with the short focusing barrel (p. 106) can be used directly on the Visoflex III, for the normal focusing range. For a near focusing range (from just over 3¼ to 2 feet) an extension ring (No. 16474) fits between the lens unit of the 90 mm. Summicron and the short focusing barrel.

The 135 *mm. Tele-Elmar f*4 can also be used with the helical focusing mount No. 16464, again after unscrewing the lens unit from the normal focusing mount. It is the rearmost thread of the lens unit which screws into the helical focusing mount. Before doing this pull the clip-on baffle ring off the rear lens barrel. (Don't lose this ring; it prevents light reflection inside the normal mount of the Tele-Elmar.) The focusing range of this combination extends from infinity down to 5 feet, with a scale of reproduction of 1 : 5.

The older 135 *mm. lenses* (Elmar, Hektor) are again used with the same helical focusing mount (No. 16464), but in this case the lens unit itself is first screwed into a No. 16472 tube. This provides the same focusing range as the 135 mm. Tele-Elmar.

The 135 *mm. Elmarit f*2.8 can be used on the Visoflex III in conjunction with its short focusing barrel for distances down to about 5 feet.

The long-focus lenses from 125 *to* 400 *mm.* (125 mm. Hektor, the 135 mm. non-tele lenses—Elmar and Hektor—in their

VISOFLEX III AND II COMBINATIONS

The Visoflex III or II (and IIA) reflex housing in effect converts the Leica into a single-lens reflex camera.

In the first place it offers two alternative viewing systems; eye level and vertically downward with interchangeable magnifiers. Further, used with a variety of adapter rings and tubes, it will take most of the lenses of a Leica for normal or close-up focusing ranges. The required adapter rings are shown in black; the number beneath them is their order number.

Some of the extension tubes and rings, shown against a shaded background, are used only to obtain an extra close focusing range.

The normal ranges and lens combination are (the figures are scales of reproduction—e.g. 0.11 = 1:9):

1. 90 mm. *f*4: ∞ to 0.11.
2. 90 mm. *f*2: ∞ to 0.11.
3. 135 mm. *f*2.8: ∞ to 0.11.
4. 135 mm. Tele-Elmar *f*4: ∞ to 0.2.
5. 135 mm. Hektor and Elmar: ∞ to 0.2.
6. 90 mm. *f*2.8: ∞ to 0.3.
7. 65 mm. *f*3.5: ∞ to 0.4.

In combinations 1–7 only the optical units of the lenses are used. Combinations 8 to 14 employ the complete lens.

8. 400 mm. Telyt: ∞ to 0.06.
9. 280 mm. Telyt: ∞ to 0.055.
10. 200 mm. Telyt: ∞ to 0.08.
11. 135 mm. Hektor and Elmar (in short mount): ∞ to 0.11.
12. 125 mm. Hektor: ∞ to 0.125.
13. 50 mm. lenses: 0.77.
14. 35 mm. lenses: 1.1.

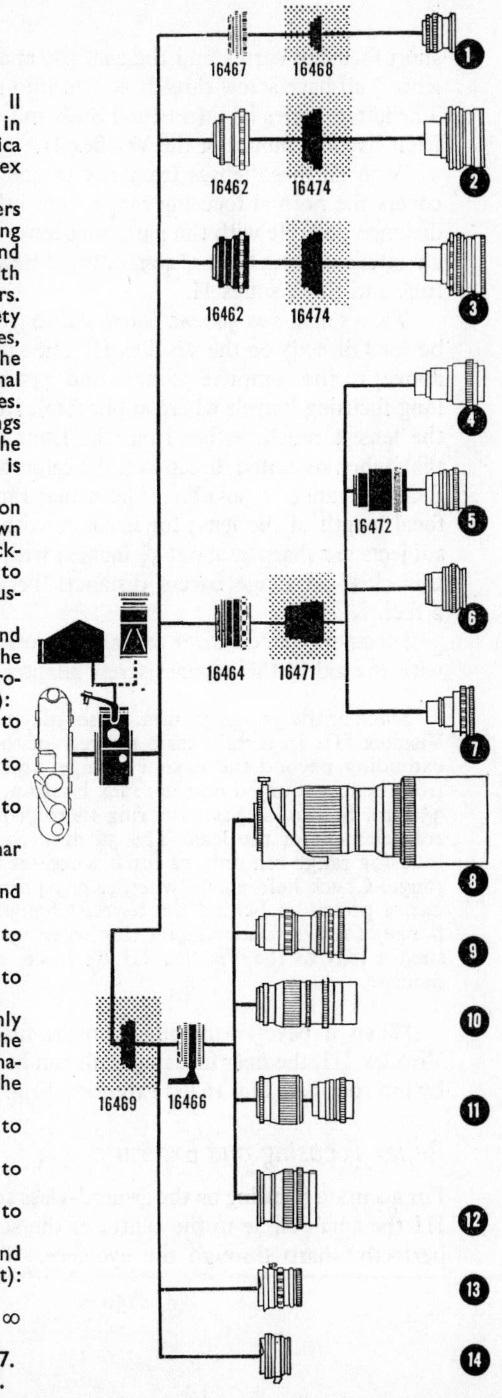

short focusing barrel, and the 200, 280 and old 400 mm. Telyt lenses) all have screw threads and fit into the No. 16466 tube. The latter carries its own tripod bush and fits directly into the front bayonet mount of the Visoflex II.

With all these lenses from 125 to 400 mm. this assembly covers the normal focusing range from infinity to the nearest distance possible with the particular lens. For closer distances an extension ring (No. 16469) is fitted between the No. 16466 tube and the Visoflex II.

The 35 mm. and 50 mm. lenses with bayonet mount can also be used directly on the Visoflex II. The same applies (as noted above) to the complete 90 mm. and 135 mm. lenses (in their long focusing barrels where applicable). In this case, however, the lens is much farther from the front mount of the Leica than when mounted directly on the camera. So only a close-up focusing range is possible. The actual range depends on the focal length of the lens; for instance with the 35 mm. lenses subjects are sharp at about 5½ inches; with the 135 mm. lenses this close-up range covers distances between about 1½ and 2 feet.

Screw-mounted lenses can also be used in the same way, with the aid of the bayonet/screw adapter ring (p. 113).

Some of the 35 and 50 mm. lenses may not fit directly on the Visoflex III. In certain cases the rear of the lens carries a ring extending beyond the bayonet flange which prevents the lens from being mounted on the reflex housing. One example is the 35 mm. Summilux *f*1.4; the ring there protects the protruding rear element of the lens. The 50 mm. Summicron with near focusing range can only be fitted when set to the near focusing range. Check beforehand whether any part of the internal lens barrel protrudes behind the bayonet flange of the lens (or the flange of the bayonet adapter ring when used); do not try to fit such a lens to the Visoflex III by force, as that would cause damage.

When a bayonet-mounted lens is fitted directly on the Visoflex III, the near focusing limit can be brought still nearer by interposing a No. 16469 extension ring.

Reflex Focusing and Exposure

For accurate focusing on the ground-glass screen of the Visoflex III the small circle in the centre of the screen should appear perfectly sharp through the eyepiece. With the right-angle finder unit most users will see this circle sharply even when wearing spectacles (the eyepiece is large enough to permit comfortable viewing).

If viewing without spectacles is preferred, correction lenses slide over the eyepiece frame.

These are available to order for certain degrees of short-sightedness (but not astigmatism).

The vertical 5× magnifier has an adjustable eyepiece. This compensates for not too serious individual eyesight variations. Rotate the mount of this until the central circle and the grain of the ground glass appear sharpest. Hold the Visoflex—without lens—so that diffused light shines into the front with the mirror down.

To fit the right-angle 4× pentaprism unit, slide it into the runners on each side of the ground-glass screen from the back. Push fully home until the catch engages. To remove, press the button at the left-hand side (seen from the back) and slide the unit off the ground-glass screen backwards. To fit the 5× vertical eyepiece magnifier, slide it over the ground-glass screen from the front or from the back. This has no special catch and can be removed by sliding off again in the direction in which it was pushed on.

The black circle in the centre of the ground-glass screen has a diameter of 1 mm. This provides an approximate check on the scale of reproduction in near shots: simply place a ruler with a millimetre scale in the subject field. If, for instance, a 9 mm. stretch of the scale appears to fill the circle on the ground-glass screen, the scale of reproduction is about 1 : 9 or 0.11.

To focus the lens, use the focusing ring of the helical mount in use, or the focusing mount of the lens itself where fitted to the Visoflex as it stands.

Always focus the lens at full aperture. This provides a more brilliant screen image and also shows the transition between sharp and unsharp more clearly.

Then stop down the lens to the required aperture immediately before the exposure.

Some of the lenses have a presetting diaphragm ring specially for reflex focusing. This is fitted on the 65 mm. Elmar, available to special order on the latest versions of the 90 mm. Summicron *f*2, and is also fitted on the 200 mm. Telyt *f*4 and the 280 to 560 mm. Telyt units.

The preset diaphragm mechanism works with two rings. One has a red dot and clicks into place at each aperture setting. This preselects the aperture, but does not actually set it. The second ring moves smoothly and has a black (or white) dot.

To preset the aperture move the red dot opposite the aperture figure. For focusing move the ring with the black dot fully to the left (when holding the camera ready for shooting). To stop down the lens to the preselected aperture move the ring to the right so that the black (or white) dot comes opposite the red dot.

Holding the Leica and Visoflex

For hand held reflex shots some modification of the way of holding the Leica with the Visoflex is necessary. For horizontal shots grip the camera in the right hand in the normal way. The right index finger now rests on the release lever of the Visoflex housing.

For focusing support the camera in the palm of the left hand, gripping the focusing mount of the lens with the left thumb and index finger. When the image is sharp, change the hold of the left hand so that the camera and Visoflex rests on the second and third fingers of the left hand, which are tucked underneath. The left thumb should lie against the back of the camera, while the left index finger steadies the lens and at the same time extends to the preset aperture ring where this is fitted. Stopping down the lens to the preselected aperture is then a simple matter of flicking the ring over with the index finger.

Release the shutter by pressing the release lever gently.

For upright shots it is still best to focus the camera while held horizontally as described above. For the exposure support the left-hand end of the camera in the palm of the left hand, with the right hand up on top and the right index finger on the release lever. The second finger of the left hand rests against the Visoflex, while the left index finger provides additional support for the lens barrel.

Again this index finger also moves the aperture ring to stop down the lens.

For shots with the long-focus lenses (125 mm. and longer) and also for close-ups it is best to mount the camera on a tripod or firm support. The Visoflex carries a tripod bush for this purpose, for English ¼ inch tripod screws.

VISOFLEX II AND IIA

The components of the Visoflex II are:

1. Right-angle magnifier.
2. Vertical magnifier.
3. Release button with setting screw.
4. Ground-glass screen.
5. Release arm.
6. Cable release socket.
7. Return lever (this is absent on the IIA).
8. Locking button for lens or adapter unit.
9. Screw or bayonet mount for fitting to camera.

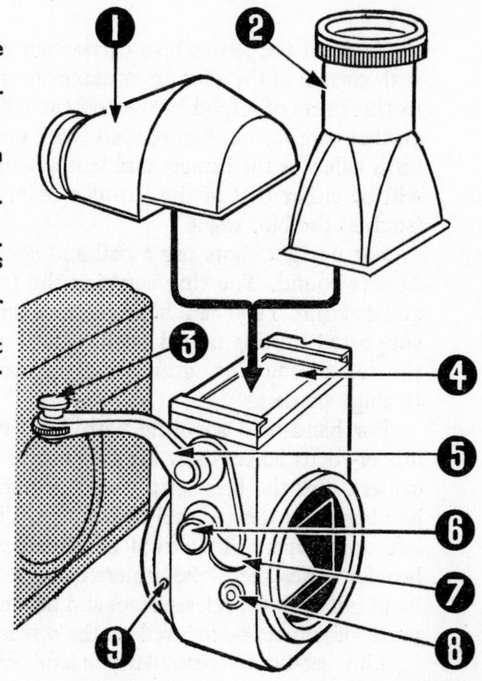

To get the Visoflex II or IIA ready for use, pull the release arm sideways and swing it forward. Also remove the eye-level finder unit if fitted (*left*). Mount the housing on the Leica just like a lens (*right*) with the bayonet (for M models) or screw mount (on earlier Leicas).

Fit the viewing magnifier by sliding it into the guide rails at the two sides of the ground-glass screen (*left*). The rim of the mounting ring carries three screws to get the housing truly lined up with screw-mounted Leicas (*right*); this is a once-and-for-all setting (p. 135).

In use, press the release buttons on the release arm to make the exposure (*left*); then press the return lever to bring the mirror to the viewing position again (*right*). This step does not apply to the Visoflex IIA with automatic return.

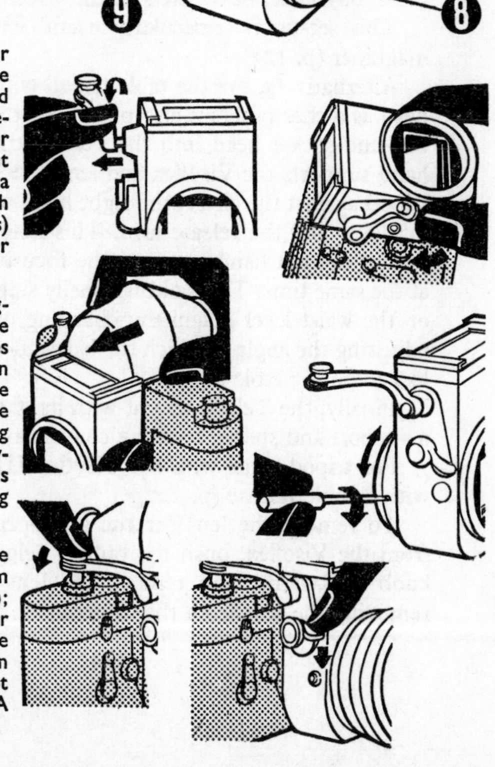

Some of the lenses also carry their own tripod bush, and with certain of the adapter or extension tubes there may be up to three sets of tripod bushes on the whole camera assembly. In that case try out beforehand (with one finger) to see which bush balances the camera and lens assembly best. Usually this will be either that of the Visoflex or of the lens adapter ring (such as the No. 16466).

For upright shots use a ball and socket head to swing the camera round. The ring carrying the tripod bush of the 280 and 400 mm. Telyt can, however, also rotate. If the assembly is supported by this tripod bush, simply slack off the screw at the top of the ring, and swing the camera and lens round through 90 deg.

For hand-held shooting with the Visoflex and one of the longer-focus lenses there are two useful ways of steadying the camera. For the first, grip your right shoulder with your left hand and rest the assembly of camera, Visoflex and lens on the left upper arm. The weight of the assembly with one of the heavier lenses keeps the camera quite steady, so that the right hand can work the release lever and advance the film. The image must, of course, be focused on the screen beforehand.

This set-up is particularly useful with the eye-level 4× magnifier (p. 123).

Alternatively, use the table tripod with the ball-and-socket head as a chestpod (see also p. 40). Fit the tripod screw of the ball-and-socket head into the bush of the Visoflex. The left hand supports the Visoflex and lens and braces it via the table tripod against the chest; the right hand works the rapid winding lever and the release arm. This hold is steady enough to permit the left hand to rotate the focusing mount of the lens at the same time. This hold is equally suitable for the eye-level or the waist-level magnifier; changing over only involves readjusting the angle at which the ball-and-socket head has to be locked on the table tripod.

Finally, the Televit mount with its shoulder stock provides a support and special focusing convenience.

For tripod shots with the Visoflex III, release the shutter with a cable release (p. 127).

To remove the lens (or the appropriate focusing mount) from the Visoflex, push the button below the mirror control knob backwards, and remove the lens or mount as when removing the lens from the camera.

The Visoflex II and IIA

The Visoflex II is a discontinued earlier version of the Visoflex III. It differs from the latter in certain operating details, but takes exactly the same lenses and extension tubes, etc., covering the same focusing ranges and scales of reproduction.

On the Visoflex II the mirror does not return after an exposure, but has to be brought down separately by a lever on the side of the housing. The design of the eye-level finder unit is different and the attachment of the housing to the camera is slightly more cumbersome.

The Visoflex IIA is an intermediate model produced for a short time. Basically it is a Visoflex II, but with the direct return feature for the mirror of the model III (and hence no mirror return lever).

Visoflex II models have also been adapted in the U.S.A. (not by Leitz) to work with a beam-splitting prism in place of the mirror. This eliminates any mirror vibration.

The Visoflex II is available with a bayonet rear mount for the Leica M cameras, and with a screw mount for the screw-mounted models. The front mount is a bayonet ring as on the Visoflex III.

The Visoflex II and IIA can only be fitted on the camera without the finder unit. So first remove the latter—in the same way as on the Visoflex III. Before mounting the housing on the camera pull the release arm outwards, away from its shaft to disengage it, and swing the arm down over the front. (A handy way of having the Visoflex II ready for mounting is to keep the lever already swung down and the eye-level finder clipped on reversed. Once the Visoflex is fitted on the camera, it is then only necessary to re-engage the release lever and reverse the eye-level prism.)

The bayonet-mounted version of the Visoflex II fits to Leica M models in the same way as a lens. The screw-mounted version screws into the lens flange of Leica models I to IIIg. If after screwing in the housing is not square to the camera, slack off the three screws around the rim of the mounting rim of the Visoflex. Align the housing exactly, and tighten the screws.

Swing the release arm back, so that it engages the shaft and rests on top of the camera release button. Adjust the setting screw on the release arm (p. 126) to ensure that the mirror is released just before the shutter. A plastic extension piece is supplied with the screw-mounted Visoflex for the release arm with older Leica models which are not the same height as the Ig and IIIg.

The same vertical 5× eyepiece magnifier is used as on the Visoflex III. The 4× eye-level pentaprism is slightly different in design, but is fitted and removed in the same way. It has an adjustable eyepiece magnifier to compensate for eyesight variations. The normal position is marked O on top of the housing; for people with normal eyesight this setting (bringing the red dot on the milled ring opposite O) should be the most suitable one. To correct short-sightedness, move the ring towards – (on the side of the finder unit); for far-sightedness move it towards +. Adjust the magnifier until the black ring in the centre of the focusing screen looks really sharp.

The eye-level finder housing also carries a white dot next to the shutter speed dial when the housing is in place. This dot serves as setting index for the shutter speeds, since the eye-level finder obscures the normal setting index.

To expose, press the release arm down in the same way as with the Visoflex III. After every shot, however, press the return lever at the side of the housing to bring the mirror down again. (There is no return lever on the Visoflex IIA; the mirror returns on its own.) The centre of the return lever carries a threaded socket to take a cable release.

For time exposures the release lever on the Visoflex IIA is removable and is replaced by a special button. Push down the button and screw it round through 180 deg.; this raises and locks the mirror. Then make the exposure with a cable release screwed directly into the camera release.

To remove the Visoflex II and IIA housings from the Leica, first remove the finder unit.

Also pull the release arm outwards and swing it forward, away from the Leica body. Then remove the housing from the camera in the same way as when removing a lens (depressing the bayonet catch on the M models).

The Visoflex II and IIA carry two tripod bushes for mounting on a tripod, for English ¼ inch and Continental ⅜ inch tripod screws respectively.

The Focorapid Mount

This is a rapid focusing mount with bayonet fitting for the Visoflex II, IIA and III to take the long-focus lenses from 135 mm. upwards. It replaces the helical focusing mounts of the lenses and permits quick focusing with click-stops at preselected settings. Its main use is in sports and similar photography where the Focorapid eliminates all reference to focusing scales or screen images—changing from for instance, the touch line to mid-field in a football match becomes an adjustment by feel and the click stops only.

The Focorapid unit takes the lens heads (optical units) of the 135 mm. Elmar and Hektor (not Tele-Elmar) or of the 200 or 280 mm. Telyt lenses. For the 135 mm. lenses an adapter ring (No. 14114) is required. For the old 200 mm. Telyt *f*4.5 the correct ring is No. 14113, and for the 280 mm. Telyt No. 14112. The lens unit of the current 200 mm. Telyt *f*4 fits directly on the Focorapid.

In all cases the Focorapid unit focuses from infinity downwards; the nearest distance with the 135 mm. lenses is as close as 2½ feet, while with the 200 and 280 mm. lenses it is about 5 feet and 9½ feet respectively. The near limit thus extends considerably closer than with the standard helical mounts for these lenses.

To mount the Focorapid on the camera plus Visoflex, first check that the rear ring of the Focorapid is correctly orientated. This is the ring with the chrome catch. The latter must be in line with the middle of the three knobs protruding from the top of the Focorapid barrel. To bring it into line if necessary, depress the catch and turn the rear ring until the catch clicks into place opposite the middle knob.

Now attach the Focorapid to the front bayonet mount of the Visoflex in the same way as a lens. The lens head itself (with adapter ring where necessary) screws into the front of the Focorapid.

Next set up the click-stops for the rapid focusing system, starting with the infinity stop.

The infinity stop is controlled by the centre knob. Slack off this knob, and carefully focus the lens on a very distant subject by moving the focusing knob in the side of the Focorapid base. The knob can also be turned for fine focusing. When the image on the Visoflex screen is really sharp, tighten the central knob.

This provides an accurate infinity setting, so that when the focusing movement is brought back to its rear limit, the lens is really at infinity. Without that adjustment, focal length variations in the lenses—now no longer compensated by the focusing mount of the lens itself—might lead to variations of the exact infinity position, and hence occasional unsharp results when setting the lens to its infinity limit without looking at the focusing screen image.

To select specific distances with the other two setting knobs (which ride in the elongated channels to each side of the centre knob) proceed as follows:

Slack off both knobs. Starting from the infinity position, advance the focusing knob until the movement picks up the first click stop and carries it along (shown by the movement of one of the knobs). Now adjust the focus to the distance required, and tighten the corresponding knob. Continue advancing the focusing knob past this click stop, until it picks up the second click stop, and set to the second required distance.

It now becomes an easy matter to focus really quickly at either preselected distance by shifting the focusing knob until the movement engages the corresponding click stop. Of course the full focusing range is still available by moving past the click stops and observing the image on the Visoflex focusing screen.

The best way of holding the camera assembly with the Visoflex is to grip the Leica with the right hand as for normal Visoflex shots. The left hand, however, supports the broad under side of the Focorapid, with the left thumb on the focusing knob.

For upright shots press the chrome catch on the rear ring of the Focorapid, and swing the Leica and Visoflex round through 90 degrees until the catch engages again. The hold of the left hand remains unchanged, only the right swings up or down. (Up is the most convenient for most people, but a second vertical position is provided for people who prefer to use their left eye for viewing).

While the near limit of the focusing range is already quite close (p. 137), still nearer distances are possible with the aid of the various extension tubes and rings as available for the Visoflex II, IIA and III (p. 129).

The Filter Turret

With the long-focus and tele lenses the number of different filter fittings required grows rapidly; in particular the Telyts take rather larger filters, and it becomes cumbersome, to say the least, to have to multiply the filter range for each lens—and to change the filters when changing lenses.

The Visoflex filter turret overcomes this by positioning the filters behind the lens and using one filter set for all the lenses. The turret has the same depth as the adapter ring No. 16466 used with the Visoflex II, III and IIA for lenses from 125 mm. upwards (p. 128) and can thus only be used with these lenses. The turret fits into the front bayonet mount of the Visoflex like a lens, and the lenses screw into the front of the turret. This arrangement covers a focusing range from infinity downwards in each case.

The turret has a removable filter disc with three holes to take 43 mm. screw-in (E 43) filters (the size used for the 50 mm. Summilux lens). Alternatively, it takes special adapters (No. 14117) to accept Kodak or other Series VI filters. The turret also carries a tripod foot with $\frac{1}{4}$ inch and $\frac{3}{8}$ inch bushes. The foot rotates to allow the camera and Visoflex to swing over from horizontal to vertical shots when the assembly is mounted on a tripod, without moving the lens.

The filter behind the lens does affect the focus slightly. This means that the image should always be focused with the filter in position—preferably the filter to be used for the shot. An acceptable alternative is to have an ultra-violet (colourless) filter in one of the filter openings—just to make sure that no opening of the turret remains empty—and to focus through the U.V. filter before switching over to another one. This assumes that all the filters in the turret are of the same thickness.

Strictly speaking, the focusing range with the filter is not precisely the same as without a filter. But as the image is focused on the screen, this is not too important.

The Visoflex I Reflex Housing

Before the Visoflex II and III housings were introduced, a rather bigger reflex housing was available for Leica cameras: the Visoflex I. This is now discontinued, since the Visoflex III offers the same versatility and is more compact and convenient for hand-held shots. The Visoflex I works on the same principle as the models II and III, showing the exact field of view and sharpness on its ground-glass focusing screen on top of the housing. It can, however, only be used for focusing to infinity with lenses of 125 mm. focal length or longer. On the other hand, fewer adapter rings are required for the tele lenses.

The Visoflex I has a tubular (or square, in the case of older models) body. The rear fits into the lens mount of the Leica. There are two versions, with a bayonet mount for the Leica M series or a screw mount for the older models. The front has a screw thread (irrespective of the camera for which it is designed) to take the mount of the 125 mm. Hektor or the Telyt lenses. Alternatively, the 135 mm. lenses (other than the Tele-Elmar and Elmarit), fitted in a non-coupled short focusing barrel, can also be used with the Visoflex I. All these fit directly, without intermediate rings or adapters.

Lenses of shorter focal length—but screw-mounted versions only—can also be fitted into the Visoflex I for close-up work.

The bayonet-mounted Visoflex I has a higher finder shoe to enable the Telyt frame finder to clear the Leica M body. When using the screw-mounted Visoflex on the Leica M with a bayonet/screw adapter, an extension shoe is required.

The body of the housing contains a movable mirror and a plunger outside the housing which raises the mirror out of the way. This plunger is shaped like the release button of the screw-mounted Leica, and also carries a thread to take a cable release.

On later models a locking nut fixes the plunger when depressed, keeping the mirror permanently raised when required.

A twin cable release is provided for simultaneously raising the mirror and releasing the shutter of the Leica. Alternatively, a cable release link from the Leica release button (not for Leica M models) screwing over the button of the housing (the tubular model only) serves the same purpose.

Above the screen a reflecting prism arrangement with a built-in 4× magnifier permits observation of the right-way-round image at eye-level. The prism head can be changed for a vertical tube or for a 90 deg. tube with a 5× magnifier; either fits into the bayonet mount above the screen.

The older model of the reflex housing has a fixed straight tube above the screen, with the magnifier, for waist-level viewing only.

A further 30 × magnifier, which can be swung out of the way, is fitted on old models for specially precise focusing on an aerial image in a clear spot in the centre of the screen.

Assembling the Visoflex I

To use the Visoflex I, fit the housing into the lens flange of the Leica like a lens.

Screw the Telyt lens into the front flange of the reflex housing.

With the twin cable release screw the milled nut at the end of one of the cables over the plunger of the reflex housing, and the other cable into the release of the Leica.

In the twin release supplied with the screw-mounted model the plungers of the two cables are permanetly fitted inside a housing. A large plunger operates both together. One of the two cables carries a black ring on the fixing nut at the bottom end. Connect the cable marked with the black ring to the reflex housing, and the plain one to the Leica. If fitted the other way round, pressing the plunger may release the Leica shutter before the mirror is fully raised and thus cut off part of the picture.

Where the cables for the screw-mounted Visoflex I are not specially marked, the heavier one of the two should go on the reflex housing.

It is also possible to screw a normal cable release over the release button part of the cable release link, to avoid camera shake when using the set-up on a tripod.

The screw-mounted tubular Visoflex I can also be used with a release link. This is a short cable with two nipples screwing over the release button of the Visoflex and the screw-mounted Leicas respectively. Here again the thicker nipple (marked with a black ring) goes over the release of the reflex housing. Depressing the button on the reflex housing end of the cable tensions but does not raise the mirror. The image can now be focused on the screen.

On pressing the release button above the camera end of the

VISOFLEX I

Black panel: The reflex mirror produces an image on the screen for focusing (*top*) until the moment of *exposure* (*bottom*).

Right-hand column: The parts of the Visoflex I reflex housing are:

1. Eyepiece.
2. Magnifier.
3. Ground-glass screen.
4. Cable release link.
5. Mirror lock.
6. Lens flange.
7. Mirror release.
8. Finder shoe.
9. Catch for rotating housing.

To align the housing (screw mounted versions), raise and lock the mirror, slacken the screws visible from the front, and rotate the housing to either side as required (p. 142).

The interchangeable magnifiers (p. 140) fit into a bayonet mount around the screen (here with an earlier version of the reflex housing). The alternatives are a right-angle magnifier (*left*), and a 45 deg. magnifier (not shown) in addition to the vertical type (here earlier version—*right*).

Left: The reflex housing will, in addition to the Telyt lenses, take the 135 mm. lenses for normal screen focusing. In that case the lens unit of the 135 mm. is fitted in a shortened focusing mount to allow for the depth of the housing (p. 139).

Right: For telephoto action shots, lock the mirror open, and use the Telyt frame finder (p. 144).

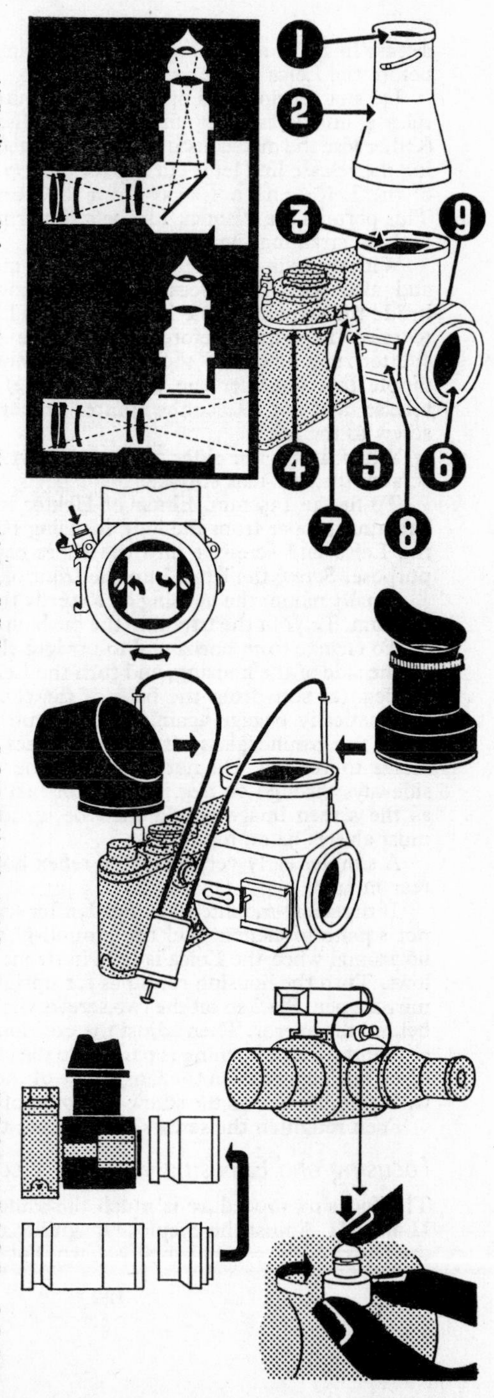

release link, the mirror swings up by spring action, immediately before the Leica shutter runs down.

Do not tension this spring-loaded button except when the release link is actually fitted to the Visoflex and the Leica. (Otherwise the mechanism may be damaged.) Also, when attaching the release link let it curve over the top of the accessory shoe of the Leica, and not away from the camera round the front. This permits the Visoflex I to be swung round for upright shots without straining the release link.

With the twin cable releases for screw-mounted Leica models, and also with the release link, the movement of the cable inside the camera nipple is adjustable. This enables the release to raise the mirror before releasing the Leica shutter. If the shutter runs down too soon, screw the small screw (inside the nipple that fits over the camera release) to the right. If the release does not release the shutter properly, screw this setting screw to the left.

When fitting the older 200 mm. Telyt *f*4.5, take care not to scratch the rear lens surface.

To fit the 135 mm. Elmar or Hektor lens, first unscrew the lens unit proper from the long focusing barrel used directly on the Leica and screw it into the short barrel available for the purpose. Screw the latter into the front of the Visoflex.

Finally mount the housing on a sturdy tripod. With the 280 or 400 mm. Telyt fit the tripod to the bush on the barrel of the lens.

To change from horizontal to upright shots, press the button on the side of the housing, and turn the Leica clockwise through 90 deg. (as seen from the back of the camera). The catch will automatically engage again. At the same time, a mask underneath the ground-glass screen also rotates to change the screen image to vertical. Do not try to tilt the whole reflex housing sideways through 90 deg. (except for hand-held shots—p. 143) as the screen image would then be upside down. The screen must always be on top.

A simpler early version of the reflex housing has no rotating rear mount.

If the screw-mounted Visoflex I, after screwing to the Leica, is not square to camera (i.e. the ground-glass screen is not truly horizontal when the Leica is held horizontally), realign it as follows. Turn the housing round as for upright shots, and lock the mirror open. Slacken off the two screws visible inside the housing behind the mirror. Then adjust the position of the reflex housing so that the frame opening is parallel to the camera base plate. The black line engraved on the lens flange of the Leica must coincide with a similar line on the screw-in mount of the housing.

Then retighten the screws, and release the mirror.

Focusing and Exposing with the Visoflex I

The focusing procedure is much the same as with the Visoflex II and III. Adjust the eyepiece magnifier until the black ring in the centre of the screen is really sharp. Focus with the lens at full aperture, and stop down afterwards to the required setting. Use the presetting ring on the tele lenses which are fitted with one (p. 131).

The clear spot in the centre of old Visoflex I models is useful for aerial focusing. In this central spot the image must appear sharp simultaneously with the crossed sighting threads. When the picture is out of focus the eye has to refocus slightly to get the one or the other sharp in the same way in which we have to readjust our eyes when looking at distant or nearby objects. Since this adaptation is largely a subconscious process, it takes a little practice to judge just when the aerial image is as sharp as the crossed threads.

For aerial focusing the high-power magnifier is used. Pull the normal eyepiece out of the reflex housing and bring the eye right up to the opening. Swing the magnifier into the field of the screen by means of the lever at the side of the tube.

Focus the magnifier by twisting the milled knob at the end of the magnifier lever until the crossed threads appear sharp. Then focus the Telyt or other lens by turning its focusing mount until the image is sharp simultaneously with the crossed sighting threads. Make sure that the reflex housing is firmly supported on a tripod or stand. Any vibration makes observation of the aerial image very difficult.

To make the exposure press the plunger of the twin cable release. At slow speeds keep the plunger depressed until the second shutter blind has closed. (That is to ensure that the mirror does not drop down in the light path during the exposure.)

With the screw-mounted Visoflex on a screw-mounted Leica camera connected with the release link, press the tensioning knob (at the end of the link over the mirror release) which preloads the mirror release. Then press the release button on the camera end of the release link. At slow speeds, keep the plunger depressed until the second shutter blind has closed.

For time exposures on the T setting, the mirror must be locked in the open position first. Unscrew the release link or cable release from the reflex housing and push down the plunger button of the housing. Lock it by pushing down the small milled ring just below the button and giving it a quarter turn clockwise. Then release the Leica shutter in the usual way. Only the normal cable release is required in this case.

On models of the reflex housing without the mirror lock, the plunger of the twin release has to be kept depressed for the required exposure time.

The 200 mm. Telyt can also be used for hand-held shots.

Press the button in the side of the reflex housing, and turn the housing to the left through 90 deg., so that the eyepiece tube points to the left of the Leica, and the special finder shoe (where fitted) of the reflex housing is on top.

Insert the Telyt frame finder (p. 122) into the finder shoe, raise the mirror, and lock it in the open position. With the cable release link it is unnecessary to lock the mirror open.

With this arrangement, which is useful for telephoto sports shots, etc., the lens has to be focused by scale, or prefocused by means of the reflex screen before locking the mirror open for the exposure.

The best way of holding the Leica for such telephoto snapshots is to support the reflex housing with the left hand, and the camera with the right.

Discontinued and Obsolete Leica Finders

Various obsolete Leica finders have been superseded by the later range or discontinued. These older models include:

The right-angle finder, for 50 mm. lenses only, shows the view at an angle of 90 deg., and is useful for inconspicuous shooting round the corner. It fits on the accessory shoe, and a small prism swings behind the rangefinder eyepiece of series II and III Leicas (a special model without prism and with a higher base to clear the rewind knob was made for the Leica I). The right-angle finder can only be used for horizontal shots, and the image is reversed left to right.

The waist-level finder, for 50 mm. lenses, shows an upright, right-way-round image from the top. It fits into the accessory shoe in two positions for horizontal and vertical shots, and carries a further accessory shoe. It is useful for low viewpoints when shooting in awkward corners where it may be difficult to get the eye behind the camera. When viewing, look into the finder with one eye so that the cross engraved on the top glass appears exactly in the circle engraved in the front glass. The waist-level finder will also serve as a right-angle finder for shooting round corners. Wide-angle models for 35 and 28 mm. lenses have a hinged negative front lens.

The earlier universal finder works similarly to the more modern model (p. 120), but shows the image reversed left to right. When used for vertical shots, turn the eyepiece knob through a quarter turn to the right, otherwise the image will be upside down. The eyepiece mask, as visible from the outside must always be horizontal, even for upright pictures. This used to be known as the VIDOM finder.

The small universal finders are handier for a limited range of lenses. Four models each cover the field of the 35 and 50 mm. lenses, together with one of longer focus (73, 90, 105 or 135 mm. respectively). The view covered by each lens is engraved on a plate inside the finder together with smaller fine frames for the reduced field of close-ups, and a cross to mark the centre.

Brilliant finders were also available for the now discontinued 85 mm. lens and the Stemar unit. The former was closely similar to the current 90 mm. model, and the latter like the 50 mm. brilliant finder.

The sports finders are an earlier version of the brilliant finders, and were made for the 73, 85, 90 and 135 mm. lenses. Some models were of a folding pattern with parallax adjustment. A special model was made for the 28 mm. wide-angle lens.

BUILDING UP AN OUTFIT

Start with the basic equipment of camera and lens, with one or two simple accessories like a filter, lens hood, and ever-ready case. This outfit is portable and usually adequate.
Acquire extra lenses and special gear only when really needed.

The range of interchangeable lenses for the Leica, with the appropriate finders, makes a formidable outfit to buy as well as to carry around. It represents an attempt to widen the scope of the Leica as far as possible. They are, however, not intended as a challenge to any Leica photographer to acquire every one of them; a Leica outfit is not a stamp collection, but a set of photographic tools to choose from.

Few photographers would indeed need all lenses; but different Leica users will probably want different ones for their particular purposes.

What, then, is a sensible way of building up a Leica outfit?

The Basic Minimum

The least we need to take straightforward pictures is the camera and one lens. This is the basic photographic equipment; it consists of the two items (and the only two apart from the film) that we cannot do without.

For the large majority of subjects a standard 50 mm. lens is fully adequate; it is, in fact, something of a universal lens.

Of the standard lenses available, the *f*2 Summicron is probably the most generally useful. It will cover an appreciable range of subjects in poor light, and in view of its high speed will make the subsequent acquisition of a high-aperture lens unnecessary.

For less ambitious photographers the *f*2.8 Elmar lens is, however, just as good; except for its smaller aperture it is in no way inferior.

If we add to this an ever-ready case (p. 31), a lens hood (p. 116) and a medium yellow or light green filter (p. 238) to fit the lens, we have a sensible basic outfit. Many Leica photographers will never need anything more.

Going Further

To extend our basic outfit, the first long-focus lens to get is the 90 mm. Elmar or Elmarit. Unless the longer 135 mm. lens is necessary for any special purpose, the 90 mm. lens is handier. Of the various 90 mm. lenses the Tele-Elmarit is the most compact one if the lens is only to be used directly on the camera. The Elmar and Elmarit are more versatile in allowing the use of the optical units of the lens for close-up work with the Visoflex housing and focusing bellows. (This is a matter of looking ahead in a choice of close-up gear—see also p. 373.)

At the other end of the range, the 35 mm. wide-angle lens at times provides a useful alternative to the standard lens. Again it is better to get the 35 mm. lens rather than the ultra-wide-angle 28 mm. one; the latter is more specialized.

With the Leica M2 to M4 the camera finder also covers the field of view of these two extra lenses, using the finder attachment for the 35 mm. lens on the M3. (With the Leica IIIg an additional viewfinder is necessary for the 35 mm. lens, and with the M1 an extra finder for the 90 mm. lens. All other Leica models—i.e. the older ones up to IIIf and the Ig—need separate finders for the alternative focal lengths.)

With the current lenses, one filter size (39 mm. screw-in) will fit all 35, 50 mm. (except Summilux) and 90 mm. and 135 mm. lenses (except the Summicron and 135 mm. Elmarit).

Individual Needs

That, then, is what we can regard as the minimum comprehensive outfit. For special interests and subjects we can, of course, modify this and, if necessary, add to it.

Thus for candid photography the 90 mm. lens is not quite so important; but a flash gun is. Nor shall we use filters much.

If our interest lies mainly in portraiture the main Leica lens to use will be the 90, or even 135 mm. one, while the wide-angle lens is unnecessary. We shall also want a tripod when the light is not good enough for short exposures.

The press photographer, who has to get pictures under any conditions, will be best served with the 35 mm. and 50 mm. *f*1.4 and the 90 mm. Summicron *f*2, together with a flash gun, to get the most out of poor lighting conditions.

In stage, circus and show photography these ultra-fast lenses are also useful, together with a unipod or similar camera support that can be used unobtrusively in the auditorium.

For colour work, supplement the basic outfit with an exposure meter, a haze filter and possibly some of the other special filters for colour films.

Pictorial photography usually calls for additional filters while in architecture the 21 or 28 mm. ultra-wide angle and 135 mm. long-focus lenses may be more suitable alternatives to the 35 and 90 mm. ones.

In copying and close-up work we shall rarely need any lenses other than the 50 mm. or 90 mm., but a whole range of close-up accessories (p. 352) is available.

Practical Limits

One consideration in building up any outfit, especially when we want to take it about with us, is portability. The camera with a battery of lenses, finders, and accessories, can become quite a burden to carry and impede rather than aid picture taking. Many of the accessories are intended for special needs and not for everyday photography.

The sensible way to start is, therefore, with the basic minimum rather than with the maximum likely to be needed. Then add further items as and when they become necessary.

One aspect of portability is the convenience with which the complete camera outfit can be carried around. While an ever-ready case is useful protection (at the cost of slower readiness in action) for the camera itself, carrying various bits and pieces around in the pockets is a nuisance and can also damage equipment, or at least lead to accumulation of dust, fluff, etc.

Once you have a well-selected Leica outfit consisting of more than the camera, a lens and a couple of filters, it is worth while stowing all the gear in a holdall universal case or gadget bag. These bags come in varying sizes from various manufacturers and accommodate the camera and accessories in compartments or clips. When choosing a gadget bag the following considerations count:

First, the inside layout should give easy access to any item without disturbing any others. At the same time the equipment should be held securely without rattling.

Second, the compartments or other internal divisions should be capable of being switched around to cater for changing outfits.

Third, get a bag large enough to leave scope for additional items likely to be acquired later on. But with a large outfit it is sometimes worth having a small as well as a large hold-all case: the small one when you want to carry little gear, and the large one for taking a more comprehensive outfit.

THE LEICAFLEX

The Leicaflex provides a direct view of the subject field and image sharpness on its integral screen.
Learn to hold the camera steady while keeping the fingers free for their proper controls.

As a single-lens reflex camera, the Leicaflex has many of the features of a combination of the Leica and the Visoflex housing. It is, however, appreciably more compact than a combination of the Leica and Visoflex could ever be. It is more convenient in use for general photography with the wide-angle to medium- to long-focus lenses (up to 180 mm.), and equipped with a number of automatic operational features.

While the Leica and Visoflex combination is a compromise (though a very effective one) for the normal range of camera subjects, extending the scope of the Leica to reflex focusing, the Leicaflex is from the outset planned for this type of photography.

The Reflex System

The heart of the Leicaflex is the reflex system—the mirror, viewing and focusing screen, eye-level pentaprism finder and automatic aperture control for the lenses. Let us look at these in turn.

The mirror is hinged, as on the Visoflex, and alternately diverts the image-forming rays from the lens to a focusing screen or lets them pass through to the film during exposure. But the Leicaflex mirror not only swings out of the way on pressing the release, but swings back equally quickly immediately the shutter has run down. While the image still disappears from the finder during the moment of exposure (in the Leica it is visible all the time), this interval is only a fraction of a second longer than the actual exposure time.

To minimize the risk of camera vibration the mirror is specially balanced and braked before it reaches the top of its movement. The residual vibration felt during shooting is due to the mirror returning to its viewing position, and can no longer affect the picture.

There are two models of the Leicaflex: the standard version and the SL (= *S*elective *L*ight measurement). The standard model has an exposure meter built into the front of the camera

ICAFLEX CONTROLS

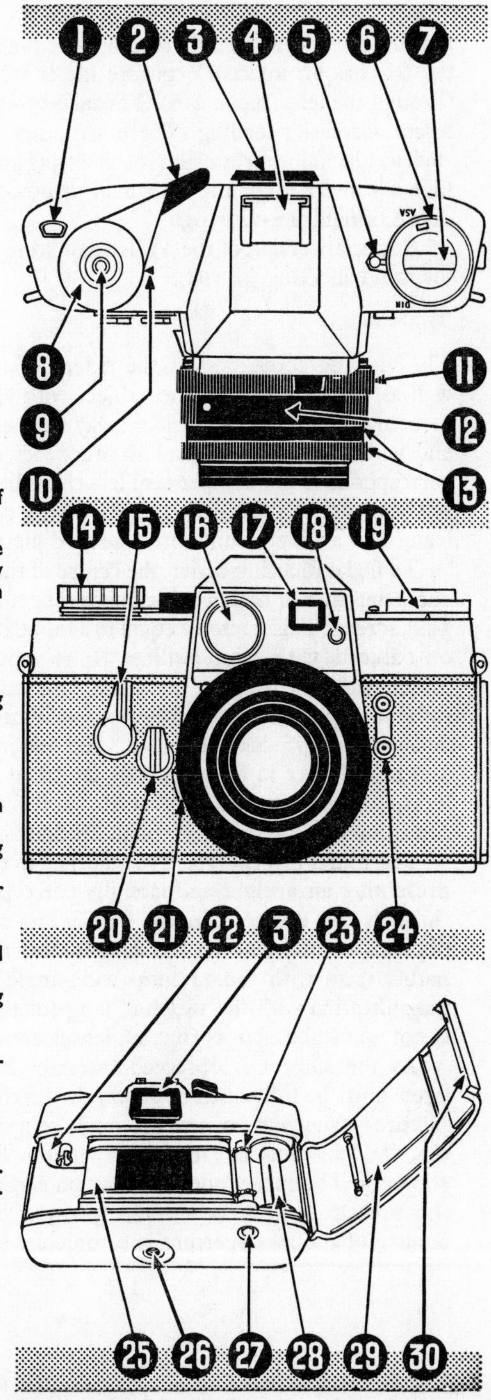

The operating features of
e Leicaflex are:

1. Film counter. (On the
rrent models this window
round and larger, as on
e Leicaflex SL—p. 151.)
2. Winding lever.
3. Finder eyepiece.
4. Accessory shoe.
5. Film speed setting
ck.
6. Film type indicator.
7. Rewind crank.
8. Shutter speed scale.
9. Release button with
ble release socket.
10. Shutter speed setting
dex.
11. Aperture selector
ng.
12. Depth of field scale.
13. Focusing mount and
stance scale.
14. Shutter speed setting
ob.
15. Self-timer.
16. Battery compart-
ent.
17. Meter cell.
18. Meter test button.
19. Film speed scale.
20. Mirror control lever.
21. Lens changing catch.
22. Cassette chamber.
23. Transport sprocket.
24. Flash sockets.
25. Film track.
26. Tripod bush.
27. Reversing button.
28. Take-up spool.
29. Pressure plate.
30. Back lock.

housing for integrated light readings over an angle of about 30°; the SL has an internal exposure meter which reads directly through the lens (see p. 226). The take-up spool is slightly different for easier loading. There are other minor differences, such as black shutter and film speed setting knobs, a very slightly higher camera body and a manual stopping-down button for depth of field pre-viewing.

A special version of the SL is adapted to take a motor drive for rapid shooting (p. 168).

The Screen

The viewing screen shows the extent of the picture area as well as the sharpness of the subject with any lens and at any focusing distance. It thus does away with all accessory finders and with finder parallax and all other viewing errors. Its area corresponds to about 8 per cent less than the image on the film, but shows what would be projected of a colour transparency framed in a slide mount with standard picture window.

To make focusing easier, the centre of the screen has certain characteristics of both a coincidence rangefinder and a ground-glass screen. This is almost equal to a rangefinder when focusing on subjects with clear outlines. It is superior to the rangefinder when focusing on fine detail and texture. It is the only reliable way of accurate observation of sharpness for close-ups and with long-focus tele-lenses. The screen is not as effective as a rangefinder in focusing objects of low contrast or in poor light, for the visual acuity of the eye is lower under these conditions than its ability to line up double outlines.

The finder incorporates a pentaprism in the camera housing, presenting an upright and laterally correct view of the screen through the eyepiece in the back. The scale of the image depends on the lens on the camera and ranges from 0.35× natural size with the 21 mm. wide-angle lens to about 3× magnification with the 180 mm. long-focus lens. The eyepiece is not adjustable, but correction lenses are available.

As the subject is observed through the camera lens, the latter must be fully open to obtain the brightest possible finder picture. Usually exposures are made at a smaller aperture, so that the lens must be stopped down after focusing and before shooting. The preset aperture ring on certain lenses simplifies this procedure with the Visoflex (p. 131); on the Leicaflex the control of the lens aperture is completely automatic.

LEICAFLEX SL FEATURES

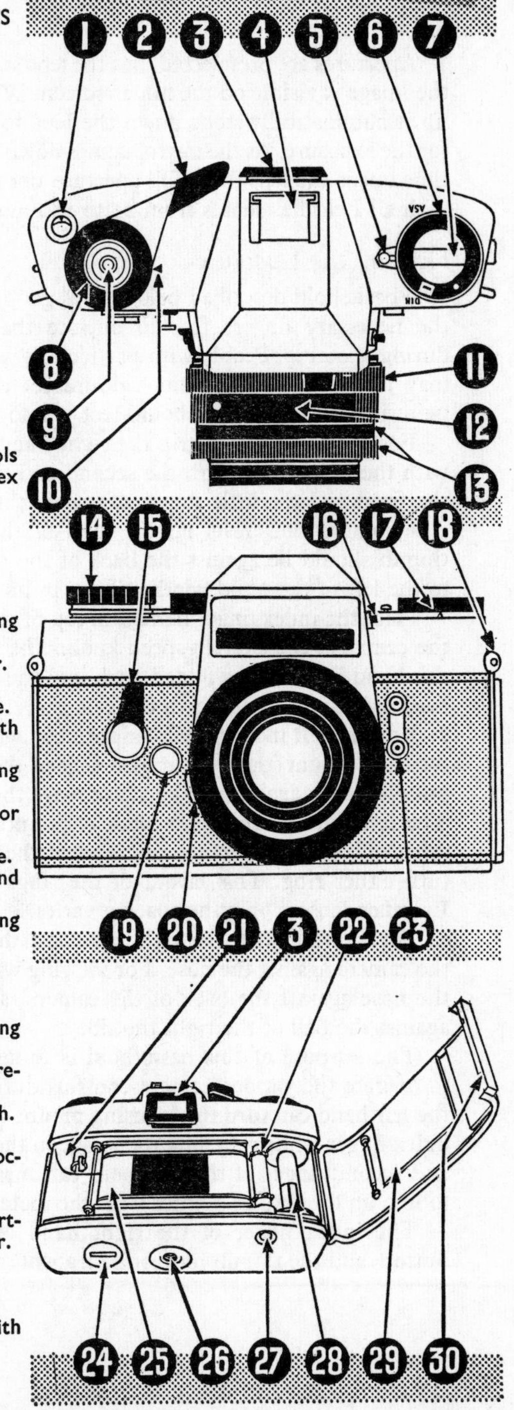

The operating controls and features of the Leicaflex SL are:

1. Film counter.
2. Winding lever.
3. Finder eyepiece.
4. Accessory shoe.
5. Film speed setting lock.
6. Film type indicator.
7. Rewind crank.
8. Shutter speed scale.
9. Release button with cable release socket.
10. Shutter speed setting index.
11. Aperture selector ring.
12. Depth of field scale.
13. Focusing mount and distance scale.
14. Shutter speed setting knob.
15. Self-timer lever.
16. Meter test button.
17. Film speed scale.
18. Eyelet for carrying strap.
19. Depth of field preview button.
20. Lens changing catch.
21. Cassette chamber.
22. Film transport sprocket.
23. Flash socket.
24. Battery compartment for exposure meter.
25. Film track.
26. Tripod bush.
27. Reversing button.
28. Take-up spool with film attachment sleeve.
29. Pressure plate.
30. Back lock.

Apertures are preselected, but the lens stays fully open while the image is visible on the finder screen. When the mirror flies up it automatically stops down the lens to its preset aperture for the exposure. As the mirror comes down again it at the same time opens the lens to its full aperture once more. This works with all Leicaflex lenses from 21 to 180 mm.

Holding the Leicaflex

The basic hold described below gives good support and leaves the necessary fingers free to operate the controls required during shooting. People with particularly large or small hands may find slight modifications desirable; the most important point is that the camera should rest comfortably in the hands.

For horizontal shots grip the right-hand end of the camera with the right hand, with the second and third fingers against the front and the little finger supporting it from underneath. The camera thus rests in the palm of the hand. The right thumb should lie against the back of the camera, the tip just to the left of the rapid winding lever in its working position.

Place the index finger lightly on top of the release button in the centre of the shutter-speed knob. The left hand, with the third and little fingers folded back into the palm, supports the base plate from underneath the camera.

Rest the left index finger comfortably against the side of the focusing mount (the front milled ring of the lens), and the left middle finger against the aperture ring (the rear milled ring). The left thumb can then switch back and forth between the other side of the aperture ring and of the focusing mount to turn either ring. This layout of the rings is the same on all Leicaflex lenses; only the spacing varies.

For viewing with the right eye, rest the left-hand end of the camera against the nose. For viewing with the left eye, rest the nose against the back of the camera, and the right cheek against the ball of the right thumb.

The purpose of this basic hold is to keep the fingers free to operate the various camera controls during shooting. Thus the left hand can turn the focusing mount with the thumb and index finger while watching the image in the finder; the thumb and second finger of the left hand can turn the aperture ring to line up the setting pointer with the meter needle (p. 161).

The index finger of the right hand operates the release button, and the thumb moves the transport lever. This thumb

LEICAFLEX HOLDS

For horizontal shots the right hand grips the right end of the camera, with the first joint of the index finger on the release button and the thumb against the transport lever. The thumb and first two fingers of the left hand operate the control rings on the lens; the other two fingers support the camera from underneath.

The vertical hold is similar for the grip of the hands on the camera; the palm of the left hand supports the camera body.

When using the ever-ready case, keep the lid well out of the way of the lens.

The neck strap wrapped round the wrists when holding the camera can provide additional steadying support. Tension the strap over the back of the neck to press the camera firmly against the head.

Press the release button with tip of the index finger only, while the middle part of the finger rests on the shutter-speed knob (*left*). For time exposures the cable release screws into the centre of the release button (*right*).

To tension the self-timer pull down the lever on the camera front. Then press the release button to set the delayed action mechanism going. The delay is adjustable according to the extent the lever is pulled down (*right*).

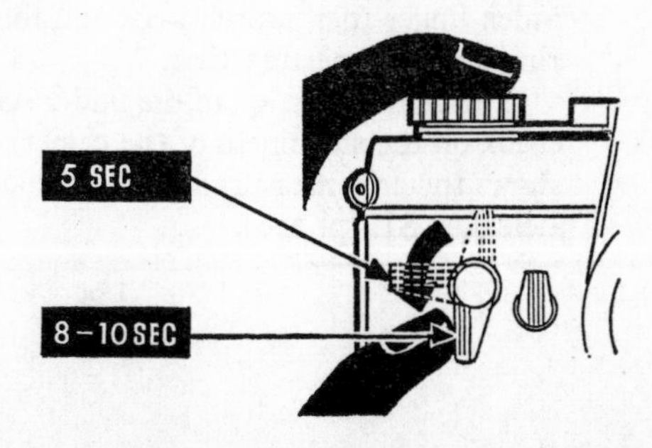

should stay to the left of the lever, so that when the latter flies back it cannot hit you in the eye. The end of the lever is black plastic to avoid breaking spectacles if it should fly back. The right index finger can also turn the shutter speed knob, together with the right thumb, again to help in lining up the needle.

People with small hands may find it more comfortable to press the little finger of the right hand against the front of the camera as well (together with the second and third fingers) instead of keeping it underneath.

It is also possible to hold the aperture and distance setting rings of the lens from the left instead of from below, but this is less steadying and a finger may obscure the meter cell.

Vertical Shots

The position of the hands on the camera remain virtually the same as for the horizontal hold just described. Turn the Leicaflex upright, so that the right hand is on top and the left hand underneath. The ball of the left thumb now supports the lower camera end, and the back of the right thumb steadies it against the forehead. The same fingers operate the controls as before.

Holding the camera upright with the right hand underneath and the left hand on top is generally less comfortable and less steady, for both hands tend to be cramped in the wrist. When viewing with the left eye, the transport lever also sticks into your mouth.

Additional Supports

The camera strap, which fits the eyelets of the Leicaflex in the same way as of the Leica (p. 31), can also help to steady the camera during shooting.

Alternatively the table tripod, braced against the chest (p. 40) or against the right shoulder, keeps the camera specially steady. The right hand here holds the Leicaflex in the normal way, but the third and fourth fingers of the left hand curl around the ball-and-socket head on the table tripod, which is also supported by the palm of the left hand. The thumb and index finger then switch back and forth between the focusing ring and the aperture ring.

The central portion of the finder screen can provide a useful check on the steadiness of the camera hold (see p. 158). It also shows the area measured by the through-the-lens meter of the Leicaflex SL (p. 226).

The Leicaflex has a tripod bush in the base plate, centrally below the lens. This takes a standard $\frac{1}{4}$ inch tripod screw.

The camera can also stand on a flat surface such as a table top. To level the camera, fit (or extend) the lens hood on the lens and place a $\frac{1}{16}$ inch thick spacer ($\frac{1}{8}$ inch with the model SL) between the rim of the hood and the supporting surface. That keeps the camera steady and firm.

Keep the front of the lens near the edge of the table to avoid the latter intruding into the field of view. The front of the lens should be not more than 3 inches (with the 50 mm. lens) or $2\frac{1}{2}$ inches (with the 35 mm. lens) behind the edge of the supporting surface.

Releasing

To release the shutter smoothly while holding the camera, press down the release button in the centre of the shutter-speed knob. The first joint of the index finger should rest on the knob; when pressing, flex this joint only, so that nothing else but the button gets pressed. Do not arch the finger to clear the shutter knob.

Instead, use the latter as the support for the index finger, to avoid transmitting pressure to the whole camera. Keep a firm grip with the right hand on the camera body, with the latter wedged firmly into the palm of the hand. Do not allow the camera to slide down in the hand while pressing the release.

Since the hold for vertical pictures is substantially the same, pressing the release there again requires the same operation.

After every shot advance the film with the winding lever. In its working position, this lever sticks out roughly backwards. To advance the film, swing out the lever fully as far as it will go to the front, and let it move back. Keep the right thumb behind the lever during this return movement. It is better not to let the lever fly back, particularly when viewing with the left eye, as the lever may otherwise hit you in the eye. The Leicaflex transport lever cannot advance in short strokes.

To swing out the lever, the right hand has to partly release its grip on the camera (the left hand keeps it supported). Push the lever forward and out with the thumb, pressing the middle and third finger of the right hand still against the front of the camera body.

Then grip the right-hand end of the camera firmly again with the index finger on the release button.

The transport lever advances the film and re-tensions the shutter, and also advances the film counter. This is visible through the window next to the transport lever, and partially obscured by the latter in the starting position of the transport movement. To check the number of exposures on the counter simply push the lever aside to its rest position next to the finder housing. Always keep the lever in the rest position when not using the camera, as this also switches off the exposure meter circuit.

The film counter indicates the number of the frame ready for the next exposure. The release button is always locked until the film is fully advanced and the lever has returned to its starting position.

The film is transported by a sprocket wheel inside the camera, and winds itself up on the take-up spool (driven through a friction coupling) with the emulsion side facing outwards. This is the same as with the rangefinder Leica models (both the bayonet-mounted M-types and the old screw-mounted series).

For time exposures a cable release screws into the threaded socket in the centre of the release button.

The Self-timer

The self-timer or delayed action release is the larger of the two levers on the camera front, below the shutter-speed knob. It is set in the same way as on the Leica M2 to M4 (p. 53), but to set the mechanism going, press the release button itself. The self-timer then takes 4–10 seconds to run down—according to how far it was pulled down in the first place—before it releases the shutter.

Once the self-timer has been tensioned, the shutter cannot (as on the Leica M models) be released independently of the self-timer. While the lever itself can be tensioned at any time, the timer can only be set into operation with the shutter tensioned—since otherwise the release button is blocked.

In addition to self-portraits and similar delayed action shots, the self-timer is also useful for releasing the shutter at slow speeds with the camera held in the hand.

LEICAFLEX OPERATION

**Focus the image in the central spot on the screen.
The viewfinder also shows the shutter speed selected and the meter needle and matching pointer for the coupled exposure control.**

Viewing, focusing and even exposure setting with the Leicaflex is centred around the viewing screen and eye-level finder system. The screen shows the extent of the image field, the sharpness of the picture, the shutter speed selected and the aperture adjustment on the lens for correct exposure, as indicated by the built-in exposure meter.

Viewing and Focusing

To see the whole finder screen, keep the eye as close as possible to the eyepiece at the back of the camera. The exit pupil of the eyepiece is sufficiently far back to allow even spectacle wearers to take in the entire screen area when looking straight into the eyepiece lens.

Eyepiece correction lenses are available to compensate for special eyesight defects. They fit over the rectangular eyepiece mount at the back. But it is usually better to view with spectacles, when no correction lenses are required.

The sharpness of the image is observed on the central circle in the finder field. When the lens is not correctly focused the image appears unsharp in this field. It also appears unsharp on the surrounding screen area which is a special microgrid focusing screen on the Leicaflex SL. (On the standard Leicaflex the image usually appears sharp as there the surrounding screen does not have a focusing surface.)

The central circle is filled by a pattern of special microprisms which break up an out-of-focus image by deflecting the image-forming rays in all directions. When an image is grossly out of focus multiple images appear, though they are not sharply defined as with a rangefinder. Bright image points in particular seem broken up into four- or six-pointed stars.

As the lens setting gets nearer to its correct point the image looks unsharp and appears broken up by a grainy pattern—the microprism grid. At the point of maximum sharpness the image becomes clearest, and the grainy pattern abruptly vanishes. This disappearance of the grain effect gives the most distinct indication of the point of maximum sharpness—more distinct than with a normal ground-glass screen.

During focusing on an area of regular texture the grid pattern and the texture between them produce a *moiré* effect. This moves with the slightest movement of the camera, and thus appears to "shimmer" in the focusing spot. As long as this shimmering persists, the image is not perfectly focused.

This shimmering effect is also useful for testing the steadiness of your camera hold (p. 152). Focus on a regularly patterned surface—a brick wall at some distance, or a net curtain at closer range—and adjust the lens until the *moiré* effect is strongest.

Then try out various camera holds to see with which one the *moiré* pattern appears most stationary.

Watch this shimmering carefully when focusing subjects with bold outlines. If the outline is contrasty, it may look sharp to the eye even when slightly out of focus. The graininess and shimmer of a dark edge against the light background, however, immediately shows up the slightest lack of sharpness of the screen image.

For focusing adjust the front ring of the lens with the left thumb and index finger when holding the camera as described on p. 152. This ring also carries the distance scale, engraved in red for feet, and in white for metres. When the image is sharply focused the correct distance appears opposite the white triangular mark on the adjacent fixed ring.

In practice the distance scale is rarely needed—except in very poor light, when focusing on the microprism spot becomes too uncertain.

Depth of Field Pre-viewing

The Leicaflex SL has a special aperture control button on the camera front between the lens mount and the self-timer. When you press this button, the lens is stopped down manually to the pre-selected stop (when this is smaller than the maximum aperture). On releasing the button, the lens iris opens again fully; it closes down of course during the exposure.

The purpose of this button is to give a rough visual idea of the depth of field on the screen with the lens stopped down to the aperture to be used. This is useful for instance to estimate how far to open the lens to make sure of an unsharp background.

.EICAFLEX SHOOTING

The elements of the iewing screen as visible hrough the finder eyepiece of the Leicaflex are:

1. Large aperture mark.
2. Microprism grid.
3. Meter needle.
4. Screen.
5. Matching or setting ointer.
6. Small aperture mark.
7. Shutter speed scale.

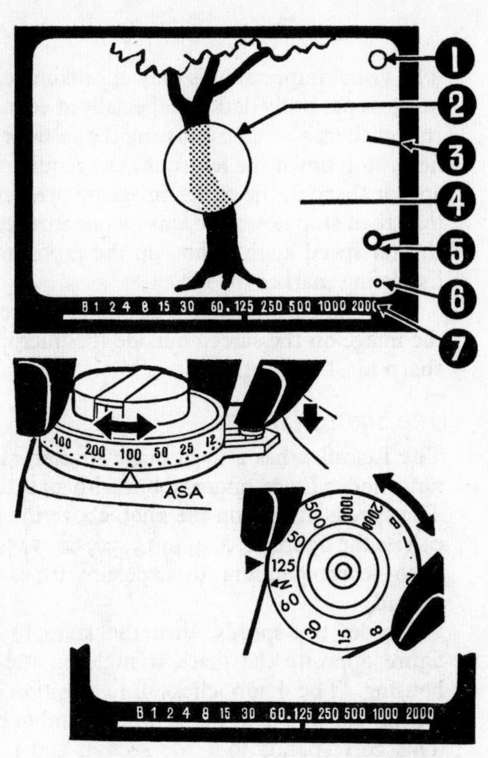

Before shooting (and referably after loading— . 166) set the film speed. Depress the catch next to he rewind crank and turn he speed ring to the ppropriate figure (*left*).

Preselect the shutter peed on the speed knob. This is also visible on the cale below the viewing creen (*right*).

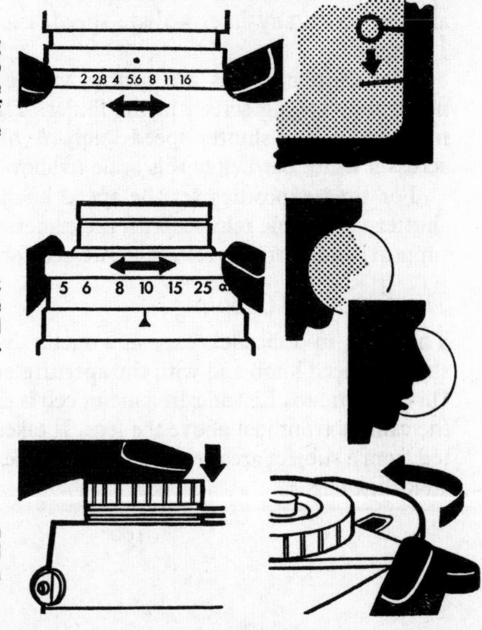

Turn the aperture ring n the lens (*left*) to line up he matching pointer in the inder with the position of he exposure meter needle right).

Turn the focusing mount of the lens (*left*) until the nsharp area in the central ocusing spot becomes comletely sharp (*right*).

Press the release button o expose (*left*); then wind n the film and re-tension he shutter (*right*).

The visual impression is only approximate, because the screen image is naturally darker, especially at very small apertures. As a rule of thumb when estimating the stop for a required depth of field, stop down the lens until the required near and far limits appear sharp in the screen image on pressing the pre-view button; then stop down the lens by one further stop. Then use the shutter speed knob to line up the exposure meter needle with its setting marker (p. 162).

The standard Leicaflex has no such pre-view button, since the image on the screen outside the microprism circle is fairly sharp most of the time.

The Shutter Speeds

The Leicaflex has a focal plane shutter, similar to that of the rangefinder Leica cameras, but with an extended setting range. The speeds are set on the knob above the winding lever. This carries the figures 1, 2, 4, 8, 15, 30, 60, 125, 250, 500, 1000 and 2000—corresponding to exposure times from 1 to 1/2000 second.

To set the speeds, turn the knob to bring the required figure opposite the black triangle on the top of the camera housing. The knob clicks into position at all the marked settings, as well as at the lightning symbol between 60 and 125. This corresponds to 1/100 second and is the fastest shutter speed for electronic flash shots (p. 258). The shutter knob can also be set to any intermediate speed, except between $\frac{1}{4}$ and $\frac{1}{8}$ second.

The shutter speeds are further visible on a scale underneath the viewing screen in the finder. This carries the same numbers as the shutter speed knob. A black pointer moves across a white bar below this scale to show the set speed.

For time exposures set the speed knob to B. Release the shutter via a cable release (with the camera mounted on a firm support) and keep the release depressed for the required time.

The Exposure Coupling

The built-in Leicaflex exposure meter is coupled with the shutter speed knob and with the aperture setting of the lenses. On the standard Leicaflex the meter cell is the small window on the camera front just above the lens. It takes in the light reflected from a subject area corresponding to the view of the 90 mm. Leicaflex lens.

On the Leicaflex SL the meter cell is inside the camera and measures the light through the lens. The measuring area is the central microprism circle on the focusing screen. The meter view is one-sixth of the angle across the screen diagonal; with the 50 mm. lens the meter thus reads an angle of just under 8°. This method of meter reading is very selective and is particularly useful for close-up work (where the meter of the standard Leicaflex cannot be used in the normal way). The technique of through-the-lens metering is described in more detail on p. 226.

The light falling on the cell controls an electric current which causes a pointer to move down along the right-hand side of the viewing screen in the finder. The stronger the light, the farther the pointer moves down.

To convert this light measurement into an exposure setting, a second matching pointer has to be superimposed with the measuring pointer. The movement of the matching pointer is linked with the exposure settings of the camera and provides the exposure coupling. There are three such linkages: the shutter speeds, the film speeds and the aperture.

The film speed (p. 190) is set on the ring surrounding the rewind crank at the left-hand end of the camera. This is best done immediately after loading the film.

The shutter speed knob is similarly linked with the setting pointer. Other things being equal, more light from the subject means that the shutter must be set to a faster speed (shorter exposure) to match the setting marker with the meter needle.

Thirdly, the matching pointer is controlled by the aperture selector ring on the lens. This linkage is via a lever visible near the top of the bayonet ring of the standard Leicaflex (and near the bottom on the Leicaflex SL) when the lens is removed.

The lever rides on a cam in the back of the lens. The cam is linked with the aperture ring of the lens. Setting the lens to a smaller aperture therefore makes the matching pointer move in the same way as turning the shutter knob to a faster speed.

The lens aperture itself is only pre-selected (p. 152), and the lens iris closes down to the selected stop on shooting.

With the camera set to the correct film speed, this is therefore the procedure for exposure settings with the coupled Leicaflex meter:

First, preselect a shutter speed to be used. For normal subjects 1/60 or even 1/125 second is advisable to avoid camera shake.

Second, view the scene through the finder and turn the aperture ring of the lens until the matching pointer (with the circle at the end) is superimposed on the meter needle. The latter should exactly bisect the circle.

Then—once the image is sharp on the screen—shoot.

If movement of the aperture ring cannot bring the matching pointer into line with the meter needle, the shutter speed may have to be modified. If in poor light that leads to too slow an exposure for steady hand-held shots, use a solid support.

Depth of field or other considerations may call for a specific aperture setting. There preselect the aperture, and bring the matching pointer into line with the meter needle in the finder by turning the shutter-speed knob. And if any combination for correct exposure is unsuitable for other reasons, alternative combinations are set by changing whichever setting (aperture or speed) needs modification, and adjusting the other control (speed or aperture respectively) to match the setting pointer with the meter needle again.

Double Exposures

In principle the film transport and shutter tensioning on the Leicaflex is linked in the same way as on the Leica M models (p. 52). For intentional double exposures the procedure is similar, too.

After tensioning the film by turning the rewind crank in the direction of its arrow (to take up slack in the cassette) depress the reversing button in the base of the camera. Keep the button pressed down while also holding the rewind crank with one hand, and wind the lever to tension the shutter.

The pressure on the reversing button during this operation disengages the film transport shaft, so that the second exposure is made on the same frame of film—which remains stationary behind the lens—as the first.

After such a double exposure the next transport movement may not fully advance the film to the next frame. To avoid a partial overlapping of two pictures, it is wise to make a blind exposure. Set the shutter to 1/2000 second, the lens to its smallest aperture and press the palm of one hand firmly over the front of the lens to shut out all light while releasing. Then advance the film again and continue shooting normally. The film counter does not advance during the tensioning of the shutter for the second exposure when the film stays stationary; it will, however, advance after the blind exposure.

The Mirror Control

During the exposure the mirror of the Leicaflex swings out of the way for an instant (p. 148). On the standard Leicaflex (but not the SL), it can also be locked up permanently—for example when using the older 21 mm. ultra-wide-angle lens (p. 176).

The mode of the mirror action is controlled by a lever next to the lens.

For normal operation this lever points upwards; the mirror then returns down immediately after every exposure. On turning the lever sideways the mirror does not return after the exposure (nor after the following transport movement), but does remain available for viewing before the exposure to be made.

This action is independent of whether the shutter is tensioned or not when the lever is turned sideways.

Turning the lever down releases the mirror to swing out of the way, provided the shutter is tensioned. If the shutter is not tensioned, the mirror swings up the next time the winding lever is pulled—and stays up.

To get the mirror back into the viewing position before the shutter is tensioned, turn the control lever to point up again. The mirror then returns automatically. If the shutter is tensioned, the mirror returns automatically after the next exposure.

As this wastes a frame, switch the mirror lever back (to bring the mirror down) before tensioning the shutter.

The mirror can also be brought down by hand after tensioning the shutter if it is vital not to lose the frame. Turn the mirror lever up and remove the lens from the camera. Gently pull down the small lever visible just inside the left-hand edge of the lens mount opening. This is not generally recommended; it is best to avoid touching any part of the internal camera mechanism by hand.

Loading

The Leicaflex can be loaded with standard 35 mm. cassettes (p. 181), but not with the Leitz N cassettes. The back of the Leicaflex opens fully. The loading procedure is somewhat different from that for the Leica.

First open the camera. Press the button in the centre of the locking ledge at the left-hand end (as seen from behind), and slide the ledge upwards. The camera back now swings open on its hinge.

To the left of the film track and aperture is an empty chamber with the shaft of the rewind crank protruding into it. This takes the cassette. To the right are the transport sprocket

—a shaft with a ring of teeth at each end to engage the film perforations—and the take-up spool. The latter is built into the camera. On the model SL the take-up spool has a red bottom flange with a series of segments pointing up towards the centre of the spool.

Both the transport shaft and the spool are linked with the film transport mechanism, but the spool can also rotate on its own, being coupled by a friction drive which acts like a slipping clutch.

Before inserting the film raise the rewind crank by pushing the shaft protruding into the feed chamber upwards. On the standard model turn the take-up spool by its milled flange to bring one of the slots in the spool to the top. (There is no need for this on the model SL.)

Inserting the Film

Pull about 2 or 3 inches of film out of the mouth of the cassette. With film bought in standard cassettes, this film leader is already trimmed down to half width for easier loading into Leica M and other cameras.

Holding the cassette in the right hand, push the beginning of the film leader into the slot of the take-up spool. On the Leicaflex SL hook the film leader into one of the prongs of the red take-up spool sleeve. The film leader should point towards the film aperture, with the *back* against the spool core. On the standard Leicaflex push the film fully into one of the white slots in the black spool core; the arrows show the direction of the film.

Then draw the cassette with the film across the film track and drop it into the film chamber. The spool knob of the cassette must point towards the bottom of the Leicaflex.

Push back the rewind crank, turning it in the direction of the arrow on it until the crank goes fully home, with the shaft engaging the spool inside the cassette. Unfold the crank and turn it gently in the direction of the arrow to tension the film inside the cassette.

This at the same time pulls the cassette mouth into line with the film track. This mouth must point towards the film aperture in the track, and not upwards—otherwise the film may jam.

Close the camera back. On the Leicaflex SL push the back against the body; it snaps in automatically. With the earlier

ICAFLEX LOADING

Open the camera back pressing the button in e locking ledge and slid- the latter upwards ft); push up the rewind ank in the cassette cham- r (*right*).

Hook or thread the n leader into the slot of e take-up spool (*left* on e model SL, *right* on the rlier Leicaflex).

Draw the film across e track and insert the ssette in the chamber ft), then push down the wind crank (*right*).

Close the camera back. e locking ledge is slid wn only on the earlier icaflex.

Advance the film by rking the lever and ernately pressing the utter release (*left*) until e film counter indicates . 1 (*right*).

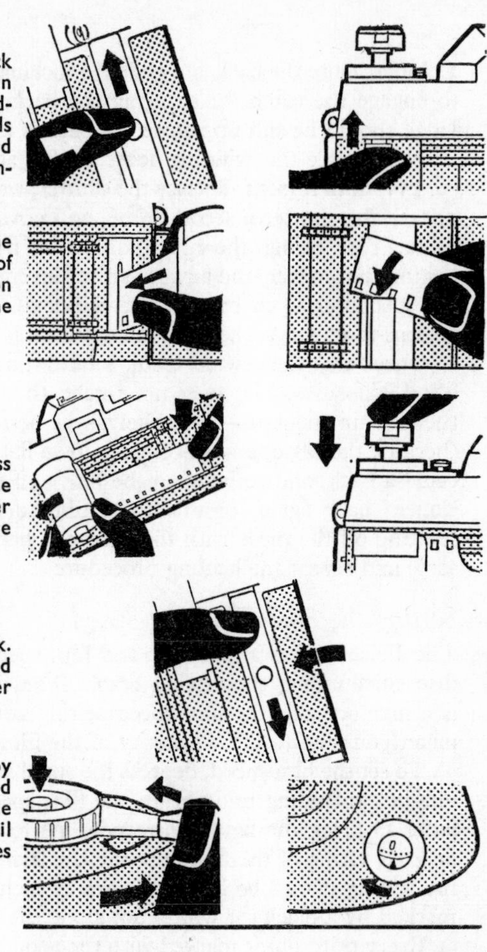

NLOADING

Press in the reversing tton (*left*), then unfold e rewind crank and wind ck the film (*right*).

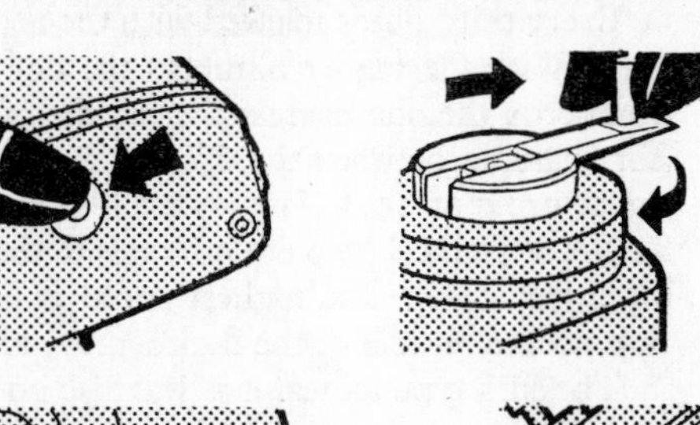

Stop winding when the n counter stops moving ft), then open the camera d remove the cassette ght).

Leicaflex close the back and slide the locking ledge downwards to engage the catch for securing the back. Here the locking ledge should be slid up before the back is closed.

Next work the winding lever as for advancing the film (p. 155) until it locks. Release the shutter, work the lever again, release the shutter a second time, and advance the film once more. This brings the first usable film frame into position behind the shutter, and advances the film counter to No. 1 (the dot just after O in the counter window). The film counter returns to its start when the camera back is opened.

Check that the rewind crank rotates during these first two blind exposures. If it does not rotate, the film may have left the take-up spool or—more likely—the perforations have torn (because the cassette was not lying down flat before closing the camera back, and so jammed the film). In that case open the camera back again, re-attach the film to the take-up spool (cutting off the piece with the damaged perforations if necessary) and repeat the loading procedure.

Setting the Film Type and Speed

The Leicaflex has a film type and film speed indicator in the disc surrounding the rewind crank. The film type indicator is a memory aid; the film speed setting adjusts the exposure meter coupling to the sensitivity of the film loaded (p. 163).

To set the film speed, depress the small shiny button on the tongue protruding underneath the film speed disc. Turn the latter to bring the figure corresponding to the required ASA or DIN rating of the film opposite the triangular index below the setting disc. The latter engages at each film speed value, marked by a black (or white) dot along the rim.

Every third dot is marked with the actual value on the ASA scale. With the higher numbers the dot corresponding to the number is the one nearest the middle of the engraved figures (for example between the 6 and the first 0 of 1600, or below the centre 0 of 100). The lowest film speed that can be set is 8 ASA or 10 DIN (two dot intervals to the right of the figure 12 on either scale). The highest speed is 6400 ASA (three dots beyond the middle of the figure 3200) or 39 DIN.

The film type indicator is the disc on top of the film speed ring. There are four symbols: a divided black-and-white field for black-and-white film, a red sun symbol for daylight reversal colour film, a light bulb for artificial light reversal colour film and the word NEG for negative colour film. Turn the indicator disc by its small lug to bring the appropriate symbol opposite the film speed setting catch next to the film speed ring.

Unloading

The Leicaflex film counter can advance up to No. 42, and thirty-six-exposure cassettes of film sometimes yield thirty-seven or even thirty-eight exposures. When the film counter has reached No. 36 (or No. 20 with a twenty-exposure film) advance the film carefully from shot to shot to avoid tearing the film out of the cassette. Any resistance—even in the middle of a transport movement—indicates that the film is finished and must be rewound.

To unload the film press in the reversing button in the camera base. Once pressed, this stays down.

Unfold the rewind crank and turn it in the direction of the arrow. During rewinding the film counter runs back to 0 again. About three divisions beyond 0 the film pulls off the take-up spool; there is a slight resistance at this point. To avoid drawing the beginning of the film fully into the cassette, stop rewinding here (the film counter also stops moving).

Open the camera back as for loading, pull up the rewind crank, and let the cassette drop out of its chamber.

Partly Exposed Films

Subject to the different preparation of the camera during loading and unloading, changing partly exposed films in the Leicaflex follows the same procedure as for the Leica M models (p. 82). Remember to reset the film speed indicator for the new film if appropriate.

Cutting off exposed lengths for processing is slightly simpler on the Leicaflex than on the Leica M models, since the film track is freely accessible through the fully opening back.

In practice, cutting off exposed film lengths is rarely worth while (p. 83). But should it become necessary, advance the film by a blank frame, take the camera in a darkroom and open the back. Hold the camera with both hands so that the thumbs lie on the film track over the back of the perforated film edges. Press on the film near the transport sprocket with the two index fingers. Push the thumbs towards the index fingers, thus pulling out more film from the cassette to form a loop. Hold up this loop (by the edges) with two fingers while the camera is standing lens down on the table, and cut through the film near the cassette.

Draw the film off the take-up spool, pulling directly away from the back. Keep one hand near the spool to stop the film from curling up on itself as the end leaves the spool. Loosely roll up the film and either wrap it up light-tight or load it into the developing tank (which should be prepared handy in the darkroom).

Finally the remaining film in the cassette can be prepared for reloading. Remove the cassette from the camera, pull out about 3 inches of film, trim a new leader (p. 189) and reload in the usual way. Note that the film counter (during opening of the camera back) has returned to its starting position. Hence the counter is no longer a reliable indication of the coming end of the film. So advance the film carefully after each shot, ready for any resistance that indicates its end. Cutting off the film in this way wastes a length equivalent to about 6–8 exposures.

The Leicaflex Motor

A special accessory for the Leicaflex SL is a battery-powered motor drive intended for sports photography and similar purposes where rapid shooting is important. The motor can be used only with a special version of the Leicaflex SL—labelled SL/MOT—which has certain modifications for electric and mechanical couplings. These include three contacts to link with the motor circuit, a drive shaft for the take-up spool and release couplings. The motor permits shooting at 3 to 4 exposures per second.

A release button on the front of the motor keeps the unit cycling as long as the button is depressed. There is a film counter at the back and two switches at the back and at the side respectively. The switch at the rear selects the number of exposures (20 or 36) for which the motor runs, while the one at the side switches over from manual to motorized camera operation. There is also remote control socket to take a cable for remote releasing by wire or even by wireless.

Assembling the Camera and the Motor

First load the battery magazine. This is in the left-hand side of the motor (as seen from the back). To remove, press in the cut-out at the rear and pull out the magazine.

Open the magazine by unscrewing the two milled screws (for instance with a coin) and lift off the cover. The 10 batteries (preferably alkali-manganese size AA) go into the magazine facing alternate ways. The positive pole of each battery must lie against the brass contacts marked with a + sign, the negative base of the batteries against the springs inside the magazine. (If the batteries are inserted the wrong way round the motor won't run.)

Place the cover over the battery magazine (with the screws) so that the grooves on one side line up with the grooves on the magazine base. Press the two halves together (against the spring pressure) and tighten the retaining screws. Then push the magazine full home into the battery compartment of the motor—it will only go in one way round.

LEICAFLEX MOTOR

The motor for the Leicaflex SL (a special version of the camera) fits to the camera base, being held in position by a screw engaging the tripod bush. The camera and motor then form a complete and self-contained assembly.

Features of the camera base of the special Leicaflex SL model for motor coupling (*left*) and of the top of the motor unit (*right*):

1. Take-up drive shaft of camera.
2. Reversing button.
3. Release shaft (locked by the catch 8 of the motor when the latter is switched to motor operation).
4. Release coupling.
5. Electrical outlets of shutter contacts.
6. Drive shaft of motor.
7. Shaft to operate reversing button.
8. Function lock for manual or motor operation.
9. Screw to fit into tripod bush of camera.
10. Electrical contact on motor.

Further features, seen from the front of the motor:

11. Release button.
12. Tripod bush.
13. Battery magazine.
14. Second tripod bush in motor base.
15. Screw for attaching the motor to the camera.

The battery magazine comes apart on unscrewing the two retaining screws with a coin. It takes 10 size AA batteries of 1.5 volts.

Rear and side features:

16. Exposure counter.
17. Catch of battery magazine.
18. Remote control outlet.
19. Changeover switch for motorized and manual operation.
20. Presetting switch for No. of exposures run and for rewinding.

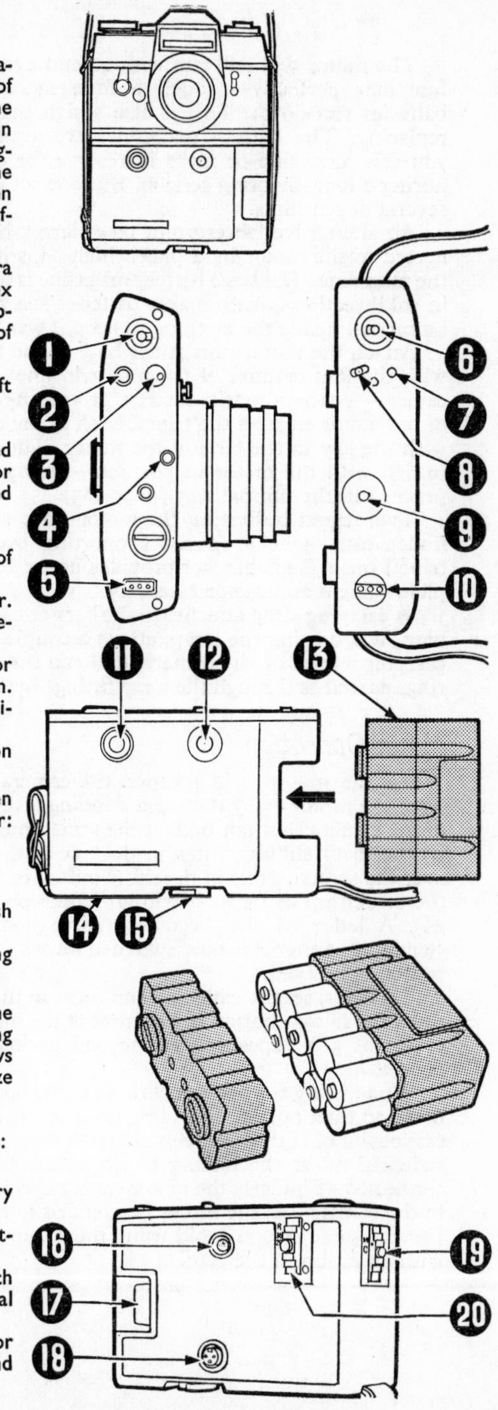

The motor will still run with 12 and even with 9 volts, so it functions perfectly—though a little more slowly—when the batteries run down. This is also a sign that the battery needs replacing. The battery magazines are available separately, so you can carry one or more in reserve for quick interchanging during a long shooting session. But one set of batteries lasts for several dozen films.

An alternative battery unit takes larger batteries and is connected to the motor by a plug which clips into place instead of the magazine. The large battery magazine is useful when shooting in cold weather (which makes batteries less active) and can then be carried inside the clothing to keep it warm.

Attach the motor unit at the base of the SL/MOT camera—with the film counter of the motor in line with the rear of the camera—so that the tripod screw protruding from the upper end of the motor engages the tripod bush in the camera base. Secure with the key in the base of the motor. The camera can now be loaded with the motor in position—simply open the back and proceed in the normal way (page 163).

Two tripod bushes on the motor—one at the front and one underneath—take a special supporting bracket with its own tripod bush. This bracket provides better balance for the complete camera and motor assembly.

A carrying strap attaches to the bars at each side in the motor base. When using the strap, attach a couple of split rings to the carrying eyelet of the camera, and run the strap through those rings as well as through the strap fittings in the motor base.

Motor Operation

When the motor is in position the camera can operate either from the motor or by the rapid winding lever and release button of the camera (but not both at the same time). This is controlled by the black sliding switch in the side of the motor. To change over the switch, press in the shiny button in the centre and move the switch up as far as it will go (white dot opposite the letter M). A letter M also becomes visible underneath the sliding switch. The motor is now switched on while the camera release button is blocked.

To shoot, set the exposure and focus in the normal way. Then press the release button in the front of the motor. The latter now cycles at 3–4 exposures per second as long as the button is depressed.

When using the camera with a motor, take exposure readings first and then push the winding lever of the camera back into its rest position. If the lever is pulled out, the motor is automatically switched off as the linking to circuit inside the camera is disconnected. (Similarly the motor cannot cycle unless it is attached to the camera—as the motor is intended to run only under load. For the same reason avoid using the motor—except to test it—without a film in the camera.)

Before starting to shoot, however, move the sliding switch in the back of the camera to the figure 36 or 20 (opposite the white dot) according to the number of exposures on the film loaded in the camera. After 20 or 36 exposures the motor automatically cuts out. If the switch was set to 20 exposures with a 36 exposure film, moving the switch to the figure 36 cuts the motor in again and it runs until the end of the film.

To make single exposures between two motorized series, move the change-over switch at the right of the motor to bring the white dot opposite the letter C (camera). A letter C now also appears above the sliding switch. In this position the motor is switched off and the camera can be operated in the normal way by pressing the release button and advancing the film with the rapid winding lever.

The motor drive can be used at all shutter speeds from 1 to 1/2000 second, but not with the B setting.

To unload the camera move the sliding switch in the back to the letter R. This resets the film counter in the back to 0 and also disengages the film transport of the camera by pushing against the reversing button in the base. Now rewind the film in the normal way with the rewind crank and reload the camera. After loading switch the rear sliding switch back to 36 or 20 again. The film counter of both the camera and the motor automatically return to 0 during this sequence of operations, so that they run in synchronism.

However, avoid running shorter film lengths in the camera than the motor is set for. It does no serious harm, but if the film in the camera reaches its end (before the film counter has reached the end of its run and before the motor stops running), the film perforation gets torn. At that point of the film this is no great harm, and in any case the film perforation tears before the film can be torn out of the cassette.

Remote Control

The socket in the centre of the back takes a standard 3-pin plug (as used for tape recorders and other audio equipment) with a cable to connect to a remote control unit. This contains four further 1.5 volt batteries as well as a remote film counter. In operation, the counter advances by 1 every time the camera motor advances the film in the camera. This enables you to keep a check on the number of exposures made even when controlling the camera from some distance away. The batteries in the unit drive the remote film counter, so that the motor batteries are not deprived of extra power. A small button on the remote control unit resets the counter to zero.

Another way of remote control is by wireless signals. This requires a suitable receiver and transmitter system. The receiver must have a relay which closes when the signal is given by the transmitter; the motor then cycles once for an intermittent signal or continuously for a continuous signal.

LEICAFLEX LENSES

The Leicaflex uses a special series of lenses with focal lengths ranging from 21 to 180 mm.
Certain Leica M lenses can be used on the Leicaflex with an adapter mount.

Like the rangefinder Leica models, the Leicaflex can be used with a range of lenses of various focal lengths to cope with different subject conditions (p. 98). The focal lengths available extend from 21 to 180 mm. All (except the early versions of 21 mm.) are coupled with the exposure setting system (aperture control linkage) of the Leicaflex and show the field of view taken in on the Leicaflex screen, so that no supplementary or accessory finders are necessary.

In addition certain Leica lenses can be mounted on the Leicaflex via a conversion adapter; this is useful with the Telyt series.

The effective range of focal lengths for the Leicaflex is thus the same as for the rangefinder Leica models.

All Leicaflex lenses are coated (p. 97) and the lenses above 50 mm. are marked with their actual as well as their nominal focal lengths (p. 86).

While the lenses for the rangefinder Leicas were produced at various times over a period of more than forty years, all the Leicaflex lenses were designed together for this camera. They therefore have a closely similar layout of the control rings and scales.

The rearmost ring (the one nearest to the camera) sets the apertures, next to it is a fixed ring with the depth of field scale. Another movable ring in front of that is the focusing mount with the distance scale in feet and metres.

The 35 and 50 mm. lenses have clip-on lens hoods which can be reversed over the front of the lens when not in use (No. 14164).

The 21 mm. lens has a clip-on square hood supplied with the lens, while the longer focal lengths have built-in extending hoods similar to the hoods of some of the longer-focus Leica lenses (p. 118).

In the optical design the Leicaflex lenses differ significantly from the rangefinder Leica types. In particular the wide-angle and standard lenses have an increased back focus (distance

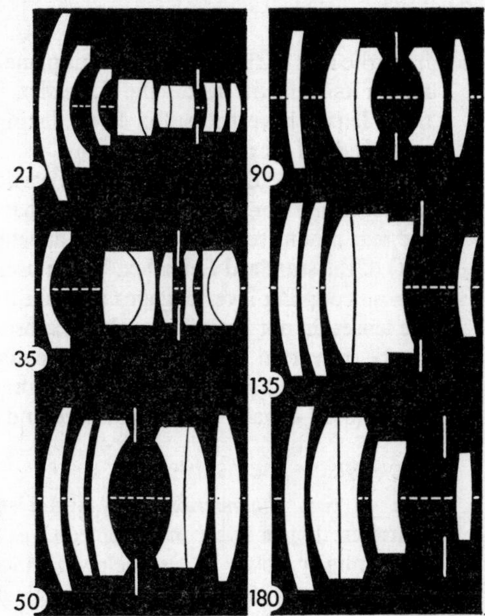

The lens constructions shown here represent (not to scale) the optical layout of the six lenses specially designed for the Leicaflex camera.

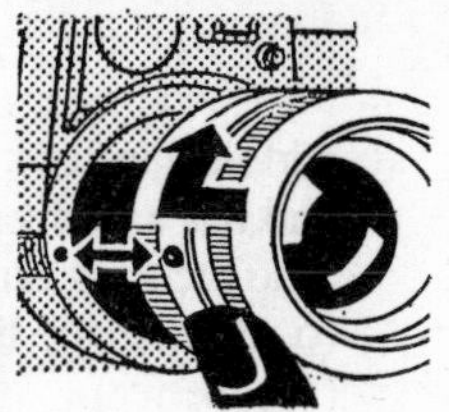

To change a Leicaflex lens, depress the lens catch, turn the lens anti-clockwise and lift off (*left*). To fit another lens, line up the red dot on the mount with the red dot on the camera, push the lens home and turn clockwise to engage the catch (*right*).

Before fitting the earlier 21 mm. Super Angulon-R, raise the mirror in the Leicaflex with the mirror control lever (*left*). On the lens itself push down the locking lever to the white dot (*right*).

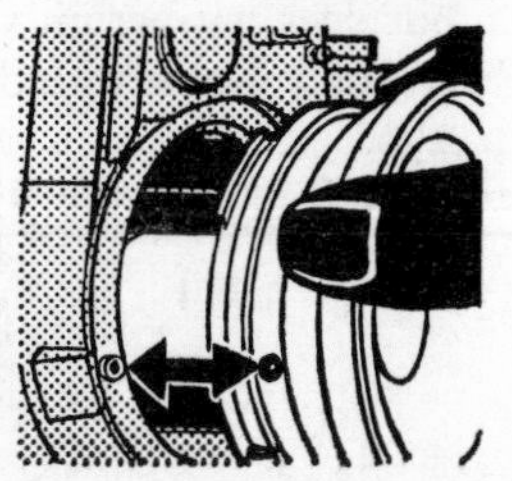

Insert the Super-Angulon in the Leicaflex, keeping the red dots carefully lined up (*left*). Push the lens home and slide the locking lever up to the red dot (*right*).

from the rear of the lens to the film plane) to accommodate the mirror movement inside the Leicaflex. In their designation these lenses have the suffix R to distinguish them from the rangefinder Leica units.

There is one difference between earlier and later Leicaflex lenses. Lenses produced before 1968 have a single cam inside the rear mount to couple with the aperture control system (p. 161) of the standard Leicaflex. When used on the Leicaflex SL (whose coupling lever engages the cam in a different position) the lenses do not permit complete exposure coupling. But they can be converted to a dual cam by the manufacturer. Leicaflex lenses produced from 1968 onwards come with two cams and can be used equally on the standard and the SL models.

The Lenses Themselves

The 50 *mm. Summicron-R f*2 is the standard lens for the Leicaflex. It is a five-component unit of six elements, focuses from infinity down to just below 20 inches (0.5 metres) and stops down to *f*16. The horizontal angle of view is 38 deg., the vertical angle 26 deg.

The nearest focus setting provides a scale of reproduction of just over 1 : 7.5.

The 35 *mm. Elmarit-R f*2.8 is an inverted telephoto type of wide-angle lens. It is a four-component unit of six elements and has a horizontal angle of view of 54 deg. (38 deg. vertical). The focusing range goes from infinity down to about 11 inches (0.28 metres), the nearest marked distance being 12 inches (0.3 metres).

The largest scale of reproduction at the near focusing limit is about 1 : 5.

The 21 *mm. Super Angulon-R f*4 is an inverted telephoto design with a sufficient back focus to permit viewing and focusing via the screen of the camera. It covers an 81 deg. horizontal angle of view (60 deg. vertical) and focuses to 8 inches (0.2 metres). It stops down to *f*22 when the depth of field covers from infinity to 16 inches.

An earlier version, the 21 mm. Super Angulon-R *f*3.4, is optically very similar to the 21 mm. Super Angulon *f*3.4 for the rangefinder Leica, but does not permit viewing on the Leicaflex screen. This lens is only usable with the standard Leicaflex, *not* the SL. See p. 176.

The 90 *mm. Elmarit-R f*2.8 is the first of the long-focus lenses, with a 22 deg. horizontal and 15 deg. vertical angle of view. It is a four-component, five-element lens of the same applications as the 90 mm. Elmarit for the rangefinder Leica models.

The nearest focus is 20 inches (0.7 metres) and the largest scale of reproduction just under 1 : 6. The lens stops down to *f*22.

The 100 *mm. Macro-Elmar f*4 is intended for use with the Leicaflex bellows only, and has no focusing mount although it has the same bayonet mount as the other Leicaflex lenses. It is optimally corrected for near distances (p. 410).

The 135 *mm. Elmarit-R f*2.8 corresponds both in construction and applications to the 135 mm. Elmarit *f*2.8 for the Leica M models. It consists of five elements assembled in four components, has a horizontal angle of view of 15 deg. (10 deg. vertical) and stops down to *f*22. Its nearest focusing distance is 5 feet (1.5 metres) with a scale of reproduction of about 1 : 9.

The 180 *mm. Elmarit-R f*2.8 is also a five-element, four-component unit with a horizontal angle of 11 deg. and vertical angle of 7½ deg. Its applications are similar to the 200 mm. Telyt, since its focal length is only 10 per cent shorter. It has, however, twice the speed of the Telyt. The nearest focusing distance is 7 feet (2 metres), with a scale of reproduction of just over 1 : 9.

Lens Changing

The Leicaflex lens mount is a bayonet fitting, similar in principle (but not in dimensions) to the bayonet mount on the Leica M series. The lens-changing catch is on the side of the reflex housing part of the camera, next to the mirror control lever (standard model) or the depth of field pre-view button (model SL—where the changing catch is in red plastic).

When fitting a lens to the Leicaflex SL (other than one bought specially for it) check that it has two aperture cams inside the rear mount (p. 174).

To remove a lens from the Leicaflex, press this catch back towards the camera body, grip the lens by the middle milled ring (the one carrying the depth of field scale) and turn the whole lens anti-clockwise until the red dot on this ring is opposite the bayonet catch. The lens can now be lifted off.

To attach another lens, hold it by the same central ring and place it over the camera mount so that the red dot on the lens is opposite the red dot (of the bayonet catch) or the bayonet catch on the camera. Push the lens against the camera mount, and turn clockwise until the catch engages.

This automatically also engages the preselector aperture ring and meter coupling.

When carrying lenses separately from the Leicaflex, cover up the rear and front with the appropriate caps to protect them against damage.

Working with the early 21 mm. Super Angulon-R

The original version of this lens does not have the increased back focus to enable it to clear the reflex mirror in the Leicaflex. When fitted on the camera, the rear element of the lens is only about $\frac{3}{8}$ inch in front of the film plane.

To permit fitting of this Super Angulon-R, the mirror of the standard Leicaflex therefore has to be locked out of the way first with the mirror control lever (p. 163). The fitting of the lens is also a little different from the other Leicaflex lenses. To prepare the lens for insertion, move the crescent-shaped lever along the aperture ring against the direction of its red arrow. The lever must be opposite the white dot beyond the red dot to the right of the depth of field scale.

Now insert the lens in the Leicaflex, very carefully keeping the red dot on the lens in line with the red dot on the camera mount. If this alignment is correct, the larger flat surface on top of the rear lens barrel is horizontal just below the swung-up mirror of the camera.

The lens cannot be inserted in any other way without fouling part of the internal camera fittings.

Next press the lens firmly against the camera body. Push the crescent-shaped locking lever in the direction of the red arrow on it, until it stops between the bayonet catch on the camera and the red dot on the lens mount. The lens is now ready mounted.

This older Super Angulon-R *cannot be fitted to the Leicaflex SL* (even with the mirror raised).

As the reflex screen is not available for viewing or focusing, a separate 21 mm. wide-angle brilliant finder is used in the accessory shoe on top of the camera.

To remove the lens, slide the crescent-shaped locking lever down opposite the white dot on the lens barrel. Then lift the lens out of the camera, taking special care not to knock the projecting rear barrel against any internal camera fittings. Always put the black cap over this rear barrel when the lens is not on the camera, to protect the protruding glass element against damage.

The removal of the mirror also blacks out the exposure meter needle and shutter speed scale in the finder. So exposures for the older Super Angulon-R have to be set beforehand, for instance with the 50 mm. lens in the camera. After setting the speed and aperture with the meter needle, memorize the aperture figure selected on the preselector ring of the standard lens.

Then replace the standard lens by the Super Angulon-R, and set the aperture ring of the latter again to the same figure noted before.

Alternatively, a separate exposure meter can be used and its indications transferred to the shutter knob and the aperture scale.

This ultra-wide-angle lens has a bulging-out front component. This is particularly liable to lead to internal reflections and ghost images when reached by strong direct light. So always use the lens with its screw-in lens hood—there is no need to remove it except when fitting a filter (for which the hood acts as a retaining ring).

Leica M Lenses on the Leicaflex

One reason, already mentioned, why normal Leica M lenses cannot be used on the Leicaflex is that the distance from the lens flange to the film on the latter camera is greater than on the M models. This so-called optical register on the Leica M models is 27.8 mm., but 47 mm. on the Leicaflex. This is, however, still less than the register of a Leica M camera with the Visoflex III or II housing (68.8 mm.). By using a 21.8 mm. spacing ring it becomes possible to convert the Leicaflex into a unit with the same optical dimensions as a Leica M camera plus a Visoflex II or III housing.

Such an extension ring is the Leicaflex/Leica adapter (No. 14127). It carries a Leicaflex bayonet mount on one side, and a Leica M bayonet ring on the other.

Mount the converter ring on the Leicaflex like a normal Leicaflex lens.

The front of the converter ring can now take any of the lenses or combinations of lenses and adapter tubes or mounts available for the Visoflex III (or II or IIA) housing, as listed on p. 127.

For focusing from infinity downwards this thus covers focal lengths from 65 to 400 mm., and still shorter focal lengths for close-ups and macrophotography (see also p. 375). Even the focusing bellows II can be combined with the No. 14127 adapter ring.

Rational Combinations

While the Leicaflex/Leica adapter ring provides many additional combinations of optical units which can be used on the

Leicaflex, not all are equally versatile. We can class them into two groups:

(*a*) lens combinations which genuinely extend the scope of the Leicaflex system; and

(*b*) combinations which are equivalent or inferior in convenience and versatility to corresponding specific Leicaflex units.

As long as we are concerned with continuous focusing from infinity down, the first group covers mainly the Telyt lenses. The 180 mm. Elmarit-R *f*2.8 has almost the focal length of the 200 mm. Telyt, but there is no Leicaflex equivalent of the 280, 400 and 560 mm. Telyt lenses. So the latter, with the No. 14127 Leicaflex/Leica adapter plus No. 16466 ring (p. 130) or the Televit mount (p. 425) genuinely increase the Leicaflex scope in telephotography.

For close-ups the 100 mm. Macro-Elmar *f*4 covers a range of magnification scales equivalent to that of the 65 mm. Elmar *f*3.5 used with the No. 16464 helical focusing mount plus the No. 16471 extension tube. The 100 mm. Macro-Elmar has to be used with the Leicaflex bellows, which is more convenient. The 100 mm. lens is, however, better for close-up work—in terms of perspective—than the 65 mm. (p. 373).

This leaves the 90 and 135 mm. lenses of the Leica M. Here the use of the Leicaflex/Leica adapter offers no advantage over the corresponding Elmarit-R lenses of the same focal length on the Leicaflex. These combinations are therefore of interest mainly to Leica photographers who have the Leica M lenses and have acquired a Leicaflex camera. The Leica M lenses can then be used on the Leicaflex as well and so make it unnecessary to acquire immediately the corresponding focal lengths in the Leicaflex range and so duplicate the optical equipment of the two cameras.

Against this, the combinations with Leica M lenses do not offer the facilities of exposure coupling and automatic aperture control of the Leicaflex lens range. Only in close-up and macrophotography does the greater versatility of the Leica M lenses, when used with the appropriate close-up mounts, score again over the presently available combinations of Leicaflex optics (p. 375).

One other Leica M item which offers certain advantages over the Leicaflex equipment is the Focorapid quick-focusing mount (p. 136). This is suitable exclusively for the 200 and

LEICAFLEX AND LEICA ADAPTATIONS

The features of the Leicaflex/Leica adapter ring No. 14127 are:

1. Front bayonet mount for Leica lenses.
2. Aperture ring with scale.
3. Coupling cam.
4. Rear bayonet mount for Leicaflex.
5. Bayonet catch.

The optical register or distance from the front flange to the film plane of the Leicaflex plus the ring No. 14127 is equal to that of a Leica M camera plus the Visoflex II or III housing.

Together with the adapter ring No. 16466 this directly takes the 200, 280 or 400 mm. Telyt lenses. Alternatively any other Leica M lens combinations suitable for the Visoflex II or III housing can be used.

With the ring No. 14127 and the Focorapid unit the optical units of lenses from 135 to 280 mm. can be used with appropriate adapter rings.

When working with the Leicaflex/Leica adapter ring, set the exposure with the aperture simulator ring on the adapter. Then transfer the aperture value from this ring to the control ring of the lens in use.

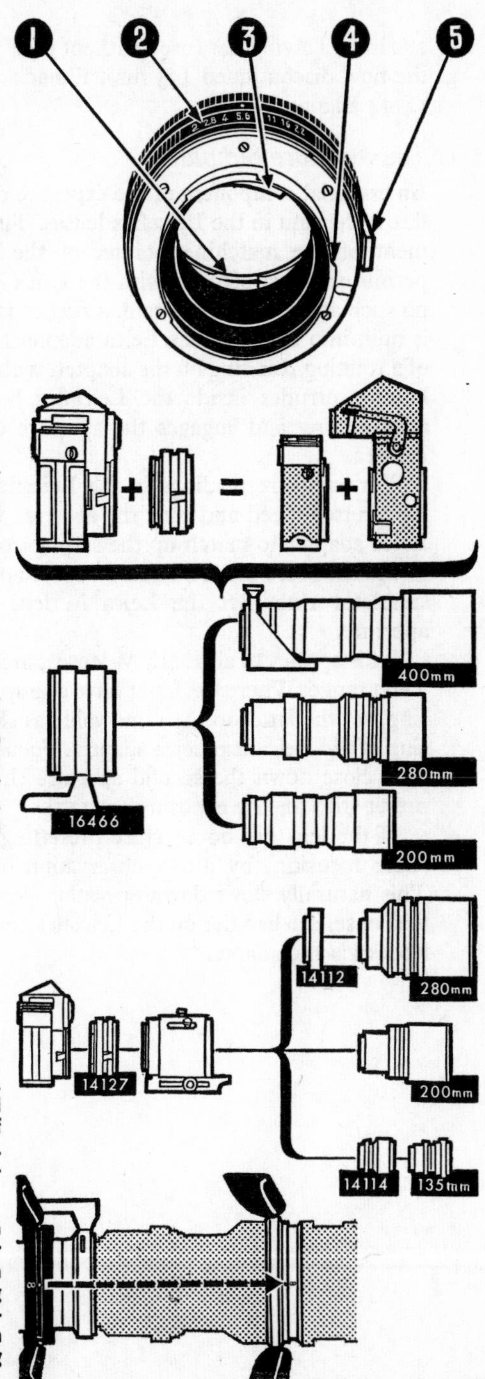

280 mm. Telyt lenses (used without their focusing mounts) and the now discontinued 135 mm. Elmar and Hektor in the No. 14114 adapter ring.

The Aperture Simulator

An essential component of the exposure coupling of the Leicaflex is the cam in the Leicaflex lenses. This controls the movement of the matching pointer of the exposure meter. To permit exposure settings with the Leica M lenses, which have no such aperture control cam, a ring to take over this function is built into the Leicaflex/Leica adapter No. 14127. It consists of a rotating rear ring on the adapter, with a coupling cam. The latter protrudes inside the Leicaflex bayonet mount of the adapter ring and engages the aperture coupling lever in the camera.

For exposure readings in the Leicaflex therefore preselect the shutter speed and turn the aperture ring of the Leicaflex/ Leica adapter to match up the setting pointer with the needle of the exposure meter. Then note the aperture shown on this simulator ring. Set the Leica M lens in use to the same aperture.

This applies to all Leica M lenses, including, of course, the Telyt range. Where the latter have a simple aperture presetting ring, set the latter to the same value as shown on the aperture ring of the Leicaflex/Leica adapter. Focus at full aperture, and then close down the second aperture ring on the lens to the preset stop for the exposure (p. 132).

If the lens has no aperture presetting, stop down the lens (after focusing) by direct observation of the aperture scale. This naturally slows down operation—one reason why Leicaflex lenses are handier on the Leicaflex than the use of Leica M lenses via the adapter.

FILMS FOR THE LEICA

Use medium-speed films for all-round work, fast films in poor light, and fine-grain films for big enlargements.
Negative colour film yields any number of colour prints or transparencies; reversal film produces a single transparency.

The Leica uses, as we have seen, standard perforated cine film, 35 mm. wide, with sixty-four perforations per foot along each edge of the strip.

This film is available in several forms for the Leica.

Standard cassettes hold sufficient 35 mm. film for thirty-six or twenty exposures plus a little extra for a film leader and trailer. This allows for loading the cassette into the Leica (altogether the length is about 63–67 inches, or 160–170 cm. for thirty-six exposures). The leader and trailer are suitably shaped to facilitate loading. These cassettes are generally reloadable.

Darkroom refills are prepared thirty-six exposure lengths of film with leader and trailer, ready for loading into a standard cassette or Leitz N cassette in the dark.

Daylight refills are largely similar to darkroom refills, except that they are wound up on a centre spool, with a strip of black paper over the last few turns. This allows the refill to be loaded into cassettes by daylight.

Bulk film is packed in uncut lengths of about 16 to 100 feet (5–30 metres). Suitable strips can be cut off and loaded into either standard or Leitz N cassettes (p. 182). This is the cheapest way of using film in the Leica (but the Leitz N cassettes cannot be used in the Leicaflex).

Standard Cassettes

Standard 35 mm. film cassettes are sold ready filled with film for immediate loading into the Leica. These cassettes are usually made of metal or plastic. Although not designed for reloading, they can be refilled, a few times at any rate, with a fresh length of film.

Colour film is usually sold in standard cassettes only, holding twenty or thirty-six exposures. Where the film has to be sent to the makers for processing, it must be returned in its original cassette.

A standard cassette consists of three main parts: the centre spool, the outside shell, and the lid (sometimes two lids).

The centre spool carries the film and consists of a hollow core with two flanges, and a knob at one end. Inside the core, near the plain end, there is a cross bar or similar fitting to engage the peg of the rewind knob.

The spool also carries a slot with a spring to hold the film end. With some makes the slot has no spring, but is wider on one side than on the other, and the film end has to be wedged in with a piece of cardboard. Other spools again carry a retaining spring attached to the core.

The outside shell has a light-tight velvet-lined slit through which the film leaves the cassette. The lid fits over the top of the outer shell and has a hole large enough for the knob of the centre spool to pass through. Some makes of cassette have a removable lid at each end.

The Leitz N Cassette

Standard cassettes are usually perfectly satisfactory, but have one drawback. The film has to pass through the velvet-lined slit and rubs against the velvet all the time. After a few reloads this may easily collect small particles of grit.

In the Leitz N cassette the film travels along a curved channel instead of a slit. This channel is fully light-proof, and can be opened into a wide slit once the cassette is inside the camera. Opening is accomplished by turning the key which locks the bottom of the Leica. The film thus freely passes in and out of the cassette while the camera is closed.

There is also an earlier version of the Leitz N cassette; the B cassette. The two are very similar in construction, and identical in manipulation. The main distinguishing feature is that the B cassette has a black button on the top, while the N cassette has a cromium-plated one. The N cassette also has a pin protruding from the bottom of the outer shell. The N cassette is 2.2 mm. shorter than the B; the cassette centre spool is identical and interchangeable between the two.

The N cassette will fit all Leica models, but not the Leicaflex; the B cassette will only fit the Leicas from I to IIIg.

The components of the Leitz N cassette are an outer shell, an inner shell, and the centre spool (p. 183).

The outer shell is a hollow cylinder with a hole in the bottom, and no top. It has a safety spring fixed to one side with a locating peg which projects inside the cylinder. Pushing the spring out also pulls out the locating peg. A second fixed peg projects into the cylinder opposite the spring. The outer shell also has a slit in the side, about $\frac{3}{8}$ inch wide.

CASSETTES

Black panel: The standard cassette (*top*) consists of a shell, a lid, and a centre spool (p. 181). The Leitz N cassette (*centre and bottom*) consists of an outer and an inner shell, as well as a spool (p. 182).

The B cassette is virtually identical in appearance and manipulation. It does not, however, fit the Leica M cameras (The N cassette fits all models of the Leica).

A. Opening button of inner shell.
B. Spool knob.
C. Safety spring.
D. Inner shell visible through slit.
E. Outer shell.

Right-hand column (*from top to bottom*): To load with a darkroom refill, attach the end of the film to the centre spool, and wind up the film. A hand winder or bench winder (p. 190) will speed up spooling. Then assemble the cassette (pp. 185, 186).

When using bulk film, a trimming template is useful to ensure a correctly trimmed film leader and end (p. 189). The piece left on the bulk roll can be used as the leader for the next length. No trimming of the leader is required with the Leica M1 to M3.

To measure out bulk film, use a board of the right length and clip one end of the film to it before cutting the other (p. 188). Alternatively, use locating pins in the table edge.

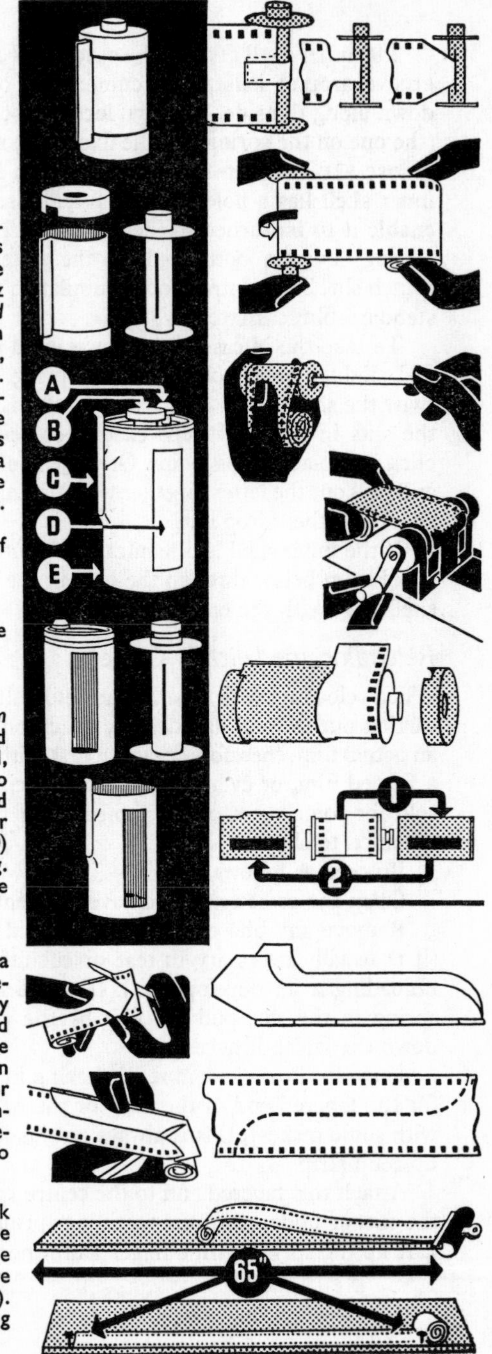

The inner shell fits into the outer shell and carries a locating groove around half the circumference of the top rim, and down along the side. The two locating pegs of the outer shell (the one on the spring and the fixed one) move in this locating groove and between them hold the two shells together. The inner shell has a hole in the top and also a small button (to enable it to be turned inside the outer shell for opening and closing) but no bottom. Like the outer shell it carries a ⅜-inch slit. The centre spool is similar to the centre spool of a standard film cassette.

To take the N cassette to pieces hold it in the right hand, and slightly pull back the safety spring. With the left hand twist the shell round clockwise (by means of the button) until the slits in the two shells exactly coincide. The spring will click into place at this point. Grip the knob of the centre spool, and pull out the latter together with the inner shell. The centre spool will then drop out.

If the inner shell is difficult to pull out, press on the centre spool from below through the hole in the bottom of the outer shell (e.g. with the end of a pencil).

Reloading the Leitz N Cassette

When reloading with a darkroom refill, all operations must be carried out in total darkness by touch only. Before reloading an actual film, therefore, practise first with a dummy film (e.g. a fogged film, or even a waste strip of cinematograph film as sold for some types of toy projector) of the right length and trimmed to shape.

Proceed as follows.

Open the cassette and remove the centre spool.

Remove any bits of film still attached to the centre spool (it is usually necessary to tear or cut off the film end when unloading it for development). If a piece of film is held by a spring in the slit, pull the film by the pointed end, cutting down the width if necessary.

Unwrap the darkroom refill packing in total darkness. Feel for the tapered end of the film (or the narrow tongue of film with some makes); this is always on the outside of the rolled-up refill strip.

Attach this tapered end to the centre spool, pushing it into the slit, or underneath the retaining spring on the spool core. Lift up the spring with a finger nail if necessary.

The aim of this is to anchor the film securely to the centre spool so that it cannot detach itself at the end of the run through the camera. Otherwise the film cannot be rewound and the Leica could only be unloaded in the darkroom.

It is important to fix the film the correct way round. When holding up the centre spool in the right hand with the attached film end in the left so that the emulsion side faces you, the knob of the spool must point downwards.

To find the emulsion side, touch the edge of the film with the tip of the tongue; the emulsion side sticks to the tongue while the back of the film does not. In the refill the film is in any case rolled up with the emulsion on the inside.

Next wind the film up on the centre spool with the emulsion side inwards.

Be careful not to touch either the emulsion side or the back of the film with the fingers; always hold the film by the edges. Wind up the film tightly.

When the full length is spooled up, the flanges of the spool should just project above the film. But do not try to tighten it up afterwards by rolling the spool tight; this often causes scratch or stress marks where tiny particles of grit or even dust rub against the film.

A hand winder or mechanical winder (p. 190) helps to spool up the film evenly.

Assembling the Cassette

Wind up the whole length, and slightly bend back the last ⅜ inch (1 cm.) of the beginning.

Then push the full centre spool, knob first, into the inner shell. The beginning of the film must lie in the slit, so that it can be pulled out later on.

Next push the inner shell with the spool, bottom first, fully into the outer shell. The slits of the two shells must be accurately in line.

Pull out about two inches of the beginning of the film through the slit. This is where bending back the end of the film makes it so much easier to grip. If the beginning of the film has for any reason got lost, turn the knob of the centre spool *anti-clockwise*, until the film start can be felt through the slit.

Finally, close the cassette light-tight by twisting the inner shell *anti-clockwise*, by means of the small fixed button, until it locks. At this point the letter Z on the top of the inner shell is next to the spring on the outer shell.

The beginning of the film now protrudes through the slit of the outer shell and can, sometimes with a little effort, be pulled out when required. Sharply bend back about $\frac{1}{8}$-inch of the end, to stop it from accidentally sliding back into the cassette.

Write or scratch the type of the film on the end of the leader; with some films the name is already perforated into the leader. If not needed immediately in the camera, wrap up the cassette in black paper and keep it in a suitable container (e.g. the original tin).

It is always useful to have several ready loaded cassettes at hand, with one or more types of film.

Daylight Refills

Daylight refills are easier to handle (though somewhat more expensive) than darkroom ones, since the film is already wound up on a centre spool.

To reload a cassette with a daylight refill, open it as before and take out the centre spool. Remove all wrappings, and break the seal of the full spool.

Insert the spool into the shell of the cassette in the same way as a darkroom refill (p. 184). Pull out the first couple of inches of the paper leader through the slit.

Then close the cassette.

Pull out the paper leader until the first 4 inches of the film protrude from the slit and remove the paper.

Bend in the last $\frac{1}{8}$ inch of the film and turn the knob anticlockwise to pull all but an inch of the film back into the cassette, until required for loading.

As its name implies, the daylight refill can be loaded into the cassette in daylight. But too strong a light, or too long an exposure to it will eventually fog a film even when it is in its daylight refill.

Therefore always load the cassette in subdued light, e.g. in a dark corner.

Reloading Standard Cassettes

The drawback of using reloaded standard cassettes is, as mentioned, the danger of scratches. Therefore don't reload the same cassette more than about three or four times. Also make sure that the cassette is strongly made; some makes leave a lot to be desired in this respect.

First, open the cassette. Pull off the top lid (the one with the knob of the centre spool protruding through it) and take out the centre spool.

If both lids are at any time removed from a cassette with two lids, the top of the shell is the side on which the velvet slit points clockwise.

Some cassettes have the lid fixed to the shell with a strip of adhesive cellulose tape; when reloading such a type have a similar strip of adhesive tape ready cut at hand for resealing.

Attach the tapered end of the darkroom refill to the centre spool. Where the centre spool has a wedge slit, push the end into the narrower side of the slit, wrap the protruding end on the other (wide) side of the slit round the cardboard wedging piece, and tuck back into the slit.

It may sometimes be necessary to trim the end of the film to a tongue, $\frac{3}{8}$ inch (1 cm.) wide and about $\frac{5}{8}$ inch (1.6 cm.) long, with this type of centre spool.

Alternatively, attach the film end by means of a piece of cellulose tape pulled through the slit with the film end.

Spool up the film until only approximately 2 inches of the specially-shaped leader of the film are left. Hold the spool firmly with three fingers of the right hand to stop it from unrolling. The leader of the film should protrude between the thumb and index finger.

Insert the centre spool in the cassette, plain end first, carefully guiding the leader into the velvet-trapped slit.

Finally push the lid over the cassette, leaving the knob to protrude. Turn the knob anti-clockwise until only about 1 inch of the leader protrudes from the cassette slit. But to be on the safe side, bend in about $\frac{1}{8}$ inch of the film end first, to stop it from accidentally sliding back into the cassette.

With daylight refills, pull out the paper leader in the first place until the film appears. Then pull away the paper and wind the beginning of the film back into the cassette except for the bent-back end.

The Leitz 250 Cassette

The Leica 250 (p. 78) takes special cassettes which hold 33 feet (10 metres) of film, to yield 250 exposures at a loading. These cassettes are similar in principle to the Leitz N cassette, though of course, correspondingly larger. They are loaded in much the same way, except that bulk film (below) is always used.

When attaching the film end, do not anchor it too securely, as the film has to be completely wound off the feed cassette after exposure.

Bulk Film

Bulk film has the advantage of being cheaper than any other way of buying film for the Leica. We can also load cassettes with less than thirty-six exposures if we choose. It is, however, less economical to load short lengths, since the proportion of waste for the leader and end of the film becomes greater.

Loading bulk film consists of measuring out the correct length of film, trimming the ends, spooling it up on a cassette spool, and loading into the cassette.

The length of film required for thirty-six exposures is about 65 inches (165 cm.), including an allowance for the trimmed beginning and end.

For shorter lengths allow 1½ inches (3.8 cm.) per exposure and add 10½ inches (26.5 cm.) for the beginning and end. Thus for twelve exposures we should need $18 + 10\frac{1}{2} = 28\frac{1}{2}$ inches, or about 72 cm.

There are several ways of measuring out the required length in the dark.

The simplest is to use a plywood strip about 1⅜ inches wide and of the right length. Clip one end of the film from the bulk roll to the end of the strip with a bulldog or similar clip, emulsion side away from the wood, and unroll the film along the strip. Cut off the film level with the other end of the strip, and clip to the wood with a second bulldog clip.

An alternative method is to mark off the correct length along the edge of the work bench or table with two notches, nails, or drawing-pins. With the left hand pull the film off the bulk roll, holding the latter in the right hand, so that the film stretches from one mark or drawing-pin to the other. Hold down the right-hand end of the film, and gently let the left-hand end roll up on itself. Then cut it off the bulk roll at the right-hand mark. Wrap up the bulk roll in its light-tight packing and put it away.

Trim one end of the film so that it tapers to a point from each edge, about 1–1½ inches (3 cm.) from the end. Avoid cutting into any perforation holes. Some types of cassette need a tongue about ½ inch wide and ⅝ inch (1.6 cm.) long.

Fix the film end to the centre spool of the cassette, and wind the film up on to the spool (p. 185). Insert into the cassette and close the cassette.

Pull out about 4½ inches (11 cm.) of the film. Cut this film down to about half width for 4 inches, taking care not to cut through a perforation hole. Then turn the knob of the centre spool anti-clockwise to pull the trimmed leader strip back into the cassette, with about ½–1 inch (1.5–2.5 cm.) protruding.

The Trimming Template

To facilitate accurate trimming of the two ends of the film in the dark, a trimming template is useful. This consists of two pieces of metal about 5 inches (13 cm.) long, hinged along their length. They taper to a point at one end, while the other corresponds to the shape of the correctly trimmed film leader.

To trim the cassette end of the film, inset the latter between the plates so that the two teeth protruding from the bottom plate engage two perforation holes. The tapered end should point towards the end of the film, and may be about ¼ inch (0.5 cm.) away from it. Close the template, and cut off the film along the tapered edges with a sharp knife or a pair of scissors.

For the Leica M1 to M3 the film leader protruding from the cassette can be cut off square. With the screw-mounted Leicas the film leader must be trimmed to make loading easier. This again can be done with the template. Insert the film as before, but with the cut-away end of the template level with the end of the film. When the film end points to the left and the hinge is on top, the emulsion side of the film must face away.

Hold the template in the left hand, and cut away the protruding part of the film on the right with a knife. Start cutting from the shoulder, not from the end.

The Leica M4 and MDa do need a trimmed film end. The usual leader trim will do, but a much simpler trim is possible. With the film end pointing towards you, emulsion side down, slit down the middle of the film for about an inch and cut off the right hand one of the two tongues so formed.

A special trimming template is required for the Leica 250 cassette as the leader is longer there.

Spooling Aids

For easier spooling of the film on to the cassette core use a hand winder. This is a rod with a slot in one end.

Hold the cassette spool with the attached film end in the left hand, and insert the slotted end of the winder into the plain end of the spool. Then simply wind up the film by turning the rod. This makes it easier to maintain the film under constant tension.

The Leitz mechanical winder serves the same purpose, but is more convenient. It screws to the darkroom table or bench and consists of a bracket to hold the cassette spool, and a handle to turn it.

To use the winder, attach the film end to the cassette spool in the usual way. Pull back the spring guide, pull out the handle, and insert the spool with the knob away from the handle. Push the latter in again and let the spring guide bear on the edges of the film. Turn the handle to spool up the film; the spring guide automatically ensures correct tension.

When guiding the film on to the spool, do not touch either the emulsion surface or the back; hold the film by the edges.

The Leitz mechanical winder will also accept the spools of Leitz 250 cassettes; it is, in fact, the only satisfactory way of winding a 33-foot length on to a Leitz 250 spool.

Cassettes may even be loaded from bulk film in broad daylight with the help of a suitable magazine loader. There the bulk roll is contained in a light-tight magazine, and the protruding end is attached to the cassette spool by daylight. The spool is then inserted into the shell of the cassette, the latter fitted into the cassette chamber, and the loader closed. After winding on the required length of film, a knife cuts off the film between the magazine and the cassette.

Film Speed

Now for the films themselves.

We have a great number of different makes and kinds to choose from, but they sort themselves into a few fairly well defined types characterized by film speed, grain, gradation, and colour sensitivity.

The film speed tells us how much light the film needs to produce an image. Slow (less sensitive) films need more light or more exposure than faster (more sensitive) types.

The actual speed is measured sensitometrally by the film manufacturer and expressed by a number or letter. There are two main types of speed numbers, or exposure indices, as they are often called.

FILMS

Speed measures the sensitivity of the film to light. Fast films permit short exposures, small apertures, and are suitable for poor light conditions. Slow films need good light, larger apertures, or longer exposures.

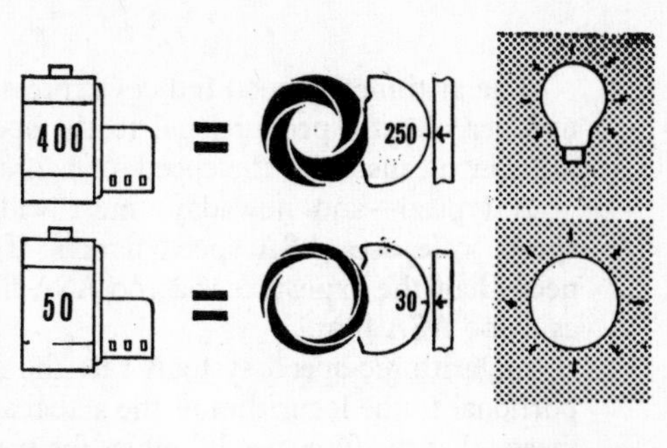

Grain and resolution determine the fineness of the image structure. Coarse-grained films permit only lower enlargements than fine grain films, and will resolve less detail.

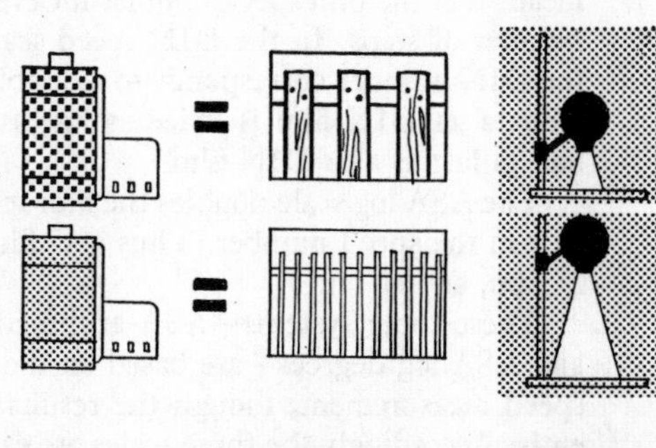

Gradation tells us how the film reproduces brightness differences. For general photography we use films of normal gradation, but for copying and similar subjects with no half-tones a contrasty (hard gradation) film is better.

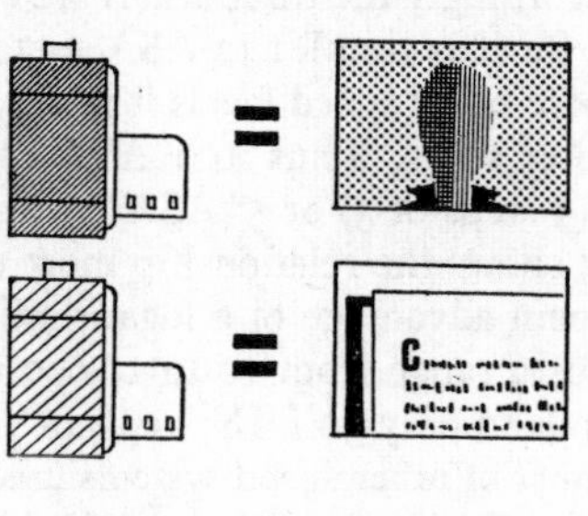

Colour sensitivity determines the way in which the film translates the brightness values of different colours into black and white. Most Leica films are panchromatic, i.e. sensitive to all colours. Orthochromatic films (not sensitive to red) are used for special purposes like fluorography, while positive film (blue sensitive only) is used for copying.

PAN

ORTO

POS:

The arithmetic speed indices express the speed by a plain number directly proportional to the speed. Twice as high a number means twice the speed, or half as much exposure.

A typical—and nowadays most widely used—arithmetic speed scale uses ASA speed figures. Thus a 200 ASA film needs half the exposure of a 100 ASA film, or twice as much as a 400 ASA film.

Logarithmic speed systems rate the speed by a scale proportional to the logarithm of the actual speed. In practice that means that the film speed doubles for every increase of a given number of steps. In the DIN speed scale an increase of 3 in the DIN number corresponds to a doubling of the film speed. Thus a 21 DIN film is twice as fast as an 18 DIN film, or half as fast as a 24 DIN film.

The ASA log scale doubles the film speed for every increase of 1 in the speed number. Thus a 5° film is twice as fast as a 4° film, and so on.

These three systems—ASA arithmetic figures, DIN steps and ASA log degrees—are based on the same method of film speed measurement, though the results are expressed differently. Accordingly the three scales are easily inter-convertible. The rule for it is simple: 12 ASA = 12 DIN = 2° ASA log. To compare other speed levels it is only necessary to progress in doubling steps. Thus 100 ASA (8 times the speed) = 21 DIN (3 steps of 3) or 5° ASA log (3 steps of 1). The table on p. 445 shows the relationship more clearly.

The main advantage of a logarithmic scale is its compactness. Thus a range from 10 to 10,000 in arithmetic numbers corresponds to only 30 DIN steps, or 10 ASA log steps.

A number of other speed systems used to be current, but are nowadays virtually obsolete. These include logarithmic BS degrees and Scheiner degrees. Both follow the same principle as DIN steps, but are about 10 units higher. Weston and GOST figures are arithmetic, too; numerically they can be taken as roughly the same as ASA numbers.

The practical purpose of film speed ratings is to provide a figure that can be set on an exposure meter or used in an exposure table. When used in this way the speed ratings published by film manufacturers lead to exposure recommendations that give the film the minimum correct exposure. Until a few years ago film speed ratings incorporated a considerable "safety factor"; that is to say, they led to exposure recommendations higher than the minimum necessary for a correctly exposed picture. This was intended to provide some latitude against under-exposure, though this degree of over-exposure usually yields grainier and slightly less sharp negatives. Some film manufacturers still quote speeds with such safety factors; that is the reason why the speed quoted for certain films in the table on p. 463 may not agree with that published by the manufacturer.

Graininess

On speed alone, the fastest films would seem to be the best to use. High-speed films, however, tend to show the grain, or image structure, when the negative is enlarged. The tones then no longer appear smooth and even, but are broken up in minute irregular dots, corresponding to the original particles of silver salt in the sensitive layer of the film.

The degree to which we can enlarge a negative before the grain becomes disturbing depends largely on the size of these silver halide crystals. Whenever possible, therefore, we shall choose a film with the finest possible grain, particularly if we want big enlargements. Unfortunately, fine-grain films are mostly slow, and high-speed films, as already mentioned, comparatively coarse grained.

The choice of film, then, becomes a compromise. Use a slow type (for fine grain) when the light is good enough (e.g. outdoor shots, and especially landscapes, in summer). Load with a fast film when the light is poor—e.g. indoors, or theatre subjects—or when the subject calls for very short exposure times (fast action shots, sports, etc.).

The finer the grain, the more easily the film can record small image detail. When the grain becomes coarser we lose some of this detail—the so-called resolving power of the film is reduced and small detail is lost.

Resolution and Exposure

While the grain and resolving power largely depend on the film, careless exposure technique can increase graininess and reduce resolution.

Every subject needs a certain minimum exposure to produce an acceptable negative. We can usually give quite a lot more exposure than this minimum amount and still obtain a good enough image, since the film has a certain exposure latitude.

Such over-exposure, however, increases the graininess of the image, and also increases the effect of scattered light within the sensitive layer of the film.

When light passes through the film some of it is reflected

from the surface of the silver halide crystals on to neighbouring grains, which also become exposed. The image of any point of light therefore spreads slightly. This effect shows up strongly when the negative is greatly over-exposed. Any image points very close to each other then tend to overlap and the finer detail in the negative disappears with a further over-all loss of resolving power.

To keep the graininess low and record finest detail on a negative, we therefore have to avoid over-exposure (p. 215).

Gradation

The film reproduces the light, medium and dark subject tones as light, medium and dark greys.

At the moment when we take the picture the sky of a view may be, say, fifty times as bright as a tree trunk in the foreground. But on the negative the sky may be only twenty times as black (as the negative reverses the tones) or it may be a hundred times as black.

The way in which the film reproduces such brightness differences depends on its gradation. A soft gradation or soft working film will give a lower image contrast, while a hard-gradation film will give a higher contrast. The actual contrast also depends on development, but under the same conditions two films may still react differently in this way.

There is also another aspect to gradation. The maximum possible image contrast on the film is itself limited to a useful ratio of about 150 : 1. Below a certain level everything is just transparent film, and above another level—150 times as black—all tones appear more or less uniformly black. A soft gradation film can thus reproduce a much higher subject contrast—it will cover many more subject tones within its range than a hard film which can cover only a few tones.

For subjects of great contrast we therefore need a soft film, and for subjects of little contrast a hard film. Most films are of normal or soft gradation, and will cover the large majority of subjects. But with subjects of particularly low contrast (e.g. copying, photomicrography, etc.) it is useful to load the Leica with a specially hard film.

Colour Sensitivity

Modern panchromatic miniature films are fairly evenly sensitive to all visible colours, and will therefore reproduce them in their correct tone value of grey. Certain panchromatic films react especially strongly to red and render deep red subjects brighter than they appear to the eye. They are specially suitable for photography in artificial light.

Films of uneven colour sensitivity are available for special purposes.

Orthochromatic films—insensitive to red, but more sensitive to green and blue—are used in fluorography (p. 454) to photograph the greenish fluorescent X-ray screen images.

Blue sensitive films are used for copying of monochrome originals (p. 420) where colour sensitivity is unimportant, and also for printing film strips (positive film).

One merit of blue-sensitive film is the fact that we can load cassettes and also handle the film by an orange darkroom light to which the film is comparatively insensitive. Panchromatic films, with their full colour sensitivity, must be loaded in complete darkness. While deep green pan darkroom lamps are available, they are not really safe when the film is exposed to them for any length of time.

With orthochromatic film a deep red light can be used.

Infra-red films, used for infra-red photography (p. 453) are sensitive to violet, blue, and again to red and also infra-red rays.

Film speed to some extent depends also on the colour of the light by which we take the picture.

The effective speed of most films is less in the comparatively yellowish artificial light than in daylight which is richer in blue. Highly red sensitive pan films lose about one-quarter to one-third of their speed. Ordinary pan films lose somewhat more in sensitivity.

Positive and copying films, which are only sensitive to blue light anyway, are merely one-quarter as fast by lamplight. That matters little, as in copying we can take our time.

The Film Base

The sensitive layer of a film is very thin and flimsy; to stand up to normal handling it is therefore coated on a flexible support or base.

This is usually cellulose acetate, also known as safety film (in contrast to old cellulose nitrate which used to be dangerously inflammable—and is no longer made).

The film base of 35 mm. films usually incorporates a grey or blue-grey dye to cut down halation. When the light passes through the sensitive layer of a film, some of it is reflected back from the rear surface of the film support, and exposes the film a second time, forming an indistinct, halo-like image round the main image.

This halation effect is similar to scatter of light in the emulsion (p. 194), and impairs the definition of the negative. It is most noticeable with bright image spots. The dye in the film base absorbs most of the light passing through it.

In addition a number of modern 35 mm. films carry an almost opaque dye layer on the back. This still further reduces the reflection of light from the rear of the film support, and thus gives virtually complete anti-halation protection. This additional dye layer disappears during development.

The Films Available

Films for the Leica fall into the following general groups.

High-speed films of the faster type have speeds of 200–400 ASA. They are panchromatic, some of them excessively sensitive to red, of soft gradation and normal graininess. They are most suitable for photography under difficult lighting conditions (artificial light, theatre, circus, night) and for subjects requiring fast shutter speeds.

High speed films also serve well as all-round negative material, provided the degree of enlargement desired is not too great for the comparatively coarse grain.

Special ultra-fast emulsions go up to 1200 ASA, but are intended for extreme conditions only, since they are appreciably grainy.

Medium-speed films provide an average measure of most film characteristics, and are thus the ideal all-round material. They come in speeds of 100–200 ASA—about half as sensitive as high-speed films—are of normal gradation, and appreciably finer grain. Medium-speed films are suitable for all types of subject where the maximum film speed is not essential.

Fine-grain films are slower still, about 50–100 ASA. With their very fine grain, the negatives will yield enlargements up to eight diameters without special processing. They are of normal gradation and panchromatic sensitivity, and are suitable for most average subjects.

Extra-fine-grain films below about 50 ASA are specially useful for outdoor shots in good light, such as landscapes and other subjects which are to be enlarged to large size prints.

Many extra-fine-grain films tend to give comparatively contrasty negatives, but will reproduce the finest subject detail.

A special feature of fine-grain and extra-fine-grain films is an exceptionally thin emulsion layer. This reduces light scatter in the emulsion, and yields greater image sharpness—often referred to as "acutance"—in addition to the fine grain inherent in the emulsion.

Copying films and positive films are similar to extra-fine-grain films in character, but even more contrasty and slower. Generally no film speed is indicated. These films are used with special lighting set-ups where exposures are determined by preliminary tests (p. 421).

Copying films, employed for copying and recording, are mostly blue-sensitive only. Certain types may be panchromatic or orthochromatic for copying coloured originals.

Special copying films are available for microfilming—copying book pages, newspapers, and documents on to 35 mm. film for subsequent enlargement back to natural size.

Positive films are mainly used for printing film strips from Leica negatives and are analogous to printing papers rather than negative materials. They give positive transparencies for projection, but may also be used for copying.

Reversal films produce first the negative and then the positive on the same film and serve for making positive transparencies by direct exposure in the camera. The idea is to develop the film to a negative, bleach out the image, and then use the remaining silver salts to form the positive image. The price of the film usually includes the cost of processing.

In structure, reversal film is thus similar to negative film (and most negative films can be processed by reversal), but its characteristics such as speed and gradation are specially suited to reversal processing.

Types of Colour Film

Ordinary black-and-white film gives monochrome negatives and prints. In addition, a whole range of colour films is available for the Leica to give pictures in full natural colours.

Colour films fall into two groups. The first—and more modern—kind resembles black-and-white film. On exposure and development it produces a negative which will yield prints or enlargements. The significant point is that both the negatives and prints are coloured.

The negative reproduces all the colours of the subject in their complementary colours. In other words, a green field looks pink, flesh tones come out greenish blue, while blue skies are yellow brown. Apart from that, the colour negative looks much like any other negative: dark subject tones are light, and light ones dark.

To obtain colour enlargements, the colour negative is enlarged in the same way as a black-and-white negative, but on a special colour printing paper. The procedure is similar, too; as the colour print reacts to all colours, we need, however, special methods of controlling the colour of the printing light.

The second kind of colour film is reversal stock. Like black-and-white reversal film, it yields a positive image which in addition shows the full colours of the subject.

Reversal film requires only one lot of colour material and often fewer stages in processing to produce the final picture. The latter is thus cheaper than with negative colour film. On the other hand, these transparencies have to be projected for the best effect or put through a viewer.

Transparencies and Prints

A fundamental difference between transparencies and prints in colour—as in black-and-white—is the tone range of the image.

The brightest and darkest tones on a print are determined by the greatest and least amounts of light that the paper can reflect. In practice the extreme limits are about 90 and 3 per cent respectively, giving a tone range of 30 : 1. No highlight can be more than thirty times as bright on a print as the deepest shadow; often the ratio is nearer 20 : 1.

In a transparency the tone range depends on the relative amount of light transmitted by the different parts of the image which in theory can be unlimited. In practice this may reach 200 : 1, a tone range corresponding to quite a contrasty subject.

In a print, therefore, the tones of the subject may have to be compressed. The print cannot reproduce them all correctly and the result appears dull. A transparency, however, shows the subject in its full brilliance and looks much more life-like. That is probably one of the reasons why colour transparencies are still popular and are likely to remain so, despite the fact that we now have quite a number of negative-positive colour processes.

Negative colour film, though more expensive to use, offers

COLOUR FILM

Nearly all colour films carry three emulsion layers sensitive to blue, green, and red (usually filter layers stop blue light from reaching the lower layers). Blue (e.g. the sky), therefore records only in the top layer, green in the middle layer, and red in the bottom one. In the positive picture the densities are reversed and replaced by complementary dye images —yellow, magenta, and blue-green. These combine to re-create the original colours (p. 200).

Negative colour film yields a colour negative in complementary colours; this is printed on colour paper to give a positive colour print.

Reversal colour film combines the negative and positive stages in one and yields positive colour transparencies.

Colour film is available in different types, balanced for daylight and artificial light respectively. Daylight type film is used for out-of-door shots, and also with blue-coated bulbs and electronic flash.

Artificial light film is balanced for Photoflood or for high-power studio lighting. Other light sources need filters in either case. With negative colour films the matching of the film to the light source is less critical.

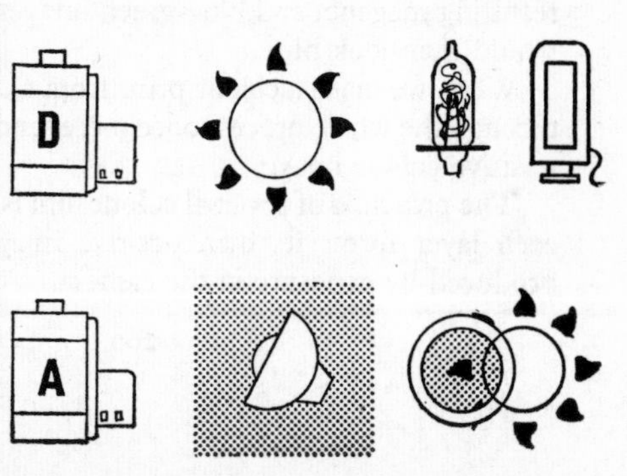

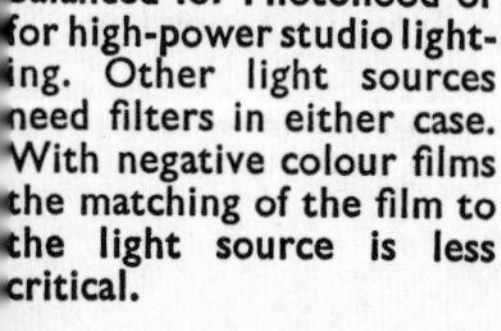

considerably wider scope for control over the final effect in a way similar to black-and-white printing. We can obtain any number of enlargements—in any desired size—from one colour negative, as well as normal black-and-white prints on ordinary printing paper. That is a useful way of judging the quality of a set of colour negatives before colour printing.

Some makers of reversal colour film offer a print service which yields fixed-size colour enlargements. In some cases the user can even make his own prints on reversal colour paper. High-quality prints from colour transparencies require a more complicated process which often involves re-photographing the transparency. Colour transparencies are, however, just as easy to make from colour negatives as colour prints; positive colour film is available for the purpose.

How Colour Film Works

On nearly all modern colour films the picture consists of dyes. Only three dyes are used—yellow, magenta, and bluish green—and their various combinations reproduce nearly all the colours in nature. To be able to do this the dyes have to deal individually with the main groups of subject colours.

The colour film carries three sensitive layers on top of each other, instead of the one of monochrome film. The uppermost layer is sensitive only to blue light, the second layer reacts only to green, and the bottom layer only to red. (A filter layer below the top coating prevents any blue light from reaching the two layers underneath.) During processing to a colour negative the images in the three layers are developed yellow, magenta, and blue-green respectively.

Any blue part of the subject only records in the top layer, and thus becomes yellow in the colour negative (p. 199). Similarly, red subjects only form an image in the bottom layer, and appear blue-green. And a yellow object would record in both the green-sensitive and the red-sensitive layer. The resulting magenta and blue-green images on top of each other would then look blue.

When we make a colour print from a colour negative, we go through the whole process once more, ending up again with the positive colour image.

The principle of reversal colour film is the same, except that each layer forms its own positive image from the negative produced by exposure in the camera.

Colour Film Characteristics

Colour films are somewhat slower than black-and-white films; the fastest colour film corresponds to a medium speed to fast black-and-white one. But most colour films are about the speed of fine-grain black-and-white emulsion—on the average around 50–64 ASA.

Colour films also yield finer grain. Although the colour image is based on the grain structure of a silver image, the dye images are individually much lighter than the silver images they are based on. The grain when the dye images are superimposed, is thus less apparent even at high degrees of enlargement.

Daylight and Artificial Light Films

To reproduce the colours of the subject faithfully, the relative sensitivities of the three layers have to be carefully balanced for the colour of the light.

Artificial light is much more red as compared with daylight. If we expose a colour film balanced for daylight by the light of a Photoflood lamp, everything will have a red tinge.

We therefore have several types of colour film.

Daylight type film (sometimes labelled type D or type T) gives the best results in bright, slightly diffuse, daylight.

Photoflood type film (usually labelled type A) is designed for use with Photoflood lamps.

Tungsten type film (sometimes called type B or type K) is balanced for high efficiency studio lighting.

The two types of artificial light type film are only slightly different. A Photoflood film used by tungsten studio lighting will give a somewhat warmer colour rendering than normal, while a tungsten film exposed with Photofloods gives colder colours.

We can sometimes readjust the colour balance with the help of a colour conversion filter (pp. 272, 484).

These different emulsions and conversion filters are specially important with reversal film where only the conditions at the time of the exposure control the colour rendering. With negative film, where the balance can be corrected in printing, the matter is less critical. Most makes of negative colour film are in fact available in a universal emulsion—for use in daylight or artificial light as required.

Colour Character

The colour rendering of a colour film is characteristic of the film itself. Since all colours are produced by three basic dyes only, no colour film will ever reproduce colours 100 per cent accurately. The actual colour fidelity is thus something of a compromise which varies from make to make. This therefore gives rise to a different colour interpretation by various films.

We cannot say that one is more correct than another, we can only notice that they are different, each having its own character. One type may reproduce skies in particularly deep blues, another may be characterized by a wide range of pastel shades in green, or may show reds with a particular hue.

Which interpretation we like best is a matter of taste. We can try different makes in turn, exposing them strictly according to the makers' instructions, and comparing the results to see which suits us most. Then stick to the process chosen and get to know it really well. This is the best way to learn what can be expected from the material.

Storing Films

Unexposed films deteriorate to some extent during storage. The main effect is a loss of speed. The film should therefore be used within two to three years of manufacture. The makers generally stamp an expiry date on the packing; beyond that date they will not guarantee the film, although it may still be in good condition. To be on the safe side, double the exposure when using stale films after their expiry date.

The colour sensitivity may also alter, though that is of importance only with colour film. There the different layers may not lose speed at the same rate, thus upsetting the colour balance. Make a special point of exposing and processing colour stock as soon as possible after buying it. Do not leave it in the camera for months after it has been exposed.

The keeping qualities of film depend largely also on storage conditions. Store films in a cool, dry place, well away from fumes, strongly smelling substances and the like. A film should not be left in the camera too long. It is better to cut off and develop the exposed portion, than to hold on to it for several months.

Special storage conditions for film may be necessary in the tropics (p. 299).

CAMERA TECHNIQUE

The viewpoint determines perspective, the focal length of the lens governs the scale of the image.
Depth of field depends on aperture, subject distance and focal length. Every lens carries a depth of field indicator.

Photography with the Leica and Leicaflex, as with any other camera, is a straightforward business.

However, when we want to get the most out of every exposure, we shall be more successful if we know the factors that make a good picture. We must learn how to control them by choosing the best lens, camera settings, exposures, etc.

That is the technique of picture taking.

Distance and Lens

The Leica, like any miniature, is essentially at its best with nearer views. Go close to the subject, so that it fills the picture area. The nearer the view, the larger the image.

With the Leica, we can also control the image size by selecting a lens of the appropriate focal length (p. 98).

With the Leica M2 to M4 use the finder frame selector lever to get a preliminary idea of the best focal length to use.

In the Leicaflex the screen shows directly how much the different lenses take in of a scene.

Use the universal finder with the other Leica models to determine which lens to employ. View the scene through the finder, and adjust the latter until the area framed just includes the right amount of view. Then use the appropriate lens.

If the reading on the universal finder is half-way between two marked focal lengths, use the shorter-focus lens.

Perspective

The distance also affects the perspective. This is the appearance of depth that a subject shows in a picture, usually by the different scale on which nearer and more distant parts are reproduced. It depends on the relative distances of different parts of the subject from the camera. The closer the subject, the more marked will be the perspective.

In a shot of, say, two similar trees at 20 and 40 feet respectively from the camera, the nearer tree, being only half as far away as the farther one, will loom up twice as large. But 200 feet from the first tree, the differences in distance is only some 10 per cent. The trees will both look much the same size—which they are—and will not show any appreciable separation.

The perspective effect is comparatively slight.

Something similar happens when we take a picture of a face at close range (p. 324). The nearer portions, such as the nose and chin, appear out of proportion to the neck and ears. Such an exaggerated view is rarely attractive and is often (incorrectly) referred to as distorted or wrong perspective.

Genuine perspective distortion does exist, but only occurs with ultra-wide-angle lenses (slightly with the 28 mm., and more with the 21 mm. lens). It appears as a "spreading" of the image near the edges of the picture. A row of columns will, for instance, show the individual columns widening at each end of the row, and the faces in a large group photograph taken with an ultra-wide-angle lens appear distorted at the edges of the group. This is due to the fact that the lens records the image over such extreme angles still on a flat piece of film while pointing in a fixed direction. When we look at the scene, our eyes sweep over it from end to end, looking in different directions all the time. To eliminate this distortion, which is independent of the optical design of the lens, we would need at least a curved film plane.

When using ultra-wide-angle lenses, avoid having objects of easily recognizable proportions near the edges of the view. (This applies to solid objects; the windows in, for instance, the flat frontage of a building would not suffer from this type of distortion.) Also, keep the camera level; tilting it up or down exaggerates this ultra-wide-angle perspective distortion.

The long-focus lens brings subjects close—analogous to a telescope or binoculars—and the perspective appears subdued.

The perspective is determined by the viewpoint, but the scale of the view depends on the lens. The pictorial effect is often a matter of suitably combining the two.

Thus we may enhance the apparent depth of a subject by going close and using a wide-angle lens to cover the field. That separates foreground elements from the middle distance and background. The near, wide-angle, view sets them off against each other by increased perspective. This holds for near landscapes as much as for industrial pictures of machinery—whenever we have a great mass of detail that makes sense only when resolved into planes at different distances.

Conversely, a subject of appreciable depth will appear better with the perspective subdued. So go farther back, and increase the scale of the image by using a longer-focus lens. This

The relative size in which different objects are reproduced in a picture depends on distance. Near objects loom larger than distant ones. The greater the difference, the greater the feeling of separation and perspective (p. 203).

Perspective depends entirely on the viewpoint. From a close viewpoint, a tree may look twice as high as another farther away. From a distant viewpoint, the relative separation between the trees is less important, and they both look equally tiny.

If we use a long-focus lens—or enlarge a portion only of the negative—the picture may show the trees large again, but their relative size is still the same. The effect of perspective is subdued, if not lost.

Black panel: Even from a fixed viewpoint the choice of lens may, however, still influence the perspective effect. This is particularly the case when we tilt the camera (p. 204). A normal or wide-angle lens will cover the whole subject and the over-all convergence of verticals appears fairly violent. Over a smaller image angle as taken in by a long-focus lens, the over-all convergence is less and the effect is not so disturbing.

Tilting the camera for ultra-wide-angle shots also emphasizes the perspective distortion occurring with extremely short focal lengths (p. 204).

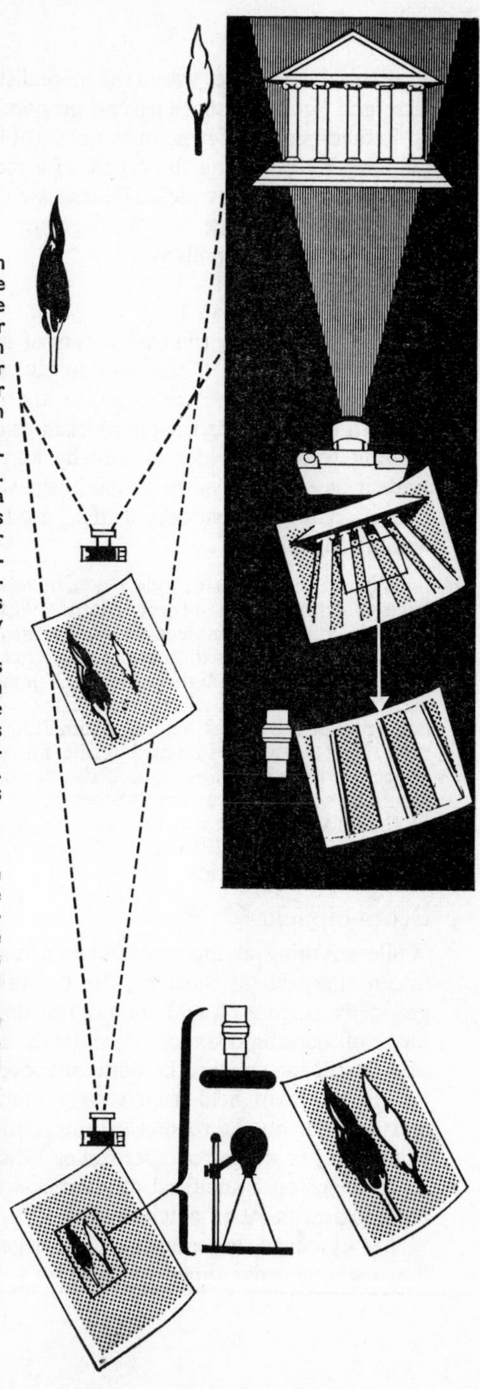

applies to portraiture, where the more distant viewpoint shows faces and figures in more natural proportions.

Remember the viewpoint is responsible for that effect, not the lens. By enlarging the centre of a picture taken from the same position with a wide-angle lens, we shall still get the same result. But the image will need greater enlargement, with a consequent loss in quality.

Focusing

With most subjects, the easiest way of focusing is to use the rangefinder (p. 46). There we simply sight the subject and turn the focusing lever or ring until the two images fuse.

With the Leicaflex the microprism grid in the centre of the viewing screen provides an equally easy means of focusing, since it directly shows the actual image sharpness. The operation of setting the lens may in this case be a little slower than with a rangefinder.

With series I Leica models, which have no rangefinder, we have to estimate the subject distance, either by pacing or, for subjects less than six feet away, by measuring. With a little practice it is possible to guess the distance reasonably exactly.

A useful aid is to sight an average person through the Leica viewfinder and see at what distance he or she just fills the finder height with the Leica held horizontally. This is usually about 10–12 feet with the standard finder for 50 mm. lenses. If the image fills only half the height of the viewfinder field, the subject would be somewhere around 22 feet away; similarly a person will fill the finder from the waist to the top of the head at about 4½ feet. With the finders for different focal lengths, these distances would be altered in proportion.

Depth of Field

While anything at the exact focused distance will be reproduced sharpest on the film, the definition deteriorates only gradually in front of, and behind, this distance. Over a certain range of focusing distances—the depth of field—this unsharpness is still too small to be noticeable even on enlargement.

The depth of field itself is very much under our control and depends on the theoretical unsharpness we are prepared to tolerate, as well as on aperture and distance settings.

In choosing a standard of sharpness the final print is the most logical point at which to start.

Let us assume we enlarge a Leica negative of 1 × 1½ inches (24 × 36 mm.) five times, to a print of 5 × 7 inches. The ideal

DEPTH OF FIELD

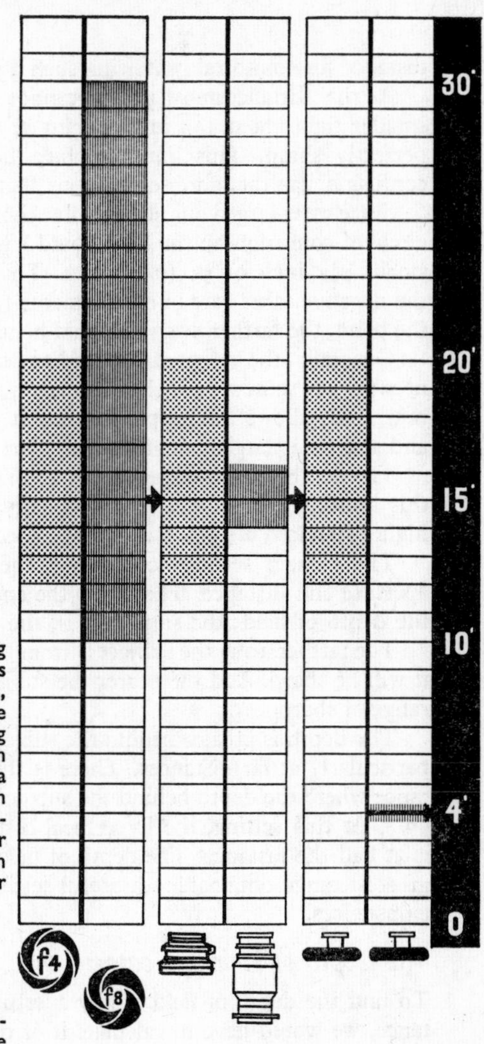

The factors affecting depth of field are the lens aperture, the focal length, and the focusing distance (p. 208). Thus stopping down increases the depth of field (*left*); while using a lens of longer focal length decreases the depth available (*centre*). At closer subject distances the depth is less than at medium or far distances (*right*).

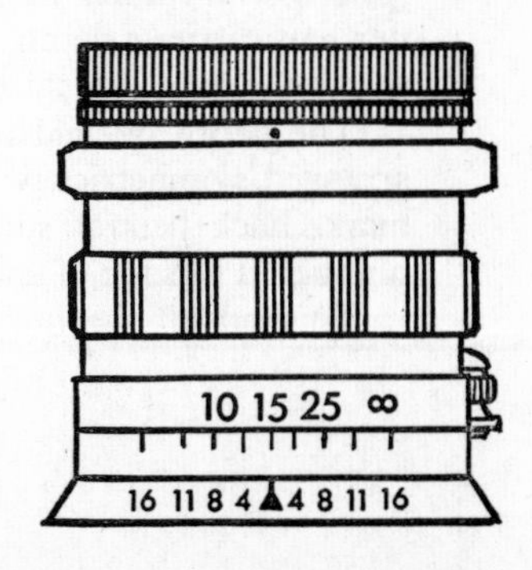

The depth of field indicator is a scale of aperture numbers arranged symmetrically at each side of the focusing mark of the lens. During focusing, the distance scale moves past the depth indicator. The distances opposite any two corresponding aperture numbers indicate the depth at that setting and aperture. In this example, with the lens set to 15 feet, the sharp zone is from about 12 to 20 feet at *f*4, and from 10 to beyond 25 feet at *f*8.

distance for comfortably viewing such a print is 10 inches.

At this distance most people cannot distinguish anything smaller than about $\frac{1}{100}$ inch; a blur of that size will appear perfectly sharp. This limiting blur, the so-called circle of confusion, can therefore serve as our standard of sharpness.

Since we enlarged our negative five times, the corresponding circle of confusion on the film would have to be five times as small, $\frac{1}{500}$ inch or $\frac{1}{20}$ (0.05) mm. This basic sharpness of the negative takes care of enlargements to any size; the larger the print, the farther away it should be viewed.

Generally, the accepted standard of definition for miniature negatives is somewhat higher, namely $\frac{1}{750}$ inch or $\frac{1}{30}$ (0.033) mm. This allows for people peering at a print more closely and also for enlargements from only part of the negative.

The depth of field tables in this book (p. 464) are based on this limiting blur of $\frac{1}{750}$ inch. For very exact work an even higher standard of $\frac{1}{1000}$ inch may be used.

The camera settings controlling the depth of field are aperture and distance. The larger the aperture, the shallower the depth of field; the smaller it is, the greater the depth.

The farther away the subject is from the Leica, the more of it will be sharp. And the nearer the subject, the narrower the range of sharpness.

The depth is greater behind the subject than in front of it, particularly at far distances. There is thus one focusing distance where the depth behind the subject just reaches infinity (∞). At this setting, the hyperfocal distance, the near limit is at half the distance. The depth of field then represents the greatest range obtainable—a useful setting under certain circumstances.

The Depth of Field Indicator

To find the depth of field at any aperture and focusing distance, we would have to calculate it or obtain it from a table (p. 464) every time. To simplify things, each Leica and Leicaflex lens carries a depth of field indicator, which automatically shows the approximate zone of sharpness at a glance.

The depth of field indicator consists of a series of lines arranged symmetrically on either side of the focusing index mark. Each pair of such lines is marked with an aperture number. The scale of lines is next to the distance scale.

To read off the near limit of the depth at any distance

setting, find the distance opposite the required aperture to the left of the focusing index (as seen from the front of the camera). The far limit is the distance opposite the corresponding aperture line to the right of the focusing index (p. 207).

For example, with the standard 50 mm. lens focused on 8 feet, and used at *f*5.6, the left-hand *f*5.6 line will point to about 6½ feet, and the right-hand *f*5.6 line to about 10 feet.

The cut-outs in the rangefinder frame of the Leica M2 and M3 are an even simpler indicator for quick checking (p. 49).

Optimum Settings

We can also use the depth of field indicator to find the most suitable distance and aperture for a required depth zone.

Determine first the near and far limits within which the subject should be sharp (e.g. by focusing on each with the rangefinder and reading off the corresponding distances). Then adjust the focusing lever or ring until one of the aperture lines is opposite the near limit, and the corresponding second aperture line is opposite the far limit.

This automatically sets the lens to the best possible distance. The aperture number of the lines which most nearly embrace this range is the figure to which we have to set the lens.

For instance, we may have to bracket a subject where the nearest part is 12 feet, and the farthest point 30 feet away. We find that with the 5 cm. lens we can just cover this range within the *f*8 lines of the depth of field indicator.

This, then, is the stop to use, while the focused distance is automatically set to just beyond 15 feet.

The depth of field suggested by the indicator may not always agree with the value in the tables on pp. 464–482. The reason is that the indicator cannot be as accurate as the tables; in addition in the case of some early lenses the standard of sharpness taken as a basis may be different.

Changing the Standard

To use a higher standard of sharpness for more accurate work, take the depth of field for the next larger aperture.

Thus the depth indicated in the tables is based on a standard of $\frac{1}{750}$ inch. For a standard of $\frac{1}{1000}$ inch, with the lens at, say, *f*5.6, use the depth limits given for *f*4, which are correspondingly smaller. Alternatively, use the depth at *f*5.6 and then stop down to *f*8 to increase the sharpness near the limits.

Zone Focusing

Focusing, quick as it is the with Leica, does take a couple of seconds, and in this time we may miss fast-moving subjects.

By utilizing the depth of field we can dispense with focusing.

Select a suitable distance range within which the subject is likely to move, and set the appropriate aperture and distance (and of course the shutter speed) beforehand. Then just follow the subject in the finder and shoot whenever it looks right. As long as the action takes place between the near and far limits foreseen, it will be in focus.

A card with suitable focusing zones written down (see also p. 463) will easily slip into the back of the ever-ready case.

Depth Focusing in Practice

Depth focusing frequently becomes something of a compromise between the smallest desirable aperture (for maximum sharpness) and the largest practicable one. Often the only way to get over the difficulty is to take the subject from farther away—when the depth of field becomes greater, and, in the case of action, the shutter speed required is slower.

Sometimes we need a minimum of depth of field, e.g. to make a portrait stand out against an unsharp background. In such a case, go as near as possible, and focus accurately, using a large aperture to reduce the available depth of field.

Finally it is not always good policy to utilize the full depth of field. For instance, we may be taking a distant landscape with a foreground stretching fairly near. To obtain the maximum depth, we would have to focus on the hyperfocal distance, so that both near and distant parts are reasonably sharp. Neither, however, will be as sharp as if we focused directly either on the foreground, or the distance, itself.

If, say, the range of mountains in a view are the real subject, it may be better to set the lens to infinity and put up with a slightly blurred foreground. But for a sharp picture of a climber on a rock some 20 feet away, focus at 20 feet. This will give a sharper image of the figure than focusing at 40 feet to get both him and the mountains within the depth.

Depth with Different Lenses

Depth of field also varies with the different lenses.

The long-focus lens enlarges the image; the latter therefore has to be sharper. Consequently the depth of field with long-focus lenses is much less than with the standard lens; the longer the focal length, the shallower the depth at any aperture. This decrease is very rapid, and long-focus lenses thus call for accurate focusing, especially with the Telyt lenses.

Yet the shallow depth of field also has a practical advantage: it makes differential focusing easier (p. 210). If we want to take, say, a portrait, using a long-focus lens, the background will be really blurred even at longer camera distances, whilst it may still be comparatively sharp with the standard lens. In this particular case the long-focus lens help to separate the different planes of the subject and give depth to the picture.

Conversely, a wide-angle lens will yield a much greater depth of field. If we are prepared to put up with the smaller scale of the image, the 35 mm. lens is therefore ideal for subjects which call for deep focusing zones at large apertures.

An approximate visual estimation of the depth of field is possible on the finder screen of the Leicaflex SL by using the aperture pre-view button on the front (see p. 158).

Soft Focus

We do not always want the pin-sharp definition of the Leica lenses. With some types of landscape shots a certain amount of softness of the image may improve the pictorial effect of the photograph. Similarly, in portraits, especially of women and children, a slightly soft definition will help to subdue the texture of the face and tone down wrinkles.

This softness of the picture is not the same as an out-of-focus or movement blur, but looks more like a slightly unsharp image on top of a sharp one. The unsharp image is somewhat larger, and the outlines of the subject therefore appear to spread slightly, softening, but not destroying, the definition of the picture.

We can obtain soft-focus effects in Leica shots with soft-focus attachments or with a soft-focus lens.

Soft-focus attachments consist of plain glass or plastic discs, to be mounted in front of the lens, with a series of concentric circles engraved or embossed on the surface. These circles slightly diffuse the rays of light passing through the disc, and thus spread the image.

This is particularly noticeable in the light parts, and bright highlights tend to overflow into adjacent shadow areas. The whole picture, in addition to the softness produced, acquires a characteristic luminous quality. This is specially effective where the highlight areas are small and the contrast between bright and dark is great, as in against-the-light shots and portraits with the outlines of the subject rimmed by a halo of light.

Stopping down the lens cuts out the diffusing effect of the outer rings on the soft-focus attachment and thus increases the sharpness.

Diffusion attachments may even be home-made, such as a plain glass disc with vaseline circles smeared on, or a screen of fine black silk (e.g. nylon stocking) or wire. With such mesh screens the diffusion depends on the closeness of the fabric and the thickness of the strands; stopping down will not affect the definition.

Mesh-type screens spread the light in well-defined directions parallel to the mesh. Bright lights may get a four-pointed star-like halo instead of an even, round one.

With the Thambar soft-focus lens (p. 112) the central part of the lens forms the sharp basic picture image, while the outer portions produce the superimposed unsharp image. The contribution of each, and thus the degree of softness, can be controlled by stopping down the lens and by using the special centre stop provided.

We can relax our standard of definition (p. 208) when working out depth of field for soft-focus shots. Generally, take the depth of field to be the same as if the lens were stopped down to its next smaller stop. Thus, at say *f*5.6 the depth may be assumed to be the same as at *f*8 without soft focus.

The image will of course be less sharp. But it will be practically as sharp within the limits of this increased depth of field, as at the distance the lens is actually focused on.

EXPOSURE TECHNIQUE

The correct exposure needed depends on the light, the subject brightness, and the film speed.
The same exposure can be obtained by different combinations of aperture and shutter speed. The choice depends on the depth of field required, and on the subject movement we have to deal with.

To take a picture, we have to expose the film to the action of a given amount of light in order to record the image.

The exposure in the camera is a combination of the lens aperture and shutter speed. Both govern the amount of light that acts on the film. The larger the aperture and the longer the exposure time, the more light the film will get.

In practice we still obtain the same result if we reduce the exposure time (use a shorter shutter speed) and open up the aperture to compensate for the loss of light, or if we reduce the aperture and use a correspondingly slower shutter speed.

Exposure Factors

The exposure required depends on the sensitivity (p. 190) of the film and on the light coming from the subject.

The latter factor in turn depends on the light falling on the scene—the time of day and year, weather, or number and strength of lamps we are using—and on the brightness of the subject itself.

To find the correct exposure to use, we have to measure or estimate this light by means of an exposure meter (which is really a light meter) or by exposure calculators or tables. In the Leicaflex the exposure measurement is part of the procedure of setting the aperture and shutter speed.

Which particular aperture-time combination we are going to choose also depends on whether conditions call for a definite aperture or a definite shutter speed.

Thus when the subject needs a great depth of field, the aperture is the governing factor (p. 208); we have to choose a comparatively small stop and suit the exposure time to it.

For fast movement where a high shutter speed is essential, we have to suit the aperture to the exposure time.

Some subjects need a short exposure time and a small aperture. If the lighting conditions are not good enough to allow for both, we may have to compromise and put up with a certain loss in quality in order to secure a picture.

Aperture Scales

The various apertures or stops are marked on the Leica lenses by a series of aperture numbers or *f*-numbers. The smaller the number, the larger the aperture.

The maximum aperture of the lens is in addition marked on the front mount (e.g. 1 : 2 on the Summicron, 1 : 4 on the 135 mm. Tele-Elmar).

The *f* numbers on the aperture scale are so arranged that each stop lets through twice as much light as the next higher number. On the current Leica lenses this series of numbers (the so-called international scale) covers the stops *f*1.4, 2, 2.8, 4, 5.6, 11, 16, 22.

The lens at *f*5.6 passes twice as much light as at *f*8, or half as much light as at *f*4. Thus to get the same exposure, we have to halve or double the shutter speed, respectively: 1/60 second at *f*5.6 is equivalent to 1/30 second at *f*8, or 1/125 second at *f*4 and so on. (On current models the shutter speeds follow a similar "halving" scale throughout—p. 42.)

The maximum aperture does not always fit into the above aperture scale. Thus *f*3.5 of some earlier Summaron and Elmar lenses is slightly larger than *f*4; *f*4.5—also of now discontinued lenses—is slightly smaller than *f*4. But in practice these apertures can be taken as more or less equal to the nearest values of the aperture series.

Older Leica lenses carry the European aperture scale which covers the stops *f*2.2, 3.2, 4.5, 6.3, 9, 12.5, 18.25. These are in-between values to the international scale. But here, too, each step from one number to the next higher halves the light passed. Some of the maximum apertures again do not fit into the series.

The aperture numbers represent a mathematical relationship between effective lens diameter and focal length. The two scales are therefore *not* two systems in the same sense as we have a British and metric system of measurement. They are rather two arbitrary series of quantities arranged in one of the quoted scales of stops for convenience. They are derived from one and the same system of expressing lens apertures.

Exposure Latitude

When we expose a shot in the Leica, too little light would not record all parts of the picture, while too much would blacken the film all over.

There is an appreciable region between this "too little" and "too much", where the exposure affects the film evenly in proportion to the brightness of the subject tones. Throughout that region we get a negative that we can regard as correctly exposed. This range of correct levels is the exposure latitude.

The latitude takes care of minor, and sometimes even major, exposure errors. If in doubt we can always give a little more exposure; the negative will be somewhat darker, but perfectly usable, since it will still produce a good print.

All the same, the exposure latitude is not a fixed quantity. It is less with contrasty films than with soft-gradation type materials, and it is always less with contrasty subjects than with flat ones. The greater the contrast, the more accurate must be the exposure.

Even within the limits of the latitude, over-exposure will not yield the best possible negative, as it coarsens the grain (p. 193), and decreases the resolution of the film. Avoid over-exposure especially with ultra-speed films.

The ideal exposure, to make sure of the maximum resolution and finest grain for really big enlargements, is therefore one that is just sufficient to record the detail of the shadows or dark portions of the subject. To expose with such accuracy an exposure meter is desirable; preferably calibrated individually (p. 220).

Exposure Tables

Exposure tables show a series of factors corresponding to the various light and subject conditions. Thus we may have one factor for the time of day or year, another one for the subject and weather, and one for the film speed. Adding up or multiplying the factors gives the appropriate exposures.

An exposure calculator works on the same principle, but uses discs which have to be set according to the conditions.

Choosing the appropriate factors is to some extent a matter of guesswork. The tables are, nevertheless, quite accurate for most subjects since they define the factors fairly closely.

With a little practice it becomes quite easy to memorize the most important exposure conditions and to estimate the exposure without reference to the tables at all.

A useful short-cut to guessing the exposure is to work out the basic correct value for a standard subject. Let us take an average case: an outdoor group of people in hazy or diffused sunshine in the early afternoon in summer. This would require 1/250 second at *f*11 on a medium speed 100 ASA film.

Taking this as a starting-point, we can then modify the basic exposure for different conditions. Thus cloudy weather would call for at least twice the exposure, so would the same subject in autumn instead of summer. Cloudy weather *and* autumn may require four times as much, i.e. either 1/60 second at *f*11 or 1/250 second at *f*5.6. Similarly we should have to double the exposure for a slower film of 50 ASA.

Such a series of doubling factors is much easier to remember than an elaborate table and is handy for making allowances when conditions change during shooting.

Using Exposure Meters

A reliable way of determining the correct exposure is of course to measure the intensity of the prevailing light. Exposure meters are used for this purpose and are available either as separate units or as special meters to fit on top of the Leica M cameras and couple with the shutter speed setting (p. 221). The Leicaflex models have their exposure meter built in. Before discussing the use of these special meters, let us briefly see what an exposure meter is and does, and how it has to be used.

An exposure meter can measure either the light falling on the subject or the light reflected from it. Accordingly, there are incident light and reflected light meters.

The usual photo-electric meter consists of a light-sensitive photo-electric cell connected to a microammeter. When light falls on the cell, it generates electricity or increases the current in a measuring circuit. The pointer of the microammeter indicates the strength of this current and thus the intensity of the light falling on the cell. Usually an attached scale or calculator shows the corresponding exposure values.

To use a reflected light meter, point it at the subject from the camera position, and take a reading to find the exposure required. As some exposure meters cover a larger field of view than the camera lens, go nearer to the subject when taking a reading.

With outdoor shots the bright sky may unduly influence the meter and cause it to indicate too short an exposure. So point the cell slightly downwards to exclude the sky from the view.

The cell of the meter gives an average reading of the brightness of the scene in front of it. That is good enough for subjects

EXPOSURE METERS

The measuring methods shown here apply primarily to a separate exposure meter, but are valid (with exception of incident light measurement) also to the Leicaflex with its built-in meter.

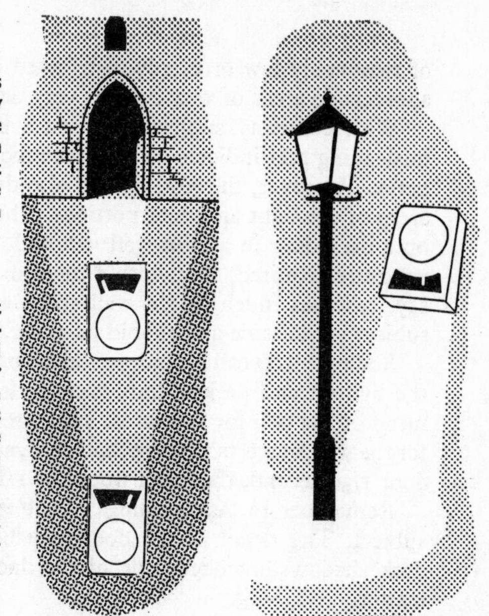

A reading depends not only on the actual brightness of highlights, and shadows, but also on their relative areas (*left*). With contrasty subjects it is better to take separate readings and use a mean value (p. 218).

With special subjects, e.g. outdoor shots at night take a reading from a well-illuminated part of the scene (*right*).

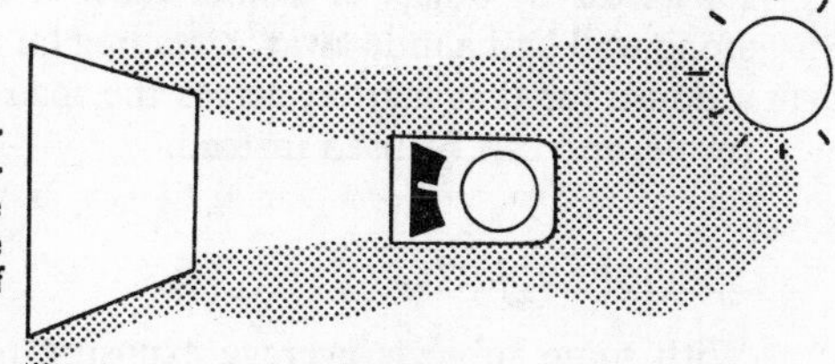

Highlight readings, taken on a white card illuminated by the same light as the subject, peg the exposure to the highlights instead of the shadows.

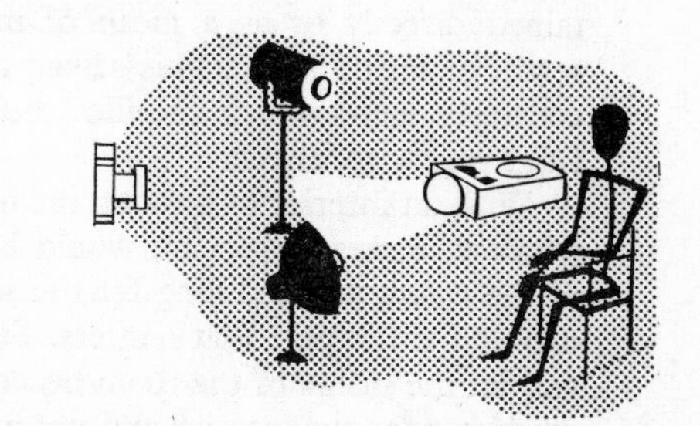

Incident light meters measure the light falling on the subject instead of that reflected from it. They are pointed from the subject position in the direction of the camera.

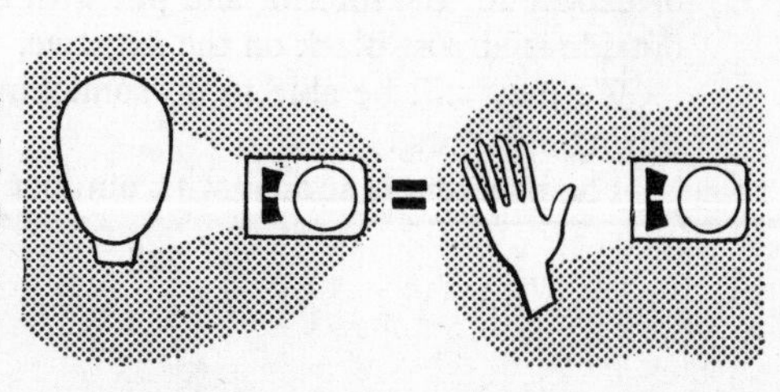

In colour photography a modified highlight reading taken on the face or other flesh tone, gives the best results (p. 219) and ensures that the skin tones always come out the same.

of reasonably low or evenly distributed contrast, i.e. with no appreciable areas of very light or very dark.

With contrasty subjects such an average reading can be misleading and indicate an exposure too short for the darker parts. Moreover, the reading will also depend on the relative areas of the light and dark portions. Thus a close-up reading on a dark door in a light wall will be lower (indicating more exposure required) than with a more distance view showing, say, twice as much bright wall space as door area. Yet the subject is the same and should be given the same exposure.

Such subjects call for independent close-up readings of both the lightest and darkest important parts. Then work out the mean of the two for the actual exposure. Thus if the reading for the wall suggests 1/500 second at *f*8, and the reading for the door 1/30 second, the mean would be 1/125 second.

Remember to take readings of the *important* parts of the subject. The detail of the door may be important, but the dark shadow down one side of the door post is unlikely to matter.

When a subject is too far away for close-up readings, look for a near-by object of similar tone. If the subject includes a stone wall half a mile away, a reading on another stone wall, or a house for that matter, across the road would give a similar result, and can be used instead.

Special Subjects

With some subjects average exposure readings, whether obtained directly or as a mean of independent high and low readings, are of no use. This is likely to be the case with specially contrasty views which the film could not reproduce in their full tone range, anyway.

With an interior of a room, including the view outside one window, a mean exposure would be too short for the detail of the room, and too long for the scene outside. In that case expose for the part that matters. Either photograph the view and let the inside of the room become a dark silhouette mass, or expose for the interior and put with the fact that the scene outside is almost black on the negative.

We may still be able to do something to help by shading during enlarging.

The problem is similar with outdoor shots at night.

Highlight Meters

The idea of exposing for the highlights of contrasty scenes can be extended even to normal subjects. Instead of taking an average, take a close-up reading of the brightest area of the scene.

Naturally, the meter will now indicate a shorter exposure than for an average reading. This highlight reading, therefore, has to be multiplied by a suitable factor to give the correct exposure. That factor is usually about 4× by 6×; we can easily find it by specially calibrating the meter with test exposures (p. 220). With an ordinary scene the darker portions will then be reproduced darker, according to their actual tone in relation to the brightest highlight.

The main advantage of this method is that the highlights always come out in the same brightness in every exposure.

This is particularly useful with reversal colour film where the bright tones are the most important ones, as they show up colour faults due to wrong exposure.

To standardize conditions still more we can use an artificial highlight of fixed brightness (such as a 6-inch square piece of white card) for every exposure meter reading. Hold up the card near the subject so that the light falls on it from the same direction as on the subject. Bring up the meter close to the card until the needle shows the maximum reading; take care not to throw a shadow on the card. This reading, multiplied by a suitable factor, then indicates the correct exposure.

With outdoor exposures there is no need to hold the card near the subject at all, provided the light falls on the card from the same direction as on the subject.

Incident Light Meters

Some highlight meters have a translucent diffusing disc fitted over the cell, and can be pointed directly at the light source from near the subject. The exposure factor will be different, but the principle of use is the same.

This is, in fact, the simplest type of incident light meter. We can, however, go a step further, and measure the average light falling on all parts of the subject facing the camera.

For this purpose the exposure meter has to be fitted with a translucent hemisphere or cone (which may be detachable) over the photo-electric cell, and pointed at the Leica from the position of the subject. The cone then collects the light from every direction within an angle of 180 deg., and indicates the total effect. Again we would have to multiply the reading by a suitable factor.

Such incident light measurement is, of course, an average reading, and it does not work for subjects of extreme contrast. There independent readings (p. 218) are the only practicable method. It is, however, very useful for set-ups with reasonably evenly balanced artificial lighting. It is then much more reliable than reflected light readings, as the cone receives comparatively little light from any effect lamps and none at all from the background. It is the ideal way of determining the exposure for colour shots by artificial light.

Meter Calibration

The one adjustment necessary on exposure meters before taking readings is the film speed setting. Most modern meters are scaled in ASA or DIN exposure index numbers (p. 192) and often in both. Nowadays these are fairly reliable; simply set the meter to the rated speed of the film in the Leica, and go ahead.

Older meters frequently used very unreliable and arbitrary film speed ratings. Even modern meters of the same make and type may indicate different exposures due to manufacturing tolerances.

In practice the variation is not serious. But for accurate work, especially colour photography, calibrate the particular meter used individually. This will also show the correct factor when using the instrument as a highlight or incident light meter.

The method is simple enough.

Choose an average subject, for instance a portrait out of doors. Take a normal reflected light reading by pointing the meter at the sitter from about half the camera distance. Set the meter to the rated speed of the film in the Leica, and note the exposure indicated.

Make a series of exposures, using the reading obtained as a basis, with additional shots at one, two and three stops larger and smaller. For instance if the meter reading suggests 1/125 second at *f*5.6, take a set of pictures with 1/125 second at *f*2, 2.8, 4, 5.6, 8, 11 and 16.

Develop the film and examine the negatives. From the results it should be easy to determine the best setting.

If the negative taken at *f*5.6 is the best, the rated speed of the film (e.g. 100 ASA or 21 DIN) is the correct one to use for that particular meter.

If the negative taken at *f*8 is correctly exposed, double the speed rating: set the meter to 200 ASA or 24 DIN with that film. The fact that the film package is labelled 100 is immaterial; we are concerned with the practical meter speed of the film. Similarly, if the best negative is that taken at *f*4, halve the speed rating and use the meter set to 50 ASA or 18 DIN.

One test like this will usually settle the effective meter speed for most films. For if a 100 ASA film has a meter rating of 50, a 160 ASA film will need a setting of 80, and so on.

It is, however, advisable to make a separate test with each type of colour film to be used, since here exact exposure is much more important. Though colour film is expensive, such tests are a big saving in the long run by eliminating future failures due to incorrect exposure. This also yields valuable information about the peculiarities of different types of colour film.

To obtain the factor for highlight or incident light measurement take appropriate additional readings, using the highlight method. Then compare the exposure indicated with the original value. For instance if the first reading gave 1/125 second at *f*5.6 and the highlight reading 1/125 second at *f*11, the factor is 4×.

The easier way of using these factors it to amend the meter speed accordingly. Instead of 100 ASA in this case, the high light meter speed would be 25.

When making separate tests with colour film, it may be more convenient to find the highlight meter speed directly, rather than via the normal speed.

The Coupled Leicameter MR

A special meter is available for the Leica M models and can be coupled with the shutter speed dial of the camera. The operation of taking a reading then automatically sets the correct shutter speed.

To fit the meter to the Leica M, first set the camera speed dial to B. Rotate the milled setting ring of the meter anticlockwise as far as it will go, so that the index line on the ring coincides with the foot of the bent arrow on the meter housing. Lift up the ring and turn it a little farther. Now push the whole meter into the accessory shoe so that the setting ring comes to lie above the speed dial. Push the meter fully home in the shoe; then turn the ring clockwise until it drops down and engages the notch of the speed dial. The ring may have to be eased to and fro a little for full engagement. The meter is now coupled to the camera.

Since the milled setting ring covers the shutter speed dial, the speeds themselves are now read off the large disc on top of the meter. Its scale carries numbers from 1000 (for 1/1000 second) to 1 second in geometric or doubling intervals (with a red dot to correspond to 1/50 second for synchronizing electronic flash—p. 258).

On turning the ring further, it stops at the marking B-2. The camera shutter is now set for time exposures. The ring can turn further on lifting up to disengage it from the shutter speed dial. The limit of the scale is reached with 120, corresponding to 120 seconds.

The figures from B-2 to 120 indicate the length of time exposure required for a given exposure reading in poor light. These exposures have to be timed or counted separately while the shutter is held open on the B-setting of the camera, with the cable release.

On turning the milled setting ring back again, it re-engages the shutter speed dial as the B-2 setting is reached.

To use the meter, first set it to the speed of the film in the camera by turning the central disc until the appropriate speed in one of the windows is opposite the index line. The windows give speeds in logarithmic DIN and ASA (arithmetic) index numbers.

The speed to be used for a particular film can, of course, be determined by a test series of individual calibration exposures (p. 220).

The marked film speed setting range covers ratings from 6 to 3200 ASA (and 6 to 36 DIN). There are two ASA windows to avoid inconvenient bunching up of the ASA numbers.

Use whichever window is more convenient or includes the actual speed figure of the film in use.

When the Leicameter MR is mounted on the camera, its cell takes in the same view as the 90 mm. lens. When taking a reading push the finder frame selector lever inwards (towards the lens) to see the area the meter measures. For the reading

LEICAMETER MR

Black panel: The parts of the MR meter are:—

1. Film speed setting.
2. Aperture scale.
3. Battery test index.
4. Sector scale.
5. Meter switch.
6. Range knob.
7. Shutter speed scale.
8. Shutter speed index.
9. Index line.
10. Setting ring.
11. Meter needle.
12. Battery test switch.
13. Meter cell.

Right-hand column: To mount the meter on the Leica M, first turn the setting ring to its limit (*top*), lift, and turn farther (p. 221); then insert the meter in the shoe.

Finally turn the setting ring back to engage the Leica speed dial.

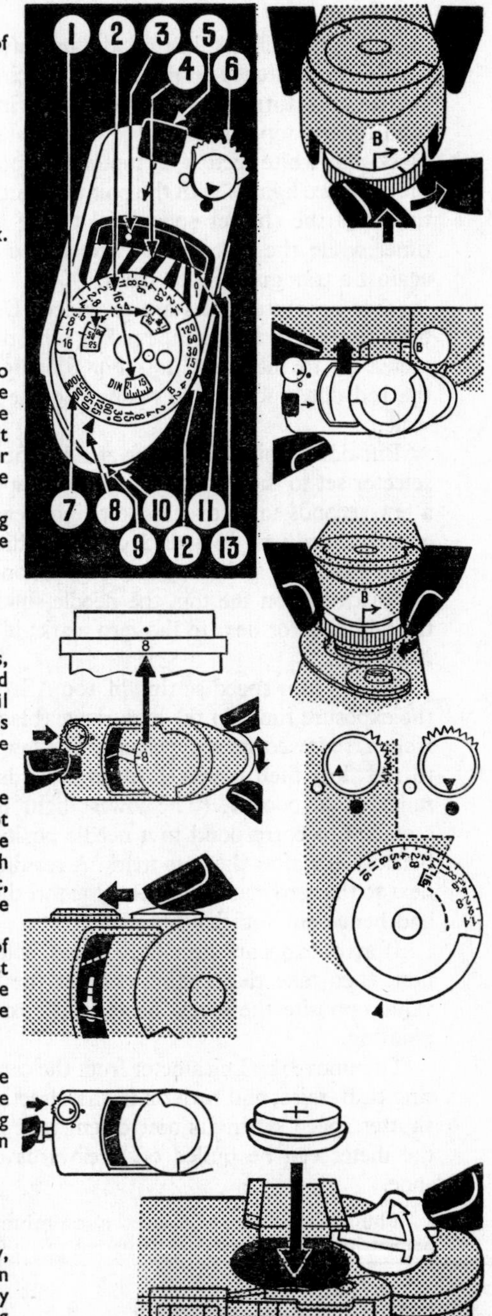

When taking readings, press the meter switch and turn the setting ring until the lens aperture set is opposite the meter needle (p. 222).

In poor light set the range knob to the red dot and use the red aperture scale; in bright light switch the knob to the black dot, and use the black aperture scale (*right*).

To check the state of the battery push the test switch; the meter needle should swing to the white dot (*left*).

Earlier versions of the Leicameter MR have the meter switch protruding from the side; it works in the same way.

To change the battery, open the swing-out lid in the meter base. The battery goes in with the lettering on top.

itself press the black key on the top inwards. This frees the needle and switches on the measuring circuit. Then, with this key pressed, turn the setting ring to bring the aperture to be used on the top disc opposite the pointer of the meter. The black-and-white sectors on top of the housing help in aligning the aperture figures with the pointer position. This at the same time sets the shutter speed dial to the appropriate exposure time, while the disc on the meter also shows the exposure against a triangular index mark.

Two aperture scales are provided. Use the black one for bright subjects, taking the reading with the knob on top of the meter set to the black dot. For dim light turn the knob to the red dot, and set the reading to the aperture on the red scale.

But don't point the meter at a bright light with the range selector set to the red dot. If this has happened, the cell needs a few seconds to recover its low-light sensitivity before giving accurate readings. As a quick check on this, set the meter range to the black dot and cover the cell with one finger. On pressing the black key on the top, the needle should return at least to the white sector next to the zero mark; if necessary, wait until it does so.

With a film speed setting of 100 ASA and aperture at *f*16, the exposure times in the high range (black dot setting) extend from 1/1000 second to ½ second. The low range (selector knob to red dot) then covers ⅛ to 60 seconds—a total measuring range of 60,000 : 1. (The lowest light measurement is here assumed to correspond to a needle position opposite the first black sector after the zero mark. A reading in the white sector next to the zero mark is too near the threshold of the instrument and hence not sufficiently reliable.)

If a set exposure time is required, select the shutter speed first, then take the reading and set the lens aperture to the value opposite the sector on the scale to which the needle is pointing.

To remove the Leicameter from the camera, turn the setting ring to B, raise, and turn on in the direction of the arrow. The shutter speed setting is now disengaged from the camera and the meter can be pulled off backwards out of the accessory shoe.

The Leicameter MR uses a cadmium sulphide cell in a measuring circuit carrying a current provided by a battery. This is a miniature mercury cell (PX 13 or PX 625), and lasts about a year or more in normal use.

To check the state of the battery slide the horizontal black rectangular key on the front of the meter housing towards the cell. The needle in the window on top should then swing out exactly over the white spot just beyond the middle of the scale. If the needle no longer reaches this spot, replace the battery.

The drain on the battery in use is very small, since the measuring circuit is only switched on while pressing the measuring key in the side. When the battery nears the end of its useful life it gives out fairly suddenly.

To change the battery, slide aside the panel marked with an arrow in the base of the meter, next to the fixing foot. (Do this while the meter setting ring is set to one of the time exposures and hence not in the way of the sliding panel.) Replace the battery by a new one, inserting the latter so that the side with the coloured ring goes in first.

The side marked with the + sign and the type number must be visible before closing the panel again. When closing, check that the edge of this cover engages the protruding ledge on the front of the meter.

If the measuring movement is correctly set, a meter reading with a piece of black paper pressed tightly against the front of the cell should make the needle point exactly to the zero mark.

If the indicating needle—with the battery in good working order, checked as mentioned above—consistently fails to line up with the zero mark, it can be realigned with the setting screw. This is on the underside of the meter, below the measuring key and surrounded by the figure 0 and two arrows. In practice such resetting should very rarely be necessary.

An earlier version of the Leicameter MR has the meter operating switch protruding from the side. It works in just the same way as the current version (handier for the Leica M4) with the switch on top.

The Leicameter MC

This is a predecessor of the MR and uses a selenium cell which covered the whole of the front of the meter. The cell has a wider angle of view (55 deg.) and does not permit such precise reading of smaller subject areas. The measuring range is not quite so wide, but can be extended with an amplifying cell which clips on the meter.

The selenium cell needs no batteries, and the circuit is switched on all the time.

To fit the meter to the Leica M cameras proceed in the same way as for the Leicameter MR. Film speeds are set in the same way, too. To take a reading it is not necessary to press any measuring switch or key.

Exposure times up to the limit of the normal low range (selector set to the red dot) are read off as with the Leicameter MR. To extend this setting an amplifying (booster) cell slides into the guides in front of the meter cell from above. With the booster cell in position the red aperture scale is used, but the exposures must be multiplied by 6 (or open up the lens by 2½ stops). An additional index mark with the symbol of the amplifying cell shows the correct setting directly.

The Leicameter MC is also suitable for incident light measurements. For this a rectangular opal disc is supplied which slides into the frame in front of the cell. The meter is then used off the camera. Take the reading by pointing the meter at the camera (p. 219). The reading can be used directly without multiplying it by any highlight factor.

For incident light readings in poor light, the amplifying cell also has a diffusing screen which slides into the frame around the front of the cell. Slide it in from the side.

When using the amplifying cell always set the range switch of the meter to the red dot.

An earlier version of the Leicameter, the model M, was slightly larger in size. The two ranges were obtained by opening or closing a cover in front of the cell, instead of a switch. The amplifying cell plugged into the side of the meter, and increased the sensitivity fourfold. The first models also indicated old-style Weston speeds, but had no amplifier index.

The Leicaflex Meter

The Leicaflex uses a photo cell similar to that of the Leicameter MR, i.e. a cadmium sulphide cell which requires a battery. The location of the cell—and also of the battery—differs on the two Leicaflex models. The operation of the meter system in conjunction with the coupled aperture speed controls of the Leicaflex has already been described on p. 160.

While the earlier Leicaflex has its cell mounted outside the camera (in front of the pentaprism housing), the cell of the Leicaflex SL is inside the camera body. The cell of the earlier Leicaflex takes in a field of view equivalent to that of the 90 mm. long focus lens. This is a reflected light meter, primarily for average readings from the camera position, and gives reasonably correct exposures with about 90 per cent of subjects normally encountered.

The advantage of any built-in meter is of course that the meter cannot be lost and it does not have to be handled separately. Having the system coupled with the camera settings greatly speeds up shooting. But wherever the meter has to go for special readings—independent highlight and shadow measurement, etc.—the camera has to go as well. And we have to view through the camera finder while taking such readings, to see and line up the matching pointer with the meter needle.

LEICAFLEX SL METER

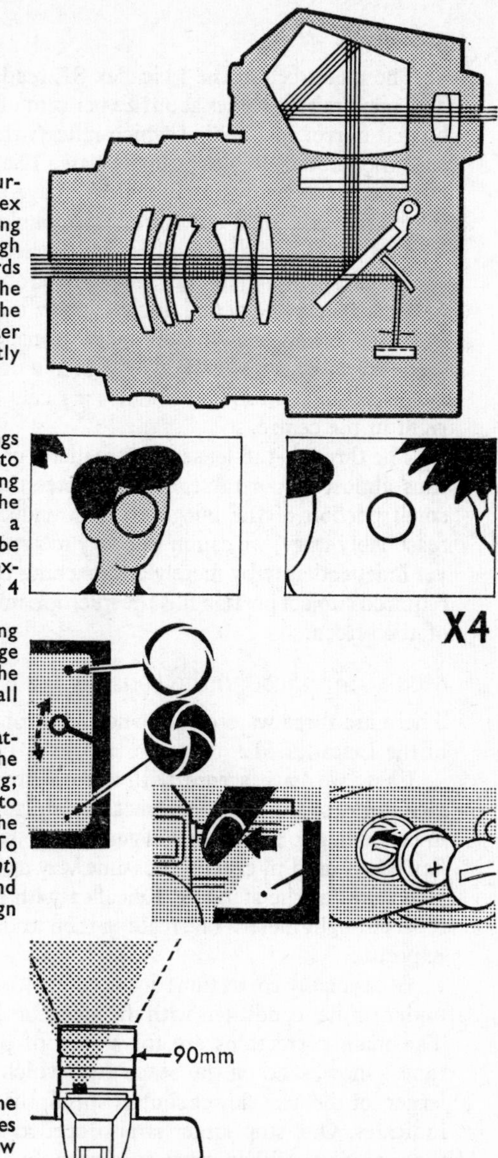

In the exposure measuring system of the Leicaflex SL part of the light reaching the mirror passes through and is deflected downwards by a second mirror into the meter cell in the base of the camera. This way the meter measures the light directly through the lens.

For selective readings arrange a medium tone to come into the measuring circle in the centre of the screen (*left*). Where a bright tone has to be measured, multiply the exposure time obtained by 4 (2 stops larger—*right*).

Moving the matching pointer towards the large spot or circle opens the aperture, towards the small spot it closes down.

To test the meter battery press the button at the side of the prism housing; the needle should point to the bottom spot in the finder screen (*centre*). To change the battery (*right*) unscrew the cover and insert a new cell, plus sign to the front.

OLD LEICAFLEX METER

The external cell of the older Leicaflex meter takes in the same angle of view as the 90 mm. lens.

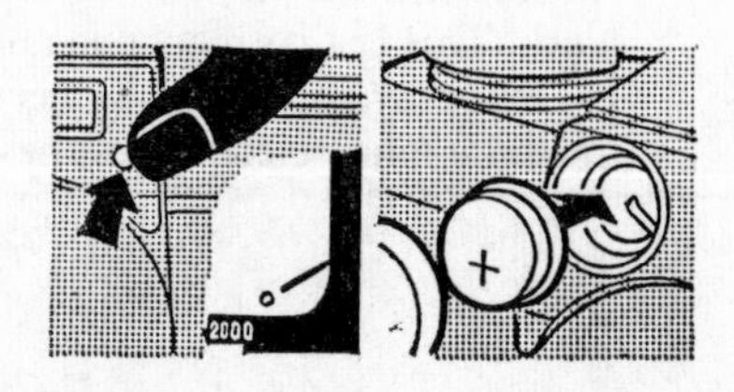

The meter battery is tested (*left*) and changed (*right*) in the same way as for the Leicaflex SL, but the test button and battery cover are differently located.

The meter cell of the Leicaflex SL reads through the lens. The main mirror passes about 22 per cent of the light to a small hinged mirror just behind which reflects the light beam down onto the photo cell in the camera base. The cell reads the light intensity in virtually an equivalent image plane. Further, the cell receives the light only through an angle equivalent to one-sixth of the film diagonal. The cell therefore "sees" a subject area corresponding to the central microprism circle on the finder screen. The actual angle of view depends on the lens: with the 50 mm. lens the cell takes in just under 8 deg.; with the 180 mm. lens it would take in about 2 deg. Hence the meter measures the light in only about 5 per cent of the picture area, right in the centre.

The through-the-lens exposure meter of the Leicaflex SL is thus almost a spot meter. It integrates the light over only a small portion of the image area. Provided image details are reasonably large, we can in this way measure them simply and yet independently by merely approaching the subject until the required subject portion fills the microprism circle in the centre of the screen.

Measuring through the Lens

There are three ways of utilising the through-the-lens facility of the Leicaflex SL.

First, we have scenes with reasonably evenly distributed brightnesses—for instance street scenes, landscapes, sports and in fact about 90 per cent of all general subjects. Here the Leicaflex SL is used in exactly the same way as any other exposure meter and as the standard Leicaflex with its external average reflected light meter. The reading then leads directly to correct exposures.

Occasionally corrections are needed—they are also required under similar conditions with the meter of the earlier Leicaflex. The main corrections are for scenes of predominantly light tones (snow, sand on the beach etc.) which need one lens stop larger (or the next slower shutter speed) than the meter reading indicates. One stop larger is also needed for colour shots on reversal film of low-contrast scenes (e.g. outdoors in dull weather). Otherwise the colour transparency tends to be rather dark. This last correction is not necessary with negative films.

Secondly, where the subject has reasonably large areas of medium tone, select one of these areas for measurement. Thus in a landscape a lawn or field makes a good medium tone, in a portrait choose dresses etc. which should record as a medium tone in the final picture. And if the scene has predominantly dark tones, again look for a suitable medium tone and take the reading from that. If necessary go closer to the subject until an area of the required tone just fills the central measuring circle.

As we are here selecting a medium subject tone, exposure corrections are rarely necessary.

If no suitable medium tone is available, read either a light or a dark tone—but with a deliberate correction. If the reading is made from the lightest tone (e.g. snow or sand) use an exposure of 2 lens stops larger for negative film, and one lens stop larger for reversal colour film (especially when no great contrasts are present).

If the reading is taken from a very dark tone such as a dark dress, a tree trunk etc. stop down the lens by 1 to 2 stops. For we are now measuring something which should be dark in the picture; on exposure without correction it would record too light, as the meter is calibrated to indicate correct exposures with medium subject tones.

Finally, with very contrasty subjects take the camera sufficiently close to the scene to measure both the brightest and the darkest area in turn in the measuring circle. For the correct exposure set the aperture (or speed) control halfway between the extreme values recorded.

This method can even be used for measuring the lighting balance in for instance a portrait or commercial studio set-up: separately read the light intensity of the subject portions which are most brightly lit and most deeply in shadow. If the ratio is more than 1 : 4 to 1 : 8 for black-and-white film and more than 1 : 2 to 1 : 4 for colour film (three stops and two stops respectively) direct extra fill-in light into the shadow areas.

The through-the-lens metering system offers virtually all the advantages of a separate exposure meter with much more precise aiming facilities for selecting exactly the subject area to be measured. Only incident light readings are not possible. But a measurement of a properly selected medium tone gives the same result in practice. So while a separate meter is often more versatile than an average reflected light meter built into the camera—as in the older Leicaflex—such a separate meter no longer has this advantage over the through-the-lens metering system of the Leicaflex SL.

Through-the-lens measurement becomes practically the only reliable way of taking readings of close-up subjects. There the camera is often so near and the lighting so concentrated on the one spot that it becomes difficult to aim a separate meter correctly. With the through-the-lens meter of the Leicaflex SL this is no problem—the microprism circle defines the measuring field.

Checking and Changing the Battery

The Leicaflex exposure meter is powered by a small battery. On the model SL this is housed in the camera base and on the earlier standard model inside the front of the pentaprism housing. The cell is behind a circular cover with either a screw slot or a milled ring. To change the battery, unscrew this cover and let the old battery drop out.

The correct type to use is a PX 625 mercury cell, carrying a white ring on one side.

Insert the new battery so that the white ring faces the contact spring inside the compartment. Before screwing the cover back, the type number of the battery and the + sign should be visible on top.

A PX 13 battery—the same as for the Leicameter MR—can also be used. This has a yellow-green ring; the main difference between it and the PX 625 is that the latter is more constant in output at low temperatures.

To check the state of the battery look through the camera viewfinder and press the small button in the left side of the pentaprism housing (model SL) or next to the meter cell itself (standard Leicaflex). The needle should swing down to point at the small black circle or ring in the lower right-hand corner of the screen. The mercury battery in the Leicaflex should last at least one year. Avoid however leaving the camera standing in strong light for long periods; the cell then needs a few minutes to recover before it can give correct readings in subdued light.

When not in use, keep the Leicaflex with the tensioning lever in its rest position. This switches off the meter circuit; otherwise the cell draws current from the battery, especially in bright light. The first models of the Leicaflex had no such switch in the winding lever; there it is best to keep the camera in a reasonably dark place when not in use.

The Choice of Shutter Speeds

The best shutter speed to choose depends on two factors: camera movement and subject movement.

However steadily we hold the Leica, a certain amount of movement is inevitable when we press the release. With a short enough exposure, the effect of this movement will be sufficiently slight not to register.

Most people can hold the Leica reasonably steady, under favourable conditions, to obtain sharp pictures at 1/60 or 1/50 second. This is the slowest speed we can regard as safe for hand-held shots. Some photographers may occasionally be able to hold the camera still for slower exposures, but a firm support such as a tripod is generally advisable for anything longer than 1/30 second.

With long-focus lenses, too, shorter exposure times are desirable for hand-held exposures. Since the long-focus lens magnifies the image, and the Leica is less evenly balanced with those lenses, any blur is greatly enlarged. The slowest safe speed with the 135 mm. and 200 mm. lenses is around 1/250 second, and it is best to use a tripod whenever possible.

Shutter Speed and Movement

When we take a picture of a moving subject, its image on the film will move during the exposure and produce a blur. The exposure time must then be short enough to ensure that this blur is too small to be noticeable—it must, in fact, be smaller than the circle of confusion (p. 208).

The slowest permissible shutter speed that will effectively "arrest" a moving subject in this way is thus governed by the image movement on the film, and depends on the speed and direction of the subject, and the scale of the image on the film.

The faster the subject moves (the greater the distance it covers in a given time), the greater will be the distance which its image covers. If we can arrest a cyclist going at 10 miles per hour with an exposure of 1/125 second, we should need 1/250 second at 20 miles.

The larger the image on the film, the greater is also the blur due to the movement. We shall get a larger image if we go closer, or if we use a long-focus lens; the effect is the same in either case. Thus a car 50 feet away, taken with a 50 mm. lens, will come out more or less the same size on the film as 90 feet away with the 90 mm. lens.

In both cases the car is about 300 focal lengths away from the Leica. The shutter speed we need is inversely proportional to the distance in focal lengths, provided we enlarge more or less the whole negative in each instance.

Finally, the image will seem to move farthest (and blur most) when the subject rushes right across the field of view. There we need the fastest shutter speeds. On the other hand, a car directly approaching (or, for that matter, directly driving away) will not move to either side. The image on the film only grows as the car comes nearer—the movement is much smaller. We can use considerably slower shutter speeds (some four to five times as slow) and still get a sufficiently sharp picture.

When the car comes towards the camera at an angle, the shutter speed required will be somewhere between the two extremes, depending on the angle of movement.

Movement Distortion

Occasionally, we shall find a curiously distorted image on negatives of fast-moving subjects. The most obvious case is that of squashed or elongated shapes, such as oval wheels on cars and other vehicles.

This distortion is due to the way in which the shutter exposes the film inside the Leica, moving across the negative as a slit (p. 42). If this slit moves in the same direction over the film as the image, the latter chases the shutter. As a result, the subject may appear to spread out in length without becoming unsharp. Similarly, if the image on the film moves against the direction of the shutter blinds, the object will look squashed in the picture.

The Leica shutter runs from right to left (as seen from behind the camera). If the subject runs from left to right, the image, being upside down and reversed, also runs from right to left, and will appear elongated. Anything moving from right to left will, for the same reason, appear compressed.

When we hold the Leica vertically with the subject moving horizontally, the shutter runs at right-angles to the image. This causes an even more obvious distortion, for any moving object appears to lean forward or back.

With the Leica held so that the shutter runs downwards (i.e. when the right hand is above the left) the lower part of the negative (with the top of the subject) is exposed later than the top of the negative (with the bottom of the subject). During that interval the upper part of the object in motion will have moved forward in relation to the lower parts, and the object as a whole appears to lean forward.

With the Leica held so that the shutter runs upwards, the image will appear to lean back.

Generally, the elongation or compression of the image is

MOVEMENT

The shutter speed we need to arrest a moving subject depends on the distance and direction of the subject as well as on its speed.

At greater distances we can use a slower shutter speed than when we are nearer (p. 231). At right-angles to the direction of the movement we need a faster speed than when the subject is approaching at an angle or coming directly towards the Leica.

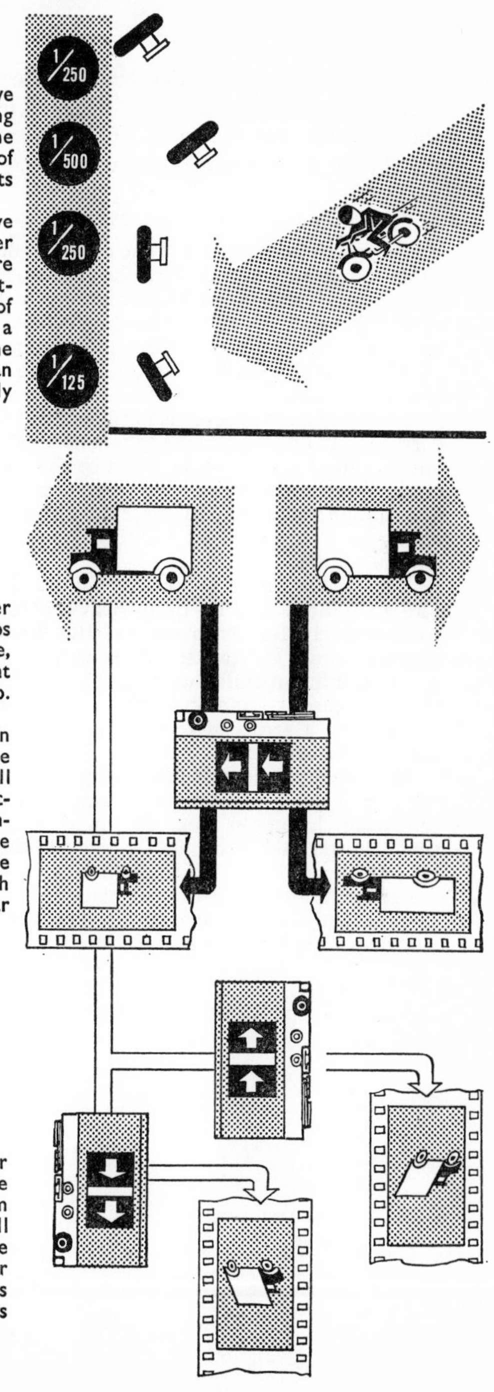

As the Leica shutter exposes the film in strips instead of all at once, various types of movement distortion may occur (p. 232).

If the subject moves in the same direction as the shutter, the image will move in the opposite direction and appear compressed on the negative (*left*). Conversely, if the image moves along with the shutter, it will appear elongated (*right*).

When the shutter moves at right-angles to the image, the latter will seem to lean over (p. 232). It will lean forward if we hold the Leica so that the shutter travels down (*left*), it leans back if the shutter travels upwards (*right*).

by no means obvious. The leaning effect, however, is, and may add to the impression of speed. Preferably the subject should lean forward, so if the Leica has to be held vertically, the shutter should move downwards.

Reciprocity and Time Exposures

So far we have assumed that the doubling or halving of exposure times for a subject of given brightness can be compensated exactly by closing down or opening up the lens aperture by one stop. This reciprocity relationship between the light intensity and exposure time is valid throughout most of the shutter speeds of fractions of a second. It does not quite hold, however, at longer exposure times.

In theory an exposure of, for instance, ¼ second at *f*1.4 should correspond, if we stop down to *f*4, to 2 seconds, at *f*8 to 8 seconds and at *f*16 to ½ minute. In practice the shot may require at *f*4 around 3 seconds, at *f*8 about 15–20 seconds and at *f*16 as much as a minute and a half. In effect the film behaves as if it had lost speed when exposed at lighting levels requiring such long exposure times.

This is known as reciprocity failure. Its extent varies from film to film; it can be quite heavy with some materials and comparatively less with others. But it very rarely arises at exposure times shorter than ¼ second.

Some film manufacturers publish correction factors when their films are exposed under these conditions. If no such factors are known, a series of test exposures will establish necessary exposure adjustments.

Reciprocity failure is disturbing with colour film—not only because of the limited exposure latitude, but because the colour rendering changes as well. So where possible, aim at exposure times shorter than ¼ second. Or take additional shots of the same subject exposed for two to eight times the time suggested by meter reading or exposure calculation. (Since the need for this can arise only with comparatively static subjects, there is usually sufficient time for such a procedure.)

FILTER TECHNIQUE

Filters modify the way in which the film translates colours into tones of black, white, and grey.
Filters correct colour reproduction, or produce special effects.
Extra exposure is required with a filter.

To a certain extent we can control the way black-and-white film interprets colours of nature in tones of grey. This we do with the help of coloured filters placed in front of the lens.

A filter modifies the light that reaches the film by transmitting rays of its own colour more than rays of other colours. Thus objects of the same or similar colours as the filter become lighter, and opposite colours darker on the final picture.

An orange filter, for instance, will brighten orange or red parts of the subject and darken blue portions. A green filter will make green areas appear lighter and red ones darker.

Correction and Effect Filters

Such control over the tones of the image is useful for two purposes. We can correct imperfections in the tone reproduction of the film, or we can purposely reinterpret tone values to create special effects.

In the first case we speak of correction filters, and in the second case of effect filters.

An example of filtering for correction is the use of yellow filters in landscape photography (p. 305). The film is more sensitive to the blue of the sky than our eyes are, and thus tends to reproduce this colour rather light. As a result clouds will not show up very strongly. A yellow filter darkens the sky and increases the contrast between it and the white clouds.

Special correction filters are available for colour photography (p. 272).

As an instance of effect filtering we may use a red filter in architectural shots (p. 321). This makes the sky appear much darker and dramatically sets off yellow stonework against it.

Effect filters are often used as contrast filters to create tone contrasts where the subject shows colour contrast.

Thus a red object and a green background will, correctly reproduced, have much the same brightness value, and appear as similar tones of grey in the picture. To differentiate them, we may distort the tones by using either a green filter, which will make the subject appear dark against a light background, or a red filter, which will show up the subject as light against dark.

This method is of particular use in copying (p. 412) and photomicrography, where the colour values are irrelevant as long as they stand out from each other.

Filter Factors

Since the filter cuts down the light that reaches the film, we must give more exposure to compensate. The exposure increase is quoted in terms of a filter factor (p. 483). Each filter has a different factor which also depends on the colour of the light, and the exact colour sensitivity of the film.

Thus filter factors for yellow and red filters are lower in artificial light, which is comparatively yellowish, than in daylight. Similarly, certain high-speed panchromatic films which are specially sensitive to red light will need a lower factor with the same red filter than more evenly balanced films.

Filter factors are usually quoted as approximate values. There is not much point in attempting to allow for them more exactly than we can determine the exposure; in accuracy closer than about 20 per cent is wasted. In other words, we can ignore odd fractions in factors above 4; increasing the exposure 4½ times has much the same effect as increasing it 4 times or 5 times.

We may, however, control the result to some extent by using higher or lower factors than those recommended. A low factor —under-exposing the picture—accentuates the darkening effect of the filter, while a high factor, through over-exposing, emphasizes the brightening up role.

For instance, if we want to differentiate red roses against green foliage, under-exposure with a red filter will make the blooms appear normal against unnaturally dark leaves. Over-exposure (a high factor) will make the blooms appear very light against normal leaves.

Generally under-exposure increases the contrast between the tones to be separated by filtering. Over-exposure decreases it, and makes the filter less effective.

The Leitz Filter Fittings

Leica filters are available in several types of mounts to fit the different Leica lenses (p. 483).

The standard filter fitting is a 39 mm. screw-in mount (E39) which fits most current lenses except certain high-aperture and telephoto types. The filter can be used together with the lens hood, as the latter clips on to the outside rim of the lens (p. 116). The outside diameter is 42 mm., and these lenses will take 42 mm. push-on filters. They are, however, less firm.

The current filter mounts are also available without filters, to take filter glasses for colour photography etc.

The larger current lenses take large-diameter screw-in filters. These screw into the front lens mount.

Some of the screw-mounted Leica lenses, especially the older types, take a 36 mm. push-on mount (A36) which has a clamping ring and screw to hold it firmly. Slip such a filter over the lens mount, and tighten the screw. Fit the filter in such a way that the screw is underneath the camera, and does not interfere with the finder. The front of the filter will take the lens hood.

Some of the newest large-diameter Leica M lenses and all Leicaflex lenses have a screw-in retaining ring to take so-called Series filters—plain glasses with metal rims. To fit a Series filter, unscrew the front ring (marked with the appropriate Series number), drop the filter disc into the front of the lens and screw the ring back again. Do not screw in too tightly—otherwise the ring may be difficult to remove again. Unscrew by gripping one edge of the ring only—and not the two opposite edges. This avoids distorting the rather springy ring.

Series VI fittings take $1\frac{5}{8}$ inch (41.3 mm.) diameter filter discs and have a screw thread of 44 mm.

Series VII take 2 inch (50.8 mm.) diameter discs and have a screw thread of 53.5 mm.

Series VIII take $2\frac{1}{2}$ inch (63.5 mm.) discs and have a screw thread of 66.2 mm.

Series IX take 3 inch (75 mm.) discs; these are used only on the later 21 mm. Super Anqulon-R *f*4 of the Leicaflex and are held in place by a clip-on lenshood.

The front of the 21 mm. Super Angulon and 28 mm. Elmarit for Leica M cameras takes 48 mm. screw-in filters, but Series VII filters can be placed over the front of the lens and held in position by the lens hood. The old 21 mm. Super Angulon-R for the Leicaflex uses the screw-in lens hood as the retaining ring for the Series VIII filters.

Series filters are standard sizes available from a number of manufacturers and sometimes in special absorptions for certain purposes.

A special aperture setting ring No. 16621 is available for the screw-mounted 50 mm. Elmar *f*3.5. This fits over the front of the lens and engages the aperture lever; a rotating rim linked with the lever takes the filter.

This permits changing the aperture of this lens by rotating the filter—without removing it.

When the screw-in supplementary lenses are used on a 36-mm. lens front they protrude in front of the lens. A special intermediate ring then takes the push-on filter.

Special adapter rings are available for using the 39 mm. screw-in filters on 36 mm. push-on lens mounts of older lenses (No. 13154) and on the 50 mm. Summitar lens (No. 13078). Other adapter rings take Summitar filters on 36 mm. lens mounts or on 39 mm. screw-in mounts. These rings cut out some unnecessary duplication of filter sets that have to be acquired when older lens types are in use. They are not, however, advisable for ultra-wide-angle lenses, since the mount may cut into the lens field.

Screw-in mounts for the older Summaron, Elmar and Hektor lenses also used to be made, but these mounts are now mostly discontinued.

The Leica Filter Range

Leitz filters are made of solid glass dyed in the mass, and are thus impervious to damp or tropical climates. They are ground parallel to a high degree of accuracy.

The range includes a series of yellow filters, a yellow-green, an orange, a red, a blue, and an ultra-violet filter.

Filters of other makes, in particular types not included in the Leica range, can be fitted in the special filter mounts made for the purpose. Such filters may, of course, be used directly if they are already bought in a push-on mount of the right size.

Although there is quite a selection of Leica filters, we won't need them all at once. In fact, for general photography a yellow-green is quite sufficient. To this may be added one or two of the others as necessary for special purposes.

The yellow filters Nos. 0, 1 *and* 2, serve mainly as correction filters and will darken blue skies, increasing the contrast between sky and clouds. The effect is greatest with the No. 2 filter, and slightest with the No. 0.

The yellow filters also improve snow scenes in sunshine by darkening the usually bluish snow shadows. The daylight filter factor ranges from 1½ to 2½.

The yellow-green filter acts similarly to the yellow as far as blue skies are concerned, and in addition darkens reddish colours, such as skin tones. People at the seaside, taken through the green filter will look really sunburnt.

In artificial light, too, the green filter improves the tone rendering of the skin. Due to the reddish-yellow quality of lamplight, faces normally tend to look pale and textureless, particularly with highly red-sensitive pan film.

Avoid using a green filter with freckle-faced sitters; it accentuates freckles. The proper filter to eliminate such skin blemishes is a yellow (No. 1) or orange one.

In landscape shots the green filter brings out the brilliance of green grass and foliage, which otherwise are inclined to come out rather dark. The factor is about 3.

The orange filter is really an effect filter. It appreciably darkens the blue sky, and produces dramatic stormy effects.

In distant landscapes the orange filter penetrates atmospheric haze and shows the view much clearer than the unaided camera lens. On the other hand, this filter will bleach skin tones and destroy textural detail. It has a factor of 4–5.

The light red filter acts in the same way as the orange filter, but the effect is stronger. The filter factor is correspondingly higher, too, being in the region of 10–15.

The medium and deep red filters are designed for infra-red photography with infra-red film (p. 453).

The blue filter is intended for artificial light portraiture with certain high-speed films of increased red sensitivity. Normally such films make faces look too pale, blue eyes too dark, and little or no differentiation between lips and skin. The blue filter reduces the excess red response of the film to yield a more balanced rendering. The factor is about 1½.

The ultra-violet filter holds back ultra-violet radiation. Its special application is in mountain photography at high altitudes above about 7,000 feet. There even a yellow filter will darken the sky excessively.

The ultra-violet filter is important in alpine photography also because the Leica lenses are corrected mainly for visible light. This correction is not as good for ultra-violet rays. In regions where the light is rich in such rays, the sharpness of the image may therefore deteriorate slightly unless the ultra-violet rays are filtered out.

The ultra-violet filter is useful in colour photography, to reduce the blue cast in distant views due to haze (p. 272).

Normally, the ultra-violet filter needs no exposure increase.

The Polarizing Filter

Occasionally, a subject includes disturbing reflections of light from shiny surfaces such as glass, china, polished or varnished furniture, painted articles, and even water. These reflections can be reduced with the help of a special filter.

Light is not coloured by being reflected, but it acquires a different property; it becomes polarized. The reflection is strongest at a certain angle depending on the reflecting material. With glass the ideal angle of reflection should be around 35 deg. This change is not visible to the eye, but a polarizing filter can stop such polarized light.

Through the polarizing filter, reflections appear stronger or weaker as we rotate the filter. In one position they may disappear altogether; with the filter turned through 90 deg. they will be there in their full strength.

To use the polarizing filter, look at the subject through it, and rotate the mount until the result appears right.

The Leica polarizing filters carry a series of numbers engraved on the mount, signifying angles of rotation. Note the number on top, and fit the filter over the lens with the same number pointing to the top of the Leica. With the screw-in polarizing filter the filter disc rotates in the mount for orientation after screwing in the filter.

One version of the polarizing filter has the filter set in a rotating swing-out mount, complete with lens hood. This is hinged to a ring which clamps on the lens mount.

To use this polarizer mount the ring over the camera lens, so that the locking screw is at the bottom. Tighten the screw to secure the ring. Swing the filter up as far as it will go, view the scene through the finder and rotate the filter itself by the milled ring until the effect is right. Then swing down the mount to bring the filter in front of the lens. As this swings the filter through 180 deg., the effect will now be the same over the camera lens as it was in front of the finder.

In addition to light reflected from shiny surfaces (but not from metal) the blue light of the sky is also partly polarized. The polarizing filter will therefore darken blue skies without affecting other colour values. This is specially useful in colour photography for darkening the sky, but works equally well with black-and-white film.

The effect is greatest when shooting at right-angles to the sun. The Leica polarizing filter has a factor of 3.

LIGHTING TECHNIQUE

Side lighting adds life and shows up modelling.
Against-the-light shots can create striking pictorial results.
Artificial light, being fully under our control, lends itself well to special lighting effects.
Always keep direct light out of the lens.

Photography is the art of drawing with light. Its images are patterns of light and shade, created by the lighting as much as by the subject.

Most of the time we shall depend on daylight, which we have to take more or less as we find it. Indoors and at night we can use lamps. That is a bit more cumbersome, but the direction, angle and effect of the lighting are fully under control, and we can vary them at will.

Lighting Outdoors

The best outdoor lighting for most subjects is sunlight coming more or less from the side. This picks out highlights, and casts well-defined shadows, showing up the different planes of the subject. It is the liveliest type of illumination; it gives modelling, and throws texture into relief.

The more brilliant the sun, the deeper the shadows. On a hazy day the haze scatters enough light to give the shadows a certain luminosity, but when the air is clear, and there are no clouds in the sky, everything not directly lit by the sun will come out almost black. In such a case look for reflecting surfaces, such as the brightly lit wall of a house, to throw light into the darker parts of the scene, especially with near subjects.

Suitable choice of lighting can also accentuate the background or subdue it by keeping it in deep shadow. That may mean waiting until the light is right, but it's often worth the time.

When the sun comes from behind the camera, the subject gets the most light. But there is very little shadow, and the result looks somewhat lifeless and flat.

As we are dealing with brightly lit areas only, such views will, however, need less exposure.

Against the Light

When we point the Leica into the light, shadows loom large, especially when the sun is low, and near objects form intriguing shadow patterns on the foreground. Highlights are small, but brilliant in comparison with the dark areas. Frequently the light forms a bright halo around the subject, and translucent objects like leaves show up as if luminous themselves, as they are lit from behind.

Against-the-light shots are, in fact, among the most successful subjects for creating a pictorial effect out of silhouettes and brilliant outlines.

Watch the sun, though; it must never shine directly into the lens. Otherwise the glare will cause ghost images by reflections from inside the optical system, and spoil the brilliance of the picture by degrading the shadows with scattered light.

While coated lenses are much less prone to this trouble, even they cannot cope with light shining directly into them. Therefore shield the lens, either with a lens hood (p. 117) or by standing in the shade of a doorway or tree. Often one hand or a hat held by somebody else will serve to shade the lens. But see that the hat or other shield does not appear in the picture.

Since the shadow areas are large as well as dark, give a little more exposure. But not too much—about twice normal—for the subject is very contrasty and over-exposure will destroy all detail in the highlights. When using a meter, take a highlight reading (p. 219).

With close-ups some extra light in the shadows will be desirable to prevent them coming out completely black. Use a white sheet or suitable reflector, or even a synchronized flash bulb (p. 267).

Against-the-light shots also lend themselves well to soft-focus effects. A soft-focus lens or lens attachment (p. 211) tends to spread the bright highlights a little into adjacent shadow areas, turning the crisp and hard scene into a more softly luminous view.

Diffused Light

When the sky is overcast, most outdoor pictures will be dull. Yet sometimes the very flatness of the scene may make a picture; not a bold and solid one, but something more like a sketch, consisting largely of light and medium greys.

Such high-key effects are often attractive, provided the subject itself is fairly light in tone. Avoid excessive detail in this case. When there is not sufficient light and shade to give clarity and boldness, simple subjects are more successful.

Allow plenty of exposure to record sufficient detail in the darker parts of the scene.

Lighting with Lamps

Household lamps are much weaker than sunlight, and generally call for longish time exposures. They are quite adequate for pictures of inanimate subjects.

For shots at 1/25 second or faster, more powerful Photoflood or studio lamps are necessary. Photoflood lamps are the size of an ordinary 75 watt household lamp, and are overrun to give more light.

A Photoflood No. 1 consumes 275 watts but burns as brightly as a 750–800 watt lamp, while a Photoflood No. 2 gives 1,500 watts worth of light for only 500 watts.

As a Photoflood No. 1 only burns for about two hours under this strain (six hours for a No. 2 lamp) it should be switched on for only a few seconds for the exposure itself. The best way of doing this is to run the lamps at half power while setting up the lighting, and switch over to full power (e.g. with the help of a series-parallel switch) when everything is ready. This warms up the filament more gradually, and extends the life of the bulb. It is, in fact, better for the lamp than switching on from cold every time.

When using Photofloods, avoid overloading the circuit, or the fuses will blow. On a 230 volt mains supply, a normal 5 amp. lighting circuit will carry up to four No. 1 or two No. 2 Photofloods. If more lamps are required, connect them to a 10 or 15 amp. power point.

The wiring must be heavy enough to carry the current, too. Cabtyre or similar rubber-covered cables stand up best to hard wear, even if trodden on.

For frequent use, high-power studio lamps are more profitable. They are available in various sizes, from 250 watts upwards. Though more expensive than Photofloods, their burning life is several hundred hours.

A 1,000 watt studio lamp also gives out almost as much heat as, and gets considerably hotter than, a 1,000 watt fire. So keep the lamp away from things that might scorch easily or even catch fire, such as thin paper shades, flimsy fabrics, and the like.

Reflectors and Spotlights

For greater efficiency, photographic lighting units have reflectors to direct most of the light on to the subject.

The reflector may be white or silvered cardboard, but aluminium ones are more durable.

The choice of the reflector influences the character of the illumination. Large and shallow reflectors give a widely spread flood of light, while smaller deep reflectors give a narrower and more directional beam.

Polished reflectors concentrate the light more than matt ones, but the latter produce less glare and are more comfortable.

Spotlights consist of a lamp placed behind a collector lens; they give a concentrated beam and are useful for effect lighting.

Certain types of Photoflood lamps exist with a reflector-shaped internally silvered bulb; this acts as a spotlight by itself. High-power quartz-iodine lamps also often come complete in reflector units to yield directed light beams.

Exposure with Lamps

As we know just how much light a lamp gives, we can work out exposures more accurately than for daylight shots.

The exposure itself depends on the number and strength of the lamps as well as their distance. It also depends on the direction of the light and on the subject brightness.

These factors can easily be tabulated in a suitable exposure table or some type of exposure calculator.

The light on a subject falls off rapidly with increasing distance. An object 2 yards from a lamp gets only one-quarter as much light—and thus needs four times as much exposure—as if it were 1 yard away. At 3 yards the brightness is only one-ninth; it is inversely proportional to the square of the distance.

When the angle between the direction of the lamp and of the Leica is more than 45 deg. the effective light is reduced. And when the lamp shines directly from the side or even behind the subject, it produces lighting effects, but makes no useful contribution to the general illumination. Such effect lights are therefore ignored for exposure determination.

Finally, a light subject in a small brightly painted room obviously reflects more light than a dark subject in a large dark hall. While most exposure figures refer to average subjects, they need adjustment for special conditions.

To get the exposure required with two or three lamps at the same distance, add up their wattages. If the lamps are at different distances, add up the reciprocals of the exposure required with each separately, and turn the result round again to get the correct exposure.

For instance, if one lamp needs 1/30 second by itself, and the other 1/60 second, the combined exposure would be 30/1 + 60/1 = 90/1, turned round 1/90 second. In practice it is more reliable to set 1/125 second and open the lens aperture by half a stop.

With whole seconds turn the numbers into fractions and add up, then turn round again. Thus where the separate values are 5 and 3 seconds respectively, the sum of the fractions is $\frac{1}{5} + \frac{1}{3}$ or $\frac{8}{15}$, which gives $\frac{15}{8}$ or about two seconds.

If the second lamp needs more than five times as much exposure by itself as the main lamp, ignore the weaker one altogether. It won't appreciably affect the exposure.

Avoid set-ups—especially for colour shots—requiring long time exposures. There reciprocity failure effects can upset exposure calculations (p. 234).

Lighting Balance

Lamps are directional, they brilliantly light up whatever faces them, and cast deep, dark shadows.

A subject may look all right to the eye, but it will photograph too contrasty. The visual effect should appear appreciably flatter than the result intended, since we can see shadow detail even when the film can no longer record it satisfactorily. Except for certain dramatic lighting effects, such shadows therefore have to be brightened to balance the lighting.

The simplest way of doing that is to use a reflecting screen to throw some light into the shadows. The screen may be white cardboard or a white sheet or even a towel, or else a piece of card covered with silver paper. Put this fairly close to the subject to derive the maximum effect from it.

Alternatively, use a second lamp. If it is of the same strength as the main light, keep this fill-in light about one and a half times to twice as far from the subject, to get the best lighting balance. This will give a brightness range of about 3 : 1 or 4 : 1 between highlights and shadows. For colour shots (p. 224) that is the maximum permissible contrast; preferably the difference should be even less.

FLASH TECHNIQUE

Flash can be the sole light source in a shot, or it can supplement daylight or other illumination such as lamps.
The Leica synchronization is adjustable to allow for different types of flash and different shutter speeds.

An artificial light source of a special type is the flash bulb. Unlike an electric lamp which burns continuously, a flash bulb lights up for only a fraction of a second in an intense flash, giving enough light to take one picture. This light comes from a miniature explosion of aluminium or zirconium wire burning in an atmosphere of oxygen.

The amount of light that a flash bulb yields depends on the quantity of aluminium in it, and is accurately determined for each type of bulb.

Every flash bulb will yield one flash for one exposure, and is discarded afterwards.

A flash bulb, therefore, is a store of light in standard portions, which we can utilize whenever required.

The only electrical side of flash is the current—derived from a small battery—needed to ignite the charge in the bulb. With flash bulbs we are thus independent of available lighting conditions and of any outside electrical supply.

We can use one or more flash bulbs as the sole source of lighting for our pictures. Alternatively, we may combine the flash with other lighting—daylight or electric lamps—either as the main source or as auxiliary light.

We can even use flash to supplement sunshine in certain types of outdoor shots (p. 267).

Firing the Flash

The batteries to fire the bulbs are contained in the battery case of a suitable flash holder which also takes the flash bulb. The flash holder may be mounted on the camera to make a handy unit.

The firing circuit of the flash gun uses mostly a small 15 to 30 volt anode battery (as fitted in hearing aids) and a capacitor. The latter is able to store up electrical energy until required for use. The battery charges the capacitor; on closing the circuit the capacitor discharges through the bulb and fires the flash.

The main advantage of this system is that it wastes very little current. Only just enough is used to fire one flash. When the battery is almost exhausted, it will still charge the capacitor with the same amount of electrical energy, though it may take a few seconds more to do so. One battery thus lasts for many hundreds of flashes, and will fire the bulb reliably every time. The voltage of the discharge is high enough to fire not only one but several flash bulbs simultaneously.

Actually most flash bulbs can be fired with a voltage as low as 3 volts, and old flash guns used to work directly with 3 to 6 volt cells. However, the battery must then yield a sufficient firing current, and partly exhausted batteries—even if still good enough for use in a pocket torch—lead to unreliable flashing and synchronization.

Taking Flash Pictures

The flash of a flash bulb lasts about 1/200 to 1/20 second. The ideal way of using flash is to synchronize this period with the opening of the shutter, using contacts built into the latter.

Put a flash bulb in the flash gun, and mount the latter on the camera. Connect to the shutter by a flash cable plugged into the appropriate socket (marked with a bulb symbol). Set the shutter speed and aperture.

Sight the subject, and press the release button. This automatically closes the firing circuit at the right time through the flash contacts of the Leica and releases the flash during exposure.

The flash holder need not be attached to the Leica; we may connect it, or even several flash holders, by means of extension cables, and hold the flash or flashes some distance away for various lighting effects.

Older Leica models (I to IIIc) which do not incorporate flash contacts may be fitted with built-in or external synchronizers and used in the same way.

Alternatively, we can take pictures by the open flash method. That involves opening the shutter on B or Z, firing the flash by means of a separate firing switch on the flash holder, and closing the shutter again. Naturally the camera must be mounted on a tripod.

Safety Points

Always use a reflector. This not only utilizes the light more efficiently, but also protects the photographer behind the camera from injury if a bulb should shatter. The risk is very small, and nearly all bulbs carry a safety coating of lacquer. But they have been known to blow up and can then be dangerous at close range. For the same reason, use a safety shield of transparent or translucent plastic for close-up flash shots.

Many modern flash bulbs carry an indicator spot on top of the bulb. If the bulb is in order, this spot should be blue. Never use a bulb where that spot has turned pink; the danger of shattering is appreciable in such a case.

Never fire synchronized flash bulbs from the electric mains. This may damage the camera, give serious electric shocks, and may blow the fuses. Even with open flash only a few of the largest bulbs are suitable for high-voltage firing.

Flash Bulb Characteristics

Bulbs available for flash photography differ in their light output, the duration of the flash, and their firing delay.

The light output is usually stated in lumen-seconds and measures the effective light a bulb yields.

The flash duration is the time during which the flash stays alight. In practice we are interested in the effective flash duration. This is the time during which the flash is above its half-peak intensity, i.e. where the brightness of the flash is more than half its maximum or peak brightness. The light before the flash builds up to this half-peak, and when it dies down again, does not contribute appreciably to the exposure.

As the shutter of the Leica uncovers the negative in strips synchronized flash shots need a long enough flash duration to last the time while the shutter blinds travel across the film. Special long-flash bulbs are available and can be used for flash shots at all shutter speeds up to 1/2000 second. They are the only fully satisfactory type of bulb for synchronization at fast speeds with the Leica or Leicaflex shutter.

Other types of flash bulbs have a limited use when we have no focal plane bulb at hand. While focal plane bulbs stay evenly bright during their effective flash duration, other flash bulbs build up to a peak and die down again fairly rapidly. The negative is therefore not exposed evenly.

The firing delay is the time the flash takes to build up to its half-peak intensity after firing. With some types of bulb, the peak delay is more important, i.e. the time the flash takes to reach its greatest brightness.

NEW PICTORIAL VALUES

As the pioneer miniature, the Leica led the way in the break-away from conventional pictorialism. We do not have to content ourselves with arranged pictures that are static for long enough to be recorded at leisure.

Leica photography can keep pace with any subject. Leica pictorialism therefore utilizes the elements of movement of the live subject, as well as unusual aspects and viewpoints. Its aim is to concentrate on the parts instead of the whole (p. 250), to record the striking rather than the pretty qualities of the subject. We deal with spontaneous glimpses of our surroundings and show them in patterns of shapes and dynamic outlines.

Our camera is not bound by tradition—often based on the limits of the medium—to an established style. Its only style is freedom from laid-down rules; we get at the core of the subject in the most telling way.

Leica pictures thus have an intimate quality about them portraying everyday reality. Whether we are looking at the delicate tracery of trees (pp. 252, 255), a new perspective of shapes and patterns of scenery (pp. 253, 254), striking lighting effects, or odd impressions of uncommon subjects (pp. 251, 256), we are interpreting something of life in a changing scene.

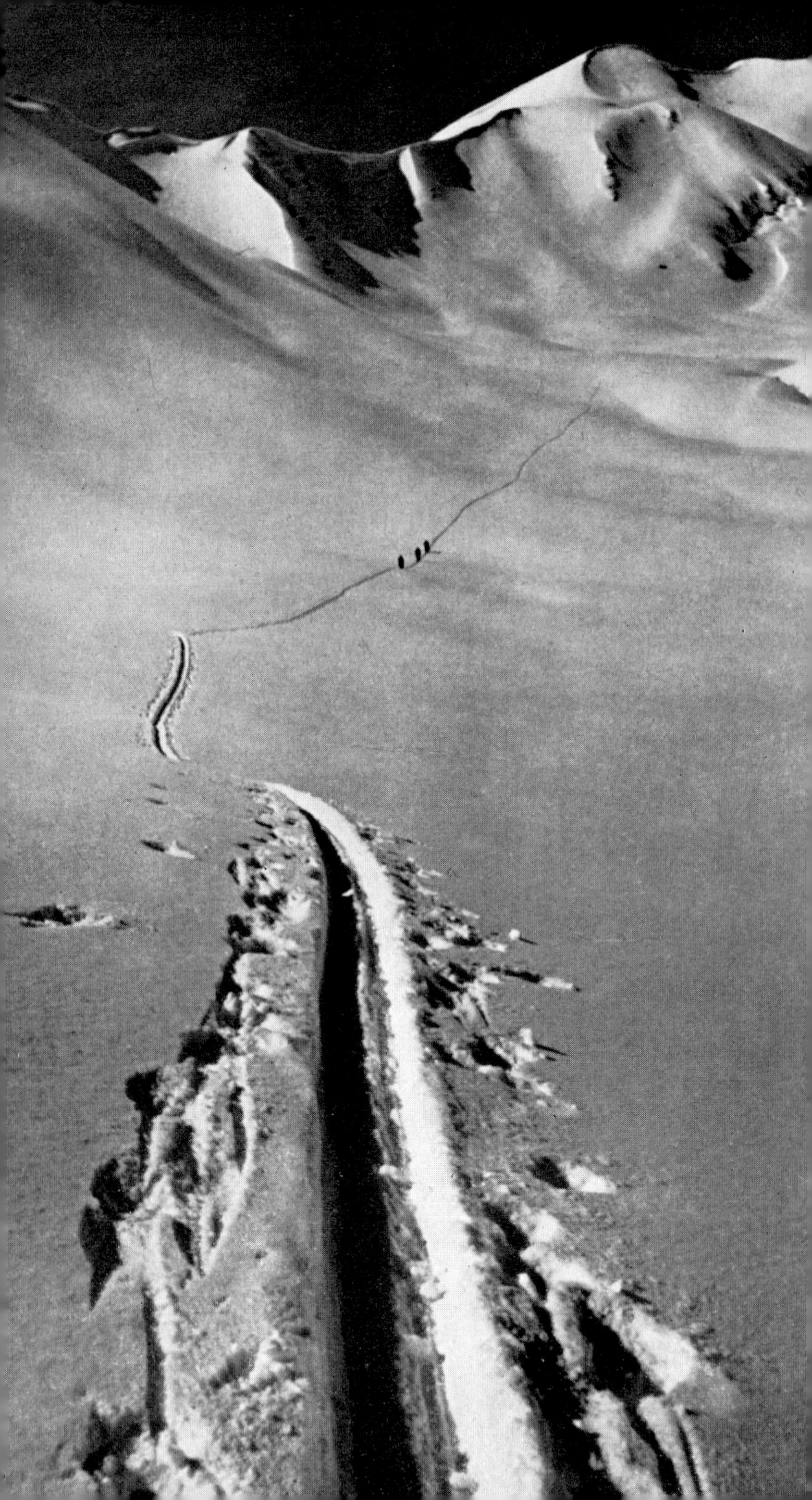

Page 249: Racing boats. 50 mm. lens, fine-grain pan film, yellow filter, 1/50 sec., *f*5.6. Photo: *P. Cornelius.*

Page 250: Fountain in Sheffield. 50 mm. lens, fine-grain pan film, 1/1000 sec., *f*11. Photo: *J. Sadovy.*

Page 251: Statue on Chelsea Embankment, London. 50 mm. lens, fast pan film, 1/100 sec., *f*8. Photo: *J. Sadovy.*

Page 252: Church in the mist. 90 mm. lens, fine-grain pan film, 1/20 sec., *f*12.5. Photo: *L. Himpelmann.*

Page 253: Flooded fields. 35 mm. lens, fine-grain pan film, 1/100 sec., *f*5.6. Photo: *A. Tritschler.*

Page 254: Ski trail. 35 mm. lens, fine-grain pan film, light yellow filter, 1/100 sec., *f*9. Photo: *A. Tritschler.*

Page 255: Forest. 135 mm. lens, fine-grain pan film, 1/100 sec., *f*9. Photo: *A. Tritschler.*

Above: Beach at Costa Brava, Spain. 35 mm. lens, fast pan film, deep yellow filter, 1/100 sec., *f*16. Photo: *J. Sadovy.*

Flash duration and firing delay are important factors in synchronizing the flash bulb with the Leica shutter. They are measured in milliseconds (thousandths of a second).

Flash bulbs, other than focal plane types, are thus often classified by their firing delay. Slow (class S) bulbs have a peak delay of 30 milliseconds, medium (class M) bulbs take 20 milliseconds, and fast bulbs of short flash duration take 7–9 milliseconds.

Flash bulbs also vary in size and in the type of caps with which they are fitted. Modern bulbs for amateur use—and, in fact, for flash shots at fairly close range—are quite small and have the contact wires protruding directly from the glass base. There are two types of these so-called capless bulbs: the European type and the American (AG–1 type). Flash guns for each kind must have suitable fittings.

Small focal plane bulbs usually have a metal bayonet cap with a single centre contact. This fits into appropriate bayonet sockets. They resemble certain types of motor-car headlamp bulbs. Larger flash bulbs may have an Edison screw cap, similar to some types of household bulbs. These are mostly used for professional photography for lighting large areas.

Electronic Flash

Ordinary flash bulbs can be used once only. There is also electronic flash which may be used repeatedly.

With electronic flash the light is derived from a high-voltage electric discharge inside a special flash tube. Such a tube will give several thousand flashes, lasting about 1/500 to 1/2000 second each.

The advantage of electronic flash is its short flash duration, which will arrest the fastest movement, and the low cost per flash. Small electronic flash units are quite compact and can fit into the accessory shoe of the Leica or Leicaflex. The light output is, however, rather low. More powerful units become bulky and expensive. Really large units are mainly suitable for studio use.

Electronic flash units may be powered from rechargeable miniature accumulators, dry batteries, and/or from the electric mains.

The firing delay of most electronic flash units is negligible, being about one-hundredth that of a flash bulb. This is classified as class X.

Leica Synchronization

The Leica cameras made since 1950 are fitted with built-in flash contacts which close the firing circuit of any flash gun connected to the camera and thus synchronize the flash to the shutter opening.

The Leica M models carry two separate synchronizing circuits, with their own sockets for flash bulbs and electronic flash. The sockets are marked respectively with the symbol of a flash bulb and of a lightning arrow.

For flash bulbs of the focal plane type and classes S and M connect the flash gun to the flash socket below the accessory shoe, marked with the symbol of a bulb. This gives a firing delay of about 18 milliseconds at all shutter speeds. The usable speeds depend on the bulb, and go up to 1/1000 second with focal plane bulbs, or 1/30 second with smaller class M bulbs.

For electronic flash use the second flash socket next to the finder eyepiece, marked with a stylized flash of lightning. This is suitable for shutter speeds from 1 to 1/50 second. (The actual exposure time—if the flash is used by itself—depends, of course, on the flash duration.)

Current Leica M models do not carry a shutter speed figure on the dial for 1/50 second. There is, however, engraved a lightning symbol (similar to that below the electronic flash socket) which corresponds to the 1/50 second setting. The first Leica M3 models have shutter speeds including the 1/50 second setting, so no lightning arrow on the shutter dial is provided.

Flash units connected to the electronic flash socket on the Leica M models receive their firing impulse the moment the first blind is fully open. This is therefore perfect for the negligible firing delay of electronic flash. However, since the flash is so short, the shutter blind must fully uncover the film; and the fastest speed at which this occurs is 1/50 second. At shorter exposure times, with the shutter opening travelling across the film as a slit, only a strip of the film would be exposed by the flash.

The two synchronizing circuits are independent, and both can be used at the same time. That means that we can connect both an electronic flash unit and a gun for flash bulbs to the Leica M models. Provided the shutter speed is slower than 1/50 second (as mentioned above) both types of flash will synchronize for the same picture.

The flash socket of the Leica M1 to M3 takes special plugs, and not the standard 3 mm. co-axial plugs of most flash units. The plug also incorporates a bayonet locking device.

The special Leica M plugs are provided with the Leitz flash gun; for other guns (including electronic flash) appropriate connecting cables are available with the M plug at one end, and a female co-axial plug at the other.

Plastic cover buttons are available for the flash sockets of the Leica M as protection against dust. Also, keeping one button in the socket not in use at any time prevents accidental connexion of the flash cable to the wrong socket.

The flash arrangements of the Leicaflex are similar, but the slowest speed at which the blinds are fully open is 1/100 second. This is marked on the shutter knob by a lightning symbol.

The flash sockets are on the camera front and take standard 3 mm. coaxial plugs, as do the sockets of the M4.

Synchronizing Leica g Models

On the Leica Ig and IIIg there is only one flash socket. The shutter speed setting here automatically governs the synchronization. Class M and FP bulbs are correctly synchronized at all speeds from 1/60 to 1/1000 second. Just set the shutter to the required speed, and the flash contacts will close on releasing about 20 milliseconds before the second blind begins to move.

For electronic flash, set the shutter speed dial to one of the arrow marks. The flash contacts then close when the first blind has reached the end of its travel and the film is fully uncovered at the instant when the flash is fired. The black arrow mark stands for 1/50 second, and the red mark for 1/30 second.

The red arrow mark is also used for synchronization of all types of flash at slow shutter speeds of 1/30 to 1 second. In that case set the fast speed dial to the red arrow mark, and the slow speed dial to the required speed.

At the B setting of the main shutter speed dial the flash circuit will equally fire electronic units and bulbs.

The flash socket of the g, f, and converted earlier models also take flash plugs with a bayonet fitting. These look similar to the flash plugs for the Leica M models, but are not interchangeable with the latter. Again, connecting cables are available for electronic and other flash units with a standard 3 mm. co-axial flash plug.

Standard 3 mm. co-axial flash plugs *can* be connected directly to the flash socket on screw-mounted Leica models. They are then pushed over the centre of the flash socket, ignoring the bayonet fitting. This is less convenient, and the plug is not secured in position.

The Synchronizing Settings of Leica f Models

The flash contacts on Leica models If, IIf, and IIIf are adjustable for different firing delay times at different shutter speeds. To set the synchronization for the bulb and shutter speed in use, move the synchronizing dial underneath the main shutter speed dial so that the required number appears in the cut-out. The synchronization numbers are given in the table on p. 470.

Then just connect the flash gun or unit to the camera, insert the flash bulb, and expose. The shutter and flash contacts will do the rest.

The flash synchronizing circuit of the Leica If to IIIf models contains two sets of contacts. One is worked by the release button and one by the shutter speed dial.

Pressing the release closes the first contact. The rotating axis of the speed dial then closes the second contact to complete the firing circuit when the dial has travelled a certain distance. The point at which the second contact closes is adjusted by the synchronizing dial according to the required firing delay. The longer the firing delay of the flash bulb, the earlier must the contact be closed.

The shutter speeds that can be used still depend upon the type of flash employed. Thus focal plane bulbs (and certain large flash bulbs) can be used at all speeds up to 1/1000 second; smaller bulbs with a short flash duration and electronic flash can only be synchronized at 1/50 second or slower—when the shutter fully uncovers the film. In all cases the synchronizing dial setting fires the flash at the correct point during the shutter release cycle.

The numbers themselves do not signify delay times; they merely specify the position of the firing contact in relation to the shutter speed dial.

There are two types of flash-synchronized Leica *f* models. The later ones with the shutter speeds of 1/25, 1/50, 1/75 second, etc., have the synchronizing settings engraved in red.

The earlier models, with the shutter speeds on the main speed dial of 1/30, 1/40, 1/60 second, etc., have the synchronizing settings engraved in black.

Both types are equally efficient, but different settings are needed in each case for the various shutter speeds. Leica models of the c series can be converted into the corresponding f models. They are then fitted with a synchronizing system identical to that of the f models with black synchronizing dial.

This applies to camera models with serial numbers above 400,001 (also between 360,000 and 400,000, though those are no longer being converted).

Leica models with serial numbers below 360,000 were at one time also synchronized internally by Leitz, being fitted with a synchronizing dial like the type f models. They are used in the same way, but the settings required are different. See p. 470.

Synchro-contacts also used to be produced for earlier non-

SYNCHRO-FLASH

The Leica M has two flash sockets. The X-socket next to the finder eyepiece serves for electronic flash while the second one (M-socket) fires most other flash bulbs at the right time.

The Leicaflex has also two sockets for the two types of flash, but on the camera front (p. 150).

On the Leica IIIg synchronization is automatic. Fast shutter speeds synchronize normal flash bulbs, while the arrow settings (1/50 and 1/30 second) synchronize electronic flash.

The Leica If, IIf, and IIIf models have a synchronizing dial. To adjust the flash synchronization move this dial to the required number.

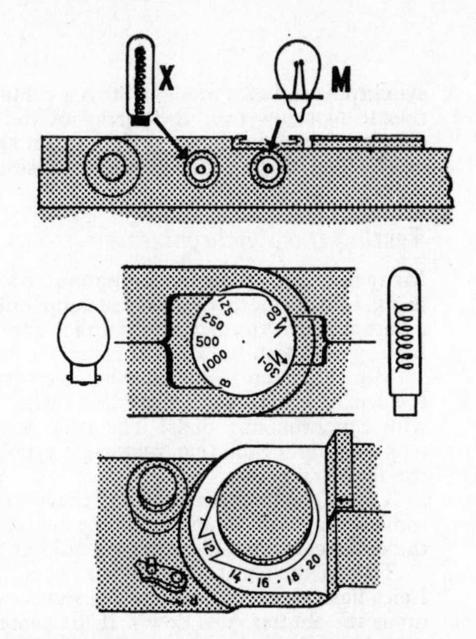

Focal plane bulbs (*solid curve*) have a long peak to cover the full time during which the shutter is travelling. The firing circuit closes before the shutter opens, to allow for the firing delay. Normal bulbs (*dotted curve*) have a shorter peak, and thus under-expose the ends of the negative at fast speeds.

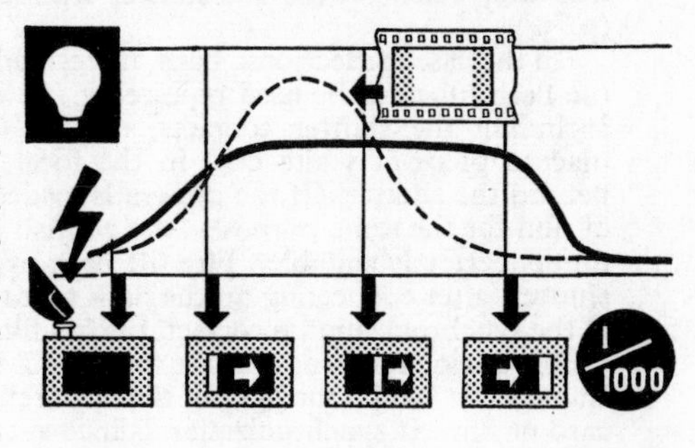

Certain types of fast-firing bulbs have a short peak and small firing delay (*left*). They can only be synchronized at 1/50 or 1/25 second and the firing circuit must close when the shutter is nearly open. Electronic flash has practically no firing delay and must be fired when the shutter is fully open.

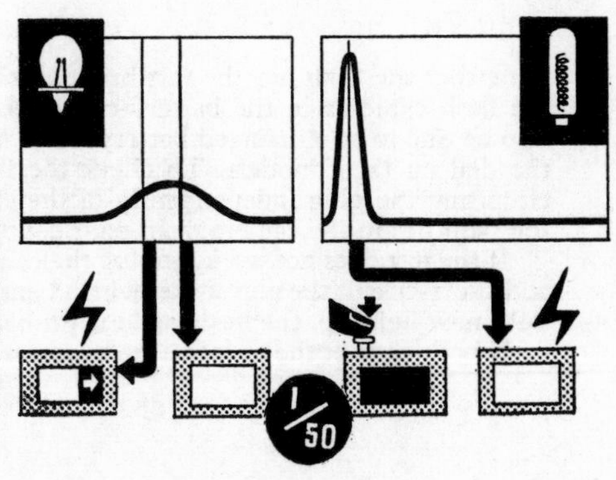

synchronized Leica models. Such a contact consists of a contact release to screw over the thread of the release button, and a contact ring which fits over the shutter speed dial. The rotation of the dial during the exposure closes the firing circuit for synchronization.

Testing the Synchronization

Many flash guns allow for testing the flash bulb and circuit before firing. Usually there is a small test lamp built into the gun; pressing a button makes this lamp light up for a fraction of a second if the battery and flash bulb are in order.

More elaborate testing may be necessary to check, for instance, the synchronization of series f and earlier screw-mounted Leicas with synchronizing dials. The best way is to insert a 6 volt 0.05 amp light bulb (e.g. motor-car type) in the gun in place of the flash bulb.

To test the battery circuit and the flash cable, short-circuit the camera plug with a pin, simultaneously touching the centre and the outer contacts. The bulb should light up momentarily.

To test the shutter synchronization, connect the gun to the Leica flash socket and release the shutter. The bulb should light up as the shutter runs down. If the camera is loaded with film, stop down the lens to its smallest aperture and cover it with the lens cap. Then rewind the shutter without advancing the film (p. 54).

In the case of electronic flash, no test lamp is necessary, since the flash tube can be used repeatedly. To test the whole circuit including the shutter contacts, remove the camera lens and place a piece of white card in the focal plane of the camera behind the shutter. (If the camera is loaded, sacrifice one frame of film for the same purpose—the whitish emulsion layer of the film is perfectly suitable.) Fire the flash by releasing the camera shutter (after connecting up the flash unit to the camera socket). If the synchronization is correct, the full film area should become visible during releasing; i.e. the flash should illuminate the entire frame as shown by the light of the flash reflected from the white card or film. If synchronization is incorrect, the image area will appear cut down at one side or the other.

Fault Tracing

If neither the flash nor the test bulb light up, look for faults in the flash cable or in the battery-capacitor circuit. Failure may also be due to an exhausted battery, or to an incorrect setting of the dial on the f models. To check the flash cable, try short-circuiting the plug independently of the shutter. If this works, the fault lies in the camera or in poor contact in the socket.

If the test does not work, unplug the cable from the flash gun, and short-circuit the gun socket with a bent wire. Should the test bulb now light up, the flash cable is probably damaged.

If both ends of the negative are unexposed or under-exposed, the flash bulb was not suitable for use at that shutter speed. A slower speed is then required, or a bulb giving a longer flash, such as a focal plane type.

If the left-hand end of the negative (viewed the right way round) is blank or very thin, the flash fired too late. This may be due to a run-down battery, but more likely incorrect synchronization, with the dial setting too low on models If, IIf, or IIIf.

If the right-hand end of the negative is under-exposed, the flash fired too early or was too short (see above). Where the flash is early, use a lower setting on the synchronizing dial.

Where the flash fires, but the negative is blank, the synchronizing dial setting is too high, and fires the flash before the shutter starts moving. Alternatively, the dial may have been set to fire the flash right at the end of the exposure, as for electronic flash. With the Leica M use of the wrong flash socket will produce blank or only partly exposed negatives; the same will occur through using electronic flash at a fast shutter speed with the Leica IIIg.

Exposure with Flash

When taking flash pictures of average subjects we usually know beforehand what shutter speed, film and bulb we are using.

The two main variable factors remain the flash distance and aperture. These two are inversely proportional, for the farther away the flash is from the subject, the less light reaches it, and the larger the aperture needed.

We can therefore control both aperture and distance simultaneously by a product of the two. This product of distance in feet times *f*-number, known as the flash guide number or the flash factor, provides a simple exposure guide for most type of flash shots.

To find the aperture required, simply divide the guide number by the flash distance. To find the correct flash distance (e.g. if a fixed aperture is called for to obtain adequate depth of field) divide the guide number by the aperture.

The guide number itself depends on the film speed, bulb and shutter speed, and the tables on pp. 485–486 give values for various film-flash combinations.

The beauty of the guide number system is that it is easily memorized; if we stick to one film and bulb we just have to remember a few numbers, according to the shutter speed to be used.

The only other point we have to think about is to use one stop larger for dark subjects or shots outdoors at night, and one stop smaller for bright subjects or surroundings.

Exposure for Several Flashes

With two flash bulbs the operation is almost as simple.

Where one of the bulbs is used only as effect light ignore it altogether.

Where both bulbs light up the subject from more or less the same direction as the camera, work out the aperture for each. If there is more than two stops difference between them, use the smaller stop. If the difference is less than two stops, add up the *f* numbers and multiply the sum by 0.7 to get the aperture to use.

For example, with two similar bulbs of guide number 100 at 10 and 15 feet from the subject, the apertures are 100 ÷ 15 and 100 ÷ 10, or *f*6.6 and *f*10. The stop to use is then $0.7 \times (10 + 6.6) = 11.6$, or approximately *f*11. If the bulbs are 6 and 15 feet away, the apertures are *f*16 and *f*6. The difference is nearly three stops, so ignore the larger stop and use a setting of *f*16.

Lighting with Flash

The most straightforward way of taking synchronized flash shots is to have the flash gun mounted on the camera. It is also the quickest and often the only way for candid shots, as well as for Press and action photography in general.

From the point of view of lighting, the result tends to be a little dull. All the light comes from the front, there is very little modelling. If other light (e.g. weak daylight or electric light) is available, arrange for this to come from the side to relieve the flatness of the illumination. Provided this outside light is not too strong, it should not affect the flash exposure.

Keep all parts of the subject at more or less the same distance from the camera. As the intensity of the light falls off rapidly with increasing distance, the foreground would tend to be grossly over-exposed and the more distant parts come out too dark.

With busy backgrounds, therefore, set up the subject some distance in front of the background, and the latter will merge in complete darkness.

Where conditions allow, fire the flash away from the camera. Hold the gun high to one side, so that the light comes downwards at an angle of about 45 deg. This gives more natural shadows. Other light available for the shadow side helps.

With static subjects we can use open flash and fire it from anywhere we like. In such a case we can even fire several flashes, one after another, at the appropriate distance from the subject, and obtain the same result as with multiple extension flashes.

This method is particularly useful for illuminating large interiors.

Bounce Flash

For very soft and even illumination, specially suitable for larger groups, fire the flash at a light wall or ceiling, utilizing the reflected light.

If such a group is distributed through the depth of a room, point the flash gun so that the foreground receives only reflected light from the ceiling, while direct light reaches the more distant parts.

This "bounce-flash" illumination needs either a stronger flash bulb or a larger aperture than direct light. The best way of calculating exposures is to work them out for the distance the light travels to the foreground—i.e. flash to ceiling plus ceiling to subject—and use one stop larger than for a direct flash at the same distance.

The evenness of bounce-flash lighting also makes it eminently suitable for colour photography.

Multiple Flash

With two or more flashes the possibilities of lighting arrangements are greatly increased.

Two flashes can be used on the camera with two flash holders, but this is rarely necessary, since one large bulb generally gives the same result as two smaller ones. The extra light output of two large bulbs (e.g. PF100) may, however, be useful for specially large subjects and outdoor shots at night, as well as for colour film.

The extra bulbs, in separate reflectors, are usually linked to a main flash gun and fired from the capacitor of the latter. There are a number of such outfits on the market. Similar arrangements are possible with several makes of electronic flash outfit.

An alternative way is to fire only one flash from the camera, and use subsidiary firing circuits, controlled by photo cells, for the other flashes. The photo cells of these so-called slave flash units respond to the light from the main flash to fire their own flashes.

With slave flash set-ups use the appropriate synchronizing outlet for the camera-fired flash (bulb or electronic), but with a shutter speed no faster than 1/30 second, to allow for the slave firing delay.

The most practical two-bulb set-up consists of one flash on the camera, and a second flash, considerably nearer to the subject, connected to the camera with an extension cable. The second flash is directed somewhat downwards on the subject from one side.

This is a good way to obtain fairly even illumination for colour shots.

Alternatively, the second flash is useful with subjects of appreciable depth. The first flash bulb then lights up the foreground, while the additional flash helps to illuminate the more distant areas.

If both flashes are on extension leads, we can use lighting schemes similar to those applicable to tungsten or Photoflood lamps.

Three flashes will permit full-scale professional portrait set-ups with all their effects.

Mixed Flash

Daylight or even artificial light may serve as supplementary lighting to a flash bulb. The role of the two can, however, be completely reversed: the flash is equally suitable as fill-in lighting for an essentially daylight or Photoflood shot.

Such a supplementary flash would, of course, have to be synchronized, otherwise any movement would register while the shutter is open, and produce ghost images.

Fire the flash from about twice the distance that would be needed at that aperture if the subject were lit by flash illumination alone.

A supplementary flash may also illuminate the background or produce special effects; for instance a flash bulb placed in an empty grate might simulate the impression of a fire burning in the fireplace.

In the same way it can reinforce a weak light source actually included in the picture, e.g. a candle. Such shots will then look as if they had been taken by candlelight. The flash must light up the subject from the same direction as the light source it reinforces, so as to avoid double shadows.

When combining flash bulbs with other sources for colour shots, the quality of the flash light must balance the colour of the other light.

Sun Flash

In outdoor shots taken against the sun the contrast is often so great that the film is unable to deal with it. A flash can then light up the shadow side sufficiently to give a well-balanced result.

For this purpose the flash must not be too strong, or it will kill the sunshine effect and look unnatural.

The flash should never be obvious in the picture. To work out the correct flash exposure under these conditions, determine the daylight exposure for the brightly lit parts of the subject. Use double the guide number for the flash at that shutter speed and aperture, firing the flash at the appropriate distance.

For instance the sunlit subject by itself may need an exposure of 1/125 second at *f*11. If we use, say, a PF24 bulb to illuminate the excessively dark shadow side, the guide number may be 70. Double the guide number (140) and fire the bulb from 12–13 feet away.

If the bulb is too strong for the distance at which the picture is to be taken, one or two thicknesses of a handkerchief will help to reduce the intensity.

The same technique works when the flash supplements diffused daylight; assume double the guide number the flash would need by itself.

Flash and Sky Tones

There is one special case of using flash out of doors and combined with sunlight. Frequently we are up against a brilliant sky. The use of an orange or red filter would darken the sky, but also make, say, a sun-burned athlete at the seaside look pale and pasty-faced.

The way to deal with this is to set the Leica for an exposure about one-fifth to one-tenth that required for the subject in sunshine (e.g. 1/125 second at *f*22 instead of at *f*8). Look up the guide number for the flash bulb used and fire the flash at the recommended distance.

The result shows the subject apparently normally lit, but with a greatly under-exposed, dark sky.

COLOUR TECHNIQUE

Colour films are slower and need more accurate exposure than black-and-white. Avoid too contrasty lighting.
Use daylight type film for outdoor shots, and artificial light type with Photofloods or studio lamps.

Taking colour photographs does not differ greatly from using black-and-white film. Both materials are loaded into the Leica in the same way. Focusing, shooting, and unloading are much the same, too.

The special points with colour are exposure and lighting.

Exposure in Colour

Average colour films are about as fast as an extra fine grain type black-and-white film; some are still slower. The fastest colour emulsions correspond to medium-speed black-and-white ones. So colour pictures generally call for reasonably good light, or larger apertures and/or slower shutter speeds in poor light.

Reversal colour films, like any other reversal film, need very accurate exposure. The final density of the image directly depends on the exposure in the camera; we have no printing stage at which we can compensate for variations in the density. Over-exposed colour shots yield thin, washed-out transparencies, while under-exposed pictures look excessively dark and heavy.

In addition, wrongly exposed colour pictures—reversal and negative-positive alike—also show distorted colours. The three layers of the colour film are designed to give an optimum colour rendering within a severely limited range of densities. Under- and over-exposure therefore may upset the colour balance quite apart from giving degraded and desaturated colours respectively.

With colour negative film, sufficient exposure is necessary to record both detail and colour gradation in the shadows. An under-exposed negative may yield acceptable black-and-white prints, but is useless for colour prints.

Using Exposure Meters

Generally the colour values in the lighter tones are the more important ones, since they show up distorted colours most clearly.

For this reason exposures are best determined by a highlight or incident light exposure meter (p. 219). This ensures that the light tones at least receive correct exposure every time, leaving the shadows to take care of themselves. Where only reflected light readings are possible (e.g. with the Leicaflex) appropriate corrections are necessary (p. 228).

Dark colours usually appear degraded (i.e. mixed with black) when we see them, anyway, so a greater or lesser degree of degradation is of no serious consequence. In the lighter tones where colours are often nearly saturated hues, a slightly greater desaturation (mixture with white) considerably reduces the brilliance and tone of a colour.

Exposure tables are reasonably satisfactory with colour film, provided the conditions are straightforward—e.g. sunshine outdoors or Photofloods indoors. They are less reliable where we have to use any discretion in estimating conditions such as overcast or cloudy weather, which may vary considerably in its light value.

Negative colour film does have somewhat more latitude. We can allow for slightly too dark or too light negatives by adjusting the printing exposure, as with black-and-white negatives. While this will also correct the saturation and purity of the colours in the light tones, it may not rectify wrong colour balance. Therefore aim at getting the exposure as nearly correct as possible. The meter can here be used in the orthodox way for reflected light readings.

For consistent results, sacrifice one colour film to make a series of test exposures to settle once and for all the best speed rating to employ with the particular exposure meter (p. 220).

Colour Lighting

Choose comparatively flat lighting for colour shots. Out of doors wait for hazy or slightly overcast sun. If the sun is too brilliant, arrange one or two large reflecting screens to light up the shadows. These screens may well be cream or even yellow, since sun shadows tend to be blue, especially if there are few or no clouds in the sky.

When using lamps, again keep the lighting balance even and avoid excessive contrast. Usually front lighting, slightly from one side of the camera, is best. Use a reflecting screen for the shadows.

The aim of colour lighting should be to keep the contrast fairly low. The range, particularly with artificial light, should not be more than about 4 : 1. Check with an exposure meter: the brightest parts should reflect no more than four times as much light as the darkest areas of any importance.

This is the main difference in approach to black-and-white and to colour photography. Where we have to rely on tones of black, grey, and white only to produce a picture, we try to arrange the masses and tones to form patterns of brightness. The greater the contrast, the more pronounced the patterns.

In colour photography we can create our patterns with colours, and lighting contrast takes a secondary rôle. A red poppy in a field will appear lost in its surroundings on black-and-white film; we can only differentiate between them by selective lighting or filtering. On colour film we obtain full colour contrast with hardly any lighting contrast.

The Film and the Light

Be sure to use the right type of film for the available light. Daylight subjects need daylight type film, artificial lighting type A or Tungsten film.

Take special care not to mix light sources of different colour quality, e.g. clear flash with daylight. Mixed lighting yields uneven colour rendering; parts of the picture will show a distinct colour cast. The effect is often more disturbing than a slight but even colour cast over the whole view, since we tend to notice the even tint less. This applies equally with the universal type colour negative film.

Physicists measure the colour quality of a light source by its colour temperature in degrees Kelvin (i.e. absolute degrees). With a Photoflood or tungsten lamp that is in practice fairly near to the absolute temperature of the filament. An overrun Photoflood burns at a higher temperature and thus yields light of a higher colour temperature (3400° K) i.e. richer in blue than studio lamps (3200° K) or household lamps which give still more reddish light (2300–2800° K).

Neon or similar discharge lamps may register in quite a different colour from what they appear. These lamps deviate in their spectral characteristics from ordinary lighting and are liable to affect the colour film in an unpredictable way. Thus a green outdoor advertisement may well turn out deep blue, or an orange neon light deep red.

For outdoor shots at night load the Leica with daylight type colour film. This conveys the warmth of the street lamps better than artificial light film which records too cold.

Flash takes a special position as light source for colour shots. Flash bulbs with a colour temperature of 3800–4000° K do not match up with either daylight (5400–6000° K) or Photofloods. Here we can use either daylight type or type A film with a correction filter. Flash bulbs may be used with artificial light type negative colour film, as there the colour rendering can be balanced in printing. But ordinary flash bulbs still must not be mixed with other light sources.

Special flash bulbs are produced by all makers for colour photography. They are bulbs of the standard range (p. 470) with a blue-tinted protective layer (instead of a clear one) over the glass, adjusting the colour of the flash to match daylight. The blue bulbs can therefore be used with daylight type colour-film (and mixed with daylight as supplementary lighting —p. 267). The firing characteristics of such tinted bulbs are the same as of the corresponding clear bulbs. The light output is often also matched; some smaller bulbs are only made now blue-tinted and recommended for black-and-white and colour work.

Electronic flash resembles average daylight in colour, and can quite safely be used with daylight type film.

Filters for Colour

Daylight type colour films are balanced to give the best results with light of a specific standard quality. Ordinary daylight varies appreciably in colour, according to the weather, time of day, and even the subject. Generally such colour variations are characteristic of the time and place of the subject. After all, why should we try to turn, say, the orange tinted hues of a summer evening into the brilliant whites of midday?

The colour film reproduces the variations of the sunlight from the yellowish early morning and late afternoon illumination to the brilliant white of the middle of the day. It also shows up the differences between the delicate pastel shades of a spring scene, the rich greens and browns of a summer subject, the multi-coloured hues of the autumn, and the comparatively yellowish and brownish-purple tones of a view in the winter.

With black-and-white film we have to translate all these subtle changes in terms of gradations of grey; in colour we see the whole range in its natural tones and colour contrasts.

When lighting conditions produce definitely unwanted colour effects, we can correct the colour rendering by using filters in a way similar to that used in black-and-white photography.

With reversal film any such correction must take place before the exposure. Once the film has recorded its image, there is little we can do about it; except perhaps to bind up the transparency with a faintly coloured sheet of celluloid—a clumsy method.

Negative colour films do not need taking filters to the same extent, since the colour balance can, within certain limits, be corrected during printing.

Never use the same taking filters for colour photography as for black-and-white film. The latter filters are much too strong and would merely yield a picture with an almost even over-all colour.

General Correction Filters

The filters we are most likely to need are the ultra-violet filter and a very special pale yellow haze filter.

The former is useful under much the same circumstances as with black-and-white film, namely mountain photography, and also distant views. These often tend to have a slight bluish tint; the filter then yields warmer and more pleasant colours.

Use the haze filter or the so-called Skylight filter (Wratten 1A) when the effect of the ultra-violet filter is insufficient.

Colour pictures taken on dull days, especially indoors, frequently also come out too blue. Again the haze filter improves the colour balance.

The blue sky has a much higher colour temperature (over 8000° K) than standard daylight (5400° K). Subjects in shadow lit by light from the sky only therefore need a strong haze filter to avoid too blue a rendering.

The polarizing filter is also suitable for use with colour film to control the depth of the sky tone in outdoor shots (p. 240).

Colour Conversion Filters

Colour conversion filters radically alter the colour balance of the light, and enable daylight type colour film to be used in artificial light and vice versa.

Preferably use the colour conversion filters recommended

THE GROWING HUMAN INTEREST

To the modern photographer people become more important than places. Where pictures used to be preoccupied with the scene, and people were incidental embellishment, the human interest is the subject of the Leica and the scenery the background. The pictures are isolated, but characteristic, moments sliced out of the activities of men, women and children around us. They may be any moments, as long as they are true to life—caught when they really occur, and not staged for the photographer.

We therefore have to go after life; we may be looking at children playing (*above*), the young and the old having fun (pp. 276, 277), or just the many anonymous characters that drift past our lens in streets (pp. 274, 279), restaurants, clubs (p. 275), parks (p. 280)—wherever we may be with the Leica or Leicaflex.

We see the excitement of great occasions, and the unnoticed moods of day-to-day existence, happy, touching, or sordid—provided they are interesting. And they nearly always are, for most people are interested in the behaviour and doings of other people.

The Leica or Leicaflex is ready for them all the time, and records in pictures what we can see when we keep our eyes open.

CATERPILLAR

Page 273: Glasgow children. 50 mm. lens, fast pan film, 1/200 sec., *f* 11. Photo: *J. Sadovy.*

Page 274: Going home. 50 mm. lens, fine-grain pan film, orange filter, 1/200 sec., *f* 8. Photo: *J. Sadovy.*

Page 275: At the London Jazz Club. 50 mm. lens, fast pan film, 1/100 sec., *f* 2. Photo: *J. Sadovy.*

Page 276, *top*: Snowball fight. 50 mm. lens, negative colour film, 1/200 sec., *f* 4.5. Photo: *A. Tritschler.*

Page 276, *bottom*: Jitterbug. 50 mm. lens, fast pan film, 1/200 sec., *f* 1.5. Photo: *J. Sadovy.*

Page 277: Fun fair. 35 mm. lens, fast pan film, 1/500 sec., *f* 3.5. Photo: *K. Hutton.*

Page 278: On the beach. 50 mm. lens, fine-grain pan film, light yellow filter, 1/200 sec., *f* 5.6. Photo: *A. Tritschler.*

Page 279: Three in company. 50 mm. lens fine-grain pan film, 1/100 sec., *f* 5.6. Photo: *J. Sadovy.*

Above left: Rain in the park. 50 mm. lens, medium-speed pan film, 1/100 sec., *f* 5.6. Photo: *J. Sadovy.*

Below left: More rain. 50 mm. lens, fine-grain pan film, 1/100 sec., *f* 4.5. Photo: *A. Tritschler.*

by the makers of the film; mixing makes of film and filters may produce a wrong colour balance.

Colour conversion filters for adapting daylight type films to artificial light sources are generally pale blue or mauve in colour. They appreciably lower the speed of the film, corresponding to a filter factor of about 4.

Conversion filters for using artificial light type films (Photoflood or type A and tungsten type) in daylight are yellow or amber and have a filter factor of about $1\frac{1}{2}$.

These filters are makeshift means only, to get over the need for changing films just for a few shots by a different type of light. For the best colour balance, however, use the correct film for the light.

Colour Casts

Subject tones are influenced by the colour of the light reflected from the surroundings. The most familiar example is that of a figure sitting on a lawn; the grass reflects green light on to the face and produces a greenish tinge or colour cast over parts of it.

The effect is similar to that of mixed lighting (p. 270), and so is the remedy—avoid it! Spread a white or neutral coloured sheet over the lawn and put the subject on that.

In the same way, a red brick wall will reflect red light, or water with a clear sky above it will reflect blue. Indoors too, the walls, furnishings, and curtains of a room reflect light of their own colour.

Colour casts are most disturbing when their origin is not included in the picture. They are less obvious when the reflection is of a similar colour to the subject area on which it falls. Thus on skin tones we can tolerate reddish or orange reflections but not blue or green ones which at the best make a face look somewhat sickly.

Colour Selection

The greatest temptation, once we have a colour film in the Leica or Leicaflex, is to go out and look for the most colourful subjects to take.

That is natural enough, but it is not the way to use colour creatively. Colour harmonies depend on careful selection and blending of a few tints and their various hues rather than on including every colour of the rainbow in strength.

Judicious selection is all the more important as colour films tend to reproduce colours more saturated and brilliant than we see them. So avoid violently clashing colours; their discord will appear emphasized in the colour picture. Look for subjects with a dominant tone or two and variations of hues and tints on these tones.

Brilliant colours should be used in small doses for the greatest effect.

Naturally, we cannot go around changing the colours in the scenes we want to photograph; our colour film is not a paint box. But we can choose the lighting; soft light gives the best colour pictures not only because it reduces the lighting contrast but also because it mellows the colours.

Do not have the colour distributed evenly throughout the subject area. Arrange neutral toned backgrounds to set off colourful foreground area, or (more rarely) vice versa.

This also assists in separating the colour picture into its different planes. Natural conditions tend to help here; for instance in landscapes atmospheric haze makes the distance look more bluish, while near objects appear warmer. If the effect is too pronounced, use a haze filter (p. 272), but do not over-filter it.

This recession of tones is often an asset in landscape photography (p. 305). It creates and accentuates depth where it has been subdued by the perspective of long-focus lenses, or the over-all sharpness of extensive depth of field.

A view that is sharp from the foreground to the distance, but gradually changes from warm to cold colours, corresponds more closely to our impression. For we invariably remember a subject as a whole, but see it in parts, assembled in the mind by our habit of letting the eye rove or scan over the scene in front of us.

The lighting has a similar effect: directly lit areas show the most saturated colours. A shadowed background will therefore appear subdued in colour as well as in brightness.

Colour Perspective

Our eyes, like a simple camera lens, tend to refract cold blue and green rays of light more than the warmer yellow and red ones. The latter therefore appear to be nearer.

The Leica lenses are mostly corrected for this difference in refraction, but the effect appears again when we look at a colour picture.

This produces an impression of perspective which we can accentuate by suitably choosing the colour scheme.

Accordingly, aim to have cold colours in the background, and warmer ones in the foreground rather than the other way round. A girl in a red or brown dress will appear to stand out against a blue sky because of this colour perspective as well as in consequence of any focusing trick.

But put the same person in blue clothes against a brown background, and the figure appears to recede.

In close-ups especially, a cold, greenish or bluish background lends solidity to a warm coloured subject.

The saturation of a colour has a similar effect. Brilliant saturated colours stand out against subdued ones. So keep backgrounds restrained in colour as well as in detail.

Unsharp backgrounds with patches of brilliant colours are particularly disturbing. Such patches spread when they are blurred, and thus become larger. Yet they lose none of their colour contrast; by their very uniformity of tone they seem to attract more attention.

THE LEICA APPROACH

Use the Leica to record life; be ready to shoot at a moment's notice and to make use of unexpected opportunities.
Be prepared to use plenty of film to tell all angles of the story.
Get close to fill the negative area. Concentrate on the main subject and leave out all unessential detail.

The development of miniature technique went parallel with the evolution of a miniature style of picture taking. This depends on certain mechanical features of the Leica—its load of thirty-six exposures, fast lenses and shutter speeds—as well as its portability and instant readiness to shoot.

To make the most of the capabilities of the Leica calls for its own approach. With a load of thirty-six exposures, at less than one-third of the price per shot of a standard roll film, we can be generous with the negative material. Picture taking becomes shooting almost on the spur of the moment. We don't expect thirty-six different pictures in the same sense as an eight-exposure roll film may cover eight different subjects.

That means a certain waste of film, but it is a virtue rather than a drawback of the Leica. We are free to photograph without worrying about the material. The purpose of the film reserve is to cover the many aspects and angles of the subject *as they crop up.*

Seeing Pictures

Shooting live subjects yields live pictures. Not each one of the thirty-six maybe, but a good number nevertheless. And those are the ones that tell more than anything we could obtain by traditional methods of photography.

The Leicaflex further shows what we are taking on a full-size viewing screen. This feature of the "seeing" camera makes it literally the photographic extension of our eyes. We photograph what we observe already within the frame of the final picture. The techniques of seeing with the rangefinder and the reflex camera are a little different, but the subject approach remains that of the fast-shooting miniature. So wherever we talk about the Leica in the following pages we nearly always equally imply the Leicaflex.

Technically, our approach must be simple. We have no time for the amount of preparation expended on an exposure with a larger camera; with laboriously setting up, to get everything just right. Nor is there any need for it. The depth of field of the standard Leica lenses is sufficiently large to dispense with highly critical focusing.

Again, we shall work with basic exposures for an average lighting level, and adjust the settings as necessary when the light (or the meter indication in the Leicaflex finder) changes. When in doubt, we can always take several shots at slightly different exposures.

We may modify either the shutter speed or the aperture as subject movement or depth of field demand it.

The important point is that these are running adjustments, made while shooting. The Leica is on the move, like a car, and we steer it by its controls to deal with conditions as they arise. Capture the shot that tells the story, and worry about the settings afterwards; if there is an opportunity, we can always take a second shot to make sure.

Seeing life in terms of pictures involves closely observing everything around us. We don't think merely of pictorial arrangements—almost anything alive has something pictorial about it—but we have to anticipate developing situations. Observe, and be ready; not just for one picture but for a whole series, almost as with a cine camera, to capture a story rather than an isolated view. The analogy is not so far fetched if we remember that the Leica format and the Leica camera have in a way been grafted on to motion picture stock.

So we regard the subject in terms of scenes of activity, and not in single shots of set arrangements. The scenes contain many facets which may change independently and simultaneously; we must pick on them individually to tell the story.

That brings us back to the key to the Leica style of photography: *get close to the subject*. Get closer as long as there is still unessential detail that can be left out; not only because the subject should fill the negative area to make the best of the small picture size, but also because only the close view can be sufficiently intimate.

Then concentrate on watching life and expression. Once we are on familiar terms with our subjects, we shall see life in its detail, too, and can interpret it in real Leica style pictures.

Candid Photography

The Leica way of catching life has also earned it the name "candid"—showing informal and frank pictures of things and people as they really are. That is very different indeed from a portrait as such; it is a record of personality during just one split second of its changing existence.

To be really candid we must take pictures of our subjects before they become too conscious of being photographed. We must retain control of what we want to take rather than let the decision slip across to the subjects in front of our Leica. We are out to catch life, drama, humour—genuine emotion is our end rather than self-conscious poses, hastily assumed attitudes, artificial expressions. We prefer faces to masks.

This means keeping the Leica ready to shoot at a moment's notice, carried round the neck on a short strap. When a likely shot presents itself, whip the camera up to the eye, release, and wind on for the next shot.

Carrying the Leica in this way has the advantage that we can hide it under a coat. This is impossible with the camera strap running over the shoulder (p. 31), though the latter method is quite as quick in shooting—only more conspicuous in action.

In crowds (for instance markets, fairs, and even in the street), make use of other people about as cover. The audience gathered round a soap box orator or a street market demonstrator is ideal for screening the camera.

Alternatively, sight in a completely different direction while adjusting any settings necessary, and swing round to shoot when the moment is ripe.

Use the standard lens for candid shots, load with fast film, and choose a near or medium focusing zone (p. 463). Shoot at a shutter speed of 1/125 or 1/100 second, if the light permits, to deal with most normal movement. An aperture of *f*5.6 to *f*8, with the lens set to 15 feet will allow quick shooting of the majority of candid subjects.

Many candid pictures are, of course, made with the co-operation of the subject. The way to go about it is to get him or her to do something—just to create a natural atmosphere—and expose on the run.

Watch the background and lighting too; the latter should be as simple as possible; complicated set-ups limit the viewpoints. The fast lenses will permit shots even in comparatively poor light.

Co-operation is specially important for any kind of documentary or instructional pictures such as shots in factories of machine operators at work. While some posing may be necessary, the subject will be able to say when a position is technically correct.

People may also have to keep still for slow shutter speeds like 1/4 or 1/2 second when the light is poor, e.g. indoors. Such a pose should, however, still be based on action—just ask the subject to hold it.

Children

Children don't keep still. To photograph them we may have to turn round in circles, join in their games and even crawl after them on hands and knees.

That is not such a bad thing, for a child's world is largely at floor-level. A higher viewpoint will often dwarf it. Habit may tempt us to use the Leica at its normal eye-level position, so make a point of shooting from the child's level.

Shots of children are most successful if they are caught naturally, while playing indoors or out, interested in their own games, or in the photographer.

We can keep small children in one place by such devices as a high chair, or a playpen, but they need stalking when they get older. Zone focusing is one useful way of getting over the problem of keeping them sharp and does away with the need for having to readjust the rangefinder—or the focus on the Leicaflex screen—continually.

Most of the time, however, we shall want the image to fill the frame, which means working at one or two set distances, e.g. 5–6 feet and 10 feet. The best method then is to adjust the lens to that distance and shoot whenever the child moves into focus as seen by the fusion of the rangefinder images.

Load with high-speed film, use a speed of at least 1/125 second, and set the stop to suit the light.

Unobserved shooting is an ideal way of tackling the subject when conditions are suitable, especially out of doors. If this is not possible, get the child used to the camera until it takes no further notice.

The 90 mm. Elmarit is a useful lens for this subject; the camera can then be a little way away from the subject.

Candid shots will show the child in all its moods. Tears are as much part of everyday life as laughter, but child photographs are most pleasant when they show a happy child.

Children's emotions are comparatively simple. Although

older children like dressing up and make-believe, the very young ones are best shown for what they usually are—natural and unpretentious.

For the same reason, photograph children in their normal surroundings. Dressing them in their best clothes makes them self-conscious, while parental admonishments to sit still turns being photographed into an unpleasant occasion.

Older children will readily co-operate on picture-taking sessions. But even they soon tire of the game and lose interest. So don't force photography on to them.

We shall need a lot of light, preferably evenly distributed. The illumination will then be fairly constant however much the subject moves about. Dramatic lighting is rarely suitable, and complicated lighting schemes produce complicated and unnatural shadows.

Daylight, on a hazy day, is ideal, and is also the best lighting for colour photography.

Indoors, near the window, use reflectors or a supplementary lamp. Direct sun streaming in may also provide useful light when suitably diffused by net curtains. That leaves the background, if not too near, completely in shadow. On the other hand, the lighting tends to be flat, and the glare may cause the child to screw up his or her face. This applies to brilliant sunlight out of doors as well—never an ideal light source for pictures of people.

Where daylight is not available or strong enough, flash, and especially electronic flash with its high speed, is useful to capture all subject movement. With a flash gun mounted on the camera we can wander around at will to expose whenever opportune. The light, though comparatively flat, is always the same; it is the child that provides the life of the picture.

Animals

Photographing animals, especially pets, is much like picturing small children. We have to follow them around with the Leica and catch them on the run.

For action shots give them something to play with—such as a piece of string for a kitten—and then watch with the finger on the Leica release. Or lure the creature to a suitable spot with titbits and shoot as many pictures as possible while the animal is busy dealing with the food.

For portraits focus carefully on the eyes and use a small

THE EXPANDING SCENE

Perhaps the greatest achievement of the Leica is the way it has widened our photographic vision, bringing many completely new subjects within our range, from factory plants (p. 295) to opium dens (p. 296).

Many such opportunities are even today just beginning to be explored, recording ever new subjects for the first time. Thus every enterprising Leica photographer becomes another pioneer, constantly applying his equipment to fresh fields. There is no precedent to limit our style of seeing things, simply because there are often no precedents for our subjects.

In the variety of material that it can cover, the miniature camera with its optical equipment and accessories is unchallenged. With the high aperture lenses, selection of different focal lengths, and fast shutter speeds we are prepared for occasions and conditions beyond any other type of photographic outfit.

By day and by night (*above*), indoors (p. 290) and out, in theatres (p. 293), floor shows (pp. 291, 292), above ground and below (p. 294), the Leica records what goes on with all the realism of an impartial observer.

That is the true scope and versatility of our photographic eye, penetrating everywhere and seeing everything worth taking in.

Page 289: Easter procession at Girona, Spain. 35 mm. lens, fast pan film, 1/20 sec., *f* 3.5. Photo: *J. Sadovy.*

Page 290: Epstein's "Genesis" at the Tate Gallery, London. 50 mm. lens, fast pan film, 1/30 sec., *f* 1.5. Photo: *D. Potts.*

Page 291: Show girl behind the scenes. 50 mm. lens, fast pan film, 1/30 sec., *f* 1.5. Photo: *J. Sadovy.*

Above: Floorshow at the Pigalle, London. 50 mm. lens, fast pan film, 1/100 sec., *f* 2. Photo: *J. Sadovy.*

Page 293: Interval at the opera. 85 mm. lens, fine grain pan film, 1/5 sec., *f* 1.5. Photo: *H. Tschira.*

Page 294: In the London sewers. 50 mm. lens, fast pan film, light from one 60-watt lamp, 10 sec., *f* 3.5. Photo: *C. Hewitt* (courtesy *Hulton Press*).

Page 295: Inside the dispersion tower of artificial fertilizer plant. 35 mm. lens, fine-grain pan film, light from hand lamp, $\frac{1}{2}$ sec., *f* 6.3. Photo: *A. Tritschler.*

Above: Opium den in Siam, lit up only by the light from the oil lamp in the centre of the table. 50 mm. lens, fast pan film, 1/20 sec., *f* 1.5. Photo: *C. Hewitt* (courtesy *Hulton Press*).

enough stop to get the whole head sharp. Every hair or feather should stand out. A fine-grain film (light permitting) will make the most of the fine detail with its higher resolving power.

Attract attention by a click of the tongue just before shooting, otherwise the animals, particularly birds, may look stuffed.

Generally a long-focus lens is necessary to permit a more distant viewpoint, or the head will appear excessively foreshortened. For that reason also avoid dead frontal views of long heads. Bulldogs and cats, but few other animals, can stand any camera angle.

The long-focus lens (90 or 135 mm.) is almost essential for pictures of smaller creatures in the Zoo, since we can rarely get close enough to them. Watch the subject through the universal finder to determine the best field of view. Set the lens to *f*5.6 to *f*8, with a speed to suit the light and movement.

When photographing through bars poke the Leica lens between them (but not in wild animal or monkey cages). Choose a time of the day when the bars at the back of the cage are in shadow. Direct sun from behind the camera will also cast shadows of the bars on the animal.

Where the cage consists of close wire mesh, bring the Leica lens right up to it.

Shy animals in the Zoo or elsewhere call for a lot of patience on the part of the photographer until they get used to him. The fewer other people about, the better; days when the Zoo is crowded with visitors are useful only for shots of the really big beasts.

Travelling with the Leica

The Leica is a valuable companion on travels and holidays to capture interesting moments of the journey as well as record the places seen.

When going on foot—on walking tours or mountain climbs—it is best to travel light, since everything has to be packed in a rucksack, especially in rainy weather. The only essential items besides the camera are an exposure calculator or chart, a yellow filter, a lens hood, and a camera clamp or something similar. With the camera clamp almost anything can be utilized as a support, even a walking stick or ice axe.

As extra lenses, the 35 mm. wide angle serves for shots in confined spaces, while the 90 or 135 mm. long-focus lens allows close shots of more distant and not so easily accessible subjects.

While the 135 mm. lens may be the more useful of the two, the 90 mm. lens is lighter and takes up less space as well as being more convenient to handle. The 90 mm. Tele-Elmarit is particularly useful for its compactness.

The Leicaflex, of course, needs no extra finders; nor do the Leica models M2 to M4 and IIIg if only the 90 mm. lens is used as extra. Otherwise the universal finder is useful for previewing.

Wrap up the accessories in some clothes, but not in the bottom of the rucksack. Temporarily, items in use may stay in the pockets, provided they cannot knock against anything hard. Put lens cap and rear cover on lenses not in use.

When cycling or motor cycling, carry the Leica itself round the neck, inside the jacket, to stop it from swinging about.

In a car, weight and bulk matter less, and we can take whatever extra equipment we want, such as additional filters, lenses, and a tripod. But a holdall case or gadget bag is useful to keep all items together.

When travelling by air, however, regulations may require cameras to be packed with the registered luggage and not with the hand luggage in the cabin.

Remember to take sufficient film of the type normally used; a favourite film may not be available abroad. Even if it is available, ascertain where it is made. Films of nominally the same brand but made in different countries are not necessarily the same in characteristics, and should be treated as if they were of different makes.

When leaving the United Kingdom for a holiday abroad, carry a dealer's receipt for the Leica if bought in Britain, or a customs clearance certificate to prove that duty has been paid. Otherwise there may be difficulties at the customs on re-entry.

Visitors from abroad can usually bring their Leica or Leicaflex in with them, but must not sell it in Britain.

Most Western European countries other than Western Germany (where the Leica and Leicaflex are made) have similar customs regulations covering the import of the camera. However, they will admit it without trouble if it forms part of the personal luggage of a foreign visitor.

Some countries also impose a limit on the quantities of unexposed film that may be brought in.

In case of doubt as to any regulations, ask for advice at the appropriate consulate before going abroad with the Leica.

Climate and Lighting Abroad

Excesses of heat or cold do not greatly affect the Leica. Explorers have used it in the icy Arctic and Antarctic climates as well as on Himalayan expeditions, and found that even at temperatures around 40° below zero the Leica functioned perfectly. Nor have photographers in tropical countries had any difficulties in the blazing heat of 120° F. and over.

For extremely cold conditions the Leica should, however, be "winterized" first by the makers. This consists of replacing the oil on the moving parts by a special lubricant.

All the same do not leave the camera lying about in the sun. If the sun should shine directly into the lens, the latter will act as a burning glass and burn through the blind of the focal plane shutter and the film in no time. Apart from that, the rubberized material of the blinds may melt, and the shutter stick or at least cease to be light-tight. This danger is not limited to tropical countries.

Excessive humidity and desert sands are more serious enemies of photography. To protect the Leica, carry it in a waterproof packing, e.g. well wrapped up in oil-cloth or plastic sheeting except when actually taking pictures.

Better still, have a tin sealed with adhesive tape.

Sand is especially dangerous, so don't try to photograph a sandstorm, since the smallest grain can upset the precision mechanism. And the fine sand gets everywhere.

On a beach the camera should be wrapped up at least in a dry towel. A special waterproof case is also available.

Salt water on or by the sea is equally risky because spray is liable to blow on to the Leica camera and lens. Salt water does neither any good, therefore wipe off any spray immediately, and keep the camera in the closed every-ready case except when actually making an exposure.

When photographing in tropical countries keep all unexposed films in sealed metal containers; the small aluminium tins for the cassettes, with a strip of adhesive plaster round them, are ideal. Do not leave a film in the camera for too long, and process it as soon as possible after exposure. Films do not keep so well in the tropics.

Use adequate precautions when processing film in hot climates and keep even developed films well protected against insects and other creatures. Film-eating insects, incidentally, are not confined to the tropics; they are just as abundant in the short summer in certain Arctic countries such as Alaska and Greenland.

In central Europe, North America and other temperate countries we are used to fairly strong, but not outstandingly harsh, lighting. The sun is high in summer, but never directly overhead.

This character of the light changes farther north or south. Getting towards Arctic and Antarctic regions, the sun even at midday is lower still, and may be completely absent in the winter (in the southern hemisphere July is midwinter). In the summer, however, the days are very much longer than in the temperate zones. We can take pictures at almost any time.

The light is softer, too, and the shadows long. At the same time the colour of the light is slightly more yellowish, a fact of some importance in colour photography. A very pale blue colour compensating filter may be useful (e.g. Wratten No. 82 and 82A for Kodachrome and other daylight type reversal films).

As we go nearer to the equator, already in southern Europe, and especially in tropical countries, it gets dark very quickly once the sun has set. The lighting is harsh and the shadows especially deep in the middle of the day. The best time for photography is when the sun is slightly overcast, or when there are plenty of clouds in the sky.

Provided the shadows are well lit, exposures can be slightly shorter; they do not, however, vary a great deal in different parts of the world for similar weather conditions. Avoid exposing too near sunset or sunrise, as the strength of the light then changes rapidly.

Under unfamiliar lighting conditions in foreign countries it is often worth while to make a few exposure tests, especially with colour film, to keep a check on how things are going.

The main factor which may make estimation of exposures misleading is the amount of haze in the air. An exposure meter is more reliable here, so follow its recommendations, even if they seem somewhat different from those at home.

When making tests shoot a few typical subjects with normal exposures and repeat them, giving half and twice the usual exposure respectively. Develop the test film as soon as possible, or get it developed under specified conditions by a reputable firm, to see results before using too much film.

Make notes of every exposure, not only to remember the

technical data, but also to keep track of all the strange and new localities and subjects. After a holiday in the mountains, who can remember just which picture shows what peak?

Pictures en Route

The main problem with pictures during the journey is subject and camera movement. Trains are the worst in that respect, for the vibration is considerable.

For shots out of the window a seat near the middle of the coach is best, not over either set of wheels. Use the fastest shutter speed, and support the camera in the hand only. Do not lean the elbows against the window ledge or any other part of the carriage.

If possible, shoot out of an open window, since train windows are rarely clean. Make sure that any attachments like lens hood or filter are firmly fixed.

With such shots the foreground should not be too near since it moves past the window fastest.

The apparent subject movement is in this case our own movement in the train. This is still fastest when photographing directly out of the window. Therefore shoot at an angle in the direction of travel (or looking back).

General views are most successful when the train is travelling along an embankment. A rear coach with a platform at the back (common in some European countries and in America) provides a good viewpoint.

Pictures of fellow travellers in the train need longer exposures. Expose when the train is standing still—on the open line or at a wayside halt rather than in a covered station where the light is poor. Get somebody to hold a newspaper or something similar to reflect extra light into faces.

In a car, use the windscreen to frame the scene. Similarly, other parts of the car included in the picture, such as the bonnet or wings, will set the travel atmosphere, especially if part of the scene is reflected from the polished surface of the car. The latter type of shot needs a wide-angle lens to show enough from a close range, and to provide sufficient depth to get both the car and the reflections sharp.

At night the headlamps provide a separate light source to illuminate the view immediately in front of the car. This is particularly effective in the winter when the trees are laden with snow, or in misty or slightly foggy weather.

Movement is much smoother on board ship, though the throbbing of the engines may spoil the exposure by camera shake if the shutter speed is not fast enough. Preferably do not lean against railing or any part of the ship; in fact stand with the knees slightly bent to absorb the vibration.

Generally, pictures in a ship will be confined to activities on board. Here the wide-angle lens is needed to cover more than a small part of the ship fittings as a foreground.

Views of the sea only, or of the coastline, tend to be dull except with special lighting effects such as sunsets. The Leica shows distant ships or features of the coast much smaller than we see them. The answer is to wait until we get closer, or to use a long-focus lens.

The real cruise pictures are shots of shipping in harbour, shore life, and foreign customs and habits. In other words, we are back to close subjects, the ideal Leica field. We are more likely to be alert abroad for little details and cameos of life which we would pass over without noticing at home.

For shots from the air use the long-focus lens and a red filter to cut through the haze. Exposures can be short, since the subject has hardly any shadow detail. Sunshine is essential.

Windows are not ideally placed for photography on air-liners, since we can never shoot directly downwards. We may, however, get a better view of the ground when the aircraft is banking for a turn, e.g., just after taking off or before landing.

Cloud formations are often equally interesting. Include a wingtip, and if possible part of one of the engines, to give a foreground. Preferably use the wide-angle lens.

This lens also helps to emphasize foregrounds which usually make the picture with scenes on board trains, ships, and other vessels, especially when the space is limited. View with the universal finder to see when a change of lens is advisable.

Load with medium speed or fast film, and rely on the lens speed to cope with lighting conditions. Flash is rarely convenient, not does it yield characteristic travel pictures.

Picture Stories

With the many shots of a subject, we can often build up a story. Story-telling in pictures is, in fact, photo-reporting.

Picture stories are series of shots following a series of incidents, almost like a strip cartoon, or—to become more photographic—a motion picture film. The comparison is not so far fetched, for we can make up a story in, if not a film, at least a film strip.

The nucleus of a story is an idea or a message. It can be built up from a promising exposure series, or it may be planned beforehand.

In planning a series we have to go about it much like a motion picture producer, basing it on a script which sums up the essential points. The shots themselves tell the story, similar to the sentences in a written description. We have to think in scenes and sequences of scenes, rather than subjects.

The choice of viewpoint and distance helps to present the story. Thus, long shots or general views establish the setting, serving as a sort of introduction. Medium shots begin to isolate the subject itself, telling what is taking place where. Close-ups draw attention to the detailed points, and in fact carry the main weight in story telling.

The photographic treatment should, of course, show variety, not only in viewpoint, but also in approach. The scenes should follow each other smoothly, though not too uniformly. A series of eye-level views, for instance, can be relieved by appropriate low-angle shots; let the Leica look up, down, and around the subject. At the same time, the series must hang together, technically as well as pictorially; so keep to even lighting and exposure levels.

While the script itself is a valuable guide towards disciplined picture taking, it should not lay down routine in too much detail. We are, after all, reporting things as we see them, while noticing all sorts of unforeseen details and incidents.

A picture series needs plenty of film. We may have to expose several times as many shots as we can use, so as to cover the subject from all aspects, and also to make sure of plenty of alternative shots when required.

The series really becomes a story only when it is finished. We can then edit the material; select the exposures to be used, arrange them in order, fit in subsidiary or linking shots to keep the story flowing, check continuity, and see that each picture makes a point. The final sequence of the pictures is hardly ever the same as the order in which they were taken, rearrangements are nearly always required to control the pace at which the story unfolds and to picture the place where it is happening. In fact action series frequently have to be built up of shots taken from several sequences.

LEICA PICTORIALISM

The Leica way is to take quick glances at reality rather than detached and carefully arranged views.
Look for unconventional pictorial aspects and life in a scene.
Use the universal finder to select the best lens to employ.

Pictorial photographs, whether carefully arranged views, formal portraits, or compositions according to classical rules, have long been associated with large cameras. These are subjects where the speed and versatility of the Leica are normally unnecessary and where a larger image size may be an advantage.

The Leica and especially the Leicaflex can still tackle such pictures. By setting it up on a tripod and operating in a fashion similar to that used with those older cameras we shall get reasonably similar results. The full-size viewing screen of the Leicaflex—but also the Visoflex used on the Leica—permit accurate composition.

Using a 35 mm. camera in that way for general photography seems somewhat odd—if only because it is slowed down to the placid pace of a studio camera. But the subject is also slow, there is plenty of time for arranging it, setting up lamps where required, and for changing our mind and starting all over again. That is a genuine photographic style, though it may not be Leica style.

Leica pictorialism differs from this traditional approach. In place of the thoughtful but somewhat remote view, we take a number of quick penetrating glances. We are looking at many parts rather than a single whole.

The Leica can experiment with unconventional aspects which the larger camera could never get down to, to investigate. Our pictorialism, too, then tends to have a candid style; like a sketch book more than a canvas. With this difference: each sketch can in itself be a fully-fledged picture.

Live Landscapes

The Leica approach to landscapes is to concentrate on near points rather than broad over-all views. The latter not only tend to be monotonous, but the fine image detail reproduced is often near the limit of the resolution of the film. In addition the aerial haze may reduce contrast and clarity of detail in the distance.

Let us then look closer at the near scene. We shall discover several things. Firstly, lack of clarity in the distance no longer matters, it does in fact become an asset.

The farther away the subject is, the more restricted its tone range becomes. A nearby rock will show every cranny and corner in sharp relief; black in the shadows, and bright where the light strikes it. The detail is well above the limit of the resolution of the film. At a greater distance the shadows appear less dark and the highlights less brilliant. In long-range views the intervening atmosphere scatters light into the shadow areas and the subject becomes slightly hazy.

This atmospheric depth is a great help in separating the planes of a subject, it gives a feeling of nearness and distance. With the help of filters (p. 235) we can ourselves control the way in which the film reacts to the atmosphere.

Secondly, and more important, the landscape is alive. It is not just a collection of fields and hills, houses and woods, but of stirring leaves, moving trees, rippling water and also people and animals.

With the Leica we can capture this movement by watching for it. Again one shot may not do it, but several will—looking at the scene from different angles and making use of different patterns of light and shade.

Use a long-focus lens to get at the dominant subject if necessary. The angle of view of the 50 mm. lens is frequently too wide for an effective landscape shot; the 90 mm. is more suitable, and often the 135 mm. lens is required.

Foreground views, on the other hand, are more successful with the 35 mm. wide-angle lens, as we can get really close to the foreground and thus emphasize and even exaggerate it in perspective. This helps to separate the planes of the subject by mere difference of scale, provided the near parts dominate sufficiently and more or less fill the picture area. Focus on the nearest portion of the subject; the middle distance need not in this case be sharp, though it will be at any but the largest apertures.

Ensure the maximum detail with a fine-grain film, and with a fast enough shutter speed to arrest any motion, especially with quickly changing subjects. Trees and bushes, flowers and grass, all sway in the wind; water streams and splashes.

Reflections scintillate; especially when taken against the light.

But all these are the detailed features of the view, not the landscape as a whole, and that is how it is best recorded. Each one of the features makes a picture by itself; the background becomes the setting of the scene.

An exception is the really broad view taken with a wide-angle lens. It must still have plenty of foreground detail, but such a shot—especially a colour transparency—projected on a really big screen can re-create a breathtakingly realistic impression.

With the Leica M models the finder frame selector is also a convenient means of deciding on the area to be included and the lens to be used. With older Leicas use the universal finder for such a preview.

Close Scenery

The Leicaflex—or the Leica with the Visoflex housing—offers a novel approach to views with one of the long-focus lenses. Focal lengths from 135 mm. upwards are handy here.

With this set-up and fairly near views we get a really close look at the scenery. From 20 feet away the 200 mm. Telyt only covers a field of about 3 square feet. Yet in this area we can watch a world in miniature. In scale, the scene is reduced from trees and bushes to branches and twigs, from lakes to puddles, and from fields to tufts of grass.

The pictures then become arrangements of branches and puddles and undergrowth. The life is still there, in the detail of the close view, in the insects and small animals that inhabit this microcosm.

To photograph it, set up the camera on a tripod, and arrange the small world on the ground-glass screen. Select the viewpoint to include the desired amount on the negative, and carefully focus on the main subject. Though the depth of the subject is limited, so is its depth of field.

On the tripod short exposure times are not vital; if there is no obvious movement quite a slow speed is permissible, and allows the use of a small stop to control the zone of sharp focus.

Telephoto Views

The telephoto lenses can equally well be used for normal landscapes taken from increased distances. Again we are able to focus on the screen of the Leicaflex or reflex housing, and arrange everything to our liking. Moreover, we can photograph views which we would not be able to approach close enough to include conveniently.

Two characteristics of telephoto views are important.

Firstly, we cannot include near foreground objects since they will never be sharp at the same time as the distance. The foreground of the picture therefore has to be a long way from the Leica; it may be a matter of something like 100 feet with the 200 mm. Telyt. As a result, quite appreciable changes in camera distance and position will make surprisingly little difference in the viewpoint as seen on the ground-glass screen of the reflex housing. To find a suitable viewpoint we may have to walk quite a lot, which necessarily slows down the taking of even one picture.

Secondly, the distant foreground we can include will show no perspective worth mentioning. To separate it from the background we have to use such tricks as differential focusing at a large aperture (which in view of the limited depth of field is easy with the telephoto lenses), and also utilize the atmospheric separation of planes, tones and contrast. The technique of telephotography is discussed in more detail on pp. 423–434.

Clouds and Skies

The sky is ever important in landscapes. It is also the feature of a scene we can control most easily by judicious use of filters —yellow to give tone and bring out clouds; orange, and especially red, to bring a sense of drama to it.

The effect of the individual filters depends on the nature of the ceiling. The deep azure blue of a summer sky will come out fairly dark even with a pale filter.

The light blue of an early morning sky in the spring will require a much heavier filter to produce any depth of tone.

The direction of light counts with the clouds almost as much as with any other subject. When we are photographing more or less against the sun, the sky is so brilliant that even a deep filter will have little effect on it.

The effect chosen should fit the character of the picture. A heavily over-filtered sky is out of place with a delicate, softly-lit scene.

The cloud shape is important, too. While we associate

heavy cumulo-nimbus storm clouds with dark and stormy weather, cirrus or feather-like wisps of cloud usually go with a pale sky.

It is well to remember that orange and red filters also tend to eliminate atmospheric haze. This may give a clearer view into the distance, but at the same time destroys aerial perspective and depth.

At sunset—or at sunrise for that matter—the difference in brightness between the sky and the rest of the scene is so strong that the foreground is usually confined to a silhouette. Such a view needs pronounced shapes in the foreground, preferably trees or figures against the skyline.

Since the sky itself is usually orange just before sunset or just after sunrise, a filter has not much effect. But after the sun has gone down, the clouds are still brilliantly lit up and can be further accentuated with the help of a yellow or orange filter. Often the contrast between the cloud shapes and the background, however, is so great that this is not necessary.

Shots like this are most effective when the whole sky is full of small fleecy clouds, in a rhythmic pattern like the waves on the sea.

When the sun has gone really low, even the best lens hood won't prevent it from shining directly into the lens. So choose a time when the sun itself has just disappeared behind a cloud, with perhaps the rays fanning out visibly from the edge of the obscuring cloud. If no convenient cloud is available, look for a viewpoint where the sun can be hidden behind a suitable silhouette—a tree trunk, a figure, or even a rock—in the foreground, outlining it with a brilliant halo of light.

Life and Mood

The life of a view is not only in its movement, but also in its play of light and shade which varies according to the time and lighting we choose. It may be bold and straightforward in direct sunshine, or intriguing in its shadow patterns when we photograph with a low sun coming from the side or even the front of the camera. The changing forms of the shadows themselves are then the picture and the subject only the setting, serving no other purpose than to provide the shapes. Almost anything will do to set the mood; a fence or a gate, a back-lit tree or bush. Watch the scene, when there is time, for the patterns the shadows can create.

We can also control the effect by photographic technique. The soft-focus attachment (p. 211) will turn the factual view into a dreamlike scene of soft glowing highlights and luminous shadows. The greater the diffusion, the less real the result. This trick is most effective with the brilliant rims and halo-like outlines of an against-the-light view. But don't overdo this sort of pictorial romanticism of a bygone age; we live in a dream world no more.

The light changes with the time of the year as well as with the time of the day. The air seems to be clearest in the spring and on fine days in the late autumn. The sun does not reach a very high point even at midday, and the lighting generally appears delicate.

This becomes increasingly harsh in the summer when the sun is high up in the sky for most of the day. The shadows in the near distance become heavier, despite the greater amount of haze in the air, and the whole becomes oppressive.

But a picture taken immediately after a thunderstorm shows the full richness of tone of the scene through an absolutely clear atmosphere. Only it does not last long.

In the winter the air is clear only when it is really cold, well below freezing-point. Otherwise there is usually a mistiness about everything. As however the light is low most of the time, there is rarely any great contrast; the illumination is soft.

Apart from sunshine, rain, fog and particularly snow can themselves set the atmosphere of a photograph.

It is the very wetness of rain that makes rain pictures. Concentrate on the effects of wetness, on puddles, wet pavements or streets, and dripping objects in the foreground, for poor weather at a distance is dull. Since the light is dull, too, the best time to take a picture is when there is a slight break in the clouds, or even when the rain has just stopped and the sun comes through for a few moments.

To show up the rain itself, we can use two methods. One is to shoot from behind a window, or the wind screen of a car, with the rain running down the glass. The blurred scene in this instance corresponds to just what we see when we are out in a driving rain. Focus on the window itself, not on the view.

The other way is to stand in a doorway at least 10 feet from the nearest falling drops. Shoot against the light with a dark background behind the rain. Focus on 15 feet, and use a shutter speed of about 1/30 second, to record the drops as falling streaks rather than individual spots. Be careful not to get the Leica or the lens wet.

For shots of rainbows be ready to take them immediately the conditions appear right: when the sun breaks through during a shower.

In a view with a rainbow the sun is always behind the camera. Frequently the foreground is lit up, with more distant parts of the scene in shadow. Rainbows are generally photographable only in the early morning and late afternoon, never at midday.

Use a wide-angle lens to include any appreciable portion of the rainbow; even the 21 mm. Super-Angulon may not cover the whole of it if the sun is low.

Mist, and especially fog, softens outlines and blurs detail. As we cannot see far, it also confines us to near subjects.

Subjects become reduced to shapes and masses only. The main appeal of a fog picture is the way in which these shapes get paler and fainter as they recede in the distance.

Choose a subject which has both depth—to separate the masses into planes—and a characteristic outline to produce interesting patterns.

Have a distinctive foreground object. With its comparatively greater detail and depth of tone this will set off the progressively indistinct shapes and lighter greys of the rest of the scene. It may be the tracery of a tree, or the silhouette of a figure. Focus on this foreground; the distance—what is visible of it—will be blurred anyway.

Keep exposures short to preserve the delicate tone gradation of the subject.

Mist in the country may show special phenomena, particularly when it is not uniform. In the early morning it rises from a river or from the ground in mountain regions, and moves in patches, showing parts of the subject clearly, and part shrouded in its veil. Be on the spot early for pictures like this, for the pattern changes continually. Just around sunrise is the ideal time, with the light coming from the side or almost behind the subject, to light up the swirling mass.

Snow

Snow can serve as a background for patterns of subjects. These may be scenery, rock, bushes, or trees; or buildings and figures, with long shadows from a low sun relieving the expanse of whiteness. Or the subject may consist of tracks in the snow itself, such as ski traces or glacier formations weaving a design into it.

Snow kills scale in its patterns. A rift across it might measure a few inches or be a glacier crevasse of many feet; we cannot easily tell the difference between a small overhang or a precipice in a picture. Such scenes therefore need figures or other objects of known size to give scale.

When we get close to it, snow also has a texture. Seen against the glancing sunlight of late afternoon (which in the winter may be very early) every snow crystal sparkles and scintillates. Naturally sunshine is essential for such against-the-light shots; it also creates shadow patterns to break up the area of white.

Back-lighting is specially effective with pictures of skiers when they throw up clouds of snow on a sudden turn. At the same time the figure casts its own shadow on the brilliant powdery mass suspended in mid-air in front of it.

Concentrate, then, on foreground items; footprints in the snow, or snow-covered branches of trees. Focus on the nearest part of the subject in the picture, and use a wide-angle lens to cover as much foreground as possible. At greater distances snow just comes out as detailless white, whether sharp or not, and may look more like sand. It is the sparkle of the individual crystals that gives snow its characteristic appearance.

The contrast is usually very great. Be careful not to over-expose snow scenes in order to preserve the delicate tones of the subject. Snow shadows, on the other hand, tend to be blue, especially under a blue sky, and may record too light in the picture. There a yellow filter helps to improve the contrast and tone rendering.

The filter should not be too deep when photographing in mountain regions, as the sky will otherwise be too heavy. Some sort of filter, at least ultra-violet, is, however, essential at high altitudes, or the ultra-violet rays may impair the definition of the lens (p. 239).

The light rapidly changes in intensity during a winter day; use a high speed film to make the most of it. Alpine scenes in the summer need much shorter exposures and there a fine-grain film ensures good detail rendering.

Always use an efficient lens hood; the glare is considerable from the snow as well as from the sun.

Snow scenes are particularly effective also at night.

Falling snow is a different proposition; the light is generally dull, and the only feature of interest is the play of whirling snow flakes. Use the same technique as for falling rain (p. 309), shooting from a doorway or other sheltered spot.

A short exposure (1/250 second or faster) will arrest the flakes in mid-air, giving an impression of gently falling snow. A longer exposure (1/30 second or slower) will blur the flakes, making them look almost like a blizzard.

Buildings

Architectural photographs may try to show a building for what it is, to translate the art of the architect into a picture; or attempt to convey the character of a house or even of a whole street in its setting.

A building is a structure of stone, brick or concrete. It has shape—it is in fact a three-dimensional design with a purpose. In our Leica pictures we want to show the texture, form, and solidity of the structure, and suggest something of its function and style.

We can consider a building as a unit for a record shot, or with the Leica look at it piecemeal. And there the whole outlook changes: we get an insight into the art of the architect. We see the lines of design in tucked-away niches, the shapes of balustrades we hardly noticed before, plasterwork decorations, small sculptures and door knockers, or even the play of light and shadow on the texture of the stone from which it is built up. That is the personality of the building.

The light is no great problem, for the stones and structures will keep still indefinitely. We can take time exposures if necessary outdoors or indoors. But the lighting should be suitable for showing up the subject: use diffused light to record shape, and side light to bring out stone texture and relief. Shafts of sunlight streaming in through windows will spotlight single objects in their path and pick them out against an almost black background.

To get close to all the architectural detail we shall need at least one of the long-focus lenses; the 135 mm. unit is the most convenient one. Even the Telyt lenses may come in useful for bits and pieces in inaccessible places.

Often such long shots are indeed the only way of showing mural decorations, frescoes, and carvings that are normally

CHANGING PORTRAIT

In portraiture, too, the Leica has revolutionized the way of recording the salient features of a personality. Instead of attempting to sum it all up in one formal pose, the miniature camera concentrates on the many sides of a living character.

Our pictures may be more in the nature of snapshots as a result, but they capture the expressions of the subject in an informal atmosphere. By this candid approach the real person is reflected in his or her activities (p. 319) and surroundings (p. 318).

We have various technical aids at our disposal to achieve our end. We may shoot off series of pictures to show the changing moods mirrored in a face (*right*). We can use long-focus lenses to portray at close range the experience of life engraved in the features (p. 317), or freeze sudden moments from characteristic occupations (p. 314), and unexpected occasions (p. 316) by action shots.

And we can set the atmosphere by the use of suitable lighting effects (p. 315).

Last, but not least, the hands can be as forceful a feature of a personality (p. 320) as the face.

Page 313: The rôles of Noel Coward. 90 mm. lens, fast pan film, 1/200 sec., *f* 1.8. Photo: *J. Sadovy*.

Page 314: Card trick artist Al Torsten. 50 mm. lens, fine-grain pan film, electronic flash, *f* 5.6. Photo: *N. Bogner*.

Page 315: Actor Albert Bassermann. 90 mm. lens, fine-grain pan film, studio lighting, 1/4 sec., *f* 9. Photo: *W. Klar*.

Page 316: Shower bath. 90 mm. lens, fine-grain pan film, 1/200 sec., *f* 5.6. Photo: *A. Tritschler*.

Page 317: Spanish fisherman. 90 mm. lens, fast pan film, 1/200 sec., *f* 16. Photo: *J. Sadovy*.

Page 318: Artist in her studio. 50 mm. lens, fine-grain pan film, three 500-watt lamps, 1/10 sec., *f* 8. Photo: *W. Genzler*.

Page 319: Scottish haddock curer. 35 mm. lens, fine-grain pan film, 1/2 sec., *f* 9. Photo: *O. Marcus*.

Page 320: Old hands. 200 mm. lens, fine-grain pan film, 1/10 sec., *f* 9. Photo: *A. Tritschler*.

well out of reach, as in churches and historical buildings.

The wide-angle lenses (35 mm. and very occasionally 28 or 21 mm.) have a different use in architecture: they can cover subjects in confined spaces where it is impossible to go sufficiently far back.

The wide-angle view exaggerates perspective (p. 203) and proportions; this may be specially useful with interiors which acquire dramatic depth. Small rooms will look large, and big halls appear immense and spacious. With such shots, however, keep the foreground clear of furniture and similar objects; anything nearer than about 6 feet from the Leica will loom up huge. But when the foreground is the main subject, it is pictorially emphasized by such distortion.

A building, even taken as a whole, is rarely a completely isolated entity, but fits in—or clashes—with the place where it stands. Where the subject and its environment harmonize, the picture shows something of both, for each contributes to the character of the other.

Of the various surroundings, natural ones are the safest. Parks, gardens, or just trees, give the picture life; combined with lakes or rivers, the setting can acquire an indissoluble unity.

Decide which is the important part of the picture; if it is the building that matters, do not let the trees obscure it or the lawns and grounds dwarf it. Rather bring them in to relieve the severity which many architectural views on their own tend to have.

Where a building forms part of a street, include enough of the surroundings to establish its character. Shoot from a fairly high viewpoint to avoid large foreground area. With streets in particular the roadway tends to become too prominent.

Cars and other vehicles as well as figures form an essential part of larger expanses such as squares or market places, but should not be too near the camera.

Buildings should usually stand out against the sky. The greater the contrast between them, the more dramatic the result. The sky mostly needs to have the darker tone of the two, so use a filter, especially in sunshine. An orange or even red filter concentrates all the attention on the building.

However, this type of over-filtering has its dangers, too. Through a red filter, brickwork looks almost as white as concrete. Also, when the sun comes more or less from one side, the sky behind the building will be very deep blue already; a red filter will make it look practically black.

Colour film conveys the character even better. It shows plainly the difference between brick and marble, or between concrete and sandstone, or special types of building material such as Cotswold stone.

With colour shots remember also the colour of the shadows. If they are illuminated purely by the blue sky, they will have a definite bluish cast, while a lawn will make even a whitewashed cottage look greenish.

A high viewpoint puts things into a different perspective. The attraction of roof-tops shots is the sea of roofs and chimneys which are almost a world of their own, especially in old towns with hundreds of pinnacles, towers and buttresses.

Downward angle shots give bird's-eye views of the scene. Take such pictures when there is plenty of life down below, with cars, buses, trams and people, not empty streets.

In pictures of complete buildings, all parts should be sharp from the foreground to the farthest important point of the subject. It is only in detail shots that an unsharp background lifts the subject itself out of its surroundings.

With the Leica on a tripod, our focusing problem is not a difficult one, as we can stop down appreciably. Firstly, we shall have to shoot from some distance to cover a substantial part of the building. That means that there is quite a deep zone of sharpness.

Secondly, we can easily find the near and far limits of the field required with the rangefinder, and work out the settings from the depth indicator on the lens (p. 208).

The difficulties start with hand-held shots in lighting that is not strong enough for small apertures. Focusing then becomes a matter of compromise between depth required and depth possible under the circumstances.

A building is also something solid; look for a viewpoint, therefore, that shows two sides. The lighting will usually bring out the difference, illuminating one side more than the other.

An upright structure will look vertical only as long as the Leica is held truly level. In other words, the film must be parallel to the verticals of the building. If we cannot retreat far enough to include the top without inclining the Leica, the vertical lines will converge towards the top and make the building lean backwards.

To get over this, we can use a wide-angle lens which covers the whole height without calling for a camera tilt. It will also take in an excessive foreground area. The other way is to correct the tilt in the negative during enlarging.

If the uprights are not particularly prominent, e.g. with a statue or monument, a slightly inclined camera angle is not serious.

The effect of a tilt is smaller with a longer-focus lens. The longer the focal length, the more the perspective appears to be flattened out, and the less disturbing such a leaning image becomes. Since the verticals converge all towards one point, this convergence naturally seems less over a narrower angle than over a wide one.

For detail shots with a long-focus lens, therefore, we can safely point the Leica however we like.

A radical tilt of an angle shot, however, changes the orientation, and no longer looks uncomfortable. It is thus a permissible means of getting a pictorial effect.

Leica Portraits

A portrait is a study of that most expressive part of a person, the face. It should show a likeness to the person photographed; it must have personality and character, and above all, life.

The Leica approach to photographing people is an active one, not dependent on carefully arranged poses. Most people have enough grace to sit naturally, and if they have not, a pose will help little.

Some direction is, of course, necessary. Prepare everything, including the lighting beforehand as far as practicable. But avoid too complicated arrangements. In daylight, a reflector on the shadow side, indoors a couple of Photofloods will form a basic set-up.

Watch, then, the expression and the effect of the light on the face. Make exposures from different directions and angles while the sitter is talking and doing things.

Half or even a whole Leica load of thirty-six exposures is not too much film for a sitting. The first shots will rarely be successful, but they get the interest away from the camera.

Have sufficient light on the subject to allow reasonably fast shutter speeds to catch live expressions.

Portraits are best taken with a long-focus lens such as the

90, 125 or 135 mm. one. The 90 mm. Summicron $f2$ is specially useful because of its high speed. Even for groups the 90 mm. lens is advisable.

The long-focus lenses give close-up views at greater subject distances. They thus avoid the apparent distortion of features resulting from too close a viewpoint. In fact, take portraits from at least 6 feet (2 metres) away. At this distance the standard 50 mm. lenses cover a three-quarter length portrait, the 90 mm. lens a head-and-shoulder view, and the 125 or 135 mm. lens little more than the head. The 90 mm. is thus the ideal all-round portrait lens.

With carefully arranged set-ups the ground-glass screen of the reflex housing becomes desirable for viewing and focusing. This also permits the use of the 200 or 280 mm. Telyt lens for large close-up shots.

With the Telyt lens, the Leica is no longer on top of the subject, but becomes a detached observer, well out of the way some 20 feet from the sitter. To some extent that relaxes the stiffness of a formal portrait, for the subject will take less notice of the camera, and will yield more natural pictures.

The 125 mm. Hektor is specially designed to be used with the reflex housing in this way; in a smaller studio the great distance required with the Telyt is not possible, and this Hektor lens (or the 135 mm.) is the only feasible alternative.

For head or head-and-shoulders pictures set up the Leica at the same level as the head. Low-angle and high-angle views tend to over-emphasize the chin or forehead respectively. However, a high viewpoint can also be attractive where the model looks up into the Leica.

Avoid high-angle shots of people with a large expanse of bald head, and also with short-necked sitters. On the other hand, do not choose too low a camera angle for people with a pronounced chin or a long neck.

Long-focus lenses yield only a limited depth of field zone. This is often a real asset in portraiture, since it allows us to concentrate on the head only, and merge the background into a general blur. By focusing the 125 or 135 mm. lenses at full aperture, it is even possible to get only the plane of the face itself sharp, with the ears already noticeably blurred. This gives the face a degree of roundedness characteristic of portrait shots with a studio camera.

For such highly differential focusing the Leica must, of

course, be mounted on a tripod; the reflex housing provides a convenient way of checking the point of maximum sharpness exactly.

Differential focusing can easily be carried too far. It is not a universal trick to be applied to every portrait, but should be limited to head-on views where the eyes look straight into the camera. And it is the eyes which must be sharpest.

A sharp image, however perfect technically, is not always pleasing in portraiture. The Leica lenses show up every detail of the skin and wrinkles of a face—a desirable quality optically but not necessarily flattering aesthetically.

We can subdue this texture rendering by soft lighting, or by softening the definition by means of a soft-focus lens or attachment (p. 211).

Soft focus is usually the more successful method in portraiture. Soft lighting—unless it is high-key lighting—tends to be dull. Soft definition gives a pleasanter result and still retains the modelling and liveliness of a picture.

The degree of softening desirable depends on the subject and on the lighting, but is also a matter of taste.

The bolder the lighting, the more marked will be the effect of the soft focus lens. With comparatively even lighting, the picture may need an appreciable degree of softening in order to show up as such, as there are no contrasty boundaries across which the light would visibly spread. Against-the-light shots gain a specially luminous quality in this way.

The Thambar soft-focus portrait lens (p. 112) is considerably more tricky to use than a soft-focus attachment, and needs a fair amount of experience to make the most of its capabilities. The degree of softening in particular should be carefully watched. This changes more rapidly at large apertures than at small ones. A further complication is the fact that the softening —being due to intentional lack of spherical correction in the lens—is not even over the negative area, but increases towards the edges. The extent of this also depends on the aperture.

The best way to gain experience in using the Thambar is to make a series of experimental shots, varying both the aperture and the position of the subject in the field of view.

The centre stop again alters the situation completely. The nature of the softening changes, as well as the degree. With the stop, the effect becomes more uniform over the negative area from the centre to the corners. In addition, the apparent superimposition of a sharp and unsharp image gives way to a more over-all softening of definition and gradation.

Pictorially, the most useful range is between *f*2.2 and *f*3.2 without the centre stop, and *f*3.2 to *f*4.5 with the stop.

When making tests, it is necessary to enlarge the negatives; the effect is difficult to judge reliably on the film, or even on contact prints.

Like differential focusing methods, soft-focus is a means only to an end. Don't start softening every picture just for the sake of soft focus.

THE LEICA AT FULL PACE

With its fastest lenses the Leica will cover any subject in almost any light by which we can see enough ourselves.
At full aperture focus accurately with the rangefinder.
Allow for speed, distance, and direction of the subject in selecting shutter speeds in action shots.

While competent over the whole of its wide scope, the Leica naturally excels in those fields where subject and lighting conditions demand fast lens power, high shutter speeds, and all-over optimum performance. Many such subjects test the Leica to the limit, and can in fact only be tackled with a camera like the Leica.

High shutter speeds will enable us to take action subjects of all types, from sports and games to races, and other forms of rapid movement.

High lens speeds make the best of poor light, even indoors, and permit really short exposures under better conditions.

By combining ultra-fast lenses and shutter speeds we can deal with action shots at night, in the theatre, circus or ballet. Such a combination with the 50 mm. or 35 mm. (for wide-angle shots) Summilux and the 90 mm. Summicron (or the earlier 85 mm. Summarex) lenses will cover practically any subject under the most unpredictable taking conditions.

High-speed shooting with special accessories like the Leicavit rapid winder brings split-second picture sequences within the Leica range.

Night Life

The fast *f*1.2 and *f*1.4 lenses of the Leica will take pictures almost as long as there is enough light to see. With the aid of a high-speed film we can photograph in reasonably good artificial room lighting. That covers anything from family shots at home to restaurants and street scenes.

Our style need not be any less candid; though the slower shutter speeds necessary will also call for a more leisurely approach. At *f*1.2 to *f*2 there is not enough depth for zone focusing, so use the rangefinder carefully. Get a good support for the arms to hold the Leica steady, and take shots as they come, at 1/15 or 1/30 second at full aperture. This may mean waiting at times for moments of comparative inaction, but indoors there is rarely a great deal of excessive activity. People may play cards, talk to each other, or just listen. In any case, they will be relatively relaxed and at ease.

Flash is not ideal for such shots. It destroys the homely atmosphere and makes the picture look like a press photograph. Also the fuss it involves draws attention to the photographer and his gear; he is no longer an unobtrusive observer, but becomes something of a performing intruder.

Night life out of doors is less intimate, though just as interesting. We look equally unobtrusively at strangers. There is life too, sometimes gay and brilliant, sometimes furtive and sordid, but rarely humdrum. And it is photographable where there is sufficient light for short exposures: in the bright spots under street lamps, in front of brilliantly-lit shop windows, in cinema and theatre foyers, and the illuminated main streets —especially with ultra-speed films.

The light attracts people, who will be constantly coming out of the darkness and disappearing again like moths around a lamp. Usually there the light is good enough for shots at 1/30 second at *f*2 on a high-speed film.

Where the light is weaker, try to catch scenes with comparatively little movement to permit slower speeds. People lounging about, waiting for other people, will often keep still for several seconds. Couples on park benches may be motionless for longer, though less likely to go for bright spots.

Even fast-moving traffic has to come to a dead stop at traffic lights, and may wait quite a while before moving off again.

At night, the limited depth of field at full aperture matters little. Focus on the nearest bright area; that should be sharpest. The background need not be sharp; the night hides most of the detail.

Focus by scale if the view is not bright enough to see plainly in the rangefinder.

Infra-red flash is useful for unobserved shooting. Load the Leica with infra-red film and fit an infra-red lamp filter (e.g. gelatine) in front of the flash gun. The flash will then be almost invisible.

For really colourful night life go to the fairground. Photograph the crowds at the side shows, the illuminated pavilions, and the roundabouts. Many of these subjects are bright enough for exposures up to 1/125 second at *f*2 or *f*1.4.

Expose when people are really near to the lamps. If possible, get the stallholder's permission to shoot from inside the stalls;

CHILDREN IN OUR TIME

One great difference between children and adults is the freedom with which a child runs through its emotions. Most of the time children are thoroughly unrestrained and unvarnished: we can photograph them with the same honesty with which they are exhibited.

The younger a child, the more small occurrences of an ordinary day become special events. This wealth of impressions and experiences crowding in on the young mind produces every imaginable uninhibited reaction, compressed into almost too short a time for a grown-up to take notice.

This, then, is ideal picture material for the Leica. Our worry, more often than not, is to keep up with the pace of it all, rather than wait for things to happen. We can shoot off whole loads of film to capture the countless expressions, gestures, and activities. In that way we get a true picture of how a child's personality is made up of so many individual facets.

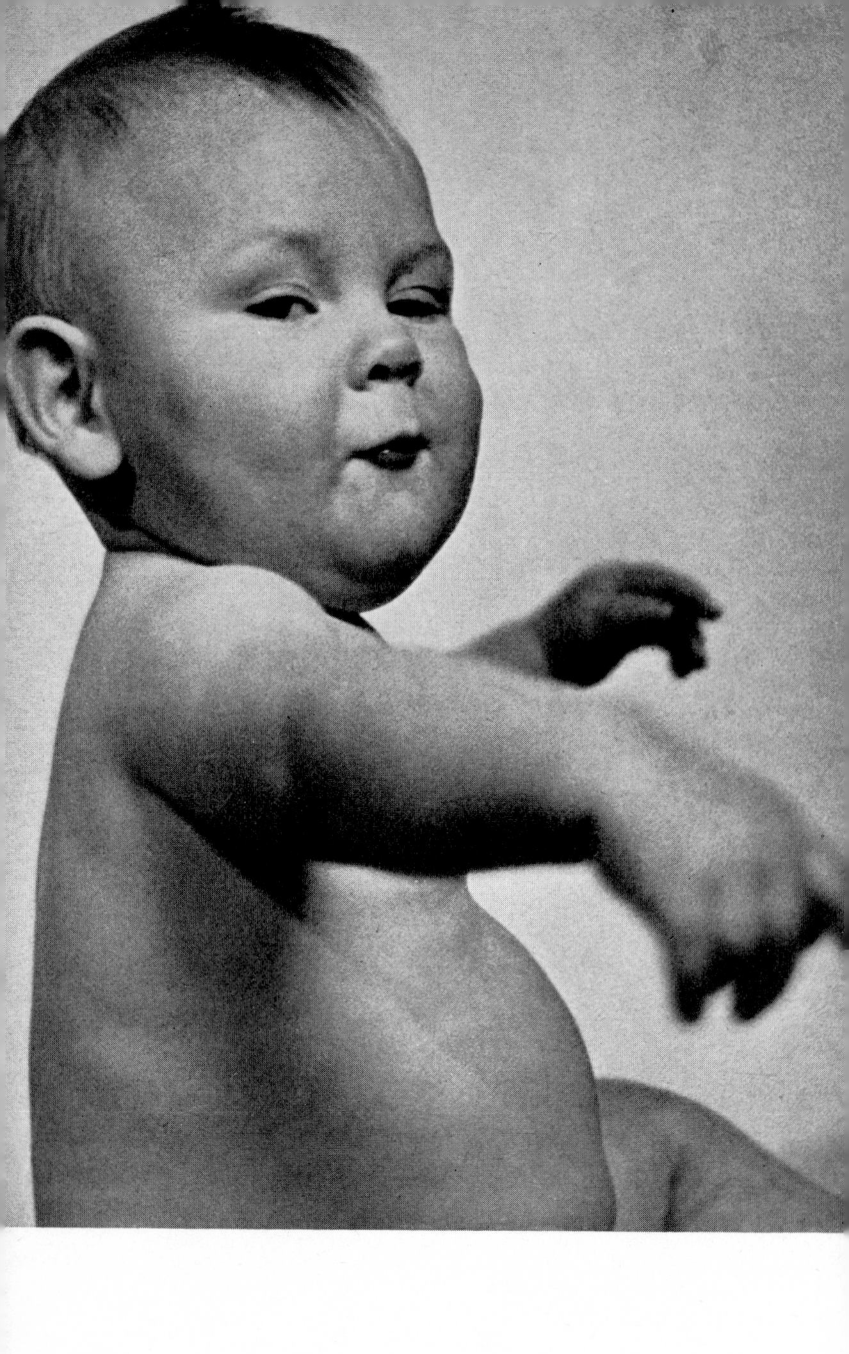

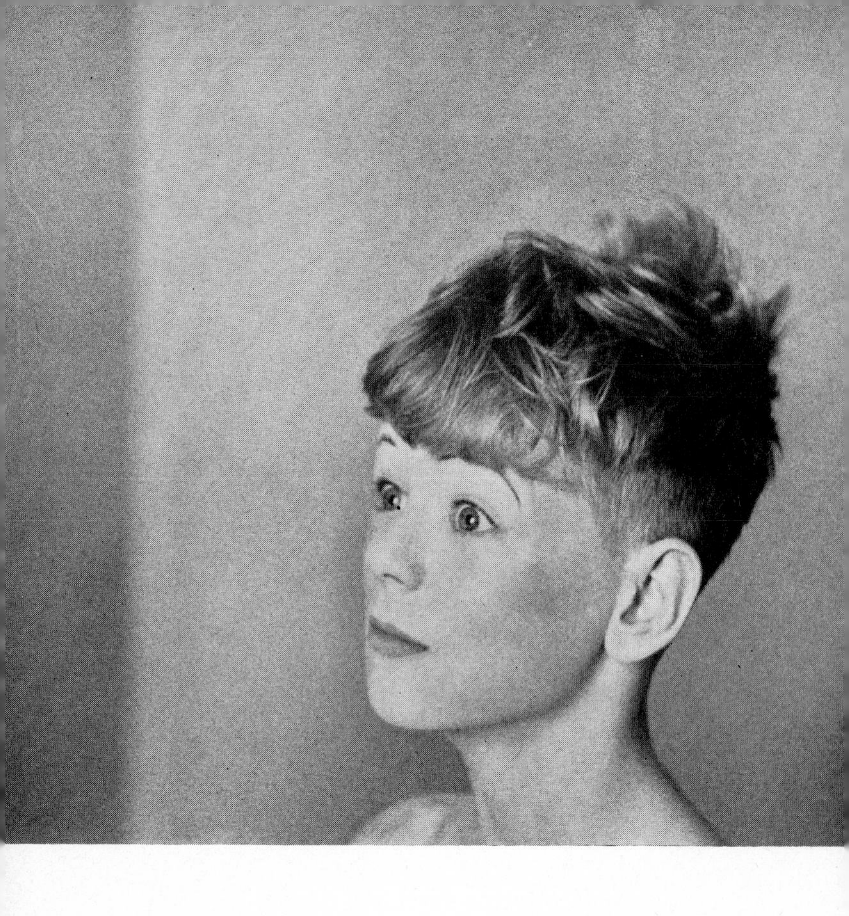

Page 329: Gossip and giggles. 35 mm. lens, medium-speed pan film, 1/20 sec., f 4.5. Photo: *C. Hewitt* (courtesy *Hulton Press*).

Page 330: Out of depth. 50 mm. lens, fast pan film, 1/100 sec., *f*8. Photo: *J. Sadovy*.

Page 331: In the shallows. 90 mm. lens, fine-grain pan film, 1/60 sec., *f*4.5. Photo: *F. Klaus*.

Page 332: Mother and child. 85 mm. lens, fine-grain pan film, 1/50 sec., *f*2. Photo: *A. Tritschler*.

Page 333: Child and child. 35 mm. lens, fast pan film, 1/200 sec., *f*11. Photo: *J. Sadovy*.

Page 334: Attention attracted. 50 mm. len s, fast pan film, ordinary room lighting, 1/100 sec., *f*2. Photo: *J. Sadovy*.

Page 335: Attention distracted. 50 mm. lens, fine-grain pan film, two electronic flash units (1/5000 sec.), *f*9. Photo: *A. Tritschler*.

Above: Make-up for the school play. 50 mm. lens, fast pan film, 1/60 sec., *f*2. Photo: *D. Potts*.

hide in an inconspicuous corner to avoid attracting attention.

The strings of lamps on the big dipper and the roundabouts and gyro-swings make attractive patterns, but usually need a time exposure to show some detail.

Try taking pictures of the roundabouts in motion; open the Leica shutter and keep it open while everything goes round and the lights record as bizarre traces on the film.

Night Views

Lens speed is less important with static subjects at night like quiet streets, without much life in them. Such scenes show shapes rather than detail. The latter gets lost in the darkness, and the outlines of large masses take on fantastic forms, relieved by pools of light.

The light makes the picture. It may consist of neon lamps and advertising signs, modern lamp standards, quaint gas lights, flood-lit buildings, old-world corners, or rows of illuminated windows in a block of flats.

The lights themselves can create the pattern of the picture, or they may illuminate the scene around them. The light alone will register with quite short exposures, but the surroundings will need time exposures. The longer the exposure, the deeper the Leica can penetrate into the darkness. But with long times the lamps will be greatly over-exposed and come out as shapeless blurs, generally with a sort of halo, as the light spreads around the image.

Strong lamps can also cause flare, ghost images of lamps in another part of the picture, often surrounded by a large circle. It is caused by internal reflections in the camera lens, and is liable to occur usually diagonally opposite the image of the lamp itself. Therefore avoid including very bright and near light sources; try hiding them behind trees, or even a figure in the foreground. Shifting the camera position a little to the left or right may do the trick.

Lamps just outside the picture area may also cause flare spots, so use an efficient lens hood for all-night pictures. If a lamp is very near the edge of the field of view and only just outside it, screen if from the lens by means of a hat or something of the sort held in the right posision.

This risk is reduced with the Noctilux *f*1.2 lens which is designed to yield the minimum of flare even when shooting scenes including light sources.

The exposure itself may take anything from a few seconds in brilliant floodlighting to several minutes for views under a weaker gas lamp. The exact time is largely a matter of experience; but quite appreciable over or under-exposure will still yield acceptable pictures. (But allow for reciprocity failure —p. 234.)

For readings with the Leicaflex SL point the camera so that one or two lamps or a well lit area falls into the measuring circle in the finder screen.

When using a separate exposure meter, point it at the pool of light under a lamp from close by, or point it at the lamp from directly underneath for a highlight reading (p. 219).

People walking past the camera will not register during a lengthy exposure. Any foreground figure you wish to include must stay still all the time. Screen the lens while cars are passing, as their lights will register as brilliant streaks.

Night shots are particularly effective after rain, as such pictures combine the atmosphere of poor weather with the pictorial quality of night views. Rain adds sparkle and life, and the reflections on wet pavements and puddles multiply the pattern of the lights.

As there is more reflected light about, exposures can be shorter, too. At the same time, take extra care to shield the lens from stray reflections, and also from drops of rain.

Snow also improves night shots by relieving the darkness of street and pavement surfaces. Look for quiet back streets where the traffic has not churned up the road too much.

Trees, with heavy piles of snow on their branches, look well if taken just in front of a street lamp against the light.

Light fog or mist has a special charm of its own. It diffuses the harsh light of the street lamps into the shadows, so that the whole scene acquires a gentle luminosity. The picture becomes a series of outlines and shapes, increasing in blackness as they recede from the light source.

The misty air also shows up shadows cast by objects such as lamp posts in the foreground. Hide the lamp behind a tree to photograph the solid beams of light stabbing into the fog.

Night-type shots are often most successful at dusk. On the one hand, the streets with the lamps have already a nocturnal character, on the other, there is still sufficient light in the sky to record as a faint grey tone instead of an inky blackness.

This state of affairs only lasts about 15–20 minutes.

Action Technique

Action means speed in terms of timing and camera manipulation, as well as subject movement. We must be ready to expose at a moment's notice with prepared camera settings (aperture, distance, and focusing zones—p. 210).

A shutter speed table (p. 463) is the most accurate guide to the correct speed required to arrest subject movement. But an easily memorized system helps greatly in a hurry.

For instance a subject moving at 15 miles per hour across our field of view (e.g. a sprinter, a cyclist, a slow car, etc.) 30–40 feet (10 metres) away would need a shutter speed of 1/125 second. That is equivalent to a slowly running figure 15–20 feet (5 metres) or a walker 8 feet (2.5 metres) away, or again a galloping horse, a faster car or slow train (30 miles per hour) at 70 feet (20 metres).

Then simply halve the exposure time for double the basic distance, or double it at half the basic distance.

If the subject is coming towards the camera, reduce the basic shutter speed to 1/30 second and use 1/60 second for oblique movement.

With long-focus lenses divide the basic shutter time by the magnifying power of the lens. Thus with the 90 mm. lens 1/125 second becomes approximately 1/250 second; with the 135 mm. lens 1/500 second (as the Leica has no 1/300 second) and so on.

If the light is not good enough for a suitable small aperture (to cover the depth required) with a sufficiently fast speed to deal with the movement, we have to compromise between the extent of image movement and the error in focusing that we are prepared to tolerate.

We can make do with slower shutter speeds by taking the picture from farther away. This also permits a larger aperture to achieve the required depth of field. However, this only works if we use the whole of the negative. When enlarging only part, or using a long-focus lens, we more than lose any advantage gained by the greater distance.

Other tricks to capture action with a comparatively slow speed include shooting the subject head-on—where the apparent movement is less (p. 231)—and following the subject with the Leica, swinging the camera round while releasing.

In this way, the subject will be sharp against a blurred background, enhancing the impression of speed. The swinging movement must be steady, not jerky, keeping the subject in the centre of the finder field. The sports and brilliant finders (p. 122) are ideal for this. Move the whole body from the waist upwards, not just the hands holding the Leica.

This method is limited to subjects moving as a whole in one direction at the same speed; e.g. racing cars, but not race-horses, where the legs move separately and will come out blurred in the picture.

The Right Moment

At its top speed the Leica shutter moves much faster than the eye can react. It then freezes action which we can only perceive as continuous movement.

To capture such subjects needs anticipation, by pressing the release just a fraction of the second before the instant we want to arrest. The shutter will then open at the right moment for the action.

A whirling dancer, for instance, may face the Leica when we press, but by the time the shutter begins to open, the picture only shows her back. To secure the shot, expose while her back is turned, before she turns round the next time.

The faster the movement, the more important this technique of anticipation. Often the moment to expose becomes a matter of guesswork—supported by experience. Fast film advance is also important. With the appropriate Leica models the rapid winder (p. 346) or motor drive (pp. 168, 348) is there a useful means of securing a number of shots in quick succession and increases the chance of capturing the most favourable instant.

Studying the action beforehand, where possible, will of course help by showing what is likely to happen. It should also provide some indication of the distance and shutter speeds that will be required.

The right moment itself varies with different types of action subjects. In sports shots it is the instant of maximum tension just before or at the climax of, say, a jump. It is the facial expression of intensive concentration as much as the pose of the body that tells the story.

At the same time such moments are often dead points as far as action is concerned. The movement itself may be at a standstill for a fraction of a second, as at the top of a leap, or at the extremity of pulling back before throwing a javelin, ball or weight. In fact such dead points will not require as fast a shutter speed as the movement just before or after.

With dancers and similar rhythmically moving subjects, the right moment is usually an instant of relaxation during the movement. The action itself may be fastest at that point, but it covers the most graceful parts of the flow of motion.

A large depth of field zone is useful, but not really essential for most kinds of action photography. If the light is too poor use more accurate focusing methods at larger apertures.

For shots where the subject has to pass a fixed point, such as a finishing line in a race, simply focus on that point, and release when the subject is in the right position. Alternatively, set the lens to a suitable distance, watch through the range-finder eyepiece, and expose when the subject fuses into focus.

We can even follow the subject in the rangefinder, though this requires a little more practice, particularly if the movement is erratic. A useful trick is to "race ahead" with the rangefinder, i.e. in following the movement, go a little beyond the subject and wait for the latter to catch up before releasing.

Taking Sports

Sports fall into well-defined groups with similar problems, like team games, field sports, contests and so on.

The way we tackle the types as well as the individual sports depends also on our own opportunities of movement. An amateur present as a spectator is less likely to have permission to roam about than a press photographer.

When covering sports, carry your gear in a holdall case. Alternatively, reserve one empty pocket—of jacket or overcoat—for each lens (standard and medium long focus) and another separate one for a frame finder covering both focal lengths, in order to be able to change over quickly. That is much more convenient than a hold-all camera case. Thoroughly brush the pockets free of dust beforehand, then there is no need to put lens caps on every lens.

The reflected image frames of the Leica M finders (and the IIIg) are particularly handy here.

Organized games, such as contest between teams (football, hockey, etc.) usually take place out of doors. In most cases we are up against fast action anywhere within a defined but large field. We shall need a long-focus lens, exposing at full aperture with the fastest shutter speeds to eliminate camera shake.

Close-ups from the side or ends of the field, on or behind goal lines, give really fast action shots. Follow the ball, puck or other missile in the finder; it is the focal point of the game.

In cricket or baseball, where the focal point of action is around fixed portions in the middle of a very large field, we can mount the Leica with a long-focus lens on a tripod for greater steadiness.

In races, where we have to photograph one or several subjects moving at a fairly uniform speed, close low-angle shots, nearly head-on, at a range of about 5 to 20 yards, are most effective near the finishing line.

For jumps in races like steeplechasing and hurdling, a low viewpoint produces the best pictures. Release just as the horse or runner appears over the fence or hurdle, making use of the dead point (p. 340). For spills, shoot as the horse and rider come adrift.

With sports where the action is largely confined to one spot (throwing, shooting, golf), concentrate on the expression of the player—it sums up the efforts of judging position, speed and movement. A series of close-ups of the face, taken with a long-focus lens from a safe distance, may be more telling than any phase of the action—which in many cases could easily be posed in the right position.

Shows

In the theatre, circus, and at cabarets we are up against some of the photographically most challenging conditions: action combined with poor light.

The most successful way of dealing with the subject is to utilize the light of spotlights reserved for star turns. There even fast acts can be captured with 1/500 second at *f*2 or *f*1.4 in a circus or music hall.

The role of the Leica is that of a story-teller, following the turn or the plot on the stage, and shooting during the performance (but get permission first). With some experience we may be able to anticipate, or at least instinctively feel, when something important is about to happen. It is, however, a help to go and see the show beforehand, and note down picture-making opportunities.

At a play, there is little arranging to be done. The story unfolds itself on the stage in front of us. All we have to do is to expose and keep exposing.

The best viewpoint for pictures in the theatre is the front row of the dress circle, or the eighth to fifteenth row in the stalls. Farther away, we can rarely fill the Leica negative.

Choose a seat half-way between the centre and the edge of the row. Dead centre views are less interesting.

Views of the whole stage are apt to be disappointing, especially in the larger theatres. Dramatic grouping, from the stage point of view, is far from ideal for photography, since producers try to spread out the actors well over the stage.

The only exception are operatic or musical scenes where the whole stage is crowded. Use the 50 mm. lens to cover the whole stage; from farther away a long-focus lens is essential.

Otherwise, try to capture smaller and closely-knit groups of two or three actors. For views of actors or small groups use a long-focus lens, such as the 90 mm. Summicron. From farther away, we may have to use the 135 mm. lens, though its smaller maximum aperture limits its use to brilliantly spotlit single figures. Even then 1/25 or 1/30 second will be the shortest practical exposure time. To steady the camera, lean the elbows against the arms of the seat, or use a unipod support.

With the Leicaflex SL make sure that only the stage (and none of the black surround) fills the central measuring circle of the finder screen. The reading will then yield reasonably correct exposures.

In the front row of the circle, the balustrade provides a firm support, and will allow even exposures of 1/8 to ½ second at static moments on the stage. That is particularly useful at operatic performances where the lighting may be greatly turned down, but there the singers will also stand comparatively still for seconds on end during an aria.

We can utilize the lighting tricks on the stage to enhance the effect. They set the mood of the play, and can equally well set the atmosphere of the photograph—provided they are not too dim. Stage scenes lit in colours are, however, best left alone. The lighting is already reduced when colour effects come into play, and the colour makes it weaker still. Greens and deep blues are worst in this respect. In any case, such scenes depend on the colour harmony on the stage, something which our black-and-white film could not record even if the light were strong enough. And colour film—except perhaps the fastest types—is too slow for that type of subject.

Cabarets staged in restaurants and night clubs are on a much more intimate and informal scale. We can shoot individual turns from close range, with settings only just indicated or altogether absent. For singers go as near as possible, but keep farther away for dancers.

Here, too, the lighting mainly consists of spotlights. The subject is best lit when the spots come from more or less behind the camera viewpoint. Against-the-light shots, however, show silhouettes of dancing girls and other figures with dresses brilliantly lit from behind.

With a floor show we can usually move about to get a favourable view, shooting from the side as well as from the front. Even flash may be allowed.

Ice shows, where the movement of the skaters tends to be unpredictable, call for specially quick camera manipulation. As following a figure in the rangefinder, shooting to and fro across the ice, is not easy, focus on a fairly narrow fixed zone. At the same time be prepared to shift the zone forward or back at a moment's notice, for skaters rarely perform the same turn twice in exactly the same spot.

Memorize three or four distance settings which can be switched at a glance on the focusing scale. Then change from zone to zone whenever necessary, almost while following the subject. The important point is that we must switch from one definite setting to the next, without attempting to track the subject in the rangefinder. The latter serves merely to show when the subject moves into sharp focus within its zone. The Televit (p. 425) or the Focorapid unit (p. 137) used with the Visoflex II or III is ideal for this purpose.

Ballet

Dancers express themselves by figures of movement. The action may be fast or slow, but it is constantly changing. The Leica has to slice out sections from this sequence and tell the story of the ballet by a series of shots, each summing up one stage of the flow, like one beat of the rhythm of the dance.

In ballet photography rapid shooting is thus more important than ever to put over something of the continuity of the action, to capture as many of the expressions of hands, arms, and patterns of bodies on the stage as possible.

The fastest shutter speed the light will allow is usually necessary. On the other hand, a certain amount of movement blur, especially of dresses, helps to enliven a photograph of a whirling dancer where it might otherwise have looked posed. Ballet does, of course, include almost motionless poses, but they lead up to or away from genuine high-speed action.

Many ballet productions are unfortunately lit in colour which limits the amount of photography possible during a performance. If a photo-call or demonstration for the benefit of the Leica can be arranged, we can use flash.

Use a couple of large professional electronic units of 500 or 1,000 joules. The portable electronic flash outfits are insufficient to light up anything more than shots at close range. Two or three 1,000-joule units will provide sufficient lighting for action shots in colour or daylight-type film.

In synchronizing the lamps with the Leica, keep all triggering cables well out of everybody's way.

Quick Shooting Technique

Advancing the film with the Leica film transport takes about a second. After a little practice it should be easy enough even without taking the eye from the finder eye-piece.

This is perfectly adequate for subjects where we would expose once every few seconds.

For a really rapid series, however, such as a cycle of a single movement, we must be able to shoot much more quickly. The ideal accessory here is the motor for the Leicaflex (p. 168) or for the Leica M2 (p. 348). But even a rapid winder attachment speeds up the film transport—especially with the older screw-mounted Leicas which have no winding lever. In this way we can follow, for instance, the graceful leap of a springboard diver from the board to the water. Similarly, time and motion studies for industrial and scientific photography are well within the scope of the Leica.

Some movements cycles, of course, take place even faster. To photograph these subjects, we have to shoot the cycle over several times to cover every phase.

Use fast shutter speeds for motion studies, for the individual pictures must be sharp. The slowest usable speed is 1/125 second. This may call for powerful light sources, since many of these subjects have to be taken indoors.

Electronic flash may also be used, provided the sequence is not too rapid. The unit must be powered by a high-tension battery and designed for quick recharging. Some outfits of this kind charge up the capacitor for the next flash in a fraction of a second; a portable accumulator unit may take anything up to a quarter of a minute.

The Leicavit Rapid Winder

A special accessory for picture series to increase the rate of shooting is the Leicavit rapid winder. The model MP fits the Leica M1 and M2 (but not the M3). It is, in fact, identical with the Leicavit fitted on the Leica MP.

For screw-mounted Leicas an alternative model is available, and fits models of serial numbers from 360,000 onwards (cameras numbers 360,000 to 399,999 have to be adapted by the makers).

It consists of a special base plate (to take the place of the normal base plate) with a built-in winding handle which works the film transport from below. With the Leicavit winder, therefore, one hand can work the film transport while the other releases the shutter, at the rate of two exposures a second, or even faster.

To fit the rapid winder, load the Leica in the usual way, but mount the rapid winder on the camera bottom instead of the standard base plate. In place of the orthodox locking key, the rapid winder has a radial lever at one end. Move this from "auf-open" to "zu-closed."

With cameras of serial numbers up to 622,251 the base plate lock in the camera body must be changed. For that purpose unscrew the two screws next to the cassette chamber, fit the locking plate supplied with the Leicavit, and screw down again.

Make the usual initial blind exposure after loading. Then fold the winding handle out of the base, until it locks in position, pull the handle to the left (i.e. towards the rewind knob end of the Leica) as far as it will go, to engage the transport shaft, and let go. The camera is now ready to shoot.

When using the rapid winder, the Leica is held slightly differently from the way described on p. 31. The grip of the right hand remains the same, but the left edge of the Leica is pressed into the left palm between thumb and index finger. The left index finger stretches along the front of the camera, while the second finger grips the winding handle. This applies to both horizontal and vertical shots.

The grip does not allow for focusing, but in rapid sequence shots there is never time for that between exposures. Focus normally beforehand, or use focusing zones (p. 210).

To make rapid sequence shots, simply release the shutter with the right index finger, pull the handle to the left with the left index finger, release again, and so on. The important point is that the handle must be pulled to the left all the way, otherwise the film will not advance fully. If there is any doubt, try pulling a second time.

Always let the handle return to its original position before pressing the release, otherwise the pull of the winder may shift the film slightly during exposure, giving blurred shots.

LEICAVIT

The main parts of the Leicavit are:

1. Folding handle.
2. Locking button.
3. Camera lock.

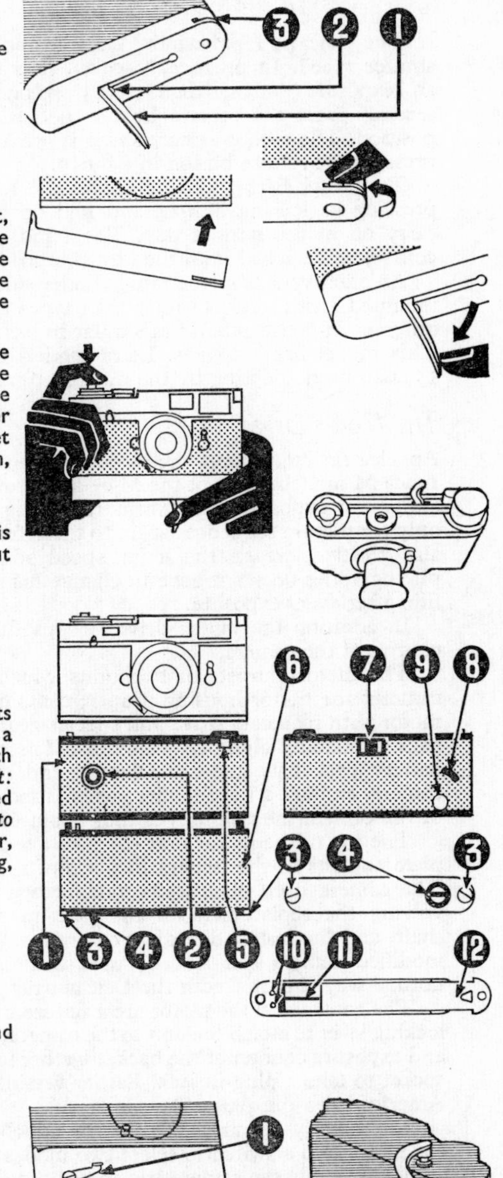

To attach the Leicavit, fit it to the bottom of the camera like the baseplate and move the lock to the closed position. Unfold the winding handle.

To shoot, press the release button to take the picture then pull the handle with the left index finger as far as it will go and let it fly back. Expose again, to start the next cycle.

The old rapid winder is similar in principle, but different in construction.

THE M MOTOR DRIVE

The motor drive consists of a motor housing and a battery housing which attach to the camera. *Left*: Front view of exploded units. *Right* (*from top to bottom*): Rear of motor, base of battery housing, top of battery housing.

1. Motor housing.
2. Release button.
3. Locking screws
4. Selector switch.
5. Locking lever.
6. Battery housing.
7. Remote control and external supply sockets.
8. Exposure counter.
9. Counter setting.
10. Contact pins.
11. Batteries.
12. Battery cover.

The main controls of the pre-war spring-powered motor are:

1. Release lever.
2. Winding key.
3. Transmission arm.
4. Exposure counter.

The Leicavit rapid winder can theoretically be used at any shutter speed. In practice, however, it is not advisable to use an exposure longer than 1/125 second—preferably 1/250 second—since the camera hold is not as firm as the normal position. The risk of camera shake is greater, particularly when pressing the release button in a hurry.

To change back to single exposures, release the handle by pressing its locking button, and fold up into the body. Then carry on in the normal way. The rapid winder must not, of course, be detached until the film is unloaded.

An older version of the rapid winder suitable for early screw-mounted Leica models (other than types c and f) is somewhat different in construction but similar in principle and operation. This model has a trigger. Leica models of serial Nos. below 159,000 need adapting by the manufacturer.

The Motor Drive

An electric motor unit produced by Leitz in the U.S.A. fits Leica M models—except the M3—and provides both automatic and rapid exposure and transport cycling. This is useful not only for picture sequences at up to three frames per second, but also greatly increases the action speed of the camera since the photographer does not have to change his grip to transport the film after every exposure.

In addition the motor drive is a useful means for remote control of the camera.

The motor consists of two units which fit together to the camera: the motor housing proper, containing a direct current motor with planetary drive and special gear train; and a power pack containing eight 1.5 volt cells. The complete motor and battery pack have the same length and depth as a Leica M camera, and are a little higher; when attached to the underside of the camera the assembly is thus about 6¼ inches high.

The top of the motor unit contains a modified Leica M base plate and fits to the camera in place of the normal base plate. The camera itself also needs modification by the makers, involving the replacement of the take-up spool and transport shaft, and the installation of an internal shutter trip lever. The modified camera can still be used without the motor in the normal way (but not with the Leicavit rapid winder).

The controls on the motor are a release button on the front, a locking lever to attach the unit to the camera, and a setting button and exposure counter at the back, together with a remote control socket to take a plug-in jack. Earlier versions have a socket for American two-pin plugs (flat pin type).

The battery housing contains the attachment bolts to fit to the motor and a switch to select two modes of operation.

To assemble the camera and motor remove the base plate of the modified camera and fit the motor housing in its place. Before attachment move the locking lever round to the front of the motor housing, and swing to the back to lock the housing to the camera.

Check that the battery housing is correctly loaded. Let the locking screw farthest from the control switch in the base drop down and pull off the sliding cover in the top. Insert eight heavy-duty size AA (or No. U7) cells, lining them up with their poles pointing in the directions shown inside the housing. Then slide the cover back into place and push the locking screw through. Attach the battery housing to the motor so that the white dot on the rim of the housing lines up with the white dot on the motor housing just below the release button. The contact pins of the battery housing must connect with the contacts in the base of the motor. Screw down the retaining screws tightly.

Before using the camera it must be loaded with the motor unit removed. Insert the film in the usual way, but do not fire off any blind exposures. Merely advance the film by one frame once it is correctly threaded. Turn the milled knob of the special take-up spool fitted in the camera clockwise to lock it in the depressed position. Do not release the shutter.

Press the release button on the motor once or twice to make sure that the driving shaft lines up with the slot in the transport shaft of the camera. Attach the motor as described above and lock it in place on the camera. Now make the two blind exposures—either with the normal transport lever of the camera or with the motor. Set the film counter of the camera to O.

The motor can only be attached when the camera shutter is fully tensioned, the take-up spool locked down and the motor operated after attachment of the battery housing.

The motor can be set to run off a sequence of any number of exposures. Slide the setting button in the back of the motor to the right until the exposure counter next to it indicates the number of exposures required. This can be up to the full 36 exposure load of a cassette.

Select the mode of operation with the switch in the base of the battery housing. This has three positions: Off, H and L. At the H setting, pressing the release button on the motor, makes the latter cycle (releasing the shutter and advancing the film) at up to three frames per second with shutter speeds above 1/125 second. At slower speeds the framing rate of course slows down. The other setting, marked L, cycles the motor at one frame per second because it receives only half the battery voltage. This setting is recommended for lower shutter speeds and whenever a high cycling rate is not necessary; the motor is much quieter then.

One set of batteries usually provides sufficient power to expose about 20 films.

With any selected exposure sequence the motor keeps cycling as long as the release button on the front is depressed. It stops either on releasing the button or when the pre-selected exposure series reaches its end. This is shown by the exposure counter running back from the set number to zero. At this point the whole motor circuit cuts out and can be reset by setting the counter to a new exposure series.

The motor also cuts out if more exposures have been set on the counter than are left on the film. When this happens, turn the selector switch to "Off" and rewind the film in the usual way.

If the motor should jam remove the battery housing from the motor. Set the camera to a fast speed and switch to H. Wait about half a minute and hold the battery housing and motor pointing in opposite directions while touching the contacts on the motor with the contact pins on the battery housing. This reverses the motor to clear the blockage. Make sure that the camera shutter is tensioned and refit the battery housing to the motor.

Always switch off the motor by the selector switch in the base of the battery housing when not required. Exhausted batteries wind the motor more slowly, so giving direct indication of when they need renewal. The motor will also operate sluggishly if the film cassette has been distorted in any way, thus opposing the smooth passage of the film through the cassette slot.

A separate D.C. power source can be plugged into the coxial socket next to the remote control socket on the back of the motor. This can be an accumulator, or a set of batteries. One use of this is in cold weather—which affects the efficiency of batteries—when a separate battery case can be carried in a pocket and connected to the camera motor by a cable.

A clockwork spring motor also used to be available for screw-mounted pre-war Leica cameras—but not types c, f or g. This fits on the bottom of the camera in place of the base plate and connects to the release button of the camera by means of a transmission arm. Operation is by pressing a release lever on the front of the motor, after winding the latter with a key in the base. The motor provides up to 12 exposures at one winding and can be used with shutter speeds faster than 1/20 second.

Remote Control

The motor drive also lends itself to operation by remote control. For this purpose a two-wire cable or flex with a suitable plug (see also p. 348) at one end and a switch at the other plugs into the remote control socket in the back of the motor. Owing to the comparatively high internal resistance of the motor system, it accepts quite long remote control connections without loss of operational reliability. A normal 3 amp or 5 amp type lighting flex up to several hundred feet long can be used. Alternatively the motor can be released by radio signals via a receiver in which the signals operate a relay. This is again connected to the remote control socket on the motor.

If the camera is linked with an electronic flash unit, remote-controlled exposures are possible even at night—for example with photo traps in nature photography, to get shy animals to take their own pictures. Such a trap consists of a carefully camouflaged platform with a sensitive remote control switch (connected to the camera motor) fitted underneath.

The camera is set up nearby and focused on the platform. When the animal treads on the latter, it takes its own picture.

Such a system is equally suitable for birds, as the weight required to close the contact can be very finely adjusted.

Whenever the Leica is set up out of doors in such arrangements, make suitable provision to protect it from rain and other weather risks. The camera controls must of course be pre-set and the lens focused on an appropriate distance.

A distant release also used to be available for the pre-war Leica models. This clipped over the camera to bear on the release button, and carried a winding drum to clamp over the film transport knob. Operation was by two cords, one for the release and one for the winding drum.

Under-water Photography

As a sport of comparatively recent origin, under-water photography of sea animals has become popular. Especially on the Mediterranean coast shallow water makes the colourful marine life easily accessible. Coral reefs of the Pacific islands provide an equally prolific, though (in view of octopuses, man-eating sharks, and similar creatures) more dangerous hunting ground.

Apart from the diving or under-water swimming gear, we need a water-proof case for the Leica. This must have a window in front for the lens, and some means of releasing the shutter and, if possible, winding the film, from the outside. A viewfinder should be fixed to the outside of the case, since the Leica finder would be too difficult to use.

The shutter speed and aperture have to be preset, about 1/125 second at *f*2 would be right. The light rapidly gets weaker the deeper we go. Therefore work as near as possible to the surface. Set the distance to 15 feet; owing to the higher refractive index of water, objects about 20 feet away will be sharpest at this setting.

For pictures at greater depths, where a proper diving suit is necessary, a powerful electronic flash outfit, appropriately synchronized to the Leica, will provide sufficient light. This is also suitable for colour shots on daylight type colour film. Under-water colour photographs by daylight tend to be disappointing, since the water filters out an appreciable part of the spectrum of sunlight.

Under-water shots need not be limited to the sea cost; we can also take them in ponds and rivers.

A suitable way of getting such pictures is to construct a longish water-tight box with a glass bottom, and mount the Leica in the back. The latter stays above the water surface, while we explore the under-water life through the glass bottom. In this case the Leica view- and rangefinder can be used to measure the effective distance and to observe the scene.

A bait in front of the box will attract fish.

CLOSE-UP EQUIPMENT

The distance gauges are the simplest means of copying at fixed distances and scales of reproduction.
With the focusing stage, bellows, reflex housing, and Reprovit the subject can be accurately focused on a ground-glass screen.
The Leicaflex is particularly versatile at close range.

Close-up accessories bring the subject nearer to the Leica than its focusing limit of about 3½ feet or 1 metre. The various instruments for this purpose cover taking distances down to a few inches, reproducing subjects at life-size and even larger.

Close-ups require accurate focusing, and in view of the limited depth of field (p. 206) the use of the Leica rangefinder is very restricted. Similarly the parallax of the normal Leica finder does not allow precise viewing at such close range.

All the more advanced close-up accessories therefore incorporate some means either of focusing the lens exactly at the required subject distance, or of placing the subject accurately at a fixed distance from the lens. At the same time they show directly the actual limits of the field of view.

The Leicaflex with screen focusing and through-the-lens viewing is ideal for all close-up photography.

The Close-up System

We can classify Leica close-up equipment in two groups.

The first comprises the simple close-up gear using increased lens-to-film distances, like the close-up focusing mounts and the close-up stands, and distance gauges used in conjunction with a special sets of extension tubes.

The close-up gear of the second group constitutes a system of its own for more advanced close-range work, scientific macrophotography, and copying.

A close-up photography set-up here consists of:

A viewing and focusing unit (reflex housing, focusing stage).

One or more fixed or variable extension units if required (extension tubes or focusing bellows).

A suitable support to facilitate setting up the equipment.

Any one of the focusing units can be used with any one of the extension units and any suitable support. This provides a very flexible method of building up and organizing a close-up photography outfit. By a suitable combination of units we may cover a continuous range of magnifications up to ten

TRUE TO NATURE

Successful animal portraits rely on expression (p. 357) even more than human faces, for at first glance similar animals tend to look much more alike. With pets at home, or creatures at the Zoo, we can study their personality and take pictures at comparative leisure.

Wild life photography, however, like hunting, calls for a lot of patience and perseverance. But the trophies are pictures of life instead of corpses, skins, and antlers. The free animal world does not trust man, and is wary of revealing its secrets.

To be unnoticed observers, we have to hide particularly well; frequently only the Leica itself is admitted into the presence of the animal. We have to shoot either from a distance with telephoto lenses (p. 356), or operate the camera by remote control to capture a rare glimpse of a rare creature like a heron (*above*).

With animals, series photography really comes into its own, for it tells us fascinating details of their life and habits as a live documentary picture of nature. At the same time we can, with the help of electronic flash, follow events that occur too fast for observation by eye. Many of these activities are of scientific interest, like the manner in which a swallow flies to its nest (*left*), or the proof that a bat rolls over sideways a split second before landing upside down (*opposite*).

Such series are not of course genuine sequences (for that we should require a high-speed cine camera), but the story is pieced together from many attempts at synchronizing the flash with the Leica at slightly different instants.

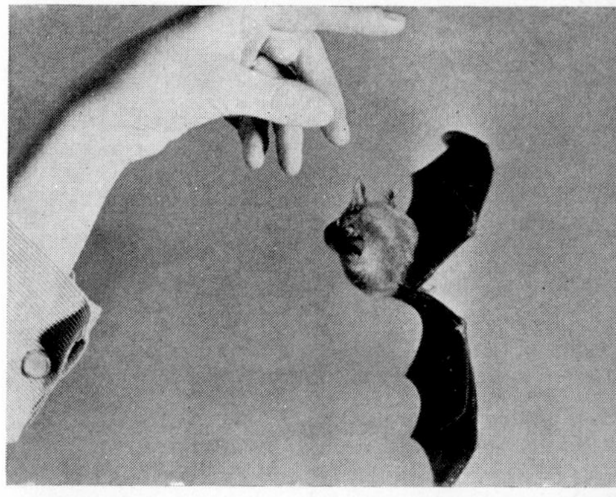

The animal world, especially in the lower orders, sports a much greater range of sizes, as well as variety of forms. A close look reveals harmless insects as amazing monsters equal to the wildest fantasies of science fiction. They come before the Leica locked in deadly combat (p. 358), menacing in appearance (p. 359), or else of a rare beauty and perfection surpassing the great works of man-made art (p. 360).

Some of these close-ups we may have to stage with either dead or doped creatures to keep them absolutely still during photography. But we can also use flash which is short enough not to harm the insect during the moment of exposure, to obtain genuine action pictures of miniature life.

Page 353: Heron flying in to land on nest. 400 mm. lens, Leica operated by remote control. Fine-grain pan film, 1/15 sec., *f*22. Photo: *W. Wissenbach.*

Page 354: Swallow approaching nest to feed its young. 135 mm. lens in reflex housing, pan film, electronic flash (1/5000 sec.), *f*11. Photo: *G. Schützenhofer.*

Page 355: Hoof-nosed bat landing. 200 mm. lens with extension tubes, fine-grain pan film, electronic flash (1/5000 sec.), *f*12.5. Photo: *L. Dorfmüller-Laubmann.*

Above: Red deer calling. 400 mm. lens, pan film, 1/2 sec., *f*22. Photo: *H. Behnke.*

Opposite: Zebra at Belle Vue Zoo, Manchester. 50 mm. lens, fine-grain pan film, 1/100 sec., *f*5.6. Photo: *J. Sadovy.*

Page 358: Fighting stag-beetles. 135 mm. lens in reflex housing, fine-grain pan film, electronic flash (1/5000 sec.) *f*11. Photo: *W. Wissenbach.*

Page 359: Head of grasshopper. 135 mm. lens with reflex housing and universal focusing bellows, fine-grain pan film, 4 sec., *f*22. Photo: *H. Cordes.*

Page 360: Peacock butterfly. 135 mm. lens in reflex housing, fine-grain pan film, electronic flash (1/5000 sec.), *f*16. Photo: *W. Wissenbach.*

times. Even this is a limit of convenience; at greater magnifications a microscope happens to be more practical.

Finally, at any scale of reproduction we can photograph the subject in the most efficient way that suits the conditions.

The Leicaflex close-up system is simpler, as the camera incorporates the necessary precision viewing and focusing features. Also, the Leicaflex lenses from 35 to 90 mm. focus nearer than corresponding Leica lenses and can go closer still with supplementary lenses. For large-scale close-ups, extension mounts or the bellows unit can be used with a number of Leica lenses.

The Close-up Stand

The close-up stand is a comparatively simple close-up unit for all Leica models with 50 mm. lens (except Summarit or Summilux) for near shots at fixed scales of reproduction of 1 : 1 (same-size), 1 : 1.5, 1 : 2, and 1 : 3. It is particularly suitable for copying small originals (miniature transparencies at 1 : 1) and close-ups of small objects. A focusing magnifier with ground-glass screen helps to check exact sharpness, and field masks outline the subject area. It used to be known as the BEOON stand.

The outfit consists of a stand with movable column carrying a camera platform, a series of extension tubes labelled A, B, C, and D, a bayonet/screw adapter ring, and a series of field masks. The front of the extension tube A has a bayonet fitting; the back, and also the back and front of the other tubes have screw threads. The top of the camera platform also has a screw mount like any screw-mounted Leica lens.

To assemble the stand for use with Leica M models, screw the bayonet/screw adapter ring over the top of the camera platform, ready to take the camera. Fit the lens into the bayonet mount of the extension tube A. For close-ups at 1/3 reduction this tube is used by itself, and screws directly over the mount underneath the camera platform.

When fitting the lens, line up the red dot or mark on its bayonet mount with the red dot on the mount of tube A. To remove the lens, first push the button on the rim of tube A diagonally upwards to free the bayonet lock.

For close-ups at 1/2 reduction (1 : 2) screw the extension tube B into the back of the tube A, and screw this combination to the camera platform. For close-ups at 1 : 1.5 combine tube A with tube C, and for same-size use tubes A and D.

Fit the appropriate field mask into the base of the stand. The hole in the front lip of the mask fits over the locating pin on the base, the rear lip goes underneath the clamping ring on the base of the column. No field mask is used for 1 : 3 reductions; the base itself outlines the field covered. The 1 : 1 field mask carries locating ridges for accurate centring of mounted colour slides. A guide in the underside of the base centres film strips.

It does not matter whether the object to be photographed is placed on top of the field mask or underneath (the former position is more convenient when copying colour slides). The focusing adjustment provides the necessary compensation for the exact object plane.

Adjust the focusing magnifier by holding it up against the light, and moving the magnifier lens in or out while looking through it. When correctly adjusted, the small engraved circle in the centre of the ground-glass screen should appear sharp. The magnifier thus provides some eye-sight correction.

Place the stand on top of the subject to be copied (or put the latter inside the field frame). When copying transparencies or negatives, mount the whole assembly on a light box (with a sheet of opal glass illuminated from underneath by lamps) or on a glass stage. In the latter case a white card underneath the glass plate can be used to reflect light up through the transparency.

Place the focusing magnifier unit over the top of the camera platform. The magnifier fits into the outer bayonet mount (not the camera mount of the adapter ring) on the platform. Focus the image on the ground-glass screen by turning the milled ring at the top of the column to lower or raise the movable part of the column. Do not, however, touch the eyepiece setting of the magnifier. When the image is exactly sharp, lock the column by the locking screw at the back. At the rear of the movable column engraved figures 1 : 1, 1 : 1.5, etc., indicate the approximate position for the different close-up ranges.

It is usually most convenient to leave the camera lens set to infinity; but when copying card-mounted slides a near setting of the lens gives just that extra magnification to compensate for the slightly smaller masked slide format.

Next remove the magnifier, and fit the Leica to the bayonet mount of the bayonet/screw adapter on top of the camera platform. The procedure is the same as for fitting a bayonet-mounted lens; when removing the camera press the bayonet catch on the camera body in the normal way.

CLOSE-UP STAND

The main components of the close-up copying stand are:

1. Screw flange to take the camera.
2. Extension tube B, C, or D for different scales of reproduction.
3. Extension tube A, used by itself or in combination with one of the other tubes.
4. Leica lens.
5. Subject field mask.
6. Extending column.
7. Adjusting ring to raise or lower the column.
8. Locking knob.
9. Base plate, also acts as field mask for 1 : 3 reductions.
10. Guides in base for film strips.

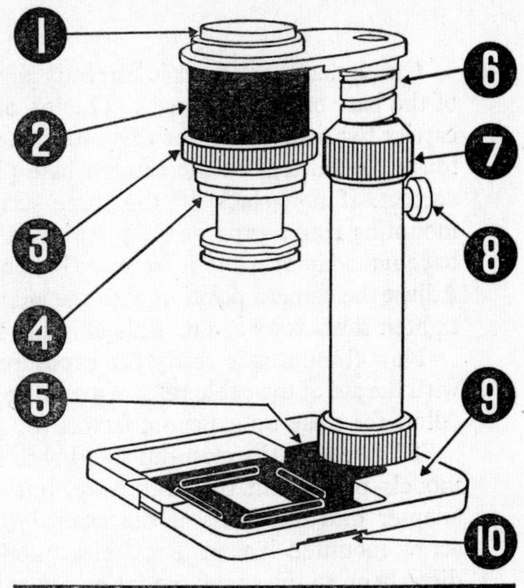

When assembling the close-up copying stand for Leica M models, the camera fits to the top of the platform with the aid of a bayonet/screw adapter, and the lens fits directly into the extension tube A (*left*). With screw-mounted Leica models the camera screws directly to the top of the platform, and the bayonet/screw adapter ring is used to fit the screw-mounted lens into the extension tube A (*right*).

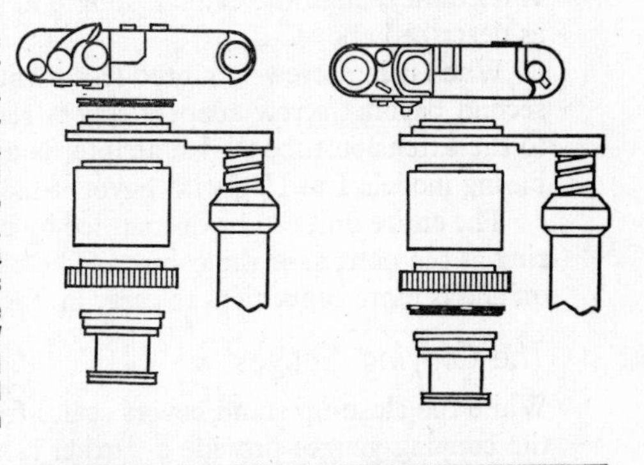

In practice the subject is first focused on the ground glass screen of the focusing unit placed on top of the close-up stand. Then the Leica camera replaces the ground-glass screen and focusing magnifier for the exposure. Use a cable release.

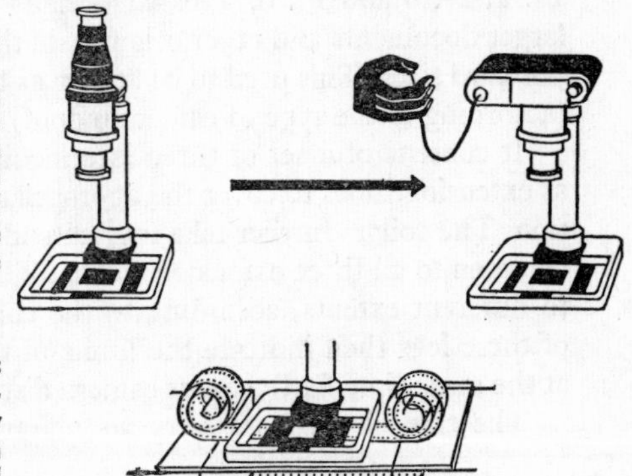

Colour transparencies and film strips are illuminated from underneath by a white card placed at an angle below a supported glass plate, which takes the copying stand.

Check that the camera is correctly aligned with the aperture of the base or the field mask. The top of the camera platform carries two white dots for this purpose. When these dots just touch the bottom of the camera base plate, the alignment is correct. If not, slack off the three screws in the rim of the mounting ring on top of the platform (the one into which the bayonet adapter ring is screwed) with a thin screwdriver. Adjust the camera position with the aid of the white dots, and tighten the screws again. This only has to be done once.

Now the outfit is ready for exposure. Release the shutter with the aid of the cable release to ensure maximum steadiness. Allow for close-up exposure factors (p. 419).

To assemble the close-up stand with screw-mounted Leica models proceed in the same way, but fit the bayonet/screw adapter into the front of the extension tube A, to take the screw mounted lenses. The Leica (models I to IIIg) screws directly on to the screw mount on top of the camera platform. If necessary, align the camera square to the frame of the base as described above.

When using screw-mounted lenses with Leica M models, a second bayonet/screw adapter ring is required to fit the lens to the extension tube A. No adapter is used at all when combining models I to IIIg with bayonet-mounted lenses.

The entire unit can be dismantled by unscrewing the milled ring at the bottom of the column. The base frame then comes off and is more convenient to carry in, for instance, a briefcase.

The Copying Gauges

While the close-up stand covers scales from 1 : 1 up to 1 : 3, the copying gauges provide a further range of fixed scales of 1 : 4, 1 : 6 and 1 : 9. This is specially suitable for copying larger documents and other originals in the quarto, octavo and postcard sizes. This used to be known as the BOOWU or BOWUM (according to the type of camera mount) outfit.

It consists of a set of three intermediate collars which act as extension tubes to cover the appropriate scales of reproduction. The collars further take four extendible legs, these being common to all three extension collars. The legs are pulled out to different extents, according to the collar in use. The tips of these legs then indicate the limits of the subject area, and at the same time fix the exact camera distance.

The extension collars carry an engraved indication of the

DISTANCE GAUGES

Black panel: The copying gauges (formerly known as the Boowu set) are a set of extension collars that go between the camera and the lens. Extendable legs screw into the collars and indicate the exact field of view taken in by the camera, as well as accurately determining the plane of sharpest focus. A filter and lens hood can be fitted in front of the lens; the latter is usually desirable in all copying work.

The copying gauges are available in either a screw or a bayonet-mounted version for the two types of Leica models.

Right hand column: The copying gauge set uses three extension collars, one for each fixed scale of reproduction covering the subject fields shown here.

In addition to copying, the copying gauge can also be used for hand-held close-ups (*right*), made by approaching the subject until the required portion of it is in the plane of the tips of the legs.

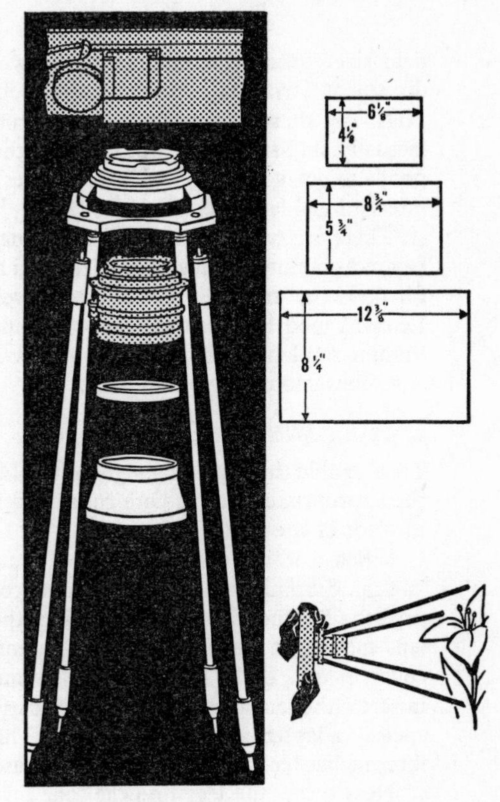

Two older types of distance gauge for screw mounted Leica models only are the Behoo (*left*) for fixed scales of reproduction from 1 : 3 to 1 : 1.5 and the Belun (*right*) for same-size copying. Both use extension tubes between the camera and the lens, and distance gauges which fitted to the front of the lens. They are now replaced by the close-up and copying stand described on p. 361.

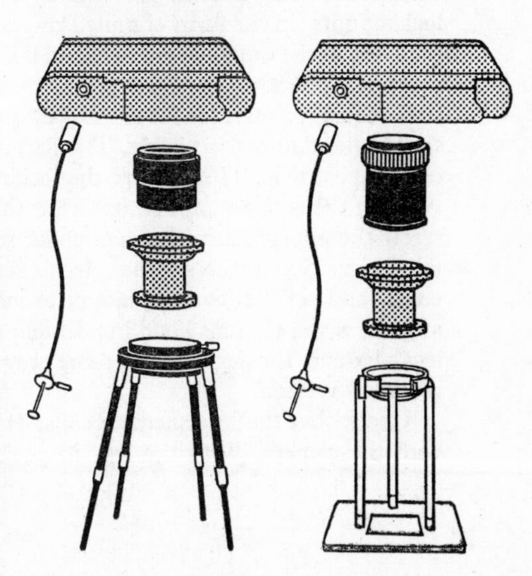

field size covered (in millimetres) as well as the appropriate document format according to the German DIN standard. DIN A4 there corresponds approximately to quarto size (actually slightly larger: $8\frac{1}{4} \times 11\frac{3}{4}$ inches); DIN A5 corresponds to octavo (in fact, $5\frac{3}{4} \times 8\frac{1}{4}$ inches), and DIN A6 is the international large postcard size ($4 \times 5\frac{3}{4}$ inches).

There are two versions of the copying gauge outfit, for the bayonet-mounted Leica M models, and a discontinued model for the screw-mounted Leicas respectively. The outfit for the Leica M models takes the bayonet-mounted 50 mm. Elmar or Summicron lenses; the version for screw-mounted Leicas takes any screw-mounted 50 mm. lens.

Exposing with the Copying Gauge

To assemble the copying gauge for the Leica M models, select the appropriate intermediate collar and fit it into the camera in place of the lens.

When working with the 50 mm. Elmar (or the collapsible 50 mm. Summicron) fit the lens in its collapsed position. Engage the bayonet fitting at the back of the lens barrel (not the lens mount) in the front bayonet mount of the intermediate collar in use. If the rigid 50 mm. Summicron is to be used, unscrew the lens unit itself from the barrel and screw it into a special adapter ring (No. 16508). This then fits into the intermediate collar. Fit any filter to be used and the lens hood.

Next screw the legs into the four threaded sockets on the extension collar. Extend the legs by slacking off the lower locking nuts (in the form of milled rings) and pull out each leg until one of the numbers engraved on it is visible. This number must correspond to the DIN number engraved on the extension collar; for instance for the DIN A5 collar extend the legs so that the figure 5 is visible. The legs click into place in the correct positions. Then secure the locking nut on each leg.

With the screw-mounted outfit for the older Leica models screw the appropriate extension collar into the lens flange of the Leica. Screw the 50 mm. lens (not collapsed) into the collar, and set the focusing mount to infinity and lock it. Fit any filters and the lens hood in position, and then screw in the legs. Extend the legs in the same way as for the bayonet-mounted version.

Check that the intermediate collar is properly squared up with the camera. With the legs in position the camera base should be parallel with a connecting line between the tips of the lower two legs. If the camera is not properly squared up, slack off the black clamping screws in the side of the extension collar, adjust the latter, and tighten the screws.

To take close-ups with this outfit, set up the whole assembly on top of the document or other material to be copied, making sure that the relevant matter is within the tip of the legs.

The copying gauge outfit is easy to carry dismantled in a briefcase.

When illuminating the original be careful to avoid shadows of the legs falling on the actual original. If it proves impossible to eliminate the shadow of one leg, this leg can be removed; the unit is still sufficiently steady on three legs.

Always release the camera shutter with the cable release.

Earlier Distance Gauges

Two outfits were available for scales of reproduction from 1 : 3 to 1 : 1 previous to the close-up stand: The BEHOO outfit (for scales from 1 : 3 to 1 : 1.5) and the BELUN same-size gauge.

The BEHOO outfit consists of a universal clamping ring which fits over the front of the lens mount, together with a set of three extension tubes for the three scales of reproduction, and four adjustable legs which screw into the underside of the clamping ring. The outfit is used with the screw-mounted 50 mm. Elmar *f*3.5 lens with a front mount diameter of 36 mm. Apart from the fact that the legs fit in front of the lens, the principle of operation is the same as with the copying gauge (p. 364). The extension tubes, however, go between the lens and the camera, and are thus suitable only for the screw-mounted Leica models.

An older version of the outfit had different clamping rings for each scale of reproduction.

A similar set of extension tubes and distance gauges was produced for use with the 35 mm. Elmar lens. The shorter focus lens makes the whole set-up more compact.

To assemble the outfit, remove the camera lens and screw it into the appropriate extension tube, then screw the extension tube into the lens flange of the Leica. Set the focusing mount to ∞ (infinity) and lock.

Screw the four legs into the appropriate holes of the clamping ring. Those are marked 1.5, 2, 3 and V (the latter for the BEOOY gauge—p. 368). The legs, at the proper extension, cover the right subject area. Make sure that all four legs are screwed into similarly marked holes.

Fit the clamping ring over the lens mount, aligning the subject area within the legs with the negative area in the Leica.

Extend the legs to the appropriate marks for the scale of reproduction to be used (p. 366).

The BELUN gauge is similar to the BEHOO gauges, but consists of an extension tube for same-size reproduction. It uses a special clamping ring, and three legs fixed to a base plate with a cut-out of the same size as the Leica negative.

Two versions are available, for use with the 50 mm. Elmar and Summar, and with the Summitar lenses respectively. An early model was also designed for the 35 mm. Elmar.

When taking pictures of flat objects, place the base plate over the object so that the latter is within the cut-out.

The plane of sharpest focus is the bottom face of the base plate. To photograph subjects like coins, raise the whole assembly so that the surface of the coin is in the same plane as the underside of the base plate. Stop down to as least *f*8.

Three supplementary lenses were also available at one time for the 50 mm. Elmar *f*3.5 lens. These screw into the inside front mount of the lens and cover subject distances from 39½ to 10¾ inches (100 to 26 cm.), the distances being measured from the back of the camera.

A special BEOOY distance gauge was also produced for use with the supplementary lenses, similar to the BEHOO gauge. It uses the same clamping ring to fit on the front of the lens, and the legs of the gauge screw into the bushes marked V on the clamping ring. When extended to the appropriate length, the tips of the legs indicate the limits of the field of view and the plane of sharpest focus.

The Close-up Focusing Mount

The close-up stands and gauges are very useful for extremely near subjects at fixed distances, but rather limited with subjects just below the 3½ feet limit of the normal focusing range of the standard lens.

The close-up mount for the Leica M2 and M3 permits precision focusing with a camera rangefinder for hand-held shots between about 3 feet and 20 inches. It works with any of the collapsible 50 mm. bayonet-mounted lenses (50 mm. Elmar *f*2.8, also the discontinued Elmar *f*3.5 and the collapsible 50 mm. Summicron *f*2).

The mount itself is an extension tube which fits into the Leica and carries a helical focusing mount. It also has an attachment with two lenses to fit in front of the viewfinder and rangefinder windows, to adapt the field of the viewfinder and convert the rangefinder to the near distance range. The helical mount is marked in distances as well as in scales of reproduction from 1 : 15 to 1 : 7.5.

To use the close-up focusing mount, collapse the lens and inset it into the front of the close-up mount by the bayonet barrel (not the normal bayonet mount).

CLOSE-UP MOUNTS

The near focusing adapter unit for the Leica IIIg consists of a supplementary lens and a rangefinder adapting wedge which fits over the top of the camera. The viewfinder shows the correct view over the whole range from 35 to 20 inches.

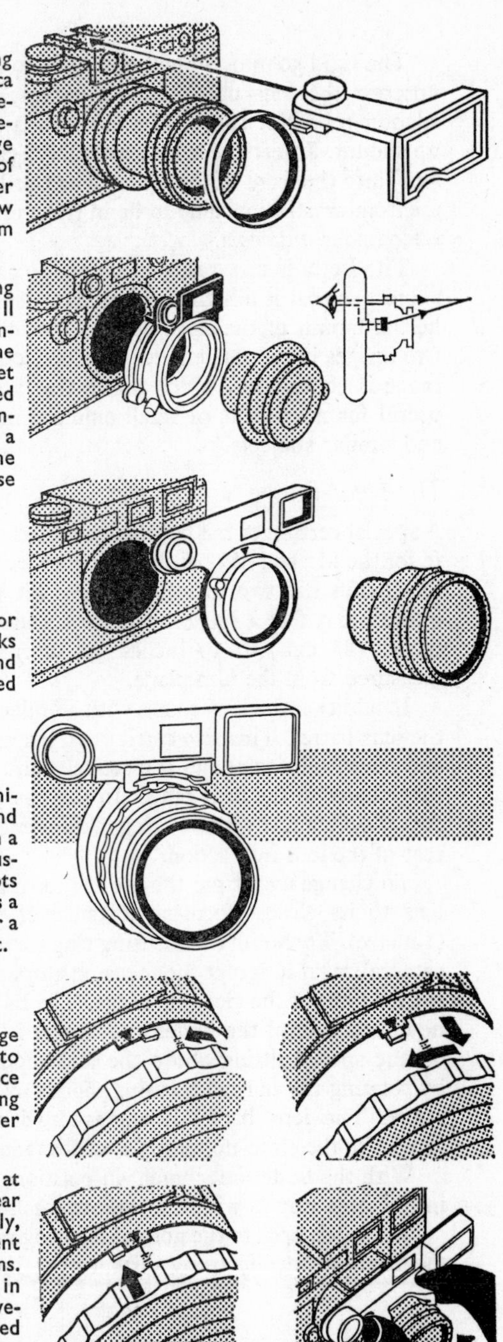

The close-up focusing mount for Leica models II to IIIf is a focusing extension tube which takes the lens for shots from $3\frac{1}{2}$ feet to 16 inches. An attached viewfinder mask compensates for parallax, while a prism wedge adapts the rangefinder to the close distances (p. 371).

The close-up mount for the Leica M2 and M3 works on the same principle, and uses the bayonet-mounted 50 mm. lenses.

The near-range Summicron of the Leica M2 and M3 is in effect a lens with a built-in close-range focusing mount. For near shots between 19 and 35 inches a finder adapter slides over a fitting on the lens mount.

To bring the near range into action, set the lens to its normal closest distance (*left*), and pull the focusing ring outward to lift it over the focusing stop (*right*).

Let the ring engage at the far limit of the near focusing range (*left*). Finally, push the finder attachment in position above the lens. Until this attachment is in place, the focusing movement of the lens is locked (*right*).

The rigid 50 mm. Summicron can also be used; in this case unscrew the lens unit from its mount, and fit it into the adapter tube No. 16508. The latter then goes into the close-up mount. Insert the whole assembly (close-up mount plus lens) into the front of the Leica. The two lenses of the attachment automatically come to lie in front of the viewfinder and rangefinder windows.

The Leica is now ready to shoot. To expose, approach the subject so that it fills the field of view of the finder. Turn the helical mount of the close-up unit (*not* of the lens) until the two images in the rangefinder eyepiece coincide. The focusing range is continuous, which makes this accessory particularly useful for near shots of small animals, machine components and similar subjects.

The Near-Range Summicron

A special version of the bayonet-mounted 50 mm. Summicron *f*2 for the M2 and M3 has in effect such a close-up mount built in. It thus has two focusing ranges: the normal range from infinity to 3 feet 4 inches (1 metre), and near range from 35 inches (88 cm.) to 19 inches (48 cm.). The distances are measured from the film plane.

In addition the lens comes with a finder adapter to fit on to the lens barrel. This also carries two lenses for the viewfinder and rangefinder windows respectively, and adapts the coupled rangefinder to the near range. In this case, however, the process of switching over also brings a different focusing cam at the rear of the lens into action.

To change over from the normal to the near range, set the lens to its closest focusing distance of just under 3½ feet (1 metre). Then pull the focusing ring forward (away from the camera), turn it across the focusing stop, and let it engage at the far limit of the close-up range. The focusing movement is now locked until the finder attachment is pushed in position on the special fitting above the lens mount. Focus the lens by rotating the normal focusing mount over the vailable near range. The lens barrel is engraved with distances in feet (inches in the close-up range) as well as metres.

With the finder attachment in position, the camera is used in the same way as with the close-up mount (p. 368).

To switch back to the normal focusing range, set the lens to the farthest near focusing distance (34 inches or just below

0.9 metres). Then pull the finder attachment away towards the front. Finally pull the focusing ring forward again, turn it past the focusing stop, and let it drop back at the nearest distance of the normal focusing range (3 feet 4 inches or 1 metre).

The lens cannot be set from the near to the normal focusing range while the finder attachment is in position. Nor can the finder attachment be removed unless the lens is set to the far limit of the near focusing range. Equally, never try to remove the lens with the finder attachment still in position; the two must always be fitted or removed separately. (Removal or fitting of the lens with the finder attachment on it to the camera is obstructed by a small locating peg at the rear of the attachment.)

The main advantage of this near-range Summicron lens is that there is no need to carry alternative focusing mounts or adapter tubes; the finder attachment is the only accessory required for close-up focusing.

Near Focusing with Screw-mounted Leicas

A close-up focusing mount, working on a similar principle is available for series II and III Leicas (up to IIIf, but not IIIg). This works in a similar way to that for the M models, and used to be known as the NOOKY mount.

The mount is again an extension tube which screws into the Leica and carries a helical focusing mount. This is connected with a prism wedge to fit in front of the rangefinder window and a mask which adapts the field of the viewfinder.

The front of the mount takes the bayonet barrel of the camera lens. There are three versions of the close-up focusing mount, one for the 50 mm. Elmar *f*3.5, one for the Summicron *f*2 and Elmar *f*2.8 and one for the 50 mm. Summitar or Summar *f*2. The third model will also take the older 50 mm. Hektor *f*2.5.

The helical mount is marked in scales of reproduction from 1 : 17.5 to 1 : 6.5 or 8. For distances, etc., see p. 471.

To use the close-up focusing mount, unscrew the Leica lens and screw the close-up mount in its place. Screw this right home, so that the wedge and mask come to lie accurately in front of the rangefinder and viewfinder windows respectively.

Collapse the lens, pushing its focusing mount to the front, clear of the bayonet barrel. Insert the bayonet barrel in the bayonet catch of the close-up mount and turn to the left to lock it. The Leica is now ready to shoot.

Since the focusing mount is directly coupled to the rangefinder of the Leica, we can focus continuously over the whole range from 3½ feet to 16 or 20 inches. To expose, approach the subject so that it fills the field of view of the finder. Turn the helical mount of the close-up unit (*not* of the lens) until the two images in the rangefinder eyepiece coincide and release the shutter.

The alternative way of focusing, particularly when a given scale of reproduction is required, is to set the helical mount to the appropriate figure first. Then approach the subject until the double image in the rangefinder eyepiece fuses into one, and take the picture.

Use only the centre of the rangefinder image for focusing.

The Leica IIIg, owing to its finder layout, cannot be used with this focusing mount. Instead the near focusing unit for this camera, covering a range from 35 to 20 inches, uses a special supplementary lens and a rangefinder attachment. The latter converges the rangefinder beams and corrects the field of view for parallax.

The unit can be used with all the 50 mm. lenses that have an E39 screw-in filter mount (since the supplementary lens screws into this); special adapter rings are used with lenses having a 36 mm. front mount diameter (No. 13154) and for the 50 mm. Summitar (No. 13078). These are, in fact, the same as the filter adapter rings (p. 238).

Fit the rangefinder attachment by pushing the bracket into the rear of the accessory shoe, as far forward as it will go, and fix by screwing down the clamping screw. This brings the more or less rectangular window of the rangefinder attachment actually a little way in front of the viewfinder and rangefinder windows.

The camera is now used in exactly the same way as for more distant views, focusing the subject through the rangefinder. The distance scale, of course, is no longer valid, but since we focus with the rangefinder anyway, this is not a vital handicap.

At one time a fixed scale 1 : 4 close-up mount (OMIFO) used to be available for the 90 mm. Elmar *f*4 lens. This is an extension tube, like the close-up mount, but has a fixed length of just over 8 inches (22.5 cm.). The scale of reproduction is 1 : 4, covering objects about 17½ inches (44 cm.) from the front of the lens. This can be used with screw-mounted Leica models from II up to and including IIIf.

A pair of wedges and a mask plate fixed to the mount fit in front of the view- and rangefinder windows, adjusting the finders for the subject distance. The mask plate automatically allows for the parallax.

To take close-ups with the OMIFO mount, unscrew the camera lens, screw in the mount, and then screw the 90 mm. Elmar lens into this. Set the lens to infinity (∞). Approach the subject, observing it through the rangefinder until the double images fuse into one, and make the exposure.

A similar fixed close-up mount for a scale or reproduction of 1 : 4 has been produced for the 50 mm. lenses.

Neither of the 1 : 4 close-up mounts is in production.

Equipment for Large-scale Close-ups

For a really near focusing range—with scales of reproduction of about 1 : 2, same size, and the various magnifications—very precise focusing is vital. And it must be visual focusing, which means observation of the image formed by the lens on a ground-glass screen.

Large-scale close-ups and macrophotography therefore involve the use of a focusing unit—the reflex housings or the focusing stage—and suitable extension units to increase the length-to-film distance (focusing mounts, extension tubes or extension bellows).

Two systems for working in this manner were produced for the various Leica models, and existed for a long time side by side. One consists of the reflex housings and the focusing bellows, and the other comprises the focusing stages with extension tubes. Of these the reflex housing and bellows combination is more convenient and quicker in operation, and is the only system now available.

The focusing stages with their associated gear are more cumbersome, but equally accurate. They are now discontinued, though the focusing stage survives in a special version in the Reprovit copying outfit (p. 399).

Either system provides a comprehensive close-up outfit of great versatility.

Which Lens?

For close-up work with the reflex housing, focusing mounts and bellows (or the Leicaflex) lenses of focal lengths from 35 to 135 mm. can be used. At close range the scale of reproduction matters primarily, and the scales obtainable with several of the focal lengths overlap.

The choice of the best lens is dictated by perspective and subject distance.

For a given scale of reproduction, the shorter the focal length the shorter the lens-to-subject distance (and also the film-to-subject distance). At very near distances, however, the amount of space available between the camera and the object for illumination is restricted.

Further, at too close range perspective effects become exaggerated, even for small subjects.

For example, at half-size reproduction (scale 1 : 2) with a 50 mm. lens, the object would be about 6 inches in front of the lens. With a 135 mm. lens the object distance for the same scale would be around 16 inches. If the subject has any depth, nearer details will look appreciably larger in proportion to more distant ones (even though the separation between such details may only be an inch or two) at the closer distance. So for a more natural rendering of small objects at fairly large scales of reproduction, between say 1 : 8 and 1 : 2—a long-focus lens is distinctly preferable.

Thus for photography between same-size and ¼ natural size a 135 mm. lens is the best choice.

A 90 mm. lens is a good second best, especially when used with a focusing mount like the No. 16464, since the required focusing extension (lens-to film distance) is less. This determines the range of scales. The largest scale of reproduction with the No. 16464 mount and the 135 mm. Tele-Elmar or Elmar lenses is 1 : 5, but with the 90 mm. Elmar or Elmarit it is 1 : 3—and with the 65 mm. Elmar over 1 : 2. 5. The latter lens is thus useful to cover the widest possible range of scales; but the 90 mm. Elmar and Elmarit units are the best all-round solution. That is also why 100 mm. was chosen for the Macro-Elmar *f*4 with the Leicaflex bellows (p. 410).

At reductions of more than 1 : 5 the lens-to-object distance with a 135 mm. lens becomes too long for a convenient camera set-up, especially when copying or when the Leica is mounted on a column above a baseboard.

The shorter-focus lenses again come into their own at magnifications larger than 1 : 1. To achieve a 1½× magnification with a 50 mm. lens requires a lens-to-film distance of some 5 inches, with the 90 mm. lens of 9 inches and with the 135 mm. lenses as much as 13½ inches. The latter two extensions are beyond the range even of the model II bellows.

At very large image scales perspective problems no longer arise. This is because the depth of field is so small that only object details in more or less a flat plane can be photographed. The zone of sharpness just cannot cover any useful extension in depth.

To sum up, therefore, choose one of the 90 mm. lenses for close-ups between same-size and about 1 : 8—especially if the focusing bellows are available. Choose a 135 mm. lens if only subjects from same-size to 1 : 4 reduction are to be covered. Use shorter focal lengths (50 to 65 mm.) for greater reductions and when copying, especially if the camera cannot be set up very far from the subject. Again use the 50 mm. or even shorter-focus lenses for macrophotography at scales of reproduction larger than life-size.

Deliberately omitted so far have been depth-of-field comparisons with different lenses. This is because at the scales of reproduction discussed the depth of field depends very largely on the scale and hardly at all on the focal length of the lens. Thus to all intents and purposes the depth of sharpness available when photographing a same-size reproduction is the same for all lenses of focal lengths from 35 to 135 mm. See also table on p. 488.

Close-ups with the Reflex Housings

The Visoflex III (and also the models II and IIA) also act as a 41 mm. extension tube. When used with the focusing mount No. 16464 it permits focusing from infinity down to 1 : 2.5 to 1 : 5 with the 65 to 135 mm. lenses respectively (p. 128).

Still closer ranges are possible by using an extension tube No. 16471: up to nearly same-size with the 65 mm. Elmar, larger than half-size with the 90 mm. Elmarit and around 1 : 2.5 with the 135 mm. Tele-Elmar or Elmar (the latter with an adapter tube No. 16472). In all these cases the optical unit only of the lens is used and screwed directly into the focusing mount No. 16464 or the extension tube No. 16471.

The scope with the mount No. 16464 is not as wide as with the model II bellows. But this focusing mount is much more compact than the bellows, and often more convenient when carrying the Leica and close-up equipment on location.

Appropriate close-up ranges are also available with the lens units of the 90 mm. Elmar and the 90 mm. Summicron, but the near limit is not so close. With the Elmar lens, used in the mount No. 16467 and two extensions tubes No. 16468, the largest scale of reproduction is 1 : 3.2; even three rings No. 16468 can be used to get down to about 1 : 2.5.

The 90 mm. Summicron, in its short mount with an extension tube No. 16474, gives a largest scale of 1 : 4.5. Additional rings No. 16474 extend the range in the same way as the ring No. 16468 with the 90 mm. Elmar.

Further, any bayonet-mounted Leica lens can fit directly into the front of the Visoflex III (or II or IIA) housing. With the 50 mm. lenses this gives a scale of reproduction of 1 : 1.3, or same-size when a ring No. 16469 is placed between the lens and the Visoflex.

With the 35 mm. lenses the scales are larger than same-size: 1.2× magnification with the lens directly on the Visoflex and 1.4× with the No. 16469 ring. Here, however the rather short lens-to-object distance (about 2¼ inches) makes working less convenient; the same scale of reproduction can be obtained with the 65 mm. Elmar and the model II bellows at almost twice the lens-to-subject distance.

The same applies to the 2× magnification obtainable with the 28 mm. Elmarit on the Visoflex (it can only be mounted with the No. 16469 ring, as otherwise the rear of the lens fouls the mirror). Here the lens-to-object distance is only about 1 inch.

The 90 mm. lenses mounted directly on the Visoflex III in their normal focusing mounts provide a largest reproduction scale of a little over half-size. With the 135 mm. lenses the largest scale is 1 : 2.5. With these lenses and an extension ring (Nos. 16471, 16468, or 16474 as applicable) still closer distances and larger scales are possible. These extension rings fit between the lens unit itself and the normal focusing mount of the lens (see also p. 489).

The Visoflex I reflex housing (p. 140) also acts as a 2½-inch (62.5 mm.) extension tube, and may be used for large-scale close-ups with any of the shorter focus Leica lenses in screw mounts.

Thus with a 50 mm. lens it yields images about 1.25 times life size. With the 35 mm. Summaron or Elmar, the magnification obtained is 1.8 times, while the 90 mm. and 135 mm. lenses yield images on a scale of about 1 : 1.5 and 1 : 2.2 respectively. In all cases higher magnifications are possible by using extension tubes.

The Focusing Bellows

Working with extension tubes has one drawback: each tube covers only a limited range of subject distances. To change from one range to another means changing extension tubes.

The focusing bellows provide a continuously variable extension of a much wider range. There have been three models: the original large bellows intended for use with the Visoflex I housing, the current bellows model II for the Visoflex III, II and IIa, and the Leicaflex bellows (p. 409).

The model II bellows extends to 3¾ inches (9.5 cm.) and

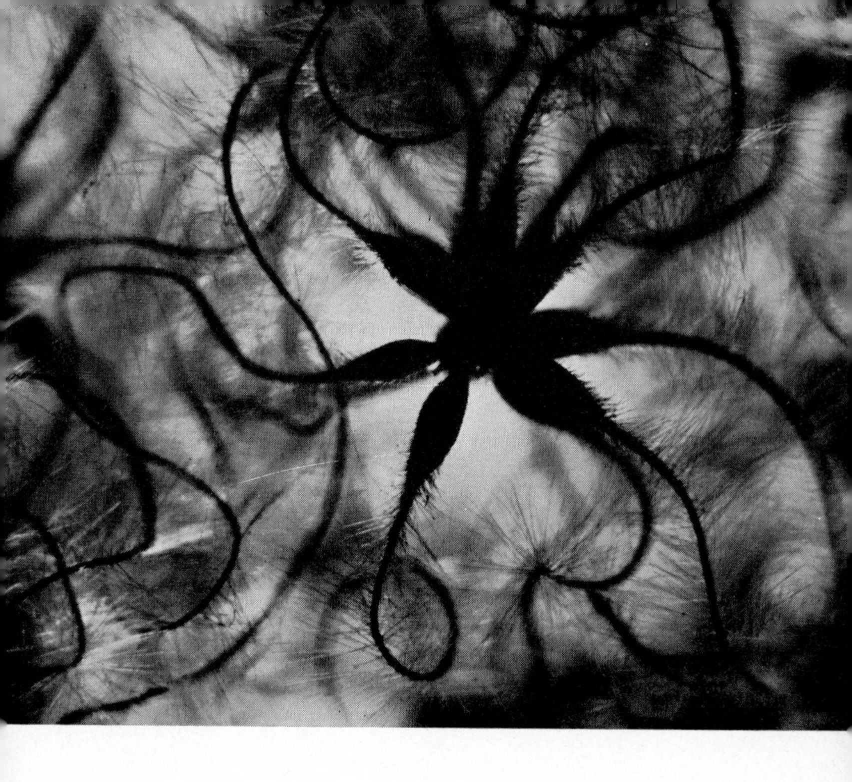

STILL CLOSER TO NATURE

The extensive range of Leica close-up gear takes us within inches of our subject, and reveals a remarkable world of small detail. Yet the new scene is far from chaotic; it exhibits an amazing degree of ordered beauty.

The almost abstract silhouettes of some seeds (*above*) or of a dandelion with a few blades of grass (p. 380) are in themselves as dramatic pictorial arrangements as any large-scale impressionistic set-up. The shapes of common wild flowers or fungi (pp. 378, 379, 382) need but the seeing eye of the Leica to become artistic patterns superior to anything we could create in a studio. And a close view of an ordinary thistle (p. 381) or a much magnified fly's eye (p. 383) shows the patterns of nature in a new light. Even the almost geometric regularity of a piece of wire netting rich with hoar frost (p. 384) becomes alive in its thousands of tiny ice crystals.

Our vision through the magnifying lens of the Leica may be more confined physically, but it is wider than ever pictorially. This miniature world is highly exclusive in its fantastic aspects; we can observe its striking forms on a table-top set-up, in a bit of a hedge, a patch in a garden or a field, or any hidden corner of nature we care to look into.

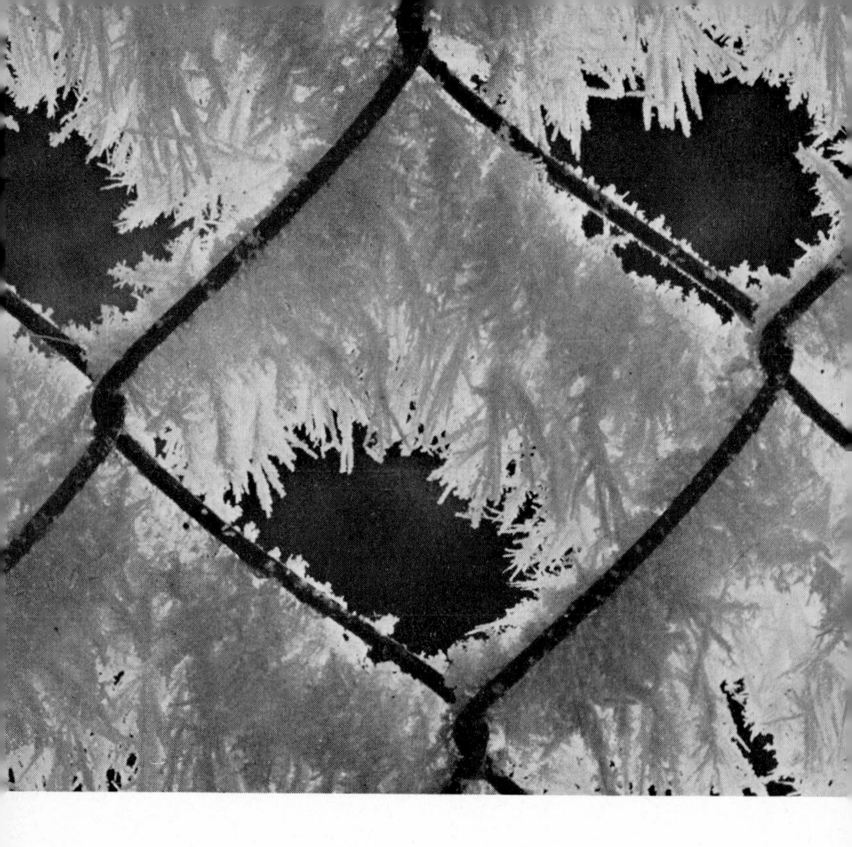

Page 377: Seeds of clematis. 50 mm. lens in reflex housing with focusing bellows, fine-grain pan film, 5 sec., *f*22. Photo: *A. Tritschler.*

Page 378: Crocus. 135 mm. lens in reflex housing with focusing bellows, fine-grain pan film, 1/40 sec., *f*9. Photo: *A. Tritschler.*

Page 379: Bluebells. 135 mm. lens in reflex housing with focusing bellows, fine-grain pan film, 1/20 sec., *f*12.5. Photo: *A. Tritschler.*

Page 380: Dandelion seed stalk. 135 mm. lens in reflex housing with focusing bellows, fine-grain pan film, 1/20 sec., *f*9. Photo: *A. Tritschler.*

Page 381: Thistle cluster. 135 mm. lens in reflex housing with focusing bellows, fine-grain pan film, 1/60 sec., *f*9. Photo: *A. Tritschler.*

Page 382: Fungi. 135 mm. lens in reflex housing with focusing bellows, fine-grain pan film, 1/5 sec., *f*18. Photo: *A. Tritschler.*

Page 383: Eye of a fly, magnified 80 times. 35 mm. lens in fully extended focusing bellows with three extension tubes, fine-grain pan film, electronic flashes from 4 inches distance, *f*18. Photo: *H. Wildenhain.*

Above: Hoar frost on wire netting. 200 mm. lens in reflex housing, fine-grain pan film, 1/20 sec., *f*12.5. Photo: *A. Tritschler.*

consists of a guide rail with a rack-and-pinion movement. On one side a knob moves the front of the bellows forward and back. Underneath the rail a second rack and pinion moves the member carrying a $\frac{1}{4}$ inch and a $\frac{3}{8}$ inch tripod bush. When mounted on a tripod or other stand, the whole camera and bellows assembly can be moved with this second knob. This is useful for focusing at very close range.

One side of the guide rail carries a scale of magnifications from 0 to 1, which applies to the 90 mm. lenses (except Summicron). The scale further carries exposure factors (p. 419) marked in red.

The other side of the rail has a millimetre scale from 0 to 95, marked in green. This can be used—with reference to the tables on p. 490—to set up specific scales of reproduction with various lenses.

The front movable panel takes the adapter rings for the various lenses. The rear panel has a bayonet mounting ring to fit into the bayonet flange of the Visoflex II housing. The combination can, of course, be used with either the Leica M or the screw-mounted Leica models; in the latter case the screw-mounted version of the Visoflex II is required to take the camera.

The bayonet mounting ring on the rear panel can rotate through 90 deg. and engages in two positions for horizontal and upright shots.

Changing round therefore involves rotating the Leica and the Visoflex as one.

The movable front part of the bellows, just below the actual lens panel, also carries two holes to take a bellows lens hood. To fit this, slide the two mounting rods into the holes on the front of the bellows unit, and secure the small clamping screw. The rear of the bellows lens hood clips on the front of the lens mount in the same way as the normal lens hood; it fits the lenses with a 42 mm. outside front diameter. An adapter ring is available for older-type lenses with 36 mm. front mount. The front of the bellows can take masks and other accessories for special effects.

Assembling the Bellows and the Visoflex II to III

Mount the bellows unit on a tripod or firm support. Mount the Visoflex on the camera and fit the viewing magnifier on top. For close-up work it is often more convenient to use the vertical magnifier—especially when the camera assembly is mounted on a vertical stand to point downwards.

Check that the red dot on the movable bayonet ring in the rear panel is opposite the red dot on the rear panel itself. If the two are not lined up, press in the catch at the side of the rear panel and rotate the ring to line up the red dots. Fit the camera plus Visoflex on the bellows unit. This simply involves placing them together so that the red dot on the Visoflex is opposite the red dot on the rear panel, and turning through a small turn to engage the bayonet lock.

Now the lens can be fitted. Any screw or bayonet-mounted lens from 35 to 135 mm. can be used, but the various lenses need different mounting rings. These screw into the front panel of the focusing bellows.

The 35 *mm. and* 50 *mm. bayonet-mounted* lenses require the No. 16596 mounting ring. The lenses are fitted directly into this ring.

The 35 *mm. and* 50 *mm. screw-mounted* lenses require the No. 16590 mounting ring, and screw into the latter.

The scales of reproduction obtained with the screw and bayonet-mounted lenses of the same focal length are not the same. The bayonet-mounted lenses yield a higher maximum magnification. The screw-mounted lenses can, however, be used with the bayonet/screw adapters, and then fit into the mounting ring No. 16596.

The 65 *mm. Elmar*, the lens units of the 90 mm. Elmar, and Elmarit, and the lens unit of the 135 mm. Tele-Elmar are used with the mounting ring No. 16558. For the 135 mm. Hektor and Elmar an adapter tube No. 16472 is also required (this is the same as is used for these 135 mm. lenses on the Visoflex II with the universal focusing mount 16464).

The 90 *mm. Summicron* needs a mounting ring No. 16598; here again only the lens unit itself, unscrewed from the focusing mount, is used.

The 125 *mm. Hektor* is used with the mounting ring No. 16572, again utilizing only the lens unit itself.

The 135 *mm. Elmarit* (lens unit only) is used with the mounting ring No. 16598.

Other bayonet-mounted lenses can be fitted in the ring No. 16596, and other screw-mounted lenses into the ring No. 16590. With the longer focal lengths this yields larger maximum magnifications than the use of the special adapters,

OCUSING BELLOWS II

Black panel: The main arts of the focusing ellows for the Visoflex II r III housing are:

1. Locating holes for ellows lens hood.
2. Catch for rotating he Leica and Visoflex II or I assembly.
3. Rail.
4. Front adapter ring interchangeable).
5. Locking knob for ellows movement.
6. Front focusing knob.
7. Data scale on rail.
8. Knob for movement f the whole bellows as- embly on the tripod nounting piece.

Right: The small focus- ng bellows mounted on he Leica and Visoflex III, vith the bellows hood ttached to the front.

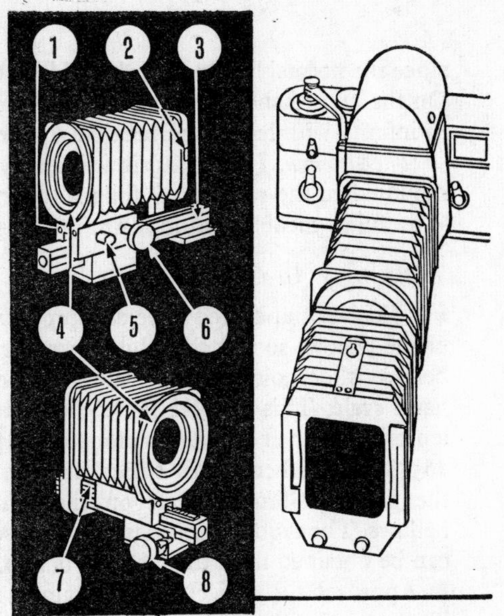

The small focusing bel- ows, used with the Viso- lex II or III covers a wide ange of scales with the lifferent lenses. The main nes—with required mount- ng rings—are shown here. With the 35 and 50 mm. enses the ring No. 16596 s for bayonet mounted enses and the ring No. 6590 for screw mounted enses. In combinations No. , 5, 6, 7 and 9 the optical nit of the lens only is used. The obtainable scales are:

1. 35 mm. lenses: 2.1 to .7
2. 50 mm. lenses: 1.4 to .2
3. 65 mm. Elmar: ∞ to .6
4. 90 mm. *f*2.8 and *f*4: ∞ o 1
5. 135 mm. Tele-Elmar: ∞ to 0.77
6. 90 mm. *f*2: 0.04 to 1
7. 200 mm. Telyt *f*4: ∞ o 0.33
8. 125 mm. Hektor: ∞ o 0.65
9. 135 mm. Hektor and Elmar: ∞ to 0.75.

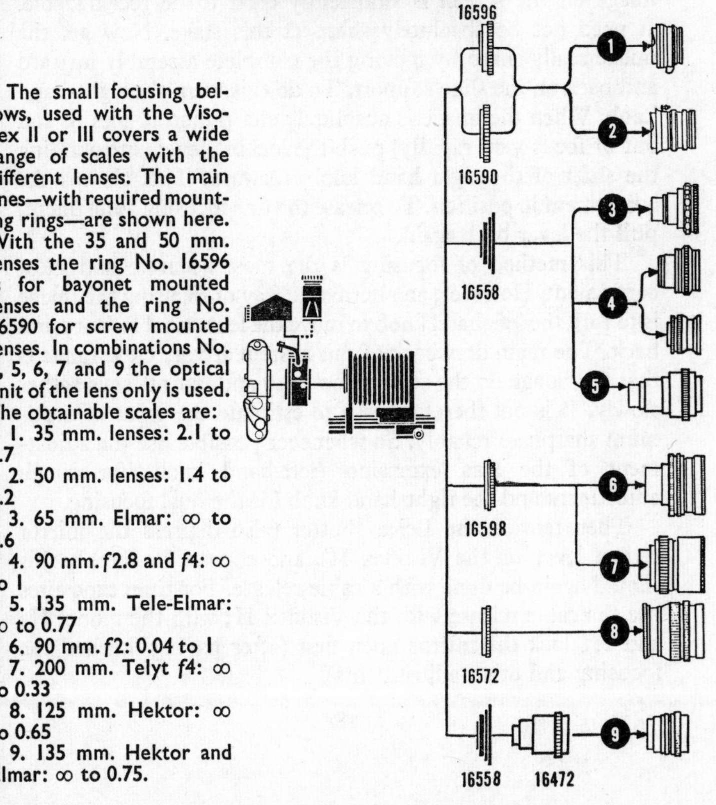

since the normal lens mount also adds to the overall extension. On the other hand, the complete assembly cannot be focused to infinity with lenses shorter than 65 mm.

The 200 *mm. Telyt f*4, again using only the lens unit, can be mounted in the ring 16598 for really long-distance close-ups —useful in medical and industrial photography.

Working with the Bellows

For close-ups at a fixed scale of reproduction extend the front of the bellows so that the white arrow head on the rear of the bellows slide points to the scale of reproduction on the left-hand scale. This is valid for the 90 mm. Elmar or Elmarit lenses, with their lens units mounted in the adapter ring No. 16558. For other lenses select the appropriate position on the green millimetre scale on the right-hand side of the bellows. The required settings for given scales of reproduction can be obtained from the table on p. 490.

Approach the subject with the camera assembly, so that the image on the screen is sufficiently clear to be recognizable. It need not be absolutely sharp at this stage. Now get the image really sharp by moving the complete assembly forward and back on the slide support. To do this, turn the right-hand knob. When the image is absolutely sharp (and it goes in and out of focus very rapidly) push the locking lever, surrounding the shaft of the right-hand knob, forward. This clamps the adjustment in position. To release the fine focusing adjustment, pull the lever back again.

This method of focusing is the most accurate and most convenient. However, an alternative way of focusing the image is to turn the left-hand knob to move the lens panel forward and back. The main drawback of this system at very close range is that the image on the screen goes into and out of focus rather slowly. It is not therefore easy to estimate the point of maximum sharpness reliably. So whenever possible use the adjustment of the lens extension (left-hand knob) for rough adjustment and the right-hand knob for the final focusing.

Then tension the Leica shutter (also depress the mirror return lever on the Visoflex II), and expose. Preferably this should again be done with a cable release. For time exposures use the cable release with the Visoflex II; with the model IIa and III lock the mirror open first (after having finished the focusing and other adjustments).

LARGE FOCUSING BELLOWS

Black panel: The main parts of the universal focusing bellows are:

1. Rear panel.
2. Front panel.
3. Rear platform.
4. Tripod screw for focusing stage.
5. Focusing knob.
6. Scale for 50 mm. Elmar (early models).
7. Rack and pinion carrier.
8. Guide rail.
9. Scale for 135 mm. lenses.
10. Tripod screw for reflex housing.

Right: A bellows lens hood (p. 390) can be mounted on the front of the focusing bellows to exclude stray light.

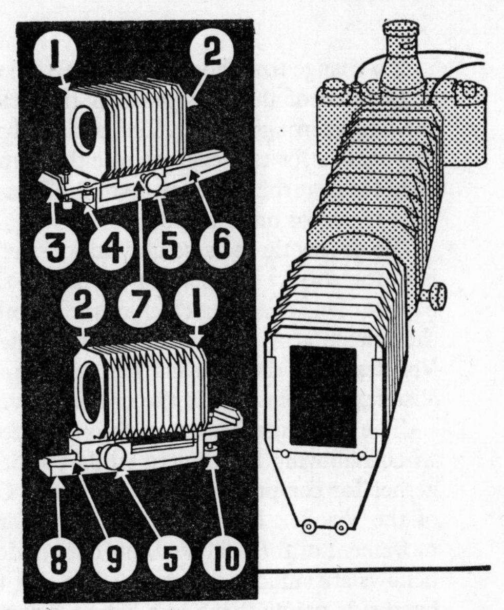

The focusing bellows, used with the Visoflex I, take a wide range of lens and extension tube combinations.

With the 135 mm. lenses mounted in an adapter tube No. 16580 L and screwed into the screw mounting ring No. 16590, the focusing bellows cover a range from infinity to same-size reproduction.

The lens unit of the 125 mm. Hektor lens fitted into the adapter ring No. 16572 covers the same range.

Screw-mounted lenses from 35 to 90 mm. fit directly into the screw ring No. 16590 to give a range of magnification up to 6.2 times with the shortest focal length. Bayonet mounted lenses can be fitted in the adapter ring No. 16596.

The lens unit only of the 90 mm. Elmar lens, fitted in the adapter ring No. 16558 and screwed in to the screw ring No. 16590 covers a focusing range from half size to 2× magnification.

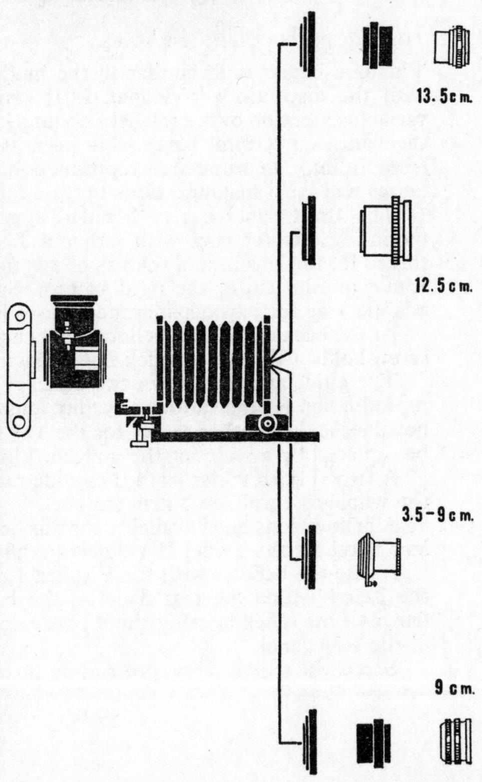

To change from horizontal to vertical shots, press the catch at the side of the rear panel of the bellows unit and rotate the Leica through 90 deg. The rotating bayonet mounting ring responsible for this engages at either setting. This avoids the need for disturbing the set-up of the focusing bellows mounted on a tripod or other stand.

To dismantle the assembly make sure first that the camera is in the correct position for horizontal shots. Then press the bayonet lens-changing catch of the Visoflex (in the side below the release arm) and uncouple the camera together with the Visoflex from the focusing bellows. Separate the camera and Visoflex combination in the normal way.

The horizontal camera position on the bellows is important when removing the camera while the bellows are pushed together for comparatively distant shots. Otherwise the bottom of the Visoflex II or III is likely to foul the front focusing movement of the bellows. This danger does not arise once the bellows are sufficiently extended so that the index on the left-hand side points to 0.3 or a higher figure on the scale.

The Large Focusing Bellows

This is a bigger unit, similar to the model II bellows, for use with the discontinued Visoflex I. It provides a continuously variable extension over a range of about 5½ inches (14 cm.). With the various 135 mm. lenses this permits continuous focusing from infinity to same-size reproduction, while shorter focus lenses will yield magnifications up to 6.2 times.

The front panel has a threaded aperture to take a screw mounting adapter ring with either a Leica lens thread, or a thread for the lens unit of the 125 or 135 mm. lenses, the 90 mm. Elmar or Elmarit, or the rigid 50 mm. Summicron. A bayonet adapter ring for bayonet-mounted lenses is also available.

At the back of the rear bellows panel a platform with a tripod screw holds a Visoflex I reflex housing with the Leica attached.

The guide rail also carries two scales. One shows the scale of reproduction for the various 135 mm. lenses used with the reflex housing, and the other serves for the 125 mm. Hektor (this can be replaced by a scale for the 90 mm. Elmar).

A tripod bush underneath the guide rail serves for mounting the whole assembly on a firm support.

A bellows lens hood available for this bellows is similar to the lens hood for the model II bellows (p. 385).

To use the bellows with the Visoflex I, mount the latter with the Leica behind the rear panel of the bellows unit. The lens flange of the reflex housing should bear against the raised flange of the rear panel.

Screw the tripod screw protruding through the rear platform

into the bush of the reflex housing. Tightening the tripod screw will automatically press the reflex housing against the rear panel of the bellows, ensuring a light-tight join.

The camera may be adjusted for horizontal or vertical shots in the normal way on the reflex housing (p. 143).

This unit is specially intended for use with the 135 mm. Elmar and Hektor lenses. To mount the lens, unscrew it from its focusing mount, and screw it into the adapter tube No. 16580 which in turn screws into the thread of the mounting ring No. 16590.

The scale at the left of the guide rail (marked f = 135 mm.) indicates the scale of reproduction at any distance and, on the latest models, the exposure factor (p. 419) in red.

Instead of the 135 mm. lens with adapter tube, the mounting ring No. 16590 will take any other screw-mounted Leica lens except the 125 mm. Hektor which needs a special ring No. 16572. This takes the optical unit of the lens, and then permits continuous focusing from infinity to same-size reproduction. The 90 mm. Elmar and Elmarit can be used either in its normal form, or the lens unit only may be mounted in a special adapter tube No. 16558. The two alternatives give different reproduction ranges.

Similarly the 50 mm. Elmar can be used on the screw ring.

The bayonet adapter ring No. 16596 is used for all bayonet-mounted lenses (Leica M) while the rings Nos. 17672 and 16598 take the lens unit of the 50 mm. (rigid) and 90 mm. Summicron.

The 135 mm. Tele-Elmar, again using only the lens unit, will also go into the adapter tube No. 16558.

Finally, the mounting ring 16598 can be used with the lens unit of the 90 mm. Summicron, the 135 mm. Elmarit and the 200 mm. Telyt $f4$. The latter again provides really long-distance close-ups.

For very high magnifications extension tubes can be mounted on the front plate of the bellows unit before screwing in the lens.

The Focusing Stage

The focusing stage consists of two principal parts:

a base plate with two tripod bushes and lens range, and

a sliding stage, moving in machined guides, with a camera holder and a ground-glass screen housing. The ground-glass screen is at exactly the same distance from the front of the focusing stage as the film plane of the Leica.

The lens flange will take one of several helical focusing mounts for use with different 50 mm. Leica lenses.

A series of extension tubes serves for macrophotography.

In use, the subject is carefully focused on the ground-glass screen, and the latter then slid aside to bring the camera in position behind the lens.

There are two versions of the last design of the focusing

stage (also known as the Focoslide): for screw-mounted Leica models (OOBAZ, or No. 16602 W), and for the bayonet-mounted Leica M series (OOTGU, or No. 16679 A). They differ mainly in the fittings to hold the camera.

To fit Leica M models to the OOTGU focusing stage, first move the sliding stage so that the ground-glass screen housing is above the lens opening in the base plate. Place the camera body in position over the bayonet fitting so that the top edge lines up with the oblique line on the sliding stage. Rotate the camera body clockwise to engage the bayonet lock. When removing the camera first depress the lens-changing catch.

To fit Leica models I to IIIg to the OOBAZ focusing stage turn the milled nut of the shaft that holds the spring-loaded clamping arm, so as to let the arm move up and swing clear of the sliding section. Move the latter so that the camera opening is above the lens opening in the base plate. Slack off the milled screw of the camera stop below the ground-glass screen housing, and push the camera stop bracket outwards.

Place the camera body in position, base plate against the base with the tripod bush, so that the screw lens flange engages in the circular recess in the sliding stage. Swing the spring-loaded clamping arm back over the camera, push down with the milled nut, and turn the latter through 90 deg. to secure.

Finally push the camera stop bracket against the camera base plate and tighten the milled locking screw. This adjustment of the camera stop bracket is only necessary once for any particular camera model. (A rubber ring is also supplied to fit over the stepped part of the stop bracket with older Leicas up to IIIb which have a slightly shorter body.)

With both focusing stages further manipulation is virtually identical.

Mount the focusing magnifier with its bayonet mount over the ground-glass screen housing, and adjust the eyepiece until the focusing mark on the screen is sharp. There is a choice of three focusing magnifiers: the vertical 5× type, and the 5× right-angle and 4× 45 deg. types for when the vertical magnifier is not easily accessible. These are identical with the magnifiers available for the Visoflex I housing (p. 142). For special work a vertical 30× fine focusing magnifier is also available.

To move the ground-glass screen housing or the camera in position above the lens opening, push the catch next to the ground-glass screen housing, and slide the sliding stage over.

Fitting the Lens

Various 50 mm. lenses can be used, each requiring a separate helical focusing mount. Strictly speaking, the screw-mounted lenses are specified for the OOBAZ stage and bayonet mounted ones for the OOTGU stage, but the helical focusing mounts are interchangeable between the two models.

In all cases fit the lens into the appropriate helical mount, and screw the latter into the lens opening of the base plate.

FOCUSING STAGE

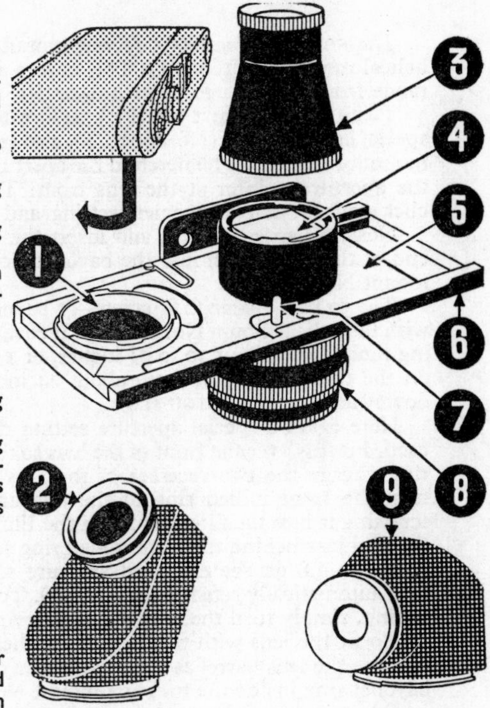

The parts of the focusing stage for the Leica M are:

1. Bayonet mount to take the M camera body.
2. 45 deg. focusing magnifier.
3, Vertical focusing magnifier.
4. Ground glass in ground-glass screen housing.
5. Sliding stage.
6. Stage base.
7. Locking catch.
8. Helical focusing mount with lens.
9. Right-angle focusing magnifier. The three alternative focusing magnifiers are identical for all models of the focusing stage.

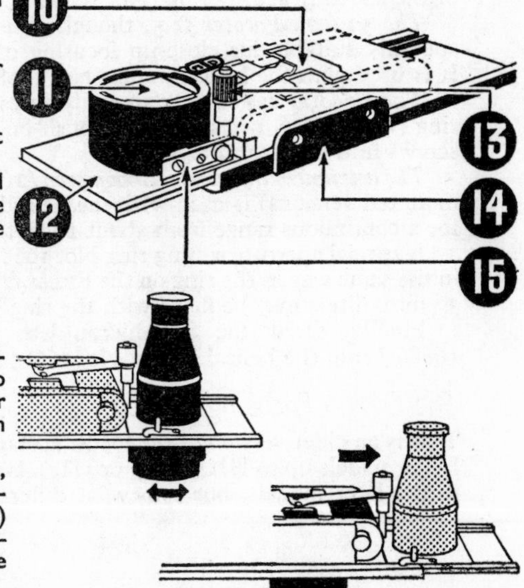

The focusing stage for Leica models Ig, IIIg, and earlier differs in certain minor aspects.

10. Clamping arm to hold the camera in place.
11. Ground-glass screen housing.
12. Sliding stage.
13. Locking ring for clamping arm.
14. Base plate.
15. Camera alignment stop.

The same magnifiers and mounts are used as for the focusing stage taking the Leica M.

In use, slide the ground-glass screen housing into position above the lens for focusing on the screen (*left*).

To make the exposure, slide the camera into position above the lens (*right*) and release the shutter—preferably with the cable release.

The 50 *mm. Elmar f*3.5 (screw-mounted) is used with the helical mount No. 16609 D. This covers a continuous focusing range from about 41 to 9¼ inches, or 1/18 to 1/2 reductions.

To fit the lens first set the aperture to *f*8, and mount the special aperture ring (No. 16620 T), also set to *f*8, over the front mount of the lens. The notch in the aperture ring should engage the aperture pointer at the lens front. The aperture ring has click stops for more convenient setting, and also acts as lens hood.

Next, collapse the lens, and insert the bayonet fitting at the end of the lens barrel into the bayonet ring inside the focusing mount No. 16609 D.

The 50 *mm. Elmar f*2.8 (screw- or bayonet-mounted) is used with the helical mount No. 16608 C. It covers a continuous focusing range from about 30 to 9¼ inches, or 1/13 to 1/2 reductions, on the OOBAZ stage; or from about 24 inches (1/10 reduction) downwards on the OOTGU stage.

Here again a special aperture setting ring (No. 16622 R) is used. Fit this over the front of the lens so that the two lugs of the ring engage the two recesses of the lens aperture ring. Then turn the front milled ring of the attachment clockwise, thus screwing it into the filter mount of the Elmar lens. Finally, turn the ring just behind the front milled ring so that the arrow head points to 2.8 on the engraved aperture scale (screwing in the ring automatically sets the lens to *f*2.8). To change the aperture setting, simply turn the milled ring carrying the aperture scale.

To fit the lens with this ring in the helical focusing mount, collapse the lens barrel as with the Elmar *f*3.5, and insert in the bayonet ring inside the focusing mount No. 16608 C.

Filters can also be used (39 mm. mount) with the aid of a filter screw ring No. 16614 R. Screw the filter into the rear thread of the filter ring, and then screw the combination into the front of the aperture setting ring (No. 16622 R).

The 50 *mm. Focotar f*4.5, though an enlarging lens, is also specially suitable for close-up focusing on the focusing stage. It is used with the helical mount No. 16688 U.

The Focotar has already an easily accessible aperture setting ring (which also takes 36 mm. push-on filters), and simply screws into the mount as it is.

The lens unit of the 50 *mm. Summicron f*2 (i.e. the rigid, bayonet-mounted versions) is used with the helical mount No. 16685 R for a continuous range from about 10 feet to some 10 inches.

A special aperture setting ring No. 16686 J is used, and fitted in the same way as the ring on the Elmar *f*2.8 (p. 348). Similarly, 39 mm. filters may be fitted with the ring No. 16614 R.

Finally, screw the Summicron lens unit with ring No. 16686 J into the helical mount No. 16685 R.

The Oozab Focusing Stage

This is an older version of the focusing stage for screw-mounted Leica models up to IIIf (not Ig or IIIg). It is similar in principle to the later models, but somewhat different in design—which

The parts of the focusng stage for the Leica up to nodel IIIf are:—

1. Spring clamp.
2. Lens opening in stage with light-trapping rings n latest models).
3. Right-angle focusing nagnifier.
4. 45 deg. focusing magnifier.
5. Vertical focusing nagnifier.
6. Ground glass in round-glass screen housng.
7. Alignment stops.
8. Sliding stage.
9. Stage base.
10. Intermediate focusng mount (for 50 mm. Elmar *f*3.5).
11. 50 mm. Elmar *f*3.5 ens (retracted).
12. Diaphragm ring.

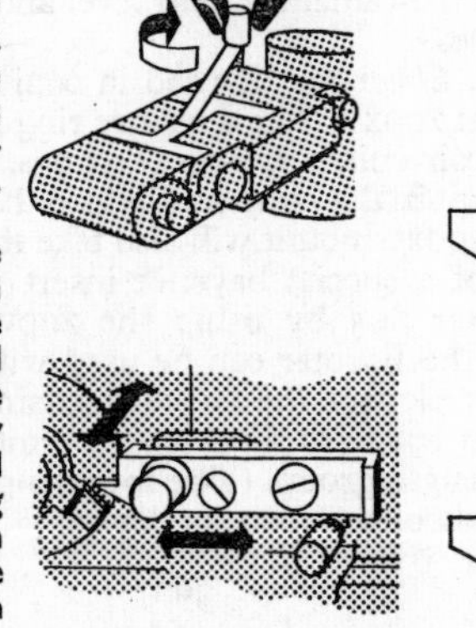

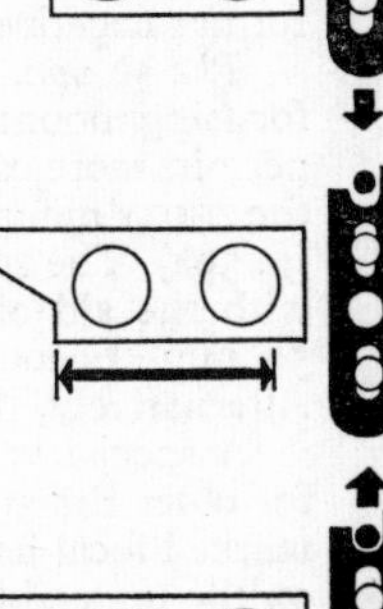

Left-hand column: The spring clamp holds the Leica firmly in place on the stage (*top*); the alignment stops position the camera accurately (*bottom*—see p. 396).

Right-hand column: The latch next to the screen housing controls the stage movement (p. 396). Pulled out (*top*), the sliding stage can be withdrawn. Half-way in, the slide can be moved from focusing to taking positions (*centre*), and with the stop pushed in the slide is locked in position for focusing (*bottom*).

changed slightly from time to time. It is suitable for certain 50 mm., 90 mm., and 135 mm. Leica lenses.

The same focusing magnifiers are used as for the OOBAZ and OOTGU stages (p. 394).

To fit the camera to the focusing stage, slacken off the screw of the spring-loaded clamping arm, and loosen the screws of the camera stop above the screen housing. The eyepiece magnifier of the Leica rangefinder (p. 67) must be set to ∞.

Fit the camera (without lens) so that the lens flange engages the cut-out in the sliding stage. Place the clamping arm over the camera back, and screw down.

Withdraw the sliding stage with the camera from the base plate after pulling up the latch (p. 395). Align the Leica accurately, parallel to the focusing stage itself. Then adjust the camera stop so that it bears against the top left-hand edge of the Leica, and tighten the milled screw. The small screw next to it adjusts the camera stop to the height of the Leica. Finally fit the sliding stage back into the base plate.

Once the camera stop is set for the particular Leica model in use, it needs no further adjustment.

Older focusing stages require adjustment by the makers to take the later Leica models.

A modified version for the Leica IIIg also takes all other earlier models.

Finally depress and lock the knob which pushes down the clamping arm to hold the Leica really firmly.

The latch by the side of the ground-glass screen housing limits the movement of the sliding stage. Pulling the latch upwards, away from the base of the focusing stage, completely frees the sliding stage. The latter can then be slid out of the base plate in the direction of the camera (for aligning and also for cleaning).

When the latch is half-way down it serves as a stop against which to move the sliding stage for focusing. Fully pushed in, the latch locks the stage for focusing.

A second latch at the side of the base plate can be used to lock the sliding stage when the camera is in shooting position. This is essential when the camera is held level and used to take vertical format negatives.

The 50 *mm. Elmar f*3.5 is used in conjunction with a helical focusing mount ZOOXY. The aperture ring No. 16620 T (p. 394) permits more convenient aperture settings. The lens is fitted into the ZOOXY mount in the same way as into the mount No. 16609 D (p. 394). The ZOOXY mount will also take the 50 mm. Elmar *f*2.8 with the aid of a special bayonet insert ring (ZOOYM), or the 50 mm. Focotar *f*4.5 by using the ZOOVX screw ring insert. Alternatively, the Focotar can be used with the ZOOWL mount.

A special version of the helical focusing mount is required for older Elmar lenses of focal length groups 1 to 3, or with no marked focal length group. (The focal length group is engraved on the underside of the focusing lever.)

With the 50 *mm. Summitar or Summar* lenses a different focusing mount (ZISUM) is required.

With the 90 *mm. Elmar* lens a special short focusing mount COOED is required. This screws directly into the lens flange of the focusing stage, and takes the lens unit only of the Elmar.

The 135 *mm. lenses* are used similarly to the 90 mm. Elmar, directly on the focusing stage. Here again, only the lens unit is utilized.

This is screwed into a short focusing mount No. 16495 while a 2-inch (50 mm.) ZOOMF extension tube is used between this mount and the focusing stage.

The 90 mm. and the 135 mm. lenses can be used in their original coupling mounts if an extension tube is fitted between the focusing stage and the lens.

It is not advisable to mount either lens directly on the focusing stage, since the rangefinder coupling barrel may foul the sliding stage at certain settings.

The focusing bellows can also be used with the old (OOZAB) focusing stage, and early models of the bellows carried a scale for the 50 mm. Elmar used with this combination. The focusing stage is not, however, as convenient to use with the focusing bellows as the reflex housing, and the later focusing stages are not suitable for fitting to the bellows at all.

Macrophotography

With most of the lenses used on the focusing stages the nearest focusing limit yields a scale of reproduction between 1 : 2 and 1 : 2.5. Still larger close-ups are possible with the aid of extension tubes No. 16689 V that screw between the OOBAZ or OOTGU focusing stage and the helical focusing mount.

One such tube No. 16689 V permits close-ups down to about natural size; two tubes yield magnifications up to nearly 1½ times, and three tubes can go up to 2 times.

Similar increases in the focusing range for the 50 mm. lenses are possible with extension tubes No. 16615 and the OOZAB focusing stage. A special set of 7 mm., and 30 mm. tubes, marked respectively B, F, and G is supplied with the ZISUM helical mount for the 5 cm. Summitar and Summar lenses.

Various other manufacturers also produce extension tubes with Leica flange and thread in assorted sizes.

A combination of enough tubes will theoretically produce unlimited magnifications, though the practical limit appears to be around 10 times. At higher magnifications a microscope is more convenient, particularly as the exposure increase (p. 419) becomes very great. In addition, the risk of reflections inside the tubes increases.

The Focusing Turret

This close-up focusing accessory was the predecessor of the focusing stage and served the same purpose.

It consists of a round base plate with a tripod bush at one

end, and two Leica lens flanges in the centre and at the other end respectively. The base plate carries a circular rotating stage plate with a camera clamping arm and a ground-glass screen housing. Rotating the stage plate brings either the screen or the Leica in position above either of the lens flanges in the base plate of the turret.

The lens flanges will take an intermediate helical focusing mount which in turn takes the bayonet mounting of the collapsed 5 cm. Elmar or Summar lens, similar to the arrangement used in the focusing stage.

The extension tubes or the lens flanges will also take other lenses, from the 24 mm. Micro-Summar to the 135 mm. lenses.

Stands and Supports

A firm support is important for close-up work, partly because of the long exposures involved, and partly because even very slight movement may upset the focusing settings.

The copying stand No. 16707 is designed for vertical downward view. It consists of a $40\frac{1}{2} \times 20\frac{1}{2}$ inch baseboard with a 31 inch column $1\frac{1}{4}$ inches (32 mm) in diameter. The column has a guide rail and takes an arm with a camera platform. A knob-operated friction drive raises and lowers the arm; there is also a quick release. Except for the form of the camera platform this arrangement closely resembles the baseboard and column of the (now discontinued) Leitz Valoy II enlarger.

On the camera platform a tripod screw can fit into either of two threaded holes which hold it captive. The upper hole (in the wide part of the platform) is for mounting the Visoflex II or III housing by its tripod bush; the Leica M camera is then aligned to point vertically downwards with the aid of the two upper locating pegs in the platform. Alternatively, the platform takes the Leicaflex (which is lined up against the two lower locating pegs) or one of the focusing stages (again lined up against the lower pegs). The hole in the lower part of the camera platform holds the focusing bellows which are lined up to point vertically downwards by the grooves machined into the platform.

With the camera fixed to the upper part of the platform, the arm movement can vary the distance from the film plane to the baseboard between about $6\frac{3}{4}$ and 31 inches (17 and 79 cm). The column also rotates in its socket for shooting downwards over the edge of a table to obtain greater film-to-subject plane distances. The whole stand is easily dismantled into the arm, column and baseboard.

Carrying arms were also available to fit the columns of the Valoy and Focomat Series I enlargers to take the camera for photographing down on the baseboard.

Other copying stand accessories which used to be available include a table clamp No. 17508 Z which clamps to the edges of tables etc. and takes a Valoy II enlarger column. This holds close-up gear via the Valoy arm (No. 16748 F) or the arm of the copying stand.

Also available at one time was a portable copying outfit consisting of a collapsible stand, ball and socket head, and focusing stage with special arm. The stand has a 24½ inch vertical column held to a base frame with brackets and struts. The whole unit packs away in a 4 × 6½ × 17 inch canvas bag.

For horizontal or oblique upward or downward views a suitable stand may be used, with the camera assembly mounted on a ball-and-socket head. The camera assembly and the ball-and-socket head may equally well be attached to an arm for use on a vertical enlarger or similar column.

Various other table and floor stands for medical photography and similar fields are equipped with multiple joints and columns, to hold the Leica at any height and angle.

The Reprovit Outfits

These are complete copying and close-up outfits with a baseboard, column, arm, focusing stage, focusing lamphouse, and lighting unit. Currently, only a Reprovit IIa outfit is available; a Reprovit I outfit formerly made was in effect a focusing stage with carrying arm mounted on a column fixed to a baseboard. Such an outfit can still be made up from the component parts and a focusing lamphouse added.

On the Reprovit IIa a special model of the focusing stage with bellows and fitted with a 50 mm. Focotar lens moves up and down the column for different subject distances and scales of reproduction. A scale alongside the rack-and-pinion focusing movement on the bellows shows scales of reproduction, subject distances (measured from the baseboard to the film plane in the camera) and exposure increase factors.

The carrying arm which moves up and down on the column incorporates two further features. The first is a magnetic relay which releases the shutter of the Leica via a cable release by remote control. This eliminates the risk of camera vibration during exposure, and also permits the camera shutter to be opened and closed by an exposure timer which plugs into the base of the column. The camera shutter in this case is set to B, and the timer can control exposures automatically from 1/10 to 60 seconds.

The second feature is a focusing lamp house. This consists of a projection lamp which illuminates the ground glass screen of the screen housing via a mirror. The latter is fitted inside a right-angle tube which clips on top of the ground glass screen housing and lines up with the lamp house when the screen is in the focusing position. The lamp then projects an image of the screen on to the baseboard. Focusing marks on the centre of this screen show whether the image is sharp, while other marks spaced at one centimetre and one inch apart provide a method of measuring the scale of reproduction. At the same time the area of light projected on the subject indicates the exact field of view.

For the exposure the focusing stage slides across to bring the camera into position behind the lens. This at the same time switches off the projection lamp and stops down the lens (which was at full aperture at focusing) to 11.

A four-lamp lighting unit, mounted on a tubular metal support, forms part of the Reprovit IIa outfit and evenly illuminates the baseboard. Special screens fit over the top of the lamp reflectors to protect the lens from light spill (especially at the smaller scales of reproduction where the lamphouse is near the top of the column). The four-lamp lighting unit automatically switches on when the focusing stage moves from the focusing to the exposure position.

With the 50 mm. Focotar lens the Reprovit IIa covers scales of reproduction from 1 : 19 up to same-size. With two extension tubes No. 16615 the range increases to magnifications of 2 : 1. For still bigger magnifications and macrophotography a 24 mm. Repro-Summar *f*4.5 lens is available; with three extension tubes this permits magnifications up to 7 : 1.

For really large originals the whole column can swing round on the baseboard for projecting on the floor.

Additional accessories like a ball-and-socket head, extra extension tubes, and various object stages and light boxes (p. 402) for copying books, negatives, transparencies, radiographs, and all sorts of other opaque or transparent originals further increase the versatility of the outfit.

To use the Reprovit, assemble the outfit and lamps, and set

REPROVIT IIa

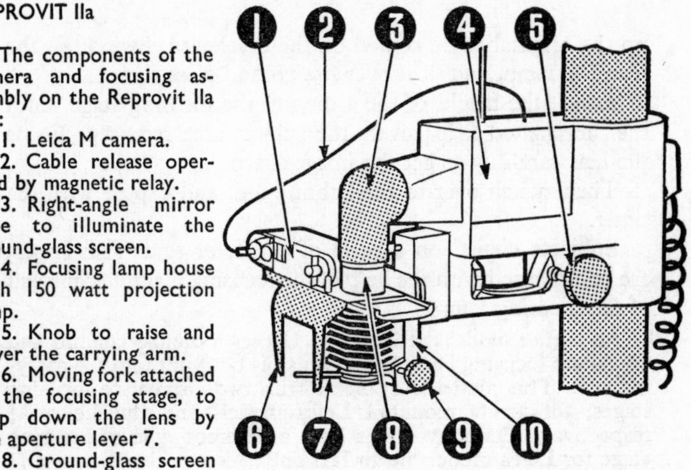

The components of the camera and focusing assembly on the Reprovit IIa are:

1. Leica M camera.
2. Cable release operated by magnetic relay.
3. Right-angle mirror tube to illuminate the ground-glass screen.
4. Focusing lamp house with 150 watt projection lamp.
5. Knob to raise and lower the carrying arm.
6. Moving fork attached to the focusing stage, to stop down the lens by the aperture lever 7.
8. Ground-glass screen housing.
9. Rack-and-pinion fine focusing knob.
10. Reduction, distance and exposure scale.

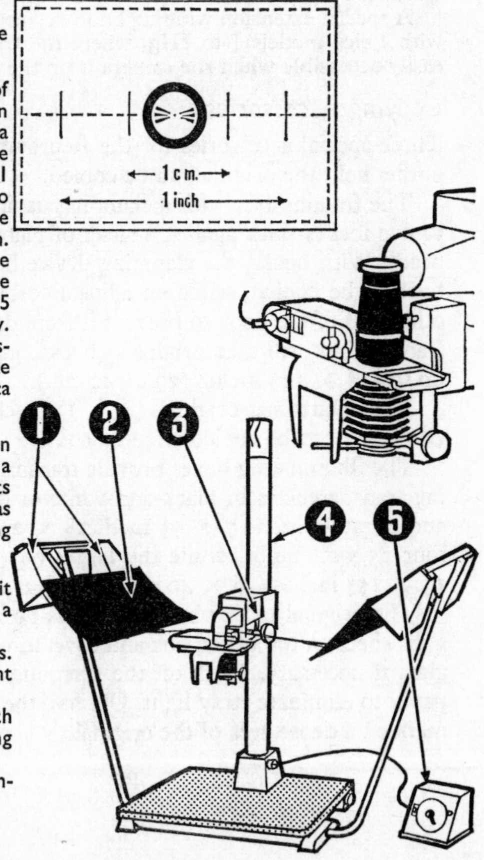

The projected image of the ground-glass screen on the baseboard shows a focusing mark in the centre and distance marks for 1 centimetre and 1 inch to facilitate determining the exact scale of reproduction. The dotted inner frame represents the limit of the field of view for a 23 × 35 mm. framed transparency. The outer frame corresponds to the image size recorded on the Leica negative.

For visual focusing on the ground-glass screen, a vertical 5× magnifier fits on top of the screen, as with the normal focusing stage.

The complete Reprovit IIa outfit incorporates a four-lamp lighting unit.

1. Lamps and reflectors.
2. Screens against light spill.
3. Carrying arm with lamp house and focusing stage.
4. Column with counterweight inside.
5. Timer.

up the original to be copied on the baseboard. Switch on the focusing lamp, and fit it over the ground-glass screen.

Adjust the height of the arm with the focusing stage, until the illuminated field covers the subject area required. Focus the lens carefully to get the image sharp.

Then switch over to the lighting unit and expose with the timer.

Subjects copied on a scale of 1 : 2, or same size larger, are best focused with the help of the focusing magnifier instead of the focusing lamp.

An earlier model the Reprovit II uses a double column and a separate focusing lamp house which is not built into the carrying arm. This model is available with two alternative focusing stages, for screw mounted Leica models and the Leica M respectively. Earlier versions have a different type of focusing stage for Leica models up to IIIf only. Also on the Reprovit II the magnetic relay release is not built-in, but is a separate unit which is suspended from the lamp house bracket.

A special extension winding knob makes film transport easier with Leica models I to IIIg, where the transport knob is not easily accessible when the camera is on the stage.

Copying Accessories

Three special accessories for the Reprovit and other copying outfits hold the originals to be copied.

The framing box with a clamping device presses books up to five inches thick against a sheet of plate glass from underneath. With books, the clamping device holds the part of the book to be copied, while an adjustable bracket supports the other half of the book to prevent it from dropping down. The framing box will take originals (books, journals, documents) up to 11¾ × 16½ inches (29 × 42 cm.).

With quarto size originals (8¼ × 11¾ inches or 21 × 29 cm.) two pages can be copied simultaneously.

The illuminating boxes provide transmitted light for copying transparencies in black-and-white or colour, X-ray films, and negatives. The 7 × 9½ inch (18 × 24 cm.) box contains four 25 watt bulbs, while the larger box for subjects up to 14 × 15¾ inches (36 × 40 cm.) uses four 60 watt bulbs.

The original to be photographed is positioned on the opal glass sheet on top of the box and covered with a sheet of plate glass if necessary. Mask off the surrounding area with black paper to eliminate stray light. Observe the projected focusing mark on a dense area of the original.

COPYING STAND

The features of the compact copying stand are:

1. Camera locating pegs.
2. Camera platform with holes for tripod screw.
3. Baseboard.
4. Camera arm.
5. Quick release lever.
6. Knob to raise or lower the carrying arm.
7. Column.

The upper hole in the camera platform takes the Leicaflex or the Visoflex II and III housings (*left*); the lower hole takes the focusing bellows (*right*).

OLDER COPYING OUTFITS

The Reprovit II outfit has a separate focusing lamphouse which fits over the ground-glass screen.

1. Focusing lamphouse.
2. Ground-glass screen housing.
3. Catch plate.
4. Aperture lever.
5. Automatic lamp change-over switch.
6. Sliding stage.
7. Rack-and-pinion focusing movement.
8. Magnetic camera release (a separate accessory).
9. Extension winding knob for Leica IIIg and older models.

The Reprovit II outfit (*left*) has a somewhat different lighting unit from the IIa.

The table clamp No. 17508Z can be used to fix the Valoy II column to any convenient table top, for use with the appropriate camera carrying arm.

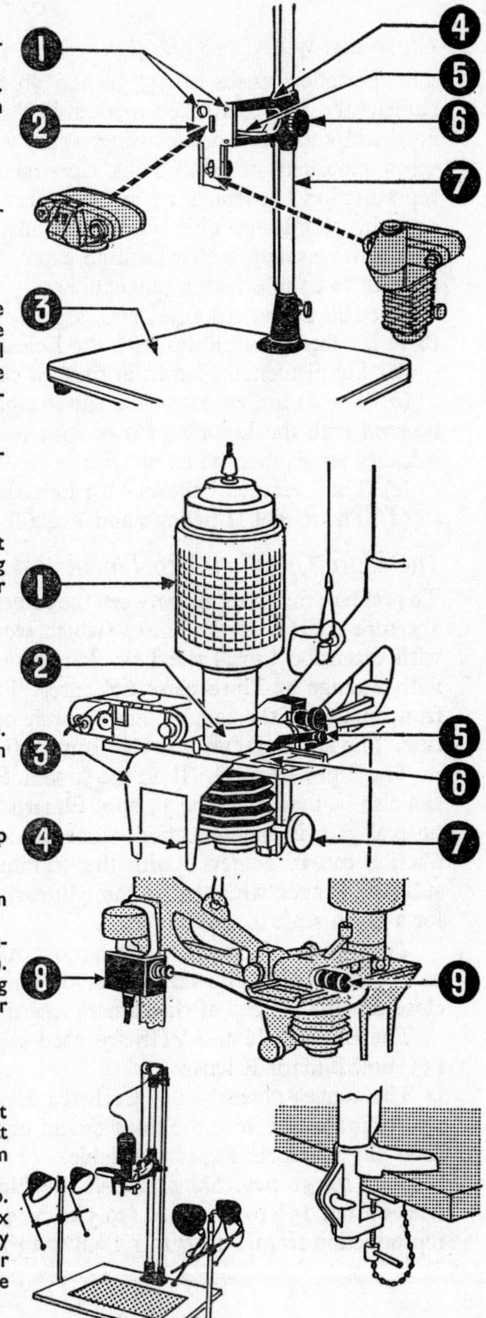

Close-ups with the Leicaflex

The Leicaflex lenses of 35, 50 and 90 mm. focus down to sufficiently close distances to permit close-ups in the range covered by the close-up focusing mount with the Leica M and screw-mounted models. Thus close shots with a scale of reproduction between 1 : 5 and 1 : 7 become possible at the near focusing limit. This is a specific advantage of the single-lens reflex system, since such an extended focusing range is difficult to couple with a rangefinder.

For still nearer distances and larger scales of reproduction there are four possibilities with the Leicaflex:

(*a*) Supplementary lenses in front of camera lenses;

(*b*) The Leicaflex extension tube combination (which can be used with the Leicaflex lenses with or without the supplementary lenses mentioned above);

(*c*) The Leicaflex bellows with Leicaflex lenses;

(*d*) The model II bellows and Leica lens units.

The Elpro Close-up Attachments

To preserve the coupling between the camera and the automatic aperture control of the lenses (which would not be possible with extension tubes) the Leicaflex provides closer distances with a range of Elpro close-up lenses. These screw into the front mount of the camera lens in place of the filter retaining ring. The latter screws into the front of the Elpro lenses.

The Elpro VIa and VIb fit the 50 mm. Summicron R. They can also be used with the 35 mm. Elmarit R, but here provide no real gain in magnification, since the same scale of reproduction can be achieved with the 50 mm. lens. The shorter subject distance with the 35 mm. Elmarit-R is no advantage for a given scale of reproduction.

The Elpro VI lenses have a groove near the front of the mount to take the clip-on lens hood. This now fits on to the close-up lens instead of the camera lens mount.

The Elpro VIIa and VIIb are used with the 90 mm. and 135 mm. Elmarit-R lenses.

The ranges given below are listed as lens-to-subject distances, measured from the front mount of the Elpro lenses, to show the actual clear space available.

With the 50 mm. Summicron-R the Elpro VIa covers distances from 15½ to 8 inches (39.5 to 20.5 cm.) and scales of reproduction from 1 : 7.7 to 1 : 3.8 (0.13 to 0.26).

LEICAFLEX CLOSE-UPS

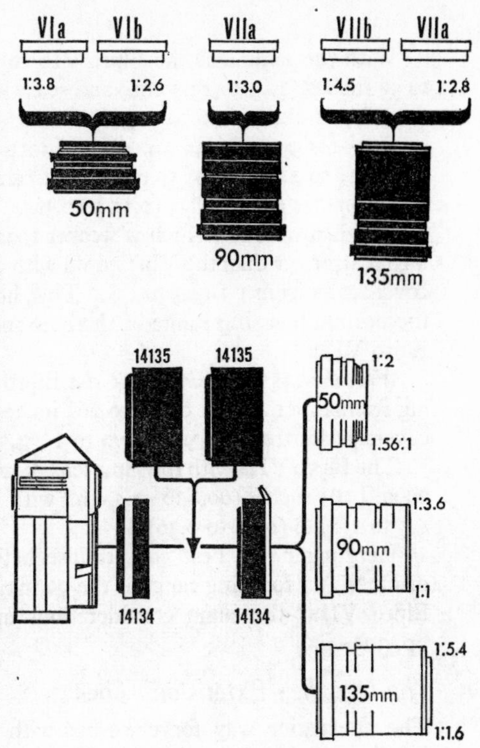

The Elpro supplementary lenses extend the near focusing range of the 50, 90 and 135 mm. lenses of the Leicaflex. The figures against the lens show the largest obtainable scale of reproduction.

The extension tubes also reduce the near focusing limit of the Leicaflex lenses. The basic unit is the No. 14134 tube which consists of a front and a rear component which screw together and carry a bayonet ring at the back and a bayonet fitting at the front for attachment to the camera and to the lens respectively. The total extension obtained by the No. 14134 combination is 25 mm.

When the two halves are screwed apart, one or more additional tubes No. 14135—each of 25 mm. length—can screw in between the two halves. The lens extension is thus increased in steps of 25 mm.

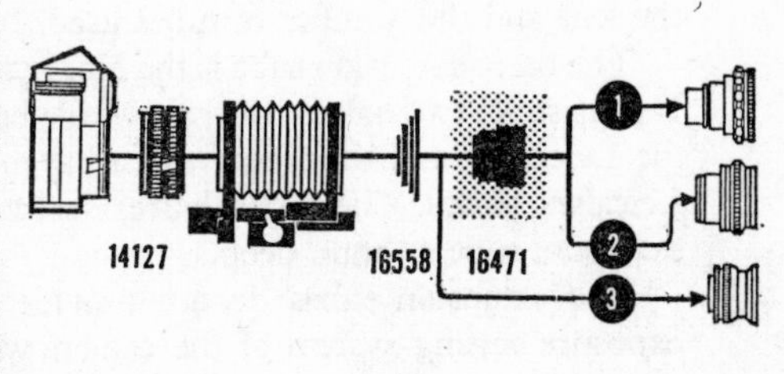

With the Leicaflex/Leica adapter ring No. 14127 on the Leicaflex, the model II bellows unit and all lenses that fit it can be used. Instead of the bellows the helical focusing mount No. 16464 can equally cover a range of close-up scales. In both cases a No. 16471 extension tube provides still nearer distances. The most useful combinations ranges are:

1. 65 mm. Elmar: ∞ to 1.6.
2. 90 mm. *f*2.8, optical unit only: ∞ to 1.
3. 90 mm. *f*4, optical unit only: ∞ to 1 (cannot be used with No. 16471 tube).
4. 90 mm. *f*2.8, optical unit only: ∞ to 0.3.
5. 65 mm. Elmar: ∞ to 0.42.

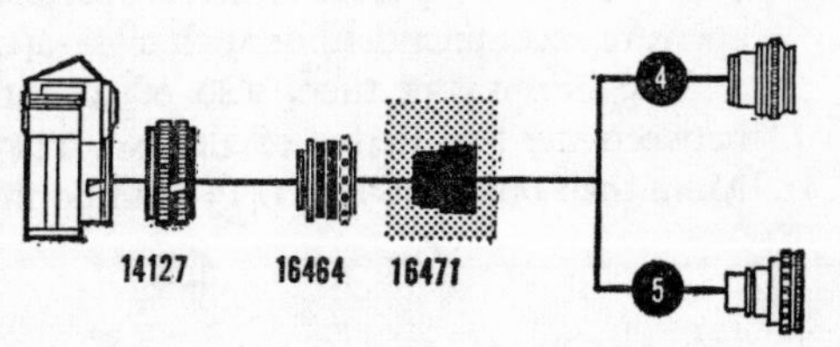

With the same lens the Elpro VIb covers distances from 8 to 5⅜ inches (20.5 to 13.5 cm.) and scales of reproduction from 1 : 3.8 to 1 : 2.6 (0.26 to 0.39).

With the 90 *mm. Elmarit-R* the Elpro VIIa covers subjects from 23¼ to 11¼ inches (59 to 28.3 cm.) and scales of reproduction from 1 : 6.7 to 1 : 3 (0.15 to 0.34).

The Elpro VIIb (which is weaker than the VIIa, while the VIb is stronger than the VIa) would with the 90 mm. Elmarit R cover scales from 1 : 14.5 to 1 : 4. This, however, fully overlaps the normal focusing range of the lens and the range with the Elpro VIIa.

With the 135 *mm. Elmarit-R* the Elpro VIIb permits focusing from about 4½ feet down to 26½ inches (135 to 67 cm.) and covers scales from 1 : 9.9 down to 1 : 4.5 (0.1 to 0.22).

The Elpro VIIa with the same lens permits focusing between 24 and 16¼ inches (60.6 to 41.5 cm.) with image scales from 1 : 4.5 to 1 : 2.8 (0.22 to 0.36).

Here again the best compromise between lens-to-subject distance and focusing range is the 90 mm. Elmarit-R with the Elpro VIIa; the same considerations apply as outlined on pp. 373–4.

The Leicaflex Extension Tubes

The alternative way for close-ups with the Leicaflex lenses is to increase the lens extension with the No. 14134 and 14135 extension tubes. This allows the Leicaflex to reach scales of reproduction up to about 1½ times natural size, according to the lens and the number of tubes used.

The basic extension tube is the No. 14134 combination ring. It consists of two halves, the rear with a bayonet ring to fit into the Leicaflex, and the front with a bayonet fitting to take the Leicaflex lenses. These two halves screw together to yield an extension tube 25 mm. deep.

The extension tubes do not provide for coupling of the exposure setting system of the camera with the lens aperture control. However when the No. 14134 tube is mounted in the Leicaflex, the setting marker of the exposure meter is adjusted to give correct exposures with an aperture *f*11; this is the lens aperture recommended for such close-ups.

The No. 14135 tube, also of 25 mm. length, screws in between the two halves of the No. 14134 combination ring. More than one tube No. 14135 can be fitted in this way.

LEICAFLEX
CLOSE-UP RANGES

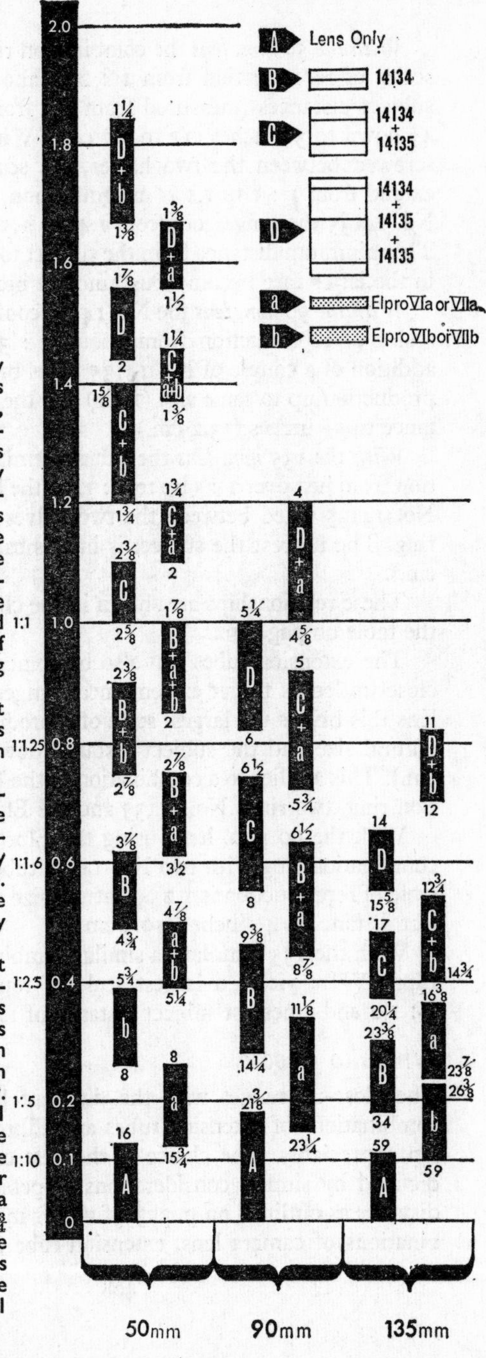

The vertical bars show the close-up range, in terms of scale of reproduction, for the different combinations of extension tubes and Elpro supplementary lenses with different Leicaflex lenses. The figures against the top and the bottom of each bar indicate the subject distance, measured from the front of the lens. (This gives a good indication of the amount of space available for lighting etc.)

The key at the top right identifies the combinations themselves (marked with letters against the bars).

Not all possible combinations are shown, since some duplicate the functions of others—especially with the 90 and 135 mm. lenses. In such cases the preferred alternative only is given.

Note that the subject distance for any combination of extension tubes plus supplementary lenses is always shorter for a given scale of reproduction than with extension tubes only. (For example a scale of 1 : 1 can be reached with the 90 mm. Elmarit-R and the No. 14134 ring plus a pair of No. 14135 tubes—at a subject distance of 5¾ inches. However with the same combination of tubes plus the Elpro VIIa lens the image distance at a 1 : 1 scale is only 4⅝ inches.)

With the 50 *mm. lens* the combination ring No. 14134 yields scales of reproduction from 1 : 2 to about 1 : 1.6, covering subject distances (measured from the front of the lens) from 4¾ down to 3⅞ inches (12 to 9.7 cm.). With a No. 14135 tube screwed between the two halves, the scales of reproduction extend from 1 : 1 to 1.1 × magnification, and with two tubes No. 14135 the range goes from 1.44 to 1.56 times natural size. The minimum distance from the subject to the front of the lens in the latter case becomes just under 2 inches (4.7 cm.).

With the 90 *mm. lens* the No. 14134 combination ring covers scales of reproduction from about 1 : 3.6 to 1 : 2.2. The addition of a couple of No. 14135 tubes brings the scale of reproduction up to same size (1 : 1) and the nearest subject distance to 5¼ inches (13.2 cm.).

With the 135 *mm. lens* the tubes permit scales of reproduction from just over 1 : 5 up to 1 : 1.5—the latter with two tubes No. 14135 fitted between the two halves of the combination ring. The nearest the subject is in this case is 14 inches (35.4 cm.).

These relationships are shown in the chart on page 407 and the table on page 492.

The extension tubes can also be combined with the Elpro close-up lenses to get extreme near ranges. With the 50 mm. lens this brings the largest scale of reproduction up to 1.84 × natural size and the subject distance down to 1¼ inches (3.2 cm.). This applies to a combination of the No. 14134 combination ring, two rings No. 14135 and the Elpro VIb.

With the 90 mm. lens, using the Elpro VIIa lens and the combination ring with two No. 14135 tubes added the largest scale of reproduction is 1.2 × natural size and the nearest subject distance is 4⅛ inches (10.3 cm.).

With the 135 mm. lens a similar combination, but with the Elpro VIIb, yields a largest scale of reproduction of about 1 : 1.2 and a nearest subject distance of 11 inches (27.8 cm.).

Which to Choose

The close-up ranges with the different lenses and different combinations of extension tubes and Elpro attachments overlap appreciably. The choice of the best combination is again dictated by similar considerations of perspective and subject distance as outlined on p. 373. If two or more alternative combinations of camera lens, extension tube and close-up lenses are at hand for a given scale of reproduction it is usually best to choose the longer lens and a combination with extension tubes in preference to Elpro lenses. This provides in every case the largest amount of space between the camera set-up and the subject, for convenient manipulation of lights and also for a better perspective. Thus the 90 mm. lens is the most convenient one to use for scales of reproduction between 1 : 1 and about 1 : 4. The 135 mm. lens gives even bigger lens-to-subject distances (which may however become inconveniently long).

For close-ups at larger than natural size the available lens extension (with or without the extension tubes) favours the use of the 50 mm. lens—it is the only one which can reach magnifications of 1.8 ×.

With the 50 mm. lens the ranges of reproduction scales of the different combinations run with comparatively little overlap to cover a continuous range up to 1.8 ×. With the 90 mm. lens the overlap between different combinations is greater and in fact combinations using the Elpro VIIb are superfluous since they do nothing which is not covered by combinations of the extension tubes and Elpro VIIa.

With the 135 mm. lens on the other hand the Elpro VIIa is less advisable in combination with the extension tubes because this supplementary lens tends to upset the optical correction of the camera lens at the closest subject distances.

The Leicaflex Bellows

The bellows unit for the Leicaflex is similar to the model II bellows for the Visoflex but incorporates various special features. An octagonal bellows connects a front and a rear ring. The front ring runs forward and back by a rack-and-pinion focusing movement. This adjusts the lens-to-film distance, controlled by a milled knob on the left-hand side (as seen from the back of the camera). The base of the front unit moves above a graduated scale, consisting of a rotating square rod which permits four different scales to be brought into view:

(*a*) A millimetre scale from 0 to 100. Since the minimum extension of the bellows unit is already 42 mm. ($1\frac{5}{8}$ inches) the maximum extension is $5\frac{5}{8}$ inches or 143 mm.

(*b*) A scale labelled 90 mm. carrying scales of reproduction from 0.5 to 1.5 (the actual extension goes beyond those limits) and a scale of exposure factors at the magnifications with the 90 mm. Elmarit-R lens.

(*c*) A scale marked 100 mm. with magnifications from 0 to 1 for the 100 mm. Macro-Elmar *f*4, plus exposure factors.

(*d*) A scale for the 135 mm. Elmarit-R with magnifications up to 1.05 and again exposure factors.

The scales are switched round by simply turning the milled knob at the end of the scale rod.

Below the main track is a base which again moves forward and back and carries a ¼ inch and ⅜ inch tripod bush. This base is mounted on a tripod; on turning the right-hand knob the whole bellows and camera assembly moves forward and back for adjustment of the subject-to-lens distance. The movement range is here 68 mm. or just under 2¾ inches. The left-hand knob can be locked by a lever.

To assemble the bellows unit and the camera, attach the camera to the rear bayonet ring with the red dot on the rear bellows panel opposite the lens catch on the camera. Push together and turn the camera clockwise to engage the lock. To remove, disengage the lens lock of the camera in the usual way and turn anti-clockwise.

Once the bellows is mounted on a tripod or a stand, the camera can swivel through 90° for upright or horizontal views. For this purpose press the chrome lever—below the camera fitting—inwards; the rear ring then rotates and engages in two positions. The lens is fitted into the front bayonet ring in the same way as on a camera.

The following lenses can be used:

The 100 *mm. Macro-Elmar f*4 is specially designed for close-up work with the Leicaflex bellows, and has no focusing mount as the bellows movement is used for focusing. This combination provides a continuous focusing range from infinity to same-size reproduction. This is thus the ideal combination for most close-up work—also because the longer focal length at any given scale of magnification offers better perspective rendering of the subject.

The 35 *mm. Elmarit-R* covers magnification of 1.2× (with the bellows fully retracted) up to 4.1× with the bellows fully extended. With the lens itself focused on its nearest distance the magnification increases to just over 4.5×.

With this lens there are however certain practical limitations. While the magnification obtained is very high, the lens-to-subject distance becomes very short. At maximum magnification there is only ⅛ inch between the front lens mount and the

LEICAFLEX BELLOWS

The controls and components of the bellows are:

1. Lens mount.
2. Cable release socket.
3. Aperture lock.
4. Rotating scale.
5. Index point.
6. Focusing knob for lens.
7. Aperture opening ring.
8. Camera mount.
9. Release catch for upright and horizontal shots.

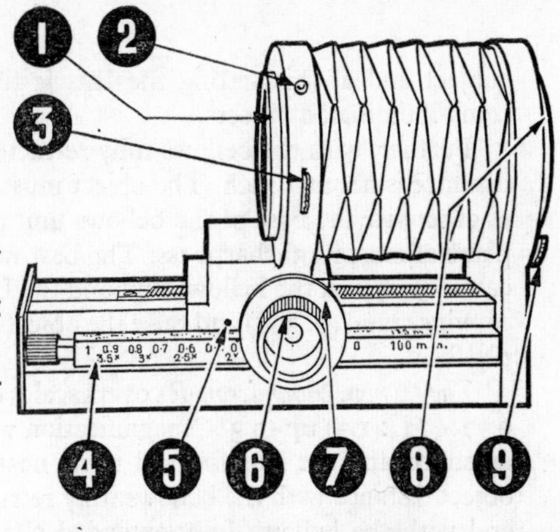

Attach the camera to the rear bayonet ring in the usual way (*left*); fit the lens into the front bayonet mount of the bellows (*right*).

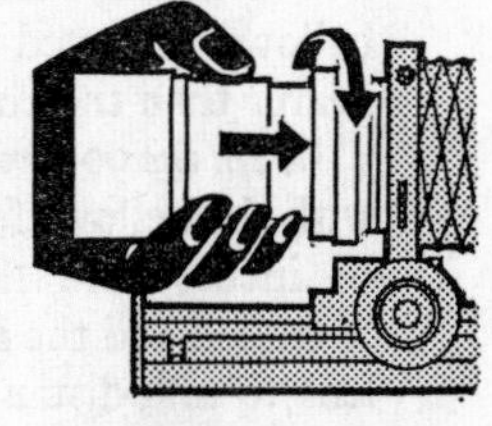

On pressing the ring surrounding the front focusing knob the lens opens to its maximum aperture (*left*). On releasing the ring, the lens closes down to its set stop (*right*).

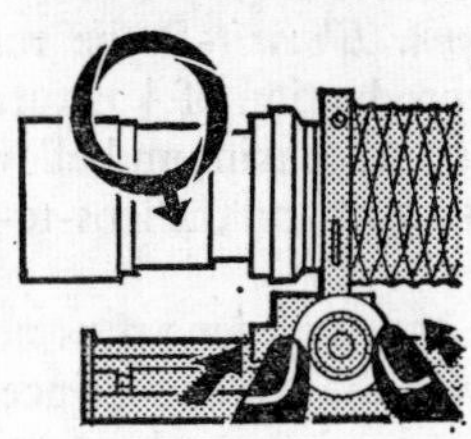

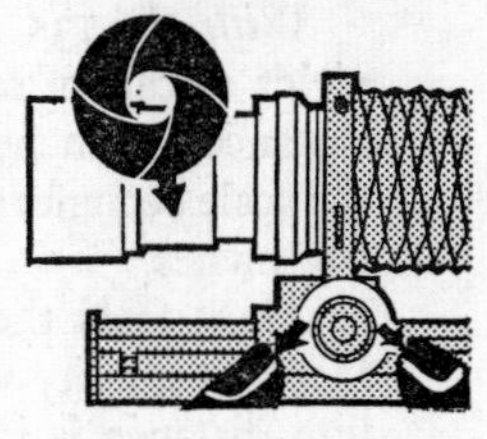

The lens can be locked at full aperture by pressing the ring and at the same time pressing down the locking lever.

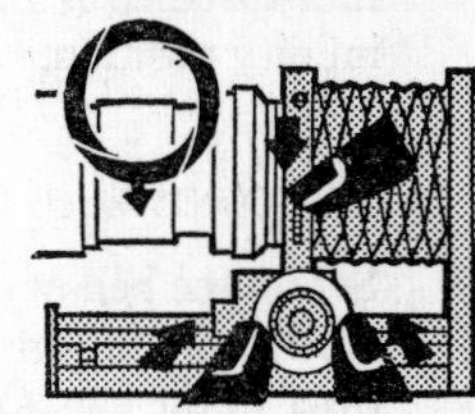

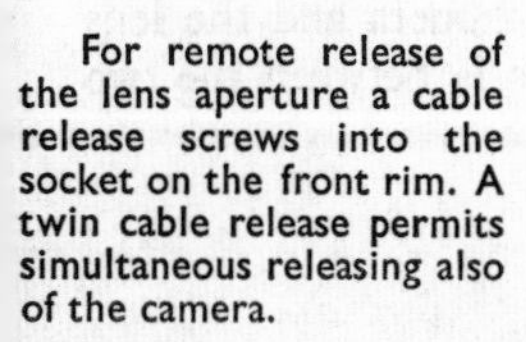

For remote release of the lens aperture a cable release screws into the socket on the front rim. A twin cable release permits simultaneous releasing also of the camera.

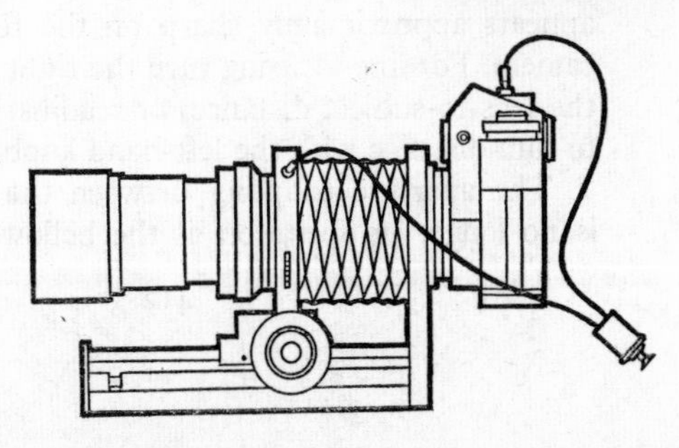

subject and at this setting the lens is thus suitable only for trans-illuminated objects.

Further, with the bellows fully retracted, the lens-to-object distance is about 1 inch. The object must thus be fairly small, as otherwise the base of the bellows unit protrudes behind the plane of maximum sharpness. The best way of working in this case is to mount the bellows unit and the Leicaflex on a vertical copying stand (p. 398) and raise the object on a small adjustable platform.

The 50 *mm. Summicron-R* covers scales of reproduction from 0.77× (1 : 1.3) up to 3× magnification with the bellows fully extended and the lens focused to its near limit. The lens-to-object distance with the bellows fully retracted is here 3 inches and with the bellows fully extended about ¾ inch. With the bellows retracted the plane of maximum sharpness is again nearer than the end of the bellows base.

With the 90 *mm. Elmarit-R* the image scale is 0.45× (1 : 2.1) with the bellows fully retracted (subject-to-film distance about 9½ inches) and 1.75× magnification with the bellows fully extended and the lens at its nearest distance setting. The front lens-to-film distance is then 3 inches.

With the 135 *mm. Elmarit-R* the fully retracted bellows yields a scale of reproduction of ⅓ natural size (lens-to-object distance 23½ inches). At maximum bellows and lens extension the scale becomes 1.15 : 1 and the lens-to-object distance about 10½ inches.

Apart from the 100 mm. lens thus none of the lenses can focus on infinity with the bellows—since after all the lens-to-film distance is increased by at least 42 mm. in front of its infinity position.

Close-ups with the Leicaflex Bellows

Set up the bellows on a tripod or firm stand, extend the lens to the required magnification (as marked on the rotating scale for three of the lenses). Then approach the subject until the image appears approximately sharp on the focusing screen of the camera. For fine focusing turn the right-hand knob (adjusting the lens-to-subject distance) or readjust if necessary the lens-to-film distance with the left-hand knob.

The aperture coupling between the camera and the lens is no longer in operation as the bellows is between the two units. So the bellows has a separate preset aperture control which works with all the lenses.

Normally the lens is stopped down to its working aperture, as set by the aperture ring. To focus at full aperture, press the black ring—surrounding the left-hand focusing knob—inwards. This operates a spring-loaded lever system which acts on the aperture coupling to open the iris diaphragm. On releasing the black ring, the lens returns to its working aperture.

For more protracted focusing and viewing the aperture can also be arrested in its full open position. Press in the aperture control ring, and push in the lever protruding from the rim of the front standard of the bellows, before releasing the black ring.

This aperture lock can now be released in two ways. The first is to depress fully the black ring on the focusing shaft; the chrome lever jumps out of the rim of the front panel again and the lens closes down. The same can be achieved by a cable release which screws into the cable release socket on the rim of the front panel. Even twin cable release operation is possible as with the old Visoflex (p. 140) and certain other units: adjust the action of the two cable releases so that the aperture lock is released before the camera shutter. A single pressure on the twin cable release then closes down the lens and takes the picture.

One special point arises with the 90 mm. and 135 mm. Elmarit-R lenses of the Leicaflex. These are telephoto designs with a shorter back focus than the focal length. One result of this is that close-ups need higher exposure correction factors than would be required from the usual calculation based on scale of reproduction (p. 419). The correct factors are marked on the scales at the side of the bellows for the 90 mm. and 135 mm. lenses.

With the Leicaflex SL the through-the-lens light measurement automatically allows for the exposure factors.

The Leicaflex with the Leica Focusing Bellows

The Leicaflex/Leica adapter ring No. 14127 mounted on the Leicaflex yields the same front flange-to-film distance as the Visoflex II or III on a Leica M; so this combination can be used with the focusing bellows model II and all lenses available for the latter (p. 386). In convenience this is inferior to the use of the Leicaflex bellows, but is cheaper when a Visoflex bellows unit and Leica lenses are already available.

The Leicaflex and the Leicaflex/Leica adapter No. 14127 can also be used with the focusing mount No. 16464 and the lenses with extension tubes taken by the latter (p. 375).

When working with the close-up combinations involving the Leicaflex/Leica adapter ring No. 14127, the aperture simulator ring is again used as described on p. 180.

It is also feasible to combine the Leica M lenses with the Leicaflex/Leica adapter ring and the No. 14134 and 14135 extension tube set. In practice it is however a little pointless to acquire the extension tube set if one only has the Leica M close-up accessories.

CLOSE–UP TECHNIQUE

The depth of field is very small at near distances.
Use even illumination for copying, and strongly directional light for texture rendering.
Large close-ups need increased exposure.

When we have a really close look at things, the features we observe are far more intimate; we examine subjects not as a whole, but in detail and often piecemeal. It is no longer the shape of a face or a hand that interests us, but the wrinkles and pores of the skin; the petals of a rose, rather than the rosebush.

Close-up photography is therefore largely texture photography. A successful close-up shot nearly always depends on its reproduction of texture. We have to arrange our focusing and lighting with that end in view.

Near Focusing

Although the various close-up accessories of the Leica all permit quite accurate focusing, the depth of field is very small. Most close-ups will therefore need small lens apertures to make the most of the depth of field. The depth is particularly shallow with very near subjects; with shots between 18 and 36 inches from the Leica we can still cover a depth of a few inches and photograph objects like flowers, small animals, and miniature art objects.

In every case focus on the nearest plane of importance. Calculate the depth required from the tables (p. 488); the visual image on a screen is usually too dim at small apertures to assess the sharpness accurately.

While the depth of field is limited, the depth of focus, i.e. the latitude in lens setting, becomes considerable. In other words, the image grows sharper or less sharp only very slowly for an appreciable movement of the lens.

This makes it difficult to find accurately the point of maximum sharpness.

To get over this, either use a high-power magnifier on the focusing screen or move the whole camera bodily forward and backwards (p. 388).

A further alternative is to employ an adjustable specimen stand. This is a small platform mounted on a column which slides up and down in a sleeve fixed to a base. The height of the platform is adjustable by means of a micrometer screw or a rack-and-pinion mechanism.

Lighting for Close-ups

Where miniature subjects are lit by fairly diffused daylight or artificial illumination, lighting presents no problems different from those of larger subjects. For effect lighting, however, normal lamp set-ups cover too large an area.

A concentrated light source such as a spotlight or two is then more convenient to handle. We can adjust the width of the beam as well as its exact direction and accurately screen off any part of the subject—or the camera lens—that we do not want to illuminate.

This type of arrangement is specially handy with table top and similar subjects, e.g. advertising close-ups.

At the other extreme, document copying and also certain types of medical and technical photographs call for very even lighting. The ideal way of achieving this kind of lighting is to use a ring illuminator, set up in front of the subject, with the camera lens photographing through the centre of the ring. The resulting illumination is completely shadowless.

Texture Lighting

Very near shots are, in view of the much reduced depth of field, mostly limited to comparatively flat subjects. To reproduce texture, we have to bring out depth by suitable lighting.

For this purpose low-angle side light shows up any small unevenness in the surface by casting long shadows which throw every detail into bold relief. The result is specially effective with surfaces like stone, leather, wood, fabrics and also coins and plaques.

The best light source is a spotlight to pick out the texture, with a fill-in lamp to illuminate the shadows created by folds in cloth or other draped materials.

With reflecting surfaces like metals, china, porcelain, and also silk and satin, plastic rendering depends largely on the sheen of the material. To bring this out use a spot of flood light from a high angle, supplementing it if necessary with a fill-in lamp. The main light should show up the shape and solidity of the object in terms of catchlights as well as its surface construction.

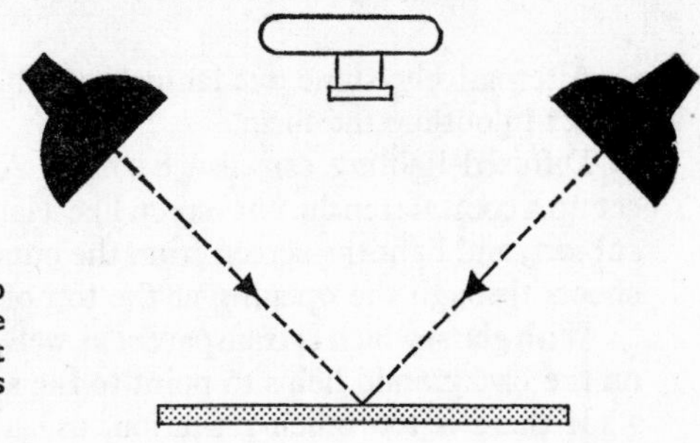

When copying, set up the lights to illuminate the subject area evenly without reflections into the lens (p. 420).

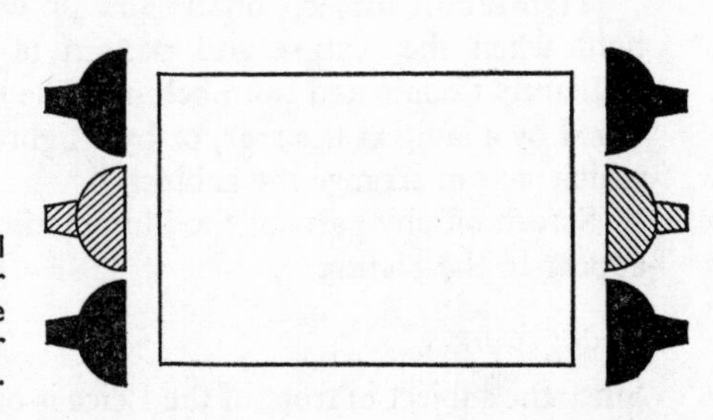

Use two lamps for small originals, or four for larger ones, in the latter case arranging them at the four corners of the field covered.

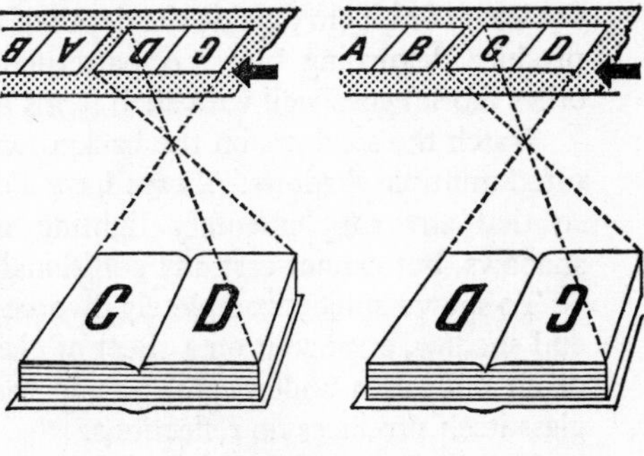

When mircrofilming books, make sure that pairs of pages are recorded in their correct sequence (*right*), and not transposed (*left*) on the film (p. 422).

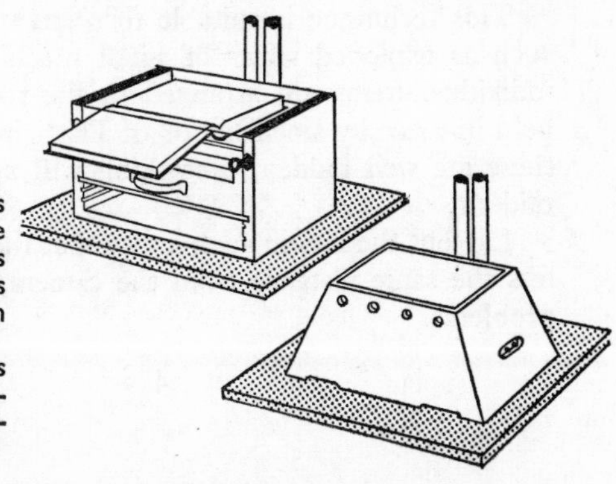

The framing box (*left*) is a special accessory for the Reprovit outfits, and holds books and similar originals flat in the correct position for copying (p. 416).

The light box (*right*) is used to illuminate transparent originals when copying, e.g. radiographs, etc.

Alternatively, shine two lamps from the two sides on to the object to outline the form.

Diffused lighting can also be used. A good method is to set up a conical translucent screen like a lamp shade around the subject, and light the screen from the outside. The Leica then shoots through the opening at the top of the cone.

With glass, which is transparent as well as shiny, the shadow on the background helps to point to the solidity of the article.

If there is too much reflection, use a polarizing filter (p. 240) to reduce the glare.

Translucent subjects often show up well taken against the light when the texture and pattern of the object appears brilliantly illuminated from behind. The lighting may be provided by a lamp at the rear, or by a light box (p. 402) against which we can arrange the subject.

Screen off any parts of the illuminating surface that might appear in the picture.

Backgrounds

Since the subject in front of the Leica is on quite a small scale, we can conveniently use artificial background screens of white or grey card. This is useful with close-ups of plants where the leaves or bloom outside the depth of field of the lens would produce disturbing blurs. A patterned background (silk or other fabric) goes well with such items as jewellery.

Watch the shadows on the background, and avoid complicated multiple shadows. Always have a dominating main light so that any supplementary lighting only lightens up the shadows, but cannot cast any additional ones.

To show a subject completely divorced from its background and shadow, arrange it on a sheet of glass, with a white sheet or an unlit area underneath. Set up the lighting so that the glass itself produces no reflections.

This technique is suitable for certain industrial subjects, such as exploded views of small machinery or tools. The individual items are arranged in the required position and held in place by small lumps of Plasticine or wax. Provided these are well hidden, everything will appear suspended in mid-air.

Lay out the bits in such a way that they are all at more or less the same distance from the camera, to reduce focusing problems.

Live Subjects

Daylight permits instantaneous exposures at quite small apertures. With Photofloods the near lamp distances required may be inconvenient because of the heat of the lamps.

The ideal light source is synchronized flash. Detach the flash gun from the Leica, though, and direct it separately at the subject. When mounted on the camera, the area lit up at close range may not be the same as that covered by the lens.

Insects in their glass cases and the smaller fish in aquaria are best tackled with a near focusing mount or focusing bellows, photographing through the glass. Additional lighting will have to come through the same glass. Place a flash gun as near as possible to the side of the case, adjusting the light so that none reaches the camera lens directly.

Exposure Factors

With pictures taken at a larger scale than 1: 10 the lens extension increases rapidly and the nominal lens aperture no longer corresponds to the effective aperture. We then have to increase the exposure.

The most convenient way of working out the compensation required is to use exposure factors based on the scale of reproduction (see table on p. 472). For quickly calculating the factor on the spot, find the degree of magnification (fractional for close-ups at less than natural size), add 1 to the number, and multiply the result by itself.

For example on a scale of 1 : 2 (i.e. $\frac{1}{2}$) the factor is $\frac{1}{2} + 1$ multiplied by itself $= 1\frac{1}{2} \times 1\frac{1}{2} = 2\frac{1}{4}$, or roughly 2. Similarly, for a large close-up at $3 \times$ magnification the factor is $(3 + 1) \times (3 + 1) = 16$.

This does not apply strictly to true telephoto lenses (like the 90 mm. Tele-Elmarit, the 135 mm. Tele-Elmar or the Telyt series), nor with the long-focus lenses of the Leicaflex. With telephoto lenses the factor is increased; with the 135 mm. Tele-Elmar increase the factor obtained by about $\frac{1}{5}$ (so that, for instance, a factor of 16 becomes about 19×). With the 90 mm. Tele-Elmarit and the 200 mm. Telyt—if used for close-up work—increase the factor by $\frac{1}{3}$. See also p. 413.

With the 35 mm. Elmarit R of the Leicaflex the factor can be ignored over the whole focusing range of this lens.

At magnifications beyond 1 : 1 reproduction the factors rise very rapidly, so that time exposures may become necessary. In that case the factor may need further modification to allow for reciprocity failure (p. 233).

Copying

Copying technique is easily standardized. We are dealing with flat subjects, so we do not need any depth of field, except possibly to cover up errors of focusing. It is better not to stop down the lens beyond *f* 11; most Leica lenses give their optimum definition around *f* 5.6.

The most suitable lens for copying is the 50 mm. Elmar or Focotar. It is the standard lens for which most copying accessories are designed, while the Summicron and Summitar also work with the distance gauges and some other units.

The lighting for copying must evenly illuminate the subject field. For small subject areas two lamps at opposite sides of the original are sufficient. For larger originals we may need four lamps, one at each corner.

The lamps should shine on to the field at an angle of about 45 deg. and be more or less level with the Leica. This ensures that no light is reflected into the lens as glare from the copying surface (that might be the case with a narrower angle of incidence). A lower angle lights up the edges more than the centre.

Where it would be inconvenient to carry a lamp set-up, use open flash, and fire one bulb from each side in succession while the shutter is open.

For transparent originals like radiographs, colour transparencies, and lantern slides, the light box provides even, diffused illumination.

Films and Filters

For copying from black-and-white line originals (diagrams, documents, printed matter) use a non-colour sensitive copying film. This yields extremely fine grain and high contrast and resolution.

For coloured originals use panchromatic film; usually such subjects are continuous tone originals (paintings, postage stamps, etc.) and the negative contrast can be lower. An extra-fine grain film is really ideal there, and will also serve for black-and-white half-tone subjects like photographs.

For copying in colour, use colour film balanced for artificial light (Type A, B, Tungsten) with the appropriate illumination.

Filters are required when copying old documents on yellowish paper. There pan film with a deep yellow or orange filter increases the contrast between the background and the writing.

Contrast or strong effect filters may also be necessary to differentiate between tones when copying coloured originals on black-and-white film. Thus a yellow centre in a deep green postage stamp would normally appear too faint to show sufficient detail of the engraving. A deep green filter will lighten the green and darken the yellow.

Similarly, a blue postmark on a red stamp may obliterate some of the detail, but will disappear through a blue filter.

When copying monochrome originals of a colour other than black, use a complementary filter (e.g. green for a red original) to increase the contrast.

Exposure Tests

Copying exposures depend greatly on subject conditions, and require preliminary tests.

Make exposures on a short length of the copying film, based on meter readings or exposure tables (use a film speed of 8–16 ASA). Take a series of shots in much the same way as when calibrating an exposure meter (p. 220). With a more or less standard set-up one such test for each type of film used will be sufficient.

To find the exposure on different occasions, use an exposure meter to measure the brightness of a piece of white paper laid down in place of the original. Once the correct exposure for a given meter reading is known, you can deduce the time required at different meter readings. The exposure meter will also indicate the correct exposure with different lamp set-ups.

Remember to allow for changes of aperture, the filter factor to use with the light employed, and also for the exposure factor at different scales of reproduction (p. 419). Some allowance may also be needed for specially light or dark originals.

Microfilming

Microfilming is a process of copying whole books, sets of plans, diagrams, correspondence or newspaper issues over a given period of time, on to 35 mm. film. The purpose of microfilming is to record the material in a form which is easily filed, yet takes considerably less room to store than the originals and is readily accessible for reference.

Microfilming technique is essentially standardized copying. The Reprovit outfits make the work most convenient, but the copying gauges will do an equally good—if slower—job of it.

To make the record most useful, it needs a little planning. Matters are simplest if all exposures are similar, as with the pages of a book. Work out how many exposures will be required, and divide them up evenly among a number of rolls of film. For instance a 250-page book will take eight thirty-six-exposure rolls, making thirty-two exposures on each. The few odd exposures left over on every roll are a reserve for mistakes, spoilt shots, and also to leave a little film at the beginning and end for handling.

Make exposure tests to get averything right first and then proceed to copy the pages one by one. Once the Leica is focused, no changes will be necessary.

The framing box (p. 402) holds books flat against a glass sheet for every exposure and thus ensures accurate reproduction. With small books (up to octavo size) you can copy two pages at a time. Place the book the same way up as the Leica; i.e. it should read the right way when looking through the viewfinder in the normal way. This ensures that the pages are recorded in the right order (p. 417).

With documents of assorted sizes it is often better to leave the focus setting undisturbed. Set it for the largest original to be copied, and photograph small ones in pairs. This eliminates recalculation of exposure factors, and speeds up the work. Even if the original does not fill the whole negative every time, it should reproduce perfectly satisfactorily.

Filing and Reading Microfilms

Keep microfilms in complete uncut rolls in labelled tins; do not cut them up into strips.

To refer to any exposure the film may be put through a microfilm reader or a transparency viewer, or a miniature projector. Although the image is a negative one, that should not interfere with reading. If there are a lot of photographs, it may be better to prepare a positive film strip.

Individual negatives can be enlarged as required.

As the complete roll receives quite a lot of handling, treat the film with a suitable scratch-proofing solution or a film varnish for greater protection.

TELEPHOTOGRAPHY

The Telyt lenses in focal lengths from 200 mm. upwards provide large-scale views of very distant subjects.
As both viewing and focusing have to be accurate, the tele lenses are used invariably with a reflex viewing system.
Telephotographs require a firm support for adequate camera steadiness.

While medium long-focus lenses up to 135 mm. are still useful for average subjects and normal camera technique—including focusing and viewing through the combined view and rangefinder—the applications of the tele lenses for the Leica are more special. In terms of image scale and angle of view, the Telyt lenses of focal lengths from 200 to 560 mm. follow directly the medium long-focus lenses. The high image magnification of the Telyt lenses however makes them particularly suitable for distant and very distant subjects, covering on the one hand details of otherwise inaccessible objects and on the other long-range action, such as sports, wild life photography and special telephoto perspective effects.

With this shift in applications of the longest lenses comes also a notable change in technique which justifies a special approach to telephotography. These differences can be considered under three headings:

(*a*) focusing and viewing;
(*b*) exposure;
(*c*) image contrast and quality.

Tele Focusing and Viewing

Very long focal lengths mean reduced depth of field (p. 206) and narrow angles of view. This calls for much more accurate focusing—even at greater distances—than with the normal and medium long focus lenses. The narrow angle of view also means that you must aim the camera much more precisely to get exactly what you want in the picture.

For both these purposes the view- and rangefinder of the Leica M models ceases to be sufficiently accurate when using lenses of 200 mm. focal length or more. The Telyt lenses are therefore intended exclusively for viewing and focusing with the aid of the Visoflex reflex housings (or of course the Leicaflex). On the Visoflex screen the image is magnified in proportion to the power of the tele lens; hence both image sharpness and the subject field are always accurately visible. With tele subjects on the other hand the rangefinder advantage of more instant readiness for action is less important.

All the current versions of the Telyt lenses have a diaphragm presetting ring to permit focusing at full aperture before stopping down (p. 131).

Exposure and Image Quality

The narrow angle of view of the tele lenses also means that steady aiming of the camera becomes more difficult unless it is reasonably firmly supported. For the longest focal lengths (400 and 560 mm.) tripod mounting is almost indispensable; with the 200 and 280 mm. lenses hand-held shooting is still possible under favourable circumstances. There are usually several tripod bushes to choose from (see also p. 134); with the 560 mm. Telyt and the Televit unit (p. 425) it may be useful to employ two tripods to give greater steadiness.

Camera steadiness is equally important because the risk of camera shake increases in proportion with the magnification of the tele lens. Hand-held shots with the 200 mm. lens already need 1/250 second or faster speeds. The magnification of the image equally affects the shutter speed required to stop movement (p. 339).

The image quality of telephoto shots is determined not only by the optical quality of the lens but also by the contrast reducing effect of atmospheric haze. The extent to which this intrudes depends on weather conditions but image detail in long-range views tends to be considerably flatter because of the light scattering haze. For this reason tele views—especially of landscapes and extreme range subjects—are best taken through a filter: orange with black-and-white or a light to medium haze filter with colour film. (In the latter case the haze filter also counteracts the blue cast usually seen in distant views.) For extreme haze penetration a red filter or even an infra-red filter and infra-red film (pp. 195, 453) may be necessary.

Ways of Using Telyt Lenses

With the Visoflex housings. The 200, 280 and older 400 mm. Telyt lenses have a screw thread to fit directly to the front of the Visoflex I and also fit the Visoflex II and III with the aid of the No. 16466 adapter tube (p. 130). This is suitable for all static subjects (with the assembly mounted on a tripod) or even some action subjects. For hand-held shooting use the camera holds described on pp. 40 and 134.

Without the Visoflex. For hand-held action shooting with the 200, 280 and 400 mm. *f*5 (the latter the obsolete type) Telyt lenses it is also possible to mount the lens directly on the camera without the reflex housing. For this purpose an extension tube No. 14024 is needed. This has the same length as the Visoflex I, or the Visoflex III (or II) plus the No. 16466 adapter. This tube also carries a special accessory shoe to take one of the Telyt frame finders (p. 122).

There are two versions of this extension tube: the 63.5 mm. tube No. 14024 for Leica M cameras and the tube No. 14023 (which is 62.5 mm. long) for screw-lens Leica models. Both these tubes have a $\frac{1}{4}$ inch tripod bush. There also used to be two further versions with a $\frac{3}{8}$ inch bush (No. 14043 N for Leica M models and No. 14039 J for screw-lens Leicas). There is no frame finder for the 280 mm. tele lens.

In replacing the Visoflex housing this extension tube makes the Leica and Telyt assembly somewhat lighter. But aiming the camera with the frame finder is much less accurate than with the Visoflex III (or II) and on the balance it is worth using the reflex housing, even if it weighs slightly more. With the replacement tube and the frame finder distances also have to be set by estimation.

With the Televit. This is a rapid focusing mount with hand grip and gun stock shoulder support. It takes the lens unit of the 280 mm. or the 400 mm. *f*5 Telyt lenses as well as the 400 mm. Telyt *f*5.6 and 560 mm. *f*5.6 lenses. The latter two can only be used with the Televit system. The Telyt is always used in connection with the Visoflex III or II reflex housing.

With the Leicaflex. If the 200 to 400 mm. (the *f*5 version of the later) Telyt lenses are used with the Leicaflex/Leica adapter No. 14127 and the adapter No. 16466, the image can be focused on the screen of the Leicaflex in the usual way (pp. 178–179). The Leicaflex and the adapter No. 14127 can also be used with the Televit mount, though with certain reservations (p. 432).

The Televit

This combined holding and focusing arrangement for the Telyt lenses consists of three parts: the rapid focusing mount,

No. 14136 and iris tube No. 14137 (used only for the 400 and 560 mm. Telyt *f*5.6 lenses) and the shoulder stock.

The rapid focusing mount consists of a hand grip carrying a tube, with a second tube sliding inside it. A fine-focusing knob, operated by the left thumb, moves the second tube in and out while the mount is held in the left hand. A button on the front of the grip releases the whole movement for rapid adjustment.

The focusing extension provided by this arrangement is 60 mm. (2⅜ inches). With the 280 mm. Telyt this permits focusing down to 6½ feet or 2 metres (giving a maximum scale of reproduction of 1 : 4.8), as compared with the near focusing limit of 19 feet with this lens in its normal focusing mount, used directly on the Visoflex housing.

With the 400 mm. Telyt lenses the near focusing limit is 13 feet (4 metres) and the maximum scale 1 : 6.8. This compares again with 25 feet (8 metres) of the 400 mm. Telyt *f*5 in its normal mount. The near limit with the 560 mm. lens is 25 feet (8 metres) and the maximum scale 1 : 9.5.

The iris tube fits into the front of the rapid focusing mount and carries an iris diaphragm and a presetting ring. This tube is used with the 400 and 560 mm. Telyt *f*5.6. lenses (which screw into the front) and stops down the lenses from *f*5.6 to *f*32. The presetting ring engages at each aperture number and also at half stop settings (except between *f*22 and *f*32).

The shoulder stock is a bent metal rod which slides within a tube for length adjustment and fits into a socket in the rear of the rapid focusing mount. When assembled, it helps to support the mount with the camera, Visoflex and lens against the shoulder.

Assembling the Televit

Attach the Visoflex II or III to the Leica, and fit the 4× eye-level magnifier. (The 5× vertical magnifier is less practical, since the Televit assembly is normally used at eye level.) Fit the camera and Visoflex to the bayonet mount at the rear of the Televit focusing mount. The assembly can swivel from horizontal to vertical shots on simply pressing the lever on the top of the focusing mount, just above the bayonet ring. The lever locks the Visoflex in three positions: for horizontal shots and for vertical shots towards either side of the horizontal position (select whichever is more convenient).

To fit the 280 mm. or the 400 mm. *f*5 Telyt lenses unscrew

TELEVIT MOUNT

The components of the Televit rapid focusing mount when assembled are:

1. Telyt lens.
2. Aperture setting ring of iris tube 4.
3. Aperture pre-setting ring.
4. Iris diaphragm tube or the 400 and 506 mm. Telyt *f*5.6 lenses.
5. Bayonet locking ring o secure the iris tube to he focusing mount 6.
7. Horizontal / vertical orientation lock.
8. Leica and Visoflex III or II) assembly. (Alternatively the Leicaflex with the he adapter ring No. 14127 can be used).
9. Near distance focusing stop.
10. Far distance focusing stop.
11. Release button for rapid focusing.
12. Hand grip.
13. Fine focusing knob.

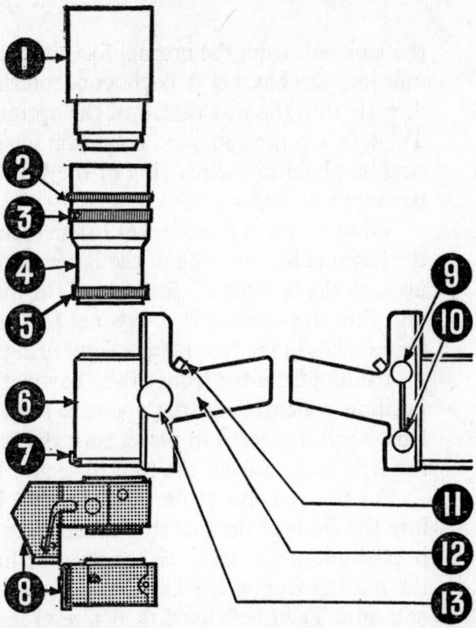

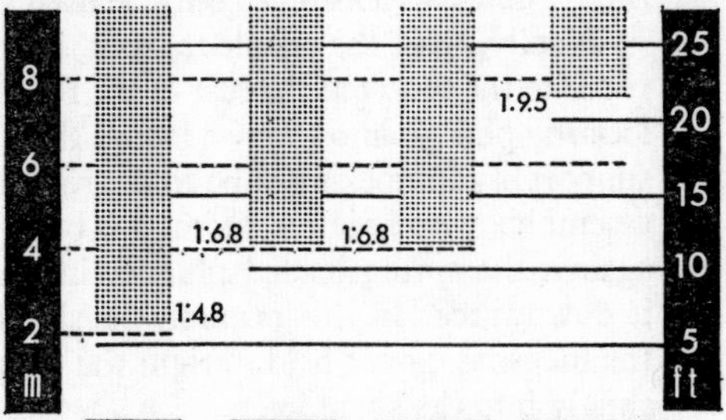

The Televit mount can be used with any of the Telyt lenses from 280 to 560 mm. The lens unit only of the 280 mm. Telyt and of the 400 mm. *f*5 (discontinued) lens fit directly into the front of the focusing mount with the aid of a bayonet ring No. 14138. The 400 mm. *f*5.6 and 560 mm. *f*5.6. Telyt lenses fit into the front of the iris tube which is then attached to the focusing mount. The shaded bars show the near focusing ranges and maximum image scales with the different arrangements.

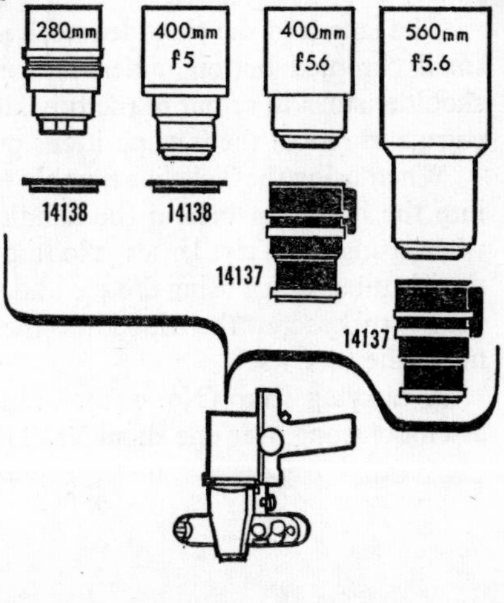

the lens unit from the normal focusing mount. Then screw the unit into the No. 14138 bayonet adapter ring. This ring screws directly into the rear thread of the optical unit of the 400 mm. Telyt *f*5. On the 280 mm. Telyt first unscrew the milled facing ring just behind the iris ring of the lens and fit the No. 14138 bayonet ring in its place.

To fit either of these lenses to the focusing mount, first turn the bayonet locking ring of the latter so that its red dot is lined up with the red dot on the body of the mount. Now fit the lens unit into the front of this bayonet locking ring, so that one of the notches in the No. 14138 adapter ring fits over the small peg protruding from the front of the bayonet locking ring. Select a position which brings the aperture scale to the top. With the lens correctly seated in place, turn the bayonet locking ring to the left (as seen from the top) to secure the lens.

For the 400 and 560 mm. Telyt *f*5.6 lenses fit the iris tube into the front of the focusing mount in the same way—place it in position so that all three red dots are lined up, and then turn the locking ring to the left to secure the iris tube. The 400 or 560 mm. Telyt lens itself then screws into the front of the iris ring. These two lenses can only be used with this arrangement.

Finally, to fit the shoulder stock, insert the thin end of the rod into the socket at the rear of the focusing mount so that the locating pins go into the two lateral slots. The curved shoulder support of the stock must be to the right of the focusing mount assembly, when viewed from the back. Push the rod home against the spring loaded plunger inside the socket and turn it downwards. In this position the shoulder stock locks. With the focusing mount held upright the curved shoulder piece fits snugly into the shoulder.

The length of the shoulder stock is adjustable: pull out the small chromed button underneath and slide the rod of the shoulder stock in or out of the tube, letting the chrome button engage in one of the four positions provided.

When using the Televit assembly on tripod, screw the latter into the bush just behind the handle of the focusing mount, when using the Telyt lenses (280 mm. and 44 mm. *f*5) without the iris tube. When using the 400 and 560 mm. *f*5.6 Telyts with the iris tube, screw the tripod into the appropriate bush underneath the tube itself.

A carrying strap (No. 14130) can hold the whole Televit assembly slung over one shoulder. The strap carries two metal

USING THE TELEVIT

With the 280 mm. lens unscrew the optical unit, remove the facing ring from the larger thread behind the aperture rings, and replace it by the No. 14138 bayonet ring.

The 400 or 560 mm. Telyt *f*5.6 lenses go directly into the iris tube.

To attach the iris tube to the focusing mount, line up the red dots on the tube, the mount, and the bayonet locking ring (*left*). Then turn the locking ring (*right*).

To attach the shoulder stock press the mounting piece into the key hole of the back of the Televit mount (*left*). To adjust the length of the shoulder support, extend the rod in its tube (*right*).

To open the filter slot press the ribbed section on the inner tube (*left*); then fit a series VII filter into the holder (*right*).

Hold the Televit mount in the left hand (*left*) so that the right hand is free to operate the camera release. For focusing the left thumb bears on the focusing knob (*right*) while the index finger presses the quick release when necessary.

To preset focusing stops move one or both locking nuts along the slot (*left*) after focusing the lens to the required distance (see p.431). To swing the camera for vertical shots, press the catch on top of the focusing mount (*right*).

With the heavier lenses mount the assembly on a tripod by the bush underneath the iris tube (*left*).

To preset the aperture on the iris tube depress the chrome button on the rear and move it to the required stop. To stop down before shooting turn the front ring to the left as far as it will go (*right*).

When shooting, support the lens.

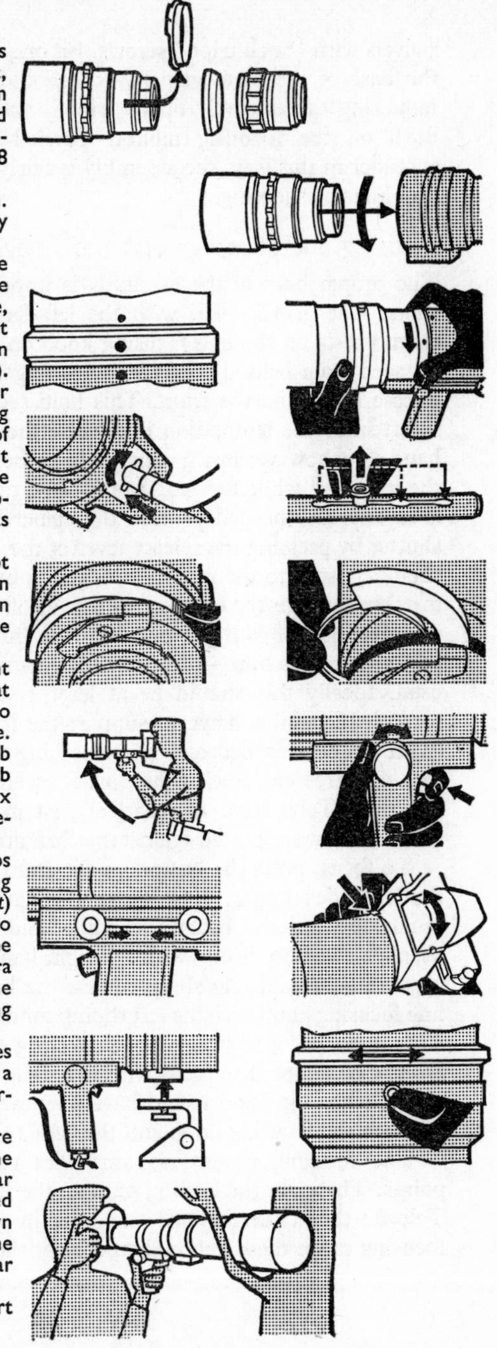

swivels with $\frac{1}{4}$ inch tripod screws. Fit one of these swivels into the base of the hand grip (which should never be used for mounting the assembly on its tripod) and the other into the bush on the focusing mount. Carried hanging from one shoulder in this way, the assembly is fairly easy to raise to the shoulder for shooting.

Focusing and Shooting with the Televit

The proper hold of the assembly is important for hand-held shots. The grip is held with the left hand, so that the left thumb rests on the fine focusing knob on the right-hand side (as seen from behind) and the index finger is on the focusing release button on the front. This hold seems unusual at first sight, since the temptation is to seize the grip with the right hand. It is however much easier to hold the Televit steady with the left hand while focusing at the same time. The right hand is in any case needed to hold the camera and to release the shutter by pressing the release lever of the Visoflex. Adjust the shoulder stock to the required length to be able to view comfortably through the eyepiece of the Visoflex.

Hand-held shooting is possible with this arrangement with lenses up to 400 mm.—provided a fast enough shutter speed is used. Ideally this should be at least 1/500 or even 1/1,000 second. If possible however support the front end of the lens (with the hood pulled out) on something solid—a railing, the fork of a tree etc. Such a support is essential with the heavy 560 mm. Telyt lens. Alternatively, sit in an armchair, with the left elbow supported against the chair arm.

To focus, press the button on the front of the handle with the left index finger. Now move the handle and the whole mount forward and backwards while holding the camera and Visoflex assembly firmly with the right hand. When the image appears approximately sharp release the button and turn the fine focusing knob with the left thumb for maximum sharpness. This knob has a ribbed rubber covering for easier gripping. Do not be tempted to focus with the right hand; this is much slower since the hand would have to move back and forward between the focusing knob and the camera release.

The focusing mount also provides two preset focusing points. These are the locking nuts on the left hand side of the Televit; they slide forward and back in a slot. For the full focusing range these knobs should be at the very ends of their slot. To select a specific far focusing distance, focus the lens accurately on the subject at the distance. Then move the front locking knob backwards in its slot until it is against the front screw head visible in the slot. Tighten the locking knob in this position.

For a near focusing limit again adjust the lens accurately to the selected distance and move the rear locking knob (after slacking it off) forward in its groove up against the rear screw head inside the groove. On pressing the focusing button on the handle you can now rapidly move the mount forward and back between the two selected positions. This is handy when shooting long-range sports, for refocusing rapidly between two fixed points.

These preset focusing limits of course need re-establishing every time for different subjects and for different lenses. With some of the Telyt lenses on the Televit the far focusing limit of the mount itself may in fact go beyond the infinity position. In that case the rear preset stop can be used to arrest the focusing movement at the infinity setting.

The setting ring of the preset aperture system on the 280 mm. Telyt (p. 131) is within easy reach of the left hand index finger when this lens is mounted on the Televit. So after preselecting the aperture to be used with the presetting ring (with the red dot) and after focusing, stretch out the left hand index finger and move the setting ring (with the white dot) upwards until it comes to the mechanical stop of the preselecting ring. With the 400 or 560 mm. *f*5.6 lens, use the right hand to stop down the iris ring—this is the front milled ring on the iris tube and is turned anticlockwise (as seen from behind). To preselect the aperture to be used press the chrome button (with the red dot) on the presetting ring—the rear milled ring on the iris tube—and move the ring to bring the red button opposite the aperture required. Then move the front ring—with the white dot—fully clockwise to open the iris for focusing and viewing.

The inner tube of the focusing mount also has a filter slot. This is visible above the tube, just in front of the bayonet ring by which the tube is attached to the Visoflex, when the tube is slightly extended. To open the slot press in the small ribbed section at the right of the cut-out and raise up the filter holder. This takes series VII filters which are pushed in until the spring grips them. Then swing the holder back into the tube again. This is the only way of using filters with the 400 and 560 mm. Telyt $f5.6$ lenses and it is the more convenient way also with the 280 mm. and the 400 mm. $f5$ lenses (which require very large screw-in filters for the front of the lens). When using a filter, always focus with the filter in position.

To dismantle the Televit unit unscrew and unlock the various lens units and bayonet rings. To remove the shoulder stock from the mount, press the mount with its front end—and preferably with the iris tube still in place—against your body. Pull the curved shoulder piece of the support towards you and twist to disengage it from the socket. Set the shoulder stock to its shortest extension first. This is a good way to hold the Televit assembly when inserting the shoulder stock in its socket.

The Televit with the Leicaflex

The Leicaflex camera with the No. 14127 Leicaflex/Leica adapter can also fit on the back of the Televit mount in place of the Visoflex and Leica M. For this combination the Leicaflex SL is preferable because it shows more even illumination of the finder screen. With the earlier Leicaflex the view appears dark in the corners of the screen, especially with the longest focal lengths. With this earlier Leicaflex model this is due to the finder optics; the image on the film is evenly illuminated. Also, the finder screen appears grossly blurred except when the lens is accurately focused; the image sharpness is however easy to observe and adjust on the central microprism area.

The Televit assembly partly obscures the view of the standard Leicaflex meter cell. So take exposure readings with a normal lens on the Leicaflex camera, before fitting and using the Telyt lenses and the Televit. This problem does not arise of course with the Leicaflex SL.

Telephoto Subjects

For long-range action subjects the Televit with the 280 or 400 mm. Telyt lenses is the best combination. With the 280 mm. lens especially, the Televit mount with its shoulder stock is handy enough to be held steady for shooting from the hand and for following moving subjects. With the preset focusing stops (p. 431) it becomes particularly easy to switch rapidly from one distance to another. The same facility is also available with the Focorapid mount and the 200 or 280 mm. Telyt lenses

p. 136). When shooting action subjects remember also to allow sufficiently fast shutter speeds (p. 339).

For long range action it is generally best to aim at capturing movement across the line of sight rather than approaching or receding. This is in direct contrast to the normal recommendations for action shots (p. 232) and arises from the fact that telephoto views tend to compress the prespective, so the separation between, for instance, sprinters nearing the finishing tape appears to be largely lost—they all seem the same distance away. A side view, even though it requires a faster shutter speed, shows their different placings more clearly.

The 200 and 280 mm. Telyt lenses can also be used for action shots without the Televit, by simply mounting the lenses on the front of the Visoflex housing—with the No. 16466 adapter ring when the Visoflex II or III is used. Brace the camera and lens assembly against the body with the table tripod and ball-and-socket head (p. 40).

The same perspective forshortening also arises in static views. It tends to make such views flat and devoid of depth. On the other hand this foreshortening can also yield interesting effects when you look for it deliberately: for example the crowding together of cars in a long shot looking down on a busy road.

Very distant backgrounds are made to appear much larger compared with foreground objects—simply because the latter also have to be quite distant away to appear as foreground in the tele view. Particularly dramatic examples are sunset or moonrise shots which show the sun or moon only just above the skyline and gigantic in size compared with trees or other objects on the horizon. This horizon is then the foreground of the view.

Static long-range tele views are best taken on a clear day after rain. Avoid shooting in the middle of a hot day, since the moving currents of warm and cooler air introduce unsharpness. There is no way of avoiding this; a fast shutter speed may cut out the unsharpness due to the air movement, but not the loss of image quality due to the optically inhomogeneous atmosphere.

Any lack of optical homogeneity in the object space affects telephoto views much more than pictures taken with shorter focal lengths. Hence filters must be of the best possible optical quality. For the same reason, do not shoot through window panes with a long focus lens. The resulting pictures invariably lack definition. Always open the window (where this is possible—or forget about the picture where it is not) before taking tele views through it.

Near-range Telephotography

The Telyt lenses are also useful for close ups of small scenes from medium distances (see p. 306). Here the comparatively close near focusing limits obtainable with the Televit mount are useful (p. 426).

However when the 200 to 400 mm. Telyt lenses are used without the Televit mount, reduced near distances are also possible with extension tubes. The nearest focusing distance of the 200 mm. Telyt is 10 feet (3 metres) but for nearer distances 15 mm. extension tubes (N. 14020) are available. With one tube the 200 mm. Telyt will focus from 10 feet to 5½ feet, and with two tubes from 5½ feet down to 4 feet to yield a maximum image scale of 1 : 5.

With the 280 mm. Telyt one 15 mm. tube covers a focusing range from 19 to 9 feet, and two rings from 10½ to 7 feet to give a scale of about 1 : 6.5. (This is almost as good as the near limit with the Televit mount.)

With the 400 mm. Telyt one 15 mm. tube shortens the nearest focusing distance to 16 feet, two tubes to 11½ feet.

Since the depth of field (p. 206) is also extremely limited, an aperture of at least *f*8 to *f*11 will be necessary at these distances. This applies equally when using the Telyt lenses near their closest limits on the Televit mount.

PHOTOMICROGRAPHY

In photomicrography, the micro-attachment and microscope replace the optical system of the Leica. The image is focused by the microscope.
The standard system yields $\frac{1}{3}$ of the magnification of the microscope: $\frac{1}{2}$ or full magnification systems can be used in special cases.

One of the applications of the Leica in science is recording photographically the views seen through a microscope. The uses of photomicrography are manifold, from research in natural history to medical and forensic investigations. The Leica micro-equipment described in this introduction to the field is applicable to a whole range of general and specialized microscopes and techniques.

Among the advantages of the 24 × 36 mm. picture against the larger negative sizes generally employed for this type of work, is the economy of negative material. Thus the Leica is specially suitable for extensive picture series and for colour shots on many materials which are available only in the miniature size.

There are various ways of taking photomicrographs. In all of them the microscope and the optical system of a micro-attachment take the place of the Leica lens. The image is focused by means of the microscope, and observed through a focusing telescope or on the screen of the reflex housing or focusing stage.

The Mikas Micro-Attachment

The micro-attachment consists of a housing which carries a swing-out prism, a right-angle focusing telescope, and a diaphragm shutter with speeds from 1 to 1/125 second, B and T. A connecting tube with an optical 1/3 reducing system screws into the top of the housing and in turn carries the Leica. Below the housing a special ring is screwed in to take the microscope eyepiece. A Periplan 10 × eyepiece is mostly supplied with the attachment, though other eyepices may be used for special purposes.

The magnification on the negative is one-third of the microscope magnification. A three-diameter enlargement of the negative will therefore show the full nominal magnification.

This is the generally most useful arrangement. For special cases, alternative connecting tubes are available to take the place of the tube with the 1/3 reducing system. Those alternatives yield reductions of 1/2 and full size, thus requiring only a two-diameter enlargement or a contact print respectively, to show the full nominal magnification of the microscope in the picture. The purpose of this arrangement is that it allows us to vary the field of view. The 1/3 system yields the largest subject field with the smallest magnification, while the 1/1 system covers the smallest field at normal microscope magnification on the negative.

The resulting magnification on the print is the product of the magnifications

M (objective) × ×M (eyepiece) × M (enlarger) × 1/3 (or 1/2 or 1).

As the focusing telescope is used to view the subject, it incorporates three engraved hairline frames. The outer frame then shows the field of view with the 1/3 system, the middle frame the field with the 1/2 system, and the smallest frame the subject area with the 1/1 system. The connecting tube of each system carries the reduction figure (1/3 ×, 1/2 × or 1 ×) engraved on it.

To assemble the set-up, screw the appropriate connecting tube into the thread of the diaphragm shutter and tighten the locking ring. Screw the wide end of the tube into the Leica in place of the lens. Unscrew the ring below the housing, insert the microscope eyepiece and screw the ring together with the eyepiece back on to the attachment. (Usually the micro-attachment is supplied complete with eyepiece.)

Finally, insert the whole assembly with the microscope eyepiece vertically into the tube of the microscope.

The normal position for the focusing telescope is in the same sagittal axis in which the stage of the microscope is fixed. To turn the telescope round, slacken the locking ring above the shutter, and swing the focusing telescope into the required position.

The micro-attachment has two cable release sockets. The one mounted at the rear of the body takes the cable for moving the right-angle prism. The other socket on the shutter takes a cable to operate the diaphragm shutter.

Exposing with the Micro-Attachment

Adjust the focusing telescope by turning its milled eyepiece mount until the hairline frames are sharp. Then insert the object slide in the microscope and readjust the illumination as required.

Focus the image visually through the focusing telescope by means of the focusing mechanism of the microscope. Check the field of view at the same time, using the hairline frame corresponding to the reducing system employed.

Set the Leica shutter to B, and open it by means of a cable release with fixing screw (p. 44). Then swing the right-angle prism out of the optical path with a second cable release and lock this also by its fixing screw. Finally make the exposure by opening the diaphragm shutter by a third cable release.

The prism has to be swung out of the way if we want to utilize the full light for the exposure. The normal prism of the MIKAS diverts about 25 per cent of the light. If observation of the field is necessary during the exposure (living and moving objects) special prisms can be built in which divert as little as 5 per cent.

After the exposure, release the prism, and close the Leica camera shutter. Then advance the film for the next shot in the normal way.

The cable releases of the diaphragm shutter and of the viewing prism can be operated together by means of a release coupler

MICRO-ATTACHMENT

The Milas micro-attachment (optical system with microscope in *black panel*) consists of:

1. Body.
2. Connecting tube.
3. Leica thread.
4. Diaphragm shutter.
5. Cable release for shutter.
6. Focusing telescope.
7. Release coupler.
8. Microscope eyepiece.
9. Eyepiece retaining ring.

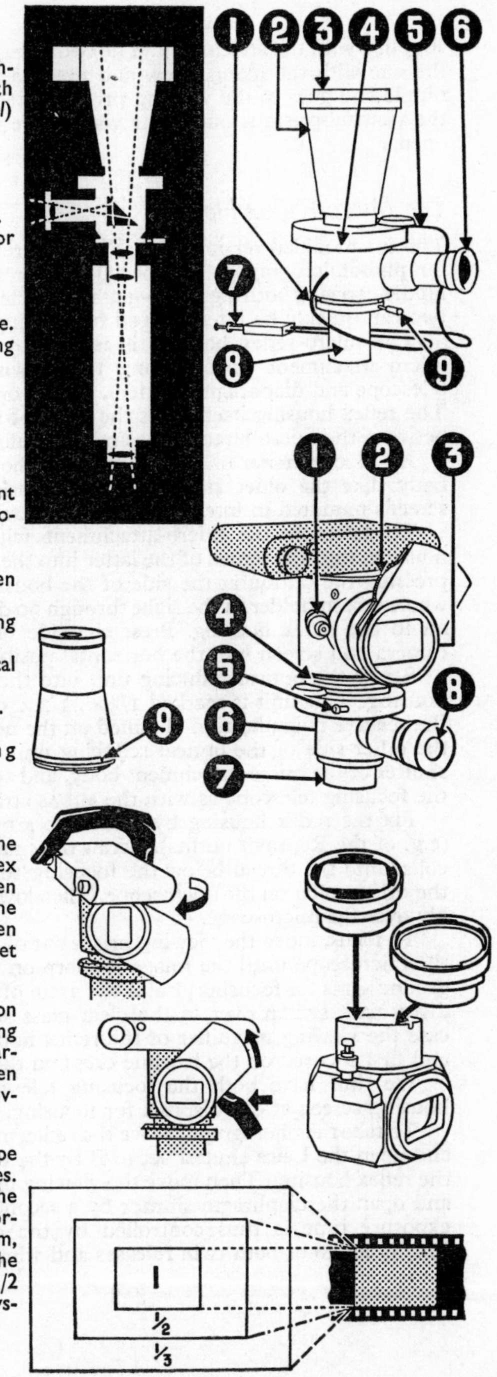

The Mikas attachment can be used with the micro-reflex housing (p. 436):

1. Mirror release.
2. Revolving screen changer.
3. Catch for rotating reflex housing.
4. Intermediate optical system.
5. Diaphragm shutter.
6. Body.
7. Light-excluding collar.
8. Focusing telescope.
9. Screen magnifier.

Left: To mount the Leica on the micro-reflex housing, set the screen vertical and screw in the camera body (p. 438). Then rotate the housing to set the screen horizontal.

Right: An earlier version of the micro-reflex housing used interchangeable clear- and ground-glass screen units in place of the revolving screen changer.

The focusing telescope shows three frame lines. The outer one indicates the field of view with the normal 1/3 reduction system, the other frames give the subject field with the 1/2 and full-magnification systems.

supplied with the attachment. The two releases are not the same, the one with the fixing screw and the wider milled ring at the nipple end goes to the viewing prism socket. That ensures that the viewing prism is out of the way before the diagram shutter opens.

The Micro-Reflex Housing

This is a modified version of the Visoflex I reflex housing (p. 140) for photomicrography. Its special feature is a rotating screen holder carrying both a ground-glass and a clear-glass screen. The two can quickly be interchanged by rotating the holder.

The micro-reflex housing is used in conjunction with the micro-attachment (incoporating the viewing prism, focusing telescope and diaphragm shutter), and an optical reducing unit. The reflex housing itself takes the place of the connecting tube between the micro-attachment and the Leica.

An older version of the micro-reflex housing had a square body (like the older standard reflex housing) and alternative screens mounted in interchangeable holders.

To assemble the micro-attachment with the micro-reflex housing, turn the screen of the latter into the upright position by pressing the button at the side of the housing and moving the whole screen holder to the right through 90 deg. Screw the Leica on to the reflex housing. Press the side button and turn the camera and screen into the horizontal position again.

Screw the optical reducing unit into the front of the reflex housing. This unit is marked 1/3×, 1/2× or 1×, according to the relative magnification obtained on the negative. Then screw the other side of the optical reducing unit into the diaphragm shutter of the micro-attachment body, and adjust the position of the focusing telescope as with the MIKAS attachment.

Fix the reflex housing by a suitable arm to a rigid column (e.g. of the Reprovit outfits). Screw the smaller light-excluding collar into the thread below the focusing telescope and mount the other collar on the microscope. Then lower the whole assembly over the microscope.

To focus, move the viewing prism out of the way, and adjust the microscope until the image is sharp on the screen. Use the ground glass for focusing; but if the grain of the screen becomes disturbing, switch over to the clear-glass screen. In the latter case the viewing magnifier of the reflex housing must be used, and first focused on the hairline cross on the screen.

We thus have both the focusing telescope and the reflex housing screen at our disposal for focusing.

To take the photograph, move the reflex mirror out of the way and open the Leica shutter set to B by the twin cable release of the reflex housing. Then move the viewing prism out of the path and open the diaphragm shutter by a second twin release. The exposure time is thus controlled by the diaphragm shutter. Finally let go of both twin releases and wind the film on.

KAVAR-MICRO ATTACHMENT

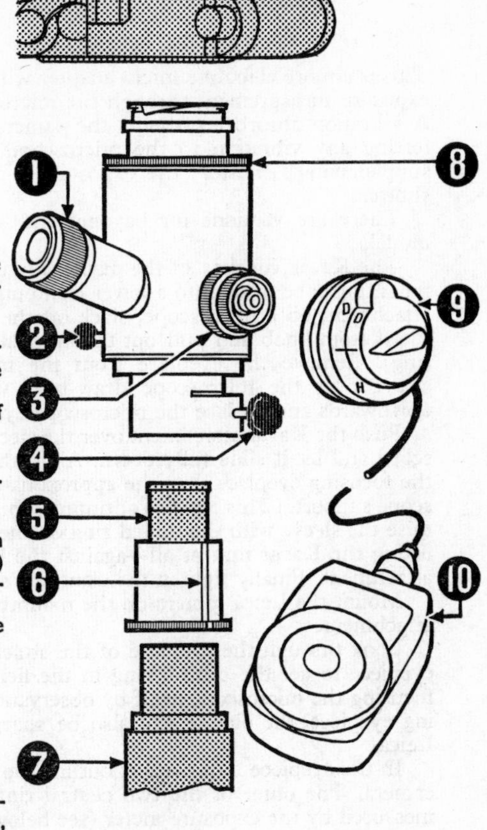

The components of the Kavar attachment and set-up on the microscope are:

1. Focusing telescope.
2. Prism control lever to divert the light into the photo cell.
3. Optical system of measuring light beam.
4. Clamping knob.
5. Microscope eyepiece.
6. Clamping sleeve.
7. Microscope.
8. Mounting plate (with bayonet fitting for camera) in vibration damped support.
9. Cadmium sulphide cell probe.
10. Exposure meter.

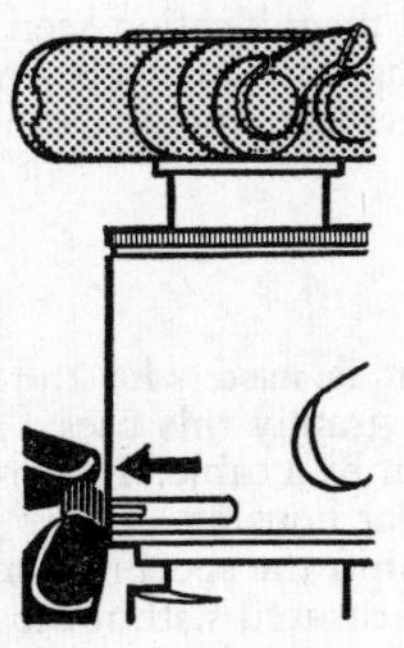

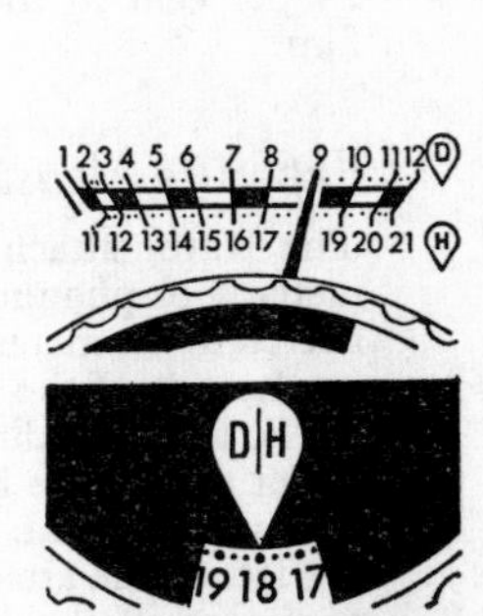

For mounting the attachment on the microscope, first remove the eyepiece, fit the clamping sleeve over the draw tube and replace the eyepiece. The Kavar attachment then fits over the sleeve and is clamped tight. The upper end directly takes the Leica M camera, while the exposure meter cell clips on to the exit of the measuring optical system.

Left: For taking exposure meter readings push the lever in the side of the tube backwards; this diverts the light into the meter cell.

Right: Read off the position of the meter needle, set the D/H index to the same number and read off the exposure time opposite a previously established calibration *f*-number (see p. 440).

The Kavar Micro Attachment

This is a more elaborate micro adapter with provision for direct exposure measurement through the microscope optical system. A vibration absorber prevents the camera shutter from transferring any vibration to the microscope set-up. There is no supplementary shutter; the exposure is made with the Leica shutter.

There are versions for bayonet and screw-mounted Leica models.

The Kavar consists of the main body unit, with an eyepiece mounting tube fitted into a lower clamping ring. To mount the attachment on a microscope, slack off the clamping screw with the bottom knob and pull out the inner sleeve (with the milled ring). Remove the eyepiece from the microscope, push the sleeve over the microscope draw-tube with the milled ring downwards and replace the microscope eyepiece.

Push the Kavar attachment over the sleeve now on the microscope and let it slide fully down. Align the attachment so that the focusing eyepiece is in the approximate plane of the microscope support. (This ensures optimum vibration damping.) Now raise the sleeve with the milled ring on the draw-tube—without lifting the Kavar unit at all—against the bottom of the micro-attachment. Finally tighten the clamping screw.

Mount the Leica camera on the mounting ring on top of the attachment.

Look through the eyepiece of the attachment and focus the eyepiece to get the central ring in the field of view sharp. On focusing the microscope itself by observation through the viewing eyepiece, the picture will also be sharp on the film in the Leica.

In the eyepiece four corners outline the view taken in by the camera. The outer of the two central rings indicates the field measured by the exposure meter (see below).

As with the MIKAS attachment, the image is photographed at about 1/3 of the visual magnification seen through the eyepiece. The latter receives its light through a beam splitter which diverts 25 per cent to the eyepiece and the other 75 per cent to the film.

Exposure Measurement

The Kavar attachment is used with the Microsix L exposure meter. For photomicrography this uses a measuring probe connected to the meter unit by a cable. The probe fits on to an outlet on the side of the Kavar housing.

To take a reading, shift the specimen on the microscope stage to get the area to be measured within the outer central circle in the eyepiece field. Then push back the lever (with the knob) at the left of the attachment. This rotates the beam splitter inside to divert all the light coming through the microscope to the measuring probe of the meter—the image disappears in the eyepiece.

Now read off the light value (pointer position) on the scale of the exposure meter.

After setting this value on the meter calculator disc, the correct exposure time is read off against an *f*-stop value established beforehand as a calibration number or exposure reference index.

This requires a calibration test of an exposure series of a given subject on the film to be used. After the film is processed select the best exposure and note the exposure time used. Locate this time on the exposure scale of the Microsix L and note the aperture figure opposite it with the meter set to the light-value measurement of the subject. This aperture becomes the calibration value.

After taking a meter reading allow the control lever of the beam splitter to return gently into the forward position. Now the light from the microscope is again split between the viewing eyepiece and the camera.

Other exposure meters can also be used on the Kavar attachment, but usually the lens system inside the measuring opening has to be removed by unscrewing the outer milled ring. The cell may also need masking off. The meter now takes in the light from the whole of the field of view and not just from the marked circle. Calibration test are naturally required.

The Single Exposure Housing

In photomicrography especially we may at times want to make single exposures, e.g. for individual test exposures on special films, where it would be inconvenient and wasteful to load the Leica with a whole length of film for the sake of one shot.

For this purpose a Leica single-exposure housing used to be available at one time—it has been discontinued for a long time. It consists of a light-alloy housing with the standard Leica lens mount on the front, and a ground-glass screen at the back. The screen is interchangeable for a film holder to take single exposure lengths of film.

The housing also carries tripod bushes, and an accessory shoe for viewfinders. It has no shutter. A diaphragm shutter is used which fits on to the front of the lens, and has shutter speeds from 1 to 1/25 second as well as a time setting. This is in fact Leica photography without a Leica camera.

To load the film holder, remove the lid, and in the darkroom insert a piece of 35-mm. film about 1⅝ inches (4 cm.) long. Press the lid firmly into the holder; it is then ready for use.

Set up the single exposure housing with a lens (and extension tubes or other accessories) screwed into the mount, and fix the shutter in front. Open the shutter for a time exposure, and focus the image on the ground-glass screen at the back. Close the shutter, remove the ground-glass screen and fit the film holder in its place. Pull out the slide, and make the exposure.

Neither the lens nor the shutter are of course needed when using the single exposure housing with the micro-adapter.

The Single Film Holder

We can also make single exposures on short pieces of film in the Leica by using the single film holder—also now discontinued. This is a thin metal frame to take a 3¼-inch length of film, and fits in position in the back of the Leica. It has to be loaded and unloaded from the camera in the darkroom.

When inserting the loaded holder into the camera, put it in together with a sheet of thin card to protect the film surface. Then slowly withdraw the card.

Two models were available, one to fit type f and type c Leicas, and one for the older Leica models I, II, III, IIIa, IIIb.

The single film holder cannot be used with the later Leica models which have a "finger" in the base plate to keep the film in position (p. 72). This finger would interfere with the holder; a special base plate is, however, available.

STEREO PHOTOGRAPHY

Stereo pictures require two shots from slightly different viewpoints, corresponding to the views of each eye. The Stemar unit automatically and simultaneously takes both pictures side by side on the 24 × 36 mm. Leica frame.
The depth effect is recreated when each eye sees its corresponding picture.

Leica photographs, like any picture on a flat surface, reduce the solid world around us to a two-dimensional plane. The Leica with its one lens does not see depth. At the best we can suggest it by various tricks like differential focusing and suitable lighting. But we are still looking at a flat image.

Visually we perceive depth and look "round" objects because each eye sees its own view. The two views differ mainly in the relative position of near and far objects. The brain fuses the separate impressions into a three-dimensional picture.

We can reproduce this photographically by taking two pictures from separate viewpoints corresponding to our two eyes. On presenting one picture to each eye, the brain will again fuse the two images.

In theory the two viewpoints should be the same distance apart as our eyes, i.e. about 2½ inches or 6.5 cm. In practice it is better to reduce this distance for very near subjects, and to increase it for very far ones if possible.

To view the stereo picture we can either use a stereo viewer, or for larger audiences, project the two images on a screen. The latter method requires special viewing spectacles to ensure that each eye sees only its own view.

Stereo photography is thus very suitable for transparency materials, and especially colour. The transparencies can also be printed from negative film. Suitable stereo viewing arrangements exist for paper enlargements.

At the camera end, the stereo images are produced in the Leica by a special pair of lenses taking the place of the single standard lens. An alternative method is to use a beam splitter in front of the normal lens. An even simpler way is to move the Leica sideways through the appropriate distance between two exposures of the same subject.

The Leica Stereo System

The key to Leica stereography is the Stemar twin lens unit. This consists of two 33 mm. (1¼ inch) *f*3.5 lenses mounted side by side in a unit which fits as a whole into the lens flange of the Leica cameras like any other interchangeable lens. The two individual lenses are carefully matched, and are coupled so that they focus together—over a range from infinity down to 3½ feet. The whole unit is also coupled to the Leica rangefinder; a lever at the side of the Stemar unit serves for focusing, similar to the focusing lever of the standard 50 mm. lenses.

In addition, the iris diaphragms of the two lenses are similarly coupled, and an aperture control stops down both lenses simultaneously. The smallest aperture is *f* 11.

The Stemar unit is available in two versions: with the standard screw mount to fit all Leica models from I to IIIg; and with a bayonet mount to fit the Leica M. The screw-mounted Stemar can, of course, be used on the Leica M with the aid of the bayonet/screw adapter.

The separation of the lenses of the Stemar unit is approximately ¾ inch; this is considerably smaller than the interocular distance, but is quite sufficient for close subjects between 3½ and 10 feet. In fact, under those conditions the normal 2½ inches separation is liable to produce exaggerated perspective effects.

For greater distances, a prism attachment is available which fits in front of the Stemar and increases the effective separation of the two viewpoints to 2⅞ inches (72 mm.).

The prism attachment also acts to some extent as a lens hood; a separate twin lens hood is available for the Stemar lenses when used by themselves. The lenses will also take a pair of special screw-in filters.

The great merit of this system is the fact that changing over from the normal to stereo photography takes no longer than changing the lenses. It is therefore possible to take stereo and ordinary pictures alternately at will on the same film.

A stereo pair consists of two images 18 × 24 mm. (usually masked down to 16 × 23 mm. for projection or viewing) side by side, and correctly aligned and level with each other. The pair thus takes up exactly the same space as a standard frame.

Fitting the Stemar Unit

To take stereo pictures, simply screw the Stemar into the Leica mount. The unit couples with the rangefinder like any Leica lens, and is focused by the focusing lever at the side.

When focusing, press in the serrated infinity lock inside the

STEMAR

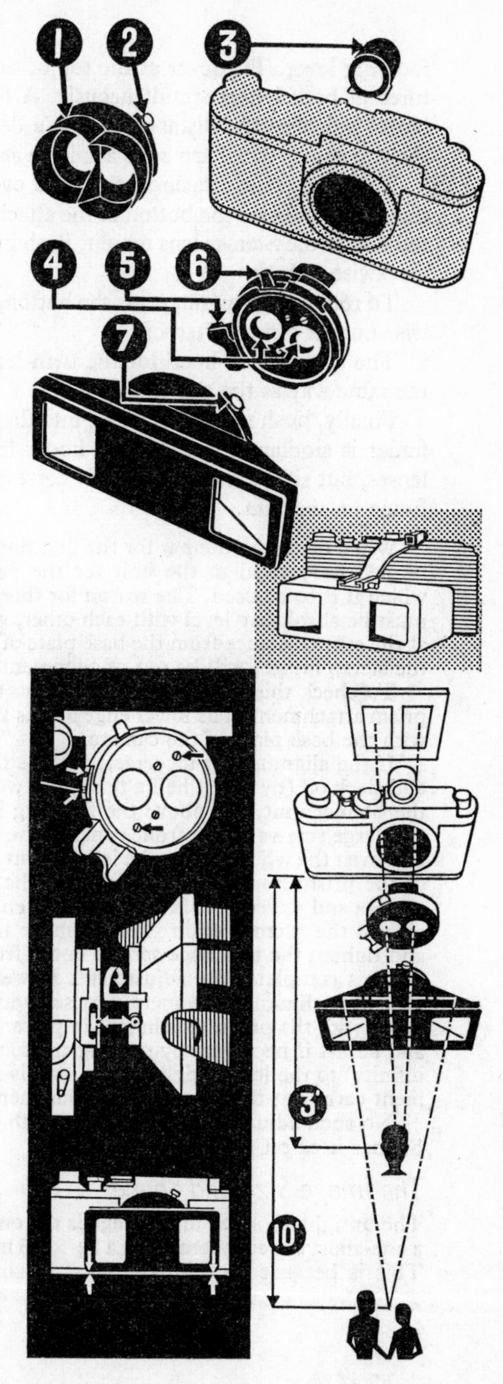

The parts of the Leica Stemar stereo unit are:

1. Twin lens hood.
2. Locking button.
3. Stero brilliant viewfinder.
4. Twin 33 mm. stereo lenses.
5. Focusing lever.
6. Coupled aperture lever.
7. Locking button on prism unit.

The old Stereoly attachment consisted of a beam-splitting system which fitted in front of the camera lens (p. 448).

Back panel: To align the Stemar twin-lens unit horizontally on the camera, screw it in place, and slack off the locking screws (*top*). Then fit the prism unit (*centre*) in the bayonet mount, and align the edge of the prism attachment accurately with the bottom edge of the Leica (*bottom*). Retighten the screws (p. 446).

Right-hand column: The Stemar unit by itself is intended for subjects between 3 and 10 feet, and over 10 feet with the prism unit. The convergence of the optical axes is arranged to place the frame or stereo window at 3 and 10 feet respectively.

focusing lever. The lever at the top of the unit sets the apertures of both lenses simultaneously. A focusing scale on the barrel indicates the distances, while a depth of field scale on the rim shows the sharp zone available at any distance.

To fit the prism attachment, place it over the Stemar unit so that the red dot on the button of the attachment is opposite the red dot on the Stemar lens mount. Push into position, and turn clockwise to lock.

To remove the prism, press the button, and turn anti-clockwise until it can be lifted off.

The special lens hood for the twin-lens unit is attached in the same way as the prism unit.

Finally, push the stereo finder into the accessory shoe. This finder is similar to the brilliant finder for the 35 or 50 mm. lenses, but shows the field of view corresponding to the stereo frame on the film.

When using the Stemar for the first time, an adjustment may be necessary to align the unit for the particular camera with which it is to be used. The reason for this is that the two lenses must be absolutely level with each other, with their optical axes at the same distance from the base plate of the Leica. Otherwise the stereo images will be out of alignment.

To check this, screw the Stemar into the Leica, and fit the prism attachment. The lower edge of this should now be parallel with the base plate of the camera.

If the alignment is incorrect, remove the prism attachment, and slack off (by about half a turn) the two screws at the side of the Stemar unit, just above the focusing lever. Also loosen the two large screws in the front panel of the unit. Refit the prism, and twist the whole unit to the left or right until the bottom edge of the prism housing is parallel with the base plate. Hold the camera and stereo unit firmly, and tighten the two screws at the side of the Stemar again. Then remove the prism attachment, and tighten the two large screws in the front.

This completes the adjustment. However, it is advisable to check the alignment frequently by screwing the Stemar into the Leica with the prism attachment in place. Line up as described, and adjust if necessary by moving the focusing lever (locked at infinity) to the left or right. If the unit is seriously out of alignment carry out the complete re-adjustment.

No such adjustment is necessary with the bayonet-mounted Stemar used on the Leica M.

The Image Size and Shape

The upright 18 × 24 mm. image is the only possible format for a one-short stereo system with a 24 × 36 mm. miniature camera. This is because the film transport mechanism necessarily advances the film by a full frame every time. That is the most fundamental argument in favour of this image shape.

There are, however, also other valid reasons to justify this choice of an upright picture. A stereo photograph depends for its effect on the presence of a series of subject planes receding from the foreground into the distance. The upright format includes more foreground (at the expense of the left and right margins) from the same viewpoint than a horizontal shape would, and can thus accommodate a greater depth of subject. To cover the same depth in a horizontal picture of the same area, we should have to take the subject from a lower viewpoint, which would compress the foreground and thus reduce the impression of the third dimension.

For this reason a pair of 24 × 36 mm. stereo images (as obtained with the discontinued stereo slide) is less favourable. (The field size in either case is the same, for the 33 mm. Stemar lenses each cover the same view on an 18 × 24 mm. frame as the standard 5 cm. lens on an upright 24 × 36 mm. negative.)

Stereo Practice

The purely mechanical side of stereo photography with the Stemar outfit is as simple as with a standard Leica lens. There are only two points to remember:

Firstly, use the Stemar unit by itself for shots between about 3½ and 8–10 feet. Use the Stemar with the prism attachment for subjects extending appreciably beyond 10 feet.

Secondly, increase the exposure (equivalent to ½ stop larger) when using the prism attachment.

The best subjects for stereo pictures are those extending well in depth. With semi-distant and distant views see that there are distinct foreground objects around 10–25 feet away to provide the nearer subject planes. Check on the depth of field indicator that the depth of the subject does not exceed the depth of field available. In stereo shots everything should as far as possible be sharp; a blurred foreground is specially disturbing. So stop down the lenses if necessary.

Distant views without any prominent foreground do not yield effective stereo pictures.

For nearer views taken without the prism attachment choose subjects that recede evenly rather than consisting of one object at a given distance. The presence of subject planes at different distances is in fact responsible for the impression of depth.

At close range the background need not be absolutely sharp, but the depth of field should still cover everything near the camera.

Take special care to hold the camera truly horizontal, without tilting it to either side. On the other hand, pointing it up or down does not matter. Align a prominent vertical edge of the subject with the side of the frame in the brilliant stereo finder to ensure proper levelling. When taking pictures from a tripod, check the correct camera position with a spirit level.

When taking pictures without the prism attachment, always fit the special twin lens hood in front of the Stemar.

Avoid awkward cuts into a foreground object by the edges of the frame. People with their legs partly cut off, an arm with the hand just outside the picture area, etc. look bad enough in a normal two-dimensional picture, but are far more disturbing in a stereo shot. Either cut radically into foreground objects, or not at all.

With stereo there is no need to rely on special lighting effects like heavy cross shadows to provide depth. Modelling and also atmospheric depth will of course, enhance the stereo effect, but avoid too contrasty lighting. The shadows must never be completely black—especially with colour film. Stick to more even lighting arrangements, and make sure of full exposure

In fact, make it a rule to expose black-and-white film at one stop larger, and colour film (reversal as well as negative) at half a stop larger, than for ordinary shots. In the case of colour film this yields a slightly light transparency which is easier to view in a viewer and more suitable for projection where the polarizing filters already reduce the image brightness.

The Stereoly Attachment

The Leica Stereoly attachment splits the image before the rays of light enter the lens. The film again records two upright stereo images 18 × 24 mm. side by side on the standard 24 × 36 mm. frame.

The attachment consists of an optical prism system which fits over the front mount of the 50 mm. Elmar *f*3.5 or Summar lenses. The front of the attachment has two openings 2½ inches apart. A bracket, fitting into the accessory shoe of the Leica and into a special shoe on the attachment, holds the whole unit together. Clamping screws secure the bracket in each shoe.

Since the bracket obscures the view of the viewfinder and rangefinder of series II and III Leicas, it carries a separate viewfinder of its own. A different bracket is available for series I Leica models.

Before taking stereo pictures, slacken the clamping screw of the front shoe on the attachment. Estimate the subject distance and focus the lens. Tighten the clamping screw, and expose.

STEREO VIEWING

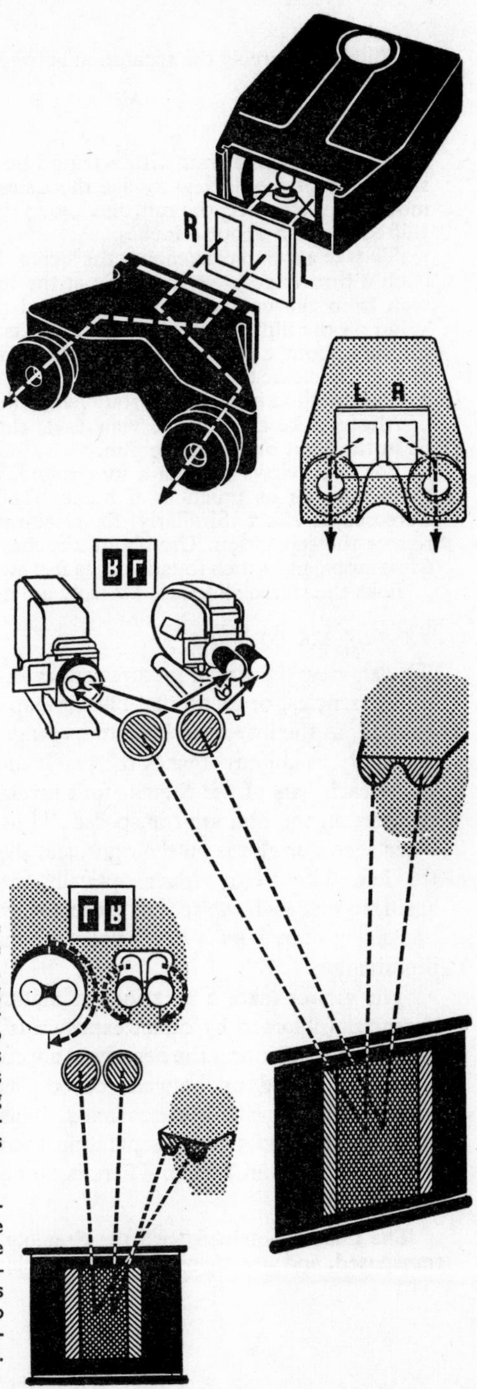

The images produced by the Stemar unit are transposed; the Leitz stereo viewer transposes them again optically so that each eye sees its correct image. A non-transposing viewer (*right*) is required to view the untransposed pictures produced with the Stereoly attachment.

For screening each image is projected through one lens of a twin-lens unit, with the light passing through two polarizing filters oriented at 90 deg. to each other. The two images on the screen are thus polarized, and on viewing through polarizing spectacles each eye sees only its own image.

When projecting untransposed stereo pairs, the twin lens unit must be turned through 180 deg.—or the polarizing filters each through 90 deg.—to interchange the polarization of the images (p. 452).

With the Stereoly the separation between the viewpoints cannot be changed.

The Stereo Slide

This is a horizontal rail with a tripod bush. The rail carries a slide with a tripod screw to take the Leica. The slide itself can move sideways along the rail, and allows the whole camera to be shifted through about 6 inches.

To take a stereo pair, mount the stereo slide with the Leica on it on a firm tripod. Set the slide at the left end of the rail (as seen from the back of the camera) and take the first picture. Wind on the film. Move the slide towards the centre of the rail through about 2½ inches without changing any of the camera settings, and take the second picture.

This method is limited to stationary subjects.

Always take the left-eye view first; the negatives will then be in the right order on the film.

For open views without a foreground, the separation of the shots may be as much as 6 inches for a more pronounced stereoscopic effect. Similarly, for close-ups nearer than 6 feet reduce the separation. Use about 2 inches (5 cm.) for subjects 6 feet away, and 1 inch for subjects 3 feet away.

Both the stereo slide and Stereoly are now discontinued.

Viewing Stereo Shots

We can view the stereo pictures either in the form of positive transparencies, or as prints. The former is the more effective method, as the increased brightness range of a transparency—especially in colour—makes the result more effective.

As each lens of the Stemar unit inverts its image, the two pictures on the film are transposed. Thus the left-hand view, when seen upright, is on the right, and the right-hand view on the left. The Leitz viewer optically transposes the images again, so that each eye sees its correct view. A detachable lamp housing powered by a dry battery provides uniform diffuse illumination.

The viewer takes 2 × 2 inch miniature slides. The transparencies (obtained by direct exposure of reversal film in the camera or by printing the negatives) are cut up into individual, pairs and bound up between cover glasses or mounted in suitable frames with a stereo mask. This masks each image down to 16 × 22.5 mm., separating them by a black centre strip ⅛ inch (3 mm.) wide. There is no need to cut the stereo pairs in two.

The images obtained with the Stereoly attachment are not transposed, and are therefore not suitable for viewing in this viewer. Viewers are available for the purpose without an optical transposing system; alternatively the single images may be cut apart and mounted with the left image on the right and the right image on the left. This requires great care in alignment.

Shots made by means of the stereo slide are mounted in frames 1⅝ × 4 inches (4 × 10 cm.) for full-frame miniature stereo viewers. Make sure that the centres of the frames are just 2½ inches apart (even if the exposures were made with a different separation).

When printing stereo negatives enlarge the left- and right-eye views to exactly the same degree and make sure the prints are of the same density. The enlargements should not be more than 2½ inches wide. Mount them on a card 2½ × 5¼ inches (6 × 13 cm.) with the centres 2½ inches apart, for viewing in a print viewer.

Bigger enlargements mounted farther apart need special viewing device with a mirror or prism system to bring the two views together. This permits enlargement of parts of the negatives.

When mounting make sure that the prints are accurately aligned relative to each other, and that they are correctly transposed for the viewing system used.

Stereo Projection

The stereo viewer can only be used by one person at a time; in a group you have to pass it round from hand to hand together with the transparencies. For larger groups the only practical way of presentation is thus projection.

Polarizing filters (p. 240) serve to separate the two images on the screen and to ensure that each eye sees only its own picture. The stereo transparencies are projected by a twin lens system similar in principle to the Stemar. A polarizing filter in front of the left lens polarizes the light in one plane, while a similar filter in front of the right lens polarizes the light passing through the right image in another plane at right-angles.

Each member of the audience wears a pair of polarizing spectacles with polarizing filters oriented in the same way as those on the projection lenses. Thus the left eye, looking through the left filter, sees the left image. The left filter, however, cuts out the right-hand image. In the same way the right eye sees only the right-hand image.

Two projection lens systems are available. The 50 mm. Elmar *f*3.5 twin lens unit is suitable for smaller projectors (it was specially designed for the Leitz Prado 100 and 250 models). The unit carries built-in polarizing filters, and has provision for individual or coupled focusing of the two lenses. Vertical and horizontal adjustments permit accurate alignment of the images on the screen.

The unit for more powerful projectors (e.g. Leitz Prado 250 and 500) consists of a diverging prism system with two 85 or 100 mm. Hektor *f*2.5 projection lenses mounted in front. Each lens has its own filter, and can be focused separately.

Always project stereo transparencies on a silver or other metallized screen. The matt and beaded types are unsuitable, as they depolarize the light falling on them. Arrange the audience reasonably near to the centre of the screen.

Both projection units can be used for untransposed stereo pairs as obtained with the Stereoly attachment. In that case simply turn the Elmar twin lens unit round through 180 deg., or turn the filter on each lens of the Hektor unit through 90 deg. This again matches the polarization of the left-eye image (now on the right) with the viewing filter in front of the left eye, and the right-eye image with the right-hand filter.

The Stereo Window

When viewing stereo transparencies in a viewer or on the screen, the frame of the image also assumes an apparent position in space. This depends primarily on the convergence of the optical axes of the two lenses on the camera.

With the Stemar outfit the apparent plane of this stereo frame or window is arranged to be about 3 feet in front of the Leica when the Stemar unit only is used. With the prism attachment mounted on the Stemar unit the stereo window appears to be about 10 feet from the Leica.

The stereo window is thus always well in front of the subject, this is usually the best arrangement. For special purposes it can; however, be quite effective to bring the scene out in front of this "window" towards the viewer.

While we cannot alter the optical alignment of the Stemar, a certain amount of control is possible in mounting the transparencies.

To do this, paste a strip of black paper over the centre strip of the mask, so as to increase the width of this strip by 1–2 mm. At the same time cut away the outer edge of each mask aperture right to the extreme edge of the image. The exact dimensions will be a matter of trial and error, but the result approximates that obtained by reducing the convergence of the taking lenses, and the window appears some way behind the foreground of the subject. Do not, however, carry the process too far; a window altogether behind the subject is unnatural.

Not every subject is suitable for this treatment. In particular, the edges of the image frame must not cut into any foreground object. Otherwise a human figure may, for instance, appear to stand in front of the window with the legs cut off by the window.

INVISIBLE RADIATION

Use special film for infra-red work, with filters to eliminate all visible light. The lens needs refocusing.
Ultra-violet photography utilizes reflected ultra-violet radiation or fluorescence of substances illuminated by ultra-violet.
In fluorography the Leica photographs X-ray screen images for mass medical surveys.

By utilizing invisible ultra-violet, infra-red, and X-rays, we are able to follow phenomena we could not observe otherwise. Many of these are suitable, and some specially suitable for recording with the Leica.

The two ways of seeing with invisible radiation are direct observation (as in infra-red photography) and indirect observation by photographing the effects of the rays (such as fluorescence phenomena with ultra-violet or X-radiation).

Infra-Red

Certain films are sensitized to respond to infra-red rays as well as to parts of the visible spectrum (p. 195). The infra-red sensitivity is considerably lower than the visible sensitivity, therefore we have to cut out all visible light by a deep red or infra-red filter.

Since Leica lenses are not corrected for infra-red, refocus the camera under these conditions utilizing the infra-red focusing mark (p. 88).

The main applications of infra-red photography are the examination of documents and pigments, and of living tissues.

Sets of different inks and pigments indistinguishable by ordinary light may have greatly varying reflectivities towards infra-red rays. Infra-red photographs will then show up the difference. They may be used to detect forgeries such as signatures added afterwards to letters, philatelic fakes made by painting in parts of stamp designs, and the like.

Medical infra-red photographs utilize the fact that certain skin tissues are transparent to infra-red rays. This permits the study of subcutaneous blood vessels and also of skin diseases.

Light sources for infra-red photographs may be tungsten or Photoflood lamps, or carbon filament and other infra-red therapy illuminators. The latter are especially rich in infra-red radiation. The filter factors for infra-red filters will therefore be lower.

Ultra-Violet

All photographic films are sensitive to ultra-violet radiation. However, we rarely use such radiation for direct photography. Ultra-violet photographs mostly utilize the fluorescence of certain substances. This is the ability to emit visible light when illuminated by ultra-violet rays.

An ultra-violet photography set-up consists of a quartz lamp to produce the ultra-violet rays, with a lamp filter (UG2 or Wratten No. 18A) to cut out all visible light.

The pictures are taken in total darkness, with an ultra-violet absorbing filter over the Leica lens. This cuts out all ultra-violet radiation, transmitting only the fluorescence light from the subject. A suitable filter is the Leitz UVa or light yellow No. 0 filter—though the latter will slightly affect the colour of the fluorescence image.

Focus the Leica by ordinary light.

Such pictures will show up forgeries, chemical erasures from documents, as well as a large number of hidden stains. They are therefore specially useful in forensic photography and in the examination of questioned documents.

At times direct ultra-violet photography will provide the required information. The subject is then photographed by ultra-violet rays to show absorption or reflection characteristics of the surface. In this case a UG2 filter is used over the lens.

Take care to shield the lens from the light source; no direct light from the ultra-violet lamp must reach the film.

Use the Elmar lenses only for direct ultra-violet photography. Other lens types, especially fast lenses like Summicron, Summitar, etc., contain glasses of high ultra-violet absorption.

Ultra-violet radiation in photomicrography has the advantage of giving higher image resolution, due to the short wavelength of the illumination. All visible light must naturally be excluded, except during focusing.

Fluorography

Fluorography is the photography of fluorescent X-ray screens. The image on the screen is produced by invisible radiation, but recorded by visible light.

The technique consists of photographing the screen with a miniature camera. In view of the large number of exposures that can be made in rapid succession, this method is particularly suitable for mass surveys of population groups, e.g. for early detection of tuberculosis. The miniature radiographs themselves cannot give the complete story, but they indicate which cases require further examination.

The best set-up consists of the Leica placed about 3½ feet from the screen. A sheet of lead glass between the screen and camera absorbs all X-rays. Enclose the space between the Leica and the screen with a conical or similar tube to eliminate extraneous light. Preferably fix the Leica lens in a panel at the back of the tube. The camera itself can then be removed rapidly for changing the film.

Fluorography calls for the fastest lenses such as the 35 or 50 mm. *f*1.4 Summilux or *f*2 Summicron, or 50 mm. Noctilux *f*1.2.

Use fast panchromatic film, or one of the flurographic films specially produced for this purpose. These are orthochromatic with a high sensitivity to the green fluorescence of the screen.

Exposure times will depend on the X-ray tube and screen used, on the lens and film as well as the chest thickness which the X-rays have to penetrate. Once the set-up is calibrated by test exposures, the chest thickness of the patient remains the only variable.

Expose by switching the X-ray tube on and off; the Leica shutter remains open on B or T.

For identification, a small illuminated panel next to the screen carries the reference number of each exposure.

HIGH-SPEED ACTION

Electronic flash will arrest ultra-high speed subjects.
For accurate timing, use the subject itself to release the flash by suitable triggering.
Stroboscopic flashes can be used to record successive phases of rapid movement on one frame.

With normal action subjects the Leica will arrest or "freeze" most movement by its top shutter speed of 1/1000 second. For investigation and analysis of really fast movement, this speed is inadequate, but combining the Leica with one or more electronic flash units, turns it into a high-speed action camera.

With such equipment we can follow the effect of falling drops and splashes of liquid, fast moving machinery and in certain conditions even the behaviour of bullets on impact.

The different types of electronic flash units have a flash duration around 1/500 to 1/5000 second. The shortest exposures are associated with low-output, high-voltage flash units; to get more light we have to link up several small units rather than use one large outfit.

Special micro-flash equipment for exposures of the order of 2-20 microseconds (1/50,000 to 1/500,000 second) is available with an output of about fifty joules.

With high-speed flash exposures the shutter fulfils no timing function. In all cases the shutter must be fully open while the flash takes place; either use a speed of 1/50 second or slower, or open the shutter for a time exposure.

Synchronized Firing

Where we can follow the movement to be recorded visually, we may take the picture in the orthodox way with the flash synchronized to the Leica and expose by pressing the release at the right time.

This is the simplest method, but calls for some practice in anticipation. The timing is far from reliable since it depends entirely on the photographer.

Synchronized firing is, however, perfectly suitable for all subjects involving periodic movement provided it does not matter what phase of the cycle we record.

Keep all outside light down to a minimum, to avoid double exposure. If necessary, use the flash at very close range and stop down the lens.

Independent Firing

Exposing high-speed subjects by synchronized flash becomes a matter of guesswork when the movement is too fast to follow by eye, and there independent firing is more successful.

These methods depend on mechanical, acoustic, and optical triggering. The subject itself sets off the flash and thus takes its own pictures.

For such photographs the Leica is set up as for open flash photography (p. 247), and focused on the point at which the picture is to be taken. Use a wide-angle lens for optimum depth of field. Eliminate all outside light as far as possible; ideally the shots should be taken in total darkness, but with a dark background a limited amount of light is permissible.

Mechanical triggering can take place by means of a trip wire or a spring contact, which is closed on impact. This works with falling objects or other subjects with a sufficiently great movement inertia.

For acoustic triggering a microphone picks up the sound of impact or other noise associated with the movement (e.g. the firing of a shot). An amplifier feeds the impulse directly into the synchronizing leads of the electronic unit.

Optical triggering methods use a photo-cell with a small beam of light focused on it. The moving subject interrupts the light on the photocell, and thus generates a current which after amplification actuates the circuit of the electronic flash.

This method can also be used to fire subsidiary "slave" units. On releasing the main flash, the light acts on a photo-cell circuit which in turn fires any number of subsidiary units.

A special way of triggering useful for drops and similar subjects falling into water, uses two electrodes. They are positioned just above the surface of the liquid; when the latter is disturbed it makes contact across the electrodes.

Timing Delay

Electronic flash, like a flash bulb, has a certain firing delay (p. 257) though this is very small (5-20 micro-seconds). While the delay is too short to have any effect on synchronization with the shutter of the Leica itself, it does influence the timing of high-speed flashes. In practice it is most convenient to consider the timing delay of the set-up as a whole and allow for it accordingly.

With mechanical firing, the timing delay depends largely on the play of the mechanism. We can adjust this to some extent, e.g. by varying the tension of the trip wire.

The Leica should cover a field a little beyond the trip wire; the exact direction may be found by trial and error.

A microphone offers the greatest timing adjustment, since we can take it closer to or farther away from the source of the sound. In this way we may cover the different stages of disintegration of a bursting balloon or the impact of a rubber ball. The farther the microphone is from the balloon, the later the flash will go off.

Photo-cell triggering is almost instantaneous and the delay depends mainly on the firing delay of the flash tube.

Stroboscopic Flash

With ordinary electronic flash units the capacitor has to charge up for several seconds between flashes. Stroboscopic units can flash up to 200 times a second with a flash duration of 10 microseconds.

Stroboscopic flash can be used to illuminate rapidly rotating or oscillating subjects like machine parts. With careful adjustment of the flashing rate to the speed of rotation, each flash lights up the subject in the same phase of its movement. The machine will then appear to stand still when it is running at speeds up to 10,000 revolutions a minute; and can thus be photographed like a still subject.

Multiple Strobe Shots

Stroboscopic flash lamps are also useful for analysis of more irregular movements, e.g., a leap of a dancer, or the movement of a golf club during a stroke. The pictures are really multiple exposures on one frame of film, taken with the shutter open. Each flash then registers one phase of the action.

For such shots the Leica must be set up in a nearly darkened room, pointed on a black background. Focus on the line along which the subject is to move, and start the stroboscopic flash unit. Open the shutter on B, and hold it open while the subject passes the camera, or goes through its movement cycle.

According to the flashing rate employed, the images will overlap each other to a greater or lesser extent. The slower the rate, the smaller the overlap (if any); a fast rate, on the other hand, shows more intermediate phases.

FACTS AND FIGURES

OLDER LEICA MODELS

While the current Leica models are described in detail on p. 26, this comparative table summarizes the main differences of the earlier models. Up to 1938 the various Leicas carried different designations in the U.S.A.

Many of the changes made in the models of any one of the three series were internal ones of detailed construction; often the general specification remained largely the same. The model IIIc, for instance, covers several slightly different cameras.

Model Germany	*Model* U.S.A.	*Year*	*Shutter Speeds (sec.)*	*Rangefinder*	*Salient Features*
Older Models					
I	A	1924	1/20–1/500	No	Lens fixed, shorter
I	B	1926	1–1/300 (Compur)	No	body, built-in finder, no flash
	C	1930	1/20–1/500	No	Lens interchangeable but mount not standard, no flash, shorter body
	E (Standard)	1932	1/20–1/500	No	Standardized lens mount, otherwise as earlier Leica I
II	D	1932	1/20–1/500	Yes	No flash, shorter
III	F	1933	1–1/500	Yes	body, separate view
IIIa	G	1935	1–1/1000	Yes	and rangefinder eyepieces
250	FF	1934	1–1/1000	Yes	No flash, takes 33 feet of film
IIIb		1938	1–1/1000	Yes	No flash, shorter body
IIIc		1940	1–1/1000	Yes	No flash and no film
IIc		1948	1/30–1/500	Yes	indicator
Ic		1949	1/30–1/500	No	
IIIf		1950	1–1/1000	Yes	Synchronizing dial
IIf		1951	*1/25–1/1000	Yes	
If		1952	*1/25–1/500	No	
72		1954	1–1/1000	Yes	72 exp. 18 × 24 mm.
IIIg		1957	1–1/1000	Yes	Brilliant-frame
Ig		1957	1–1/1000	No	finder

*Earlier models: 1/30–1/500.

LEICA FINDERS

The range of finders covers all the lenses of the Leica. We can have a separate finder for each lens, or cover almost every lens with one finder.

Finder	*Focal Lengths Covered*	*Parallax Adjustment*
Universal*† (VIOOH, VIDOM)	35, 50, 73, 85, 90, 105, 135 mm.; also 28 mm. with attachment	Lever at back
Small Universal*	35, 50 mm. plus either 73 *or* 90 *or* 105 *or* 135 mm.	Horizontal lever at back (none on early versions)
Brilliant	21 *or* 28 *or* 35 *or* 50 *or* 85* *or* 90 *or* 135 mm. *or* stereo*	85, 90, 135 mm.; milled disc
Frame*	35, 50, 73, 90, 135 mm.	Rear sight
Wide angle*	28 *or* 35 mm.	None
Wide-angle attachment	35 mm. (bayonet, M3)	Automatic compensation by camera finder
Sports*	73 *or* 90 *or* 135 mm.	Early models only
Waist level*	28 *or* 35 *and/or* 50 mm.	None
Right angle*	50 mm. only	None
Telyt frame	200 *or* 400 mm.	Rotating rear sight
Visoflex I*	125 to 400 mm.; any for close-ups	None required
Visoflex II*, III	65, 90 mm., and longer; any for close-ups	None required

*Obsolete models. †Some of the focal lengths are available only on certain early models.

LEICA LENSES

This table shows the leading particulars of the Leica lenses that are, or used to be, produced by the makers of the Leica, together with available mounts (S = screw mount for models I to IIIg, B = bayonet mount for series M models). The screw mounted versions except the Telyts—are discontinued. The angles refer to the full 24 × 36 mm. frame; they would be slightly smaller for the effective 23 × 35 mm. frame utilized in a mounted colour transparency.

Lens	*Focal Length*		*Full Aperture*	*Angle of Field*		*Mount*	*Magnif. compared with 50 mm. lens*
	mm.	*in.*	*f*	*Hor.*	*Vert.*		
Current Lenses							
S. Angulon	21	⅞	3.4	81°	60°	B	0.42
Elmarit	28	1⅛	2.8	65°	46½°	B	0.56
Summaron	35	1⅜	2.8	54°	38°	B, S	0.7
Summicron	35	1⅜	2	54°	38°	B, S	0.7
Summilux	35	1⅜	1.4	54°	38°	B	0.7
Elmar	50	2	2.8	38½°	26½°	B, S	1
Summicron	50	2	2	38½°	26½°	B, S	1
Summilux	50	2	1.4	38½°	26½°	B, S	1
Noctilux	50	2	1.2	38½°	26½°	B	1
Elmar	65	2⅝	3.5	30°	21°	†	1.3
Elmar	90	3½	4	22½°	15°	B, S	1.8
Elmarit	90	3½	2.8	22½°	15°	B, S	1.8
Summicron	90	3½	2	22½°	15°	B, S	1.8
Tele-Elmarit	90	3½	2.8	22½°	15°	B	1.8
Tele-Elmar	135	5⅜	4	15°	10°	B	2.7
Elmarit	135	5⅜	2.8	15°	10°	B	2.7
Telyt	200	7⅞	4	10½°	7°	S	4
Telyt	280	11	4.8	7⅓°	5°	S	5.6
Telyt	400	15¾	5.6	5°	3½°	††	8
Telyt	560	22	5.6	3½°	2½°	††	11.2
Obsolete and Discontinued Lenses							
S. Angulon	21	⅞	4	81°	60°	B, S	0.42
Summaron	28	1⅛	5.6	65°	46½°	S	0.56
Hektor	28	1⅛	6.3	65°	46½°	S	0.56
Summaron	35	1⅜	3.5	54°	38°	B, S	0.7
Elmar	35	1⅜	3.5	54°	38°	S	0.7
Elmar	50	2	3.5	38½°	26½°	B, S	1
Hektor	50	2	2.5	38½°	26½°	S	1
Summitar	50	2	2	38½°	26½°	S	1
Summar	50	2	2	38½°	26½°	S	1
Summarit	50	2	1.5	38½°	26½°	B, S	1
Xenon	50	2	1.5	38½°	26½°	S	1
Hektor	73	2⅞	1.9	27½°	18½°	S	1.5
Summarex	85	3⅜	1.5	24°	16°	S	1.7
Thambar	90	3½	2.2	22½°	15°	S	1.8
Elmar	105	4⅛	6.3	19½°	13°	S	2.1
Hektor	125	5	2.5	16½°	11°	S	2.5
Elmar	135	5⅜	4	15°	10°	B, S	2.7
Hektor	135	5⅝	4.5	15°	10°	B, S	2.7
Elmar	135	5⅜	4.5	15°	10°	S	2.7
Telyt	200	7⅞	4.5	10½°	7°	S	4
Telyt	400	15¾	5	5°	3½°	S	8
Stemar	33	1¼	3.5	*27°	*40°	B, S	*1

*On each 18 × 24 mm. stereo frame.
†Special screw mount for use only with the helical focusing mount No. 16464 on Visoflex II and III.
††Special screw mount for use on Televit.

FILM SPEEDS

Among currently quoted speed figures the ASA ratings are arithmetical, in other words the speed is directly proportional to the speed index. DIN speeds are logarithmic, every 3 degrees increase representing a doubling of the speed. The ASA and ISO (proposed international standard) logarithmic figures double the speed for every increase of 1 degree.

These figures compare speed ratings for minimum correct exposures (revised ASA, BS, and DIN standards).

ASA & BS Arith.	*DIN*	*Weston (old)*	*BS Log*	*ASA & ISO Log.*
10	11	8	21°	1.5°
12	12	10	22°	2°
16	13	12	23°	
20	14	16	24°	2.5°
25	15	20	25°	3°
32	16	24	26°	
40	17	32	27°	3.5°
50	18	40	28°	4°
64	19	50	29°	
80	20	64	30°	4.5°
100	21	80	31°	5°
125	22	100	32°	
160	23	125	33°	5.5°
200	24	160	34°	6°
250	25	200	35°	
320	26	250	36°	6.5°
400	27	320	37°	7°
500	28	400	38°	
650	29	500	39°	7.5°
800	30	650	40°	8°
1000	31	800	41°	
1300	32	1000	42°	8.5°
1600	33	1300	43°	9°

LEICA FILMS

Film	Speed Index ASA	DIN	Grain	Colour Sensitivity
Fast and Ultra-Fast Film				
Adox KB21	200	24	m	Pan
Adox KB27	800	30	m	Red pan
Agfa Isopan ISS	200	24	m	Red pan
Agfa Isopan Record ...	1300	32	m	Red pan
Ansco Super Hypan ...	500	28	m	Pan
Ferrania P. 33	160	23	m	Red pan
Ferrania P. 36	320	26	m	Red pan
Gevaert Gevapan 33 ...	250	25	sf	Pan
Gevaert Gevapan 36 ...	500	28	m	Red pan
Ilford H.P.3, H.P.4	400	27	m	Red pan
Ilford H.P.S.	800	30	m	Red pan
Kodak Tri X	400	27	m	Pan
Kodak 2475 Recording	1600	33	m	Pan
Orwo NP27	400	27	m	Pan
Perutz 21	200	24	sf	Pan
Perutz 27	500	28	m	Red pan
Medium Speed Films				
Gevaert Gevapan 30 ...	125	22	sf	Pan
Ilford F.P.4	125	22	f	Pan
Kodak Plus X	160	23	sf	Pan
Orwo NP20	80	20	sf	Pan
Fine Grain Films				
Adox KB17	40	17	f	Pan
Agfa Isopan F	40	17	f	Pan
Ferrania P.30	80	20	f	Pan
Gevaert Gevapan 27 ...	64	19	f	Pan
Ilford F.P.4	125	22	f	Pan
Perutz 17	40	17	f	Red pan
Extra Fine Grain Films				
Adox KB14	20	14	ef	Pan
Agfa Isopan FF	16	13	ef	Pan
Ferrania P 24	20	14	ef	Pan
Ilford Pan F	50	18	ef	Pan
Kodak Panatomic X ...	32	16	ef	Pan
Orwo NP15	25	15	ef	Pan
Infra-red Films				
Eastman Infra-red	40*	17*	—	Infra-red
Gevaert Infra-red	50*	18*	—	Infra-red
Reversal Films				
Adox UKB17	40	17	f	Pan
Gevaert Dia Direct ...	25	15	f	Pan
Kodak Direct Pos. Pan	80	20	sf	Pan
Negative Colour Films				
Agfacolor CN17S	40	17	—	Universal
Ferraniacolor NM64 ...	64	19	—	Universal
Gevacolor N5	40	17	—	Daylight
Ilford Colorprint	80	20	—	Universal
Kodacolor X	80	20	—	Universal
Reversal Colour Films				
Agfacolor CT 18	50	18	—	Daylight
Agfacolor CK 20	80	20	—	Tungsten
Anscochrome 50 Daylight...	50	18	—	Daylight
Anscochrome 100 Daylight	100	21	—	Daylight
Anscochrome 100 Tungsten	100	21	—	Photoflood
Anscochrome 200	200	24	—	Daylight
Anscochrome 500	500	28	—	Daylight
Ektachrome X	64	19	—	Daylight
Ferraniacolor 28	50	18	—	Daylight
Gevacolor R5	50	18	—	Daylight
H.S. Ektachrome	160	23	—	Daylight
H.S. Ektachrome B ...	125	22	—	Tungsten
Ilford Colorslide	32	16	—	Daylight
Ilford Super Colorslide ...	64	19	—	Daylight
Kodachrome II Daylight ...	25	15	—	Daylight
Kodachrome II A	40	17	—	Photoflood
Kodachrome X	64	19	—	Daylight
Perutz Color C18	50	18	—	Daylight

*With deep red filter.

The most important 35 mm. black-and-white films are grouped here according to their main applications.

The film speeds refer to daylight and are values for minimum correct exposure; these do not necessarily agree with the manufacturer's rating in all cases.

High speed films usually have medium grain (m); medium speed and slower films yield semi fine (sf) or fine (f) grain images. Certain films, especially copying materials, produce exceptionally fine grain (ef).

The main colour films available for the Leica are grouped as negative and reversal colour films.

The film speeds quoted apply when the material is used by the light for which it is balanced. "Tungsten" colour balance here refers to 3200°K, "Photoflood" to 3400°K.

FOCUSING ZONES

For candid photography, action shots, and similar subjects, pre-set focusing zones are useful, as they save time over focusing the Leica (p. 210). The zones are not as exact as the depth of field tables, but are easy to remember and to set in a hurry.

These zones cover the four focal lengths most likely to be used for snap-shooting.

Zone	*Focus*	*Stop*	*Focus*	*Stop*
	50 mm. Lenses		*90 mm. Lenses*	
Near 9–12 ft. (2.5–3.5 m.)	10 ft. (3 m.)	*f*4	10 ft. (3 m.)	*f*11–12.5
Medium 12–20 ft. (3.5–6 m.)	15 ft. (5 m.)	*f*4	15 ft. (5 m.)	*f*11–12.5
Far 20 ft.–∞ (6 m.–∞)	30 ft. (10 m.)	*f*5.6–6.3	30 ft. (10 m.)	*f*16–18
	35 mm. Lenses		*135 mm. Lenses*	
Near 7–20 ft. (2.6 m.)	10 ft. (3 m.)	*f*5.6–6.3	—	—
Medium 25–40 ft. (7.5–12 m.)	—	—	30 ft. (10 m.)	*f*16
Far 40 ft.–∞ (12 m.–∞)	—	—	75 ft. (25 m.)	*f*16–18
Extreme 10 ft.–∞ (3 m.–∞)	20 ft. (6 m.)	*f*5.6–6.3	—	—

SPEEDS AND ACTION

Shutter speeds needed to take sharp pictures of moving subjects depend on the subject speed as well as on the subject distance and focal length of the lens (see p. 230).

With different Leica lenses it is most convenient to define the subject distance in terms of the focal length. Therefore first look up (*top table*) how many focal lengths the subject is away, and find the shutter speed needed for different subjects in the *lower table*.

The speeds apply to movement across the field of view of the Leica. For subjects directly approaching or receding (p. 230) four times these exposures will still yield a sharp image (e.g. 1/30 instead of 1/125). For obliquely moving objects twice the given speeds may be used. With Leica models marked with different shutter speeds use the nearest marked figure (e.g. 1/100 for 1/125 second).

The speed of 1/2000 second is available only on the Leicaflex.

Lens		*Approx. Subject Distances Corresponding to Focal Lengths* 60	120	250	500	1000
28 mm.	ft.	6	12	25	50	100
	m.	1.8	3.5	7.5	15	30
35 mm.	ft.	7	14	30	60	120
	m.	2.1	4.2	8.5	17	35
50 mm.	ft.	10	20	40	80	160
	m.	3	6	12	25	50
85 or 90 mm.	ft.	18	36	75	150	300
	m.	5.5	11	23	45	90
135 mm.	ft.	27	55	110	220	450
	m.	8.3	16	33	65	135
180 or 200 mm.	ft.	40	80	160	330	650
	m.	12	25	50	100	200
400 mm.	ft.	80	160	330	650	1300
	m.	25	50	100	200	400

Subject	*Camera Distance (Focal Lengths)* 60	120	250	500	1000
Walking people (2–3 m.p.h.)	1/125	1/60	1/30	1/15	1/8
Running people (5–7 m.p.h.)	1/250	1/125	1/60	1/30	1/15
Sprinter (10 m.p.h.)	1/500	1/250	1/125	1/60	1/30
Cyclist, trotting horse, bus in town, fast sailing boat, motor boat (12–15 m.p.h.)	1/500	1/250	1/125	1/60	1/30
Slow train, car, motor cycle, galloping horse (30 m.p.h.)	1/1000	1/500	1/250	1/125	1/60
Fast train or car (50–60 m.p.h.)	1/2000	1/1000	1/500	1/250	1/125
Sports plane (100–200 m.p.h.)	—	1/2000	1/1000	1/500	1/250
Air liner (400–500 m.p.h.)	—	—	1/2000	1/1000	1/500

DEPTH OF FIELD

Aperture		Depth of Field for 50 mm. (2 inch) Lenses with Leica Focused on (feet and inches)					
		3½	4	5	6	7	8
f 1.2	from	3–5½	3–11	4–10½	5–10	6–9½	7–8¼
	to	3–6½	4–1	5–1½	6–2	7–2¾	8–4¼
f 1.4	from	3–5¼	3–11	4–10¼	5–9¼	6–8½	7–7¼
	to	3–6¾	4–1	5–2	6–2¾	7–4	8–5½
f 2	from	3–4¾	3–10¼	4–9½	5–8½	6–7½	7–6
	to	3–7¼	4–1¾	5–2¾	6–4	7–5	8–6½
f 2.8	from	3–4	3–9½	4–8½	5–7¾	6–6	7–4½
	to	3–8	4–2½	5–3½	6–5¼	7–7	8–8½
f 4	from	3–3½	3–9	4–7½	5–5½	6–3	7–1
	to	3–9	4–3½	5–5	6–8	7–11	9–3
f 5.6	from	3–2¾	3–8	4–6	5–3	6–0	6–9½
	to	3–10¼	4–4¾	5–7½	6–11	8–3½	9–9
f 8	from	3–1½	3–6½	4–3½	5–0	5–8	6–4
	to	3–11½	4–7½	6–0	7–6	9–1	10–11
f 11	from	2–11½	3–4½	4–1	4–8½	5–4	5–11
	to	4–2½	4–10½	6–5	8–2	10–0	12–1
f 16	from	2–10	3–2	3–9	4–3½	4–9	5–3
	to	4–7½	5–5	7–6	10–0	13–2	17–3
f 22	from	2–8	2–11	3–4½	3–11	4–4	4–8½
	to	5–0	6–3	9–0	12–6	17–9	26–6

Aperture		Depth of Field for 50 mm. (2 inch) Lenses with Leica Focused on (feet and inches)					
		10	15	25	50	100	∞
f 1.2	from	9–7	14–0	22–6	41–0	68–0	210
	to	10–6	16–2	28–5	65–0	190	∞
f 1.4	from	9–5	13–10	22–0	39–0	64–0	180
	to	10–8	16–4	29–0	69–6	225	∞
f 2	from	9–3	13–5	21–0	35–0	55–0	120
	to	11–0	17–6	32–6	90–0	600	∞
f 2.8	from	9–0	12–10	19–6	32–6	47–6	90–0
	to	11–4	18–0	34–9	112	∞	∞
f 4	from	8–8	12–3	17–8	27–3	37–6	60–0
	to	12–0	20–0	43–0	300	∞	∞
f 5.6	from	8–2	11–3	16–2	23–9	31–0	45–0
	to	12–10	22–6	53–0	∞	∞	∞
f 8	from	7–6	10–0	13–8	19–9	23–0	30–0
	to	15–0	30–0	150	∞	∞	∞
f 11	from	7–0	9–3	12–0	15–9	18–8	23–0
	to	17–8	39–0	∞	∞	∞	∞
f 16	from	6–0	7–6	9–4	11–6	13–0	15–0
	to	30–0	∞	∞	∞	∞	∞
f 22	from	5–4	6–4	8–0	9–4	10–4	11–6
	to	76–6	∞	∞	∞	∞	∞

The depths of field indicated in this table for the standard 50 mm. (2 inch) Leica and Leicaflex lenses (and also the tables on pp. 466–482) are based on a circle of confusion of $\frac{1}{30}$ mm. ($\frac{1}{750}$ inch). The depth of field indicator on some lenses may be based on a larger circle of confusion; that would give different values.

To find the depth at any aperture and distance, look up the horizontal row of double figures corresponding to the aperture used. Then trace across to the column for the subject distance and read off the near limit (row "from") and the far limit (row "to") of the depth of field.

Example: We want to know the depth of field available with the lens focused on 8 feet and stopped down to f 11. Trace the rows for f 11 across to the column corresponding to 8 feet: the near limit is 5 feet 11 inches, the far limit 12 feet 1 inch.

For the Elmar f 3.5 at full aperture use the same figures as for f 4.

Older Leica lenses carry Continental aperture markings (p. 214). With those lenses use the next larger aperture shown in the tables (e.g. f 8 for f 9). While the actual depth at f 9 is slightly greater than at f 8, this matters little in practice; we are erring on the safe side.

For close distances nearer than 3½ feet or 1 metre (with the 50 mm. lens of the Leicaflex) find the depth from the table on p. 488 for the scale of reproduction; the latter can be found in the table on p. 492.

DEPTH OF FIELD

Aperture		Depth of Field for 50 mm. (2 inch) Lenses with Leica Focused on (metres)					
		1	1.25	1.5	1.75	2	2.5
f 1.2	from	0.99	1.22	1.47	1.70	1.94	2.40
	to	1.02	1.27	1.53	1.80	2.06	2.61
f 1.4	from	0.98	1.22	1.46	1.69	1.93	2.38
	to	1.02	1.28	1.55	1.82	2.08	2.63
f 2	from	0.98	1.21	1.44	1.67	1.89	2.34
	to	1.03	1.29	1.57	1.84	2.12	2.68
f 2.8	from	0.97	1.19	1.42	1.65	1.86	2.29
	to	1.04	1.31	1.59	1.87	2.16	2.76
f 4	from	0.95	1.17	1.39	1.60	1.81	2.20
	to	1.06	1.32	1.63	1.93	2.24	2.88
f 5.6	from	0.93	1.14	1.36	1.55	1.74	2.10
	to	1.08	1.35	1.68	2.01	2.35	3.06
f 8	from	0.90	1.10	1.29	1.47	1.65	1.94
	to	1.12	1.42	1.78	2.15	2.54	3.41
f 11	from	0.87	1.06	1.23	1.39	1.55	1.83
	to	1.17	1.53	1.92	2.40	2.83	3.96
f 16	from	0.83	0.99	1.14	1.28	1.41	1.64
	to	1.27	1.70	2.20	2.78	3.48	5.35
f 22	from	0.77	0.90	1.04	1.16	1.26	1.44
	to	1.42	1.98	2.79	3.60	4.85	9.45

This table shows the depth of field for the 50 mm. (2 inch) Leica lenses in metres, corresponding to the table in feet and inches opposite.

To find the aperture and focusing distance required for any given depth of field zone, look for a pair of figures which approximately cover the depth required. Then check the column in which they are, to find the focusing distance. Trace across to the left-hand edge of the table to find the aperture.

Example: We want to cover a zone of sharp focus from 4 to 10 metres. The nearest pair of figures covering these limits is 3.20 and 10.4 metres. They are in the 5-metre column, and in the row for *f* 8. We therefore focus on 5 metres, and stop down to *f* 8.

If the focusing distance is known, it becomes simpler still: trace down the appropriate distance column until the near and far limits cover the field, and trace across to the left-hand edge to find the aperture needed.

Aperture		Depth of Field for 50 mm. (2 inch) Lenses with Leica Focused on (metres)						
		3	4	5	7	10	20	∞
f 1.2	from	2.86	3.77	4.64	6.28	8.64	15.2	63
	to	3.15	4.27	5.43	7.86	11.9	29.3	∞
f 1.4	from	2.83	3.70	4.58	6.20	8.45	14.6	54.0
	to	3.19	4.30	5.50	8.05	12.3	31.8	∞
f 2	from	2.78	3.62	4.41	5.88	7.90	13.1	37.5
	to	3.26	4.48	5.76	8.57	13.6	43.0	∞
f 2.8	from	2.70	3.49	4.22	5.36	7.30	11.5	27.0
	to	3.38	4.70	6.14	9.45	15.9	77.0	∞
f 4	from	2.59	3.30	3.95	5.10	6.53	9.70	18.8
	to	3.57	5.08	6.80	11.1	21.4	∞	∞
f 5.6	from	2.45	3.08	3.64	4.60	5.72	8.11	13.3
	to	3.87	5.70	8.00	14.6	39.4	∞	∞
f 8	from	2.28	2.80	3.20	4.02	4.85	6.30	9.40
	to	4.40	6.95	10.4	27.5	∞	∞	∞
f 11	from	2.08	2.52	2.88	3.45	4.05	5.08	6.80
	to	5.36	9.72	18.9	∞	∞	∞	∞
f 16	from	1.83	2.16	2.42	2.82	3.20	3.81	4.70
	to	8.30	26.8	∞	∞	∞	∞	∞
f 22	from	1.59	1.84	2.02	2.28	2.54	2.90	3.40
	to	25.4	∞	∞	∞	∞	∞	∞

DEPTH OF FIELD

Aperture		Depth of Field for 21 mm. (⅞ inch) Lens with Leica Focused on (feet and inches)							
		⅔	1	1½	2	3	4	10	∞
f3.4	from	0–7¾	0–11¼	1–4¼	1–9	2–6	3–1	5–7½	13–0
	to	0–8½	1–0¾	1–8½	2–4½	3–11	5–9	43	∞
f4	from	0–7½	0–11	1–3¾	1–8	2–5	2–11	5–2	10–6
	to	0–8½	1–1¼	1–9	2–6	4–4	6–6	210	∞
f5.6	from	0–7½	0–10¾	1–3	1–7	2–2	2–8	4–5	8–0
	to	0–8¾	1–1¾	1–10	2–8	4–9	8–0	∞	∞
f8	from	0–7¼	0–10¼	1–2	1–5½	1–11	2–3	3–5	5–3
	to	0–9	1–2¾	2–0¾	3–3	7–0	16–9	∞	∞
f11	from	0–7	0–9½	1–1¼	1–4	1–8½	2–0	2–10	4–0
	to	0–9½	1–4	2–5	4–0	12–0	∞	∞	∞
f16	from	0–6½	0–8¾	0–11½	1–2	1–5	1–7	2–1	2–8
	to	0–10½	1–7¼	3–5	8–0	∞	∞	∞	∞
f22	from	0–6	0–8	0–10	1–0	1–2	1–4	1–8	2–0
	to	1–0	2–0	6–0	∞	∞	∞	∞	∞

Aperture		Depth of Field for 21 mm. (⅞ inch) Lens with Leica Focused on (metres)							
		0.2	0.3	0.5	0.7	1	1.2	2.5	∞
f3.4	from	0.19	0.28	0.44	0.59	0.79	0.92	1.52	3.9
	to	0.21	0.32	0.57	0.85	1.35	1.73	6.9	∞
f4	from	0.19	0.27	0.43	0.58	0.77	0.88	1.42	3.3
	to	0.21	0.33	0.59	0.89	1.43	1.88	10.3	∞
f5.6	from	0.18	0.26	0.41	0.54	0.70	0.79	1.20	2.3
	to	0.22	0.34	0.64	1.01	1.77	2.5	∞	∞
f8	from	0.18	0.25	0.39	0.50	0.63	0.70	1.01	1.70
	to	0.23	0.36	0.71	1.19	2.42	4.1	∞	∞
f11	from	0.17	0.24	0.35	0.45	0.55	0.60	0.81	1.20
	to	0.24	0.40	0.86	1.68	6.0	∞	∞	∞
f16	from	0.16	0.22	0.31	0.36	0.44	0.48	0.61	0.80
	to	0.27	0.48	1.33	5.6	∞	∞	∞	∞
f22	from	0.15	0.20	0.27	0.32	0.37	0.40	0.49	0.60
	to	0.30	0.60	3.0	∞	∞	∞	∞	∞

Depth of field values in feet and inches (*top table*) and in metres (*bottom table*) for the 21 mm. (⅞ inch) Super-Angulon wide-angle lenses (see also pp. 464–465). The distances from ⅔ feet (8 inches) to 1½ feet or 0.2 to 0.5 metres apply to the Super-Angulon-R of the Leicaflex.

DEPTH OF FIELD

Aperture		*Depth of Field for 28 mm. (1⅛ inch) Lenses with Leica Focused on (feet and inches)*							
		2	2½	3	4	5	8	15	∞
*f*2.8	from	1–10½	2–3½	2–8½	3–6	4–3	6–3	9–9	28–0
	to	2–2	2–9	3–4½	4–8	6–1	11–2	32–0	∞
*f*4	from	1–10	2–3	2–7¼	3–4	4–0	5–8½	8–7	20–0
	to	2–3	2–10	3–6	5–0	6–8	13–4	60–0	∞
*f*5.6	from	1–9	2–1½	2–6	3–1	3–8	5–1	7–3	14–0
	to	2–4	3–0½	3–10	5–7¼	7–9	18–6	∞	∞
*f*6.3	from	1–8½	2–1	2–5	3–0	3–6	4–10	6–8	12–0
	to	2–4¾	3–1¾	4–0	6–0	8–6	24–0	∞	∞
*f*8	from	1–8	2–0	2–3½	2–10	3–4	4–5¼	6–0	10–0
	to	2–6	3–4	4–3½	6–8	10–0	40–0	∞	∞
*f*11	from	1–6¾	1–10¼	2–1¼	2–6½	2–11	3–8¾	4–9	7–0
	to	2–9½	3–10¾	5–3	9–4	17–6	∞	∞	∞
*f*16	from	1–5	1–8	1–10½	2–2¾	3–6	3–1	3–9	7–0
	to	3–4	5–0	7–6	20–0	∞	∞	∞	∞
*f*22	from	1–3	1–5¼	1–7½	1–10½	2–0¾	2–5	2–10	3–6
	to	4–8	8–9	21–0	∞	∞	∞	∞	∞

Aperture		*Depth of Field for 28 mm. (1⅛ inch) Lenses with Leica Focused on (metres)*							
		0.75	1	1.5	2	2.5	3	5	∞
*f*2.8	from	0.69	0.89	1.27	1.61	1.93	2.21	3.14	8.40
	to	0.82	1.11	1.83	2.62	3.55	4.67	12.4	∞
*f*4	from	0.67	0.86	1.20	1.50	1.76	2.00	2.73	6.00
	to	0.86	1.20	2.00	3.00	4.28	6.00	30.0	∞
*f*5.6	from	0.64	0.81	1.11	1.36	1.57	1.57	2.28	4.20
	to	0.91	1.31	2.33	3.82	6.18	10.5	∞	∞
*f*6.3	from	0.63	0.79	1.07	1.30	1.49	1.68	2.12	3.70
	to	0.94	1.36	2.52	4.35	7.70	15.9	∞	∞
*f*8	from	0.60	0.75	1.00	1.20	1.36	1.50	1.87	3.00
	to	1.00	1.50	3.00	6.00	15.0	∞	∞	∞
*f*11	from	0.56	0.68	0.88	1.02	1.14	1.24	1.48	2.10
	to	1.17	1.90	5.25	42.0	∞	∞	∞	∞
*f*16	from	0.50	0.60	0.75	0.86	0.94	1.00	1.15	1.50
	to	1.50	3.00	∞	∞	∞	∞	∞	∞
*f*22	from	0.38	0.52	0.64	0.71	0.76	0.81	0.90	1.10
	to	2.04	11.0	∞	∞	∞	∞	∞	∞

Depth values in feet and inches (*top table*) or metres (*bottom table*) for the 28 mm. (1⅛ inch) Elmarit *f*2.8, Summaron *f*5.6 and Hektor *f*6.3 wide-angle lenses (see also pp. 464–465).

DEPTH OF FIELD

Aperture		Depth of Field for 35 mm. (1⅜ inch) Lenses with Leica Focused on (feet and inches)							
		1	2	2½	4	6	10	15	∞
f 1.4	from	—	1-11½	2-5	3-9½	5-7¾	9-0	12-10	90-0
	to	—	2-0½	2-7	4-2½	6-5¼	11-4	18-0	∞
f 2	from	—	1-11	2-4¾	3-9	5-6	8-8	12-3	60-0
	to	—	2-1	2-7¼	4-3½	6-8	12-0	20-0	∞
f 2.8	from	0-11¾	1-11	2-4½	3-8	5-3	8-2	11-3	45-0
	to	1-0¼	2-1	2-8	4-5	6-11	12-10	22-6	∞
f 4	from	0-11½	1-10½	2-3¾	3-6½	5-0	7-6	10-0	30-0
	to	1-0½	2-2	2-8¾	4-7¼	7-6	15-0	30-0	∞
f 5.6	from	0-11½	1-10	2-3	3-4½	4-8½	7-0	9-3	23-0
	to	1-0½	2-2¼	2-7½	4-10½	8-2	17-8	39-0	∞
f 8	from	0-11	1-9	2-1½	3-2	4-3½	6-0	7-6	15-0
	to	1-1	2-3¾	3-0	5-5	10-0	30-0	∞	∞
f 11	from	0-11	1-8	2-0	2-11	3-11	5-4	6-4	11-6
	to	1-1¼	2-5	3-4	6-3	12-6	∞	∞	∞
f 16	from	0-10½	1-7	1-10½	2-7¼	3-4	4-3½	5-0	7-6
	to	1-1¾	2-8½	3-9	8-7	30-0	∞	∞	∞
f 22	from	0-10	1-5½	1-8½	2-4¼	2-11	3-8	4-1¾	5-9
	to	1-2½	3-1½	4-8	13-1	∞	∞	∞	∞

Aperture		Depth of Field for 35 mm. (1⅜ inch) Lenses with Leica Focused on (metres)							
		0.3	0.6	1	1.5	2	3	5	∞
f 1.4	from	—	0.59	0.97	1.42	1.86	2.70	4.22	27.0
	to	—	0.61	1.04	1.59	2.16	3.38	6.14	∞
f 2	from	—	0.58	0.95	1.39	1.18	2.59	3.95	18.8
	to	—	0.62	1.06	1.63	2.24	3.57	6.80	∞
f 2.8	from	0.29	0.57	0.93	1.36	1.74	2.45	3.64	13.3
	to	0.31	0.63	1.08	1.68	2.35	3.87	8.00	∞
f 4	from	0.29	0.56	0.90	1.29	1.65	2.28	3.20	9.40
	to	0.31	0.64	1.12	1.78	2.54	4.40	10.4	∞
f 5.6	from	0.29	0.55	0.87	1.23	1.55	2.08	2.88	6.80
	to	0.31	0.66	1.17	1.92	2.83	5.36	18.9	∞
f 8	from	0.28	0.53	0.83	1.14	1.41	1.83	2.42	4.70
	to	0.32	0.69	1.27	2.20	3.48	8.30	∞	∞
f 11	from	0.28	0.51	0.77	1.04	1.26	1.59	2.02	3.40
	to	0.33	0.73	1.42	2.79	4.85	25.4	∞	∞
f 16	from	0.27	0.48	0.70	0.91	1.07	1.30	1.58	2.30
	to	0.33	0.81	1.77	4.35	15.3	∞	∞	∞
f 22	from	0.25	0.44	0.63	0.80	0.92	1.09	1.27	1.70
	to	0.36	0.93	2.43	12.8	∞	∞	∞	∞

Depth values in feet and inches (*top table*) and in metres (*bottom table*) for the 35 mm. (1⅜ inch) Summaron, Summicron, Summilux, Elmarit R and Elmar wide-angle lenses (see also pp. 464–465). The closest distances apply to the 35 mm. Elmarit R of the Leicaflex only.

DEPTH OF FIELD

Aperture		Depth of Field for 65 mm. (2½ inch) Elmar Lens with Leica Focused on (feet and inches)							
		3½	5	7	10	15	25	100	∞
*f*3.5	from	3–4¾	4–9½	6–7½	9–3	13–5	21–0	55–0	120
	to	3–7¼	5–2¾	7–5	11–0	17–6	32–6	60–0	∞
*f*4	from	3–4½	4–9	6–7	9–1	13–0	20–0	50–0	100
	to	3–7½	5–3	7–6	11–2	17–8	33–4	∞	∞
*f*5.6	from	3–4	4–8	6–5	8–9	12–3	18–5	41–0	70–0
	to	3–8	5–4½	7–9	11–8	19–0	39–0	∞	∞
*f*8	from	3–2½	4–6½	6–2	8–4	11–6	16–8	33–4	50–0
	to	3–10	5–6	8–2	12–6	21–6	50–0	∞	∞
*f*11	from	3–1	4–4½	5–10	7–9	10–6	14–6	26–0	35–0
	to	3–11	5–10	8–8	14–0	26–4	87–6	∞	∞
*f*16	from	3–0	4–2	5–6	7–2	9–4	12–6	20–0	25–0
	to	4–1	6–3	9–9	16–9	37–6	∞	∞	∞
*f*22	from	2–11	3–11	5–1	6–5	8–3	10–6	15–3	18–0
	to	4–4	6–11	11–5	22–6	90–0	∞	∞	∞

Aperture		Depth of Field for 65 mm. (2½ inch) Elmar Lens with Leica Focused on (metres)							
		1	1.5	2	3	5	10	20	∞
*f*3.5	from	0.98	1.43	1.88	2.75	4.40	7.85	13.0	36.0
	to	1.03	1.58	2.31	3.30	5.80	13.7	45.0	∞
*f*4	from	0.98	1.42	1.87	2.72	4.32	7.60	12.3	32.0
	to	1.04	1.59	2.15	3.33	5.91	15.6	53.2	∞
*f*5.6	from	0.96	1.41	1.83	2.64	4.05	6.80	10.5	22.0
	to	1.05	1.61	2.20	3.46	6.60	21.0	22.0	∞
*f*8	from	0.94	1.37	1.78	2.53	3.80	6.15	8.81	16.0
	to	1.07	1.65	2.29	3.70	7.28	26.7	∞	∞
*f*11	from	0.92	1.31	1.69	2.30	3.40	5.20	7.10	11.0
	to	1.10	1.74	2.47	4.13	9.40	11.0	∞	∞
*f*16	from	0.89	1.26	1.60	2.18	3.08	4.44	5.70	8.0
	to	1.14	1.85	2.66	4.80	13.3	∞	∞	∞
*f*22	from	0.85	1.19	1.48	1.97	2.67	3.63	4.44	5.7
	to	1.21	2.04	3.08	6.34	40.7	∞	∞	∞

Depth values in feet and inches (*top table*) and in metres (*bottom table*) for the 65 mm. (2½ inch) Elmar *f*3.5 lens in the Visoflex II and III reflex housing. These tables are intended mainly as a guide to the depth to be expected, since neither the 65 mm. Elmar nor the No. 16464 focusing mount carry any sort of distance scale. At close-up distances use the table on p. 488 for the appropriate scale of reproduction.

Aperture		Depth of Field for 85 and 90 mm. (3⅜ and 3½ inch) Lenses with Leica Focused on (feet and inches)						
		3½	4	5	6	8	10	12
f1.5	from	3–5¾	3–11½	4–11¼	5–11¼	7–10½	9–9½	11–9
	to	3–6¼	4–0¼	5–0¾	6–0¾	8–1½	10–2½	12–3
f2	from	3–5¾	3–11½	4–11	5–11	7–10	9–9	11–8
	to	3–6½	4–0½	5–0½	6–1	8–2	10–3	12–4
f2.8	from	3–5½	3–11½	4–10¾	5–10½	7–9	9–8	11–7
	to	3–6½	4–0¾	5–1½	6–1½	8–3	10–5	12–6
f4	from	3–5¼	3–11	4–10½	5–10	7–8	9–6	11–5
	to	3–6¾	4–1	5–2	6–2½	8–4½	10–7	12–9
f5.6	from	3–5	3–10¾	4–10	5–9½	7–7	9–4	11–2
	to	3–7	4–1¼	5–2¼	6–3	8–6	10–9	13–0
f8	from	3–4½	3–10¼	4–9½	5–8	7–6	9–1	10–9
	to	3–7½	4–2	5–3	6–5	8–8	11–2	13–6
f11	from	3–4	3–9½	4–8	5–7	7–2	8–9	10–3
	to	3–8	4–3	5–4½	6–6	9–0	11–8	14–3
f16	from	3–2½	3–8½	4–6½	5–4	6–11	8–4	9–8
	to	3–10	4–4	5–6	6–10	9–6	12–6	15–9
f22	from	3–1	3–7	4–4½	5–1½	6–6	7–9	8–11
	to	3–10½	4–6	5–10	7–3	10–0	14–0	18–3
f32	from	3–0	3–5½	4–2	4–10	6–1	7–2	8–1
	to	4–1	4–9	6–3	7–11	11–9	16–9	23–0

Aperture		Depth of Field for 85 and 90 mm. (3⅜ and 3½ inch) Lenses with Leica Focused on (feet and inches)						
		15	20	30	50	100	300	∞
f1.5	from	14–7	19–3	28–5	45–8	84–0	190	520
	to	15–5	20–10	32–0	55–6	124	710	∞
f2	from	14–6	19–0	27–10	44–6	80–0	171	400
	to	15–6	21–0	32–5	57–0	133	1200	∞
f2.8	from	14–3	18–8	27–2	43–0	73–6	145	280
	to	5–10	21–6	33–6	60–0	160	∞	∞
f4	from	14–0	18–3	26–1	40–0	66–8	120	200
	to	16–3	22–2	35–4	66–8	200	∞	∞
f5.6	from	13–9	17–9	24–9	37–0	58–0	95–6	140
	to	16–9	23–0	38–0	78–0	350	∞	∞
f8	from	13–0	16–8	23–0	33–4	50–0	75–0	100
	to	17–8	25–0	42–10	100	∞	∞	∞
f11	from	12–3	15–6	21–0	38–8	41–0	56–9	70–0
	to	19–0	28–6	52–6	162	∞	∞	∞
f16	from	11–6	14–3	18–9	25–0	33–4	43–0	50–0
	to	21–6	33–6	75–0	∞	∞	∞	∞
f22	from	10–6	12–9	16–2	20–7	26–0	31–5	35–0
	to	26–4	46–6	46–6	210	∞	∞	∞
f32	from	9–4	11–0	13–7	16–8	20–0	23–1	25–0
	to	37–6	100	∞	∞	∞	∞	∞

Depth values in feet and inches for the 85 mm. (3⅜ inch) Summarex f1.5 and the 90 mm. long-focus lenses (see also pp. 464–465).

For nearer distances with the 90 mm. Elmarit R of the Leicaflex use the close-up depth of field table on p. 488 according to the scale of reproduction obtained from the table on p. 492.

The depth of field for the now obsolete 73 mm. (2⅞ inch) Hektor f1.9 is somewhat greater. With any aperture on this lens therefore use the next higher stop values given in this and the opposite tables. Thus at f4.5 the depth of field with the 73 mm. Hektor corresponds to the figures given here for f5.6.

Aperture		Depth of Field for 85 and 90 mm. (3⅜ and 3½ inch) Lenses with Leica Focused on (metres)							
		1	1.25	1.5	1.75	2	2.5	3	4
*f*1.5	from	0.99	1.24	1.49	1.73	1.98	2.46	2.95	3.92
	to	1.01	1.26	1.51	1.77	2.02	2.54	3.06	4.10
*f*2	from	0.99	1.24	1.48	1.73	1.97	2.45	2.93	3.90
	to	1.01	1.26	1.52	1.77	2.03	2.55	3.08	4.12
*f*2.8	from	9.98	1.23	1.47	1.72	1.95	2.43	2.90	3.85
	to	1.02	1.27	1.53	1.78	2.05	2.57	3.11	4.20
*f*4	from	0.98	1.23	1.46	1.71	1.93	2.40	2.86	3.75
	to	1.02	1.28	1.54	1.80	2.07	2.61	3.16	4.30
*f*5.6	from	0.98	1.22	1.45	1.69	1.90	2.36	2.80	3.62
	to	1.03	1.29	1.56	1.83	2.11	2.65	3.23	4.45
*f*8	from	0.97	1.20	1.43	1.66	1.87	2.31	2.72	3.50
	to	1.04	1.31	1.58	1.86	2.14	2.73	3.31	4.60
*f*11	from	0.96	1.18	1.41	1.63	1.83	2.24	2.64	3.35
	to	1.05	1.33	1.61	1.91	2.20	2.83	3.46	4.90
*f*16	from	0.94	1.15	1.36	1.57	1.76	2.15	2.50	3.20
	to	1.07	1.36	1.67	1.98	2.31	3.00	3.75	5.50
*f*22	from	0.92	1.12	1.31	1.51	1.69	2.04	2.36	2.95
	to	1.10	1.41	1.74	2.08	2.47	3.25	4.13	6.50
*f*32	from	0.88	1.07	1.25	1.42	1.58	1.88	2.14	2.61
	to	1.15	1.50	1.88	2.28	2.73	3.80	5.00	8.60

Aperture		Depth of Field for 85 and 90 mm. (3⅜ and 3½ inch) Lenses with Leica Focused on (metres)							
		5	7	10	15	20	50	100	∞
*f*1.5	from	4.88	6.70	9.40	13.7	17.8	38.0	61.5	160
	to	5.13	7.30	10.7	16.5	22.8	72.5	267	∞
*f*2	from	4.80	6.63	9.20	13.3	17.1	35.3	54.6	120
	to	5.20	7.40	10.9	17.2	24.0	85.5	600	∞
*f*2.8	from	4.72	6.50	8.93	12.7	16.1	31.6	46.2	86.0
	to	5.29	7.60	11.4	18.4	25.9	119	∞	∞
*f*4	from	4.60	6.30	8.60	12.0	15.0	27.2	37.5	60.0
	to	5.46	7.90	12.0	20.0	30.0	300	∞	∞
*f*5.6	from	4.46	6.05	8.20	11.1	13.7	23.2	30.1	43.0
	to	5.65	8.30	13.2	23.0	37.3	∞	∞	∞
*f*8	from	4.30	5.60	7.50	10.0	12.0	18.8	23.1	30.0
	to	6.00	9.10	15.0	30.0	60.0	∞	∞	∞
*f*11	from	4.05	5.25	6.80	8.75	10.5	15.3	18.1	22.0
	to	6.60	10.5	21.0	47.0	220	∞	∞	∞
*f*16	from	3.80	4.80	6.00	7.50	8.56	11.5	13.1	15.0
	to	7.50	13.1	30.0	∞	∞	∞	∞	∞
*f*22	from	3.40	4.28	5.20	6.34	7.10	9.00	9.90	11.0
	to	9.40	19.3	110	∞	∞	∞	∞	∞
*f*32	from	3.00	3.60	4.30	5.00	5.45	6.50	6.97	7.50
	to	30.0	105	∞	∞	∞	∞	∞	∞

Depth values in metres for the 85 mm. (3⅜ inch) Summarex *f*1.5 and the 90 mm. long-focus lenses (see also pp. 464–465).

The depth of field for the now obsolete 105 mm. (4⅛ inch) Elmar *f*6.3 is somewhat smaller. As, however, that lens is calibrated with a Continental aperture scale, the figures here already indicate less depth than the corresponding stop values on the 105 mm. Elmar (p. 111). This difference approximately covers the loss of depth due to the slightly longer focal length.

Aperture		Depth of Field for 125 mm. (5 inch) Hektor Lens with Leica Focused on (feet and inches)						
		4	5	6	7	8	10	12
f2.5	from	3–11¾	4–11¾	5–11¾	6–11¼	7–11	9–10	11–9¼
	to	4–0¼	5–0¼	6–0¼	7–0¾	8–1¼	10–2	12–2½
f2.8	from	3–11¾	4–11¾	5–11¾	6–11	7–10¾	9–9¾	11–9
	to	4–0½	5–0½	6–0½	7–1	8–1½	10–2¼	12–3
f4	from	3–11½	4–11¼	5–11	6–10½	7–10	9–9	11–8
	to	4–0¾	5–0¾	6–1	7–1½	8–2	10–3	12–4
f5.6	from	3–11¼	4–10¾	5–10½	6–10	7–9	9–8	11–7
	to	4–0¾	5–1½	6–1½	7–2½	8–3	10–5	12–6
f8	from	3–11	4–10½	5–10	6–9	7–8	9–6	11–5
	to	4–1	5–2	6–2½	7–3½	8–4½	10–7	12–9
f11	from	3–10¾	4–10	5–9½	6–7	7–7	9–4	11–2
	to	4–1½	5–2¼	6–3	7–5½	8–6	10–9	13–0
f16	from	3–10	4–9½	5–8	6–6	7–6	9–1	10–9
	to	4–2	5–3	6–5	7–6½	8–8	11–2	13–6
f22	from	3–9½	4–8	5–7	6–5	⅞–2	8–9	10–3
	to	4–3	5–4½	6–6	7–8	9–0	11–8	14–3

Aperture		Depth of Field for 125 mm. (5 inch) Hektor Lens with Leica Focused on (feet and inches)						
		15	20	30	50	100	300	∞
f2.5	from	14–8	19–4½	28–10	46–5	86–5	204	630
	to	15–4	20–7	31–6	54–3	119	574	∞
f2.8	from	14–7	19–4	28–5	46–0	85–0	195	560
	to	15–5	20–9	31–9	55–0	122	650	∞
f4	from	14–6	19–0	27–10	44–7	80–0	171	400
	to	15–6	21–0	32–5	57–0	133	1200	∞
f5.6	from	14–3	18–8	27–2	43–0	73–6	145	280
	to	15–10	21–6	33–6	60–0	170	∞	∞
f8	from	14–0	18–3	26–1	40–0	66–8	120	200
	to	16–3	22–2	35–4	66–8	200	∞	∞
f11	from	13–9	17–9	24–9	37–0	58–0	95–6	140
	to	16–9	23–0	38–0	58–0	350	∞	∞
f16	from	13–0	16–8	23–0	33–4	50–0	75–0	100
	to	17–8	25–0	42–10	100	∞	∞	∞
f22	from	12–3	15–6	21–0	28–8	41–0	56–9	70–0
	to	19–0	28–6	52–6	162	∞	∞	∞

Depth values in feet and inches for the 125 mm. (5 inch) Hektor f2.5 long-focus lens (see also pp. 464–465).

Aperture		Depth of Field for 125 mm. (5 inch) Hektor Lens with Leica Focused on (metres)							
		1.2	1.3	1.4	1.5	1.75	2	2.5	3
*f*2.5	from	1.19	1.29	1.39	1.49	1.74	1.98	2.47	2.96
	to	1.21	1.31	1.41	1.51	1.76	2.02	2.53	3.05
*f*2.8	from	1.19	1.29	1.39	1.49	1.73	1.98	2.46	2.95
	to	1.21	1.31	1.41	1.51	1.77	2.02	2.54	3.06
*f*4	from	1.19	1.28	1.38	1.48	1.73	1.97	2.45	2.93
	to	1.21	1.32	1.42	1.52	1.77	2.03	2.55	3.08
*f*5.6	from	1.18	1.28	1.38	1.47	1.72	1.95	2.43	2.90
	to	1.22	1.33	1.43	1.53	1.78	2.05	2.57	3.11
*f*8	from	1.18	1.27	1.37	1.46	1.71	1.93	2.40	2.86
	to	1.22	1.33	1.43	1.54	1.80	2.07	2.61	3.16
*f*11	from	1.17	1.26	1.36	1.45	1.69	1.90	2.36	2.80
	to	1.23	1.34	1.45	1.56	1.83	2.11	2.65	3.23
*f*16	from	1.15	1.24	1.34	1.43	1.66	1.87	2.31	2.72
	to	1.25	1.36	1.47	1.58	1.86	2.14	2.73	3.31
*f*22	from	1.14	1.23	1.31	1.41	1.63	1.83	2.24	2.64
	to	1.27	1.38	1.50	1.61	1.91	2.20	2.83	3.46

Aperture		Depth of Field for 125 mm. (5 inch) Hektor Lens with Leica Focused on (metres)							
		4	5	7	10	20	50	100	∞
*f*2.5	from	3.92	4.87	6.74	9.50	18.1	39.6	65.5	190
	to	4.08	5.14	7.25	10.5	22.3	68.0	211	∞
*f*2.8	from	3.91	4.86	6.72	9.44	17.9	38.6	63.0	170
	to	4.10	5.16	7.30	10.6	22.7	70.9	243	∞
*f*4	from	3.90	4.80	6.63	9.20	17.1	35.3	54.6	120
	to	4.12	5.20	7.40	10.9	24.0	85.4	600	∞
*f*5.6	from	3.85	4.72	6.50	8.93	16.1	31.6	46.2	85.0
	to	4.20	5.29	7.60	11.4	25.9	119	∞	∞
*f*8	from	3.75	4.60	6.30	8.60	15.0	27.2	37.5	60.0
	to	4.30	5.46	7.90	12.0	30.0	300	∞	∞
*f*11	from	3.62	4.46	6.05	8.20	13.7	23.2	30.1	43.0
	to	4.45	5.65	8.30	13.2	37.3	∞	∞	∞
*f*16	from	3.50	4.30	5.60	7.50	12.0	18.8	23.1	30.0
	to	4.60	6.00	9.10	15.0	60.0	∞	∞	∞
*f*22	from	3.35	4.05	5.25	6.80	10.4	15.3	18.1	21.5
	to	4.90	6.60	10.5	21.0	220	∞	∞	∞

Depth values in metres for the 125 mm. (5 inch) Hektor *f*2.5 long-focus lens (see also pp. 464–465).

DEPTH OF FIELD

Aperture		*Depth of Field for 135 mm. (5⅜ inch) Lenses with Leica Focused on (feet and inches)*						
		5	6	7	8	10	12	15
2.8	from	4–11½	5–11½	6–11½	7–11	9–10½	11–9½	14–9
	to	5–0½	6–0¾	7–0¾	8–1¼	10–2	12–2¼	15–4
*f*4	from	4–11¼	5–11¼	6–11	7–10½	9–10	11–9	14–6
	to	5–1	6–1	7–1½	8–2	10–3	12–3	15–6
*f*5.6	from	4–11	5–10¾	6–10¼	7–9¾	9–8½	11–7	14–4
	to	5–1	6–1½	7–2	8–2½	10–4	12–5	15–8
*f*8	from	4–10¾	5–10¼	6–9½	7–9	9–6¾	11–5	14–1
	to	5–1½	6–2	7–3	8–3½	10–5	12–8	16–0
*f*11	from	4–10¼	5–9¼	6–8½	7–7¼	9–5	11–2	13–10
	to	5.2	6–2¾	7–4	8–5½	10–8	12–11	16–8
*f*16	from	4–9½	5–8½	6–7½	7–6	9–3	10–11	13–5
	to	5–2¾	6–4	7–5	8–6½	11–0	13–4	17–6
*f*22	from	4–8½	5–7	6–5½	7–4	9–0	10–5	12–8
	to	5–3½	6–6	7–7	8–10	11–6	14–1	18–5
*f*32	from	4–7½	5–5½	6–3	7–1	8–8	10–0	12–3
	to	5–5	6–8	7–11	9–3	12–0	15–0	20–0

Aperture		*Depth of Field for 135 mm. (5⅜ inch) Lenses with Leica Focused on (feet and inches)*						
		20	30	50	100	150	300	∞
*f*2.8	from	19–5	28–11	46–8	87–6	123	220	660
	to	20–6	31–4	54–1	116	195	550	∞
*f*4	from	19–3	28–4	45–6	83–4	115	188	460
	to	20–103	1–11	55–7	125	214	750	∞
*f*5.6	from	18–10	27–6	43–4	76–6	101	157	330
	to	21–2	33–0	58–9	143	270	∞	∞
*f*8	from	18–5	26–6	41–0	69–6	91–0	130	230
	to	21–11	34–5	64–0	177	430	∞	∞
*f*11	from	17–11	25–3	38–0	62–10	77–6	104	160
	to	23–0	37–0	72–6	270	2400	∞	∞
*f*16	from	17–2	24–0	35–0	55–0	66–8	85–9	120
	to	24–0	40–0	90–0	600	∞	∞	∞
*f*22	from	16–0	21–10	30–8	44–6	52–0	63–3	80–0
	to	26–8	48–0	130	∞	∞	∞	∞
*f*32	from	15–0	20–0	27–3	37–6	43–0	50–0	60–0
	to	30–0	60–0	300	∞	∞	∞	∞

Depth values in feet and inches for the 135 mm. (5⅜ inch) long-focus lenses (see also pp. 464–465). The depth of field figures for the maximum aperture *f*4.5 of the discontinued Hektor and Elmar lenses are approximately half-way in the extent of the zone of sharpness between the figures for *f*4 and for *f*5.6.

Aperture		Depth of Field for 135 mm. ($5\frac{5}{8}$ inch) Lenses with Leica Focused on (metres)						
		1.5	1.75	2	2.5	3	4	5
f2.8	from	1.49	1.74	1.98	2.47	2.97	3.94	4.89
	to	1.51	1.76	2.02	2.53	3.04	4.08	5.12
f4	from	1.48	1.73	1.98	2.46	2.94	3.92	4.87
	to	1.52	1.77	2.03	2.54	3.06	4.11	5.16
f5.6	from	1.48	1.72	1.96	2.44	2.91	3.87	4.75
	to	1.53	1.78	2.04	2.56	3.10	4.15	5.25
f8	from	1.47	1.71	1.95	2.42	2.88	3.80	4.66
	to	1.54	1.79	2.06	2.59	3.13	4.20	5.35
f11	from	1.46	1.69	1.93	2.38	2.83	3.70	4.55
	to	1.55	1.82	2.08	2.63	3.19	4.35	5.55
f16	from	1.44	1.67	1.89	2.34	2.78	3.62	4.41
	to	1.57	1.84	2.12	2.68	3.26	4.48	5.76
f22	from	1.42	1.64	1.86	2.28	2.68	3.45	4.20
	to	1.59	1.88	2.16	2.78	3.40	4.75	6.20
f32	from	1.39	1.60	1.81	2.20	2.59	3.30	3.95
	to	1.63	1.93	2.24	2.88	3.57	5.08	6.80

Aperture		Depth of Field for 135 mm. ($5\frac{5}{8}$ inch) Lenses with Leica Focused on (metres)							
		6	8	10	15	20	50	100	∞
f2.8	from	5.82	7.68	9.52	13.9	18.2	40.0	66.7	200
	to	6.19	8.36	10.5	16.3	22.2	66.7	200	∞
f4	from	5.77	7.60	9.38	13.6	17.7	37.5	60.0	150
	to	6.25	8.45	10.7	16.6	23.1	75	300	∞
f5.6	from	5.66	7.40	9.05	13.0	16.7	33.3	50.0	100
	to	6.38	8.70	11.1	17.8	25.0	100	∞	∞
f8	from	5.55	7.24	8.85	12.5	15.8	30.0	42.8	75.0
	to	6.50	8.94	11.6	18.7	27.3	150	∞	∞
f11	from	5.36	6.90	8.35	11.5	14.3	25.0	33.3	50.0
	to	6.80	9.41	12.5	21.4	33.3	∞	∞	∞
f16	from	5.17	6.60	7.90	10.7	13.1	21.4	27.3	37.5
	to	7.15	10.3	13.6	25.0	43.0	∞	∞	∞
f22	from	4.84	6.05	7.25	9.36	11.4	16.7	20.0	25.0
	to	7.90	11.8	16.7	37.5	100	∞	∞	∞
f32	from	4.55	5.60	6.53	8.33	9.90	13.7	15.8	18.8
	to	8.80	13.9	21.4	74.2	∞	∞	∞	∞

Depth values in metres for the 135 mm. ($5\frac{5}{8}$ inch) long-focus lenses (see also pp. 464–465).

Aperture		Depth of Field for 180 mm. (7⅛ inch) Elmarit-R with Leicaflex Focused on (feet and inches)							
		7	10	15	20	30	50	200	∞
f2.8	from	6–11½	9–11	19–9½	19–8	29–3	47–9	170	1100
	to	7–0½	10–1¼	15–2½	20–4¾	30–10	52–4	244	∞
f4	from	6–11¼	9–10½	14–8½	19–6	28–11	47–0	160	800
	to	7–0¾	10–1¾	15–3½	20–6	31–2	53–4	267	∞
f5.6	from	6–11	9–9¾	14–7	19–4	28–5	46–0	147	560
	to	7–1	10–2¼	15–5	20–9	31–9	55–0	310	∞
f8	from	6–10½	9–9	14–6	19–1	27–10	44–7	133	400
	to	7–1½	10–3	15–7	21–0	32–5	57–0	400	∞
f11	from	6–10	9–8	14–3	18–8	27–2	43–0	117	280
	to	7–2½	10–5	15–10	21–6	33–6	60–0	700	∞
f16	from	6–9	9–6	14–0	18–3	26–1	40–1	100	200
	to	7–3½	10–7	16–3	22–2	35–4	66–8	∞	∞
f22	from	6–7	9–4	13–9	17–9	24–9	37–0	82–6	140
	to	7–6	10–9	16–9	23–0	38–0	58–0	∞	∞

Aperture		Depth of Field for 180 mm. (7⅛ inch) Elmarit-R with Leicaflex Focused on (metres)								
		2	2.5	4	6	10	15	20	50	∞
f2.8	from	1.99	2.48	3.95	5.89	9.71	14.4	18.9	43.6	340
	to	2.01	2.52	4.06	6.10	10.3	15.7	21.2	58.6	∞
f4	from	1.99	2.47	3.93	5.86	9.60	14.1	18.5	41.3	240
	to	2.01	2.53	4.08	6.15	10.4	16.0	21.8	63.2	∞
f5.6	from	1.98	2.46	3.91	5.78	9.44	13.8	17.9	38.6	170
	to	2.02	2.54	4.10	6.20	10.6	16.4	22.7	70.9	∞
f8	from	1.97	2.45	3.90	5.72	9.20	13.3	17.1	35.3	120
	to	2.03	2.55	4.12	6.31	10.9	17.2	24.0	85.4	∞
f11	from	1.95	2.43	3.85	5.60	8.93	12.7	16.1	31.6	85
	to	2.05	2.57	4.20	6.46	11.4	18.4	25.9	119	∞
f16	from	1.93	2.40	3.75	5.45	8.60	12.0	15.0	27.2	60
	to	2.07	2.61	4.30	6.67	12.0	20.0	30.0	300	∞
f22	from	1.90	2.36	3.62	5.26	8.20	11.1	13.7	23.2	43
	to	2.11	2.65	4.45	7.00	13.2	23.0	37.3	∞	∞

Depth values in feet and inches (*top*) and in metres (*bottom*) for the 180 mm. (7⅛ inch) Elmarit-R *f*2.8 of the Leicaflex (see also pp. 464–465).

Aperture		Depth of Field for 200 mm. (7⅞ inch) Telyt with Leica Focused on (feet and inches)						
		10	12	15	20	25	30	50
f 4	from	9–11½	11–11½	14–11	19–9	24–4	29–1½	47–7
	to	10–1	12–1	15–2	20–5	25–8	31–0	52–7
f 4.5	from	9–11	11–11	14–10	19–7	24–3	29–0	47–5
	to	10–1	12–1	15–2	20–6	25–9	31–0	52–10
f 5.6	from	9–10½	11–10	14–8	19–5	24–1	28–10	46–8
	to	10–2	12–2	15–4	20–7	25–11	31–2	53–9
f 8	from	9–10	11–9	14–6	19–3	23–10	28–4	45–6
	to	10–3	12–3	15–6	20–10	26–4	31–11	55–7
f 11	from	9–8½	11–7	14–4	18–10	23–2	27–6	43–4
	to	10–4	12–5	15–8	21–2	27–0	33–0	58–9
f 16	from	9–6¾	11–5	14–1	18–5	22–6	26–6	41–0
	to	10–5	12–8	16–0	21–11	28–0	34–5	64–0
f 22	from	9–5	11–2	13–10	17–11	21–7	25–3	38–0
	to	10–8	12–11	16–8	23–0	29–7	37–0	72–6
f 32	from	9–3	10–11	13–5	17–2	20–8	24–0	35–0
	to	11–0	13–4	17–6	24–0	30–9	40–0	90–0

Aperture		Depth of Field for 200 mm. (7⅞ inch) Telyt with Leica Focused on (feet and inches)						
		70	100	150	200	300	500	∞
f 4	from	65–5	91–0	130	167	231	335	1000
	to	75–4	111	176	250	428	1000	∞
f 4.5	from	65–0	90–0	128	164	225	320	900
	to	76–10	112	180	257	450	1120	∞
f 5.6	from	63–9	88–0	124	157	212	295	720
	to	77–9	116	190	277	515	1640	∞
f 8	from	60–4	83–4	115	143	188	250	500
	to	81–5	125	214	333	750	∞	∞
f 11	from	57–9	76–6	101	125	147	200	330
	to	88–10	143	270	508	3300	∞	∞
f 16	from	53–7	69–6	91–0	107	130	187	230
	to	100	177	430	1530	∞	∞	∞
f 22	from	48–8	62–10	77–6	89–0	104	121	160
	to	124	270	2400	∞	∞	∞	∞
f 32	from	44–3	55–0	66–8	75–0	85–9	97–0	120
	to	168	600	∞	∞	∞	∞	∞

Depth values in feet and inches for the 200 mm. (7⅞ inch) Telyt telephoto lens (see also pp. 464–465).

DEPTH OF FIELD

Aperture		Depth of Field for 200 mm. ($7\frac{7}{8}$ inch) Telyt with Leica Focused on (metres)							
		3	4	5	6	8	10	12	15
f4	from	2.98	3.95	4.92	5.89	7.78	9.70	11.6	14.3
	to	3.03	4.05	5.08	6.12	8.21	10.3	12.5	15.7
f4.5	from	2.97	3.94	4.90	5.87	7.77	9.66	11.5	14.2
	to	3.03	4.06	5.08	6.14	8.25	10.4	12.6	15.8
f5.6	from	2.96	3.93	4.87	5.85	7.72	9.56	11.4	14.0
	to	3.04	4.08	5.10	6.18	8.30	10.5	12.7	16.1
f8	from	2.94	3.90	4.83	5.77	7.60	9.38	11.2	13.6
	to	3.06	4.11	5.16	6.25	8.45	10.7	13.1	16.6
f11	from	2.91	3.87	4.76	5.66	7.40	9.05	10.7	13.0
	to	3.10	4.15	5.25	6.38	8.70	11.1	13.6	17.8
f16	from	2.88	3.80	4.66	5.55	7.24	8.85	10.3	12.5
	to	3.13	4.20	5.35	6.50	8.94	11.6	14.3	18.7
f22	from	2.83	3.70	4.55	5.36	6.90	8.35	9.70	11.5
	to	3.19	4.35	5.55	6.80	9.41	12.5	15.8	21.4
f32	from	2.78	3.62	4.41	5.17	6.60	7.90	9.10	10.7
	to	3.26	4.48	5.76	7.15	10.3	13.6	16.6	25.0

Aperture		Depth of Field for 200 mm. ($7\frac{7}{8}$ inch) Telyt with Leica Focused on (metres)							
		20	30	40	50	75	100	200	∞
f4	from	18.8	27.3	35.3	42.9	60.0	75.0	120	300
	to	21.4	33.4	46.2	60.0	100	150	600	∞
f4.5	from	18.6	27.0	34.8	42.2	58.7	72.6	115	270
	to	21.6	33.7	40.0	61.4	104	158	770	∞
f5.6	from	18.4	26.4	33.9	40.8	56.0	68.7	95.3	220
	to	22.0	34.7	49.0	64.7	114	183	2200	∞
f8	from	17.7	25.0	31.6	37.5	50.0	60.0	85.8	150
	to	23.1	37.5	54.5	75.0	150	300	∞	∞
f11	from	16.7	23.1	28.6	33.3	42.8	50.0	66.7	100
	to	25.0	42.8	66.8	100	300	∞	∞	∞
f16	from	15.8	21.4	26.0	30.0	37.5	42.8	54.5	75.0
	to	27.3	50.0	85.5	150	∞	∞	∞	∞
f22	from	14.3	18.8	22.2	25.0	30.0	33.3	40.0	50.0
	to	33.3	75.0	200	∞	∞	∞	∞	∞
f32	from	13.1	16.7	19.4	21.4	25.0	27.3	31.6	37.5
	to	43.0	150	∞	∞	∞	∞	∞	∞

Depth values in metres for the 200 mm. ($7\frac{7}{8}$ inch) Telyt telephoto lens (see also pp. 464–465).

DEPTH OF FIELD

Aperture		Depth of Field for 11 inch (280 mm.) Telyt with Leica Focused on (feet and inches)					
		12	15	20	25	30	50
f4.8	from	11–11½	14–11	19–10	24–8	29–6	48–9
	to	12–1	15–1½	20–3	25–5	30–7	51–7
f5.6	from	11–11	14–10½	19–9	24–7	29–4½	48–5
	to	12–1	15–2	20–4	25–5	30–8	51–9
f8	from	11–11	14–10	19–7	24–3	29–0	47–5
	to	12–1	15–2	20–6	25–9	31–0	52–10
f11	from	11–10	14–8	19–5	24–1	28–10	46–8
	to	12–2	15–4	20–7	25–11	31–2	53–9
f16	from	11–9	14–6	19–3	23–9	28–3	45–2
	to	12–3	15–6	21–0	26–6	32–1	56–0
f22	from	11–7	14–4	18–10	23–3	27–7	43–6
	to	12–5	15–8	21–2	27–0	33–0	58–6

Aperture		Depth of Field for 11 inch (280 mm.) Telyt with Leica Focused on (feet and inches)						
		70	100	150	200	300	500	∞
f4.8	from	67–3	94–3	138	180	255	390	1610
	to	72–11	106	164	226	370	700	∞
f5.6	from	66–9	93–5	135	175	245	370	1380
	to	73–9	108	170	235	395	770	∞
f8	from	65–3	90–6	129	166	228	330	960
	to	76–0	111	178	253	438	1000	∞
f11	from	63–9	88–0	123	155	210	280	700
	to	78–0	118	200	290	530	1750	∞
f16	from	60–1	83–0	112	140	180	240	480
	to	82–0	130	220	343	800	∞	∞
f22	from	57–9	76–7	103	130	150	220	350
	to	88–9	142	265	465	2000	∞	∞

Depth values in feet and inches for the 11 inch (280 mm.) Telyt *f*4.8 telephoto lens (see also pp. 464–465).

Aperture		Depth of Field for 280 mm. (11 inch) Telyt with Leica Focused on (metres)						
		4	5	6	8	10	12	15
*f*4.8	*from*	3.96	4.94	5.91	7.88	9.79	11.7	14.4
	to	4.04	5.07	6.10	8.15	10.3	12.3	15.5
*f*5.6	*from*	3.96	4.93	5.90	7.85	9.75	11.6	14.4
	to	4.04	5.07	6.11	8.18	10.4	12.3	15.6
*f*8	*from*	3.95	4.92	5.89	7.79	9.70	11.6	14.3
	to	4.05	5.08	6.12	8.21	10.5	12.4	15.7
*f*11	*from*	3.93	4·87	5.85	7.72	9.56	11.4	14.0
	to	4.08	5.10	6.16	8.28	10.5	12.6	16.0
*f*16	*from*	3.90	4.83	5.77	7.60	9.38	11.2	13.6
	to	4.11	5.16	6.21	8.40	10.7	13.0	16.6
*f*22	*from*	3.87	4.76	5.66	7.40	9.05	10.8	13.0
	to	4.15	5.25	6.38	8.70	11.0	13.6	17.8

Aperture		Depth of Field for 280 mm. (11 inch) Telyt with Leica Focused on (metres)							
		20	30	40	50	75	100	200	∞
*f*4.8	*from*	19.3	28.4	37.0	45.5	65.0	83.2	142	490
	to	20.9	32.2	43.0	55.8	88.5	126	331	∞
*f*5.6	*from*	19.1	27.9	36.3	44.0	63.5	80.5	136	420
	to	21.1	32.5	44.0	57.0	92.0	131	380	∞
*f*8	*from*	18.8	27.3	35.3	42.8	59.8	74.6	119	294
	to	21.5	33.5	46.3	60.9	103	156	630	∞
*f*11	*from*	18.4	26.4	33.9	40.7	55.6	68.4	104	214
	to	22.0	34.7	49.5	65.2	116	118	3000	∞
*f*16	*from*	17.7	25.0	31.6	37.4	49.8	59.6	84.8	147
	to	23.1	37.7	54.7	76.1	153	315	∞	∞
*f*22	*from*	16.8	23.2	28.8	34.0	43.2	51.7	70.0	107
	to	24.5	42.2	66.7	93.6	250	1530	∞	∞

Depth values in metres for the 280 mm. (11 inch) Telyt *f*4.8 telephoto lens. **See also pp. 464–465.**

DEPTH OF FIELD

Depth values in feet and inches for the 400 mm. ($15\frac{3}{4}$ inch) Telyt *f*5 and *f*5.6 telephoto lenses. The depths of field for the 560 mm. Telyt *f*5.6 are approximately the same as for the 400 mm. lens at two stops larger (for example the 560 mm. lens at *f*11 has the same depth zones as the 400 mm. lens at *f*5.6.). However, no figures are given here since this lens is only used with the Televit rapid focusing mount which has no distance scale (see also pp. 464–465).

Aperture		*Depth of Field for 400 mm. ($15\frac{3}{4}$ inch) Telyt with Leica Focused on (feet and inches)*						
		25	30	40	50	70	60	80
*f*5	from	24–9½	29–9	39–5	49–2	58–9	68–6	77–10
	to	25–2½	30–3½	40–6	50–10	61–3	71–9	82–3
*f*5.6	from	24–9¼	29–8½	39–4	49–1	58–8	68–4	77–8
	to	25–2¾	30–4	40–7	50–11	61–4	71–10	82–5
*f*8	from	24–8½	29–7	39–2	48–9	58–3	67–7	76–9
	to	25–4	30–5½	40–10	51–4	61–10	72–6	83–4
*f*11	from	24–7	29–4½	39–0	48–5	57–7	66–9	75–11
	to	25–5	30–7½	41–2	51–9	62–6	73–6	84–10
*f*16	from	24–4	29–1½	38–5	47–7	56–7	65–5	74–0
	to	25–8	31–0	41–8	52–7	63–10	75–4	87–0
*f*22	from	24–2½	28–8	37–10	46–8	55–4	63–9	71–11
	to	25–11	31–4	42–3	53–9	65–9	77–9	90–0
*f*32	from	23–10	28–4	37–0	45–6	53–7	60–4	68–10
	to	26–4	32–0	43–6	55–7	68–3	81–5	95–0

Aperture		*Depth of Field for 400 mm. ($15\frac{3}{4}$ inch) Telyt with Leica Focused on (feet and inches)*						
		100	150	200	300	500	1000	∞
*f*5	from	96–10	143	188	273	428	750	3000
	to	104	158	215	334	600	1500	∞
*f*5.6	from	96–8	142	187	262	425	730	2900
	to	104	159	216	335	605	1520	∞
*f*8	from	95–1	140	182	261	400	670	2000
	to	105	162	222	353	667	2000	∞
*f*11	from	93–5	136	176	248	371	590	1440
	to	107	167	232	389	765	3300	∞
*f*16	from	91–0	130	167	231	333	500	1000
	to	111	176	250	428	1000	∞	∞
*f*22	from	88–0	124	157	212	295	420	720
	to	116	190	277	515	1640	∞	∞
*f*32	from	83–4	115	143	188	250	333	500
	to	125	214	333	750	∞	∞	∞

Aperture		Depth of Field for 400 mm. (15¾ inch) Telyt with Leica Focused on (metres)						
		8	10	12	15	20	25	30
*f*5	from	7.94	9.90	11.9	14.8	19.6	24.4	29.1
	to	8.06	10.1	12.1	15.2	20.4	25.8	31.0
*f*5.6	from	7.93	9.88	11.9	14.7	19.6	24.3	29.0
	to	8.07	10.1	12.2	15.3	20.5	25.9	31.1
*f*8	from	7.90	9.84	11.8	14.6	19.4	24.0	28.6
	to	8.11	10.2	12.2	15.4	20.7	26.1	31.6
*f*11	from	7.86	9.77	11.7	14.5	19.2	23.6	28.1
	to	8.16	10.3	12.3	15.5	21.0	26.5	32.2
*f*16	from	7.78	9.70	11.6	14.3	18.8	23.1	27.3
	to	8.21	10.4	12.5	15.8	21.4	27.3	33.4
*f*22	from	7.72	9.56	11.4	14.0	18.4	22.5	26.4
	to	8.30	10.5	12.7	16.1	22.0	28.2	34.7
*f*32	from	7.60	9.38	11.2	13.6	17.7	21.4	25.0
	to	8.45	10.7	13.1	16.6	23.1	30.	37.5

Aperture		Depth of Field for 400 mm. (15¾ inch) Telyt with Leica Focused on (metres)						
		40	50	75	100	200	300	∞
*f*5	from	38.4	47.5	69.5	90.5	166	231	960
	to	41.7	52.8	81.4	111	252	437	∞
*f*5.6	from	38.3	47.2	69.0	90.0	163	223	880
	to	42.0	53.1	82.0	113	258	455	∞
*f*8	from	37.5	46.2	66.7	85.7	150	200	600
	to	42.8	54.5	85.6	120	300	600	∞
*f*11	from	36.7	45.0	64.2	81.5	137	179	440
	to	44.0	56.5	90.5	129	367	940	∞
*f*16	from	35.3	42.9	60.0	75.0	120	150	300
	to	46.2	60.0	100	150	600	∞	∞
*f*22	from	33.9	40.8	56.0	68.7	95.3	127	220
	to	49.0	64.7	114	183	2200	∞	∞
*f*32	from	31.6	37.5	50.0	60.0	85.8	100	150
	to	54.5	75.0	150	300	∞	∞	∞

Depth values in metres for the 400 mm. (15¾ inch) Telyt *f*5 and *f*5.6 telephoto lenses (see also pp. 464–465).

FILTER FACTORS

The filter factors listed are average values for daylight (D) and for artificial light (A), e.g. Photoflood or tungsten lamps.

Leica Filter	Films and Factors			
	Pan		Red Pan	
	D	A	D	A
Yellow No. 0	1½	1½	1½	1½
Yellow No. 1	2	1½	2	1½
Yellow No. 2	2½	2	2	1½
Yellow-green	2½	2½	3	3
Orange	5	4	4	3
Light red	8	5	6	4
Medium red	15	10	12	8
Light blue	—	1½	—	1½
Ultra-violet	1	—	1	—
Polarizing	3	3	3	3

FILTERS COMPARED

Film makers often quote filter factors for their products with Wratten or Ilford filters. This comparison shows the nearest equivalent Leica filters, and also indicates what filter to use when the corresponding Leica filter is not available.

Leica Filter	Equivalent Filters		
	Ilford	Gevaert	Wratten
Yellow No. 0	Alpha (104)	1	No. 3
Yellow No. 1	Iso (105)	3	K2 (No. 8)
Yellow No. 2	Delta (109)	5	K3 (No. 9)
Yellow-green	Beta (401)	—	X1 (No. 11)
Orange	Micro 5 (202)	R578	G (No. 15)
Light red	No. 204	R599	A (No. 25)
Medium red	No. 205	R619	F (No. 29)
Ultra-violet	Q (805)	R400	No. 1A, 2B

FILTER FITTINGS

Most Leica lenses other than the high-aperture and telephoto types will take the standard 39 mm. screw-in filters. These filters also fit lenses normally designed to take A36 push-on filters, if an adapter ring No. 13154 is used. Suitable screw-in filters are provided for the larger lenses.

In addition a number of now obsolete filter mounts are listed (mainly screw-in types) which were available for standard lenses.

The current filter mounts are also obtainable empty, for insertion of any special filter.

The Series VI, VII and VIII fittings consist of screw-in rings which take loose filters of 1⅝ in, 2 in and 2½ in diameter respectively; with some lenses these filters are held in place in front of the lens by the lens hood.

Filter Fitting	Suitable for
18.5 mm. screw-in*	35 mm. Elmar, 50 mm. Elmar *f*3.5†
34 mm. screw-in*	28 mm. Hektor,† 50 mm. Summar, 90 mm. Elmar,† 135 mm. Hektor† and Elmar†
36 mm. screw-in*	50 mm. Summitar and Elmar *f*3.5, 35 mm. Elmar
39 mm. screw-in (E39)	21 mm. Super Angulon *f*4, 35 mm. Summaron (current versions) and Summicron, 50 mm. Elmar (current versions) and Summicron, 90 mm. Elmar (current versions) Tele-Elmarit and Elmarit, 135 mm. Tele-Elmar, also later Elmar and Hektor.
40.5 mm. screw-in*	73 mm. Hektor
41 mm. screw-in (E41)	50 mm. Summarit, 35 mm. Summilux, 65 mm. Elmar
43 mm. screw-in (E43)	50 mm. Summilux, Visoflex filter turret
48 mm. screw-in (E48)	21 mm. Super Angulon *f*3.4, 28 mm. Elmarit *f*2.8, 90 mm. Summicron, 200 mm. Telyt *f*4.5
58 mm. screw-in (E58)	85 mm. Summarex, 125 mm. Hektor, 200 mm. Telyt *f*4, 280 mm. Telyt
85 mm. screw-in (E85)	400 mm. Telyt
36 mm. slip-on with fixing screw (A36)	28 mm. Summaron and Hektor, 35 mm. Summaron† and Elmar, 50 mm. Elmar *f*3.5† and Summar, 90 mm.† and 105 mm. Elmar, 135 mm. Hektor† and Elmar *f*4.5
42 mm. slip-on*	73 mm. Hektor
51 mm. slip-on*	90 mm. Thambar 200 mm. Telyt *f* 4.5
Bayonet*	50 mm. Xenon
Series VI	35 mm. Elmarit-R, 50 mm. Summicron-R
Series VII	21 mm. Super Angulon *f*3.5 and 28 mm. Elmarit (in lens hood in both cases); 90 mm. Elmarit-R, 135 mm. Elmarit and Elmarit-R; 280-560 mm. Telyt in Televit.
Series VIII	21 mm. Super Angulon-R (old), 50 mm. Noctilux (in lens hood), 180 mm. Elmarit-R

*Discontinued †Old screw-mounted types

CHOICE OF FILTERS

This table summarizes the applications and effects of the Leica filters as well as of a few special kinds of filters.

Filter	*Applications*	*Effect*
Yellow No. 0, 1	Landscapes	Progressively darkens blue, e.g., skies
Yellow No. 2	Landscapes, contrast filter, e.g., for copying originals on yellow paper	Darkens blue skies lightens yellow, orange
Deep yellow	Contrast filter	Darkens blue, green lightens yellow, orange
Green	Landscapes, outdoor portraits, correct tone reproduction in copying coloured originals	Darkens blue, also skin tones, lightens green
Deep green	Contrast filter	Darkens blue, red, orange; lightens green
Orange	Architecture, landscapes, distant views, contrast filter	Strongly darkens blue (e.g., skies), also green; lightens orange and red, penetrates haze
Light red	Architecture, dramatic and distant views, contrast filter	Lightens red; darkens green, blue; penetrates haze
Medium red	Distant view, infra-red shots	Lightens red; darkens all other colours
Dark red	Infra-red shots only	Darkens all visible colours
Blue	Contrast filter	Lightens blue; darkens green, yellow, red
Ultra-violet	Alpine views	Cuts out U.V. rays

CONTRAST FILTERS

Special filters in addition to those in the Leica range may be needed for copying or photomicrography. Many other filters are also made for these purposes.

Colour	*Filter*		*Films and Factors*			
	Ilford	*Wratten*	*Pan*		*Red Pan*	
			D	*A*	*D*	*A*
Deep green	No. 404	No. 58	7	5	15	16
	No. 408	No. 61	—	15-25	—	30-40
Deep blue	No. 304	No. 47B	—	14	7	18
	No. 306	—	—	60-80	—	150
Deep yellow	No. 110	No. 12	3	2½	3	2½

FILTERS FOR COLOUR

Colour films may need special filters when used with a light source for which they are not balanced (e.g., daylight type film in Photoflood lighting).

For the best results the maker's recommended filters should be used for each film and light combination. This table lists similar conversion filters of different makes; these are, however, only approximate equivalents, and nominally similar film-filter combinations will not necessarily yield exactly the same colour rendering.

Film Used with	*Filter*			*Factor*
	Gevaert	*Ilford*	*Wratten*	
Daylight Reversal Films				
Photofloods	CTB 8 + CTB 2	351	80B	3½
Studio lamps	CTB 12	—	80A	4
Clear flash	CTB 8	351	80C	2
Clear flash (Zirconium bulbs, e.g., AG-I, PF-I)	CTB 4 + CTB 2	—	80D	1¼
Electronic flash (needed with some films for warmer rendering)	CTO 2	171	81A	1
Type A Reversal Films				
Daylight	CTO 8 + CTO2	161	85	1½
Clear flash	CTO 2	171	81C	1
Studio lamps	CTB 2	362	82A	1½
Household lamps	CTB 4	—	82C	2
Tungsten Reversal Films				
Daylight	CTO 12	161	85B	1½
Clear flash	CTO 4	—	81D or 81C	1¼
Photofloods	CTO 2	—	81A	1

FLASH EXPOSURE

This table gives the guide numbers or flash factors for exposure with various types of flash.

The guide numbers apply to black-and-white film, and to negative colour film. Electronic flash figures also apply to daylight reversal colour film.

For films of intermediate speed use intermediate guide numbers. The figures assume the use of an efficient reflector, and average subjects in medium-sized, light-walled rooms.

To find the exposure required for any flash bulb, select the guide number for the shutter speed and film speed to be used. Divide the guide number by the flash-subject distance to get the best aperture, or by the aperture to get the best distance.

Example: We may want to use a PF 24 bulb at 1/125 second with 64 A.S.A. film, and take a picture with the flash 9 feet from the subject. The guide number is 70, the aperture therefore 70/9 or approximately *f*8.

Remember to set the synchronizing dial to the appropriate figure where applicable on type f models (see p. 486).

Flash Bulb	*Shutter Speed*	*Film Speed*							
	A.S.A.	25	40	64	100	160	250	400	640
	D.I.N.	15	17	19	21	23	25	27	29
Focal Plane Bulbs	Philips PF 24, G.E. FP 6, Sylvania No. 26								
	To 1/60	62	78	100	125	155	200	250	310
	1/125	44	55	70	87	110	140	175	220
	1/250	33	40	55	66	80	100	130	160
	1/500	22	27	35	44	55	70	90	110
	1/1000	15	19	25	33	40	50	65	80
	Philips PF 45, G.E. FP 31, Sylvania No. 2A								
	To 1/60	87	110	140	180	220	280	360	440
	1/125	62	78	100	125	155	200	255	310
	1/250	44	55	70	87	100	140	170	200
	1/500	33	40	50	66	80	100	130	160
	1/1000	22	27	35	44	55	70	90	110
Class S Bulbs	Philips PF 100, G.E. No. 50, Sylvania No. 3, Osram S2								
	To 1/30	230	290	360	450	580	720	900	1160
	1/60*	160	200	250	320	400	500	640	800
	1/125*	115	145	180	225	290	360	450	580
	1/250*	80	100	125	160	200	250	320	400
	1/500*	57	72	90	112	145	180	225	290
Class M Bulbs	Philips PF 1, G.E.C., G.E., Mazda No 1, Sylvania Bantam 8								
	To 1/30	65	80	100	130	160	200	260	320
	G.E. Mazda G.E.C. etc. AG-1								
	To 1/30	60	75	95	120	150	190	240	300
	Philips PF 5, G.E.C., G.E., Mazda No. 5, M3, M5, Sylvania 25								
	To 1/30	105	130	160	200	260	320	400	520
	1/60	75	95	120	150	180	240	300	360
	1/125	50	66	80	100	130	160	200	260
	1/250	36	45	60	75	90	120	150	180
	Philips PF 38, G.E. No. 11, Sylvania 40								
	To 1/30	125	160	200	250	320	400	500	640
	1/60	85	100	125	170	200	250	350	400
	1/125	62	80	100	125	160	200	250	320
	2/250	42	50	62	85	100	125	170	200
	1/500	30	38	45	60	75	90	120	150
	Philips PF 60, G.E. No. 22, Sylvania No. 2								
	To 1/30	160	200	250	320	400	500	640	800
	1/60	105	130	160	200	250	320	400	500
	1/125	80	100	125	160	200	250	320	400
	1/250	50	65	80	100	125	160	200	250
	1/500	35	45	55	70	90	110	140	180
	1/1000	25	32	40	50	65	80	100	130
Class X Flash (Electronic)									
30–40 Joules	To 1/50**	35	45	55	70	90	110	140	180
50–60 Joules	To 1/50**	50	64	80	100	125	160	200	250
100–135 Joules	To 1/50**	70	90	110	140	180	220	280	360
200–250 Joules	To 1/50**	110	140	180	225	280	360	450	560

*On type f and syn models these speeds can only be used with the synchronizing dial set to the appropriate figure (p. 470).

**To 1/100 second on Leicaflex. Use the electronic flash outlet on Leicaflex and M models; on the Leica IIIg set the dial to one of the arrow marks.

Figures for G.E.C., G.E., and Mazda bulbs also apply to Westinghouse, Solar Electric, Amplex, West, and other bulbs of similar type numbers. The Osram bulbs listed are those of German manufacture.

Guide numbers for 1/30 second also apply to 1/25 second.
Guide numbers for 1/60 second also apply to 1/50 second.
Guide numbers for 1/125 second also apply to 1/100 second.

COLOUR FLASH

With daylight reversal colour film we have to use suitable coated blue bulbs (with suffix /97 or B). Blue bulbs or electronic flash can also be used for fill-in lighting with daylight type colour films (negative and reversal) used in daylight.

The table gives guide numbers for daylight type colour film with various types of blue bulbs and electronic flash.

The synchronization characteristics of colour bulbs are the same as for the clear bulbs from which they are derived. Thus the No. 22B bulb needs the same synchronizing dial settings as the No. 22, and the PF 100/97 the same as the PF 100 (see p. 485 and below).

Shutter Speed (Sec.)	*A.S.A.* / *D.I.N.*	25 / 15	32 / 16	40 / 17	50 / 18	64 / 19	100 / 21	160 / 23	200 / 24
Philips PF 24/97									
To 1/60		39	44	50	56	62	78	100	110
1/125		28	31	35	39	44	56	70	78
1/250		19	22	25	28	32	39	50	56
1/500		14	16	17	19	22	28	35	39
Philips PF 45/97									
To 1/60		50	56	64	70	78	100	125	140
1/125		35	39	45	50	56	70	90	100
1/250		25	28	32	35	39	50	62	70
1/500		18	20	23	25	28	35	45	50
1/1000		12	14	16	17	19	25	32	35
Philips PF 100/97, G.E. No. 50B, Sylvania No. 3B									
To 1/30		180	200	220	250	280	360	440	500
1/60*		132	140	156	180	200	265	310	350
1/125*		90	100	110	125	140	180	220	250
1/250*		60	79	78	90	100	130	156	175
Philips PF 60/97, G.E. No. 22B, Sylvania No. 2B									
To 1/30		140	156	180	200	220	280	360	400
1/60		100	110	125	140	156	200	250	280
1/125		70	78	90	100	110	140	180	200
1/250		50	56	63	70	78	100	125	140
1/500		35	39	45	50	56	70	90	100
G.E. No. 11B, Sylvania 40B									
To 1/30		100	110	125	140	156	200	250	280
1/60		78	90	100	110	125	156	200	220
1/125		56	63	70	78	90	110	140	156
No. M3B, M5B, Sylvania 25B									
To 1/30		70	78	90	100	110	140	180	200
1/60		63	70	78	90	100	125	156	180
1/125		45	50	56	63	70	90	110	125
Philips PF 1B, Mazda etc. No. 1B, AG-3B									
To 1/30		62	70	78	90	100	125	156	180
G.E., Mazda, etc. AG-1B									
To 1/30		45	50	56	63	70	90	110	125

* and **See footnotes to table on p. 469, also for alternative bulb type numbers and shutter speeds.

SYNCHRO-SETTINGS

This table shows the required settings of the synchronizing dial of earlier Leicas so fitted to synchronize the various flash types at various shutter speeds.

Shutter Speed	*Focal Plane*	*S*	*M*	*F*	*X*
Red synchronizing dial on later type f models					
1/25	16	15.5	10	0	0
1/50	13	12.5	11	4	20
1/75	7	6.5	6	—	—
1/100	4.5	4.5	4	—	—
1/200	2	2	—	—	—
1/500	1	1	—	—	—
1/1000	0	—	—	—	—
Black synchronizing dial on earlier f and converted c models					
1/30	20	20	16	4.5	2.5
1/40	15	15	11	—	—
1/60	10	10	9	—	—
1/100	7.5	7	—	—	—
1/200	5	5	—	—	—
1/500	4	4	—	—	—
1/1000	3	—	—	—	—
Black synchronizing dial on converted II syn, and IIIa syn models					
1/20	20	20	14	11	4
1/30	20	18	14	10	0
1/40	17	14	11	—	—
1/60	12	10.5	8.5	—	—
1/100	8.5	8	—	—	—
1/200	6	6	—	—	—

(Flash Bulb Class: S, M, F, X)

NEAR FOCUSING

These comparison figures indicate the maximum and minimum subject-film distances, field sizes, etc. obtainable with the various near focusing attachments and close-up mounts for focusing with the Leica rangefinder. Exact distances at the extreme (and intermediate) settings are in any case measured with the rangefinder.

	Subject Film Distance in.	Subject Film Distance cm.	Reduction 1:	Field Sizes in.	Field Sizes cm.
Close-up Mount for Leica M2 and M3 with 50 mm. Elmar or Summicron lenses in bayonet mount†					
Maximum	34⅝	88	15	14 × 21¼	36 × 54
Minimum	19	48	7.5	6¾ × 10⅝	17 × 27
Attachment with Suppl. Lens (Leica IIIg)					
Maximum	34⅝	88	15.4	14½ × 21¾	36.8 × 55.2
Minimum	20¾	53	8.3	7¾ × 11⅜	19.2 × 28.8
NOOKY Close-up Mount (Leica II to III with 50 mm. Elmar f3.5)					
Maximum	39⅝	100.7	17.5	16½ × 24¾	42 × 63
Minimum	17½	44.6	6.5	6 × 9½	15 × 22.5
SOOKY Close-up Mount Leica II to IIIf with 50 mm. Elmar f2.8 or Summicron f2)					
Maximum	39⅝	100.7	17.5	16½ × 23¾	42 × 63
Minimum*	19¾	50	8	7½ × 11¼	18.7 × 28.6
Minimum	18	45.7	6.5	6 × 9½	15 × 22.5
NOKUM Close-up Mount (Leica I to IIIf with 50 mm. Summar or Summitar f2)					
Maximum	40	101.5	17.5	16½ × 23¾	42 × 63
Minimum	18	45.7	6.5	6 × 9½	15 × 22.5

*With Summicron lens. †The same figures apply for the near-range Summicron lens on the Leica M2 and M3 models.

DISTANCE GAUGES

The various distance gauges and copying gauges for the Leica cover scales of reproduction from 1 : 9 to same-size.

The same clamping ring serves for the older 1 : 3, 1 : 2, and 1 : 1.5 gauges; the same-size gauge and the copying gauges use separate extension mounts. The supplementary lenses, the 1 : 3, 1 : 2, 1 : 1.5 gauges, and the 1 : 9, 1 : 6, 1 : 4 copying gauges use different sets of extendible gauge legs.

The older distance gauges are designed for the 50 mm. Elmar f3.5 lens; most of them will also take the 5 cm. Summar, though the leg extensions are slightly different (yellow rings instead of white). The 1 : 9, 1 : 6, 1 : 4 copying gauges will take any 50 mm. lens.

Scale (approx.)	Lens	Field Size	Legs Screwed into Bush Marked	Legs Extended to*
DIN A 4 Extension Mount, BOOWU Legs				
1 : 9	Any 50 mm. lens (set to ∞)	8¼ × 11¾ in. (21 × 29.7 cm.)	—	Ring 4
DIN A 5 Extension Mount, BOOWU Legs				
1 : 6	Any 50 mm. lens (set to ∞)	5¾ × 8¼ in. (14.8 × 21 cm.)	—	Ring 5
DIN A 6 Extension Mount, BOOWU Legs				
1 : 4	Any 50 mm. lens (set to ∞)	4⅛ × 5¾ in. (10.5 × 14.8 cm.)	—	Ring 6
Clamping Ring and 1 : 3 Extension Tube; BEHOO Legs				
1 : 3	50 mm. Elmar or Summar (set to ∞)	2¾ × 4¼ in. (7.2 × 10.8 cm.)	3	Upper ring
Clamping Ring and 1 : 2 Extension Tube; BEHOO Legs				
1 : 2	50 mm. Elmar or Summar (set to ∞)	1⅞ × 2¾ in. (4.8 × 7.2 cm.)	2	Middle ring
Clamping Ring and 1 : 1.5 Extension Tube; BEHOO Legs				
1 : 1.5	50 mm. Elmar or Summar (set to ∞)	1⅜ × 2⅛ in. (3.6 × 5.4 cm.)	1.5	Bottom ring
Special Clamping Ring, 1 : 1 Extension Tube and BELUN Gauge				
1 : 1	Most 35 and 50 mm. lenses† (set to ∞)	1 × 1½ in. (2.4 × 3.6 cm.)	—	

*White ring for 50 mm. Elmar, yellow ring (if marked) for Summar lens.

†According to marking on base plate.

Scale of Reproduction		f5.6 in.	f5.6 mm.	f8 in.	f8 mm.	f11 in.	f11 mm.	f16 in.	f16 mm.
Reductions									
1 : 20	(0.050)	6.18	157	8.85	224	12.1	308	17.7	448
1 : 18	(0.055)	5.05	128	7.17	182	9.94	251	14.4	365
1 : 17	(0.058)	4.50	114	6.43	163	8.85	224	12.8	326
1 : 16	(0.062)	4.02	102	5.72	145	7.90	200	11.4	290
1 : 15	(0.066)	3.53	89.6	5.05	128	6.95	176	10.0	256
1 : 14	(0.071)	3.09	78.4	4.41	112	6.08	154	8.84	224
1 : 13	(0.076)	2.68	68.0	3.83	97.1	5.28	134	7.66	194
1 : 12	(0.083)	2.30	58.2	3.28	83.2	4.50	114	6.55	166
1 : 11	(0.09)	1.94	49.3	2.77	70.4	3.82	96.8	5.56	141
1 : 10	(0.10)	1.62	41.1	2.32	58.7	3.18	80.7	4.62	117
1 : 9	(0.11)	1.32	33.6	1.89	48.0	2.60	66.0	3.78	96.0
1 : 8	(0.12)	1.06	26.9	1.51	38.4	2.08	52.8	3.03	76.8
1 : 7	(0.14)	0.825	20.9	1.18	29.9	1.62	41.1	2.36	59.7
1 : 6	(0.17)	0.620	15.7	0.885	22.4	1.21	30.8	1.77	44.8
1 : 5	(0.20)	0.440	11.2	0.632	16.0	0.867	22.0	1.26	32.0
1 : 4	(0.25)	0.296	7.5	0.422	10.7	0.580	14.7	0.840	21.3
1 : 3	(0.33)	0.118	4.5	0.252	6.4	0.347	8.8	0.505	12.8
1 : 2	(0.50)	0.087	2.2	0.126	3.2	0.173	4.4	0.252	6.4
1 : 1.5	(0.67)	0.055	1.4	0.079	2.0	0.110	2.8	0.158	4.0
1 : 1.33	(0.75)	0.047	1.2	0.067	1.7	0.091	2.3	0.134	3.3
Same Size									
1 : 1	(1.0)	0.031	0.80	0.043	1.1	0.059	1.5	0.083	2.1
Enlargements									
1.5 : 1		0.016	0.41	0.023	0.59	0.032	0.81	0.047	1.2
2 : 1		0.011	0.28	0.016	0.40	0.022	0.55	0.032	0.80
3 : 1		0.007	0.17	0.010	0.24	0.013	0.33	0.018	0.47
4 : 1		0.005	0.12	0.007	0.17	0.009	0.23	0.013	0.33
5 : 1		0.004	0.09	0.005	0.13	0.007	0.18	0.010	0.26
6 : 1		0.003	0.07	0.004	0.10	0.006	0.14	0.008	0.21
6.5 : 1		0.003	0.07	0.004	0.09	0.005	0.13	0.007	0.19
7 : 1		0.002	0.06	0.004	0.09	0.005	0.12	0.007	0.17
8 : 1		0.002	0.05	0.003	0.08	0.004	0.10	0.006	0.15
9 : 1		0.002	0.05	0.003	0.07	0.004	0.09	0.005	0.13
10 : 1		0.001	0.04	0.002	0.06	0.003	0.08	0.005	0.12

Image Reduction	*Exposure Factor*	*Image Magnification*	*Exposure Factor*
1 : 10	1.2	1.2 ×	5
1 : 8	1.25	1.4 ×	6
1 : 7	1.3	1.8 ×	8
1 : 5	1.5	2 ×	9
1 : 4	1.6	2.5 ×	12
1 : 3	1.8	3 ×	16
1 : 2.5	2	4 ×	25
1 : 2	2.3	5 ×	36
1 : 1.5	2.8	6 ×	49
1 : 1.2	3.5	7 ×	64
1 : 1 (same size)	4	8 ×	80
		10 ×	120

CLOSE-UP DEPTH

With close-ups, the depth of field largely depends on the actual scale of reproduction, and not on the distance and focal length of the lens used (these two factors are allowed for in calculating the scale of reproduction). This table gives the total depth in inches and mm., calculated for a circle of confusion of 1/750 inch of 1/30 mm. The point of maximum sharpness is in most cases in the middle of the depth of field zone, except at the smallest apertures and greatest reductions, where the depth in front of the sharpest plane is rather less than behind.

CLOSE-UP EXPOSURE

When we go close to a subject, the increased lens extension alters the effective aperture of the lens. We therefore have to increase the exposure by multiplying it by a factor which depends on the scale of reproduction (p. 419).

For close-ups with the Elpro lenses of the Leicaflex use the factor for the largest scale of reproduction with the *unaided* Leicaflex lens. Close-ups with the older Leitz supplementary lenses need no extra exposure.

REFLEX HOUSING

The reflex housings can, in addition to their use with the telephoto lenses (p. 123), be employed for close-ups with any of the shorter focus Leica lenses. The shorter the focal length, the greater the magnification; it can be increased in every case by the use of extension tubes (p. 375).

With the Visoflex II and III the extension tubes go between the lens unit and the appropriate mounts—16464 or 16467. The extension tube No. 16469, however, goes between the Visoflex and the lens.

In the case of the Visoflex I the extension tubes go between the lens and the housing; *this takes screw-mounted lenses.*

The lens settings usually imply the closest focusing position of the lens mount, except where an infinity setting is given. Naturally the use of the focusing mount plus the extension tubes provides a whole range of settings and scales of reproduction; the figures with the closest setting merely show the limits of the particular combination.

The focusing range for the complete 90 mm. lenses in their normal mount on the Visoflex housings is the same; the ranges with extension tubes between the lens unit and the mount vary, since different tubes are used with different lenses.

The focusing ranges of the different 135 mm. lenses are also similar when directly fitted on the Visoflex. The range with the 135 mm. Hektor and Elmar lens units (with adapter No. 16472) on the mount No. 16464 is similar to that of the 135 mm. Tele-Elmar.

Scale (app.)	*Subject-Film Distance in.*	*cm.*	*Field Size in.*	*cm.*	*Lens set to*	*Extension Tubes*
Visoflex II and III: 35 mm. Lenses Complete						
1.2:1	5.5	14.0	0.79×1.2	2×3	c.	None
1.4:1	5.7	14.5	0.67×1.0	1.7×2.6	c.	1 No. 16469
Visoflex II and III: 50 mm. Lenses Complete						
1:2.5	12.8	31.0	2.4×3.6	6×9	c.	None
1:1	8.1	20.6	0.95×1.4	2.4×3.6	c.	1 No. 16469
Visoflex II and III: 65 mm. Elmar Lens in Mount No. 16464						
1:2.5	13.0	33	2.4×3.6	6×9	c.	None
1:1.2	10.6	27	1.1×1.7	2.9×4.3	c.	1 No. 16471
1.2:1	10.6	27	0.7×1.1	1.9×2.8	c.	2 No. 16471
Visoflex II and III: 90 mm. Elmar Lens Unit only in Mount No. 16467						
1:9	39.4	100	8.5×12.7	21.6×32.4	c.	None
1:5	25	63	4.5×6.8	11.5×17.3	c.	1 No. 16468
1:3.5	20	50	3×4.5	7.7×11.5	c.	2 No. 16468
1:2.5	17.2	43.6	2.2×3.3	5.7×8.5	c.	2 No. 16468
Visoflex II and III: 90 mm. Elmar in Own Standard Focusing Mount						
1:2.2	16.2	41.5	2×3	5×7.5	∞	None
1:1.7	15.2	38.6	1.5×2.2	3.9×5.9	c.	None
1:1.1	14.1	36	1×1.5	2.6×3.9	c.	3 No. 16468*
Visoflex II and III: 90 mm. Elmarit Lens Unit only in Mount No. 16464						
1:3.5	20	50	3×4.5	7.7×11.5	c.	None
1:2	15.4	39	1.9×2.8	4.8×7.2	c.	No. 16467
1:1.1	14.2	36	1×1.5	2.5×3.8	c.	2 No. 16471
Visoflex II and III: 90 mm. Elmarit in Own Standard Focusing Mount						
1:2.2	16.5	42	2×3	5×7.5	∞	None
1:1.8	15.4	39.2	1.6×2.4	4×6	c.	None
1:1.1	14.4	36.6	1×1.5	2.6×3.9	c.	1 No. 16471*
1.1:1	14.4	36.6	0.8×1.2	1.9×2.8	c.	2 No. 16471*
Visoflex II and III: 90 mm. Summicron in Short Mount						
1:9	40	101.3	8×12	20×30	c.	None
1:4.5	24	60.8	4.2×63	10×15	c.	1 No. 16474
Visoflex II and III: 135 mm. Tele-Elmar Lens Unit in Mount No. 16464						
1:5	38.5	98	4.4×6.6	11×16.5	c.	None
1:2.5	26.8	68.2	2.2×3.3	5.6×8.4	c.	1 No. 16471
1:1.6	23.3	59.2	1.5×2.2	3.8×5.7	c.	2 No. 16471
Visoflex II and III: 135 mm. Lenses in Standard Focusing Mount						
1:3.3	acc. to lens		2.9×4.4	7.4×11.2	∞	None
1:2.4	acc. to lens		2.1×3.2	5.4×8.2	c.	None
Visoflex I: 35 mm. Lenses						
1.8:1	6.0	15.2	0.51×0.78	1.3×2.0	∞	None
4.0:1	8.6	21.9	0.23×0.35	0.6×0.9	∞	3 No. 16615
*Visoflex I: All 50 mm. Lenses***						
1.2:1	8.2	20.8	0.79×1.2	2.0×3.0	∞	None
2.7:1	10.3	26.2	0.35×0.51	0.9×1.3	∞	3 No. 16615
Visoflex I: 90 mm. Lenses in Standard Focusing Mount						
1:1.4	14.6	37.0	1.30×2.0	3.4×5.0	∞	None
1.6:1	15.0	38.0	0.60×0.91	1.5×2.3	∞	3 No. 16615*
Visoflex I: 135 mm. Lenses in Standard Focusing Mount						
1:2.2	24.7	62.7	2.1×3.1	5.2×7.8	∞	None
Visoflex I: 135 mm. Elmar and Hektor Lenses in Short Mount						
1:9	5.90	150	8.5×12.7	21.6×32.4	c.	None
1:1.5	22.2	56.3	1.4×2.1	3.6×5.4	c.	3 No. 16615

*These tubes are inserted between the lens unit and the normal focusing mount of the lens.

**The subject-film distances refer only to the 50 mm. Elmar, *f*3.5 lens. With other 50 mm. lenses (Elmar *f*2.8, Summicron Summitar, Summar) the distances are 0.4 to 0.5 inches (1 to 1.2 cm.) longer.

VISOFLEX II AND III WITH BELLOWS II

Scale Setting on Rail	Subject-Film Distance inches	cm.	Field Size mm.	Scale of Reproduction
Bayonet-mounted 35 mm. Lenses with Ring No. 16596				
0	6.3	16	11.4×17.1	2.1:1
15	6.8	17	9.6×14.4	2.5:1
32	7.4	19	8.0×12.0	3:1
67	8.7	22	6.0×9.0	4:1
95	10	25	4.8×7.2	5:1
Screw-mounted 35 mm. Lenses with Ring No. 16590				
0	6.0	15	14.0×21.0	1.7:1
29	6.8	17	9.6×14.4	2.5:1
46	7.4	19	8.0×12.0	3:1
95	9.0	23	5.3×8.0	4.5:1
Bayonet-mounted 50 mm. Lenses with Ring No. 16596				
0	8.3	21	17.0×16.0	1.4:1
31	9.4	24	12.0×18.0	2:1
57	10	26	9.4×14.4	2.5:1
95	11.4	29	7.5×11.0	3.2:1
Screw-mounted 50 mm. Lenses with Ring No. 16590				
0	8.3	21	22.0×33.0	1.1:1
19	8.7	22	16.0×24.0	1.5:1
45	9.4	24	12.0×18.0	2:1
71	10	26	9.6×14.4	2.5:1
95	11	28	8.0×12.0	3:1
65 mm. Elmar Lens with Ring No. 16558				
0	∞	∞	∞	1:∞
17	16.5	42	96×144	1:4
34	12	30	48×72	1:2
67	10.6	27	24×36	1:1
95	11	28	17×25.5	1.4:1
Lens Unit of 90 mm. Elmar or Elmarit Lens with Ring No. 16558				
0	∞	∞	∞	1:∞
23	22.4	57	96×144	1:4
45	16	41	48×72	1:2
90	14.2	36	24×36	1:1
95	14.2	36	22×33	1.1:1
Lens Unit of 90 mm. Summicron with Ring No. 16598				
0	40	102	218×327	1:9
13	22	56	96×144	1:4
35	15.8	40	48×72	1:2
80	14	35.5	24×36	1:1
95	14.1	35.7	20×30	1.2:1
Lens Unit of 125 mm. Hektor with Ring No. 16572				
25	∞	∞	∞	1:∞
54	30	75	96×144	1:4
84	21.3	54	48×72	1:2
95	20.4	51	40×60	1:1.7
*Lens Unit of 135 mm. Tele-Elmar (or 135 mm. Elmar or Hektor Lenses in Mount No. 16472) with Ring No. 16558**				
0	∞	∞	∞	1:∞
33	33	84	96×144	1:4
67	24	61	48×72	1:2
95	22	56	34×51	1:1.4
Lens Unit of 135 mm. Elmarit with Ring No. 16598				
0	155	390	650×975	1:25
95	22.3	56	31×47	1:1.3
Lens Unit of 200 mm. Telyt f4 with Ring No. 16598				
95	38.5	98	70×105	1:3

*Same-size reproduction is possible by using in addition two rings No. 16471.

The Model II focusing bellows used with the Visoflex II and III reflex housing will yield enlarged close-ups at various magnifications up to 5 times natural size, according to the lens employed. The table shows a selection of settings with various lens combinations and mounting rings; in most cases the lens unit only is used—i.e. removed from its normal focusing mount. See also p. 386.

LARGE FOCUSING BELLOWS

The larger focusing bellows used with the Visoflex I reflex housing will yield enlarged close-ups to over six times natural size. This table shows the focusing distances, field widths, and scales of reproduction.

The field width is the width of the subject area covered by the longer dimension of the Leica frame; the field height covered by the shorter dimension of the negative is two-thirds these figures.

The figures apply equally to the reflex housing on the Leica I to IIIg, as to the bayonet mount reflex housing (or the screw-mounted one with adapter ring) on the Leica M.

The scale on the left of the guide rail (marked $f = 135$ mm.) carries the scales of reproduction which apply for the 135 mm. Elmar and Hektor lenses (now discontinued) when used with the focusing bellows and reflex housing. With other lenses the scale of reproduction is different, but the figures in the table give the corresponding values for each lens.

The 135 mm. lenses are fitted (without focusing mount) into a special adapter barrel, the latter being screwed into the screw mounting ring in the front panel. All the other lenses are fitted into a bayonet mounting ring (bayonet mounted lenses) or screw directly into the screw mounting ring.

		Focusing Bellows and Reflex Housing: Left-hand (f = 135 mm.) Scale Settings 0	0.3	0.5	0.7	1.0
Lens Unit of 135 mm. Elmar and Hektor Lenses in Adapter Tube No. 16580L with Mounting Ring No. 16590						
Subject-film Distance	in.	∞	30.1	24.1	22.1	21.4
	cm.	∞	76.3	61.0	56.0	54.3
Field width	in.	∞	4.74	2.84	2.02	1.42
	cm.	∞	12.0	7.2	5.1	3.6
Scale of Reproduction		0	0.3	0.5	0.7	1.0
Lens Unit of 125 mm. Hektor Lens with Mounting Ring No. 16572						
Subject-film Distance	in.	∞	24.8	20.4	19.0	18.8
	cm.	∞	63.2	51.7	48.3	47.8
Field width	in.	∞	4.21	2.52	1.81	1.26
	cm.		10.7	6.4	4.6	3.2
Scale of Reproduction		0	0.34	0.56	0.79	1.13
Complete 90 mm. Elmar Lens with Mounting Ring No. 16590 or No. 16596** (Lens set to Infinity)*						
Subject-film Distance	in.	14.3	14.6	15.2	15.9	17.2
	cm.	36.1	37.0	38.5	40.4	43.6
Field width	in.	1.52	1.03	0.84	0.72	0.58
	cm.	3.9	2.6	2.1	1.8	1.4
Scale of Reproduction		0.93	1.38	1.68	1.98	2.43
Lens Unit of 90 mm. Elmar and Elmarit Lenses in Adapter Tube No. 16585D and with Ring No. 16590; Lens Unit of 90 mm. Summicron in Adapter Tube No. 16598 and with Ring No. 16590						
Subject-film Distance	in.	15.9	14.2	14.4	14.9	16.0
	cm.	40.5	36.1	36.5	37.9	40.6
Field width	in.	2.79	1.5	1.14	0.90	0.71
	cm.	7.1	3.8	2.9	2.3	1.8
Scale of Reproduction		0.50	0.95	1.26	1.56	2.01
50 mm. Elmar f3.5 in UYCOO Bayonet Mounting Ring (discontinued)						
Subject-film Distance	in.	8.15	8.80	9.60	10.5	11.9
	cm.	20.7	22.3	24.2	26.5	30.1
Field width	in.	1.52	0.82	0.63	0.51	0.40
	cm.	3.9	2.1	1.6	1.3	1.0
Scale of Reproduction		0.93	1.72	2.24	2.76	3.55
All Complete 50 mm. Lenses with Mounting Ring No. 16590 or No. 16596** (Lens Set to Infinity)*						
Subject-film Distance	in.	8.70	9.90	10.8	11.7	13.2
	cm.	22.0	25.0	27.3	29.7	33.5
Field width	in.	0.89	0.69	0.49	0.41	0.34
	cm.	2.3	1.5	1.2	1.0	0.86
Scale of Reproduction		1.60	2.64	2.90	3.42	4.20
All Complete 35 mm. Lenses with Mounting Ring No. 16590 or No. 16596** (Lens Set to Infinity)*						
Subject-film Distance	in.	6.70	8.10	9.10	10.1	11.6
	cm.	17.0	20.5	23.1	25.6	29.8
Field width	in.	0.60	0.40	0.33	0.28	0.23
	cm.	1.5	1.0	0.84	0.71	0.25
Scale of Reproduction		2.36	3.51	4.28	5.05	6.20

*With screw-mounted lenses. **With bayonet-mounted lenses.

LEICAFLEX CLOSE-UPS

Elpro Lens	*Ext.* Tube*	*Dist.** Setting*	*Lens-to Subject Distance* *in.*	*cm.*	*Approx. Subject Field* *cm.*	*Scale of Reprod.* *1:*	*×*
35 *mm. Elmarit-R*							
None	None	c.	10	25	14 × 21	6	0·16
50 *mm. Summicron-R*							
None	None	c.	15 7/8	40·5	17 × 26	7·7	0·13
None	4	∞	4 3/4	12·0	4·7 × 7·1	2	0·49
None	4	c.	3 3/4	9·7	3·6 × 5·5	1·6	0·61
None	4 + 5	∞	2 5/8	6·7	2·3 × 3·5	1	1·0
None	4 + 5	c.	2 3/8	6·1	2·1 × 3·1	—	1·1
None	4 + 5 + 5	∞	2	5·0	1·6 × 2·3	—	1·44
None	4 + 5 + 5	c.	1 7/8	4·7	1·4 × 2·1	—	1·56
VIa	None	∞	15 1/2	39·5	17 × 26	7·7	0·13
VIa	None	c.	8 1/8	20·5	8·7 × 13	3·8	0·26
VIb	None	∞	8	20·3	8·7 × 13	3·8	0·26
VIb	None	c.	5 3/8	13·5	5·7 × 8·6	2·6	0·39
VIa + b	None	∞	5 1/8	13·0	5·8 × 8·7	2·6	0·39
VIa + b	None	c.	3 7/8	9·8	4·4 × 6·7	2	0·50
VIa	4	∞	3 1/2	8·8	3·6 × 5·5	1·6	0·61
VIa	4	c.	2 7/8	7·3	3·0 × 4·6	1·5	0·75
VIb	4	∞	2 7/8	7·2	3·0 × 4·6	1·5	0·75
VIb	4	c.	2 5/8	6·2	2·5 × 3·8	1·1	0·90
VIa + b	4	∞	2 1/8	5·5	2·6 × 3·9	1·2	0·95
VIa + b	4	c.	1 7/8	4·7	2·3 × 3·4	1	1·0
VIa	4 + 5	∞	2	5·1	2·1 × 3·1	—	1·1
VIa	4 + 5	c.	1 7/8	4·6	1·8 × 2·7	—	1·2
VIb	4 + 5	∞	1 7/8	4·6	1·8 × 2·7	—	1·2
VIb	4 + 5	c.	1 5/8	4·1	1·6 × 2·4	—	1·4
VIa + b	4 + 5	∞	1 3/8	3·4	1·7 × 2·5	—	1·37
VIa + b	4 + 5	c.	1 1/4	3·0	1·5 × 2·3	—	1·46
VIa	4 + 5 + 5	∞	1 1/2	3·8	1·4 × 2·1	—	1·56
VIa	4 + 5 + 5	c.	1 3/8	3·5	1·3 × 1·9	—	1·67
VIb	4 + 5 + 5	∞	1 3/8	3·5	1·3 × 1·9	—	1·67
VIb	4 + 5 + 5	c.	1 1/4	3·2	1·2 × 1·8	—	1·84
90 *mm. Elmarit-R*							
None	None	c.	21 3/8	54·2	12·5 × 19	5·6	0·18
None	4	∞	14 1/4	36·1	7·9 × 12	3·6	0·28
None	4	c.	9 3/8	23·8	4·9 × 7·3	2·2	0·46
None	4 + 5	c.	8	20·2	4·0 × 6·0	1·8	0·55
None	4 + 5	∞	6 1/2	16·6	3·0 × 4·6	1·4	0·74
None	4 + 5 + 5	∞	6	15·2	2·7 × 4·1	1·2	0·82
None	4 + 5 + 5	c.	5 1/4	13·2	2·3 × 3·4	1	1·0
VIIa	None	∞	23 1/4	59·0	14·6 × 22	6·7	0·15
VIIa	None	c.	11 1/4	28·3	6·5 × 9·9	3	0·34
VIIa	4	∞	8 7/8	22·5	5·1 × 7·6	2·3	0·44
VIIa	4	c.	6 1/2	16·6	3·5 × 5·3	1·6	0·63
VIIa	4 + 5	∞	5 3/4	14·8	3·1 × 4·6	1·4	0·72
VIIa	4 + 5	c.	4 7/8	12·5	2·5 × 3·7	1·1	0·92
VIIa	4 + 5 + 5	∞	4 5/8	11·6	2·3 × 4·3	1	1·0
VIIa	4 + 4 + 5	c.	4 1/8	10·3	1·9 × 2·8	—	1·2
135 *mm. Elmarit-R*							
None	None	c.	53	135	20 × 30	9·1	0·11
None	4	∞	34	86	12 × 18	5·4	0·19
None	4	c.	23 1/2	60	7·4 × 11·2	3·3	0·30
None	4 + 5	∞	20 1/4	51·5	6·1 × 9·1	2·7	0·37
None	4 + 5	c.	16 7/8	43·0	4·6 × 6·9	2	0·48
None	4 + 5 + 5	∞	15 1/2	39·5	4·0 × 6·1	1·8	0·55
None	4 + 5 + 5	c.	14	35·4	3·3 × 5·1	1·6	0·67
VIIb	None	c.	53	135	23 × 35	9·9	0·10
VIIb	None	c.	26 3/8	67	9·8 × 14·7	4·5	0·22
VIIa	None	∞	23 7/8	60·6	10 × 15	4·5	0·22
VIIa	None	c.	16 3/8	41·5	6·1 × 9·3	2·8	0·36
VIIb	4	∞	21 1/8	53·5	7·3 × 11·1	3·3	0·30
VIIb	4	c.	16 3/8	41·6	5·2 × 7·8	2·3	0·44
VIIb	4 + 5	∞	14 3/4	37·5	4·4 × 6·7	2	0·50
VIIb	4 + 5	c.	12 3/4	32·5	3·5 × 5·3	1·6	0·64
VIIb	4 + 5 + 5	∞	12	30·4	3·2 × 5·8	1·4	0·70
VIIb	4 + 5 + 5	c.	11	27·8	2·7 × 4·1	1·2	0·82

*4 = combination ring No. 14134; 4 + 5 = ring No. 14134 with tube No. 14135; 4 + 5 + 5 = ring No. 14134 with two tubes No. 14135.

* *This refers to the focusing setting on the lens. ∞ = infinity; c. = closest lens setting.

The near focusing limit of Leicaflex lenses is generally closer than of Leica lenses. It can be brought closer still with extension tubes and supplementary lenses (p. 404).

This table gives approximate close-up distances, subject fields and scales of reproduction available with the different lenses and combinations of supplementary lenses and extension tubes. With the 90 and 135 mm. lenses this does not include every possible combination, partly because there is a certain amount of overlapping and partly because some of the combinations with the supplementary lenses do not give as good image quality as with the extension tubes.

The scales are given both as reductions (1 : 6 etc) and as magnifications (0.16 etc). Of the two the magnification figure is the more accurate one.

The distances are measured from the front of the lens to the subject plane, rather than from the film plane to the subject, to show the amount of working space available between the camera and the subject. The field sizes are also rounded off and show the subject area taken in in the finder of the Leicaflex — corresponding roughly to the masked area recorded on a colour transparency. The actual field on the film is approximately 5% longer in each direction. (The Leicaflex screen is in any case used for precise focusing and so determining the field of view taken in.)

See also the chart on p. 407 for selecting appropriate lens, supplementary lens and extension tube combinations for different scales of reproduction.

INDEX